The Archaeology of Medite

BLACKWELL STUDIES IN GLOBAL ARCHAEOLOGY

Series Editors: Lynn Meskell and Rosemary A. Joyce

Blackwell Studies in Global Archaeology is a series of contemporary texts, each carefully designed to meet the needs of archaeology instructors and students seeking volumes that treat key regional and thematic areas of archaeological study. Each volume in the series, compiled by its own editor, includes 12–15 newly commissioned articles by top scholars within the volume's thematic, regional, or temporal area of focus.

What sets the *Blackwell Studies in Global Archaeology* apart from other available texts is that their approach is accessible, yet does not sacrifice theoretical sophistication. The series editors are committed to the idea that usable teaching texts need not lack ambition. To the contrary, the *Blackwell Studies in Global Archaeology* aim to immerse readers in fundamental archaeological ideas and concepts, but also to illuminate more advanced concepts, thereby exposing readers to some of the most exciting contemporary developments in the field. Inasmuch, these volumes are designed not only as classic texts, but as guides to the vital and exciting nature of archaeology as a discipline.

1. Mesoamerican Archaeology: Theory and Practice
   Edited by Julia A. Hendon and Rosemary A. Joyce
2. Andean Archaeology
   Edited by Helaine Silverman
3. African Archaeology: A Critical Introduction
   Edited by Ann Brower Stahl
4. Archaeologies of the Middle East: Critical Perspectives
   Edited by Susan Pollock and Reinhard Bernbeck
5. North American Archaeology
   Edited by Timothy R. Pauketat and Diana DiPaolo Loren
6. The Archaeology of Mediterranean Prehistory
   Edited by Emma Blake and A. Bernard Knapp

Forthcoming:

An Archaeology of Asia
  Edited by Miriam T. Stark

Archaeology of Oceania: Australia and the Pacific Islands
  Edited by Ian Lilley

Historical Archaeology
  Edited by Martin Hall and Stephen Silliman

Classical Archaeology
  Edited by Susan E. Alcock and Robin G. Osborne

The Archaeology of Mediterranean Prehistory

Edited by

Emma Blake and
A. Bernard Knapp

Blackwell Publishing

BLACKWELL PUBLISHING
350 Main Street, Malden, MA 02148-5020, USA
108 Cowley Road, Oxford OX4 1JF, UK
550 Swanston Street, Carlton, Victoria 3053, Australia

First published 2005 by Blackwell Publishing Ltd

Library of Congress Cataloging-in-Publication Data

Blake, Emma.
    The archaeology of Mediterranean prehistory / edited by Emma Blake and
A. Bernard Knapp.
        p. cm.—(Blackwell studies in global archaeology)
    Includes bibliographical references and index.
    ISBN 0-631-23267-2 (hardback : alk. paper)—ISBN 0-631-23268-0 (pbk. : alk. paper)
    1. Prehistoric peoples—Mediterranean Region.   2. Archaeology—Mediterranean Region.
3. Mediterranean Region—Antiquities.   I. Knapp, Arthur Bernard.   II. Title.   III. Series.

    GN848.B53 2004
    909′.09822—dc22

                                                                                        2004014017

A catalogue record for this title is available from the British Library.

Set in 10 on 12.5 pt Plantin
by SNP Best-set Typesetter Ltd, Hong Kong
Printed and bound in the United Kingdom
by TJ International, Padstow, Cornwall

The publisher's policy is to use permanent paper from mills that operate a sustainable forestry policy,
and which has been manufactured from pulp processed using acid-free and elementary chlorine-free
practices. Furthermore, the publisher ensures that the text paper and cover board used have met
acceptable environmental accreditation standards.

For further information on
Blackwell Publishing, visit our website:
www.blackwellpublishing.com

For my mother (EB)

For Maria of the (western) Mediterranean, who has taught me so much about the world beyond archaeology (ABK)

Contents

List of Figures   ix

List of Tables   xi

Notes on Contributors   xii

Acknowledgments   xvi

1   Prehistory in the Mediterranean: The Connecting and Corrupting Sea   1
    A. Bernard Knapp and Emma Blake

2   Substances in Motion: Neolithic Mediterranean "Trade"   24
    John E. Robb and R. Helen Farr

3   Agriculture, Pastoralism, and Mediterranean Landscapes in Prehistory   46
    Graeme Barker

4   Changing Social Relations in the Mediterranean Copper and Bronze Ages   77
    Robert Chapman

5   The Material Expression of Cult, Ritual, and Feasting   102
    Emma Blake

6   The Gendered Sea: Iconography, Gender, and Mediterranean Prehistory   130
    Lauren E. Talalay

7   The Genesis of Monuments among the Mediterranean Islands   156
    Michael J. Kolb

8   Lithic Technologies and Use   180
    Evagelia Karimali

 9   Archaeometallurgy in the Mediterranean: The Social Context of Mining,
     Technology, and Trade   215
     Vasiliki Kassianidou and A. Bernard Knapp

10   Settlement in the Prehistoric Mediterranean   252
     Luke Sollars

11   Maritime Commerce and Geographies of Mobility in the Late Bronze
     Age of the Eastern Mediterranean: Problematizations   270
     Sturt W. Manning and Linda Hulin

12   Museum Archaeology and the Mediterranean Cultural Heritage   303
     Robin Skeates

Index   321

Figures

2.1	Some patterns of circulation of raw materials in the Neolithic central Mediterranean	28
2.2	Reconstruction of local trade networks at Passo di Corvo, Italy	32
3.1	The "timeless Mediterranean landscape": plowing with an oxen team in the Biferno Valley (central-southern Italy) in the 1970s	47
3.2	Map, with the principal sites and regions mentioned in the text	48
3.3	Rock art: "settlements/fields"	61
3.4	Rock art: "plowing"	62
4.1	Location of main sites in southeast Spain mentioned in the text	81
4.2	Location of main sites in the Aegean mentioned in the text	88
4.3	Proposed extension of Prepalatial Malia state	91
5.1	Rock-cut tomb entrance viewed from tomb interior. Sant' Andrea Priu, Sardinia	112
5.2	View toward peak sanctuary at Ketsophas, Crete	117
5.3	Row of three menhirs. Perda Longa, Sardinia	119
7.1	Various Mediterranean islands showing the major sites mentioned in the text	157
7.2	Plans of typical Mediterranean monuments	159
7.3	Plan of the palace at Knossos	162
8.1	Map of the Mediterranean with stone material sources and sites mentioned in the text	186
8.2	Blade cores and flaking production techniques	190
8.3	Main flaked tool types	196
8.4	Main ground stone tools	199
9.1	Map of the Mediterranean showing the location of principal ore deposits	219
9.2	Variety of ceramic tuyères from the Late Bronze Age primary copper smelting site Politiko *Phorades* in Cyprus	222

9.3   Copper ox-hide ingot dating to the Late Bronze Age, from the
      site of Enkómi in Cyprus   223
9.4   Silver ingots, from the Late Bronze site of Pyla *Kokkinokremos*
      in Cyprus   228
10.1 Map of regions, places, projects, and sites mentioned in the text 253
11.1 Maximum maritime visibility in the Eastern Mediterranean
      and the Aegean   277
12.1 Total numbers of museums in different Mediterranean countries   309
12.2 Cycladic figurines in the Robert and Lisa Sainsbury Collection
      displayed in the Sainsbury Centre for Visual Arts at the
      University of East Anglia, Norwich   314

Tables

2.1 The distribution and context of Lipari obsidian along a path from
     the source at Lipari to the head of the Adriatic   34
8.1 Chipped and ground stone industries: raw materials and
     production techniques   181
8.2 The main tool types encountered in Mediterranean assemblages,
     the type of activity involved, and the type of raw material used   183

Notes on Contributors

Graeme Barker took up the post of Disney Professor of Archaeology and Director of the McDonald Institute of Archaeological Research at Cambridge University in October 2004. Previously, he was Pro-Vice-Chancellor and Professor of Archaeology at the University of Leicester. His research interests have focused principally on relations between landscape and people, in Europe and the Mediterranean, in arid zones (Libya, Jordan), and now in tropical environments in Southeast Asia. He is the author, editor, or co-editor of numerous books on such topics as prehistoric farming, subsistence archaeology, the Etruscans, and desertification. His publications include *The Etruscans* (co-author, 1998); *A Mediterranean Valley* (1995); and *The Archaeology of Drylands* (co-author, 2000).

Emma Blake is Visiting Assistant Professor in the Department of Classical Studies at the University of Michigan. She received her Ph.D. in Archaeology in 1999 from Cambridge University. She was a Postdoctoral Teaching Fellow in Humanities at Stanford University, and the 2000–1 Cotsen Visiting Scholar in Archaeology at UCLA. Her research focuses on the western Mediterranean in later prehistory, and her thematic research interests include spatial theory, culture contact and change, colonialism and diaspora, megalithic monuments, ceramic analysis, and landscape studies. She spends her summers in Sicily as assistant director on the excavations at the indigenous first millennium BC site of Monte Polizzo. Her articles have appeared in *World Archaeology*, the *Journal of Mediterranean Archaeology*, the *European Journal of Archaeology*, and the *American Journal of Archaeology*.

Robert Chapman is Professor of Archaeology at the University of Reading. His principal research interests lie in the development of social inequality in Mediterranean societies from the adoption of agriculture to the emergence of the state, and the archaeological analysis of mortuary practices. He has conducted fieldwork in the Balearic Islands and southeast Spain (the Gatas project in the Vera basin). His most recent book is *Archaeologies of Complexity* (2003).

R. Helen Farr is a maritime archaeologist completing a Ph.D. at Cambridge University. Her research focuses upon exploring Neolithic maritime travel and obsidian circulation as social activities embodying local knowledge and experience. This gives rise to the exploration of general questions about social organization, knowledge and prehistoric travel. At present she is working in the central Mediterranean. She is an accomplished sailor and spends much of her spare time on the water.

Linda Hulin is a Ph.D. candidate in the Department of Archaeology at the University of Reading, researching the factors that influence the perception of exotic and non-exotic imports in local economies in the Late Bronze Age eastern Mediterranean. She has participated in a number of excavations on Cyprus (Ayios Dhimitrios) and in Israel (Aphek, Lachish, Jerusalem, Miqne, Haror) and Egypt (Tell el-Amarna). She has worked as a pottery specialist at Maroni (Cyprus) and Marsa Matruh (Egypt) and conducted survey work in the coastal western desert (Egypt). Her research interests and publications center on the Libyans of the Late Bronze Age, and social aspects of intercultural relations in the eastern Mediterranean Bronze Age. She is a contributor to *Marsa Matruh I: The Excavation* (2002).

Evagelia Karimali is an external research scholar under contract at the Institute for Mediterranean Studies (Foundation of Research and Technology, Hellas [Greece]). Previously she lectured in the Department of History and Archaeology at the University of Crete and was a research coordinator and consultant on Prehistoric and Classical Archaeology at the Foundation of Hellenic World. Currently, she is teaching in the Department of Philosophy and Social Studies at the University of Crete. Her research interests focus on Mediterranean and Aegean Neolithic prehistory, lithic technology, ethnoarchaeology, and economic archaeology. She has participated in more than twenty archaeological research projects and a number of joint research and technology programs between Greece and the USA, Bulgaria, Belgium, Cyprus, and China.

Vasiliki Kassianidou received her (honors) Bachelor's degree in Chemistry and Classical and Near Eastern Archaeology from Bryn Mawr College and her Ph.D. in Archaeometallurgy from the Institute of Archaeology, University College London. Her doctoral research focused on an ancient silver-smelting workshop located in the southwestern Iberian Peninsula. She has worked as Research Fellow at the Institute of Archaeology, UCL (on a new method for the stabilization of corroded iron). Currently she is Assistant Professor in the Department of History and Archaeology at the University of Cyprus, which she joined in 1994. She lectures in Environmental Archaeology, Archaeometry, and Ancient Technology. Her research interests include: extractive metallurgy, ancient technology, conservation of metals, and the production and trade of Cypriot copper in antiquity. She has participated in numerous excavations on Cyprus and currently is involved with two major field projects: the excavations at Politiko *Phorades* (completed and in the process of final publication), and the Troodos Archaeological and Environmental Survey Project, which she co-directs with Michael Given, A. Bernard Knapp, and Jay Noller.

A. Bernard Knapp is Professor of Mediterranean Archaeology in the Department of Archaeology, University of Glasgow. He received his Ph.D. (1979) in Ancient History and Mediterranean Archaeology from the University of California, Berkeley. He has held research fellowships at the University of Sydney, the Cyprus American Archaeological Research Institute, Cambridge University, and Macquarie University (Sydney). Research interests include archaeological theory, the archaeologies of landscape, gender and social identity, island archaeology, the prehistory of the Mediterranean (especially Neolithic-Bronze Age Cyprus), and the Bronze Age trade in metals. He co-edits the *Journal of Mediterranean Archaeology* (with John F. Cherry) and edits the series *Monographs in Mediterranean Archaeology* (both published by Equinox Press, London). His most recent monograph, co-authored with Michael Given, is entitled *The Sydney Cyprus Survey Project: Social Approaches to Regional Archaeological Survey*. Monumenta Archaeologica 21 (2003).

Michael J. Kolb is Associate Professor of Anthropology at Northern Illinois University. His research interests include complex societies, monumental architecture, and the archaeology of power and ritual. He has conducted fieldwork in Polynesia, Europe, and Africa. He is currently the director of the Na Heiau O Maui project, studying social stratification and the political economy of the Maui Kingdom in Hawaii, and is one of the international co-directors of the Elymi Project in Sicily, focusing on the rise of social complexity in early Iron Age Sicily. His publications have appeared in the journals *American Antiquity*, *Antiquity*, and *Current Anthropology*.

Sturt W. Manning is Walter Graham and Homer Thompson Chair in Aegean Prehistory at the University of Toronto, and Visiting Professor, Department of Archaeology, University of Reading. His current research interests include Aegean and east Mediterranean prehistory, cultural interconnections, the development of complex societies, radiocarbon dating, dendrochronology and dendrochemistry, and climate change processes. At present he directs archaeological fieldwork projects around Maroni in southern Cyprus: the Maroni Valley Archaeological Survey Project, and the Tsaroukkas Mycenaeans and Trade Project. Recent publications include *A Test of Time: The Volcano of Thera and the Chronology and History of the Aegean and East Mediterranean in the Second Millennium BC* (1999) and *The Late Roman Church at Maroni Petrera* (2003).

John E. Robb is Senior Lecturer at Cambridge University. He teaches and conducts research on the Neolithic and Bronze Age of the Central Mediterranean, archaeological theory, and human osteology. His current fieldwork includes long-term excavations on later prehistoric sites at Bova Marina, Calabria, Italy. His publications include *Agency in Archaeology* (co-editor, 2000) and *Material Symbols: Culture and Economy in Prehistory* (ed. 1999). He is particularly interested in questions of how everyday material culture embodies processes of agency and social reproduction, and in playing with his two small children.

Robin Skeates is Lecturer in Museum Studies in the Department of Archaeology, University of Durham. His research extends across the related fields of material culture, museum and heritage studies, and he has particular interests in the prehistoric archaeology of the central Mediterranean region, the history of archaeological collecting, and public archaeology. He is currently examining the relationship between visual culture studies and archaeology, with particular reference to prehistoric southeast Italy. His publications include *Radiocarbon Dating and Italian Prehistory* (co-author, 1994); *Debating the Archaeological Heritage* (2001); and *The Collecting of Origins* (2000).

Luke Sollars is a graduate of the University of Glasgow and is currently writing his Ph.D. thesis – concerning settlement and landscape in historic Cyprus – at the same institution. His research interests include the many facets of settlement and community, the viability of small-scale survey methods, and the considered management and presentation of archaeological data. He has, over the past four years, worked on the Troodos Archaeological and Environmental Survey Project on Cyprus, managing their data and studying their settlements.

Lauren E. Talalay is Associate Director and Curator at the Kelsey Museum of Archaeology and Adjunct Associate Professor in the Department of Classical Studies, University of Michigan. Her research focuses primarily on Neolithic figurines from Greece, the use of the body as a symbol in antiquity, and gender and feminist studies. She is the author of *Deities, Dolls and Devices: Neolithic Figurines from Franchthi Cave, Greece* (1993). She has also co-edited a book on the modern Greek poet Constantine P. Cavafy (*What these Ithakas Mean* [2002]) and is currently conducting research on the topic of archaeology and advertising in the print media.

Acknowledgments

We would like to thank Lynn Meskell and Rosemary Joyce, co-editors of *Blackwell Studies in Global Archaeology*, for their invitation to edit this volume and for their enthusiastic support. We are extremely grateful to Jane Huber, Emily Martin, and all the other staff at Blackwell, who have been helpful, patient, and supportive from beginning to end. Heartfelt thanks are due to the contributors to the volume: they have worked long and hard to provide the most up-to-date, comprehensive yet widely accessible essays on their individual topics; it has been a pleasure to work with them all.

1
Prehistory in the Mediterranean: The Connecting and Corrupting Sea

A. Bernard Knapp and Emma Blake

Introduction

For many thousands of years, the islands of the Mediterranean Sea and the lands that rim its coasts – from the Iberian Peninsula to the Levant – have nurtured some of the world's most diverse human cultures, and spawned an array of cultural developments that reverberate to the present day. The Mediterranean Sea's impact on human societies has had multiple and unpredictable consequences. For those with the strength and wherewithal, the sea has facilitated the movement of people, ideas, ideologies, technologies, and objects. The settlers in the Mediterranean have reaped the benefits of the region's rich and varied natural resources, permitting economic development and resulting in diverse, complex social systems as well as artistic and cultural achievements. In the popular imagination, the Mediterranean's absorption into the classical world in the latter half of the first millennium B.C. constitutes the defining moment in Mediterranean history. Yet this cultural integration is the exception, not the rule. Instead, it is in the periods prior to the spread of Greek and Roman culture that we can observe autonomous regions jostling for position and interacting spontaneously, a pattern that is far more typical of the Mediterranean over its *longue durée*. These earlier periods offer an important counterpoint to the relatively brief period of classical cohesiveness, and are more consistent with the political and cultural plurality of Mediterranean regions today, even if the experience of prehistory and modernity differ in virtually every other respect. The prehistory of the Mediterranean warrants study, then, and our knowledge of it is served by a very rich body of data, even if that richness increasingly has become not just a diminishing but a vanishing resource (Cherry 2003:156–158; Renfrew 2003:312).

Perhaps more readily than any other discipline, archaeology has embraced the Mediterranean as a coherent subject of study (Morris 2003). With archaeology's evidence framed in terms of the distribution of goods and cultures, the data lend themselves to studies of pan-Mediterranean interactions. In contrast, the specificities of ancient textual sources, in terms of language, content, and authorship, tend to generate more localized questions. This readiness to speak in regional terms is attested by publications such as Horden and Purcell's *The Corrupting Sea* (2000) (although the authors are historians); the recent, posthumous publication of Braudel's *The Mediterranean in the Ancient World* (2001); the *Journal of Mediterranean Archaeology*; the annual student-led conference *Symposium on Mediterranean Archaeology* (SOMA – most recently Muskett et al. 2002; Brysbaert et al. 2003); and by various graduate programs and degrees in Mediterranean archaeology within European, British, American, and Australian institutions of higher education.

Such a quest for unity in Mediterranean studies stands at odds with the perspective of Mediterranean anthropologists like Herzfeld (1987; 2001) or Piña-Cabral (1989; 1992), who maintain that the notion of Mediterranean cultural unity implies a "pervasive archaism," a "Mediterraneanism" like Said's (1978) "Orientalism." These social anthropologists thus see the quest for a pan-Mediterranean perspective as folly, making the region's cultures as exotic as those of the Orient. Mediterranean archaeology, on the contrary, increasingly is concerned with the ways that "Oriental" cultures and material culture, ideology, and iconography have impacted on the wider Mediterranean world, whether as the result of "Orientalization" (e.g., Burkert 1992; Morris 1993; Feldman 1998; Riva and Vella, n.d.) or as an example of how distance and access to the "exotic" may have served as sources of social power amongst Mediterranean elites (e.g., Broodbank 1993; Knapp 1998; n.d.).

Far from yielding a revitalized pan-Mediterranean perspective, however, more recent emphases as well as an enormous amount of new information have rendered the region's prehistory a subject far too vast for any single author to master. Recent attempts to synthesize Mediterranean prehistory (e.g., Trump 1980; Mathers and Stoddart 1994; Patton 1996; Bietti Sestieri et al. 2002) were in most respects appropriate for their time, but they are now unsatisfactory for various reasons, whether because they present tedious arrays of cultures and chronology, use a single-minded theoretical orientation stretched too tight to cover the unwieldy data, or simply seem outdated in terms of all the new publications and data that now typify Mediterranean archaeologies. One reaction to this situation has been a trend toward localized studies meant to exemplify a larger Mediterranean context (e.g., Renfrew and Wagstaff 1982; Cherry et al. 1991; Jameson et al. 1994; Barker 1995; Barker and Mattingly 1999–2000; Given and Knapp 2003). Such studies, typically based on regional field surveys, are rich in detail, provide critical sources of basic data, and have become essential for understanding micro-scale variations across the Mediterranean (various papers in Alcock and Cherry 2004). More recently, some Mediterranean archaeologists have undertaken comprehensive studies focused on a single area, whether treating basic cultural history (e.g., Dickinson 1994; Leighton 1999;

Rowland 2001) or analyzing the mechanisms behind specific phenomena of social change (e.g., Chapman 1990; 2003; Perlés 2001; Greenberg 2002; Akkermans and Schwartz 2003; Albanese Procelli 2003).

As Horden and Purcell's (2000) recent volume demonstrates, however, there is also good reason to attempt to conceptualize the heterogeneity of the Mediterranean region in holistic terms, to confront exactly why, despite the enormous variety in social lives and histories ("the differences that resemble"), we are justified in recognizing the Mediterranean as an *entity*, more than simply the southern edge of Europe or the northern edge of Africa (see also Morris 2003). There is a danger in essentializing the concept of the Mediterranean, not least because it has been marginalized by northern Europe in just this way or because, as Herzfeld and Piña-Cabral caution, we risk singularizing the Mediterranean as Europe's "other." Nonetheless, by adopting a carefully nuanced and appropriately theorized stance, we can begin to look beyond the borders that separate Europe and Africa, the Orient and the Occident, Islam and Christianity, and all the other political, social, and cultural divisions that fragment the Mediterranean region. We can examine some of the more embedded links based on commonalities of climate and geography, on social identities and interactions, and on postcolonial *mentalités* that can ultimately serve not only as a source of empowerment for Mediterranean peoples, but also as a rich and varied resource of archaeological research. Archaeologists today have already begun to move beyond these age-old divisions, and are concerned more with the social, material, memorial, and representational aspects of Mediterranean peoples and cultures, with the ways that factions, alliances, and individuals, as well as material culture, play an active role in cultural process and social change (e.g., Faust and Maeir 1999; Broodbank 2000; Robb 2001; Lyons and Papadopoulos 2002; van Dyke and Alcock 2003).

Contributors to this volume confront the notion of a "Mediterranean prehistory" by tacking between specific cultural details and broader themes, emphasizing what may characterize a particular area as "Mediterranean" rather than simply why it is unique. In so doing, we gain new insights into Mediterranean peoples' social identities, gender, and rituals; their monuments, metallurgies, and lithic technologies; their modes of commerce and patterns of rural and town settlement; their museums and cultural legacies. We seek to disentangle what links and distinguishes the prehistoric inhabitants of the Mediterranean, particularly with respect to their material and mental histories. We do so by presenting some of the central debates – theoretical and empirical – in Mediterranean prehistoric archaeology. Perennial questions about the prehistories of the Mediterranean, which revolve around issues of social complexity, trade and interaction, and subsistence practices, are considered in a manner that reflects contemporary interests in, for example, social identity, difference, multivocality, mobility and memory, the politics of archaeology, and the interface between archaeology and the public. Although the various authors emphasize current theoretical concerns, they also engage fully with the material expression of their individual topics, and employ the approaches they deem most appropriate for engaging with those topics.

The History of Prehistory in the Mediterranean

Because of the Mediterranean's immense size and the diversity of cultures it has embraced, the study of Mediterranean archaeology has become a complex enterprise influenced by a rich, if problematic, heritage. There are several major biases that have traditionally colored research on Mediterranean prehistory. These may be understood as binary oppositions along the cardinal axes of East/West and North/South.

Throughout much of the archaeological history of the Mediterranean, emphasis on the grand civilizations of the east overshadowed the multiple and complex cultures in the west and often made "Mediterranean archaeology" synonymous with "Classical archaeology" (Renfrew 1980; 2003:317–318; Snodgrass 1985; 2002; Dyson 1993). While the result was a serious imbalance in the amount of fieldwork and energy invested in the East compared with the West, this classical bias also proved to be detrimental to studying the peoples of earlier prehistory in the East as well: the lack of interest until only very recently in the Greek Paleolithic is a case in point (Runnels 2003). From Italy to the Levant and south to Egypt, Mediterranean archaeology was long associated with the study of fine arts, architecture, and ancient written sources (Akkadian and Hittite; Egyptian hieroglyphic/hieratic; Ugaritic, Hebrew, and Phoenician; Greek and Latin). The ultimate goal was to collect, classify, and describe the relevant archaeological data, to use them as witnesses to corroborate or construct historical scenarios, or simply to covet and admire them as *objets d'art*. These early stages in the history of Mediterranean archaeology were driven not only by 19th-century romantic ideals that reflected and promoted the superiority of Greek and Roman civilizations, but also by modern political developments such as the independence of Greece – and eventually Crete, Cyprus, and the Levant – from the Ottoman Empire (Silberman 1989; Baram and Carroll 2000; MacGillivray 2000; Tatton-Brown 2001).

In the western Mediterranean, by contrast and despite the existence of monuments such as Maltese "temples," Sardinian *nuraghi*, or Balearic *taulas and talayots*, the lack of high Bronze Age cultures such as the Minoan or Mycenaean, or the paucity of exotic Graeco-Roman remains, led to an approach centered on field methodology, problem orientation, cultural histories, and the quest for "explanation in archaeology" (Watson et al. 1984). More recent fieldwork and research have placed the cultures of the western Mediterranean islands and littorals in much sharper relief (e.g., Webster 1996; Balmuth et al. 1997; Tykot et al. 1999; Albanese Procelli 2003; Chapman 2003), permitting a more balanced view of the Mediterranean region as a whole.

If the East-West divide is slowly being resolved, the North-South divide has only become stronger. With Egypt as a unique exception, political and economic conditions in North Africa have limited opportunities for communication and exchange between North African archaeologists and those working elsewhere in the Mediterranean. Although foreign projects are not unknown, only native archaeologists working year round can be expected to produce data in sufficient quantities to fill out the picture of North Africa's indigenous peoples. The problem is compounded in that research agendas favor specific areas such as the rock art of nomadic Stone Age populations, or Phoenician and Greek colonies or, of course, Roman settlements, with only limited work on the intervening periods. Examples include the international team excavating Carthage, the Greek colony of Cyrene, and the Roman colony of Sabratha (White 1984; Kenrick 1986; Ennabli 1992). Notable exceptions are two projects carried out in Libya: (1) the Libyan Valley Project (Barker et al. 1996), whose frequent citing points to the potential importance of such projects; and (2) the recently published Fezzan Project (Mattingly 2003). Admittedly, in the desert and some regions of the pre-desert, the nomadic populations collided with the classical world. Yet this was certainly not true along the stretches of fertile coastal plains in modern-day Libya, Tunisia, and Morocco that had long been under cultivation and home to sedentary populations. The commonalities and differences of these groups with their neighbors elsewhere in the Mediterranean need to be explored further. In this regard, we recognize that our volume, too, is weighted toward the North, West, and East.

In both cases, these divides are underpinned by a misplaced and oversimplified emphasis on regional differences, between the East and the West in the past, and between the North and the South in the present. While there are unquestionably observable differences between, say, the early states of the Bronze Age Aegean and Levant, and the segmentary societies of southern France, scholarship has reached a stage where the diversity of lifestyles and material culture between groups within both the West and the East is far more relevant intellectually than those broad and thick-grained distinctions. Similarly, the cultural differences that separate Europe and Africa in the present day are projected back onto the past with little justification (see Mahjoubi 1997:18). Emil Ludwig's (1942:x) comment that "To the life of the Mediterranean, the Acropolis is more important than the whole history of Morocco," although sixty years old, is starkly emblematic of the sentiments still to be overcome. The southern littoral was inhabited by peoples who, like their neighbors to the north, were harvesting crops after the summer droughts, harnessing the strength of the sea, making and decorating pottery, honoring their dead with megalithic tombs: in short, confronting and adapting to the same fundamentals of Mediterranean life. The differences that matter are not North-South, but in this case between what is Mediterranean and what is not as we move further south into the Sahara, and as the influence of the sea wanes.

This brings us to a discussion of the Mediterranean Sea itself. Before we discuss in fuller detail some of the thematic and theoretical issues that unify this volume and, we believe, justify our view of the Mediterranean as a coherent spatial, cultural, and archaeological entity, we offer an overview of the Mediterranean and its physical environment. The Mediterranean landscape is one that, throughout many millennia, has been impacted by, as much as it has impacted upon, the peoples who have lived, worked, worshiped, and died there.

The Mediterranean

With an area of 2.5 million square kilometers, the Mediterranean is the world's largest inland sea. Its present configuration would have been recognizable already five million years ago, when the Atlantic Ocean finally and irreversibly broke through the land barrier that previously linked modern-day Morocco with Spain. The boundaries of the Mediterranean Sea, therefore, are clear. But how do we define "The Mediterranean," which is not just a sea but a landscape (and seascape, with islandscapes), a climate, an identity, a way of life, and much more? Most geographies define the Mediterranean region as comprising the countries that border or lie within the Mediterranean Sea, but many of these lands extend in part to, or even identify themselves as part of, other, non-Mediterranean regions: for example, France with northern Europe; Serbia with the Danube Basin; Algeria with the Sahara Desert; Syria with the Middle East. How "Mediterranean" is Slovenia with its approximately five-kilometer foothold on the (Adriatic) Sea? Portugal, while primarily Mediterranean in climate and culture, borders the Atlantic, not the Mediterranean (King et al. 1997:2–3).

In UNESCO's "Blue Plan" for economic and social planning in the countries that border or lie within the Mediterranean, with its particular emphasis on the sea and on factors that affect its coasts (e.g., urbanization, water supply, tourism), the Mediterranean is defined on the basis of both hydrological and administrative criteria (see maps in Grenon and Batisse 1989:18–19). Although these criteria produce different boundaries for the Mediterranean region, each results in a strip showing a great deal of variation in width both within and between modern-day countries. For example, using hydrological criteria (fresh water sources, land-based pollution, local coastal topography), Italy lies almost entirely within and Libya virtually without the Mediterranean. Using administrative criteria (the coastal divisions of each nation), only the island nations of Cyprus and Malta lie entirely within the Mediterranean; the only countries with a major portion of their land areas in the Mediterranean are Greece and Italy; most of Turkey, France, Spain, and the countries along the north African littoral, excepting Tunisia, lie beyond the Mediterranean.

One interesting, and archaeologically relevant, way to imagine the Mediterranean is to consider the distribution of its characteristic plant regimes. These include trees such as the Aleppo pine, the Holm oak, the olive, the pistachio, the fig, and the carob; the grape vine (although now cultivated much farther afield); and the ubiquitous shrub, maquis (distribution maps of the first four are provided in King et al. 1997:6–7). The vine and the olive, along with the fig, form part of the "Mediterranean triad"; Renfrew (1972:480–482) regarded the domestication of the olive and vine as instrumental in the "emergence of civilization" in the Cycladic islands during the third millennium B.C.

The olive is perhaps the most emblematic feature of the Mediterranean landscape. Dependent on summer droughts, able to find moisture in the most rugged limestone soils, sturdy enough to endure for centuries and still produce fruit, and with its silvery-green leaves perennially ruffling against a backdrop of terra rossa soils and the deep blue sea, the olive is the quintessential symbol of "the Mediterranean" (Brun 2003). Indicative, perhaps, of cultural stability, or at least of environmental continuity, or both, the olive provides the basis of the Mediterranean diet (along with, traditionally, salt and fish). If it is not the single most definitive criterion of the Mediterranean, certainly it is a key feature of most Mediterranean landscapes, Mediterranean lifestyles, and the Mediterranean "experience." Thus it lies at the interface between Mediterranean peoples and their environment (King et al. 1997:4). Indeed, the olive and its distinctive, aromatic oil embody the intimate relationship between people and the land and sea, so that what was artificial – the domestication of the olive and its introduction throughout the Mediterranean Basin – is at once so ingrained as to become natural. The Mediterranean landscape as we know it is a naturalized cultural construct, and thus there can be no peeling back of the olive trees and the like to reach a pure Mediterranean landscape. The olive, therefore, can be said suitably to characterize the social approaches to the study of Mediterranean landscapes and material culture adopted by many of the contributors to this volume.

Geologically, the Mediterranean region is dominated by limestone, although major outcrops of igneous rock occur on Cyprus, Sicily, Sardinia, and Corsica. Coastal plains typically are narrow, while mountains of complex and fragmented relief often rise directly from the coast (McNeill 1992). Tectonically, unstable mountain chains, old and rigid tablelands, and younger sedimentary rocks infrequently clash, which accounts for both the devastating impact of earthquakes throughout the Mediterranean, and the intensity of volcanic activity in southern Italy and the Aegean. In terms of climate, hot and very dry summers – one of the defining characteristics of the Mediterranean – are offset by mild winters, when rain falls sporadically (but on occasion, savagely, like the 192 millimeters of rain that fell in four hours and inundated the Larnaca region, in Cyprus, during the autumn of 1981). Mediterranean vegetation is one of the most original in the world: over half the 25,000 plant species that thrive there are endemic to the region (Grenon and Batisse 1989:8; King et al. 1997:8). Dominated by light woodlands and – where woodlands have been cleared – by maquis or garrigue, Mediterranean regional landscapes are as richly variegated as the human cultures that often have overgrazed, intensively plowed and deforested them. Soils tend to be very thin, and highly calcareous, usually lacking in groundwater. The lack of groundwater is in fact critical, particularly on the islands. The destructive force of soil erosion, whether natural or human-induced, adversely affects a multitude of cultural as well as natural landscapes throughout the Mediterranean. Heavy autumn or winter rains contribute to major soil losses, particularly in southern Greece, the Aegean islands, and Turkey, in southeast Spain, and all along the Levantine and North African coasts.

Nonetheless, the islands and coasts of the Mediterranean enjoy a moderate climate, an abundance and variety of mineral resources, and a cornucopia of plants and animals, all of which made the region very attractive for human settlement. The sea itself, virtually tideless and comparatively calm, typically has facilitated rather than precluded human migration and trade, although seasonal currents constrained the timing of sea travel and were forces to be reckoned with. Myth and history – as well as archaeology – bear witness to its periodic storms and dangerous currents: for example, the shipwreck of St. Paul, or the thousands of shipwrecks documented by underwater archaeologists (Parker 1992), or the currents of Scylla and Charybdis, whose tempest wily Odysseus fought to overcome. Ancient and modern mariners alike have always been wary of coastal currents and prevailing winds, offshore reefs and inshore rocks, and conscious of the need to have in store a repertoire of suitable landfalls (Altman 1988; Pryor 1988:12–24).

Most Mediterranean landscapes reveal starkly the heavy imprint of occupancy and exploitation. Human settlement, plant cultivation, and stock-grazing have contributed a great deal to the degraded landscapes that characterize many Mediterranean countries today. Thin soils, steep slopes, a vegetation vulnerable to fire, and unpredictable seasonal rainfalls all made Mediterranean ecosystems very vulnerable to human impact. The complex and dynamic interplay between cultural and environmental factors has resulted in the Mediterranean landscape so recognizable today, as well as the prehistoric landscapes we seek to conceptualize and reconstruct.

Along the littorals of the Mediterranean, especially in the east and in North Africa, some of the earliest-known "modern" humans had already settled some 100,000 years ago (Bar-Yosef and Pilbeam 2000; Lordkipanidze et al. 2000; Shea 2001). On the Mediterranean islands, recent archaeological data from Sardinia, Sicily, and Cyprus indicate that people first arrived about 12,000 years ago, and in so doing helped to drive the islands' "mini-mega fauna" (e.g., pygmy hippos and elephants, giant swans and dormice) to extinction (e.g., Cherry 1990:194–197; Vigne 1999; Simmons 2001). Reversing previous notions about the prolonged coexistence on the Balearic islands of *Myotragus Balearicus* (a small, antelope-like ruminant) with humans, a recent study (Ramis et al. 2002) argues that those islands were only settled about 4,000 years ago; thus *Myotragus* was hunted to extinction just as quickly as its counterparts elsewhere on the Mediterranean islands. Most Mediterranean lands, including the smaller islands, had been settled by the Bronze Age (after about 3000 B.C.), when the dynamics of environmental-cultural interrelations had already produced a recognizable Mediterranean landscape, about the same time that complex societies emerged in the region. Although the long history of settled life in the Mediterranean does not end there, the scope of the chapters in this volume is limited to prehistory, and to the problems and prospects that emerged during that dynamic period of development in "The Mediterranean." We turn now to more detailed consideration of these issues.

Mediterranean Archaeology: Thematic and Theoretical Issues

The scope of this volume spans the Neolithic through the Iron Ages, with some chapters reaching back into the Paleolithic. The format of an edited volume permits the breadth of expertise and plurality of vision lacking in a single-author volume, and indeed, as mentioned earlier, the topic is in any case too vast to be treated by any single author. Each chapter covers one of the major themes in the study of Mediterranean prehistory, blending both concrete examples and more general viewpoints. In each case, we have left the author's voice and perspective intact, in order to immerse the reader in the vocabulary and debates surrounding these topics. There is no attempt at total coverage, but instead the authors highlight the key issues surrounding their subject, drawing on salient concrete examples from throughout the region. Certain areas of the Mediterranean receive fuller treatment than others. Rather than attempt to standardize the chronological terminology, we have left it to the authors to provide the dates for individual regions, to demonstrate the variation in temporal periods. The result is that some regions remain "prehistoric" longer than others, so that the western Mediterranean stays within the volume's purview for centuries after Egypt, Greece, and the Levant have left it.

In order to conceptualize better the complexity of and approaches to prehistoric archaeology in the Mediterranean, we have elected to focus in this introduction only on certain issues. Contributors to this volume were not compelled to consider these issues in their own studies (although many have done so); rather they focused on several themes that give a coherence and unity not only to this volume but to the concept of Mediterranean archaeology. Amongst these issues and themes, we single out the following for discussion:

- insularity and maritime interaction;
- tradition, change and the question of identities;
- unity and diversity;
- cultural heritage in the Mediterranean.

Insularity and maritime interaction

There is a stereotype of Mediterranean cultures as backward and isolated, insular both literally and figuratively. Given that sea travel was in fact easier and quicker than movement overland, and that the sea might facilitate as well as impede travel, this position is untenable. Nevertheless, the boundedness of islands and the sharp separation of the sea underscore the distinctions between regions in a way that travel across land does not. Despite the "success" of island archaeology in furthering our understanding of concepts like insularity and adaptation (e.g., Evans 1973; 1977; Cherry 1981; 1990; Keegan and Diamond 1987; Held 1989; Patton 1996), the time is ripe to reconceptualize them and to develop a socially focused perspective that recognizes how islanders consciously fashion, develop, and change their world; how they establish their identity; and how their identities may change as the result of interaction with other islanders or non-islanders (e.g., Rainbird 1999; Broodbank 2000). As Robb (2001) emphasizes, islands are ideas, inhabited metaphors with natural symbols of boundedness. The concept of insularity must be revisited in the context of broader island-mainland or inter-island relations (Broodbank 2000). It is equally important to consider how distance and the "exotic" serve as symbolic resources as well as the essence of "otherness," how they impact on the movement of people, ideas, iconographies, and materials, and on the ideologies that enabled certain people – social groups, factions, key individuals – to establish and maintain their social position or political power and influence (e.g., Helms 1988; Gilman 1991; Broodbank 1993; Feldman 1998; Knapp 1998). Islands may be much more susceptible to exploitation than mainlands are, but because they encompass the sea they have, potentially, a much greater area to exploit. Insularity, then, is not an absolute, perennially stable, and permanently fixed state of being; rather it is historically contingent and culturally constructed, like island identities themselves. We must attempt to understand islanders from their own perspective, which incorporates both the land and the sea.

Maritime interaction involves communication between distant peoples, and social resources must be evaluated as closely as natural or mineral resources if we wish to gain a better understanding of prehistoric exchange. Although the actors of prehistoric trade remain somewhat invisible, and their ethnic identities obscure, issues of agency and entrepreneurship increasingly permeate the archaeological literature on exchange (e.g., Dietler 1998; Bennet 2001; Stein 2002). Sea trade serves many functions, from purely economic to social and ideological: it might facilitate the transfer of subsistence goods and basic commodities to rural peasants, raw materials to craftspeople, and luxury goods to rulers and elites. Maritime interaction has the potential to transform social structures, motivate political or economic development, and modify individual human needs and actions.

Mediterranean archaeologists increasingly are concerned to examine the interplay between insularity, identity, human settlement, and maritime interaction. Such factors impact on the levels and intensity of contact and mobility between island settlements and their mainland counterparts. Contributors to this volume have considered various aspects of these closely related themes:

- the social dimensions of exchange and the logic of consumption;
- changing perceptions of the sea and maritime commerce as an aspect of social orientation and geographic mobility;
- the roles of travel and geography, as social knowledge, in establishing identity;
- isolation and the avoidance of interaction as a social choice;
- the role of socio-structural change in maritime movements and settlement foundations;
- maritime interactions and the trade in stone and metals.

Tradition, change, and the question of a Mediterranean identity

A popular and romantic tendency seeks to find in the Mediterranean countryside evidence of continuity since the "dawn of time." This approach, usually by non-Mediterraneanists whose views are tainted by a condescension toward the contemporary residents of the countryside as holdovers from a pre-modern time, has been widely critiqued by anthropologists working in the region, particularly for the Orientalist flavor of such positions (Faubion 1993; Just 2000). These scholars have worked to transform this image by demonstrating that the past itself was fraught with change (e.g., Buck Sutton 1988). The present volume continues in this vein, demonstrating that, as the authors separately argue, even the most fundamental components of daily life – subsistence, settlement, religion, gender roles, and the like – underwent major transformations before the classical era.

Those changes that do occur, however, need not constitute a steady path toward progress: as we see time and again, complex societies in the Mediterranean fall as well as rise. One might argue that the very continuities observable in the prehistoric material record, in such elements as stone tool morphologies or ritual practices, offer an important corrective to our understanding of progressive social and cultural change in the Mediterranean. It is through such continuities that scholars of the Mediterranean have sought to understand the long term (Braudel's *longue durée*): the ongoing patterns of Mediterranean lifeways as well as the similarities that transect regional boundaries. The many references to Braudel's work by the authors in this volume speak to his lasting importance in making sense of continuity and change in the region.

These layerings of tradition and innovation intrinsic to Mediterranean communities, past and present, have important implications for how the region's inhabitants see themselves. The discourse of tradition and change is not limited to academics: modern-day residents of Mediterranean cities themselves rely on the notion of timeless and "authentic" rural communities in designing their own self-image, as Herzfeld (1985; 1991) has shown for Greece and Crete. Likewise, underpinning many archaeological discussions of the activities of past Mediterranean peoples is the concept of identity. Positing identities from material remains, however, is notoriously difficult, and there is increasing concern that the cultural labels archaeologists give to material cultural patterning may not have been recognized by those people in the past. We may confidently acknowledge what there is not: there is little question of a unified Mediterranean identity in prehistory. Indeed, even today, people identify themselves by village or town, by island or ethnicity, or by nation; few would label themselves as Mediterranean, except perhaps tacitly, in opposition to non-Mediterranean groups or "northerners."

An interesting exception is the recent adoption of a Mediterranean topos and identity in Israeli public discourse, as a way of conceptualizing Israel as neither "western" nor "oriental" (Shavit 1994). If we acknowledge that identities are devices employed for strategic action, we can understand better that a "Mediterranean identity" will wax and wane, to be applied when necessary. The ingredients for a common Mediterranean identity are there. Currently, however, it is of no practical use to most people in the region to define themselves along those lines. The selective construction of extra-national identities in the Mediterranean revolves around the quest for European identity on the one hand, through membership in the European Union, while, on the other hand, for the countries of North Africa, an Islamic identity prevails. We may imagine a time when it will become important to emphasize a Mediterranean identity, but that time is not yet ripe.

Contributors to this volume have addressed this topic in discussions of:

- the iconography of gendered identities;
- emergent participant identities in ritual settings;
- social transformations in diverse periods and places, both in isolation and through cultural contacts and interaction;
- social aspects of continuity and change in material culture;
- the links between present identities and the material remnants of the Mediterranean past.

Unity and diversity

Horden and Purcell (2000) have rekindled the debate over the tension between Mediterranean cultural unity and diversity. They argue that the Mediterranean region is no longer an intelligible spatial entity, and that most specialized practitioners are incapable of keeping up with Mediterranean-wide developments. In their opinion, geo-historical studies of the wider Mediterranean world, especially those that attempt to treat its status as a coherent spatial or cultural entity, are on the wane. Accordingly, if it is difficult to pinpoint unifying themes in Mediterranean social, cultural, ideological, and historical patterns, Horden and Purcell suggest that perhaps we should regard diversity in another way. To paraphrase them, it is not the resemblances, but the *differences which resemble each other* that matter. Their aim is to challenge simplistic notions of Mediterranean cultural unity – notions that equally concern social anthropologists like Herzfeld and Piña-Cabral (noted above), or archaeologists like Morris (2003) – and instead to consider how divergent forms of variation, similarity, and difference throughout the Mediterranean are interrelated. Horden and Purcell, unfortunately, seem to think that anthropology, lacking historical depth, cannot make a distinctive contribution to studies of "the Mediterranean." As Mediterranean historians, they assign a primacy to documentary studies and the ever-present "text" that goes against the grain of material culture studies specifically, and is somewhat at odds with prehistoric archaeology in the Mediterranean as well.

Mediterranean regional studies and survey archaeology increasingly engage with issues directly relevant to the concept of Mediterranean cultural unity, issues that would repay more focused archaeological attention. These include: peasant studies (e.g., Whitelaw 1991; van Dommelen 1993; Given 2000), colonialism (Lyons and Papadopoulos 2002); gender (e.g., Hamilton 2000; Talalay 2000; this volume; Bolger 2003), social identity (e.g., Sherratt and Sherratt 1998; Blake 1999), agency (Dobres and Robb 2000); ethnicity and *habitus* (e.g., Deitler and Herbich 1998; Frankel 2000; Knapp 2001). In this Mediterranean world of "connectivity," commerce, and mobility (Horden and Purcell 2000:123–172), so close to the sea and the soil alike, people such as farmers, charcoal-burners, miners, and metalsmiths held the direct technological knowledge essential for the production of "primary" commodities like fuels, grains, and metals. Specialist craftspeople had the skills needed to produce "secondary" commodities like pottery, tools, and weapons, and luxury or prestige objects. Raw materials and bulk commodities, like luxury objects, were imbued with social meaning as well as economic value. The social significance of any "commodity" is directly related to its technological and production context, as well as to its spheres of distribution and consumption. Long-term fluctuations in demand or value, and in social or peer-polity relations, ensured that the meanings and cultural perceptions of prestige goods, everyday objects, and even raw materials were constantly changing. From an archaeological perspective it can be argued that the Bronze Age cultures of Europe actively sought exotica from the Mediterranean (Sherratt 1993), while Bronze Age Mediterranean societies regarded the high cultures of the ancient Near East, including Egypt, as distant and exotic (Manning et al. 1994; Knapp 1998, n.d.). The unity, therefore, extends far beyond the rugged basics of survival in a common climate, to the consensual construction of value.

Contributors to this volume have engaged with several issues related to the unity and diversity of prehistoric Mediterranean peoples and cultures:

- commonalities and differences in the social dimensions of trade, mobility, and maritime interaction;
- the lifecycles of peasants and the role of rural economies in prehistoric agriculture;
- changing social identities and social status amongst merchants, mariners, and elites;
- the impact of mobility on social status, modes of trade, and settlement location;
- archaeological perceptions of the known (Mediterranean) vs. the unknown (Orient);
- the emergence of divergence through cultural hybridization (between indigenous island inhabitants and settler-colonists, for example), geographic mobility, etc.;
- commonalities in ritual practices, despite diversity in the belief systems underpinning those practices;
- the diverse nature of social, economic, and artistic contacts;
- iconographies and ideologies of gender;
- social aspects of lithic and metallurgical production and exchange.

The cultural heritage of the Mediterranean

Virtually every country in the Mediterranean enjoys a rich archaeological and cultural heritage and has countless areas deserving of protection, yet beyond their financial reach. The prospects for Mediterranean archaeologies loom large in this area, both in terms of research and more actively in the realm of preserving the cultural legacy of those lands where so much archaeological energy is expended. Yet the Mediterranean cultural heritage is threatened by many common problems (Stanley Price et al. 1996; Stanley Price 2003): natural forces, modern development, tourism, and the potentially disastrous impact of erosion (discussed above, under "The Mediterranean"). The agricultural policies and economic incentives of the European Union have more often exacerbated than alleviated these problems.

The development of modern housing, the building of new roads and canals, and sweeping land reclamation and conversion projects represent the main human-induced threats to the Mediterranean cultural heritage, and thus to the archaeological record. Irrigation strategies, the boring of wells, and the creation of artificial lakes or basins seriously destabilize the natural water tables: in a very short period of time, waterlogged deposits dry out and dry deposits rot. One good result of EU agricultural policies and regulations is that farmers have been forced to leave many fields fallow: when they are no longer plowed they become overgrown, erosion is much reduced, and the archaeological record effectively becomes protected. Somehow all these practices must be re-jigged toward sustainable development without unduly constraining essential agricultural production: this is a vital key to protecting the Mediterranean archaeological heritage.

Preserving the Mediterranean's archaeological heritage increasingly is linked to the development of tourism (Odermatt 1996; Sant Cassia 1999; Urry 2002; Michael n.d.), a tortured issue for archaeology. On the positive side, while tourists themselves are at least gaining a general awareness of the past as a cultural resource, they also provide – often unwittingly – considerable financial resources used to protect or conserve the archaeological record. On the negative side, the increasingly overwhelming number of visitors to heritage sites often results in substantial damage to archaeological remains. Many countries have built paths or walkways to restrict tourist access to archaeological sites. At Altamira in Spain's Cantabria province, for example, the famous Paleolithic caves with striking painted images of bison, deer, and hunters are now permanently closed to the general public, and a facsimile cave has been built as an extension to the site museum in order to satisfy tourist demand. The apparent tourist preference for monumental, often classical remains, now affects many governments' decisions regarding preservation, conservation, or restoration of archaeological sites. In fact, economic conditions in most Mediterranean countries compel government officials to support the development of cultural tourism, which of course limits the amount of resources available for new or continuing fieldwork.

The results are even more far-reaching than simple economics: tourism becomes the arbiter of a site's cultural value. Local populations become habituated to leaving their own heritage to outside market demands instead of engaging with it locally and personally, confusing cultural importance with the number of visitors. The result is that prehistoric sites, with little to show foreign tourists, become even less appreciated by local populations. The alienation of local populations from their prehistoric heritage is sometimes acute. On Malta in 1994, for example, government efforts to fence off the Neolithic temple complexes of Hagar Qim and Mnajdra as an archaeological park interfered with local practices of bird-trapping around the monuments. Vandals responded by spray-painting portions of the monuments with anti-government slogans, apparently perceiving the monuments as obstructions rather than heritage (Grima 1998:41).

Almost all Mediterranean countries now have established heritage legislation. In Cyprus, Syria, Egypt, Tunisia, Algeria, and Morocco, such measures derive from a colonial legacy. In countries such as Italy, Spain, France, and Greece, laws regulating the cultural heritage stem from a long-standing national tradition, dating back to the 19th century. In these latter cases, the law recognizes and protects the archaeological heritage as the primary basis of national pride and unity. For the most part, the focus of legislation and protections fall on monumental remains like the Maltese temples, Sardinian *nuraghi*, the Roman towns of north Africa and the Minoan palaces of Crete, or on precious art objects. Less prominent structures or sites tend to be ignored and many have been destroyed, whether accidentally or willfully, in the course of development. Such a focus on monuments has led to somewhat piecemeal protection, and as a result many archaeological landscapes are still being devastated while others have been completely destroyed.

For the countries of the northern Mediterranean, EU legislation has begun to reverse this situation: for example, the Valetta convention promotes European-wide legislation on the monitoring, documentation, and protection of the archaeological record in the face of ongoing modern development throughout Europe, including the Mediterranean. The sponsorship of well-designed field projects, equipped to analyze past systems of land use and agricultural practice, perhaps offers a more proactive way of preserving the Mediterranean's archaeological heritage. Of the many projects that might be cited, we note two that have been completed and published in exemplary fashion: (1) the UNESCO-sponsored "Libyan Valleys Project" (Barker et al. 1996) which examined farming methods in the semi-desert of Libya during the pre-Roman and Roman period; and (2) the EU-sponsored "Archaeomedes" project (Castro et al. 2000) which assessed how ongoing desertification processes in the Vera Basin of southeast Spain are related to past human activities.

The End of the Mediterranean?

Horden and Purcell frequently refer to the "End of the Mediterranean" (e.g., 2000:39–43). By this they mean the end of its study as an intelligible unity, not the end of active and dynamic research and fieldwork in Mediterranean archaeology and Mediterranean history (e.g., Abulafia 2003). Scholars involved in the study of the Mediterranean past, however, must bear in mind that their highly specialized areas of research become much more relevant when contextualized within the multicultural world of Mediterranean archaeologies. From Gibraltar in the west to the Levantine shores in the east, from the mountain chains that shadow the littorals of the northern Mediterranean to the Maghreb's Atlas Mountains and the desert cultures that lie in such close proximity to the Mediterranean's southern shores, to all the islands in the midst of this corrupting and connecting sea, there has always seemed to be limitless scope for Mediterranean archaeologies to flourish and expand.

But as we ponder the current and future role of archaeology in the Mediterranean, we must consider how we will become involved in, and react to, wider, very pressing social concerns. Archaeology as a discipline needs to respond positively and responsibly to the social and political institutions, and to the diverse public – from tourists to enthusiastic amateurs to wary taxpayers – who support archaeology and provide its relevance as well as its justification. The past is no longer the exclusive domain of institutionally situated historians and archaeologists and, as already noted, some concerned Mediterranean archaeologists (Cherry 2003: 156–158; Renfrew 2003: 312) now regard its material heritage as increasingly threatened. Their view is not without reason, and it is borne out of long experience.

Anyone who has been involved in regional field projects in the Mediterranean over the past 20–30 years cannot have failed to see how traditional, rural landscapes have become transformed by human migrations, the tourist industry, and non-sustainable "development," all issues discussed above (under "Cultural heritage"). Cherry's (2003:157) prediction of the likely ". . . near-total annihilation of the archaeological record everywhere over the period from about 1950 to 2050" is indeed dire, but it is one about which many archaeologists – particularly those whose vision remains focused on the excavation of major "sites" (e.g., Tringham 2003) – seem blissfully unaware. Given the vast number and variety of archaeological sites in the Mediterranean, and the always finite resources available for their curation and conservation, as a discipline we must decide whether and to what extent such sites should continue to be excavated, how to preserve the rapidly changing landscapes of which such sites form only one part, and how to expand the ways in which we undertake archaeological research beyond the field and without the spade. If ours is the last generation to enjoy the luxury of access to what has always seemed to be the inexhaustible and resplendent archaeological record of the Mediterranean world, then we have immediate and pressing obligations to our students, our colleagues, the public who support us, and most crucially to the future of archaeology.

The archaeological heritage of the Mediterranean world forms an irreplaceable aspect of the social memory, historical identity, and national pride of its diverse peoples, communities, and states. Regional survey projects in the Mediterranean have made major strides in documenting the landscapes and monuments that embrace this heritage and give material witness to local memory and identity. But they have perhaps been less successful in their overall attitude and response to local concerns and practices, and especially to the alternative, often contradictory and "unscientific" narratives, myths, and voices expressed by local people to explain their own past, and to help them understand the material and spatial settings in which they live. As Cherry (2003:158–159) argues forcefully, we need to develop a more responsible, less appropriating Mediterranean archaeology for the future.

REFERENCES

Abulafia, David, ed., 2003 The Mediterranean in History. Los Angeles: Getty Publications.
Akkermans, Peter M. M. M. G., and Glenn M. Schwartz, eds., 2003 The Archaeology of Syria: From Complex Hunter-Gatherers to Early Urban Societies (ca. 16,000–300 B.C.). Cambridge: Cambridge University Press.

Albanese Procelli, Rosa Maria, 2003 Sicani, siculi, elimi: forme di identità, modi di contatto e processi di trasformazione. Biblioteca di Archeologia 33. Milan: Longanesi.

Alcock, Susan E., and John F. Cherry, eds., 2004 Side-by-Side Survey: Comparative Regional Studies in the Mediterranean World. Oxford: Oxbow.

Altman, A., 1988 Trade between the Aegean and the Levant in the Late Bronze Age: Some Neglected Questions. *In* Society and Economy in the Eastern Mediterranean (ca.1500–1000 B.C.). Michael Heltzer and Edward Lipínski, eds. pp. 229–237. Orientalia Lovaneinsia Analecta 23. Leuven: Peeters.

Balmuth, Miriam S., Antonio Gilman, and Lourdes Prados-Torreira, eds., 1997 Encounters and Transformations: The Archaeology of Iberia in Transition. Monographs in Mediterranean Archaeology 7. Sheffield: Sheffield Academic Press.

Baram, Uzi, and Linda Carroll, eds., 2000 A Historical Archaeology of the Ottoman Empire: Breaking New Ground. New York: Kluwer Academic/Plenum.

Barker, Graeme, 1995 A Mediterranean Valley: Landscape Archaeology and Annales History in the Biferno Valley. London: Leicester University Press.

Barker, Graeme, and David Mattingly, eds., 1999–2000 The Archaeology of the Mediterranean Landscape. 5 volumes. Oxford: Oxbow.

Barker, Graeme, David Gilbertson, Barri Jones and David Mattingly, eds., 1996 Farming the Desert: The UNESCO Libyan Valleys Archaeological Survey. 2 volumes. Tripoli: UNESCO Publishing, Department of Antiquities.

Bar-Yosef, Ofer, and David Pilbeam, eds., 2000 The Geography of Neanderthals and Modern Humans in Europe and the Greater Mediterranean. Peabody Museum Bulletin 8. Cambridge, Mass.: Peabody Museum of Archaeology and Ethnography.

Bennet, John, 2001 Agency and Bureaucracy: Thoughts on the Nature and Extent of Administration in Bronze Age Pylos. *In* Economy and Politics in the Mycenaean Palace States. Sofia Voutsaki and John Killen, eds. pp. 25–37. Cambridge Philological Society Supplementary Volume 27. Cambridge: Cambridge Philological Society.

Bietti Sestieri, Anna Maria, A. Cazzella and Alain Schnapp, 2002 The Mediterranean. *In* Archaeology: The Widening Debate. Barry Cunliffe, W. Davies and Colin Renfrew, eds. pp. 411–438. Oxford: Oxford University Press/British Academy.

Blake, Emma, 1999 Identity-Mapping in the Sardinian Bronze Age. European Journal of Archaeology 2:35–55.

Bolger, Diane, 2003 Gender in Ancient Cyprus: Narratives of Social Change on a Mediterranean Island. Walnut Creek, CA: AltaMira Press.

Braudel, Fernand (eds. Roselyne de Ayala and Paule Braudel), 2001 The Mediterranean in the Ancient World. London: Allan Lane, Penguin.

Broodbank, Cyprian, 1993 Ulysses Without Sails: Trade, Distance, Knowledge and Power in the Early Cyclades. World Archaeology 24:315–331.

——2000 An Island Archaeology of the Early Cyclades. Cambridge: Cambridge University Press.

Brun, Jean-Pierre, 2003 Le vin et l'huile dans la Méditerranée antique: viticulture, oléiculture et procédés de transformation. Collection des Hespérides. Paris: Errance.

Brysbaert, Ann, Natasja de Bruijn, Erin Gibson, Angela Michael and Mark Monaghan, eds., 2003 SOMA 2002: Symposium on Mediterranean Archaeology. Proceedings of the Sixth Annual Meeting of Postgraduate Researchers, University of Glasgow, 15–17 February 2002. British Archaeological Reports: International Series 1142. Oxford: Archeopress.

Buck Sutton, Susan, 1988 What is a "Village" in a Nation of Migrants? Journal of Modern Greek Studies 6:187–215.

Burkert, Walter, (translated by M. E. Pinder and W. Burkert), 1992 The Orientalising Revolution: Near Eastern Influence on Greek Culture in the Early Archaic Age. Cambridge, Mass.: Harvard University Press.

Chapman, Robert, 1990 Emerging Complexity: The Later Prehistory of South-East Spain, Iberia and the West Mediterranean. Cambridge: Cambridge University Press.

——2003 Archaeologies of Complexity. London: Routledge.

Cherry, John F., 1981 Pattern and Process in the Earliest Colonization of the Mediterranean Islands. Proceedings of the Prehistoric Society 47:41–68.

——1990 The First Colonization of the Mediterranean Islands: A Review of Recent Research. Journal of Mediterranean Archaeology 3:145–221.

——2003 Archaeology Beyond the Site: Regional Survey and its Future. In Theory and Practice in Mediterranean Archaeology: Old World and New World Perspectives. John K. Papadopoulos and Richard M. Leventhal, eds. pp. 137–159. Cotsen Advanced Seminars 1. Los Angeles: Cotsen Institute of Archaeology, UCLA.

Cherry, John F., Jack L. Davis, and Eleni Mantzourani, eds., 1991 Landscape Archaeology as Long-Term History: Northern Keos and the Cycladic Islands from Earliest Settlement until Modern Times. Monumenta Archaeologica 16. Los Angeles: UCLA Institute of Archaeology.

Dickinson, Oliver T.P.K., 1994 The Aegean Bronze Age. Cambridge: Cambridge University Press.

Dietler, Michael, 1998 Consumption, Agency, and Cultural Entanglement: Theoretical Implications of a Mediterranean Colonial Encounter. In Studies in Culture Contact: Interaction, Culture Change, and Archaeology. Center for Archaeological Investigations, Occasional Paper 25. James G. Cusick, ed. pp. 288–315. Southern Illinois University Press: Carbondale, Illinois.

Dobres, Marcia-Anne, and John Robb, eds., 2000 Agency in Archaeology. London: Routledge.

Dyson, Stephen L., 1993 From New to New Age Archaeology: Archaeological Theory and Classical Archaeology – A 1990s Perspective. American Journal of Archaeology 97:195–206.

Ennabli, Abdelmajid, ed., 1992 Pour sauver Carthage: Exploration et conservation de la cité Punique, Romaine et Byzantine. Paris: Unesco/INAA.

Evans, John D., 1973 Islands as Laboratories for the Study of Culture Process. In The Explanation of Culture Change: Models in Prehistory. Colin Renfrew, ed. pp. 517–520. London: Duckworth.

——1977 Island Archaeology in the Mediterranean: Problems and Opportunities. World Archaeology 9:12–26.

Faubion, James D., 1993 Modern Greek Lessons. A Primer in Historical Constructivism. Princeton: Princeton University Press.

Faust, Avraham, and Aren M. Maeir, 1999 Material Culture, Society and Ideology. Tel Aviv: Bar-Ilan University.

Feldman, Marian H., 1998 Luxury Goods from Ras Shamra-Ugarit and Their Role in the International Relations of the Eastern Mediterranean during the Late Bronze Age. Unpublished PhD thesis, Harvard University, Department of Fine Arts.

Frankel, David, 2000 Migration and Ethnicity in Prehistoric Cyprus: Technology as habitus. European Journal of Archaeology 3(2):167–187.

Gilman, Antonio, 1991 Trajectories Towards Social Complexity in the Later Prehistory of the Mediterranean. In Chiefdoms: Power, Economy, and Ideology. Timothy K. Earle, ed. pp. 146–168. Cambridge: Cambridge University Press.

Given, Michael, 2000 Agriculture, Settlement and Landscape in Ottoman Cyprus. Levant 32:209–230.

Given, Michael, and A. Bernard Knapp, 2003 The Sydney Cyprus Survey Project: Social Approaches To Regional Archaeological Survey. Monumenta Archaeologica 21. Los Angeles: Cotsen Institute of Archaeology, UCLA.

Greenberg, Raphael, 2002 Early Urbanizations in the Levant: A Regional Narrative. London and New York: Leicester University Press.

Grenon, M., and M. Batisse, 1989 Futures for the Mediterranean Basin. Oxford: Oxford University Press.

Grima, Reuben, 1998 Ritual Spaces, Contested Places: The Case of the Maltese Prehistoric Temple Sites. Journal of Mediterranean Studies 8(1):33–45.

Hamilton, Naomi, 2000 Ungendering Archaeology: Concepts of Sex and Gender in Figurine Studies In Prehistory. *In* Representations of Gender from Prehistory to the Present. Moira Donald and Linda Hurcombe, eds. pp. 17–30. London: Macmillan.

Held, Steve O., 1989 Colonization Cycles on Cyprus: The Biogeographic and Paleontological Foundations of Early Prehistoric Settlement. Report of the Department of Antiquities, Cyprus: 7–28.

Helms, Mary W., 1988 Ulysses' Sail: An Ethnographic Odyssey of Power, Knowledge and Geographical Distance. Princeton: Princeton University Press.

Herzfeld, Michael, 1985 The Poetics of Manhood: Contest and Identity in a Greek Mountain Village. Princeton: Princeton University Press.

——1987 'As in Your Own House': Hospitality, Ethnography, and the Stereotype of Mediterranean Society. *In* Honor and Shame and the Unity of the Mediterranean. David D. Gilmore, ed. pp. 75–89. American Anthropological Association, Special Publication 22. Washington, DC: AAA.

——1988 Anthropology Through the Looking Glass: Critical Ethnography in the Margins of Europe. Cambridge: Cambridge University Press.

——1991 A Place in History: Social and Monumental Time in a Cretan Town. Princeton: Princeton University Press.

——2001 Performing Comparisons: Ethnography, Globetrotting, and the Spaces of Social Knowledge. Journal of Anthropological Research 57:259–276.

Horden, Peregrine, and Nicholas Purcell, 2000 The Corrupting Sea: A Study of Mediterranean History. Oxford: Blackwell.

Jameson, Michael H., Curtis N. Runnels and Tjeerd H. Van Andel, 1994 A Greek Countryside: The Southern Argolid from Prehistory to the Present Day. Stanford: Stanford University Press.

Just, Roger, 2000 A Greek Island Cosmos: Kinship and Community on Meganisi. Santa Fe: School of American Research Press.

Keegan, William F., and Jared M. Diamond, 1987 Colonization of Islands by Humans: A Biogeographical Perspective. *In* Advances in Archaeological Method and Theory 10. Michael B. Schiffer, ed. pp. 49–92. San Diego: Academic Press.

Kenrick, Philip M., 1986 Excavations at Sabratha 1948–1951. London: The Society for the Promotion of Roman Studies.

King, Russel, Lindsay Proudfoot and Bernard Smith, eds., 1997 The Mediterranean: Environment and Society. London: Arnold.

Knapp, A. Bernard, 1998 Mediterranean Bronze Age Trade: Distance, Power and Place. *In* The Aegean and the Orient in the Second Millennium: Proceedings of the 50th Anniversary Symposium, Cincinnati 18–20 April 1997. Eric H. Cline and Diane Harris-Cline, eds. pp. 260–280. Aegaeum 18. Liège: Université de Liège.

——2001 Archaeology and Ethnicity: A Dangerous Liaison. Archaeologia Cypria 4:29–46.

——n.d. Orientalization and Prehistoric Cyprus: The Social Life of Oriental Goods. *In* Orientalization in Antiquity. Corinna Riva and Nicholas Vella, eds. Monographs in Mediterranean Archaeology 10. London: Equinox Press.

Leighton, Robert, 1999 Sicily Before History: An Archaeological Survey from the Palaeolithic to the Iron Age. London: Duckworth.

Lordkipanidze, D., Ofer Bar-Yosef and M. Otte, eds., 2000 Early Humans at the Gate of Europe. Etudes et recherches archeologiques de l'Université de Liège 92. Liège: Université de Liège.

Ludwig, Emil, 1942 The Mediterranean: Saga of a Sea. New York: McGraw-Hill Book Co.

Lyons, Claire, and John K. Papadopoulos, eds., 2002 The Archaeology of Colonialism. Los Angeles: Getty Research Institute.

MacGillivray, John A., 2000 Minotaur: Sir Arthur Evans and the Archaeology of the Minoan Myth. London: Jonathan Cape.

Mahjoubi, Ammar, 1997 Reflections on the Historiography of the Ancient Maghrib. *In* The Maghrib in Question: Essays in History and Historiography. Michel Le Gall and Kenneth Perkins, eds. pp. 17–34. Austin: University of Texas Press.

Manning, Sturt W., Sarah J. Monks, Georgia Nakou and Frank A. DeMita Jr., 1994 The Fatal Shore, the Long Years and the Geographical Unconscious. Considerations of Iconography, Chronology, and Trade. In Response to Negbi's The "Libyan Landscape" from Thera: A Review of Aegean Enterprises Overseas in the Late Minoan IA Period. Journal of Mediterranean Archaeology 7:219–235.

Mathers, Clay, and Simon Stoddart, eds., 1994 Development and Decline in the Mediterranean Bronze Age. Sheffield Archaeological Monograph 8. Sheffield: John Collis Publications.

Mattingly, David, ed., 2003 The Archaeology of Fezzan. Volume 1: Synthesis. Tripoli: Dept of Antiquities, Society for Libyan Studies.

McNeill, J.R., 1992 The Mountains of the Mediterranean World. Cambridge: Cambridge University Press.

Michael, Angela S., In press Aphrodite's Child: Postcolonialism, Tourism and Archaeology in Cyprus. Archaeological Dialogues.

Morris, Ian, 2003 Mediterraneanization. Mediterranean Historical Review 18(2):30–55.

Morris, Sarah P., 1993 Daidalos and the Origins of Greek Art. Princeton: Princeton University Press.

Muskett, G., A. Koltsida and M. Georgiadis, eds., 2002 SOMA 2001: Symposium on Mediterranean Archaeology. Proceedings of the Fifth Annual Meeting of Postgraduate Researchers, University of Liverpool, 23–25 February 2001. British Archaeological Reports: International Series 1040. Oxford: Archeopress.

Odermatt, Peter, 1996 Built Heritage and the Politics of (Re)presentation: Local Reactions to the Appropriation of the Monumental Past in Sardinia. Archaeological Dialogues 3:95–119.

Parker, Anthony John, 1992 Ancient Shipwrecks of the Mediterranean and the Roman Provinces. British Archaeological Reports: International Series 580. Oxford: Tempus Reparatum.

Patton, Mark, 1996 Islands in Time: Island Sociogeography and Mediterranean Prehistory. London: Routledge.

Perlés, Catherine, 2001 The Early Neolithic in Greece. Cambridge: Cambridge University Press.

Piña-Cabral, Joao de, 1989 The Mediterranean as a Category of Regional Comparison: A Critical View. Current Anthropology 30:399–406.

——1992 The Primary Social Unit in Mediterranean and Atlantic Europe. Journal of Mediterranean Studies 2:25–41.

Pryor, John H., 1988 Geography, Technology, and War: Studies in the Maritime History of the Mediterranean, 649–1571. Cambridge: Cambridge University Press.

Rainbird, Paul, 1999 Islands Out of Time: Towards a Critique of Island Archaeology. Journal of Mediterranean Archaeology 12:216–234, 259–260.

Ramis, Damià, Josep A. Alcover, Jaume Coll, and Miquel Trias, 2002 The Chronology of the First Settlement of the Balearic Islands. Journal of Mediterranean Archaeology 15:3–24.

Renfrew, Colin, 1972 The Emergence of Civilization: The Cyclades and the Aegean in the Third Millennium B.C. London: Methuen.

——1980 The Great Tradition Versus the Great Divide: Archaeology as Anthropology. American Journal of Archaeology 84:287–298.

——2003 Retrospect and Prospect: Mediterranean Archaeology in a New Millennium. In Theory and Practice in Mediterranean Archaeology: Old World and New World Perspectives. John K. Papadopoulos and Richard M. Leventhal, eds. pp. 311–318. Cotsen Advanced Seminars 1. Los Angeles: Cotsen Institute of Archaeology, UCLA.

Renfrew, Colin and Malcolm Wagstaff, eds., 1982 An Island Polity: The Archaeology of Exploitation on Melos. Cambridge: Cambridge University Press.

Riva, Corinna, and Nicholas Vella, eds., n.d. Orientalization in Antiquity. Monographs in Mediterranean Archaeology 10. London: Equinox Press.

Robb, John, 2001 Island Identities: Ritual, Travel and the Creation of Difference in Neolithic Malta. European Journal of Archaeology 4:175–202.

Rowland, Robert J., Jr., 2001 The Periphery in the Center: Sardinia in the Ancient and Medieval Worlds. British Archaeological Reports, International Series 970. Oxford: Archaeopress.

Runnels, Curtis, 2003 The History and Future Prospects of Paleolithic Archaeology in Greece. In Theory and Practice in Mediterranean Archaeology: Old World and New World Perspectives. John K. Papadopoulos and Richard M. Leventhal, eds. pp. 181–193. Cotsen Advanced Seminars 1. Los Angeles: Cotsen Institute of Archaeology, UCLA.

Said, Edward W., 1978 Orientalism. New York: Pantheon.

Sant Cassia, Paul, 1999 Tradition, Tourism and Memory in Malta. Journal of the Royal Anthropological Institute 5:247–263.

Shavit, Yaacov, 1994 Mediterranean History and the History of the Mediterranean: Further Reflections. Journal of Mediterranean Studies 4:313–329.

Shea, John J., 2001 The Middle Paleolithic: Early Modern Humans and Neanderthals in the Levant. Near Eastern Archaeology 64:38–64.

Sherratt, Andrew, and Susan Sherratt, 1998 Small Worlds: Interaction and Identity in the Ancient Mediterranean. In The Aegean and the Orient in the Second Millennium: Proceedings of the 50th Anniversary Symposium, Cincinnati 18–20 April 1997. Eric H. Cline and Diane Harris-Cline, eds. pp. 329–343. Aegaeum 18. Liège: Université de Liège.

Sherratt, Andrew, 1993 What Would a Bronze Age World System Look Like? Relations between Temperate Europe and the Mediterranean in Later Prehistory. Journal of European Archaeology 1(2):1–58.

Silberman, Neil A., 1989 Between Past and Present. Archaeology, Ideology, and National-ism in the Modern Middle East. New York: Doubleday.

Simmons, Alan, 2001 The First Humans and the Last Pygmy Hippopotami of Cyprus. *In* The Earliest Prehistory of Cyprus: From Colonization to Exploitation. Stuart Swiny, ed. pp. 1–18. Cyprus American Archaeological Research Institute, Monograph 2. Boston: American Schools of Oriental Research.

Snodgrass, Anthony M., 1985 The New Archaeology and the Classical Archaeologist. American Journal of Archaeology 89:1–7.

——2002 A Paradigm Shift in Classical Archaeology? Cambridge Archaeological Journal 12:179–194.

Stanley Price, Nicholas, 2003 Site Preservation and Archaeology in the Mediterranean Region. *In* Theory and Practice in Mediterranean Archaeology: Old World and New World Perspectives. John K. Papadopoulos and Richard M. Leventhal, eds. pp. 269–283. Cotsen Advanced Seminars 1. Los Angeles: Cotsen Institute of Archaeology, UCLA.

Stanley Price, Nicholas P., M. K. Talley, and A. M. Vaccaro, eds., 1996 Historical and Philosophical Issues in the Conservation of Cultural Heritage. Malibu, CA: Getty Trust.

Stein, Gil, 2002 From Passive Periphery to Active Agents: Emerging Perspectives in the Archaeology of Interregional Interaction. American Anthropologist 104:903–916.

Talalay, Lauren E., 2000 Archaeological Ms.conceptions: Contemplating Gender and the Greek Neolithic. *In* Representations of Gender from Prehistory to the Present. Moira Donald and Linda Hurcombe, eds. pp. 3–16. London: Macmillan.

Tatton-Brown, Veronica, ed., 2001 Cyprus in the Nineteenth Century B.C.: Fact, Fancy and Fiction. Oxford: Oxbow Books.

Tringham, Ruth, 2003 (Re)-digging the Site at the End of the Twentieth Century: Large-Scale Archaeological Fieldwork in a New Millennium. *In* Theory and Practice in Mediter-ranean Archaeology: Old World and New World Perspectives. John K. Papadopoulos and Richard M. Leventhal, eds. pp. 89–108. Cotsen Advanced Seminars 1. Los Angeles: Cotsen Institute of Archaeology, UCLA.

Trump, David, 1980 The Prehistory of the Mediterranean. London: Allen Lane.

Tykot, Robert H., Jonathan Morter and John E. Robb, eds., 1999 Social Dynamics of the Prehistoric Central Mediterranean. Accordia Specialist Studies on the Mediterranean 3. London: Accordia Research Institute, University of London.

Urry, John, 2002 The Tourist Gaze. London: Sage (second edition; first edition 1990).

van Dommelen, Peter, 1993 Roman Peasants and Rural Organization In Central Italy: An Archaeological Perspective. *In* Theoretical Roman Archaeology: First Conference Pro-ceedings. E. Scott, ed. pp. 167–186. Avebury: Aldershot.

Van Dyke, Ruth M., and Susan E. Alcock, eds., 2003 Archaeologies of Memory. Oxford: Blackwell.

Vigne, Jean-Denis, 1999 The Large "True" Mediterranean Islands as a Model for The Holocene Human Impact on the European Vertebrate Fauna? Recent Data and New Reflections. *In* The Holocene History of the European Vertebrate Fauna. Modern Aspects of Research. N. Benecke, ed. pp. 295–322. Archäologie in Eurasien 6. Berlin: Deutsche Archäologisches Institut, Eurasien-Abteilung.

Watson, Patty Jo, Steven A. LeBlanc, and Charles Redman, 1984 Archaeological Explanation: The Scientific Method in Archaeology. New York: Columbia University Press.

Webster, Gary S., 1996 A Prehistory of Sardinia, 2300–500 B.C. Monographs in Mediter-ranean Archaeology 5. Sheffield: Sheffield Academic Press.

White, Donald, 1984 The Extramural Sanctuary of Demeter and Persephone at Cyrene, Libya Final Reports, Volume I: Background and Introduction to the Excavations. Philadelphia: The University Museum, University of Pennsylvania.

Whitelaw, Todd M., 1991 The Ethnoarchaeology of Recent Rural Settlement and Land Use in Northwest Keos. *In* Landscape Archaeology as Long-Term History: Northern Keos in the Cycladic Islands from Earliest Settlement until Modern Times. John F. Cherry, Jack L. Davis and Eleni Mantzourani, eds. pp. 403–454. Monumenta Archaeologica 16. Los Angeles: UCLA Institute of Archaeology.

2

Substances in Motion: Neolithic Mediterranean "Trade"

John E. Robb and R. Helen Farr

Introduction

"Trade" is an archaeological category, not an ethnographic one. It is a convenient rubric we use to discuss things moving between people, places, and groups in the past. The social mechanisms through which things circulated, however, probably rarely corresponded to our modern concept of "trade" as a disembedded, free exchange of goods. Every society, including our own, has many social mechanisms for circulating goods, ranging from avowedly utilitarian exchange to gifts and oblig- atory social presentations to marriage payments, compensation payments, inheri- tance, ritual transfers, and even disposal, scavenging, and recycling. In our capitalistic society, a commodity's transition from the "public" to the "private" sphere is accompanied by a change in modes of transaction from sale to gift; each form of transaction has its own rules, expectations, and etiquette. The famous kula cycle through which men obtained shell ornaments was only one of a number of exchange systems in Trobriand society; goods were also circulated through women's trade in clothing and foodstuffs, through a more open inter-island trade in pottery and foodstuffs, through missionaries and colonial administrators, and through inter- family redistribution and payments from commoners to chiefs in yams and other foodstuffs (Malinowski 1922; Weiner 1988). In many if not most forms of exchange, the item itself is often less important than the social relationship it creates or sig- nifies (Mauss 1990). Moreover, specific trade systems have historical trajectories on a scale of centuries, against which particular exchanges must be understood (Wiessner and Tumu 1998).

Mediterranean prehistorians have rarely dealt with trade anthropologically, that is, with a focus on social relations established through the transfer of items rather than on the objects themselves. By far most of the relevant work has been con- ducted by means of characterization studies for establishing the exotic origin of archaeological finds – portraying trade as abstract arrows on the maps. The social context of trade is not commonly discussed: most of the traded artifacts studied have been divorced from their archaeological setting, and it has generally been assumed that the social value of exotic items, tools, and raw materials was self-evident and related to their functional use. We have lost the human stories of lives being lived, journeys made, and social relations established. Only in some situations is this due to the limitations of the archaeological record; transported materials offer some of the most vivid and immediate insights into human actions if our archaeological imagination permits us to see them.

This discussion focuses on the Neolithic, conventionally defined as the period from the adoption of farming through the introduction of metals in the Copper or Bronze Ages. Although both these boundaries are more ambiguous and the chronological limits vary both according to archaeological asynchronies and to national traditions of scholarship, the period runs from some point in the seventh millennium B.C. through the early to mid third millennium B.C. Here, we begin with a brief discussion of the meaning of space in the Neolithic Mediterranean. We then review the archaeology of traded substances and trade-related places before focusing in more detail on several relatively well-contextualized trade systems, including obsidian, axes, and the use of trade in constructing local identities. There are many important questions we simply cannot answer using the data currently available, even with the best-studied trade systems. The archaeological literature on "trade," however, does provide an entrée into some of the disparate and intriguing range of institutions that must have existed in the Neolithic.

Neolithic Geography, Space, and Travel

Any account of the circulation of materials in the Neolithic world must begin by considering Neolithic social space. Space is relative to the physical and social possibilities for traversing it and what we consider archaeologically as "trade" may often be a by-product of travel and interaction undertaken for other purposes. Here, it is not possible to ignore the influence of the Mediterranean landscape. In considering it, we need to see beyond recent historical change. On land, agriculture and pastoral extensification and intensification have resulted in gradual but substantial environmental change through the Holocene. Deforestation and land reclamation in recent centuries have increased erosion, aridity, soil loss, and alluviation. Postglacial sea-level rise and local tectonic processes have changed coastlines (Pirazzoli 1996; Lambeck 1996), an effect most marked on shallow shelving coasts such as the Aegean and the upper Adriatic.

The sea has been an important avenue for communication and trade since the initial spread of Impressed Wares, which appear rapidly between 6200 and 5500 B.C. all around the northern Mediterranean coast from Corfu and Croatia to Sicily, Liguria, southern France, and Mediterranean Spain (Price 2000). Evidence of Neolithic boats in the Mediterranean is sparse. The earliest known boats from Italy are dugout canoes or log boats, found at the submerged mid-sixth millennium site of La Marmotta on Lake Bracciano near Rome (Fugazzola Delpino, et al. 1993). While these log boats provide an example of inland water transport, equally simple vessels of reeds or logs would have been used on coastal waters. As there is no evidence for sailing anywhere in this period – the earliest existing evidence for sails does not appear until ca. 3100 B.C. in the very particular context of the River Nile (Johnstone 1980:76) – it is likely that these early boats would have been paddled.

The idiosyncratic Mediterranean landscape and seascape, with island chains, archipelagos, and complex coastlines, enabled maritime travel and exploration from the middle Paleolithic onward (Broodbank 1999; Cherry 1981). Early exchange of raw materials is seen in the Melos obsidian found in pre-Neolithic levels at Franchthi Cave and dated around 11,000 B.C. The importance of geography is clearest if we assume, as is usually done, that Neolithic sailors typically traveled within sight of land. Distributions of obsidian (Robb and Tykot 2002) and material culture styles suggest that sailing routes remained within coastal envelopes where possible, though mariners were not afraid to tackle open water (for instance when crossing from Sicily to Pantelleria). The broadest contrast is between the eastern Mediterranean, where the Aegean island chains provide ample opportunities for travel networks, and the western Mediterranean, in which long peninsulas, few large islands, and greater expanses of open water led to the development of a few important "trunk routes."

Stretches of water should not be viewed solely as boundaries or obstacles for trade and exchange but equally as corridors for movement: as Grahame Clark (1965:5) noted long ago, "water presented no barrier, but on the contrary a ready medium for transport." Seafaring provided easy contact with coastal groups, perhaps easier than traversing mountains and valleys when traveling overland. Yet navigational considerations mean that the sea may be described as having a terrain or topography with passes and routes in the same way as the land has mountain passes and impasses. Not all waterways present equal accessibility at all times of the year, month, or even day, due to weather conditions, prevailing winds, currents, and tides. To take one example, a relatively short journey from Calabria across the Straits of Messina to Lipari, an important obsidian source (see below), would probably have been undertaken in the summer when the sea was calmer and weather conditions predictable. Coming from the east, crossing the Straits of Messina required travelers to deal with complex combinations of local currents and tides, exacerbated by funneling winds from the north. Mariners would have needed detailed knowledge of local conditions to judge when to proceed with crossing the strait and continuing on to Lipari; as the southward currents can run faster than a northbound vessel could be paddled, timing was crucial. Although the distances involved are small, allowing time for navigational indirectionalities, social encounters, and obsidian procurement, a trip from southern Calabria to Lipari could have taken several weeks, presumably during slack periods in the calendar of other activities (Farr 2001). Such a trip would have involved negotiating considerable uncertainties. It is a testimony to the knowledge and skill of Neolithic mariners that similar journeys were undertaken right across the Mediterranean throughout the Neolithic.

In considering travel, therefore, we need to consider geographical knowledge and social interaction as well as the mechanical means of transport. This is less readily investigated for land travel. The distribution of material culture often gives an indication of communication networks, and this in fact justifies to some extent the definition of the Mediterranean as a cultural zone. Horden and Purcell (2000) stress the fragmented yet interconnected nature of Mediterranean landscapes. The north coast of the Mediterranean is largely surrounded by rugged mountain ranges, and in Neolithic times Mediterranean France was generally linked culturally to Catalonia and Liguria rather than to central and northern France, just as coastal Croatia, Bosnia, Montenegro, and Albania typically share a coastal culture distinct from the inland Balkans. Mountain passes were sometimes desirable locations (for instance La Starza in Campania where a pass over the Apennines was occupied throughout the entire prehistoric sequence – Trump 1963).

If we are to try to understand travel in the Neolithic, it is important to be aware of our present-day notions of distance, time, and accessibility (Broodbank 2000:41); an appropriate prehistoric map would presumably require stretching and warping geography to represent travel time rather than invariant spatial relations. Both on land and sea, knowledge, spatial awareness, and navigation would have been key. Knowledge of our surroundings is gained through our perception of the landscape influenced by our existing knowledge. Especially in seafaring, where decisions must constantly be updated due to changing conditions, knowledge and skill can be seen as socially constructed and influenced. Yet the question remains as to how prehistoric people navigated across stretches of unknown land or water without maps. Bourdieu (noted in Gell 1985) uses the concept of practical mastery theory to describe familiarity with subjective practical space as opposed to objective Cartesian space. We must imagine that through oral traditions and collective memories, mental maps of a sequence of memorized images or of an idealized journey as a chain of events could be passed down, combined with external reference points such as landmarks. In the case of navigation, the cues would include knowledge of landscape and seascape (currents, prevailing winds, and wave formations), lunar cycles, star courses, and navigational lore to enable speed, drift, and heading to be reckoned (Farr 2001). For this reason Perlès (1990:26–27) has described seafaring as a specialist occupation "dependent on a minority of movement specialists to obtain non local resources" (though we would argue that such complex knowledge bases could have been maintained within an unspecialized community as well). In addition, the need for fresh water, food, shelter, or personal security may indicate necessary formations of social alliances: travelers were not moving through empty lands. The death of the famous Ice Man Otzi, who was killed by an arrow in the back, may indicate some of the social dangers of travel.

The Archaeology of Substances in Motion

The primary literature for the movement of objects around the Mediterranean in the Neolithic is vast. Archaeologically, chipped stone and axes are the best-understood transported items, but there are many finds of other stone, minerals, pottery, and natural materials being transported from their original sources. Here we can only mention some general outlines; see Perlès (1992b) and Skeates (1993) for more detailed review.

The same basic repertory of materials was transported in most Mediterranean societies: flaked stones such as flint and obsidian, ground stone axes, and a variety of other localized mineral resources such as marine shell, marble, and ochre.

Flint, chert, and obsidian were essential materials that occurred patchily. Spatially, flakable stone was circulated at three distinct geographical scales (Figure 2.1). While poor quality chert is often available even in broad, recently sedimented valleys as river cobbles, outcrops of good quality flint are much more localized and often formed the center of distributional systems ranging over 100 kilometers in radius. In Italy, for example, flint from the Monti Lessini near Verona was traded throughout the Po Valley and up the Alpine valleys; red jasper was circulated widely throughout Liguria; Gargano flint was traded westward to the Apennines and eastward across the central Adriatic islands to Croatia; the Monti Iblei in Sicily provided the major flint source for Malta, eastern Sicily, Lipari, and southernmost Calabria. Elsewhere in Mediterranean Europe a similar system of networks oper-

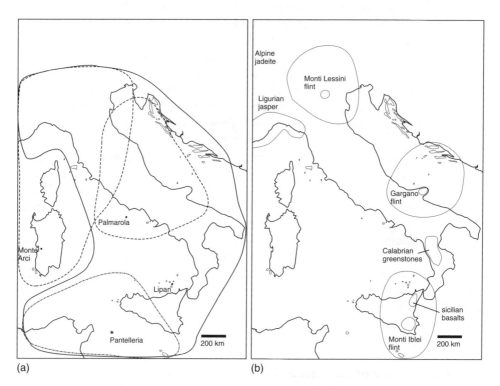

(a)   (b)

Figure 2.1 Some patterns of circulation of raw materials in the Neolithic central Mediterranean. Note that "empty" areas may simply be poorly known archaeologically. (a) Obsidian (after Tykot and Ammerman 1997); (b) Flint and other materials (after Leighton 1992 and other sources)

ated. In France, for example, Cretaceous honey-colored flint from Lombardy was found over 150 kilometers from its source (Binder 2000; cf. Mills 1983); flint in Neolithic Greece circulated in territories of approximately the same size (Perlès 1992b). Finally, obsidian, a geologically distinct natural black glass which occurs only at a few volcanic flows in Europe, was circulated over very long distances (see below).

In some locations, collecting at outcrops was intensified into actual mining. Prehistoric mines are known at Lisbon in Portugal, at Malaucene, Les Esperelles, Vigne du Cade, and Mur-de-Barrez in southern France, and in Italy at Valle Lagorara in Liguria, the Gargano peninsula in Puglia, and Monte Tabuto in Sicily (Di Lernia and Galiberti 1993: figure 24). While flint mines in Europe generally seem to be a Late Neolithic phenomenon – for instance the Millaran culture mines in southeastern Spain (Millán et al. 1991) – at least some mines such as La Defensola on the Gargano were in use from the sixth millennium B.C.

Polished stone tools were used throughout the Mediterranean and traded from the Early Neolithic (for example, Ricq de Bouard and Fedele 1993). Unfortunately, quarry sites per se are generally unknown and relatively little detailed work on axe circulation has been done (in contrast to Britain; cf. Bradley and Edmonds 1993). Typically this rubric includes at least three distinct genres of item: coarse, heavy picks and mauls made from a wide range of local pebbles; carefully shaped and polished axes made of greenstone or other stones such as diorite, rhyolite, and amphibolite; and small trapezoidal adzes and chisels usually made from greenstone. Axes were probably used for clearing land, woodworking, and possibly as hoes for digging, and may have been used in fighting as well. The smaller adzes were probably hafted as woodworking tools, but pierced examples suggest that they were sometimes worn as ornaments (Skeates 1995). Suitably hard stone for making axes is sparsely distributed (and, interestingly, is almost never found in the same geological zones as high-quality flint). Only rarely are exact sources known (e.g., the andesite source on Aigina, Perlès 1992b). Some evidence points to distinct circulation zones. For example, even when other materials such as flint and obsidian were crossing the Straits of Messina between Sicily and southern Italy, Calabrian diorite and Sicilian basalt axes rarely crossed into one another's zones. In contrast, Calabrian axes traveled much farther in the other direction, due to the lack of metamorphic and igneous stone in eastern Italy (Leighton 1992). Functional context was also sometimes important: in third-millennium Portugal, axes found in burials were made of local basalt and siltstone, while axes found in villages were of amphibolite imported from western Spain, a difference which may reflect the desire to keep the tougher stone in use (Lillios 1999a). This medium-range trade, which has been termed "utilitarian" (Perlès 1992b), contrasts with the very long-distance trade in glossy greenish jadeite axes. These were traded from their sources in the Alps throughout the central Mediterranean and western Europe.

Pottery has often been identified as a traded object, based on long-distance similarities in styles and unusual depositional contexts (for example, Malone 1985). Occasional vessels were undoubtedly taken on journeys and left in new places. Systematically documenting a trade in pottery in this period, however, has proven much more difficult. Stylistically, following the broad horizons of initial Impressed and Cardial Wares, the Mediterranean Neolithic was characterized by highly varied regional styles, at least until the later Neolithic. Even when we know from other traded goods that there was regular traffic between regions such as Sicily and Malta, few clearly exotic clay vessels can be seen. This impression is confirmed by thin-section studies: both in Greece (Perlès 1992b) and in Italy (Skeates 1992; Cassano et al. 1995), such studies have revealed few cases of pots moving very far. Such transport as can be documented was essentially short-range (as in southern France; Barnett 2000) with few exceptions. Small islands with limited geological resources are one context where pottery importation clearly occurred; both finished vessels and raw clay were imported into the Lipari Islands (Williams 1980). But generally, as makes sense for a heavy and fragile item that, in its most basic form, required neither special skills nor rare material to make, pots appear essentially to have been produced locally for local consumption.

Marine shells provide another traceable commodity. Shell exchange is known from the Mesolithic in Provence (Barnett 2000), and cardial shells may have been transported inland for decorating the earliest Neolithic pottery in the western Mediterranean. Liguria may have supplied triton shell trumpets to adjacent parts of Italy (Skeates 1991). Shells were particularly used for personal ornaments. The intensive manufacture of small shell beads, probably by specialists, is known at Franchthi Cave in Greece (Miller 1996) and at several sites in Spain (Pascual Benito 2003). Spondylus shells from the Aegean were made into ornaments and traded into central Europe (Shackleton and Renfrew 1970) as well as accumulated locally (Halstead 1993), and bracelets and half-bracelets made from similar large shells were common in Neolithic Liguria and particularly in Spain (López 1988).

Among other mineral substances, grinding stones were sometimes exchanged over distances of up to 200 kilometers to meet local deficiencies in good stone, for instance andesite querns from Aigina (Runnels 1985) and volcanic querns from Monte Vulture in Basilicata (Rossi 1983). Little work has been done on sourcing ochre, but it was used in almost all Mediterranean Neolithic cultures as a red colorant and must have been traded to areas naturally lacking in it (such as Malta: Maniscalco 1989). Cinnabar, a natural ore of mercury, was also traded widely in Iberia (López 1988). Stone was circulated for figurines including Late Neolithic and Copper Age Almerian stone figurines, Portuguese slate "idols" (López 1988) and Cycladic marble figurines (Papathanassopoulos 1996). Some clay figurines in Neolithic southern Greece may have been broken as tokens marking agreements (Talalay 1993) and it is easy to see how this would result in the transport of figurines between communities. Varied stones were also used for ornaments, including marble (Barfield 1981; Herz 1992), steatite, and various small colored stones. Serpentine bracelets circulated between Sardinia and Corsica (Lewthwaite 1983). The Iberian Neolithic is particularly rich in personal ornaments of all kinds, and finds of stone beads and bracelets are common (López 1988). A very extensive complex of shaft and tunnel mines was created to extract variscite, a greenish stone used exclusively for ornaments from the source at Can Tintoré in Gavá, just outside

Barcelona (Alonso et al. 1978). Variscite beads from here are found throughout northeastern Spain and the Pyrenees into France.

Under normal archaeological circumstances, we can track only things made from durable materials. However, there may well have been a flourishing circulation of food and other organic materials. These may have included textiles, meat crops, dried fish, fruit, nuts, drinks, drugs, and medicines (Skeates 1993). Young animals such as piglets and lambs are easily transported, and adult animals can be herded overland. Fur, feathers, antlers, and tusks would have been desirable commodities that may have been exchanged across ecological zones. This phenomenon is clearest in small island situations: for example, it is likely that stocks of large game would have been exhausted after several millennia of human occupation, hence the belief that antlers found in Maltese temples (Evans 1971) were probably imported from Sicily. Although few fish were eaten in the Mediterranean Neolithic generally, Zohar et al. (2001) report a Pre-Pottery Neolithic coastal site where fish was dried for consumption at sites inland (Bar-Yosef et al. 1991). Organic materials were probably also important as containers or for transport. By 3500 B.C. Malta would have been substantially deforested and may have obtained the larger tree trunks necessary for boat building and temple roof beams from Sicily. On a smaller scale, expertly crafted baskets are known from both Greece (Perlès 2001) and Italy (Fugazzola Delpino et al. 1993). Both desirable in themselves and more transportable than pottery, baskets and fiber bags may have been widely traded.

Finally, it seems overwhelmingly likely that salt was produced and traded extensively. Salt is a much-desired trade good in the tribal world. Rock salt was mined in Neolithic Catalonia at La Muntanya de Sal (Weller 2002). Historically, salt has also been produced by evaporation all around the Mediterranean in shallow salt pans, a method eminently feasible using Neolithic technology, which would have sustained a coastal-inland trade. The Mediterranean's salinity approaches 0.4 percent in places; the evaporation of 25–35 liters of sea water produces a kilo of salt, which in summer can be accomplished in less than a week with minimum effort using shallow basins or receptacles. The very simplicity of this method may be responsible for the lack of any evidence for it: with small-scale production, the archaeological remains would consist of little more than a few undated shallow rock basins or coastal pottery scatters.

"Normal" Trade (and a Normal Trader?)

The review above seeks to dissect the world of circulated goods by material. How would Neolithic Mediterranean trade look from the point of view of people living at a particular place? While there is a lot of variation, we can define a very general pattern (summarized in Figure 2.2 using the Middle Neolithic site of Passo di Corvo [Tinè 1983] as an example) but any estimate of quantities in circulation is entirely notional.

Among items used constantly, a typical Neolithic site would have gathered poor quality chert locally as needed, while obtaining good quality flint from up to 100

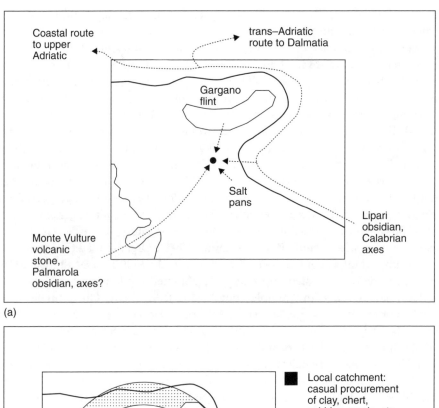

(a)

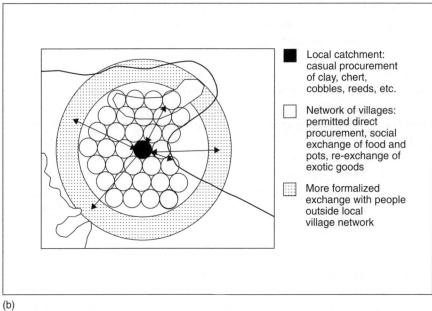

(b)

Figure 2.2 Reconstruction of local trade networks at Passo di Corvo, Italy (data from Tinè 1983). (a) Flows of sourced and other probable materials into the site; (b) Hypothetical social landscape of trade

kilometers away. Small but regular supplies were probably the case: 5–10 one-kilo nodules a year would have supplied a village with 20–30 usable flakes a day. Although we lack evidence that axes were symbols of personal identity as in the central European Linearbandkeramik (ca. 5500–5000 B.C.), axes must have been relatively common tools, and sporadic archaeological finds must belie a more extensive collection in use at any time. If half the adults possessed an axe, a typical village would have possessed 10–30 of them. Use damage and reworking show that axes both wore out and were considered worth refashioning, and one or a handful would need to be replaced each year. The quantities of other things – primarily ochre and ornaments of shell and stone, but also obsidian – would have been moving in even smaller amounts and possibly more sporadically. If we impose this picture on a social landscape, we can suggest that materials would have been brought into a site in diverse ways: e.g., from within the immediate village catchment; from other villages nearby whose people would have been well known or related through kinship (including both local goods and exotic goods re-exchanged locally); through direct procurement in areas between village territories and on the borders of inhabited areas; and through directional trade with people from outside the network of related villages, especially along major transit routes (Table 2.1).

Variations in this general pattern seem to derive from two sources. Some cultural differences in the Neolithic world can be detected even with the blunt instruments of archaeology (for example, an emphasis on ornaments in the western Mediterranean, an especially intensive use of red ochre in the Maltese temples). Secondly, some areas are marked by specialized production and abundance near source areas, for example near obsidian sources (see below), along some coastal areas with shells, and with other localized minerals. Here we should also include sites particularly used in traveling, for example the central Adriatic islands such as Palagruza (Bass 1998; Kaiser and Forenbaher 1999).

This review suggests that, quantitatively, all the exotic material moving in and out of the typical Neolithic village yearly would have fit into a couple of backpacks. While notional, this usefully highlights three facts. First, the vast bulk of exchange may easily have been in consumed rather than enduring goods, particularly animals but also including other foods, salt, skins, containers, and forest products such as furs and honey. Secondly, we should decenter the objects of trade. Even in sedentary villages, people would always have been traveling in the course of normal social life, and the circulation of small amounts of archaeologically visible things may have been a reflex of this rather than a "trade system" in itself. Thirdly, and to some extent in opposition, the small scale of trade and its social embeddedness itself added value to traded items: rather than being off-the-shelf commodities, each axe, core, or pot was a unique product of a specific human chain of social events, something with its own biography.

What of the people moving between sites? Without any convenient "capsule" such as the Bronze Age Ulu Burun shipwreck, our only vignette of a traveler comes from the "Ice Man" mummy found on the Hauslobjoch glacier at the Italian-Austrian border in 1990 (Spindler 1994). This middle-aged male, who had been killed with an arrow shot in the shoulder and left unburied before being naturally

Table 2.1 The distribution and context of Lipari obsidian along a path from the source at Lipari to the head of the Adriatic

Location	Lipari	Southern Calabria	Northern Calabria, Basilicata, Northern Apulia	Adriatic (including island sites on Tremitis, Palagruza)	Croatia
Distance from Lipari	0	83–370 km	370 km–1,133 km	1,133–1,249 km	1,249 km
Cultural context	Painted wares	Stentinello	Painted Figulina ware		Hvar wares
Amount of obsidian	>95%	50–95%	<10%–<1%	<1%	<1%
Obsidian form/Reduction strategy	• Blank cores • Debitage, roughing out flakes • Bladelets from dedicated cores • Expedient flakes	• Bladelets from dedicated cores • Expedient flakes • Core blanks and reduction debris on some sites	• Bladelets from dedicated cores	• Bladelets from dedicated cores	• Bladelets from dedicated cores
Mechanism	Collecting from sites	Direct procurement, local re-exchange of blanks and cores	Down the line/local re-exchange from trade specialists?	Down the line/local re-exchange from trade specialists?	Down the line/local re-exchange from trade specialists?
Social context	Free collection, seasonal aggregation?	Multiple contexts for obsidian use: all-purpose cutting edge and a specific institution	Specific institutions "Prestige goods" where relatively abundant?	Specific institutions	Specific institutions

Straits of Messina

mummified, has been dated to approximately 3000 B.C., at the very end of the Neolithic or beginning of the Copper Age. Found well above the tree-line and far from the nearest known settlement, he had been in agricultural areas shortly before his death. The circumstances of his death are unclear, as is his purpose in journeying, but he reminds us of the human presence in the "empty" areas between sites. He also provides us with the closest thing we have to a life assemblage of material things used at a single moment. He himself probably came from the nearby Italian valleys. He carried an axe whose metal probably originated in the Austrian Alps but which may well have been cast in Italy, judging by the style and by the traces of arsenic from metalworking in his hair. He carried a polished disk of Alpine marble, used not as an ornament, apparently, but to bind up a bundle of twine. He carried several artifacts of Monti Lessini flint; all of his other clothing and belongings were of materials found within the nearby high Alpine valleys. As a geographical capsule, the Ice Man's material goods bind space over at least 250 kilometers, and there is no indication that this was unusual. He also gives some insight into the lost Neolithic craft of traveling, with lightweight flexible containers of bark, firemaking gear, a probably medicinal fungus, expertly fashioned layered clothing suitable for a wide range of conditions in the high Alps, and a small kit of generalized tools and materials for repairs and craft-working as needed.

Obsidian as a Case Study

Obsidian has come to represent the paradigm of a prehistoric European system of long-distance trade. Chemical analysis of obsidian has become the "success story of archaeological material provenancing" (Williams-Thorpe 1995) and the Mediterranean obsidian trade is one of archaeology's most intensively investigated Neolithic phenomena (e.g., Ammerman 1979; Ammerman and Andrefsky 1982; Perlès 1992a; Tykot 1997; 1998; Tykot and Ammerman 1997; for a parallel analysis of Catalhöyük in Anatolia see Conolly 1999). Because all known sources in the Aegean (Giali, Melos) and in the central Mediterranean (Lipari, Pantelleria, Palmerola, Sardinia) are on islands, the early circulation of obsidian also provides one of the best indicators of early sea voyages, providing positive evidence of the earliest sea trade in the world (Johnstone 1980:55).

Obsidian is a natural volcanic glass that forms when viscous silica and aluminum-rich lava cools rapidly, preventing the development of a crystalline structure (Shackley 1998; Williams-Thorpe 1995). The resulting glassy quality prescribes a conchoidal fracture, far finer than that of flint. This characteristic, perhaps combined with obsidian's black luster, made obsidian widely desirable in the ancient world. Usefully for archaeologists, obsidian sources are limited, well known, and readily identified through their distinctive chemical profiles of trace elements (Cann and Renfrew 1964; Clark 1981; Shackley 1998; Tykot, 1997; 1998; Tykot and Ammerman 1997; Williams-Thorpe 1995). In addition to the identification of major obsidian sources, recent provenance work has been able to identify obsidian from distinct flows within Sardinian sources (Tykot 1997; Tykot and Ammerman 1997).

Detailed lithic studies, maritime reconstructions, and investigations of social context can add much to what has been learned from sourcing studies. The two largest, most complex, and best-studied trade networks in the Mediterranean involve the circulation of obsidian from Melos in the Aegean and from Lipari, an Aeolian island which lies to the north of Sicily.

The circulation of obsidian from Melos began in the Paleolithic, as witnessed by the presence of Melian obsidian at Franchthi Cave in the Peloponnese (Broodbank 2000:110–111). This circulation and exchange of obsidian alongside honey-colored flint and other artifacts developed during the Mesolithic and became widespread throughout Greece by the Early Neolithic in the seventh to sixth millennia B.C. (Perlès 1992b). These networks and the seafaring knowledge involved may have been crucial to the expansion of the Neolithic across the Aegean (Renfrew and Aspinall 1990). Melian obsidian was widely used across southern and central Greece, with quantities dropping off into Macedonia and Thrace, where Anatolian and central European obsidian was also available (Kilikoglou et al. 1996). Its circulation reached its peak in the Late Neolithic (later fifth to fourth millennia B.C.) before dropping with the availability of metals in the Copper Age (later fourth to third millennia B.C.). The island of Melos does not seem to have been occupied until the Late Neolithic, so it would appear that obsidian was obtained through direct procurement, possibly by specialists or itinerant middlemen (Torrence 1986; Perlès 1990). The increase of obsidian in the Late Neolithic corresponds with the first occupation of the island. The Late Neolithic obsidian network was widespread and linked Greek and central European trade networks, for example at the Late Neolithic and Early Bronze Age site of Mandalo in Macedonia (Kilikoglou et al. 1996). Perlès has suggested that opening up access to obsidian sources led to changes in exchange mechanisms; a larger quantity of raw material began to circulate in the form of large raw material blocks as well as the blank cores and bladelets (Broodbank 2000; Perlès 1990).

Obsidian use in the central Mediterranean was thought to have begun in the Early Neolithic (Ammerman 1979), although more recent evidence suggests that obsidian was used in some Mesolithic contexts (Nicoletti 1997). Unlike Melos, the main island sources were inhabited from the Early Neolithic. Lipari obsidian had a broader distribution than that from the other central Mediterranean sources, with the maximum distribution stretching from southern France and northern Italy to Croatia (Table 2.1). Lipari obsidian bladelets found in Dalmatia demonstrate connections between Palagruza, Dalmatia, and Apulia (Bass 1998; Kaiser and Forenbaher 1999). From the other sources, obsidian from Monte Arci in Sardinia was circulated across central and western Italy and into France. Both Sardinian and Lipari obsidian have been found in southern France (Roudil and Sulier 1983; Tykot 1997). The other two sources have more limited distributions: Palmarolan obsidian is found primarily in central Italy, Campania, and Puglia, with a few pieces known in the upper Adriatic. Pantellerian obsidian is found on Sicily, Malta, and in North Africa, where the islands of Pantelleria and Lampedusa may have been stepping stones between North Africa and Italy (B. Vargo, personal communication, 2003). Where obsidian from several sources was used, aesthetic qualities may have been important; in northern Italy, Lipari obsidian was preferred to Sardinian obsidian for thin bladelets, perhaps because of its greater gloss and translucency (Ammerman et al. 1990).

The form of the obsidian trade is increasingly well understood. Ammerman (1979) argued that Lipari obsidian was carried to coastal Calabria as roughed-out cores that were worked before being exchanged further. Lithic assemblages from both the west coast of Calabria (Ammerman 1979; Ammerman and Andrefsky 1982) and from the east coast (Farr 2001) contain over 90 percent obsidian. Following Renfrew and Dixon's (1976) definition of an interaction zone as "an area within which sites, within the time range considered, derived 30% or more of their obsidian from the same specific source," large areas of coastal Calabria had direct contact with the Lipari source.

Thus in both the Aegean and the central Mediterranean, material was transported as preformed cores. Although use of obsidian was somewhat earlier and more standardized in Melos, both see sharp rises in Late Neolithic circulation and sharp drops in the Copper Age. Both systems probably involved specialist tasks of procurement and manufacture. Obsidian can be seen to have been transported at high levels over quite some distances, possibly as far as 200 kilometers, after which it may have been circulated through diffusion. Obsidian "hotspots" with high amounts of obsidian at greater distances, however, may suggest villages with a greater participation in trade networks. It is important to bear in mind that many strategies for the procurement of obsidian may have been active at any one time, and that the same material, in this case obsidian, may have been treated in different ways by different groups (Roth 2000).

As obsidian traveled further from its sources, its functional niche and meaning changed (Table 2.1). In Calabria, obsidian filled a local functional role; raw material was procured directly from Lipari or internally from neighboring communities as preformed cores and finished blades and bladelets. Within this zone, obsidian did not occupy the niche of regionally circulated "formal" tools, in which fine, high quality Sicilian flint tools may be viewed. Instead, fairly small weights of obsidian were transported in a raw form; some material was then used expediently and exhaustively, but additionally, bladelets were also utilized. A material making up 90 percent of assemblages can hardly be considered a prestige good, nor was it deposited in special circumstances. As one moves into northern Calabria, the quantity of obsidian drops off sharply. Local flint supplied expedient cutting edges; when obsidian is found, it typically occurs as small, thin bladelets. If the argument in favor of the category of prestige goods applies anywhere, it is within this zone, where obsidian is common enough to be a recognized prestigious alternative, but still uncommon enough to be distinctive. As distances increase from the source, obsidian diminishes in quantity and tool size. At these distances it is hard to imagine the social niche of obsidian in places where a few bladelets are found, yet there was probably not enough in circulation to make it a commonly sought-after good.

The stereotypical form of both central Mediterranean and Aegean obsidian is blades and bladelets struck from a carefully prepared, dedicated core. Many lithicists argue that such blades must have been produced by specialists (Pelegrin 1988;

Perlès and Vitelli 1999; Conolly 1999). Such bladelets have been associated with cereal harvesting and other uses in the Near East (Conolly 1999; Quintero and Wilke 1995).

This poses the question of why Neolithic people wanted or needed obsidian in the first place. Functionally, while sharper than flint, obsidian is brittle and its edges break and blunt easily; it is primarily useful for slicing plants, animals, or other relatively soft materials. It could have been a prestige marker only when it was a moderately common minority component of an assemblage, which would have occurred in specific bands of its geographical range. Yet, paradoxically, specialized production of small bladelets was practiced relatively uniformly from the sources to the furthest extremes of the obsidian trade systems. Obsidian bladelets may have had an important social role, either because of a special function, or because of their materiality. Of the former, obsidian may have gained a certain status from a limited, possibly ritual function. It is possible that such a function may be directly related to the human body, for example, blades used for shaving, scarification, circumcision, or sacrifice, rather than daily butchery or plant processing tasks. Carter has argued that obsidian blades in the Aegean Late Neolithic and Early Bronze Age were particularly suited for these personal processes, especially shaving. In Greece, though not in Italy, they also feature in burial assemblages, possibly because of their role in processes of personal adornment and also because of the mystery surrounding their production (Carter 1994; 1997; 1998).

Neolithic Exchange in its Social Context

As a default interpretation, especially in continental studies, Neolithic Mediterranean trade has traditionally been regarded as a pragmatic affair carried on to obtain needed, desired, or self-evidently superior exotic goods. To this, New Archaeologists added the concept of "prestige goods" whose social value derived from their exotic origins and relative scarcity; such goods imparted status to their owners (Renfrew and Shennan 1982). This view has been influential in much Anglo-American work on axes (for example, Evett 1975), pottery (Malone 1985), and especially obsidian (Hallam et al. 1976). Within obsidian studies, Renfrew's work has also inspired numerous studies seeking to elucidate mechanisms of exchange such as direct procurement vs. "down the line" exchange (e.g., Ammerman and Andrefsky 1982; Ammerman and Polglase 1993; Torrence 1986). A more recent line of interpretation, which treats trade as the socially situated circulation of culturally significant objects (Bradley and Edmonds 1993; Lillios 1999b; Whittle 1996), has had relatively little impact on Neolithic Mediterranean studies (although see Pluciennik 1997; Skeates 1993).

At risk of stating the anodyne, all three approaches to exchange are valid for some situations. Trade clearly functioned to circulate unevenly distributed products and materials: axes are the best example. Nonetheless, a simple functionalist view does not explain the social relations of trade, nor the details of artifact biographies (for instance, why presumably valuable and useful tools such as axes were so often lost or deposited off sites). Nor does it tackle the thorny questions of where cultural demand for an item comes from and why some things (such as ornaments or obsidian) were desired at all. A "prestige goods" view usefully highlights the social context of trade. Mechanisms such as direct procurement or "down the line" exchange, however, have proven remarkably hard to pin down, in part due to the equifinality of their archaeological signatures. Moreover, "prestige" clearly requires a more precise specification of the cultural meaning of things; many apparent prestige goods were also functional tools, others were not necessarily of restricted access, and not all exotic objects were treated equally as prestige goods. Ultimately, too, we need to remember that terms such as "utilitarian," "pragmatic," and "prestigious" originate in our own experience of a capitalistic economy.

The variety of traded products was probably matched by an equal variety of social and cultural institutions. We are broadly in agreement with Perlès' (1992b) general distinction between the strictly local circulation of pottery, the widespread circulation of useful items such as axes, flint, and grinding stones, and the very long-range circulation of small quantities of highly valued substances. However, we probably cannot simply classify the trade in functionally useful items as "utilitarian" and that in rarer valuables as "social." Useful items such as axes are often symbolically elaborated and may be treated as valuables or heirlooms precisely because of their use-histories (Lillios 1999b), while apparent "luxuries" may have been deemed necessary to their users. Moreover, there is no necessary relationship between their use-value and the social mechanisms and relations through which they were procured. It is also clearly the case that archaeological categories such as axes include items circulated in different ways (for example, a local basalt axe vs. an Alpine jadeite axe), and some substances (for example, obsidian) demonstrably changed their meaning and use through their range.

Thus, trade must be understood in terms of how people incorporated substances in motion into a local cultural context of meaning, into a social geography. This is a formidable challenge but not an impossible one. For example, while there is no evidence for full-time, maintained craft specialists, some communities clearly put much labor into producing more of a given product than they would have needed: the Can Tintore bead greenstone mines in Spain, shell bead workshops in Spain (Pascual Benito 2003) and Greece (Miller 1996; Perlès 2001), and mariners visiting Melos (Perlès 2001) or Lipari (Farr 2001) regularly enough to maintain a body of detailed navigational knowledge. There may have been circulation specialists as well. Traded material is often not distributed homogeneously; sites such as Mulino Sant'Antonio in Campania (Albore Livadie et al. 1987) and Gaione in Emilia-Romagna (Ammerman et al. 1990) have much more obsidian than would be expected based on their distances from the sources. Such hotspots or "broker sites" suggest that some communities participated much more actively than others in exchange (cf. Perlès 1992b for Greece). The implication is that trade networks probably were a complex mosaic of direct procurement, medium-range regional trade systems akin to the kula, and local capillary diffusion. In this system, "specialization" in production or trade would have been essentially an aspect of personal identity rather than a formal division of labor.

Exchanged materials bound people together, but in very varied ways. We have described the Lipari obsidian trade above; here we turn briefly to its cultural organization. What is striking is its geography. For much of the Neolithic, from Crotone southward, Stentinello stamped pottery was used and lithic assemblages contain over 50 percent obsidian. From Cosenza province northward, painted pottery was used and the obsidian drops sharply to 10 percent or less. The drop in obsidian use coincides with one of the few places in Neolithic Italy where one can draw a sharp boundary for the pottery, and the zone south of this line coincides with areas within about two weeks' journeying time to Lipari. This implies a well-bounded network of communities whose close links integrally involved obsidian circulation. But Lipari had a dynamic history. In the Late Neolithic (later fifth to earlier fourth millennia B.C.) much more obsidian was exported from Lipari, reaching more distant destinations. This is accompanied by the demolition of any pottery-based boundaries; the new emphasis on trade was reinforced by pottery styles essentially similar throughout southern Italy (Malone 1985). The major site on the island of Lipari at this time, the Contrada Diana, was a very large plain near the harbor (Bernabò Brea and Cavalier 1960). No substantial structures were found here, but many hearths were, probably used for earth oven cooking. If we suppose that sailing was a summer activity, it is tempting to imagine a seasonal or annual convergence on Lipari combining obsidian collecting, trade and social contacts, and feasting. By the end of the Neolithic, therefore, obsidian still bound people together, but in a way very different from earlier in the Neolithic.

Traded materials also separated people, or allowed them to create geographies of difference. The best case here is Malta in the fourth to third millennia B.C. Malta's idiosyncratic pottery, uniquely florid megalithic temples, and maritime isolation give an impression of insularity and cultural difference (Stoddart et al. 1993). Malta, however, had few resources, and a constant flow of imported items – flint, axes, ochre, and perhaps animals and wood – was needed for both daily life and rituals, and trade contacts with Sicily reached their highest levels just as the temple culture appeared most different from its Sicilian neighbors. Trade contact was thus encapsulated within the construction of local difference (Robb 2001). One interpretation is that inter-group trade and rituals stressing local origins were competing principles of social action in Neolithic societies; in the fourth and third millennia, a heightened emphasis on inter-group exchange of prestigious goods was balanced in many places by new, locally idiosyncratic forms of origins rituals, a process taken to extremes on Malta.

Neolithic Mediterranean trade has a long history of almost four millennia, from the beginnings of farming societies to the threshold of the Metal Ages. A focus on traded items tends to homogenize our view of it. A focus on people and social contexts brings into sharper focus regional and historic changes in how traded items were used. We have tried to sketch out Neolithic Mediterranean trade here in general outline, emphasizing factors of cultural geography, travel, knowledge, identity, and the social use of commodities. The largest shift, indubitably, is the intensification of trade seen throughout the Mediterranean in the fourth and third millennia B.C. Although this foreshadows the Copper and Bronze Age emphasis on the circulation of metal objects (Sherratt 1994), it happens firmly within the ambit of later Neolithic societies; before copper, the preferred trade goods were obsidian, ornaments, and perhaps axes. This later Neolithic intensification of trade probably involved greater regional contact, as suggested by broad ceramic horizons, and probably more formalized trade networks. It must be seen both as an indigenous change and as stimulating rather than caused by technological developments in metallurgy. As such, it builds on longstanding Neolithic understandings about the meaning and social role of trade.

REFERENCES

Albore Livadie, C., R. Federico, F. Fedele, U. Albarella, F. De Matteis, and E. Esposito, 1987 Ricerche sull'insediamento tardo-neolitico di Mulino Sant'Antonio (Avella). Rivista di Scienze Preistoriche 41:65–103.

Alonso, Manuel, et al., 1978 Explotación minera neolítica en Can Tintoré (Gavá, Barcelona). Pyrenae 13–14:7–14.

Ammerman, Albert J., 1979 A Study of Obsidian Exchange Networks in Calabria. World Archaeology 11:95–110.

Ammerman, Albert J., and William Andrefsky, 1982 Reduction Sequences and the Exchange of Obsidian in Neolithic Calabria. In Contexts for Prehistoric Exchange. J. E. Ericson and T. K. Earle, eds. pp. 149–172. New York: Academic.

Ammerman, Albert J., A. Cesana, Christopher Polglase, and M. Terrani, 1990 Neutron Activation Analysis of Obsidian for Two Neolithic Sites in Italy. Journal of Archaeological Science 17:209–220.

Ammerman, Albert J., and Christopher Polglase, 1993 The Exchange of Obsidian at Neolithic Sites in Italy. In Trade and Exchange in European Prehistory. F. Healy and C. Scarre, eds. pp. 101–107. Oxbow Monograph 33. Oxford: Oxbow Books.

Barfield, Lawrence, 1981 Patterns of N. Italian trade, 5000–2000 B.C. In Archaeology and Italian Society. G. Barker and R. Hodges, eds. pp. 27–51. International Series. Oxford: British Archaeological Reports.

Barnett, William K., 2000 Cardial Pottery and the Agricultural Transition in Mediterranean Europe. In Europe's First Farmers. T.D. Price, ed. pp. 93–117. Cambridge: Cambridge University Press.

Bar-Yosef, Ofer., Avi Gopher, Eitan Tchernov, and Mordechai Kislev, 1991 Netiv Hagdud: An Early Neolithic Village Site in the Jordan Valley. Journal of Field Archaeology 18:405–424.

Bass, Bryon, 1998 Early Neolithic Offshore Accounts: Remote Islands, Maritime Exploitations, and the Trans-Adriatic Cultural Network. Journal of Mediterranean Archaeology 11:165–190.

Bernabò Brea, Luigi, and Madeleine Cavalier, 1960 Meligunís Lipàra. Volume I: La stazione preistorica della contrada Diana e la necropoli preistorica di Lipari. Palermo: S. F. Flaccovio.

Binder, Didier, 2000 Mesolithic and Neolithic Interaction in Southern France and Northern Italy: New Data and Current Hypotheses. In Europe's First Farmers. T. Douglas Price, ed. pp. 117–144. Cambridge: Cambridge University Press.

Bradley, Richard, and Mark Edmonds, 1993 Interpreting the Axe Trade: Production and Exchange in Neolithic Britain. Cambridge: Cambridge University Press.

Broodbank, Cyprian, 1999 Colonization and Configuration in the Insular Neolithic of the Aegean. *In* Neolithic Society in Greece. P. Halstead, ed. pp. 15–42. Sheffield Studies in Aegean Archaeology. Sheffield: Sheffield Academic Press.

—— 2000 An Island Archaeology of the Early Cyclades. Cambridge: Cambridge University Press.

Cann, J. R., and Colin Renfrew, 1964 The Characterization of Obsidian and its Application to the Mediterranean Region. Proceedings of the Prehistoric Society 30:111–134.

Carter, Tristan, 1994 Southern Aegean Fashion Victims: An Overlooked Aspect of Early Bronze Age Burial Practices. *In* Stories in Stone. N. Ashton and A. David, eds. pp. 127–144. London: Lithics Studies Society.

—— 1997 Blood and Tears: A Cycladic Case Study in Microwear Analysis. The Use of Obsidian Blades as Razors? *In* Siliceous Rocks and Culture. A. M. Bustillo and R. M. Bustillo, eds. pp. 256–271. Madrid: Consejo Superior de Investigaciones Cientificas.

—— 1998 Through a Glass Darkly: Obsidian and Society in the Southern Aegean Early Bronze Age. Unpublished Ph.D. Dissertation, University College London.

Cassano, Selene Maria, et al., 1995 Dall'argilla al vaso: fabbricazione della ceramica in una comunità neolitica di settemila anni fa. Rome: EAN.

Cherry, John F., 1981 Pattern and Process in the Earliest Colonization of the Mediterranean Islands. Proceedings of the Prehistoric Society 47:41–68.

Clark, Grahame, 1965 Prehistoric Societies. London: Hutchinson.

Clark, J. E., 1981 Multi-Faceted Approach to the Study of Mesoamerican Obsidian Trade: An Example from Early Chiapas. Paper presented at the 46th annual meeting of the Society of American Archaeology, San Diego, California, 1981.

Conolly, James, 1999 Technical Strategies and Technical Change at Neolithic Catalhoyuk, Turkey. Antiquity 73:791–800.

Di Lernia, Savino, and Attilio Galiberti, 1993 Archeologia mineraria della Selce nella preistoria. Firenze: All'insegna del Giglio.

Evans, John, 1971 Prehistoric Antiquities of the Maltese Islands. London: Athlone.

Evett, D., 1975 A Preliminary Note on the Typology, Functional Variability and Trade of Italian Neolithic Ground Stone Axes. Origini 7:35–54.

Farr, R. Helen, 2001 Cutting Through Water: An Analysis of Neolithic Obsidian from Bova Marina, Calabria. Unpublished MA Dissertation, University of Southampton.

Fugazzola Delpino, M. A., et al., 1993 "La Marmotta" (Anguillara Sabazia, RM): Scavi 1989 – un abitato perilacustre di età neolitica. Bullettino di Paletnologia Italiana:181–342.

Gell, Alfred, 1985 Cognitive Maps of Time and Tide. Man (N.S.) 20:271–286.

Hallam, B., S. Warren, and Colin Renfrew, 1976 Obsidian in the Western Mediterranean: Characterization by Neutron Activation Analysis and Optical Emission Spectroscopy. Proceedings of the Prehistoric Society 42:85–110.

Halstead, Paul, 1993 Spondylus Shell Ornaments from Late Neolithic Dimini, Greece: Specialized Manufacture or Unequal Accumulation? Antiquity 67:603–609.

Herz, N., 1992 Provenance Determination of Neolithic to Classical Mediterranean Marbles by Stable Isotopes. Archaeometry 34:185–194.

Horden, Peregrine, and Nicholas Purcell, 2000 The Corrupting Sea: A Study of Mediterranean History. Oxford: Blackwell.

Johnstone, P., 1980 The Sea Craft of Prehistory. London: Routledge and Kegan Paul.

Kaiser, Timothy, and Staso Forenbaher, 1999 Adriatic Sailors and Stone Knappers: Palagruza in the 3rd Millennium B.C. Antiquity 73:313–324.

Kilikoglou, V., Y. Bassiakos, A. Grimanis, K. Souvatzis, A. Pilali-Papasteriou, and A. Papan-thimou-Papaefthimiou, 1996 Carpathian Obsidian in Macedonia, Greece. Journal of Archaeological Science 23:343–349.

Lambeck, Kurt, 1996 Sea-Level Change and Shore-Line Evolution in Aegean Greece since Upper Palaeolithic Time. Antiquity 70:588–611.

Leighton, Robert, 1992 Stone Tools and Exchange in South Italian Prehistory: New Evidence from Old Collections. Accordia Research Centre 3:1–28.

Lewthwaite, James, 1983 The Neolithic of Corsica. In Ancient France: Neolithic Societies and Their Landscapes, 6000–2000 B.C. Christopher Scarre, ed. pp. 146–183. Edinburgh: Edinburgh University Press.

Lillios, Katina, 1999a Symbolic Artifacts and Spheres of Meaning: Groundstone Tools from Copper Age Portugal. In Material Symbols: Culture and Economy in Prehistory. J. E. Robb, ed. pp. 173–187. Carbondale, Illinois: Center for Archaeological Investigations, Southern Illinois University.

——1999b Objects of Memory: The Ethnography and Archaeology of Heirlooms. Journal of Archaeological Method and Theory 6:235–262.

López, Pilar, 1988 El Neolítico en España. Madrid: Cátedra.

Malinowski, Bronislaw, 1922 Argonauts of the Western Pacific. Routledge: London.

Malone, Caroline, 1985 Pots, Prestige and Ritual in Neolithic Southern Italy. In Papers in Italian Archaeology IV: The Cambridge Conference. Caroline Malone and Simon Stoddart, eds. pp. 118–151. International Series 245. Oxford: British Archaeological Reports.

Maniscalco, Laura, 1989 Ochre Containers and Trade in the Central Mediterranean Copper Age. American Journal of Archaeology 93:537–541.

Mauss, Marcel, 1990 The Gift: The Form and Reason for Exchange in Archaic Societies. London: Routledge.

Millán, A. Ramos, et al., 1991 Flint Production and Exchange in the Iberian Southeast, III Millennium B.C. Granada: Universidad de Granada.

Miller, Michele, 1996 The Manufacture of Cockle Shell Beads at Early Neolithic Franchthi Cave: A Case of Craft Specialization? Journal of Mediterranean Archaeology 9:7–37.

Mills, Nigel, 1983 The Neolithic of Southern France. In Ancient France: Neolithic Societies and Their Landscapes, 6000–2000 B.C. Christopher Scarre, ed. pp. 91–145. Edinburgh: Edinburgh University Press.

Nicoletti, Fabrizio, 1997 Il commercio preistorico dell'ossidiana nel mediterraneo ed il ruolo di Lipari e Pantelleria nel più antico sistema di scambio. In Prima Sicilia: alle origini della società siciliana. Sebastiano Tusa, ed. pp. 259–273. Palermo: Regione Siciliana.

Papathanassopoulos, George A., 1996 Neolithic Culture in Greece. Athens: N. P. Goulandris Foundation.

Pascual Benito, Josep Luis, 2003 Los talleres de cuentas de cardium en el Neolitico peninsula. Paper presented at the III Congreso Neolitico, University of Cantabria.

Pelegrin, J., 1988 Débitage expérimental par pression: du plus petit au plus grand. In Technologie préhistorique. J. Tixier, ed. pp. 37–53. Valbonne: Editions de CNRS.

Perlès, Catherine, ed. 1990 Les industries lithiques taillées de Franchthi (Argolide, Grèce). Volume II: Bloomington and Indianapolis: Indiana University Press.

Perlès, Catherine, 1992a In Search of Lithic Strategies: A Cognitive Approach to Prehistoric Chipped Stone Assemblages. In Representations in Archaeology. J.-C. Gardin and C. Peebles, eds. pp. 223–250. Bloomington: Indiana University Press.

——1992b Systems of Exchange and Organisation of Production in Neolithic Greece. Journal of Mediterranean Archaeology 5:115–164.

——2001 The Early Neolithic in Greece. Cambridge: Cambridge University Press.

Perlès, Catherine, and Karen D. Vitelli, 1999 Craft Specialization in the Neolithic of Greece. *In* Neolithic Society in Greece. P. Halstead, ed. pp. 96–107. Sheffield: Sheffield Academic Press.

Pirazzoli, Paolo A., 1996 Sea-Level Changes. The Last 20,000 Years. Chichester: John Wiley and Sons.

Pluciennik, Mark, 1997 Historical, Geographical, and Anthropological Imaginations: Early Ceramics in Southern Italy. *In* Not So Much a Pot, More a Way of Life. C. Cumberpatch and P. Blinkhorn, eds. pp. 37–56. Oxbow Monographs. Oxford: Oxbow.

Price, T. Douglas, ed. 2000 Europe's First Farmers. Cambridge: Cambridge University Press.

Quintero, Leslie, and Philip Wilke, 1995 Evolution and Economic Significance of Naviform Core and Blade Technology in the Southern Levant. Paleorient 21:17–34.

Renfrew, C., and A. Aspinall, 1990 Aegean Obsidian and Franchthi Cave. *In* Les industries lithiques taillées de Franchthi (Argolide, Grèce). Les industries du Mésolithique et du Néolithique initial, Excavations at Franchthi Cave, fasc. 5. Vol. II. Catherine Perlès, ed. pp. 257–270. Bloomington and Indianapolis: Indiana University Press.

Renfrew, Colin, and John Dixon, 1976 Obsidian in Western Asia: A Review. *In* Problems in Economic and Social Archaeology. G. d. G. Sieveking, I. H. Longworth, and K. E. Wilson, ed. pp. 137–150. London: Duckworth.

Renfrew, Colin, and Stephan Shennan, 1982 Ranking, Resource and Exchange: Aspects of the Archaeology of Early European Society. Cambridge: Cambridge University Press.

Ricq de Bouard, M., and F. G. Fedele, 1993 Neolithic Rock Resources across the Western Alps: Circulation Data and Models. Geoarchaeology 8:1–22.

Robb, John, 2001 Island Identities: Ritual, Travel, and the Creation of Difference in Neolithic Malta. European Journal of Archaeology 4:175–202.

Robb, John, and Robert Tykot, 2002 Ricostruzione di aspetti marittimi e sociali nello scambio di ossidiana durante il Neolitico tramite analisi GIS. Atti, Riunione Scientifica dell'I.I.P.P.

Rossi, G., 1983 Altre industrie su pietra. *In* Passo di Corvo e la civiltà neolitica del Tavoliere. S. Tinè, ed. pp. 124–130. Genova: Sagep.

Roth, Barbara J., 2000 Obsidian Source Characterization and Hunter-Gatherer Mobility: An Example from the Tucson Basin. Journal of Archaeological Science 27:305–314.

Roudil, J.-L., and M. Soulier, 1983 Le gisement néolithique ancien de Peiro Signado Portiragnes, Hérault: étude préliminaire. Congres Préhistorique de France. pp. 258–279. Paris: Société Préhistorique.

Runnels, Curtis N., 1985 Trade and the Demand for Millstones in Southern Greece in the Neolithic and the Early Bronze Age. *In* Prehistoric Production and Exchange: The Aegean and Eastern Mediterranean. A. B. Knapp and T. Stech, eds. pp. 30–43. Los Angeles: Institute of Archaeology, UCLA.

Shackleton, N., and C. Renfrew, 1970 Neolithic Trade Routes Realigned by Oxygen Isotope Analysis. Nature 228:1062–1065.

Shackley, M. S., ed. 1998 Archaeological Obsidian Studies, Method and Theory. New York: Plenum Press.

Sherratt, Andrew, 1994 The Transformation of Early Agrarian Europe: The Later Neolithic and Copper Ages, 4500–2500 B.C. *In* The Oxford Illustrated Prehistory of Europe. Barry Cunliffe, ed. pp. 167–201. Oxford: Oxford University Press.

Skeates, Robin, 1991 Triton's Trumpet: A Neolithic Symbol in Italy. Oxford Journal of Archaeology:17–31.

—— 1992 Thin-Section Analysis of Italian Neolithic Pottery. *In* Papers of the Fourth Conference of Italian Archaeology. Volume 3: New Developments in Italian Archaeology. E. Herring, R. Whitehouse, and J. Wilkins, eds. pp. 29–34. London: Accordia Research Centre.

—— 1993 Neolithic Exchange in Central and Southern Italy. *In* Trade and Exchange in Prehistoric Europe. C. Scarre and F. Healy, eds. pp. 109–114. Oxford: The Prehistoric Society.

—— 1995 Animate Objects: A Biography of Prehistoric "Axe-Amulets" in the Central Mediterranean Region. Proceedings of the Prehistoric Society 61:279–301.

Spindler, Konrad, 1994 The Man in the Ice. London: Weidenfeld and Nicolson.

Stoddart, Simon, Anthony Bonanno, Tancred Gouder, Caroline Malone, and David Trump, 1993 Cult in an Island Society: Prehistoric Malta in the Tarxien Period. Cambridge Archaeological Journal 3:3–19.

Talalay, Lauren, 1993 Deities, Dolls and Devices: Neolithic Figurines from Franchthi Cave, Greece. Bloomington: Indiana University Press.

Tinè, S., 1983 Passo di Corvo e la civiltà neolitica del Tavoliere. Genova: Sagep.

Torrence, Robin, 1986 Production and Exchange of Stone Tools: Prehistoric Obsidian in the Aegean. Cambridge: Cambridge University Press.

Trump, David H, 1963 Excavations at La Starza, Ariano Irpino. Papers of the British School at Rome 31:1–32.

Tykot, Robert H., 1997 Characterization of the Monte Arci Obsidian Sources. Journal of Archaeological Science 24:467–479.

—— 1998 Mediterranean Islands and Multiple Flows – the Sources and Exploitation of Sardinian Obsidian. *In* Archaeological Obsidian Studies. M. S. Shackley, ed. pp. 67–83. New York: Plenum Press.

Tykot, Robert H., and Albert J. Ammerman, 1997 Mediterranean Obsidian Provenance Studies. Antiquity 71:1000–1006.

Weiner, Annette B., 1988 The Trobrianders of Papua New Guinea. London: Harcourt Brace Jovanovich.

Weller, Olivier, 2002 The Earliest Rock Salt Exploitation in Europe: A Salt Mountain in the Spanish Neolithic. Antiquity 76:317–318.

Whittle, Alasdair, 1996 Europe in the Neolithic: The Creation of New Worlds. Cambridge: Cambridge University Press.

Wiessner, Polly, and Akii Tumu, 1998 Historical Vines: Enga Networks of Exchange, Ritual and Warfare in Papua New Guinea. Washington: Smithsonian Institution Press.

Williams, John Lloyd, 1980 A Petrological Examination of the Prehistoric Pottery from the Excavation in the Castello and Diana Plain of Lipari. *In* Meligunìs Lipára, Volume IV: L'acropoli di Lipari nella preistoria. Luigi Bernabò Brea and Madeleine Cavalier, eds. pp. 845–868. Palermo: Flaccovia.

Williams-Thorpe, Olwyn, 1995 Obsidian in the Mediterranean and the Near East: A Provenancing Success Story. Archaeometry 37:217–248.

Zohar, I., T. Dayan, E. Galili, and E. Spanier, 2001 Fish Processing During the Early Holocene: A Taphonomic Case Study from Coastal Israel. Journal of Archaeological Science 28:1041–1053.

3

Agriculture, Pastoralism, and Mediterranean Landscapes in Prehistory

Graeme Barker

Introduction

In the fifty years since the publication of *La Méditerranée et le Monde Méditerranéen*, Fernand Braudel's vision of Mediterranean history has been praised and criticized by historians in equal measure, the criticisms focusing particularly on his inability to demonstrate convincingly how *événements*, *conjonctures*, *mentalités*, and the *longue durée* actually related to, and impacted on, one another, particularly given the relatively short time-scales he dealt with (the sixteenth century in the case of *La Méditerranée et le Monde Méditerranéen*) (Knapp 1992). But is it possible to write such holistic histories over longer time-scales? In their remarkably ambitious and scholarly volume, *The Corrupting Sea: A Study of Mediterranean History* (2000), Peregrine Horden and Nicholas Purcell attempted to extend Braudel's Mediterranean history backward from the Middle Ages to the second millennium B.C., the Bronze Age. One of the principal threads they detect in this history is the contrast between, on the one hand, the fragmentation of the Mediterranean landscape, with very different topographies and environments lying cheek by jowl, and on the other what they term the "connectivity" or high degree of connection and contact between these different landscape components, principally because of the role of the sea in linking communities (like "frogs around the pond" in Aristophanes' famous phrase). For Horden and Purcell the principal factor that has given this fragmented region its historical unity and character has been not the *longue durée* of Mediterranean landscapes but rather people's perceptions of the constraints and opportunities offered by those landscapes, and their decisions about how to react to them. Far removed from Braudel's "underlying currents, often noiseless, whose direction can only be observed by watching them over long periods of time" (Braudel 1972:20), or Carlo Levi's immobile peasant history over which "every outside influence has broken over . . . like a wave, without leaving a trace" (Levi 1947:13; Figure 3.1), for Horden and Purcell the history of Mediterranean rural landscapes and peasant soci-

Figure 3.1 The "timeless Mediterranean landscape": plowing with an oxen team in the Biferno Valley (central-southern Italy) in the 1970s. (Photo: Graeme Barker)

eties over the past 4,000 years has to be envisaged instead as myriad historically contingent local histories, characterized above all by flux: ". . . local continuities over many generations of rural life are not to be expected" (2000:400).

Such divergent views of Mediterranean landscape history provide an ideal introduction to this chapter's exploration of Mediterranean landscape prehistory. Its purpose is to overview the prehistory of "rural economies" – especially agriculture and pastoralism – in the Mediterranean, our understanding of the physical development of the landscape in which these activities took place, and the relationships between the two. The time-scale of the chapter has to be ambitious, beginning in the early Holocene (given debates about the ways in which farming was first established in the Mediterranean), and extending through later prehistoric periods to the emergence of the archaic states of the classical world in the opening centuries of the first millennium B.C.

Foraging Seascapes in the Early Holocene

Several parts of the Mediterranean and the Balkans had acted as refuges for human populations in the most extreme conditions of the Pleistocene (20,000 years ago), and as the climate ameliorated foraging populations expanded rapidly throughout the Mediterranean Basin (see Figure 3.2 for the location of the sites mentioned in

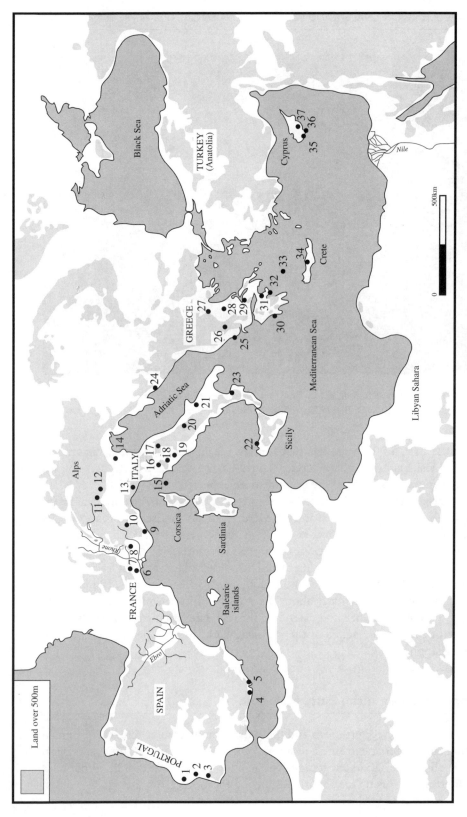

Figure 3.2 Map, with the principal sites and regions mentioned in the text: 1. Tagus river; 2. Sado river; 3. Mira river; 4. Los Millares; 5. Fuente Alamo, Gatas, Vera Basin; 6. Aberuador; 7. Font-Juvénal; 8. Sante Victoire; 9. Fontbrégoua; 10. Monte Bego; 11. Val Camonica; 12. Fiavè; 13. Ligurian sites: Castellaro dell' Uscio, Libiola, Vall Lagorara; 14. Frattesina; 15. Elba; 16. Podere Tartuchino; 17. San Marco; 18. Sorgenti della Nova; 19. Luni sul Mignone; 20. Biferno Valley; 21. Tavoliere; 22. Grotta dell' Uzzo; 23. Broglio; 24. Smilčić; 25. Asfaka; 26. Doliana; 27. Nea Nikomedeia; 28. Thessaly sites: Achilleion, Argissa, Makriyalos, Sesklo; 29. Boeotia; 30. Pylos; 31. Tiryns; 32. Franchthi Cave; 33. Melos; 34. Knossos; 35. Kissonerga; 36. Akrotiri; 37. Paraklessia

the text). From the beginning of the Holocene, about 12,000 years ago, the entire region was populated by Mesolithic societies, although the indications are of distinct settlement clusters where food resources were diverse and rich (rocky coasts adjacent to accessible unglaciated uplands, for example) rather than of equally dispersed populations (Zvelebil 1996). Furthermore, it is very likely that these early Holocene foragers made use of seagoing craft capable of coping with Mediterranean currents, tides, and winds. There are fragments of obsidian from the small Aegean island of Melos in early Holocene contexts in Franchthi Cave on the coast of mainland Greece, over 100 kilometers away (Jacobsen 1976; 1981). Several coastal cave sites like Franchthi have fish bones of deepwater species that realistically can only have been fished using offshore watercraft, rather than with lines and nets cast from shore. There is also evidence of longer, more purposeful sea crossings.

From as early as the eleventh millennium B.P. foragers were making journeys of some 90 kilometers from the Levantine mainland to the island of Cyprus, where they may have been responsible for the extinction of endemic species such as the pygmy hippopotamus (*Phanourios minutus*) and the pygmy elephant (*Elephas cypriotes*) (Simmons 1999). It is also likely (though the evidence is much debated) that Mesolithic foragers were sailing from adjacent mainlands to the west Mediterranean islands to hunt indigenous endemic species there, such as the *Prolagus sardus* (hare) and *Megaceros cazioti* (deer) on Corsica and Sardinia, where again they may have been the principal factor in the eventual demise of these species (Cherry 1990; Lewthwaite 1986; Vigne 1987). Rainbird's comment (1999:232) that Mediterranean archaeologists have overemphasized islands as "bounded landscapes" rather than thinking of them as components of a shared "broader seascape", while written in the context of debates about the insular nature of later prehistoric monument building, surely applies just as well to the world views of early Holocene foragers in the Mediterranean Basin: the "connectivity" of the Mediterranean landscape has its roots at this much earlier date.

The people using Franchthi Cave in the early Holocene hunted red deer in particular, along with aurochs (wild cattle) and pig, as well as a variety of smaller game. They also fished, probably with hook and line, and collected a wide range of shellfish. The key difference between late Pleistocene and early Holocene foraging at the cave, however, is the evidence for intensive plant gathering in the latter period. Along with numerous grindstones, the excavators recovered some 28,000 seeds from 27 species, compared with some 700 seeds from far fewer species in the late Pleistocene deposits (Hansen 1991, 1992). The primary species represented are oats, lentils, pistachio, and almond, but there were also smaller quantities of barley, einkorn wheat, and various legumes. At the Grotta dell' Uzzo cave on the northern coast of Sicily, too, a similar range of hunting and fishing strategies was augmented by gathering plants such as wild barley and legumes (Cassoli and Tagliacozzo 1995; Tagliacozzo 1994; Tusa 1996). Legumes have also been reported from early Holocene sediments in cave sites in southern France such as Fontbrégoua and Abeurador, although doubts have been expressed about their association with Mesolithic foragers (Binder 2000:120; Vaquer et al. 1986).

The cereals and legumes reported from the Mesolithic levels at Franchthi and Grotta dell' Uzzo are all morphologically wild, but it is impossible to gauge whether Mesolithic foragers were gathering these plants as wild stands, or were tending or cultivating them in some way. This is because harvesting wild, semi-cultivated or cultivated cereals by beating grains into a bag or basket consistently would have selected for brittle-rachis seeds, yielding more or less identical archaeobotanical samples. Hence the evidence could imply that a form of incipient or primitive plant husbandry was being practiced by Mesolithic foragers in the Mediterranean (Dennell 1981). The balance of probability, though, is that the cereals and legumes at sites such as Franchthi were being gathered from unmanaged wild stands (Hansen 1991; 1992). Either way, it would appear that several cultivars tradition-ally regarded as endemic to the Near East but exotic to the Mediterranean, and thus by definition assumed to have been introduced to the latter from the former by Neolithic farmers, were in fact native to the Mediterranean and were recognized by the indigenous population of foragers as a useful source of food from the beginning of the Holocene.

Sheep and goats have traditionally been regarded as primarily Near Eastern animals in terms of their natural habitats, and thus the Near East is assumed to have been the locus of their domestication. Wild goats (ibex) today are restricted to high mountains such as the Alps of the Italian/Swiss border, but ibex bones in Mediterranean faunal samples show that in the late Pleistocene and early Holocene they were much more widespread, at lower elevations (Phoca-Cosmetatou 2001). On ecological grounds it is also possible that the distribution of wild sheep extended westward from the Near East in the late Pleistocene. Bones of domestic sheep have been reported from time to time from Mesolithic sites in the Mediterranean, espe-cially the central and western parts, giving rise to discussions of the possibility of sheep being domesticated locally, or at least semi-managed by Mesolithic foragers (Geddes 1985). Another interpretation for the occasional presence of sheep bones in Mesolithic contexts was proposed by Lewthwaite (1986): that domestic sheep spread westward from early farming communities in the eastern Mediterranean as an exotic or prestige item in systems of exchange. Neither argument finds much favor in recent syntheses (e.g., Binder 2000; Zilhao 1993; 2000). Certainly the con-textual evidence is highly problematic: some bones from Mesolithic sites once iden-tified as of domestic sheep have turned out to be, on reexamination, definitely of ibex; and at many sites the likelihood of stratigraphic disturbance (for example from burrowing animals) is high, so it is quite likely that many "Mesolithic sheep" are in fact sheep bones from later contexts. Nonetheless, we should note that there is now unequivocal evidence for Mesolithic foragers corralling and feeding wild Barbary sheep in caves in the Libyan Sahara a thousand or so years before the introduction there of the domestic sheep (Cremaschi and di Lernia 1988). Hence it would be very unwise to assume with complete certainty that sheep and goats were not part of the early Holocene Mediterranean landscape, or of Mesolithic foragers' lifeways.

Through the seventh millennium (Cal) B.C., there are indications at Franchthi Cave of more intensive, multi-seasonal use, including the use of the cave for burials. There was also an increasing emphasis on shellfish collection and fishing: the main species caught was tunny, its size suggesting that people may have practiced co-operative hunts using watercraft and nets. In the Grotta dell' Uzzo, too, stratigraphic changes and other indicators such as microfauna suggest that the cave was used more intensively by the seventh millennium (Cal) B.C. There were parallel developments on the Iberian peninsula, where people concentrated about this time in quite substantial settlements along the margins of the major river estuaries such as the Tagus, Sado, and Mira, sustained by subsistence strategies strongly focused on estuarine and marine foods (Lubell and Jackes 1994; Zilhao 2000). This increasing focus on marine foods in the later Mesolithic may reflect in part the rising sea levels of the mid Holocene "climatic optimum" – bringing such foods nearer to coastal caves such as Franchthi and Uzzo – and the impact on terrestrial resources of the expansion of forests at the same time. Yet it also seems significant that the dietary shifts coincide with indications of increased sedentism and (on the evidence of burials) increased social differentiation.

In contrast with these developments in many coastal locations of what seem to have been more sedentary and more socially differentiated communities linked by sizeable social networks of kin-based contact and exchange (Skeates 2000), the interior regions of Greece, Dalmatia, Italy, southern France, and Spain sustained rather sparse, residentially mobile, presumably egalitarian, hunter-gatherers throughout the early Holocene (Zvelebil 1994). Evidence from the North African littoral is too sparse for comment.

From Foraging to Farming

The earliest definite indications of agro-pastoralism in the Mediterranean currently derive from underwater sites off the Levantine coast (Galili et al. 2002) and from the island of Cyprus, from sites such as Kissonerga *Mylouthkia* and Paraklessia *Shillourokambos*, dated to the second half of the tenth millennium B.P. (Peltenburg et al. 2000; 2001). The latter sites have produced chipped stone industries very like those of Pre-Pottery Neolithic B ("PPNB") settlements in the Levant (the first genuinely agricultural communities in that region). The excavations have also yielded a suite of cultivated plants very similar to those of the Levantine PPNB villages, such as morphologically domestic einkorn (*Triticum monococcum*), emmer (*Triticum dicoccum*), and hulled barley (*Hordeum sativum*), together with large seeded legumes (*Lathyrus/Vicia* spp.), linseed/flax (*Linum* sp.), pistachio, and various roots, tubers, and grasses. The fauna included the "farmyard suite" of animals (cattle, pig, sheep, goat, dog), all morphologically domestic, together with fallow deer. It is assumed that the livestock was introduced, the limited morphological evidence suggesting that it was brought over from the Levantine mainland as domesticated species. Given the evidence for forager visits to Cyprus (presumably from the adjacent Levantine coast) to sites such as Akrotiri *Aetokremnos* from the eleventh millennium B.P. (Simmons 1999), the indications are that an extended period of "exploration and the generation of inter-regional and seafaring knowledge" (Peltenburg et al. 2000:852) was eventually followed by purposive colonization by people from the

Levantine agricultural community. The island of Crete, like Cyprus, provides another convincing piece of evidence for the "purposive colonization" theory of the transition from foraging to farming in the Mediterranean: an agriculture-based group established itself at Knossos about a millennium after the Cypriot settlements, although there is no evidence yet for earlier forager explorations to this island (Broodbank and Strasser 1991; Hamilakis 1996).

The famous *tell* or mound villages of the alluvial plains of Thessaly in northeast Greece – for example, Nea Nikomedeia, Argissa, and Sesklo – traditionally have been interpreted as settlements of agriculturalists who had migrated into the region from Anatolia, because of their many similarities with Anatolian Early Neolithic settlements in terms of tell construction, house architecture, chipped stone assemblages, fine decorated pottery, fired clay figurines, and so on, and the convincing evidence that their subsistence was based primarily on plant and animal husbandry (Perlès 2001). The phenomenon of tells within southeast Europe has been explained in recent years as a functional response to living in landscapes prone to flooding, although the importance of symbolic ties to place is also indicated by the within-community burials, figurines (representations of ancestral figures?), and the building of successive houses in the same place (Bailey 2000). The seasonally flooded soils of the low-lying floodplains seem to have been deliberately selected by these communities for their cereal fields (van Andel and Runnels 1995; Halstead 1989). These wet and forested landscapes clearly were not well suited to animals of semi-arid open habitats such as sheep and goat, and stock-keeping was probably on a small scale. Nonetheless, as the numerous clay figurines of domestic animals imply, livestock may well have had considerable significance in other respects, for example to be maintained as a form of "social storage" on the hoof against the periodic crop failures, or as wealth to be accumulated by acquisitive individuals or groups to trade with others as live animals or to consume with them in feasts (Halstead 1987; 2000; Keswani 1994). The tells, sometimes just 2–3 kilometers apart, seem to have had populations ranging from several tens to several hundreds of inhabitants, suggesting that they can indeed be termed villages.

Alongside the similarities in material culture between the southeast European and Anatolian Early Neolithic tells, the virtual lack of any evidence for Mesolithic settlement on the alluvial plains of Thessaly has been taken as a further pointer to the Anatolian origin of these tell communities, and many scholars still prefer this interpretation (e.g., Tringham 2000). Initial Neolithic settlement at the base of tells such as Achilleion, however, seems to have been small scale, ephemeral, and probably seasonal in character. Moreover, open or flat settlements such as Makriyalos existed alongside the tells (Pappa and Besios 1999). The likelihood is that similar ephemeral sites of mobile Neolithic societies were common elsewhere in Greece, although they may not have been recognized as such (Bintliff et al. 1999). Such evidence led Whittle (1996:71) to conclude that the ". . . the Neolithic community did not spring to life fully formed. It was created gradually and unevenly over the first generations" from the existing forager population of the region.

The evidence for the foraging-farming transition at Franchthi Cave provides further ambiguities. Around 6000 (Cal) B.C. the importance of fishing peaked, coinciding with sea-level rises that would have flooded much of the low-lying land around the cave. As in earlier periods, tunny was again the main species caught. There are some indications that barley gathering diminished at the same time (Hansen 1992:162). Yet soon after these developments there is unequivocal evidence from the cave for the sudden appearance of domesticated cereals (emmer wheat, two-row hulled barley) and livestock, including sheep and goat. On the other hand, there is little evidence for change in the lithic industry, while hunting and gathering (e.g., collecting pistachio, almond, various legumes, wild grasses) continued to be practiced alongside plant and animal husbandry. On balance, the Franchthi evidence is much easier to explain in terms of the existing foraging community having developed a commitment to husbandry as a component of their subsistence behavior, rather than as the sudden displacement of Mesolithic foragers by incoming farmer-foragers. The possible context for such a sudden but partial commitment is unclear (a point to which I return), but the Franchthi scenario certainly seems to have been typical of foraging-farming transitions in the central and western Mediterranean.

Like the tells of Thessaly, the "ditched villages" of the Tavoliere plain in Apulia in southeast Italy have long been regarded as the cornerstone of the Neolithic colonist hypothesis, because they appeared to represent an early appearance of mixed farming, associated with items of material culture such as painted pottery with demonstrable links to the Greek Early Neolithic, in a region lacking convincing evidence for preceding Mesolithic settlement (Cassano and Manfredini 1983; G. D. B. Jones 1987). However, alongside other enclosure settlements with Early Neolithic pottery such as Asfaka in northwest Greece and Smilcic in Dalmatia, they can be understood as the sites of semi-mobile forager communities in the process of developing a commitment to agriculture (Skeates 2000). "Perhaps as novelties associated with food and the sharing of food (rather than as solutions to any subsistence problems) . . . these groups began – during the first quarter of the sixth millennium Cal B.C. – to accept, adopt, and disseminate this integrated 'package' throughout the zone via their pre-existing social networks of contact and exchange" (Skeates 2000:171). This process involved the exploitation of previously unused or little used (but already known) parts of the forager resource zone. Although the enclosures have often been interpreted simply as corralling devices for livestock, presumably they also served to emphasize, like the shared material culture, group identities, territorial ownership, ancestral ties to land, and so on, a new "place-based" view of the world tied to the ownership of domestic plants and animals.

The adoption of components of the Neolithic package appears to have been very slow throughout the central and western Mediterranean. Many caves in peninsular Italy and Sicily have yielded stratified sequences with evidence for foraging in the earlier Holocene followed, from about the early fifth millennium (Cal) B.C., by a mix of foraging and farming (sheep and goat herding especially). The latter was associated with Neolithic pottery and mixed lithic assemblages (Skeates and Whitehouse 1994). In the Biferno Valley, just 50 kilometers north of the Tavoliere, the first Neolithic sites are almost a thousand years later in date than the earliest Tavoliere ditched settlements; they consist of collections of pits and post-holes that suggest somewhat ephemeral structures and non-sedentary communities, associated with evidence for farming combined with foraging (Barker 1995:104–108). San Marco near Gubbio is another example of this kind of site, probably one of several encampments used through the year by a group of Early Neolithic mobile forager-farmers (Malone and Stoddart 1992). Rather similar forager-farmer societies can be discerned at this time in Dalmatia, the Po Valley in northern Italy, in Liguria in northwest Italy, in southern France, coastal Spain, but less certainly along the North African littoral (e.g., Barker 2003; Barker et al. 1990; Boschian and Montagnari-Kokelj 2000; Castro et al. 2000; Lanzinger 1996; Maggi 1997; McBurney 1967; Rowley-Conwy 1997; Vaquer 2000). Their landscape impact was essentially the same as those of the earlier foraging populations, that is, minimal (Ballais 1995; 2000; Biagi et al. 1994; Chester and James 1999; Lowe et al. 1994; Vernet 1999). These small-scale, mobile societies were characterized by segmentary tribal structures without marked ranking or differentiation in gender roles and ideologies (Chapman 1988; Robb 1994; Whitehouse 1992).

Although some scholars prefer to interpret the evidence in terms of a gradual infiltration by Neolithic farmers into the Mesolithic foragers' world (e.g., Binder 2000; Binder and Maggi 2001; Zilhao 1993; 2000), to my mind the evidence fits much better the three-stage model of indigenous acculturation proposed by Zvelebil and Rowley-Conwy (1985): (1) an "availability" phase (ca. 6000 to 5000 B.C.) when many foragers must have been in contact with farmers but made little or no changes to their subsistence behavior; (2) a "substitution phase" (ca. 5000 to ca. 4000 B.C.) when foraging was combined with farming to various degrees; and (3) a "consolidation" phase (early fourth millennium B.C.) when the commitment to agriculture throughout the region became more or less complete. This is not the place to rehearse the debates in the literature about the possible reasons why Mesolithic foragers developed their eventual commitment to farming. As Bogucki (1999:188) describes, current thinking tends to divide between "push," "pull," and "social" models. An example of the first process would be if food supplies and systems of procurement came under threat from climatic and environmental changes, or from rising populations caused by the increasing sedentism of some coastal communities. An example of the second process would be if increased sedentism brought about subtle changes in seasonal scheduling and territorial behavior, with people increasingly tied to particular places and to particular food sources, providing the context in which "manageable" resources such as domestic cereals and livestock became increasingly attractive to adopt. A social model that has been proposed (Hayden 1992; 1995) is that increasingly competitive behaviors amongst particular individuals or groups of foragers might have made new exotic foods attractive, whether for feasting or exchange. The development of "incipient" cultivating (and herding?) practices amongst Mesolithic foragers could also have facilitated transformations in *mentalités*, the "domestication of the mind" that is increasingly recognized as likely to have been the necessary underpinning of foragers becoming farmers (Bradley 1998; Hodder 1990).

New Landscapes, New Connectivities – ca. 4000–2000 B.C.

Whatever their origins, farming communities steadily proliferated in Greece during the fifth and fourth millennia (the Middle and Late Neolithic) and into the third millennium B.C. (the Early Bronze Age). Although Renfrew (1972) originally argued that southern Greece was more densely inhabited than northern Greece by the third millennium B.C., more recent fieldwork in the north, such as the Langadas Survey in Macedonia, indicates rather a process of settlement nucleation there, with fewer but larger settlements (Andreou and Kotsakis 1999). Moreover, excavations at Thessalian Late Neolithic settlements such as Assiros have produced structural, artifactual, faunal, and botanical evidence suggestive of increasing social elaboration and economic complexity, including centralized food storage (Halstead 1996). The agricultural system remained small scale and intensive, rather than large scale and extensive (Halstead 2000; G. Jones 1987). The exchange of livestock and foodstuffs within and between households to combat the vagaries of the Mediterranean climate may have provided the critical stimulus for an accelerating process of wealth differentiation and social ranking (Halstead 1992a; 1992b). Changes in faunal mortality structures indicate the increasing importance of animals on the hoof, one of the stimuli for the development of small-scale transhumance to summer grazing in the mountains at this time (Halstead 2000). Traces of ephemeral huts have been found in the mountain summer-grazing areas of recent transhumant pastoralists (e.g., Doliana in Epirus: Dousougli 1996), but most upland landscapes remained minimally disturbed or modified by human intervention (Ntinou and Badal 2000).

A process of landscape infilling throughout the Neolithic and Early Bronze Age can be observed in southern Greece, on both the mainland and the islands of the central and southern Aegean, including the first widespread evidence for the use of upland caves (Whitelaw 2000). The process of upland settlement may have been facilitated by a trend toward a drier climate that can be observed in the third millennium B.C., at the transition from the Atlantic to Sub-Boreal climatic phases, which would have favored the development of more open vegetation (Bintliff 1992). Although some of the upland sites may have been encampments of marginal communities and others were locations for rituals and ceremonies, there does seem to have been an expansion of upland pastoralism in the context of increasing economic complexity on the lowlands (Halstead 2000). Pastoralism thus seems likely to have been the main process behind the first significant (though extremely small-scale) anthropogenic disturbances that have been observed by palynologists and geomorphologists in upland test sites (Atherden 2000).

By the third millennium B.C. (the Early Bronze Age), crop husbandry in Greece certainly included the cultivation of a wide range of cereal crops and legumes (Halstead 1994:200–201). There are also charred remains of grape, fig, pear, and strawberry dried for storage. The quantities of grape pips suggest that wine production was now widely practiced, one of the behaviors by which elites differentiated themselves from the rest of the population. Domestic olives were present on Cyprus in the Chalcolithic, and earlier still in the Levant, while botanical remains and artifacts such as lamps indicate that olives were being cultivated in Greece at least by the Early Bronze Age, although domestication can be difficult to demonstrate with certainty using morphological criteria (Runnels and Hansen 1986). In *The Emergence of Civilization*, Renfrew (1972) argued persuasively that Mediterranean polyculture (the coordinated cultivation of the three tree crops: olive, vine, and fig) was established in the Aegean during the third millennium B.C., one of a series of cultural transformations at this time. Whether such polyculture was based on terracing technologies, the basis of so much vine and olive cultivation in the modern Mediterranean landscape, remains uncertain. While the technology of building reinforced earth platforms as stable surfaces for buildings on sloping terrain probably stems from the Neolithic, the use of this technique to create systems of agricultural terraces – commonly assumed from indirect evidence for the Early Bronze Age in Greece (van Andel and Runnels 1987) – has yet to be identified with any certainty (Frederick and Krahtopoulou 2000; but cf. French and Whitelaw 1999). By the Early Bronze Age, faunal samples from the eastern Mediterranean indicate the widespread use of the donkey for riding and as a pack animal, and cattle for plow traction (Croft 1991; Frankel 2000; Keswani 1994).

Later Neolithic (fifth-fourth millennia B.C.) and Chalcolithic (third millennium B.C.) societies in Italy and southern France were characterized by parallel changes (to those of Greece) in technological, social, and economic complexity (see chapter 4, this volume). They were associated with comparable changes to the landscape. Archaeological surveys and palynological studies indicate settlement infilling on the lowlands and expansion into the mountains (Barker 1995; Cruise 1991; Laval et al. 1992; Trément 1999). People were by now invariably reliant on mixed farming, the faunal samples commonly indicating a shift in the emphasis of animal husbandry toward secondary products as well as meat (Rowley-Conwy 1997). The mountains became an important component of small-scale transhumant systems from lowland settlements: the Chalcolithic ceramic repertoire, for example, includes spindle whorls and perforated strainer sherds that are presumed to have been used in cheese-making. However, they were also being exploited for other high-value commodities as well: in the Ligurian mountains, for example, there were communities mining copper at Libiola (Maggi and Vignolo 1987) and jasper at Valle Lagorara (Maggi et al. 1995), and working leather at Castellaro di Uscio (Maggi 1990).

Parallel trends in social complexity can be observed at this time in the Iberian peninsula, notably in the Millaran Chalcolithic cultures of southeast Spain (Chapman 1990; 2003; Monks 1997). One of the best examples of landscape analysis has been the Vera Valley Survey in Almeria, the arid heartland of the Millaran culture, an excellent example of modern interdisciplinary research into long-term landscape history by archaeologists and environmental scientists (Castro et al. 2000; Chapman 2003:116–143; Ruiz et al. 1992). A distinct settlement hierarchy can be observed by the third millennium B.C., with substantial fortified hilltop sites at the apex of the system. Excavations at Gatas and Fuente Alamo indicate that these communities were sustained by agricultural systems that combined localized horticulture and extensive farming on the hill-slopes beyond. It was once thought that they made use of simple check dams to trap floodwaters in the dry valleys, but the crops and associated weeds suggest instead that dry (rain-fed) farming was the norm (Ruiz et al. 1992). There is good botanical evidence for the cultivation of the vine and the fig, but olive cultivation is less certain. On the evidence of the frequency and dimensions of olive charcoal at Los Millares, it has been argued that Millaran farmers may have cultivated the olive, but Ruiz et al. (1992) suggest that polyculture was not practiced in this region until at least the second millennium B.C. Palynological studies in various parts of Spain indicate that Late Neolithic and Chalcolithic societies may, however, have started the practice of managing woodlands (*dehesas*) in order to promote animal husbandry, probably by a combination of pruning trees, grazing the understorey vegetation with sheep and goats, pigs, and cattle, and manuring the cleared ground (Stevenson and Harrison 1992).

By the third millennium B.C., therefore, several components of our concept of the "traditional Mediterranean landscape" were in place, albeit in undeveloped form: sheep and goat-dominated pastoralism; upland grazing systems, including ones characterized by seasonal transhumance; plowing with the ox-drawn ard; the use of donkeys for riding and as pack animals; the cultivation of tree crops as well as cereals and legumes; systems of forest management; and perhaps terracing. At the same time, pollen diagrams and associated paleoenvironmental indicators (such as charcoal suites from excavated sites) emphasize the tiny scale of arable and pastoral activity, and the enormous extent of the "wildscape" compared with more recent times. Nevertheless, the one consistent trend that we can observe throughout the Mediterranean by this time is the evidence that the mountains had become as much a means of communication for people as a barrier. Although on the margins of the Mediterranean world, perhaps the most eloquent example of the developing "connectivity" of the mountains by this period is the Iceman, who came to grief on his final journey over the Italian Dolomites (Fowler 2000).

The Bronze Age Landscapes of the Second Millennium B.C.

The second millennium B.C. witnessed the floruit and subsequent decline of the Minoan and Mycenaean cultures in the Aegean. These were highly stratified and economically complex societies, whose trading enterprises (and purported colonies) are likely to have had a profound impact on trajectories of social change amongst the societies of the central and western Mediterranean. Thirty years ago Colin Renfrew (1972) argued from the evidence of material remains and the Linear B tablets (the record-keeping archives of the major Aegean centers or palaces) that Minoan and Mycenaean dynastic elites accumulated and controlled the resources of their countryside (oil, wine, cereals, wool, etc.), returning sufficient foods as rations to their subservient populations (mainly bread and oil, the traditional poverty diet of the Mediterranean peasant). These elites then used the surplus to maintain themselves and their "support staff" (e.g., craft-workers in the palaces) and to trade high status commodities such as wine and textiles around the

Mediterranean in exchange especially for metal ores that Greece lacked. The tablets show that a palace such as Pylos controlled a sheep flock in the tens of thousands, but owned only a dozen or so plow oxen, each of which is named individually in the archive, suggesting that control over the means of arable production was a critical part of palace authority.

Most fundamental features of the Renfrew model remain reasonably intact, although there has been and remains intensive debate about the details. Scholars now emphasize the divergent regional trajectories of Bronze Age Greece. The scale of the "palace economy" was perhaps overemphasized, because the tablets tell us only about the territories controlled by the palaces, not the total landscape. As is the case with similar systems of record-keeping (e.g., the "production norms" of Soviet collective farms), it is difficult to tell whether what the records say *should* have happened actually *did* happen. The primary importance of wine and oil may have been for feasting and drinking ceremonies, and gift exchanges between the Bronze Age elites. Hunting probably played a similarly important role for them (Hamilakis 1996). Although the evidence for food storage at the palaces seems unequivocal (cf. Strasser 1997), opinions vary as to the role of the elites. Were they benign landlords husbanding the products of their estates in order to have emergency supplies ready for their estate workers in times of drought and harvest failure (Halstead 1989)? Or were they more akin to the worst kind of feudal landlords, intent on extracting all they could from a cowed peasantry for their own ends (Bintliff, 1982)? In fact, neither scenario is appropriate to describe the different ways in which the Greek landscape was being exploited at this time (Halstead 1992a; 1994; 1997). The royal estates were farmed "extensively," albeit in a specialized way: the arable land was cultivated for cereals and tree crops, and large flocks of sheep were maintained especially for wool, probably being grazed in systems of transhumance between winter lowland and summer upland pastures. Alongside this system, farmers within the palace territories, like those beyond them, practiced more small-scale but intensive systems of mixed farming, keeping a variety of livestock and manuring small patches of land to extract higher yields than were possible with the extensive systems of cultivation on the palace estates.

The reasons for the decline and collapse of these palace societies in the latter centuries of the second millennium B.C. are topics of serious debate (Manning 1994 provides a good summary). Some scholars have posited the potentially devastating effects of environmental factors such as the eruption of the Santorini volcano and its resultant tidal waves and ash fallouts, or a climatic shift to severe winters and summer drought (like the Medieval Little Ice Age) creating a succession of poor harvests that the palace economic systems could not cope with (most recently, Moody 2000). Others have emphasized the likely importance of internal processes of social fragmentation. Still others suggest that external and internal pressures worked in tandem. One of the problems with the environmental arguments is that in unstable landscapes and semi-arid climates such as the Mediterranean, it is difficult if not impossible for a geomorphologist to establish whether a major flood event detected in an alluvial sequence is the result of a genuine oscillation in rainfall over a sufficient number of years to represent a climatic shift of significance at the regional and human scale, or simply the result of a devastating single storm event, of the kind Zangger (1994) has postulated at Tiryns.

In the central Mediterranean, the situation was quite different. Etruria, the western side of central Italy, was rich both in fertile volcanic soils on the extensive *tufo* bedrock in the southern part toward Rome, and in copper, lead, and iron ores in the central sector, especially on the island of Elba and the adjacent "Ore Mountains" (Colline Metallifere) on the mainland. Archaeological survey evidence for demographic expansion (Barker et al. 1986; n.d.; Miari 1987; Potter 1979) coincides with pollen indicators for increases in the amount of cleared land, both on the lowlands where settlement was densest and in the adjacent mountains, although these are still very small scale compared with the clearance activities recorded after 1000 B.C. (see next section) (Attema and Delvigne 2000; Cruise 1991; Kelly and Huntley 1991). Apart from the now-disputed evidence that substantial longhouses partly cut into the rock of the Luni sul Mignone *tufo* acropolis are Bronze Age in date, most Bronze Age habitation sites in this part of Italy consisted of small clusters of wattle-and-daub huts (Anzidei et al. 1985; Potter 1976), their communities cultivating a range of cereals and legumes, and keeping a variety of stock, especially sheep and goats for meat, milk, and wool (Wilkens 1991–1992).

In the later centuries of the second millennium, however, there are indicators of a significant acceleration in social complexity in Etruria, more marked than anywhere else in Italy and presumably related to elite control of the formidable agricultural and metallurgical resources of the region. (This phenomenon was to crystallize a few centuries later in the Etruscan city states.) We can now discern distinct regional settlement hierarchies, with naturally defensible hilltops selected as the locations for the largest and most complex settlements. The best excavated example is Sorgenti della Nova in the Fiora Valley, which had substantial central buildings likely to have been either public buildings or elite residences (or both), surrounded by smaller simpler domestic structures (Negroni Catacchio 1981). The bones of old cattle and of donkeys at this site suggest that the elites at emergent centers controlled the critical means of agricultural production (plow cattle) and transport (pack animals), and there are also intriguing hints that the site was being supplied foodstuffs from the surrounding population (de Grossi Mazzorin 1998). Although Mycenaean trading posts and perhaps colonies were established on the southern coasts of the Italian peninsula from the fourteenth century B.C. onward, and a few sherds of Mycenaean pottery have been found at Etrurian Bronze Age sites, there is no compelling evidence so far that communities like Sorgenti della Nova were in direct trading contact with the Mycenaeans. Equally, there is no convincing evidence yet that olive oil and wine were being produced in Etruria at this time, though grapes were certainly eaten.

Beyond Etruria, Italian archaeological survey projects have produced evidence for population increase and settlement expansion at this time, but without the same indicators of dramatic social intensification (Balista et al. 1991–1992; Barker 1995; Malone and Stoddart 1994). In the Biferno Valley, the program of intensive fieldwalking identified over 50 locations with Bronze Age pottery. These sites divided into two major categories in their surface remains: a smaller category less than 50 meters in diameter and a larger category 50–100 meters in diameter. Excavations and geophysical investigations indicated that the former represented single huts, presumably for a single family or a few individuals, and that the latter were small clusters of huts for, say, 3–5 families. The small sites, together with "off-site" lithic material such as flint arrowheads, were distributed throughout the study area from the coast to about 1,500 meters above sea level in the Matese Apennines (where there are ski slopes today), whereas the larger sites were only in the main valley, invariably below 500 meters. The latter sites also produced evidence for cereal/legume cultivation and stock-keeping, as well as indicators of crafts such as potting, bone-working, and (on a very small scale) metalworking. The conclusion I reached was that the principal zone of permanent settlement, which had been restricted to the coastal sector in the Neolithic and Chalcolithic, extended during the second millennium B.C. throughout the main valley, with the high mountains used on a seasonal basis for hunting and pastoralism by people from the "mixed farming" settlements. The overall impression is of agricultural societies without marked social hierarchies, and with production primarily at the household level. An important focus for ritual in these societies was the underground springs in caves (Skeates 1997; Whitehouse 1992), very different from the elaborate and public ceremonialism of so many Bronze Age societies elsewhere in Europe. Burials of humans accompanied by complete or partial skeletons of sheep, dog, and cattle hint at pastoral ideologies (Wilkens 1995).

The richest settlement evidence comes from northern Italy, from the so-called Polada "lake villages" along the alpine foreland on the northern edge of the Po plain. One of the best excavated is Fiavè, a village of small wooden cabins surrounded by a substantial palisade (Perini 1987). The wealth of botanical evidence for well-integrated mixed farming systems augmented by hunting, fishing, and gathering (Jones and Rowley-Conwy 1985) is augmented by a wide array of artifacts from such sites including wooden ards, hoes, sickles, whisks, sieves, and churns, as well as canoes, paddles, bows, arrows, baskets, nets, and so on. The organic material culture of the waterlogged *terramare* ("black earth") settlements on the southern edge of the Po plain is almost as rich. The landscape was densely settled, with sites a few kilometers apart, whilst their distinct size differences (small: 1–1.5 hectares; medium: 2–3 hectares; large: 7–11 hectares) imply that these societies were linked in some kind of hierarchical relationships (Bernabò Brea et al. 1997). Although the famous rock carvings of Monte Bego and Val Camonica in the uplands behind the Polada lakeside villages (both areas rich in metal ores) cannot be interpreted as simple representations of daily life, they include motifs that appear to be settlements viewed from higher ground set amidst enclosed fields (Figure 3.3, for which see Barfield and Chippindale 1997), implying an increasing emphasis on privately held rather than communal land. Some of the fields are being plowed by oxen teams (Figure 3.4 – see Barfield and Chippindale 1997), others are being grazed by livestock, and there are also scenes of males riding, hunting, and fighting. Fields enclosed with dry-stone walls were also a new feature of Bronze Age landscapes in Dalmatia, although unlike in northern Italy there are hints in the plant remains

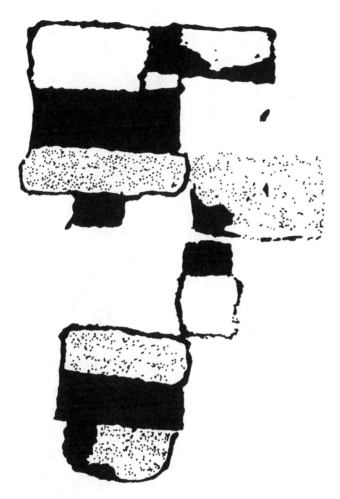

Figure 3.3 Rock art: "settlements/fields" (after Barfield and Chippendale 1997: fig. 15, reproduced by kind permission of the authors and publishers)

from the excavated sites that olive and vine cultivation was practiced in these landscapes (Chapman and Shiel 1993).

Mycenaean trade impacted most clearly on those coastal communities able to take the greatest advantage of their economic opportunities. At the head of the Adriatic, for example, the settlement of Frattesina developed as a large regional center housing a craft community that produced not just pottery, metalwork, and textiles, but also prestige items made of exotic materials such as glass paste and even elephant ivory, the latter presumably from North Africa (Bietti Sestieri and de Grossi Mazzorin 1995). The Frattesina community was maintained by foodstuffs in part supplied to it from neighboring lower-order settlements, perhaps in some kind of client relationship (Clark 1986). Broglio at the instep of Italy was another

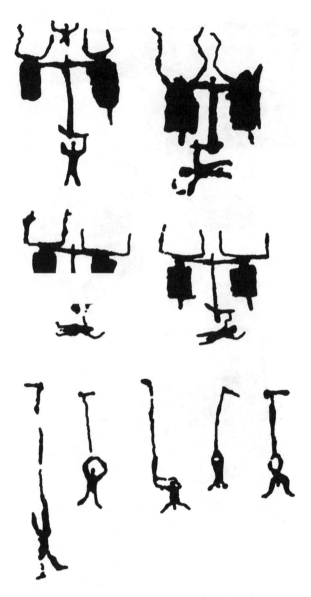

Figure 3.4 Rock art: "plowing" (after Barfield and Chippendale 1997: fig. 12, reproduced by kind permission of the authors and publishers)

regional center of craft production in close contact with the Mycenaean world: not only did its inhabitants produce wheel-made pottery copying Aegean wares but it is likely that they were familiar with, and may have produced, olive oil and wine (Bergonzi 1985; Peroni 2000).

The expansion of the agricultural landscape during the second millennium B.C. is also evident in southern France. Faunal samples from sites such as Font-Juvénal near Carcasonne reveal a decline in forest birds and a rise in open country species (Guilaine 1988). There was a contraction in forest cover and an expansion in arable indicators, together with increases in boxwood, an indicator of increasing numbers of fixed fields (Vernet 1999). The pollen and charcoal records also imply the development at this time of systems of upland forest management for valuable foods such as walnuts, hazelnuts, and chestnuts (Laval et al. 1992; Vernet 1991; 1995; 1999). The opening up of the landscape seems to have been the principal factor in a dramatic increase in hill-slope erosion that has been noted in several sediment studies (Provensal 1995).

The earlier part of the Argaric Bronze Age of southeast Spain (ca. 2300–1500 B.C.) was characterized by the emergence of highly stratified societies in an ore-rich region, much like the situation in Etruria (Chapman 2003:141–146). There are many signs of marked inequalities within and between settlements, and of competitive militaristic elites who controlled the manufacture and exchange of prestige objects (e.g., in copper, lead, and gold) and also, it seems likely, the agricultural economy (Mathers 1994). The settlement record of the Vera Basin indicates a complex political economy of regional centers and satellite communities, the latter probably in some kind of tribute relationship to the former (Castro et al. 2000:155). The main crops grown at the Vera Valley sites were barley and a variety of legumes, but the frequency of grape pips, fig seeds, and olive charcoal suggests that the cultivation of Mediterranean tree crops was now a well-established component of the Argaric agricultural economy. Ruiz et al. (1992) concluded that polyculture was a critical driver of social differentiation, and that the consumption of olive oil and wine was an important signature of elite power. Sheep and goats formed the basis of the animal husbandry systems, the flocks being kept for their milk and wool as well as meat (von den Driesch et al. 1985).

In the later phases of the Argaric Bronze Age, the production system seems to have intensified even further. Small-scale irrigation systems were developed around key settlements – sites are situated by springs and watercourses, water cisterns are increasingly common, and the botanical record includes moisture-demanding crops such as flax. The increasing evidence for the cultivation of tree crops coincides with indicators of terrace construction around hill-slope sites. The faunal samples have been interpreted in terms of an expansion in pastoralism involving small-scale transhumance from the valley-bottom settlements to the surrounding uplands. This process of agricultural intensification, however, was not without a price in the arid, fragile, and erosion-prone landscapes of Almeria. Evergreen oak forests declined, maquis developed on the lowlands and rosemary matorral in the mountains, and there are many indicators of severe gullying and sheet erosion (López 1988; Rodríguez and Vernet 1991; Rodríguez Ariza 1992; Stevenson and Harrison 1992). In the Vera Basin, arable clearance extended farther and farther from the settlements, but the weed seeds and pollen indicate how this process was accompanied by the steady expansion of degraded wasteland and saline zones (Castro et al. 2000). It seems clear from such studies that the degraded and desertic landscapes of Almeria were beginning to take shape by the end of the second millennium B.C.

The Formation of the Mediterranean Landscape

In their preface, Horden and Purcell (2000) reflected on whether they had been able to identify a specifically Mediterranean history underpinning all the particular histories they could discern within the Mediterranean Basin. They concluded that, if there is such a history, it can probably best be characterized as the constant tension between the myriad individual or local histories of this fragmented landscape, on the one hand, and on the other the "connectivity" or unifying role of the sea (hence the "corrupting sea" of their title) in bringing these "microecological" histories together and making them interact with each other in complex and ever-shifting ways. How useful is this view for understanding the development of the Mediterranean landscape in the prehistoric period? The evidence summarized here certainly does not support the thesis that the present-day agricultural and pastoral landscape, in all its essential characteristics, extended back deep into prehistory. At the same time, however, we can discern parallel as well as divergent landscape histories, and continuities as well as discontinuities. These cannot be dismissed simply as an inevitable result of the looser chronologies and imprecise data sets that prehistorians have to deal with.

As a first example, there is the increasing evidence that sea travel connected Mediterranean forager societies from the beginnings of the Holocene, long before the beginnings of farming. Conversely, the transition to farming in the Mediterranean region emerges increasingly as a complex set of "microecological" histories rather than a simple east-to-west process of colonization or acculturation. Some of the plants and animals that scholars long assumed must have been introduced by Neolithic colonists from the Near East were in fact indigenous to the Mediterranean Basin. Many foraging groups used them. Some foraging societies may have developed systems of exploitation that presaged agriculture, long before the date of the putative "Neolithic colonization." There are instances of direct colonization by agricultural groups, notably on Crete (as may also be the case with some of the west Mediterranean islands), others of a rapid switch from foraging to farming over a century or so; but many other communities appear to have combined foraging with components of agriculture for a good thousand years before becoming farmers. The latter fit uneasily with our traditional, ethnographically based assumptions of a dichotomy between, on the one hand, prehistoric foragers characterized by group-based systems of production and consumption, and associated ways of thinking about the landscape and their place within it (Hodder's *agrios* concept), and on the other, prehistoric farmers characterized by household-based systems of subsistence, land ownership, and the agriculture-based ideologies (Hodder's *domus*) (Hodder 1990). Somehow or other, Mediterranean forager-farmer societies combined both.

Whatever its origins through the periods which we classify as the Mesolithic and earlier Neolithic, and the rapidity or otherwise with which mixed farming was established in the Mediterranean, it seems increasingly likely that most prehistoric agriculture was small scale and intensive – perhaps more akin to small-holding, rather than large scale and extensive. The landscape was much more wooded than today. Through the fourth and especially the third millennia BC there is consistent evidence in most regions for agriculture expanding into upland areas, a combination of seasonal herding and shepherding from lower settlements, locally based communities developing appropriate systems of farming adapted to the new locations, and in some instances specialized communities producing high-value trade commodities like the copper miners of Libiola in the Italian Apennines. The increasing importance of the secondary products of livestock is also a clear trend through this period.

The key Mediterranean tree crops – olive, vine, and fig – were all probably part of the landscape from the beginning of the Holocene, and their fruits were consumed. The history of their initial cultivation, however, and of the development of associated pressing technologies to produce oil and wine, appears to have been just as variable and socially contingent as had been the case earlier with the use of domesticated cereal and legumes. Mediterranean polyculture, and pressing grapes and olives for wine and oil, may have developed in Greece as early as the third millennium B.C., following the practice's earlier history in the Levant. By the second millennium B.C., wine was probably being produced by many prehistoric communities in the central and west Mediterranean. The technology may have spread as part of Minoan-Mycenaean trading activities, along with the critical role of wine drinking (like horse riding and hunting), as a signature of elite behavior. In Italy the first consistent evidence for fully integrated polyculture, and for the manufacture of oil and wine, is not until the Etruscan period, from sites such as the Podere Tartuchino farm (Perkins and Attolini 1992). A frieze from a Tarquinian tomb may represent olives and vines being grown in rows mixed together with cereals and legumes (Barker and Rasmussen 1998:185), the classic *coltura promiscua* of the Mediterranean landscape described to us by Roman writers such as Columella, Pliny, Varro, and Virgil. Olive cultivation is not attested in Italy outside Etruria until the later centuries of the first millennium B.C., the period of expanding Roman hegemony (Attema et al. 1999; Barker 1995). Likewise in Spain the first clear evidence for olive cultivation comes from the Iberian Iron Age communities of the eastern littoral who were in trading contact with Phoenicians, Greeks, and Etruscans (Gilman 1992), while olive cultivation may not have been widespread until as late as 1,000–1,500 years ago in southern France, Portugal, Spain, Morocco, and Algeria (Chester and James 1999).

The development of animal husbandry has a similarly confused history. Leaving aside the debate about "pre-Neolithic herding", most Neolithic stock-keeping seems to have been small scale, involving localized movements around the settlement foci, predominantly in the lowlands. Grazing systems began to extend into the uplands, presumably on a seasonal basis, by the fourth and third millennia B.C. Cattle were being used as traction animals and donkeys as pack animals in the Near East in the fourth millennium, and the technology then seems to have spread rapidly across the Mediterranean during the third millennium. Transhumant systems of grazing large flocks of sheep and goat appear to have been part of Minoan and Mycenaean estate farming, but there was a reversion to small-scale husbandry with the collapse

of these polities (Cherry 1988). There is some evidence that elite-owned transhumant flocks were an important component of the Etruscan agricultural economy
(Barker and Rasmussen 1998:198), although large-scale long-distance transhumance mirroring the kind of state- or Church-organized systems of medieval and
recent centuries was probably not a feature of the Mediterranean landscape until
the Roman period (Barker 1989; Barker and Grant 1991; Cherry 1988).

In short, it was not until the development of the archaic city states in the
early first millennium B.C. and the beginnings of classical antiquity that the
physical characteristics of the Mediterranean agro-pastoral landscape finally took
shape in ways that would be recognizable in terms of the modern (or rather pre-
modernized) Mediterranean landscape. It is only during the first millennium B.C.,
too, that the palynological and geomorphological records finally register human
impacts on the landscape that bear any resemblance to later historical levels in terms
of widespread deforestation and erosion in both uplands and lowlands (van Andel
and Runnels 1995; van Andel et al. 1990; Attema et al. 1999; Gerasimidis
2000; Rodríguez Ariza et al. 1992; Stevenson and Harrison 1992; Trément 1999).

Having emphasized the complexity of arable and pastoral history, and of landscape formation, in Mediterranean prehistory, it is important to conclude by
emphasizing how careful we have to be in attempting to identify any causal relationships. Forbes (2000), for example, has recently addressed the assumption
underpinning so much Mediterranean landscape research that sheep and goats are
inherently prone to degrade the environment. He shows that in the southern
Argolid, the past 300 years – a time of profound economic and demographic
changes that might be assumed to have exerted enormous pressure on farmers and
shepherds to operate for short-term expediency – have in fact been characterized
by sustainable grazing regimes. This is not so say, he concludes, that Greek pastoralists always behaved with self-restraint, but rather that the onus is on scholars
dealing with periods of antiquity to demonstrate pastoral-linked degradation, not
simply assume it. As another example, Krahtopoulou (2000) concluded from a
detailed analysis of the geomorphological sequences of two adjacent valley systems
in northeast Greece that, even with her far better chronological resolution than in
much fieldwork of this kind, there was still enough doubt about degrees of correlation to be sure about the contemporaneity and duration of erosional events,
making it difficult to argue with confidence for degrees of linkage between environmental and cultural events, let alone be confident of causal relationships between
the two. Both of these studies have profound implications for the circular reason-
ing and recognition of "correlations" between environmental and cultural events
that permeate the literature (historical, archaeological, geomorphological, and
palynological) on Mediterranean landscape change.

Reflecting on these difficulties, Halstead (2000:123) concluded that ". . . the
relationships between landscape change and land use, and between land use and
human settlement, are too complex and too variable for patterns of land use to be
inferred solely from paleoecological records or for the latter to be explained solely
in terms of settlement patterns. Rather the scale and nature of land use must be
inferred through multi-disciplinary approaches." Perhaps we should add an adden-

dum to that phrase: "applied together," as in the Biferno Valley (Barker 1995), Boeotia (Bintliff and Snodgrass 1985), Dalmatia (Chapman et al. 1996), Kea (Cherry et al. 1991), Cyprus (Given and Knapp 2003), Sainte Victoire (Leveau and Provensal 1993), southern Argolid (Jameson et al. 1994), and Vera Basin (Castro et al. 2000) projects. To advance understanding of Mediterranean landscape prehistory and history significantly, we need detailed regional studies conducted by multidisciplinary teams of archaeologists, geomorphologists, paleoecologists, and historians, so that discipline-based data sets of similarly high quality can be obtained from the same study area for comparison and integration. It is difficult to see how the respective roles of people and climate in shaping the Mediterranean landscape, the issue formulated so elegantly by Vita-Finzi in 1969 and so much debated ever since, will advance significantly without such studies.

REFERENCES

Andreou, Stelios, and Kostas Kotsakis, 1999 Counting People in an Artefact-Poor Landscape – The Langadas Case, Macedonia. In The Archaeology of Mediterranean Landscapes 1: Reconstructing Past Population Trends in Mediterranean Europe. J. Bintliff and K. Sbonias, eds. pp. 35–43. Oxford: Oxbow Books.

Anzidei, A. P., Anna Maria Bietti-Sestieri, and Angelo De Santis, 1985 Roma e il Lazio dall' Età della Pietra alla Formazione della Città. Rome: Quasar.

Atherden, Margaret, 2000 Human Impact on the Vegetation of Southern Greece and Problems of Palynological Interpretations: A Case Study from Crete. In Landscape and Land Use in Postglacial Greece. Sheffield Studies in Aegean Archaeology 3. P. Halstead and C. Frederick, eds. pp. 62–78. Sheffield: Sheffield Academic Press.

Attema, Peter, and Jan Delvigne, 2000 Settlement Dynamics and Alluvial Sedimentation in the Pontine Region, Central Italy: A Complex Relationship. In Geoarchaeology of the Landscapes of Classical Antiquity. Babesch Supplement 5. F. Vermeulen and M. de Dapper, eds. pp. 35–47. Leiden: Peeters.

Attema, Peter, Jan Delvigne, and Berndt-Jan Haagsma, 1999 Case Studies from the Pontine Region of Central Italy on Settlement and Environmental Change in the First Millennium BC. In The Archaeology of Mediterranean Landscapes 2: Environmental Reconstruction in Mediterranean Landscape Archaeology. P. Leveau, F. Trément, K. Walsh, and G. Barker, eds. pp. 105–121. Oxford: Oxbow Books.

Bailey, Douglas W., 2000 Balkan Prehistory. London: Routledge.

Balista, Claudio, Gian Luigi Carancini and R. P. Guerzoni, 1991–1992 Insediamenti nell' Area della Conca Velina (Province di Terni e Rieti). Rassegna di Archeologia 10:403–410.

Ballais, Jean-Louis, 1995 Alluvial Holocene Terraces in Eastern Maghreb: Climatic and Anthropogenic Controls. In Mediterranean Quaternary River Environments. J. Lewin, M. G. Macklin, and J. C. Woodward, eds. pp. 183–194. Rotterdam: Balkema.

——2000 Conquests and Land Degradation in the Eastern Maghreb during Classical Antiquity and the Middle Ages. In The Archaeology of Drylands: Living at the Margin. G. Barker and D. Gilbertson, eds. pp. 125–136. London: Routledge, One World Archaeology 39.

Barfield, Lawrence, and Chris Chippindale, 1997 Meaning in the Later Prehistoric Rock-Engravings of Monte Bégo, Alpes-Maritimes, France. Proceedings of the Prehistoric Society 63:103–128.

Barker, Graeme, 1989 The archaeology of the Italian shepherd. Cambridge Philological Proceedings 215:1–19.

——1995 A Mediterranean Valley: Landscape Archaeology and Annales History in the Biferno Valley. Leicester: Leicester University Press.

——2003 In press Transitions to Farming and Pastoralism in North Africa. *In* Examining the Farming/Language Dispersal Hypothesis. C. Renfrew, P. Bellwood, and K. Boyle, eds. Cambridge: McDonald Institute.

Barker, Graeme, and Annie Grant, 1991 Ancient and Modern Pastoralism in Central Italy: An Interdisciplinary Study in the Cicolano Mountains. Papers of the British School at Rome 59:15–88.

Barker, Graeme, Annie Grant, Alison McDonald, and Tom Rasmussen, n.d. The Tuscania Archaeological Survey: Changing Landscapes around an Etruscan, Roman and Medieval Town in South Etruria. London: British School at Rome.

Barker, Graeme, and Tom Rasmussen, 1998 The Etruscans. Oxford: Blackwell.

Barker, Graeme, Stefano Coccia, David Jones, and John Sitzia, 1986 The Montarrenti Survey, 1985: Problems of Integrating Archaeological, Environmental, and Historical Data. Archeologica Medievale 13:291–320.

Barker, Graeme, Paolo Biagi, Gill Clark, Roberto Maggi, and Renato Nisbet, 1990 From Hunting to Herding in the Val Pennavaira (Liguria, Northern Italy). *In* The Neolithisation of the Alpine Region. P. Biagi, ed. pp. 99–121. Brescia: Monografie di Natura Bresciana 13.

Bergonzi, Giovanna, 1985 Southern Italy and the Aegean during the Late Bronze Age: Economic Strategies and Specialised Craft Production. *In* Papers in Italian Archaeology IV (ii) Patterns in Protohistory. C. Malone and S. Stoddart, eds. pp. 355–387. Oxford: British Archaeological Reports, International Series 245.

Bernabò Brea, Maria, Andrea Cardarelli, and Mauro Cremaschi, eds., 1997 Le Terramare. La Più Antica Civiltà Padana. Milan: Electa.

Biagi, Paolo, Renato Nisbet, and Robert Scaife, 1994 Man and Vegetation in the Southern Alps: The Valcamonica-Valtrompa-Valsabbia Watershed (Northern Italy). *In* Highland Zone Exploitation in Southern Europe. P. Biagi and J. Nandris, eds. pp. 133–141. Brescia: Monografie di *Natura Bresciana* 20.

Bietti Sestieri, Anna-Maria, and Jacopo de Grossi Mazzorin, 1995 Importazione di Materie Prime Organiche di Origine Esotica nell'Abitato Protostorici di Frattesina (RO). Padusa 1:367–370.

Binder, Didier, 2000 Mesolithic and Neolithic Interaction in Southern France and Northern Italy: New Data and Current Hypotheses. *In* Europe's First Farmers. T. Douglas Price, ed. pp. 117–143. Cambridge: Cambridge University Press.

Binder, Didier, and Roberto Maggi, 2001 Le Néolithique Ancien de l'Arc Liguro-Provençal. Bulletin de la Société Préhistorique Française 98(3):411–422.

Bintliff, John, 1982 Settlement Patterns, Land Tenure and Social Structures: A Diachronic Model. *In* Ranking, Resource, and Exchange. C. Renfrew and S. Shennan, eds. pp. 106–111. Cambridge: Cambridge University Press.

——1992 Erosion in the Mediterranean Lands: A Reconsideration of Pattern, Process, and Methodology. *In* Past and Present Soil Erosion. J. Boardman and M. Bell, eds. pp. 125–131. Oxford: Oxbow.

Bintliff, John, and Anthony Snodgrass, 1985 The Cambridge/Bradford Boeotia Expedition: The First Four Years. Journal of Field Archaeology 12(2):123–161.

Bintliff, John, Phil Howard, and Anthony Snodgrass, 1999 The Hidden Landscape of Prehistoric Greece. Journal of Mediterranean Archaeology 12(2):139–168.

Bogucki, Peter, 1999 The Origins of Human Society. Oxford: Blackwell Publishers.

Boschian, Giovanni, and Emanuela Montagnari-Kokelj, 2000 Prehistoric Shepherds and Caves in the Trieste Karst (Northeastern Italy). Geoarchaeology 15(4):331–371.

Bradley, R., 1998 The Significance of Monuments. London: Routledge.

Braudel, Fernand, 1949 La Méditerranée et le Monde Méditerranéen à l'Epoque de Philippe II. Paris: Libraire Armand Colin.

——1972 The Mediterranean and the Mediterranean World in the Age of Philip II. London: Fontana.

Broodbank, Cyprian, and Strasser, Thomas, 1991 Migrant Farmers and the Neolithic Colonization of Crete. Antiquity 65:233–245.

Broglio, Alberto, 1992 Mountain Sites in the Context of the Northeast Italian Upper Palaeolithic and Mesolithic. Preistoria Alpina 28(1):293–310.

Cassano, Maria, and Alessandro Manfredini, 1983 Studi sul Neolitico del Tavoliere della Puglia. Oxford: British Archaeological Reports, International Series 160.

Cassoli, P. F., and A. Tagliacozzo, 1995 Lo Sfruttamento delle Risorse Marine tra il Mesolitico e il Neolitico alla Grotta dell' Uzzo, Trapani (Sicilia). Padusa 1:157–170.

Castro, Pedro, Sylvia Gili, Vicente Lull, Rafael Micó, Cristina Rihuete, Roberto Risch, Ma. Encarna Sanahuja Yll, and Robert Chapman, 2000 Archaeology and Desertification in the Vera Basin (Almeria, South-east Spain). European Journal of Archaeology 3(2):147–166.

Chapman, John C., Robert Shiel, and S. Batovic, 1996 The Changing Face of Dalmatia: Archaeological and Ecological Investigations in a Mediterranean Landscape. London: Cassell.

Chapman, John C., 1988 Ceramic Production and Social Differentiation: The Dalmatian Neolithic and the Western Mediterranean. Journal of Mediterranean Archaeology 1(2):3–25.

Chapman, John C., and Robert Shiel, 1993 Social Change and Land Use in Prehistoric Dalmatia. Proceedings of the Prehistoric Society 59:61–104.

Chapman, Robert W., 1990 Emerging Complexity: The Later Prehistory of Southeast Spain, Iberia and the West Mediterranean. Cambridge: Cambridge University Press.

——2003 Archaeologies of Complexity. London: Routledge.

Cherry, John F., 1988 Pastoralism and the Role of Animals in the Pre- and Protohistoric Economies of the Aegean. In Pastoral Economies in Classical Antiquity. C. R. Whittaker, ed. pp. 6–34. Cambridge: Cambridge University Press, Cambridge Philological Society Supplement 14.

——1990 The First Colonization of the Mediterranean Islands: A Review of Recent Research. Journal of Mediterranean Archaeology 3(2):145–221.

Cherry, John F., Jack L. Davis, and Eleni Matzourani, eds., 1991 Landscape Archaeology as Long Term History. Monumenta Archaeologica 16. Los Angeles: UCLA Institute of Archaeology.

Chester, David K., and Peter A. James, 1999 Late Pleistocene and Holocene Landscape Development in the Algarve Region, Southern Portugal. Journal of Mediterranean Archaeology 12(2):169–196.

Clark, Gill, 1986 Economy and Environment in Northeastern Italy in the Second Millennium BC. Papers of the British School at Rome 54:1–28.

Cremaschi, Mauro, and Salvio di Lernia, eds., 1998 Wadi Teshuinat: Palaeoenvironment and Prehistory in South-western Fezzan (Libyan Sahara). Florence: Insegna del Giglio.

Croft, Paul, 1991 Man and Beast in Chalcolithic Cyprus. Bulletin of the American School of Oriental Research 282/3:63–80.

Cruise, Gillian M., 1991 Environmental Change and Human Impact in the Upper Mountain Zone of the Ligurian Apennines: The Last 5000 Years. *In* Archeologia della Pastorizia nell'Europa Meridionale II. R. Maggi, R. Nisbet, and G. Barker, eds. pp.169–194. Bordighera: Istituto Internazionale di Studi Liguri.

Dennell, Robin, 1981 European Economic Prehistory: A New Approach. London: Academic Press.

Dousougli, A., 1996 Epirus: The Ionian Islands. *In* Neolithic Culture in Greece. G. A. Papathanassopoulos, ed. pp. 46–48. Athens: Goulandris Foundation.

von den Driesch, Angela, J. Boessneck, M. Kokabi, and J. Schäffer, 1985 Tierknochenfunde aus der bronzezeitlichen Höhensiedlung Fuente Alamo, Provinz Almería. Munich: Universität München, Studien über frühe Tierknochenfunde von der Iberischen Halbinsel 9:1–75.

Forbes, Hamish, 2000 Landscape Exploitation via Pastoralism: Examining the "Landscape Degradation" Versus Sustainable Economy Debate in the Post-Mediaeval Southern Argolid. *In* Landscape and Land Use in Postglacial Greece. P. Halstead and C. Frederick, eds. pp. 95–109. Sheffield: Sheffield Academic Press, Sheffield Studies in Aegean Archaeology 3.

Fowler, Brenda, 2000 Iceman. London: Macmillan.

Frankel, David, 2000 Migration and Ethnicity in Prehistoric Cyprus: Technology as *habitus*. European Journal of Archaeology 3(2):167–187.

Frederick, Charles, and Athanasia Krahtopoulou, 2000 Deconstructing Agricultural Terraces: Examining the Influence of Construction Method on Stratigraphy, Dating and Archaeological Visibility. *In* Landscape and Land Use in Postglacial Greece. P. Halstead and C. Frederick, eds. pp. 79–94. Sheffield: Sheffield Academic Press, Sheffield Studies in Aegean Archaeology 3.

French, Charles A. I., and Todd M. Whitelaw, 1999 Soil Erosion, Agricultural Terracing and Site Formation Processes at Markiani, Amorgos, Greece: The Micromorphological Perspective. Geoarchaeology 14:151–189.

Galili, Ehud, Baruch Rosen, Avi Gopher, and Liora Kolska-Horwitz, 2002 The Emergence and Dispersion of the Eastern Mediterranean Fishing Village: Evidence from Submerged Neolithic Settlements off the Carmel Coast, Israel. Journal of Mediterranean Archaeology 15:167–198.

Geddes, David, 1985 Mesolithic Domestic Sheep in West Mediterranean Europe. Journal of Archaeological Science 12:25–48.

Gerasimidis, Achilles, 2000 Palynological Evidence for Human Influence on the Vegetation of Mountain Regions in Northern Greece: The Case of Lailias, Serres. In Landscape and Land Use in Postglacial Greece. P. Halstead and C. Frederick, eds. pp. 28–37. Sheffield: Sheffield Academic Press, Sheffield Studies in Aegean Archaeology 3.

Gilman, Antonio, 1992 Comment on M. Ruiz et al. "Environmental Exploitation and Social Structure in Prehistoric Southeast Spain" (JMA 5.1 [1992] 3–38). Journal of Mediterranean Archaeology 5(2):239–241.

Given, Michael, and A. Bernard Knapp, 2003 The Sydney Cyprus Survey Project: Social Approaches to Regional Archaeological Survey. Monumenta Archaeologica 21. Los Angeles: Cotsen Institute of Archaeology, UCLA.

de Grossi Mazzorin, Jacopo, 1998 Analisi dei Resti Faunistici da Alcune Strutture di Sorgenti della Nova. *In* Protovillanoviani e/o Protoetruschi: Ricerche e Scavi. N. Negroni Catacchio, ed. pp. 169–180. Florence: Octavo.

Guilaine, Jean, 1988 Six Millénaires d'Histoire de l'Environnement: Étude Interdisciplinaire de l'Abri Sous-Roche de Font-Juvénal (Conques sur Orbiel, Aude). Toulouse: Centre d'Anthropologie des Sociétés Rurales.

Halstead, Paul, 1987 Traditional and Ancient Rural Economy in Mediterranean Europe. Journal of Hellenic Studies 107:77–87.

——1989 The Economy has a Normal Surplus: Economic Stability and Social Change among Early Farming Communities of Thessaly, Greece. *In* Bad Year Economics: Cultural Responses to Risk and Uncertainty. P. Halstead and J. O'Shea, eds. pp. 68–80. Cambridge: Cambridge University Press.

——1992a Agriculture in the Bronze Age Aegean. *In* Agriculture in Ancient Greece. B. Wells, ed. pp. 105–117. Stockholm: Skrifter Utgivna av Svenska Institutet I Athen 4, 42.

——1992b Dimini and the "DMP": Faunal Remains and Animal Exploitation in Late Neolithic Thessaly. Annual of the British School at Athens 87:29–59.

——1994 The North-South Divide: Regional Paths to Complexity in Prehistoric Greece. *In* Development and Decline in the Mediterranean Bronze Age. C. Mathers and S. Stoddart, eds. pp. 195–217. Sheffield: Sheffield University (Department of Archaeology and Prehistory).

——1996 Pastoralism or Household Herding? Problems of Scale and Specialization in Early Greek Animal Husbandry. World Archaeology 28(1):20–42.

——1997 Storage Strategies and States on Prehistoric Crete: A Reply to Strasser (JMA 10 [1997] 73–100). Journal of Mediterranean Archaeology 10(1):103–107.

——2000 Land Use in Postglacial Greece: Cultural Causes and Environmental Effects. *In* Landscape and Land Use in Postglacial Greece. P. Halstead and C. Frederick, eds. pp. 110–128. Sheffield: Sheffield Academic Press, Sheffield Studies in Aegean Archaeology 3.

Hamilakis, Yannis, 1996 Wine, Oil, and the Dialectics of Power in Bronze Age Crete: A Review of the Evidence. Oxford Journal of Archaeology 15(1):1–32.

Hansen, Julie, 1991 Excavations at Franchthi Cave, Greece. Fascicle 7: The Paleoethnobotany of Franchthi Cave. Bloomington: Indiana University Press.

——1992 Franchthi Cave and the Beginnings of Agriculture in Greece and the Aegean. *In* Préhistoire de l'Agriculture: Nouvelles Approches Experimentales et Ethnographiques. P. Andersen, ed. pp. 231–247. Paris: CNRS.

Hayden, Brian, 1995 A New Overview of Domestication. *In* Last Hunters, First Farmers: New Perspectives on the Prehistoric Transition to Agriculture. T. D. Price and A. B. Gebauer, eds. pp. 273–299. Santa Fe: School of American Research Press.

Hodder, Ian, 1990 The Domestication of Europe: Structure and Contingency in Neolithic Societies. Oxford: Blackwell.

Horden, Peregrine, and Nicholas Purcell, 2000 The Corrupting Sea: A Study of Mediterranean History. Oxford: Blackwell.

Jacobsen, Thomas W., 1976 17,000 Years of Greek Prehistory. Scientific American 234(6):76–87.

——1981 Franchthi Cave and the Beginning of Settled Village Life in Greece. Hesperia 50:303–19.

Jameson, Michael, Curtis Runnels, and Tjeerd van Andel, 1994 A Greek Countryside. Stanford: Stanford University Press.

Jones, Glynis, 1987 Agricultural Practice in Greek Prehistory. Annual of the British School at Athens 82:115–123.

Jones, Glynis, and Peter Rowley-Conwy, 1985 Agricultural Diversity and Sub-Alpine Coloni-sation: Spatial Analysis of Plant Remains from Fiavè. *In* Papers in Italian Archaeology IV (ii). C. Malone and S. Stoddart, eds. pp. 282–295. Oxford: British Archaeological Reports, International Series 244.

Jones, G. D. Barri, 1987 Apulia I. Neolithic Settlement in the Tavoliere. London: Society of Antiquaries, Research Reports 44.

Kelly, Michael G., and Brian Huntley, 1991 An 11000-Year Record of Vegetation and Envi-ronment from Lago di Martignano, Latium, Italy. Journal of Quaternary Science 6(3):209–224.

Keswani, P. S., 1994 The Social Context of Animal Husbandry in Early Agricultural Soci-eties: Ethnographic Insights and an Archaeological Example from Cyprus. Journal of Anthropological Archaeology 13:255–277.

Knapp, A. Bernard, 1992 Archaeology and Annales: Time, Space, Change. *In* Annales, Archaeology and Ethnohistory. A.Bernard Knapp, ed. pp. 1–21. Cambridge: Cambridge University Press.

Krahtopoulou, Athanasia, 2000 Holocene Alluvial History of Northern Pieria, Macedonia, Greece. *In* Landscape and Land Use in Postglacial Greece. P. Halstead and C. Frederick, eds. pp. 15–27. Sheffield: Sheffield Academic Press, Sheffield Studies in Aegean Archaeology 3.

Lanzinger, M, 1996 Sistemi di Insediamento Mesolitico come Adattamento agli Ambienti Montani Alpini. *In* The Mesolithic. S. K. Kozlowski and C. Tozzi, eds. pp. 125–140. Forlì: XIII International Congress of Prehistoric and Protohistoric Sciences, Volume 7.

Laval, H., J. Médus, C. Parron, J. P. Simonnet, and Frédéric Trément, 1992 Late Glacial and Holocene Climate and Soil Erosion in Southeastern France: A Case Study from Etang de Pourra, Provence. Journal of Quaternary Science 7:235–245.

Leveau, Philippe, and Mireille Provansal, eds., 1993 Archéologie et Environnement de la Sainte-Victoire aux Alpilles. Aix-en-Provence: Université de Provence.

Levi, Carlo, 1947 Christ Stopped at Eboli. New York: Farrar Strauss and Co.

Lewthwaite, James, 1986 The Transition to Food Production: A Mediterranean Perspec-tive. *In* Hunters in Transition: Mesolithic Societies of Temperate Europe and their Transition to Farming. Marek Zvelebil, ed. pp. 53–66. Cambridge: Cambridge University Press.

López, G., 1988 Estudio Polínico de Seis Yacimentos del Sureste Español. Trabajos de Prehistoria 45:335–45.

Lowe, John, N. Branch, and C. Watson, 1994 The Chronology of Human Disturbance of the Vegetation of the Northern Apennines during the Holocene. *In* Highland Zone Exploita-tion in Southern Europe. P. Biagi and J. Nandris, eds. pp. 169–187. Brescia: Monografie di Natura Bresciana 20.

Lubell, David, and Mary Jackes, 1994 The Mesolithic-Neolithic Transition in Portugal: Isotopic and Dental Evidence of Diet. Journal of Archaeological Science 21:201–216.

Maggi, Roberto, 1990 Archeologia dell' Appennino Ligure. Gli Scavi del Castellaro di Uscio: un Insediamento di Crinale Occupato dal Neolitico alla Conquista Romana. Bordighera: Istituto Internazionale di Studi Liguri.

——1997 Arene Candide: A Functional and Environmental Assessment of the Holocene Sequence. Rome: il Calamo.

Maggi, Roberto, and Maria Rosa Vignolo, 1987 Libiola. *In* Archeologia in Liguria III.1. Scavi e Scoperte 1982–86. Preistoria e Protostoria. P. Melli and A. del Lucchese, eds. pp. 41–44. Genova: Soprintendenza Archeologica della Liguria.

Maggi, Roberto, Nadia Campana, and F. Negrino, 1995 Valle Lagorara (I 28): A Quarry of Radiolarite (Jasper) Exploited during the Copper and Early Bronze Ages. Archaeologia Polona 33:187–208.

Malone, Caroline, and Simon Stoddart, eds., 1992 The Neolithic Site of San Marco, Gubbio (Perugia), Umbria: Survey and Excavation 1985-7. Papers of the British School at Rome 60:1–69.

Malone, Caroline, and Simon Stoddart, 1994 Territory, Time and State: The Archaeological Development of the Gubbio Basin. Cambridge: Cambridge University Press.

Manning, Sturt, 1994 The Emergence of Divergence: Development and Decline on Bronze Age Crete and the Cyclades. In Development and Decline in the Mediterranean Bronze Age. C. Mathers and S. Stoddart, eds. pp. 221–270. Sheffield: Sheffield University, Sheffield Archaeology Monographs 8.

Mathers, Clay, 1994 Good Bye to All that? Contrasting Patterns of Change in the Southeast Iberian Bronze Age c. 24/2200–600 B.C. In Development and Decline in the Mediterranean Bronze Age. C. Mathers and S. Stoddart, eds. pp. 21–71. Sheffield: Sheffield University, Sheffield Archaeology Monographs 8.

McBurney, Charles, 1967 The Haua Fteah in Cyrenaica. Cambridge: Cambridge University Press.

Miari, Maria, 1987 La Documentazione dei Siti Archeologici dei Bacini del Fiora e dell' Albegna: Criteri di Classificazione e Analisi dei Modelli di Insediamento dell' Età del Bronzo. Padusa 23:113–145.

Monks, Sarah J., 1997 Conflict and Competition in Spanish Prehistory: The Role of Warfare in Societal Development from the Late Fourth to the Third Millennium B.C. Journal of Mediterranean Archaeology 10(1):3–32.

Moody, Jennifer, 2000 Holocene Climate Change in Crete: An Archaeologist's View. In Landscape and Land Use in Postglacial Greece. P. Halstead and C. Frederick, eds. pp. 52–61. Sheffield Academic Press, Sheffield Studies in Aegean Archaeology 3.

Negroni Catacchio, Nuccia, ed., 1981 Sorgenti della Nova: Una Comunità Protostorica e il Suo Territorio nell' Etruria Meridionale. Rome: Consiglio Nazionale delle Ricerche.

Ntinou, Maria, and Ernestina Badal, 2000 Local Vegetation and Charcoal Analysis: An Example from Two Late Neolithic Sites in Northern Greece. In Landscape and Land Use in Postglacial Greece. P. Halstead and C. Frederick, eds. pp. 38–51. Sheffield: Sheffield Academic Press, Sheffield Studies in Aegean Archaeology 3.

Pappa, M., and M. Besios, 1999 The Neolithic Settlement at Makriyalos, Northern Greece: Preliminary Report on the 1993–1995 Excavations. Journal of Field Archaeology 26:177–195.

Peltenburg, Edgar, Sue Colledge, Paul Croft, Adam Jackson, Carole McCartney, and Mary Anne Murray, 2000 Agro-Pastoralist Colonization of Cyprus in the 10th Millennium BP: Initial Assessments. Antiquity 74(286):844–853.

——2001 Neolithic Dispersals from the Levantine Corridor: A Mediterranean Perspective. Levant 33:35–64.

Perini, Renato, 1987 The Typology of the Structures on Bronze Age Wetland Settlements at Fiavè and Lavagnone. In European Wetlands in Prehistory. J. M. Coles and A. J. Lawson, eds. pp. 75–93. Oxford: Oxbow.

Perkins, Philip, and Ida Attolini, 1992 An Etruscan Farm at Podere Tartuchino. Papers of the British School at Rome 60:71–134.

Perlès, Catherine, 2001 The Early Neolithic in Greece. Cambridge: Cambridge University Press.

Peroni, Renato, 2000 In Calabria Prima dei Greci: Vent'Anni de Scavi à Broglio de Trebisacce. Archeo: Attualità del Passato 16(8):57–83.

Phoca-Cosmetatou, Nellie, 2001 Stalking the Ibex: Wild Caprid Exploitation in Southern Europe during the Upper Palaeolithic. Cambridge: Cambridge University, unpublished PhD thesis.

Potter, Timothy W., 1976 A Faliscan Town in South Etruria: Excavations at Narce 1966–1971. London: British School at Rome.

——1979 The Changing Landscape of South Etruria. London: Elek.

Provensal, Mireille, 1995 Holocene Sedimentation Sequences in the Arc River Delta and the Etange de Berre in Provence, Southern France. *In* Mediterranean Quaternary River Environments. J. Lewin, M. G. Macklin, and J. C. Woodward, eds. pp. 159–165. Rotterdam: Balkema.

Rainbird, Paul, 1999 Islands Out of Time: Towards a Critique of Island Archaeology. Journal of Mediterranean Archaeology 12(2):216–234.

Renfrew, Colin, 1972 The Emergence of Civilisation. London: Methuen.

Robb, John, 1994 Burial and Social Reproduction in the Peninsular Italian Neolithic. Journal of Mediterranean Archaeology 7(1):27–71.

Rodriguez-Ariza, M. O., 1992 Human-Plant Relationships During the Copper and Bronze Ages in the Baza and Guadix Basins (Granada, Spain). Bulletin de la Société Botanique de France 139, Actual.bot. (2/3/4):451–464.

Rodríguez-Ariza M., and Jean-Louis Vernet, 1991 Etude Paléoécologique du Gisement Chalcolithique de Los Millares. *In* Oxford International Western Mediterranean Bell Beaker Conference. W. H. Waldren and R. C. Henward, eds. pp. 1–7. Oxford: British Archaeological Reports, International Series 574.

Rodriguez-Ariza, M. O., P. Aguayo De Hoyos, and F. Moreno Jimenez, 1992 The Environment in the Ronda Basin (Malaga, Spain) During Recent Prehistory Based on an Anthracological Study of Old Ronda. Bulletin de la Société Botanique de France 139, Actual.bot. (2/3/4):715–725.

Rowley-Conwy, Peter, 1997 The Animal Bones from Arene Candide: Final Report. *In* Arene Candide: A Functional and Environmental Assessment of the Holocene Sequence. R. Maggi, ed. pp. 153–277. Rome, il Calamo.

Ruiz, Matilde, Roberto Risch, Paloma González Marcén, Pedro Castro, Vicente Lull, and Robert Chapman, 1992 Environmental Exploitation and Social Structure in Prehistoric Southeast Spain. Journal of Mediterranean Archaeology 5(1):3–38.

Runnels, Curtis N., and Julie Hansen, 1986 The Olive in the Prehistoric Aegean: The Evidence for Domestication in the Early Bronze Age. Oxford Journal of Archaeology 5:299–308.

Simmons, Alan H., 1999 Faunal Extinction in an Island Society: Pygmy Hippopotamus Hunters of Cyprus. Dordrecht, Boston: Kluwer Academic/Plenum.

Skeates, Robin, 1997 The Human Use of Caves in East-Central Italy during the Mesolithic, Neolithic and Copper Age. *In* The Human Use of Caves. C. Bonsall and C. Tolan-Smith, eds. pp. 79–86. Oxford: British Archaeological Reports, International Series 667.

——2000 The Social Dynamics of Enclosure in the Neolithic of the Tavoliere, South-East Italy. Journal of Mediterranean Archaeology 13(2):155–188.

——and Ruth Whitehouse, eds., 1994 Radiocarbon Dating and Italian Prehistory. London: British School at Rome, Archaeological Monographs 8 (and Accordia Specialist Studies in Italy 3).

Stevenson, A. C., and Richard Harrison, 1992 Ancient Forests in Spain: A Model for Land Use and Dry Forest Management in South-West Spain from 4000 B.C. to 1900 A.D. Proceedings of the Prehistoric Society 58:227–247.

Strasser, Thomas F., 1997 Storage and States on Prehistoric Crete: The Function of the Koulouras in the First Minoan Palaces. Journal of Mediterranean Archaeology 10(1):73–100.

Tagliacozzo, A., 1994 Economic Changes between the Mesolithic and the Neolithic in the Grotta dell' Uzzo (Sicily, Italy). Accordia Research Papers 5:7–37.

Trément, Frédéric, 1999 The Integration of Historical, Archaeological and Palaeoenvironmental Data at the Regional Scale: The Étang de Berre, Southern France. In The Archaeology of Mediterranean Landscapes 2: Environmental Reconstruction in Mediterranean Landscape Archaeology. P. Leveau, F. Trément, K. Walsh, and G. Barker, eds. pp. 193–205. Oxford: Oxbow Books.

Tringham, Ruth, 2000 Southeastern Europe in the Transition to Agriculture in Europe: Bridge, Buffer, or Mosaic. In Europe's First Farmers. T. Douglas Price, ed. pp. 19–56. Cambridge: Cambridge University Press.

Tusa, Sebastiano, 1996 From Hunter-Gatherers to Farmers in Western Sicily. In Early Societies in Sicily. Robert Leighton, ed. pp. 41–55. London: University of London, Accordia Research Institute, Accordia Specialist Studies on Italy 5.

van Andel, Tjeerd, and Curtis Runnels, 1987 Beyond the Acropolis: The Archaeology of the Greek Countryside. Stanford: Stanford University Press.

——1995 The Earliest Farmers in Europe. Antiquity 69:481–500.

van Andel, Tjeerd, Eberhard Zangger, and Ann Demitrack, 1990 Land Use and Soil Erosion in Prehistoric and Historic Greece. Journal of Field Archaeology 17:379–396.

Vaquer, Jean, 2000 Détection Aérienne des Camps Néolithiques en Languedoc Occidental. In The Archaeology of Mediterranean Landscapes 4: Non-destructive Techniques Applied to Landscape Archaeology. M. Pasquinucci and F. Trément, eds. pp. 61–69. Oxford: Oxbow Books.

Vaquer, Jean, David Geddes, M. Barbaza, and J. Erroux, 1986 Mesolithic Plant Exploitation at the Balma Abeurador (France). Oxford Journal of Archaeology 5:1–18.

Vernet, Jean-Louis, 1991 L'Histoire du Milieu Méditerranéen Humanisée Révélée par les Charbons de Bois. In Pour une Archéologie Agraire. J. Giulaine, ed. pp. 369–408. Paris: Colin.

——1995 Anthracologie, Biostratigraphie et Relations Homme-Milieu en Région Méditerranéenne. In L'Homme et la Dégradation de l'Environnement. S. van der Leeuw, ed. pp. 175–184. Sophia Antipolis: APDCA

——1999 Reconstructing Vegetation and Landscapes in the Mediterranean: The Contribution of Anthracology. In The Archaeology of Mediterranean Landscapes 2: Environmental Reconstruction in Mediterranean Landscape Archaeology. P. Leveau, F. Trément, K. Walsh, and G. Barker, eds. pp. 25–36. Oxford: Oxbow Books.

Vigne, Jean-Denis, 1987 L'Extinction Holocène du Fonds de Peuplement Mammalien Indigène des Iles de Méditerranée Occidentale. Mémoires de la Société Géologique de France 150(n.s.):167–177.

Vita-Finzi, Claudio, 1969 The Mediterranean Valleys: Geological Changes in Historical Times. Cambridge: Cambridge University Press.

Whitehouse, Ruth, 1992 Underground Religion: Cult and Culture in Prehistoric Italy. London: University of London, Accordia Research Centre.

Whitelaw, Todd, 2000 Settlement Instability and Landscape Degradation in the Southern Aegean in the Third Millennium B.C. *In* Landscape and Land Use in Postglacial Greece. P. Halstead and C. Frederick, eds. pp. 135–161. Sheffield: Sheffield Academic Press, Sheffield Studies in Aegean Archaeology 3.

Whittle, Alasdair, 1996 Europe in the Neolithic. The Creation of New Worlds. Cambridge: Cambridge University Press.

Wilkens, Barbara, 1991–1992 I Resti Faunistici di Alcuni Insediamenti dell' Età del Bronzo nell' Italia Centro-Meridionale. Rassegna di Archeologia 10:463–469.

——1995 Animali di Contesti Rituali nella Preistoria d'Italia Centro-Meridionale. Atti del I Convegno Nazionale di Archeozoologia: 201–207. Rovigo: Centro Polesano di Studi Storici Archeologici ed Etnografici.

Zangger, Eberhard, 1994 Landscape Changes around Tiryns during the Bronze Age. American Journal of Archaeology 98:189–212.

Zilhao, Joao, 1993 The Spread of Agro-Pastoral Economies across Mediterranean Europe: A View from the Far West. Journal of Mediterranean Archaeology 6(1):5–63.

——2000 From the Mesolithic to the Neolithic in the Iberian Peninsula. *In* Europe's First Farmers. T. Douglas Price, ed. pp. 144–182. Cambridge: Cambridge University Press.

Zvelebil, Marek, 1994 Plant Use in the Mesolithic and the Implications for the Transition to Farming. Proceedings of the Prehistoric Society 60:95–134.

——1996 Subsistence and Social Organisation of the Mesolithic Communities in Temperate and Northern Europe. *In* The Mesolithic. S. K. Kozlowski and C. Tozzi, eds. pp. 163–174. Forlì: XIII International Congress of Prehistoric and Protohistoric Sciences, Volume 7.

Zvelebil, Marek, and Peter Rowley-Conwy, 1984 The Transition to Farming in Northern Europe: A Hunter-Gatherer Perspective. Norwegian Archaeological Review 17, 2:104–128.

4

Changing Social Relations in the Mediterranean Copper and Bronze Ages

Robert Chapman

Introduction

This chapter begins with a caveat: my coverage is inevitably selective and thematic. Although technological stages are mentioned in the title, I am restricting discussion to societies in the third and second millennia B.C. I am not aiming at evenness across the Mediterranean Basin, but instead highlighting current research, new questions, conflicting interpretations, and issues that I hope will interest specialist and non-specialist alike. There is also an inevitable artificiality in the separation of this chapter from those on themes such as trade and interaction, production, feasting, technologies, settlement, and monuments: for example, social relations cannot be divorced from production activities, while settlement sizes and densities are used to support inferences of social hierarchies.

Given this caveat, I begin by presenting briefly different ways of thinking about prehistoric societies in the Mediterranean. Then I examine recent work on, and changing perceptions of, such societies in the western Mediterranean and in the Aegean. The focus is on sequences of social change and its material representation. As will become apparent, such a comparative exercise takes me out of my "comfort zone" in the west Mediterranean and involves (perhaps even embroils) me in issues that are vexing Aegean Bronze Age specialists. I hope that the approach taken in this chapter will counter any deficiencies in the detailed knowledge normally required of such specialists.

Concepts and Ambiguities

Studies in Mediterranean ethnography stress continuity, survival, stability, and conservatism in "traditional" local societies. As Horden and Purcell put it, such studies give "the impression that at least some Mediterranean societies have been frozen in time and cut off from the wider world" (2000:467) and emphasize "all that is apparently archaic, culturally and economically primitive in southern Europe" (2000:487). Such an interpretation is given support by historians such as Braudel (1972:1239), who proposed that "antiquity lives on round today's Mediterranean shores." This "antiquity" refers to the distinctive ways of life of Mediterranean societies living in different Mediterranean environments.

If the key to the past of Mediterranean societies lay in the ethnographic present, then there would be little need for either history or archaeology. While ethnographic analogies permeate archaeological practice both within and beyond the Mediterranean Basin, we have come to recognize that they are not preserved "snapshots" of antiquity, but the product of local histories, changes, and fluctuations. A more subtle use of such analogies recognizes these histories and does not deny the existence of "other" pasts.

How far do we recognize such "other" pasts in the Mediterranean? Before the advent of radiocarbon dating, many innovations such as metallurgy and megalithic tombs were argued to be the result of diffusion (whether or not by population movement) from east to west, from areas of "higher" culture in the Near East and eastern Mediterranean to the more "traditional" societies of the west. Local innovation was less important than external adoption. Nothing in the west could equal the Bronze Age societies of the Aegean, while even the first widely acknowledged state in the west, that of the Etruscans, was attributed, at least in part, to eastern influences. The widespread use of radiocarbon dating allowed us to place more emphasis on local innovation and adoption (Renfrew 1973), but the emphasis in the western Mediterranean was still on more "stable" societies living "traditional" ways of life, involving transhumance and polyculture (e.g., Barker 1981).

The nature of these later prehistoric societies has been expressed, much as elsewhere, in terms of an evolutionary scale from "simple" to "complex," although definition of the meaning of these terms is usually absent. Generally speaking, the more "complex" societies are distinguished by the largest settlements, the most imposing fortifications, and the richest burials. Using such criteria, authors refer to societies with "a measure/degree/level" of complexity, "incipient" complexity, or "greater" complexity than others that preceded them (for examples, see discussion in Chapman 2003:176–178). These societies are on a ladder of increasing complexity, but the higher rungs become noticeably narrower. When these levels of complexity are equated with neo-evolutionary stages, tribal or egalitarian societies are ubiquitous in the Neolithic, a smaller number of chiefdom or ranked societies are recognized by the Copper Age, an even smaller number become stratified by the Bronze Age, and in the same period state societies are confined to the eastern Mediterranean. "Cycles" of complexity are also recognized (e.g., Mathers and Stoddart 1994), whereby societies ascend to one of the higher rungs on the ladder, but then lose their footing and slip back to a lower/"simpler" rung.

An alternative view of prehistoric societies is critical of such fixed societal types and of the classification of societies as either equal or unequal (Chapman 2003). Inequalities are recognized in societies ranging from hunters and gatherers to states, while hierarchies based on characteristics such as age and gender are also known in so-called egalitarian societies. Such societies may exhibit variations in degrees of egalitarian relations and social practices in daily life, especially given the contradictions between such practices and the ideologies of egalitarianism that impose demands on all members of society. As Wiessner (2002:235) has put it, "egalitarianism is the outcome of complex institutions and ideologies created and maintained by cultural means which empower a coalition of the weaker to curb the strong." She goes on to argue that the variation in the nature and composition of egalitarian societies means that not only will there be several "paths" toward institutionalized inequalities, but that the nature of societies made up in this way will also vary.

This argument is important, as it suggests a potentially more dynamic picture of tension, conflict, and variation in egalitarian societies (as for example in the Mediterranean Neolithic), as well as different pathways to more stratified societies (as in the Mediterranean Bronze Age), which themselves will take on different forms. This fluidity and variation also needs to be considered for the development of the state. Although social scientists and historians have disagreed about the definition of the state, Anglo-American archaeologists in the past three decades have agreed, in the main, that such societies were at the apex of decision-making hierarchies, through which economic and political activities were specialized and centralized. There were at least two levels of specialized decision-makers above the primary producers (Wright and Johnson 1975). Past states were different from chiefdoms in that the latter lacked the bureaucracy and coercion of the former (Wright 1977). Levels of decision-making are defined in the archaeological record by the size levels in a settlement hierarchy. This has created a rather exclusive club of early states, essentially restricted to the early "civilizations."

In spite of this definitional consensus, it is recognized that, like chiefdoms, there is much variation in states studied by both archaeologists and anthropologists (e.g., Marcus and Feinman 1999:5; Keech McIntosh 1999:2). There is also debate over the sharpness of the divide between stratified and state societies (e.g., Fried 1967:185), especially given the proposal that what some call "complex chiefdoms" were in fact archaic states (Kristiansen 1991:18). Decision-making hierarchies are also not always expressed in settlement hierarchies and political hierarchies are not necessarily accompanied by economic centralization: here multiple heterarchies replace a single regional hierarchy. Indeed the extent of centralization within early states has now become a matter of individual determination rather than assumption (Stein 1998).

An alternative view of early states recognizes, as I have written elsewhere, "success for the few and oppression, exploitation and coercion for the many" (Chapman 2003:95). This view is derived from a historical materialist perspective, according to which state formation is "the emergence of institutions that mediate between the dependent but dominant class(es) and the producing class(es), while orchestrating the extraction of goods and labor used to support the continuation of class relations" (Gailey 1987:x). The power of the state is based on ideological and/or physical coercion and the private property of the dominant class is the main interest that the state is intended to protect. Such property may be natural resources (e.g., land), human labor, the means of production, or actual products. Lull and Risch (1995:100) propose that the archaeological analysis of property relations is best pursued through the analysis of differences in production and access to that production, as well as the generation of surplus: the latter is more than simply excess production, as is commonly defined, but rather the appropriation of that production by groups not physically responsible for it. This alternative view places emphasis on the structural changes that took place between kin- and class-based societies, including changes in property relations, the allocation and exploitation of labor, and the emergence of physical and ideological coercion. Such structural relations should be distinguished from the material forms taken by early state societies.

Given these different views of social change in state and non-state societies, let alone what are accepted as the criteria for defining the state, I will not present the usual sequence of Mediterranean societies trying to reach higher rungs on the neo-evolutionary ladder of complexity. Instead my focus will be on sequences of change, highlighting any evidence for tensions or conflicts, variations in structural relations, and the material representations of such relations. In line with this approach I will reverse the usual east-to-west treatment of Mediterranean societies (the former being supposedly more "complex" than the latter) and begin in the west. I am also mindful of the observation (e.g., Cherry 1984:21–22) that our understanding of the development of Aegean Bronze Age states should be seen in the context of Mediterranean societies as a whole: Why were these states present in some areas and not in others, at least until a later date? Recent research suggests that this question might be recast: How did different material forms of the state develop in different regions of the Mediterranean at different times in later prehistory?

Conflict, Exploitation, and Coercion in the West Mediterranean

Any attempt to answer these questions has to recognize the variable quality of the archaeological record in different regions of the Mediterranean. Temporal scales vary in precision according to the intensity of use of radiocarbon and tree-ring dating, while spatial patterning has to be understood in the context of the intensity of modern surface survey, which was pioneered in the Near East, adopted initially in Italy and Greece, and then developed even further in the Aegean and the east Mediterranean (Knapp 1997:19–27). Evidence of productive activities, and especially their social contexts, is still restricted in scope and quality. The chronological resolution of deposition in burial contexts is largely too coarse for the kinds of questions we wish to ask about differences of age, gender, and social position in later prehistory.

For these reasons I want to begin with the archaeological record of southeast Spain, where there has been an intensification of stratigraphic and area excavations, surface surveys, and radiocarbon dating during the last four decades (see Figure 4.1 for the main sites mentioned in the text). Settlements such as Los Millares, Fuente Alamo, Gatas, and Peñalosa are providing the higher-quality

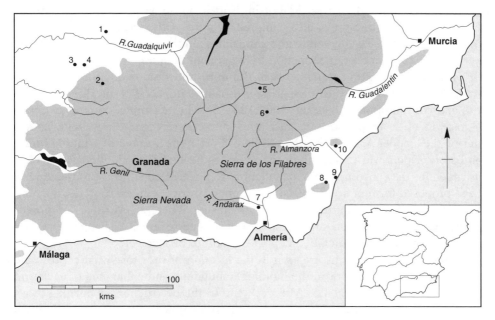

Figure 4.1 Location of main sites in southeast Spain mentioned in the text. Land over 500 m altitude shaded. 1. Peñalosa; 2. Marroquíes Bajos; 3. Albalate; 4. Alcores; 5. Cerro de la Virgen; 6. El Malagón; 7. Los Millares; 8. Gatas; 9. Las Pilas; 10. Fuente Alamo

contextual evidence that supports a radically different understanding of changing societies in the third and second millennia B.C. (for fuller details, see Chapman 2003:101–163).

The Neolithic agricultural communities that lived in southeast Spain in the two millennia prior to 3000 B.C. are known from open-air settlements, caves and rock shelters, and burial contexts. The majority of sites lack detailed contextual evidence and reliable absolute dating, while the open-air settlements are often small and ephemeral. The inference is of low density, mobile communities practicing animal and plant domestication, with little solid evidence for production beyond domestic needs. Communal burials in caves, stone cists, and circular tombs support the inference of kinship-based groups who used material items to mark out social distinctions based on age, gender, or group affiliation. There is no evidence of inequalities based on inter-generational control of productive activities.

During the third millennium B.C., or more specifically ca. 3000–2250 B.C., the period of the Copper Age, stratigraphic excavations and radiocarbon dating permit a better contextualized knowledge of the archaeological record. Site distributions and sizes suggest both an increase and an aggregation of local populations: the majority of open-air settlements were less than one hectare in size, but a small number, including Los Millares and Las Pilas, reached five hectares and there was marked discontinuity of settlement occupation in areas such as the Vera Basin. In contrast to the ephemeral and short-lived sites of the Neolithic, there was now greater sedentism and increased labor investment in domestic structures, systems of enclosing dry-stone walls, and communal tombs. Although of variable quality, the evidence for cereal cultivation and animal husbandry does not support the inference of unequal access to production between communities.

Evidence from within settlements in the third millennium B.C. has been used to propose the hypothesis of increasing inequalities in access to productive activities and consumption (Chapman 2003:126–130). For example, communal cereal storage in open-air pit clusters gave way to exclusively intra-household storage during the Copper Age, while at Los Millares Fort 1, the number of grinding stones and storage pots was greater than the numbers needed if production were solely intended for the consumption of its inhabitants. Specialized surplus production has been proposed for flint arrowheads, based upon restricted areas of production and the amount of skill required for pressure flaking. There is evidence for predominantly local production of lithics, as well as interregional exchange networks, although whether these included copper has still to be resolved.

Increased social tensions are seen in the location of sites for visual control, the investment of surplus labor in the building, rebuilding, and enhancing of enclosing wall systems (especially at Los Millares), and in the destruction or burning levels at sites such as Cerro de la Virgen and El Malagón. Whereas the communal tombs were the material embodiment of kinship group identity in the Neolithic, the situation was more complex in the Copper Age, with the investment in enclosing walls, the size of which is such that the term "fortification" seems justified. While such walls, where built, physically and symbolically defined settlement identity, differences in labor investment and grave-good consumption in the associated communal tombs suggest the existence of higher-ranked kinship groups or lineages: these groups were larger than the others and were therefore able to build larger tombs and accumulate more wealth items for deposition in the tombs (Chapman 2003:130–131; Micó 1991). In the case of Los Millares, such groups were able to locate their dead closer to the settlement. What is not yet clear is whether these groups also controlled the production of such wealth items, although the fact that they are found in other tombs might suggest not. Although the chronological control of tomb construction and use is still inadequate, it is proposed that the ideology of communal relations increasingly was being confronted with inequalities of wealth and access to production between individual groups and households.

The archaeological record of the Argaric Bronze Age has a more refined chronology, with three phases, ca. 2250–2000 B.C., 2000–1750 B.C., and 1750–1550 B.C., defined by stratigraphic excavation and radiocarbon dating on domestic and funerary contexts. The dating of human bone also enables us to measure the chronological relationship between different burial containers and grave goods, so that we can begin to assess the extent to which social relations changed through time and were symbolized in different ways. Initially there were marked disjunctions in settlement continuity and architecture, material culture, and mortuary rituals, although there is no evidence for population change. Site sizes suggest some population nucleation and in the Vera Basin overall population size may have doubled during the seven hundred years of Argaric occupation.

Analysis of plant and animal remains, grinding stones, and other macrolithic arti-facts (especially their frequencies per volume of excavated deposit at Gatas) forms the basis for proposing an increase in agricultural production by ca. 1700–1550 B.C., with the practice of more extensive, and more labor-intensive, barley mono-culture (Castro et al. 1999). The inverse relationship between site size/population and available cultivable land in the Vera Basin suggests that there was unequal access to agricultural production between the primary producers of the valley bottom and the consumers on the hilltop settlements that surrounded the basin. This is strength-ened by the evidence for the storage of instruments of production such as grind-ing stones and flint sickle blades within restricted areas of the hilltop settlements at Fuente Alamo and Gatas: experimental work shows that the concentrations of grinding stones exceeded the subsistence needs of the populations that lived in these settlements. Given the paucity of such instruments of production in the valley bottom sites, we may propose the existence of a regional political system in which the agricultural (and possibly linen) production of the valley bottom settlements was appropriated by those living in the hilltop settlements. In other words, this was a system of surplus production that, on current evidence, was primarily geared to local political and economic factors. Human labor was increased to support the appropriation of surplus and there was an increasing disparity between the labor invested in cereal agriculture and the product available to different interest groups. Social inequalities were based on differential access to land and to the means of production. This contradicts previous arguments that there was no evidence for "elite intervention in agricultural production" in Bronze Age Spain (Gilman 1991:160).

The creation of a more regional identity is seen in the standardization of pottery and metal artifacts, as well as in mortuary rituals, across an area of nearly 50,000 square kilometers of southeast Spain in which Argaric materials are present in the archaeological record. The conspicuous consumption of ornaments (especially of gold and silver), weapons, and other wealth items in intra-mural burials, along with detailed grave associations and the evidence for their location in relation to productive activities such as metalworking, has led to the proposal that there were five "levels" or "social categories" in the Argaric (Lull and Estévez 1986; Lull 2000). Inequalities are shown in differences of wealth and gender. There are examples of exclusive associations of metal objects with males or females. Weapon associations marked out a small number of adult males and are thought to sym-bolize the coercive power of the dominant group in society, while the females in this group are marked by the presence of silver diadems. Symbols of such coercion changed through time: halberds were confined to the period ca. 2000–1800 B.C., after which they were succeeded by swords (Lull 2000:581–584). In contrast, some other associations (e.g., females of the third "social category" with a dagger and awl each) stayed constant through time. Studies of kinship relations, as seen in metric analyses on skeletal remains, also suggest the existence of matrilocality, which may lie behind the changes in domestic architecture at this time (to accommodate families of related females and their husbands) (Chapman 2003:143–144).

The combination of various lines of evidence, especially relating to productive activities and the centralization of food production, cultural standardization, and the disposal of the dead, has led to the proposal of a class society in the Argaric (Lull 2000). Most recently, Risch (2002) has brought together the evidence for surplus appropriation and exploitation at Fuente Alamo with the spatial location and concentration of wealth consumption in individual tombs, arguing that this supports the inference of class divisions in different areas of the settlement, and hence a state organization. On the basis of the decision-making and administrative model of the state, the Argaric, with its two-level hierarchy, sites of only a few hectares in size, and the lack of palaces, temples, and so on, would not constitute a state. And yet it occupied an area over three times the size of Renfrew's (1975) Early State Module and it shows evidence of the main characteristics of the historical materialist definition of the state, especially in the period ca. 1750–1550 B.C.

A counter-argument, proposed interestingly by an avowed historical materialist, describes evidence of "complexity" (e.g., settlement hierarchies, hereditary elites, supra-village economic organization) as being "lacking or inadequate," while the sequence from Copper to Argaric Bronze Age was one of resolving tension between agricultural intensification and communal social institutions "not by the development of a more stable system of class stratification, but by a descent into internecine strife" (Gilman 2001:81). This argument also proposes that the standardization of Argaric pottery, metal, and mortuary rituals could just as easily have been the result of common "mental templates" that were not ideologically imposed by the Argaric ruling class (Gilman 2001:77, n.27). If that were the case, then how and why did such "templates" develop over 50,000 square kilometers in the late third and early second millennia B.C.? Such a question directs our attention not only to the beginning of the Argaric, but to the last few hundred years of the Copper Age: we need to know more about the organization of production within and between households and lineages, and the extent to which tensions were emerging between everyday social practices and communal ideologies, rather than putting our interpretive weight on general notions of "agricultural intensification." What is clear from the past two decades of research is that we now have better controlled data, both in time and space, for productive activities and social differences, as well as the relationship between them, in the period ca. 2250–1550 B.C., than in the preceding centuries of the third millennium B.C.

Southeast Spain is one of a small number of areas (see especially southern Portugal) in the Iberian Peninsula which have been argued to show a sequence of change toward increasing "complexity" from the third to the second millennia B.C. The use of this mostly undefined term is coupled with problems in its material form. For example, the number of so-called "fortified sites" in the Copper Age has increased from a handful to over a hundred during the past four decades (Oliveira Jorge 2003; Chapman 2003:168–173) and they extend beyond the areas in which "complex" societies were supposed to have developed at this time. These sites vary widely in their form, size, monumentality, energy investment, length of occupation, and use. For example, a group of major, monumental, ditched enclosures, such as Valencina de la Concepción (Seville) and Marroquíes Bajos (Jaén), include inner settlement areas of 20 and 32 hectares respectively, and outer areas of presumed cultivation and grazing, as well as tombs for the disposal of the dead. Such sites suggest both population aggregation and labor mobilization, but inferences about productive activities and social inequalities are still being developed: at Marroquíes Bajos it is proposed that there was a domestic mode of production, although there are differences in the location of textile and metal production, while the numbers of storage pits at Valencina de la Concepción have been used to support the inference of surplus production from a hinterland (although the absence of detailed data on their contemporaneity, the needs of the local population, and unequal access to production or the means of production makes this hypothesis difficult to support at present). The key point is that the organization of production and the extent of social inequalities require determination rather than the assumption that any such "fortified" or "monumental" site is a marker of a more "complex" society.

The historical materialist model of "initial class societies" and hence the state has also been used by Nocete (2001) for the Guadalquivir Valley in the third millennium B.C. The core of this state was supposed to have been in the upper part of the valley, where a small number of heavily fortified sites, such as Albalate and Alcores, were located in areas of agricultural production, defended by smaller sites exercising visual and physical control over political frontiers. This interpretation, including that of a large-scale political system linked to "primate centers" such as Valencina de la Concepción in the lower Guadalquivir Valley and beyond, is more contentious than that of the early state in the Argaric.

In the succeeding Bronze Age, contemporary with the Argaric, the settlement of Cabezo Juré, near Huelva, has yielded evidence of social asymmetries in metal production and consumption, as well as the absence of local agricultural production (Nocete 2001:111–123). In the upper Guadalquivir Valley, class relations have been inferred for the settlement at Peñalosa (Contreras 2000; Contreras et al. 1995), although the evidence is not consistent. For example, different categories of burials (themselves poorly preserved) are not associated spatially with areas in which there were differences in access to production and consumption, nor to the instruments of production. On the other hand, not all stages of metal production occur in all production areas and there is some evidence for unequal access to products such as silver.

Sites such as these, with intentionally collected data on inequalities in access to production and consumption from both domestic and burial contexts, are still comparatively rare in the Iberian Peninsula, let alone other areas of the west Mediterranean. As in Iberia, later prehistoric societies are conceived in terms of degrees and cycles of complexity, with individual societies being assigned to neo-evolutionary social types. For example, Robb (1999) uses ethnographic analogy to infer the development of "Big Men" societies in the Late Neolithic/Copper Age of Italy, while Malone et al. (1994:188) infer limited centralization before ca. 1300 B.C. in southern Italy, Sicily, and Malta, and hence not yet the development of a chiefdom society. After 1300 B.C. the presence of tombs with wealthy grave goods, the increase in defended settlements and settlement hierarchy, and the evidence for craft specialization eventually lead to the claim that Sicily was "on the brink of quite complex, chiefly societies" (Malone et al. 1994:192). There is little discussion of production and consumption, nor of surplus production (in the sense defined in this paper). For example, it is claimed that the Middle Bronze Age (late second millennium B.C.) coastal settlement of Thapsos on Sicily was "semi/proto-urban" (Malone et al. 1994:179), but there is no discussion about how its population was supported and the extent to which it comprised both producers and non-producers, let alone its relations with its hinterland.

A further example comes from the island of Sardinia (Webster 1996). Here regional, ritual integration is suggested by the 10-meter-high truncated pyramid at Monte d'Accodi in the fourth millennium B.C. and chiefdom-like societies, with more nucleated settlements and enclosure/fortification developed in the third millennium B.C. (Webster 1996:62). For the period between ca. 2300 and 1300 B.C., Webster (1996:81) infers a "non-hierarchical" or "tribal" society, given the absence of a settlement hierarchy, but "simple/petty chiefdoms" return ca. 1300–900 B.C. (1996:130–133), with more complex stone monuments and a three-level settlement hierarchy in the southwest of the island. Full social stratification and classes only emerged ca. 900–500 B.C.

This sequence of social change depends heavily on the presence/absence of settlement hierarchies and is subject to debate. More intensive radiocarbon dating is required, especially of the claimed monument sequence, while it is argued that chiefdoms were present from the beginning of the Bronze Age and that a class system developed from these chiefdoms during the second millennium B.C., with elites supported by the tribute of a lower class (Perra 1997). Such an interpretation leaves open the question as to when stratification really developed. There is evidence for larger corralling and storage facilities, but not of centralized metallurgy, by ca. 1300 B.C., but only between ca. 900 and 500 B.C. is there evidence for household specialists, and the larger, more complex monuments have evidence for greater production and storage. Such evidence would suggest a comparatively late date for stratification. But at Nuraghe Trobas, dated to the period ca. 1800–1300 B.C., there were found 28 grinding stones and 122 pestles (Webster 1996:95), possible evidence for the kind of concentration of instruments of production that we have seen in southeast Spain. Evidence such as this is rare, as are studies of the relationship between settlement/population size and agricultural potential, as have been done for the Vera Basin. Such studies would allow us to determine the extent of social inequality in Sardinia before the periods of Greek, Phoenician, and Roman expansion in the first millennium B.C.

Some scholars even dismiss the notion of stratification for such Bronze Age societies as are seen in the west Mediterranean. Given that "the elite did not retain the power to enforce unequal access to resources over long periods," the use of the term stratification is "misplaced," and it is better to think in terms of "fluid and competitive ranking rather than fixed hereditary succession to status" (Mathers and Stoddart 1994:16). The same scholars also contrast the levels of cultural development, mainly between the East and West Mediterranean Basins, during the Bronze Age: the material forms of such development included writing, institutionalized bureaucracy, monumental public and funerary architecture, representational elite iconography, and a professional standing army. But these are material forms, and not the actual structure of these societies. The extent to which west Mediterranean societies were kin or class based, with all that this implies, in the third and second millennia B.C., is a question for further research. The discussion in this section suggests a potentially more dynamic picture of social change than has previously been conceived. How does this compare with what was happening over the same period of time in the east Mediterranean? The focus of what follows is on mainland Greece, the Cycladic islands, and Crete.

Society, Material Representation, and the State in the Aegean

The theme of the "emergence of civilization" from the third to second millennia B.C. in the Aegean was given a major impetus by the seminal publication of Renfrew (1972) just over thirty years ago. Rereading this book, it is interesting to observe the ambiguity in Renfrew's discussion on the nature of Minoan-Mycenaean society. On the one hand he refers to "a number of large chiefdoms or principalities" (Renfrew 1972:363), on the other he observes that "the palace principalities can . . . be regarded as minor states, effectively organized economically, but in other respects not differing so strongly from chiefdoms" (1972:369). Using both the neo-evolutionism of anthropology and the archaeological record of Near Eastern civilizations, Renfrew found it difficult to assign the Aegean Bronze Age cultures to either the chiefdom or state levels of social evolution. For example, these cultures were "organized on a basis more complex than the usual tribal level, (but) lacked . . . some of the features of the developed state" (1972:364), had "an economic organization which rivalled in complexity that of the Near Eastern states" (1972:368) and "social stratification" (1972:377), and Mycenaean society was "something more than chiefdoms, something less than states" (1972:369).

During the past three decades there has been more of a consensus that state society developed in the Aegean Bronze Age, while still recognizing the local form(s) taken by the state in this region (e.g., Cherry 1984, 1986; Halstead 1994; Manning 1994). More problematic has been the nature of social forms preceding the state in the Aegean: for example, were third millennium B.C. societies on Crete "egalitarian," "big men," or even "chiefdoms"? Such neo-evolutionary types still tend to dominate thought. Apart from the use of these types, part of the problem stems from the material representation of social relations: in what ways were inequalities materially expressed, and how does our knowledge of the archaeological record aid or impede our inferences of such inequalities? Recent research enables us to address such issues, as well as the nature of local state societies. In what follows I will largely avoid both the problems and pitfalls of Aegean Bronze Age periodization and absolute chronology, and use the papers contained in Cullen (2001) as the most recent syntheses. Figure 4.2 shows the location of the main sites mentioned in the text.

I begin with the third millennium B.C. societies living on the Cycladic islands, mainly because of the challenges posed by comparative analysis of their settlement

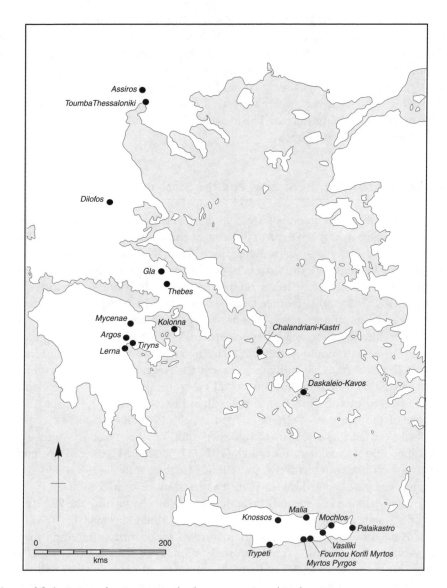

Figure 4.2 Location of main sites in the Aegean mentioned in the text

and funerary records (a problem we have already noted for southeast Spain). This task has been enhanced by the "data explosion" of the past three decades (for details, see Broodbank 2000). The settlements are less than one hectare in size, range from "farmsteads" to "hamlets" and "villages," and witness small populations dispersed among areas of cultivable land. They suggest the existence of "egalitarian" societies, but there is a change in form during the middle and late third millennium Keros-Syros culture, when what are interpreted as "major" sites of about one hectare are known from mainly coastal locations, with some evidence of craft production. At the core of sites such as Chalandriani-Kastri, and probably Daskaleio-Kavos, were dry-stone enclosures with external bastions, as well as separate settlement and cemetery areas. Interestingly, much of the evidence of craft production at the first of these sites occurs in one room within the enclosure (Broodbank 2000:215). The absence of detailed, contextual analyses of productive activities within and between the structures of such settlements, let alone of the surplus labor invested in the enclosure walls, limits our ability to assess the extent of social inequalities, apart from inferences about the outcome of trading through long-distance voyaging (Broodbank 2000:245–275).

Although the third millennium B.C. funerary evidence from the Cyclades has been known much longer, it still suffers from a paucity of both contextual data and skeletal analyses. Two observations, however, are of interest. First, Broodbank (2000:171) has argued that the mortuary rituals of the early third millennium B.C. exemplify a conflict between the expression of community identity (and hence the claim to land) through burial in cemeteries and individual claims to status through single burial with what are interpreted as "prestige" goods. Within the contemporary communal burials of southern Crete and southeast Spain, individual identity was concealed within communal burials. Secondly, the consumption of such "prestige" goods with burials increased during the course of the third millennium B.C., while their average life-span appears to have decreased, and some appear to have been deliberately "killed" (Broodbank 2000:263, 268). This is interpreted as evidence of competitive display, as the communal ideology was increasingly confronted with the outcome of individuals or households jockeying for social power. As in southeast Spain, however, the quality of both the settlement and funerary data still leaves open the extent of social inequalities on the Cyclades before the end of the third millennium B.C.

The extent of such inequalities during the same time period on Crete is also still open to debate, as is the nature of the transition to local states and their conformity with neo-evolutionary models. Given the consensus on the existence of a form of Protopalatial state society in Middle Minoan (MM) IB-II (ca. 1900–1750 B.C.), attention is then focused on the Early Minoan (EM) II (ca. 2700–2200 B.C.), EM III (ca. 2200–2100 B.C.), and MM IA (ca. 2100–1900 B.C.) periods to assess the degree to which state formation was a "discontinuous quantum leap" (Cherry 1983:33).

The nature of EM II society depends, as it does in the Cyclades and southeast Spain, on the interpretation of settlement and funerary evidence (e.g., Watrous 2001 for an overall summary). The settlements are mainly small, dispersed "hamlets" or "farmsteads," which are located in close proximity to cultivable soils. The classic analysis is that of Fournou Korifi Myrtos, for which Whitelaw (1983) proposed a division into five or six economically independent households, each with their own food production and storage areas, and none with evidence for inequalities in access to material products. More recently, small settlements at sites such as Trypeti and Vasiliki show evidence for groups of houses, some of which have store-rooms and annexes, although the preliminary information (Watrous 2001:168–171) does not allow evaluation of the extent to which there was equal access to production. Some settlements in more densely occupied areas increased in size, but none compared to the five hectares of Knossos, the architectural features of which suggest to Manning (1999:474) a "big man" or "chiefdom" organization.

Early Minoan funerary practices, as seen especially in the tholos tombs of the Mesara in southern central Crete, show the submergence of individual to communal identities, either of local lineages or clans (Branigan 1998; Murphy 1998) or individual nuclear families (Whitelaw 1983). Tholoi were located close to settlements and were the focus of a series of consumption and purification rituals. During EMII and MMIA, there is an increase in the deposition of "prestige goods" and "symbols of authority," as well as the addition of small, exclusive, areas to the tombs, suggesting to Murphy (1998:37–39) the development of "stratified ranked societies" analogous to chiefdoms, in which ritual was being used as a means of social advancement. Elsewhere Whitelaw (1983:337) discussed the differences in structural elaboration and wealth deposition in the tombs of Mochlos with respect to differences in family status. To infer chiefdoms and stratified ranking seems to be stretching such evidence too far. We might instead see the funerary evidence in much the same way as it is seen in southeast Spain, with a communal ideology and perhaps larger households and lineage groups building larger tombs and/or gaining access to greater amounts of wealth items.

Putting together this domestic and funerary evidence, there seems to be little support for anything more than competing households/lineages over most of Crete during much of the third millennium B.C., excepting the implications of the larger population at Knossos. Schoep (1999a), however, argues for what she calls "more elaborate" forms of social organization, as seen, for example, in the central authority implied by the size and architecture of Knossos, the monumental architecture of Palaikastro, the evidence for some form of administrative activities (e.g., seal stones, imprints on vases, and loomweights) and the possibility of a predecessor to the Protopalatial palace at Malia. She also notes that the earliest evidence for writing is in EMIII, a period of supposed discontinuity in settlement and tomb use after abandonment and destruction. The limited areas of excavations for both EMII and MMIA occupations, especially given the structural remodeling of such settlements caused by the subsequent Protopalatial and Neopalatial occupations, make the assessment of such evidence difficult. For Watrous (2001:215), the second phase of MMIA was the key, with the development of "palaces" and towns, the differentiated use of space for residence, storage, and craft production, and evidence of a "literate bureaucracy" for the administration of goods including sheep, wine, grain, and figs. These changes mark the beginnings of city states, but the details of their development have still to be clarified.

The nature of this early state society is now a major topic of research. Manning (1999:476–477) has argued that "Crete may in fact offer a type of mini or proto-state, or "early state" of a type different to the conventional larger states of anthropology and ancient history, and the traditional neo-evolutionary models." This reflects the difficulties in dealing with early Aegean states that were highlighted in Renfrew's (1972) analysis (see above), the recognition of variation in state societies and the extent to which one can actually divide up "stratified" and "state" societies, or "complex chiefdoms" and "archaic states" (see above).

This debate has been taken further by Knappett (1999) and Schoep (1999b; 2002; Knappett and Schoep 2000). Knappett (1999) focuses on one of the Middle Minoan states, centered on the town of Malia, where areas such as the Quartier Mu have yielded evidence of workshops for craft production, extensive storage areas, a sanctuary, and palatial architecture. He maps out the area of Malia's possible territory from the north to the south of the island (Figure 4.3) and uses analyses of pottery production to propose that there was centralized production within Malia, but non-centralized production in its territory, as seen at the site of Myrtos Pyrgos, over 30 kilometers distant on the south coast. The evidence also supports the hypothesis that exchange between regional sites was independent of palace control. Knappett proposes the existence of a decentralized state, in which there were "low levels of administrative intervention in the day-to-day economic affairs of dependent populations" (1999:631). The nature and extent of political centralization depended upon ideological coercion, rather than physical coercion and control of the regional economic base.

Schoep (2002) takes a complementary approach to Knappett, examining the evidence for productive, administrative, and ritual activities within the town of Malia. Her basic argument is that rather than there being a centralized palace authority over these activities, they were distributed in different parts of the town and under

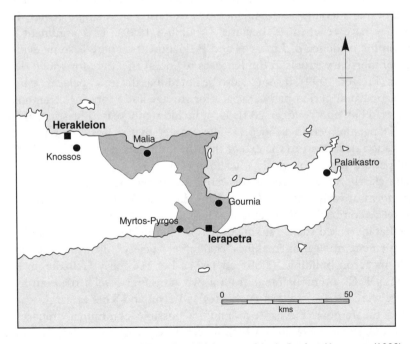

Figure 4.3 Proposed extension of Prepalatial Malia state (shaded), after Knappett (1999)

the authority of several elite groups: in other words, this was what Schoep calls "a heterarchical social landscape" (2002:117). The competition between these groups is seen also in architectural divisions, in evidence for conspicuous consumption, and in mortuary data. Neither storage nor ritual activities were confined to the "palace," nor is it clear whether this was used for elite residence (thus further bringing into doubt the validity of this term). Moving beyond the town, Schoep supports Knappett's hypothesis of the Malia state being composed largely of economically autonomous communities (2002:122).

The proposal that the first state societies in Crete were less centralized and more heterarchical than has been previously thought has wider implications. First, the degree of centralization has to be demonstrated rather than assumed. Secondly, it is perhaps not surprising that these early states such as Malia lasted about two hundred years, or six to seven generations, before a phase of widespread palace destruction in Middle Minoan II: with competing elites, economically autonomous communities in the hinterland, and the absence of physical coercion, such states were inherently unstable and had a short "life expectancy." At the same time, if we are now to understand the "palaces" in terms of ceremonial or ritual centers for competing elites, then their destruction in MMII may not necessarily have had as wide an impact on Minoan culture, economy, and society as has also been assumed.

The extent of centralization is also an issue for the succeeding Neopalatial (MMIII-LMIB, ca. 1750–1500 B.C.) and Final Palatial (LMII-LMIIIB, ca. 1500–1300 B.C.) Cretan societies. Schoep (1999b) argues for greater political and administrative centralization in the Neopalatial period, accepting the possibility that political and/or ideological dominance was exercised by a single center, Knossos, which may have reached 75 hectares (Manning 1999). This argument is based largely on the evidence of Linear A and B documents. There is some evidence for the use of mortuary rituals in the Knossos region at this time for wider ideological purposes (Preston 1999). It should also be noted that the new "palaces" constructed in the Neopalatial period had *less* space for storage and more for ceremonial/ritual activities (Rehak and Younger 2001:395), including increased feasting. By the end of the Neopalatial period Schoep (1999b) argues that political and administrative centralization decreased to the extent that the domination of Knossos, in the Final Palatial period, was ideological rather than economic.

There clearly remain many unanswered questions about both the development and the form of early states in Crete. How does the sequence of change on mainland Greece compare with Crete? In Thessaly and southern Greece, it has been argued that increased social ranking developed in the later fourth millennium B.C., with settlement nucleation making "egalitarian society" unsustainable and elites living in megaron buildings (Halstead 1994). For the Early Helladic, in the third millennium B.C., opinions range from a two- to a four-level settlement hierarchy, and there were fortifications at such sites as Lerna and Thebes, large-scale buildings, and the famous Tiryns "rundbau," a possible communal granary (Rutter 2001:111; Halstead 1994:203), which together may suggest further social inequality, but its nature is far from agreed. Also a matter of debate is the nature of the site of Manika, on the island of Euboia, which was one of the largest sites in the

Aegean at this time, even taking into account the likelihood that not all of the known area (about 80 hectares) was occupied at this time (Davis 2001:36–39). Domestic architecture in EHII was centered on courtyards and probably housed nuclear and/or extended families (Harrison 1995). Unlike Crete, there is no evidence for monumental architecture until late in the third millennium B.C.

The interpretation of southern Greek society is no less ambiguous in Middle Helladic I–II, ca. 2050/2000–1750/1720 B.C. (Rutter 2001:124–135). Current attention focuses on the island of Aegina, a source of pottery and macrolithic exports to the mainland, and the important settlement of Kolonna, with its impressive fortifications and what is claimed to be the earliest shaft grave in the Aegean: this was located immediately outside a major entrance into the lower fortified settlement and contained a warrior burial associated with goods such as a bronze sword and a gold diadem. Evidence is claimed for agricultural storage, but the extent to which this was socially appropriated is unclear. The presence of other settlements on the mainland without such features as public architecture or wealthy tombs suggests to some a settlement hierarchy, while the presence of large settlements under modern towns at Argos and Thebes may support this. The claim that Kolonna embodies the Aegean's first state (Rutter 2001:145), even preceding Crete, is potentially of great importance, but lacks definition in terms of evidence for class relations and social exploitation. For most areas of southern Greece, neither the production nor the burial evidence supports the inference of non-kinship-based social relations (Voutsaki 1997:41).

If there is a fixed point in the social evolution of Bronze Age societies on the Greek mainland, then it must surely be the construction and use of the Shaft Graves at Mycenae. Over a century after their excavation by Schliemann, however, the periodization and social interpretation of Grave Circles A and B are still the subject of debate, especially given the problems posed by the records of artifacts, their contexts, and the number and sex of buried individuals. In this paper I follow the chronological proposal of Graziadio (1988; 1991), according to which deposition in Circle B lasted from late/end Middle Helladic until the end (with one exception) of Late Helladic I, while the burials of Circle A were all interred in this last period: this means that burial took place over a period of about 100–150 years, or maybe four to five generations (ca. 1750/1720–1600/1580 B.C.). Analysis of grave size and elaboration, as well as units of wealth and known age and sex data, by Graziadio (1991) suggests that these were individuals of ascribed wealth, including high-ranking males and females. There was an increase through time in the human labor invested in the size and elaboration of the graves, as well as in the deposition of wealth items, from the initial burials in Circle B, which were more like Middle Helladic cist graves, to Graves III-V in Circle A, which contained the majority of the wealth items. As in the Argaric of southeast Spain, weapons were mostly associated with males, while diadems marked out wealthy females. Coupled with the evidence of healthier, physically larger individuals, this analysis suggests the existence of social stratification and a ruling class. Facial reconstructions (Musgrave et al. 1995) support the case for families being deposited in individual graves and for different families being deposited in different parts of the Grave Circles. There also appears to have been no match between the facial likeness and the portrait on the gold death masks from Circle A. This is an interesting observation in relation to the symbolism of mortuary rituals, as is the fact that some burials contained more weapons than could have been used at one time.

The Shaft Graves are one example of the increasing amount of wealth items deposited with burials at this time in southern Greece. They are also part of a wider tradition of reusable, multiple burials, as in the tholoi of Messenia. Voutsaki (1997) argues that this conspicuous consumption of wealth items has to be understood within the context of social and political competition. Effectively the deposition of such items enables living relatives to "retain a symbolic 'ownership' of the goods even while seemingly giving them away, sacrificing them, denying their materiality" (Voutsaki 1997:38). In this way access to such goods is restricted and they are given a value associated with the living group, becoming its "property." The status of this group is now defined through the acquisition and deposition of such exotic items. Social demand rather than control of production is the basis of this status. The central part of Voutsaki's argument focuses on the social value of such goods and she rejects the position that such value is the product of labor, as in the classic Marxian formulation. The counter-argument is that the embodiment of that labor, whether near or distant, in material objects is critical in the initial ascription of value, such that the "social" value accrued during exchange simply accentuates the initial differences of "economic" value. The manipulation of such goods as those deposited in the Shaft Graves also requires an understanding of access to, and control of, their production. If social relations were kinship-based before the Shaft Grave period, how did such conspicuous consumption come about in the first place? And how does the evidence of wealth deposition and mortuary rituals at Mycenae and other sites in the period ca. 1750/1720–1400 B.C. compare with evidence for the control of production and the development of the relations of production? Given the problems posed by the primary data from the Shaft Graves, as well as the broader theoretical issues associated with the interpretation of mortuary rituals, this last question assumes an even greater importance.

It is during the Late Helladic III period, from the fourteenth to the mid-eleventh centuries B.C., that centralized states appear to have developed and declined in southern Greece. If the social and political landscape was populated by "chiefdoms" (Shelmerdine 2001:349) before this, then the change at the beginning of the fourteenth century is argued to be a discontinuous one. It would certainly be risky to project backward the economic and administrative organization displayed in the Linear B records from Late Helladic III. There is further evidence for population nucleation (e.g., Thebes at 50 hectares, Mycenae at 32 hectares), a three-level settlement hierarchy, the investment of surplus labor in the construction of elite palaces and massive fortifications, and sometimes extensive workshops and storerooms (e.g., the 2500 square meters of storerooms at Gla) both inside and outside citadel walls (Halstead 1994; Shelmerdine 2001). Large tholos tombs decreased in number and were concentrated at the palatial centers, where it is argued they were used for the disposal of a ruling class. It is still uncertain as to how many separate states existed, especially in areas like the Argive Plain (Shelmerdine 2001:344).

The Linear B tablets refer exclusively to palatial centers and document the existence of "bureaucratic states, regulating aspects of land tenure, agricultural activity, industrial production, exchange, religious observance and perhaps military service over a large territory" (Halstead 1994:206). The manufacture and mobilization of goods and agricultural products in palatial centers (including the support of feasting for the "wanax"/king), alongside the support of specialists, servants, and officials, and the top-down taxation system are all evidence of centralized elite control. At the same time, agricultural production in the non-palatial sector was not under palatial control and there are records of more independent workers (Shelmerdine 2001:362). Although there are clearly limits to this centralization, the states of Mycenae and its contemporary palatial centers took a different form to those on Crete, which were more decentralized and which have evidence for ideological rather than physical coercion. The investment of surplus labor in mortuary rituals was clearly greater on the Greek mainland than on Crete.

The detail provided by the Linear B records of centralized economic and political control in southern Greece is such that we often pay less attention to the purely archaeological evidence for such centralization further to the north. In Thessaly, more nucleated settlements developed in the Bronze Age, with sites such as Dilofos reaching 60 hectares and including an acropolis at the same time as the Late Helladic polities in southern Greece (Andreou et al. 2001:280). There has, however, been little research on both production and exchange at this time. Farther to the north, in Central Macedonia, there is also evidence of more centralized societies during the Late Bronze Age. The 14-meter-high tell settlement at Assiros has Late Helladic III occupation with evidence of agricultural storage in excess of the needs of the site's population: this is interpreted as being part of a regional economic structure that accumulated surplus to counter unpredictable harvests and not a centralized, elite-supporting economy (Andreou et al. 2001:301). More centralized organization, however, is proposed for sites such as Toumba Thessalonikis, which has clustered houses and extensive storerooms, and fortifications including large casemates (Andreou et al. 2001:303–304). These examples suggest that future research will help us to put the Late Bronze Age societies of southern Greece within a broader comparative context, and to examine more closely the relationships between the structural form and material representation of such societies.

Conclusions

As stated at the outset of this chapter, my coverage of third and second millennium B.C. societies in the Mediterranean has, by necessity, been selective. In spite of the inevitable omissions that may have resulted, what conclusions may we draw?

First, it is abundantly clear that the last three decades have witnessed major changes in the funerary and settlement records of later prehistoric societies across the Mediterranean Basin. The "data explosion" to which Broodbank refers for the Cycladic Islands has also occurred in many other regions. Interesting comparisons are beginning to be made between, for example, northern and southern Greece in the last three centuries of the second millennium B.C., or southeast Spain and the Aegean from the third to the second millennia B.C., or the sequences of social change on islands such as Sardinia and Crete. There are still major differences in spatial and chronological resolution, the intensity of both survey and excavation, and the evidence for access to production, as well as differences of class and property. Overall the potential for comparison of social forms, their material representation and their sequences, has been markedly enhanced.

Secondly, there have been some major changes of interpretation, as well as what might be regarded as "surprises" in the archaeological evidence. Examples include the proposal that there were decentralized states and heterarchical polities in second millennium Crete, as well as an earlier state centered on the site of Kolonna and the island of Aegina. The suggestion that a form of state society existed in southeast Spain during the second millennium is also surprising. Those who might find this difficult to accept may have fewer problems with the recognition that there is now evidence for elite intervention in production in this region. Elsewhere there are suggestions of possible centralization and stratification, perhaps even relations of class. These factors provide hypotheses for future evaluation.

Thirdly, there are periods of major disjunctions in local societies, but the key to their understanding lies in the conflicts and tensions of preceding centuries. These are imperfectly defined and understood, often because of the nature of the archaeological evidence. What is clear is the need for a more incisive attack on the evidence provided by both settlement evidence of access to production and the material traces of past mortuary rituals. For example, the tensions that have been proposed between communal ideologies and emerging inequalities between households and lineages require definition.

Fourthly, we need to move away from the attribution of Mediterranean societies to rather subjective degrees of complexity, or to neo-evolutionary types, as well as reappraising the use of terms such as "palace," or "villa" in Crete, or "urban" and "semi-urban" in parts of the central and west Mediterranean. The major term that has occupied our attention in this paper is that of the state. There are clearly conflicting definitions of early states. Even following some of the more accepted archaeological indicators, as in the Aegean, there is variation in the form of such states (e.g., centralized/decentralized, physical/ideological coercion). The materialist definition may be dismissed by some, but we would do well, at the very least, to take on board the emphasis on class relations, property, inequalities in participation in production and access to consumption, exploitation, and coercion. This directs us to areas of archaeological research that are still lacking in many regions of the Mediterranean.

When we start probing a little more deeply at the use of concepts such as chiefdom and state across the Mediterranean, we realize more clearly the difficulties we still have in trying to get to grips with its distinctive archaeological record. Like the areas we have considered in this chapter, there is still division of opinion on the extent to which hereditary elites or elite controlled production existed on Cyprus during the late third millennium B.C. (compare Frankel 1988 with Knapp 1990). In the succeeding centuries, Knapp (1994:271) argues that there was a major discontinuity about 1700 B.C., when there was "transformation of an isolated, village-based culture into an international, urban-oriented, complex society." For some this signifies the emergence of the state, associated with urban-based polities, ideological and physical coercion, elite areas and burials, international trade, and so on (for the features of the archaeological record, see Knapp 1994; for the emergence of an archaic state, see Peltenburg 1996). For others, there is a real difficulty in fitting these societies into either the chiefdom or the state models. Keswani (1996) favors a heterarchical model and questions any hierarchically organized political system with a paramount urban center at Enkomi, on the east coast, arguing for two patterns of urbanization, with complex chiefdoms emerging in the southern part of the island. In contrast, Webb (2003) proposes a single administrative system and a three-level ranking, based on the evidence of seals. Given these divisions of opinion, it is once again clear that a renewed focus on inequalities in access to production, consumption, and property would help us to gain a clearer idea of the nature of changing social relations in the third and second millennia B.C.

Lastly, the view of Mediterranean societies I have proposed here is more dynamic and variable than the usual east-west divide. This differs from the ethnographic emphasis on stability and conservatism. Instead the focus has fallen on tensions and conflicts, on disjunctions, on different pathways to institutionalized inequalities, on unstable political formations, and on the material representation of social relations. There is a basis for a more complex history of Mediterranean prehistoric societies here. Some of it is undoubtedly contentious, but equally it should be stimulating and perhaps lead us in new directions.

ACKNOWLEDGMENTS

I would like to thank the editors for their invitation to write this chapter and Emma Blake for her support, encouragement, and patience as successive deadlines passed. I have learned much about Aegean prehistory by having Sturt Manning as a colleague, although he would not necessarily agree with all that I have written here. I would also like to thank Linda Hulin for discussion and information on Cyprus.

REFERENCES

Andreou, Stelios, Michael Fotiadis, and Kostas Kotsakis, 2001 The Neolithic and Bronze Age of Northern Greece. In Aegean Prehistory. A Review. Tracey Cullen, ed. pp. 259–327. Boston: Archaeological Institute of America.

Barker, Graeme, 1981 Landscape and Society. Prehistoric Central Italy. London: Academic Press.

Branigan, Keith, 1998 The Nearness of You: Proximity and Distance in Early Minoan Funerary Behaviour. In Cemetery and Society in the Aegean Bronze Age. K. Branigan, ed. pp. 13–26. Sheffield: Sheffield Academic Press.

Braudel, Fernand, 1972 The Mediterranean and the Mediterranean World in the Age of Phillip II. London: Collins.

Broodbank, Cyprian, 2000 An Island Archaeology of the Early Cyclades. Cambridge: Cambridge University Press.

Castro, Pedro, Robert Chapman, Sylvia Gili, Vicente Lull, Rafael Micó, Cristina Rihuete, Roberto Risch, and Ma. Encarna Sanahuja, 1999 Agricultural Production and Social Change in the Bronze Age of Southeast Spain: The Gatas Project. Antiquity 73:846–856.

Chapman, Robert, 2003 Archaeologies of Complexity. London: Routledge.

Cherry, John, 1983 Evolution, Revolution and the Origins of Complex Society in Minoan Crete. *In* Minoan Society. Olga Krzyszkowska and Lucia Nixon, eds. pp. 33–45. Bristol: Bristol Classical Press.

——1984 The Emergence of the State in the Prehistoric Aegean. Proceedings of the Cambridge Philological Society 210:18–48.

——1986 Polities and Palaces: Some Problems in Minoan State Formation. *In* Peer Polity Interaction and Socio-Political Change. Colin Renfrew and John Cherry, eds. pp. 19–45. Cambridge: Cambridge University Press.

Contreras, Francisco, 2000 Proyecto Peñalosa. Análisis Histórico de las Comunidades de la Edad del Bronce del Piedemonte Meridional de Sierra Morena y Depresión Linares-Bailén. Seville: Junta de Andalucía.

Contreras, Francisco, Juan Antonio Cámara, Rafael Lizcano, Cristobal Pérez, Beatriz Robledo, and Gonzalo Trancho, 1995 Enterramientos y Diferenciación Social 1. El Registro Funerario del Yacimiento de la Edad del Bronce de Peñalosa (Baños de la Encina, Jaén). Trabajos de Prehistoria 52(1):87–108.

Cullen, Tracey, ed. 2001 Aegean Prehistory. A Review. Boston: Archaeological Institute of America.

Davis, Jack, 2001 The Islands of the Aegean. *In* Aegean Prehistory. A Review. Tracey Cullen, ed. pp. 19–94. Boston: Archaeological Institute of America.

Frankel, David, 1988 Pottery Production in Prehistoric Bronze Age Cyprus: Assessing the Problem. Journal of Mediterranean Archaeology 1(2):27–55.

Fried, Morton, 1967 The Evolution of Political Society. New York: Random House.

Gailey, Christine, 1987 Kinship to Kingship. Gender Hierarchy and State Formation in the Tongan Islands. Austin: University of Texas Press.

Gilman, Antonio, 1991 Trajectories toward Social Complexity in the Later Prehistory of the Mediterranean. *In* Chiefdoms: Power, Economy and Ideology. T. Earle, ed. pp. 14–68. Cambridge: Cambridge University Press.

——2001 Assessing Political Development in Copper and Bronze Age Southeast Spain. *In* From Leaders to Rulers. J. Haas, ed. pp. 59–81. New York: Kluwer Academic/Plenum.

Graziadio, Giampaolo, 1988 The Chronology of the Graves of Circle B at Mycenae: A New Hypothesis. American Journal of Archaeology 92(3):343–372.

——1991 The Process of Social Stratification at Mycenae in the Shaft Grave Period: A Comparative Examination of the Evidence. American Journal of Archaeology 95(3):403–440.

Halstead, Paul, 1994 The North–South Divide: Regional Paths to Complexity in Prehistoric Greece. *In* Development and Decline in the Mediterranean Bronze Age. Clay Mathers and Simon Stoddart, eds. pp. 195–219. Sheffield: J. R. Collis Publications.

Harrison, Steven, 1995 Domestic Architecture in Early Helladic II: Some Observations on the Form of Non-Monumental Houses. Annual of the British School at Athens 90:28–40.

Horden, Peregrine, and Nicholas Purcell, 2000 The Corrupting Sea: A Study of Mediterranean History. Oxford: Blackwell.

Keech McIntosh, Susan, 1999 Pathways to Complexity: An African Perspective. *In* Beyond Chiefdoms: Pathways to Complexity in Africa. S. Keech McIntosh, ed. pp. 1–30. Cambridge: Cambridge University Press.

Keswani, Priscilla, 1996 Hierarchies, Heterarchies and Urbanization Processes: The View from Bronze Age Cyprus. Journal of Mediterranean Archaeology 9(2):211–250.

Knapp, A. Bernard, 1990 Production, Location and Integration in Bronze Age Cyprus. Current Anthropology 31:147–176.

—— 1994 Emergence, Development and Decline on Bronze Age Cyprus. *In* Development and Decline in the Mediterranean Bronze Age. Clay Mathers and Simon Stoddart, eds. pp.271–304. Sheffield: J. R. Collis Publications.

—— 1997 The Archaeologies of Late Bronze Age Cypriot Society: The Study of Settlement, Survey and Landscape. Department of Archaeology, University of Glasgow, Occasional Paper 4. Glasgow.

Knappett, Carl, 1999 Assessing a Polity in Protopalatial Crete: The Malia-Lasithi State. American Journal of Archaeology 103:615–639.

—— and Ilse Schoep, 2000 Continuity and Change in Minoan Political Power. Antiquity 74: 365–371.

Kristiansen, Kristian, 1991 Chiefdoms, States and Systems of Social Evolution. *In* Chiefdoms: Power, Economy and Ideology. T. Earle, ed. pp. 16–43. Cambridge: Cambridge University Press.

Lull, Vicente, 2000 Argaric Society: Death at Home. Antiquity 74: 581–590.

—— and Jordí Estévez, 1986 Propuesta Metodológica para el Studio de las Necropolis Argáricas. *In* Homenaje a Luis Siret, pp. 441–452. Sevilla: Junta de Andalucía.

—— and Roberto Risch, 1995 El Estado Argárico. Verdolay 7:97–109.

Malone, Caroline, Simon Stoddart, and Ruth Whitehouse, 1994 The Bronze Age of Southern Italy, Sicily and Malta c. 2000–800 B.C. *In* Development and Decline in the Mediterranean Bronze Age. Clay Mathers and Simon Stoddart, eds. pp. 167–194. Sheffield: J. R. Collis Publications.

Manning, Sturt, 1994 The Emergence of Divergence: Development and Decline on Bronze Age Crete and the Cyclades. *In* Development and Decline in the Mediterranean Bronze Age. Clay Mathers and Simon Stoddart, eds. pp. 221–270. Sheffield: J. R. Collis Publications.

—— 1999 Knossos and the Limits of Settlement Growth. *In* Meletemata. Studies in Aegean Archaeology Presented to Malcolm H. Wiener as He Enters his 65th Year. P. P. Betancourt, V. Karageorghis, R. Laffineur, and W.-D. Niemeier, eds. pp. 469–480. Liège and Austin: Histoire de l'art et archéologie de la Grèce antique, Université de Liège and Program in Aegean Scripts and Prehistory, University of Texas at Austin.

Marcus, Joyce, and Gary Feinman, 1999 Introduction. *In* Archaic States. Gary Feinman and Joyce Marcus, eds. pp. 3–13. Santa Fe: School of American Research Press.

Mathers, Clay, and Simon Stoddart, eds., 1994 Development and Decline in the Mediterranean Bronze Age. Sheffield: J. R. Collis Publications.

Micó, Rafael, 1991 Objeto y Discurso Arqueológico. El Calcolítico del Sudeste Peninsular. Revista d'Arqueologia de Ponent 1:51–70.

Murphy, Joanne, 1998. Ideologies, Rites and Rituals: A View of Prepalatial Minoan Tholoi. *In* Cemetery and Society in the Aegean Bronze Age. K. Branigan, ed. pp. 27–40. Sheffield: Sheffield Academic Press.

Musgrave, J. H., R. A. H. Neave, and A. J. N. W. Prag, 1995 Seven Faces from Grave Circle B at Mycenae. Annual of the British School at Athens 90:107–136.

Nocete, Francisco, 2001 Tercer Milenio antes de Nuestra Era. Relaciones y Contradicciones centro/periferia en el Valle del Guadalquivir. Barcelona: Bellaterra.

Oliveira Jorge, Susana, 2003 Revisiting Some Earlier Papers on the Late Prehistoric Walled Enclosures of the Iberian Peninsula. Journal of Iberian Archaeology 5:89–135.

Peltenburg, E. J. 1996. From Isolation to State Formation in Cyprus, c. 3500–1500 B.C. In The Development of the Cypriot Economy from the Prehistoric Period to the Present Day. V. Karageorghis and D. Michaelides, eds. pp. 17–44. Nicosia: Bank of Cyprus.

Perra, Mauro, 1997 From Deserted Ruins: An Interpretation of Nuragic Sardinia. Europeae III-2:49–76.

Preston, Laura, 1999 Mortuary Practices and the Negotiation of Social Identities at LMII Knossos. Annual of the British School at Athens 94: 131–143.

Rehak, Paul, and John G. Younger, 2001 Neopalatial, Final Palatial and Postpalatial Crete. In Aegean Prehistory. A Review. Tracey Cullen, ed. pp. 383–473. Boston: Archaeological Institute of America.

Renfrew, Colin, 1972 The Emergence of Civilisation. London: Methuen.

——1973 Before Civilization. London: Penguin.

——1975 Trade as Action at a Distance: Questions of Integration and Communication. In Ancient Civilization and Trade. J. A. Sabloff and C. C. Lamberg-Karlovsky, eds. pp. 3–59. Albuquerque: School of American Research Press.

Risch, Roberto, 2002 Recursos Naturales, Medios de Producción y Explotación Social. Mainz am Rhein: Philipp von Zabern.

Robb, John, 1999 Great Persons and Big Men in the Italian Neolithic. In Social Dynamics of the Prehistoric Central Mediterranean. R. H. Tykot, J. Morter, and J. E. Robb, eds. pp. 111–121. London: Accordia Specialist Studies on the Mediterranean 3.

Rutter, Jeremy, 2001 The Prepalatial Bronze Age of the Southern and Central Greek Mainland. In Aegean Prehistory. A Review. Tracey Cullen, ed. pp. 95–155. Boston: Archaeological Institute of America.

Schoep, Ilse, 1999a The Origins of Writing and Administration on Crete. Oxford Journal of Archaeology 18(3):265–276.

——1999b Tablets and Territories? Reconstructing Late Minoan IB Political Geography through Undeciphered Documents. American Journal of Archaeology 103: 201–221.

——2002 Social and Political Organization on Crete in the Proto-Palatial Period: The Case of Middle Minoan II Malia. Journal of Mediterranean Archaeology 15.1:101–132.

Shelmerdine, Cynthia, 2001 The Palatial Bronze Age of the Southern and Central Greek Mainland. In Aegean Prehistory. A Review. Tracey Cullen, ed. pp. 329–381. Boston: Archaeological Institute of America

Stein, Gil, 1998 Heterogeneity, Power and Political Economy: Some Current Research Issues in the Archaeology of Old World Complex Societies. Journal of Archaeological Research 6:1–44.

Voutsaki, Sofia, 1997 The Creation of Value and Prestige in the Aegean Late Bronze Age. Journal of European Journal of Archaeology 5(2):34–52.

Watrous, Vance, 2001 Crete from Earliest Prehistory through the Protopalatial Period. In Aegean Prehistory. A Review. Tracey Cullen, ed. pp. 157–223. Boston: Archaeological Institute of America.

Webb, Jennifer M., 2003 Device, Image and Coercion: The Role of Glyptic in the Political Economy of Late Bronze Age Cyprus. In Script and Seal Use on Cyprus in the Bronze and Iron Ages (Colloquium and Conference Papers 4). J. S. Smith, ed. pp. 111–154. Boston: American Institute of Archaeology.

Webster, Gary, 1996 A Prehistory of Sardinia 2300–500 B.C. Sheffield: Sheffield Academic Press.

Whitelaw, Todd, 1983 The Settlement at Fournou Korifi Myrtos and Aspects of Early Minoan Social Organisation. *In* Minoan Society. Olga Krzyszkowska and Lucia Nixon, eds. pp. 323–345. Bristol: Bristol Classical Press

Wiessner, Polly, 2002 The Vines of Complexity: Egalitarian Structures and the Institutionalisation of Inequality among the Enga. Current Anthropology 43:233–269.

Wright, Henry, 1977 Recent Research on the Origins of the State. Annual Review of Anthropology 6:379–397.

Wright, Henry, and Gregory Johnson, 1975 Population, Exchange and Early State Formation in Southwestern Iran. American Anthropologist 77:267–289.

5

The Material Expression of Cult, Ritual, and Feasting

Emma Blake

Introduction

The material expression of a ritual is arguably its least important aspect, when compared to the beliefs, inspirations, and social purposes underpinning it. This is particularly true when it comes to rituals relating to cult. Just as today a religious experience is understood to transcend the physical surroundings and material objects associated with it, so too would such experiences have done in the past. Yet it is increasingly clear that contemporary notions of such concepts as religion and the sacred may be of little help in understanding these concepts in prehistory. It is virtually impossible even to agree on the particular referents of ritual symbolism, let alone infer from those referents either the transcendent, ineffable experience of the ritual, or the tenets of the cult itself. In spite of these limitations in inference, or perhaps because of them, the acts and materiality of worship take on enormous weight. Therefore, an examination of the materiality of cult practice in prehistory is of sustained interest to prehistorians as a source of evidence on more approachable topics such as cosmology or indirectly, social structure, although these too are problematic endeavors (Garwood et al. 1991:ix).

The Oxford English Dictionary's primary definition of cult is "reverential homage rendered to a divine being or beings." It is a secondary definition emphasizing the materiality of worship "in reference to its external rites and ceremonies" that is of particular relevance to archaeology. In the case of cult activities, "Religious belief asserts the existence of some transcendental, supernatural force or power, or of several of these. It is the purpose of cult to bring the participating humans, and also sometimes those whom they represent, into some more direct relation with these transcendental realities" (Renfrew 1985:16). To achieve this connection with the divine, some type of human action is required. In his recent, ambitious, and cross-cultural study of pre-modern state-level societies, Trigger (2003:472) notes that sacrifice and prayer would have been the two most important activities of ancient cults. Sacrifices, as nourishment to the gods, involved the offering of food and drink as well as non-edible items of all kinds (Trigger 2003:483). To the degree that such sacrifices are symbolic rather than involving the literal consumption of the gift by a deity, the sacrifices can on occasion be substituted by a further symbol, a representation of the gift such as a statue of a sheep rather than a real one, or miniature bowls rather than full-sized ones.

Colin Renfrew's opening chapter in *The Archaeology of Cult* (1985) offers a sound framework for archaeological approaches to cult and ritual practices in antiquity. In it he outlines a methodology for inferring past cult and ritual behavior from the material record. Renfrew defines religious ritual as ". . . the performance of expressive actions of worship and propitiation by the human celebrant towards the transcendent being" (1985:18). What we should expect archaeologically, then, is to see in some form or other: "1) evidence for expressive actions (of prayer, of sacrifice, of offering etc.); and 2) some indications that a transcendent being is involved" (Renfrew 1985:20). Archaeologists rely heavily on the first sort of evidence: cult paraphernalia may include altars, hearths, libation tables; or offerings with recognizable forms but modified so as to be functionally useless, such as miniature bowls or deliberately broken full-sized vessels, or weapons made of soft metals. Animal sacrifices involving slaughter and immolation may be identified materially by ash and charcoal, animal bones, altars with channels for blood, and sometimes even implements such as blades for blood-letting and killing. In addition, remains of cult activities often look different from everyday activities in the location and nature of the deposition. These remains, imbued with heightened significance, may be treated more carefully. We might expect to see valuable objects left at the site, or taken permanently out of circulation by breakage, or purposefully arranged, resulting in structured depositions. We might also expect to see a clear delimiting of space, with no mixing of sacred and profane activities.

Underpinning the study of this evidence of cult activity is the assumption that it will in some way differ from non-cult assemblages. This is particularly problematic when distinguishing it from a ritual action that is not religious in nature. The potential for misreading the material remains is real, as Renfrew points out, particularly in the absence of iconography pointing explicitly to a cult, such as a representation of a god. Indeed, throughout much of Mediterranean prehistory, there is little evidence that divinities were even conceived of in anthropomorphic terms (Goodison and Morris 1998:119). Even if we can identify an activity as relating to religious worship, the nature of the beliefs underpinning that activity may be indeterminate. The problem is compounded by the fact that religions are not static: they undergo internal transformations that may not be reflected by any corresponding changes in practice. Thus the conservatism of religious imagery may mask significant changes in belief. To take a later example, the votive statuettes of the maternal Egyptian goddess Isis depicted in Roman Egypt with her infant son Harpocrates were re-signified by the fourth century A.D. as the Christian Mary and Jesus, with little change to the iconography itself (Wilfong 1997:29). Even without evidence to reconstruct the object of cult or the nature of the beliefs associated with it, nevertheless we may seek general patterns concerning the practice and social significance of the cult and associated rituals.

Ritual and Society

Lukes offers a succinct definition of ritual as "rule-governed activity of a symbolic character which draws the attention of its participants to objects of thought and feeling which they hold to be of special significance" (Lukes 1975:291) (see Knapp 1996 for further discussion of definitions). From the rich iconography relating to Minoan cults provided by the engraved scenes on sealstones, gold rings, ceramics, and wall frescoes, Warren (1988) has identified five ritual actions: dance, blood sacrifice, baetylic rituals of touching a stone, the presentation of a robe to a female deity, and the collection and presentation of flowers to a deity (Warren 1988:11–30). These depicted actions, perhaps the closest we can get to *seeing* prehistoric ritual, have a wider application in other prehistoric contexts. What is interesting is the purposive nature of these rituals as Warren presents them: the goal of epiphany, or at least some indirect divine intervention, is central, and is an aspect that is not explicit in Lukes' more general definition of ritual. The epiphany, the manifestation of the divine, may be real, or enacted, or may simply entail an action on the part of the divine as in the case of healing cults or acts of divination.

Sherratt (1991) adds another component to our understanding of prehistoric ritual in his suggestion that narcotics were an important and overlooked feature of them, accentuating chemically the sensory experiences of the ceremonies, and perhaps following Warren's approach, facilitating the encounter with the divine. Remnants of poppy-heads and an alternative function for the numerous objects identified variously as braziers, incense burners, and the like in ritual contexts from the Neolithic on support Sherratt's argument. He notes that the alcohol consumed at some of these ceremonies would have had similar psychoactive qualities (1991:55; see also Sherratt 1995).

The social role of rituals is always immanent if not explicit. It has long been observed that social structure and the forms religious practice takes among a given group are related. As physical actions, rituals can serve as mnemonic devices, aiding in the production of shared memories within a community (Connerton 1989). While ritual actions need not be repeated, they almost always are, and this is one of the mechanisms of memory-making. In practical terms, if repeated, the rituals stand a better chance of being identified archaeologically, as when we find residues of actions that have been performed over a period of time. The redundancy, in the repeating of acts and phrases, serves to naturalize the ritual and habituate the participants to the bodily experience. This "automation" has the effect of instilling further the messages inherent in the ritual itself. "Every group, then, will entrust to bodily automatisms the values and categories which they [sic] are most anxious to conserve" (Connerton 1989:102). The same spirit of reiteration is evident in the redundancy of iconography, most famously in the double axe and so-called "horns of consecration" prevalent at Minoan cult sites, and known in other forms in the

Iberian rock art and Sardinian rock-cut tombs of the Copper Age (fourth millennium B.C.) (Jorda 1991; Lilliu 1988:213–216).

Another hallmark of rituals may be archaic elements: ritual paraphernalia may change at a slower rate than other material culture. Thomas (1991:34) has suggested that these archaic elements constitute a form of inter-textuality, quotations of the past. An example is the sixth century B.C. round shrine at the site of Monte Polizzo in western Sicily, which recalls earlier Iron Age huts long since replaced by rectilinear domestic architecture (Morris et al. 2002:186). Such references to the past would also serve to naturalize the acts and messages of the cult. The naturalizing power of rituals can be overstated, however, leading to assumptions, such as Bourdieu's (1977:164), that the condition of *doxa*, in which social orders are entirely naturalized, prevailed in all ancient societies. As Smith (2001) explains, such a position overlooks the purposive nature of even the most scripted behaviors.

Functionalist approaches concerned with ritual as a mechanism for social cohesion or ideological manipulation contend with symbolic approaches that see in ritual communicable meaning (see Lewis 1980). Barrett (1991:5) has proposed a variation on the latter approach to ritual, treating it as discursive text: "Those who participate do so by accepting the disciplinary requirements of customary practice, enabling the text to be written with the symbolic elements employed in the rituals as well as upon their own physical movements and oral pronouncements." If ritual activities grant heightened significance to places and objects, the participants themselves would, based on their formalized roles and presence, be in turn re-signified. This is most clearly the case at ritual activities marking a stage in the life cycle, such as coming-of-age ceremonies that do not simply mark the transition to adulthood but in fact initiate it (see Bell 1992).

We may expect certain individuals to be responsible for carrying the knowledge of how to perform the acts of worship and interpret signs from the gods, serving as mediators between the natural and supernatural realms. We can see traces of specialized cult personnel in some of the Mediterranean's more complex societies, confirming the links between cult practices and social structure. As Whitehouse (1995:83) aptly puts it: "No one would expect to find shamans in an urban civilization, nor a specialist priesthood in a hunter-gatherer band." In the Iron Age in central Italy, there is evidence that a few individuals with specialized skills were directing cult activities. Rare individual burials containing cult-related objects have been found among many other burials lacking such objects, as in Grave 126, at Osteria dell'Osa, dated to 900-830 B.C. (Bietti-Sestieri 1992:129–131).

In early state societies that role of mediator may have been held primarily by the rulers or upper classes, thus reinforcing their political authority and social control. The relationship between religious authority and political authority does not hold in all cases: in some circumstances, such as the Israelite prophets of the eighth-fifth centuries B.C., religious power may be held by those in opposition to the political elites, and conflict may arise between these factions. Nevertheless, it is evident that those who can claim both religious and political authority will be very powerful indeed (see Mann 1986 for discussion of these sources of social power). Rituals, with the emphasis on sensory and emotive experiences, are not easy to question, and so people who have control over rituals often wield considerable social power. While private rituals constituted direct communication between individuals and the divine, public rituals displayed the privileged place of the leaders in communicating with the gods on behalf of the entire community. "The main role of public religious festivals in all early civilizations was to establish ritual connections between ordinary people and gods whose cults were controlled by the upper classes" (Trigger 2003:515). Another set of ritual activities may have been private, practiced by elites, and the esoteric rites would have had an exclusionary effect, separating this group and raising them above the rest of the population by their privileged knowledge. Thus the latter two types of rituals reinforce the social hierarchy, even if the public rituals also encourage social integration (Trigger 2003:472–521). Therefore, determining the context of ritual activities in the archaeological record will aid in understanding both social structure and the mechanisms of social control.

Feasting

Among the most common types of ritual activities that may or may not be cult-related are feasts, defined as "communal food consumption events that differ in some way from everyday practice" (Dietler 1996:89). Because feasts have received so much separate attention lately by scholars, it is worth discussing them independently of the general discussion of ritual above, although the two are closely linked. Like other rituals, feasts are most easily identified archaeologically when they occur repeatedly. The hallmarks of past feasts may include traces of food preparation (cooking pots, hearths) or merely food consumption, such as serving bowls or burnt bones. In the latter case, food may be prepared ahead of time in individual households, and then transported for consumption to the feasting site. Feasts may be differentiated from everyday food consumption by such factors as the location of the remains in a non-domestic area and the distinct nature of the deposition: for example, any materials discarded in a purposeful way, such as in stone-lined pits. It may be more difficult to differentiate between sacral feasts consumed by the living participants, and sacrifices to the divine or to ancestors, although of course in practice there need not have been a distinction between the two types, with a feast following the act of sacrifice.

In the food and drink consumed at the feast itself lies a whole economic story of the means of procurement and distribution, and the establishment of value. At feasts we might expect different food remains from those of everyday meals (such as a predominance of bones from an animal not represented in domestic contexts), but not always: societies with a limited range of diet might not be eating different food at feasts, just more of it (see Goody 1982:78). Goody notes that socially differentiated cuisines, with higher and lower cooking, with the elites consuming qualitatively different foods from the rest, are generally restricted to societies with two characteristics: one, intensive agriculture, and two, literacy. The latter feature allows for the elaboration and codification of ideas about food that are necessary for two-tiered dietary practices to work (Goody 1982:99). Similar conditions might need to be met for a society to have qualitatively different feasts from their daily diets, and these might not be readily achieved in prehistoric contexts.

Considerable work has been done in anthropology, archaeology, and ancient history on the links between food and society (Davidson 1999; Goody 1982; Wiessner and Schiefenhovel 1996), and feasting has received particular attention (Dietler and Hayden 2001; Schmitt-Pantel 1992). Feasts clearly can be a force for social cohesion: as Robertson Smith (cited in Goody 1982:11–12) wrote: "According to antique ideas those who eat and drink together are by this very act tied to one another by a bond of friendship and mutual obligation." Beyond that, commensalism always has some bearing on social relations and on the identities of the participants, whether creating them, reinforcing them, or even masking them. Thus the punctuated occasion of the feast sheds light on ongoing social roles: Who is hosting this feast? Who are the participants? Who is excluded? What kind of obligations does this event place on its participants? From the answers to these questions we may be able to determine the wider significance of the feast. Feasts serve a range of social functions. They may help raise or maintain the status of the host, and establish indebtedness in the guests that can be repaid immediately (as in the case of work-parties) or at a later date in the form of a delayed reciprocity. Inclusive feasts in which a whole community participates may reinforce group solidarity while naturalizing hierarchies within that group through such features as the uneven distribution of the food. Exclusionary feasts, limited to only a segment of a community, may accentuate social divisions and distinguish the feasting group from the rest (Dietler 2001:85–87). Distinguishing these different functions archaeologically is a challenge, but such evidence can shed light on the society and its structure that goes beyond the feasting remnants.

Figurines, Statues, and the Mother Goddess

When considering the material residues of cult in the prehistoric Mediterranean, anthropomorphic figurines stand out as rich objects of study (see also Talalay this volume). They are common in many diverse Mediterranean prehistoric contexts, and may have featured in cult activities in some areas (although there are many other possible uses for them: see, most famously, Ucko 1968, as well as Hamilton 1996 and Meskell 1998 for overview of more recent perspectives). With some notable exceptions, anthropomorphic statues from the prehistoric Mediterranean are almost universally small in size, often held easily in the hand: for example, Sardinian figurines of the Late Bronze Age and Early Iron Age (Lo Schiavo 1999; Webster 1996:198–206); Chalcolithic and Bronze Age Cypriot figurines (Knapp and Meskell 1997); and Bronze Age Cycladic figurines (Doumas 2002). The poses of the figures, often in apparent adoration or supplication, with one arm raised, or with hands crossing the chest, or clasping objects, hint at the physical actions of possible encounters with the divine. The exceptions to the small stature include some of the standing stones or menhirs, carved to resemble humans. These so-called statue-menhirs, although highly stylized, may include anthropomorphic features such as breasts and accessories such as knives. While these figures are very difficult to date, the consensus is that they span a long period, from the Copper Age (fourth or third millennium B.C.) to the Iron Age (early first millennium B.C.), and have a wide distribution, with large concentrations in Iberia, Corsica, and the Alpine region. They are often found in association with megalithic or rock-cut tombs, but may also be found in isolated locations or in alignments in natural settings. These statues, whatever they represented, must have featured in the design and significa-tion of landscapes as sacred (Whitehouse 1981).

The remarkable monumental statue from the Tarxien complex at Malta, which must have been approximately two meters high when complete, is another excep-tion. The statue is contemporary with the apex of Malta's so-called temple period, ca. 3000–2500 B.C., and is presumably of a deity, given the size: "It is rare to make monumental, larger than life-size statues unless you are referring to either a great ruler or to a deity figure" (Renfrew 1986:129). Although conventionally identified as a female, the statue bears no unmistakably female features and therefore cannot be convincingly sexed (Malone 1998:151). Some of the Cycladic figurines of the Early Bronze Age (more specifically: Early Cycladic II, 2700–2300 B.C.) are also a clear exception, with rare examples reaching 1.5 meters in height, although 70 centimeters is more common (Doumas 2002:66). In Post-Palatial Crete, ca. 1450–1050 B.C. and corresponding to the Late Bronze Age, large clay painted figures, some 80 centimeters tall, depicting females with their arms raised, are found in shrines. The distinctive rendering of the figurines, although found in groups, has led scholars to suggest that a plurality of deities was being worshiped (Goodison and Morris 1998:130–131). The remains of some 25 over life-size statues from the cemetery of Monte Prama on Sardinia are also intriguing exceptions, although they are rather late (seventh century B.C.), and, while native products, seem to be a result of external contacts with Phoenician colonists (Tronchetti 1986). There are thus few examples of monumental statues which would have served as focal points for the worship of a deity in the prehistoric Mediterranean. Smaller figurines with superhuman accessories, such as the snakes of the faience figurines from Knossos on Crete, are also likely to be deities (Goodison and Morris 1998:124–125). Finally, the recently discovered monumental plaster and reed statuary from the Pre-Pottery Neolithic B site of 'Ain Ghazal, near Amman, Jordan, is of great interest. Reaching as much as 100 centimeters high, these statues were carefully buried in pits in the floors of abandoned buildings. They are particularly surprising as they date to a period (ca. 6750–6500 B.C.) when figurines are almost universally miniature in the Mediterranean (Schmandt-Besserat 2004).

Female figurines in the Neolithic (ca. 7000–3500 B.C.) have given rise to claims to a universal mother goddess cult throughout the Mediterranean and in south-east Europe. The work of Maria Gimbutas (1982) purporting to identify a matriarchal society structured around worship of a principal deity, a "Great Goddess," has been largely discredited now, but her claims were influential for a time, and indeed remain so in the popular imagination (Meskell 1995). The popular appeal of a wide-spread cult of the mother goddess notwithstanding, the diversity of cult practices across the Mediterranean does not lend itself to such a theory, and the theory itself has been criticized for essentializing female traits (despite the celebratory tone) (Tringham and Conkey 1998). Nor does the evidence itself, the presence of the female figurines across a wide area, prove the existence of a universal cult. Similarities in iconography across regions might simply be a case of what Renfrew (1986:124) labels "structural homology," that is, "resemblance of form coming about without a direct common cause." Therefore the figurines might have arisen independently in multiple places. Moreover, the gendering of these figurines has proved to be far more complex than originally thought (see Talalay this volume). While scholars have moved away from Gimbutas' theories, the notion of a fertility cult, or at least a concern with fertility as a component of many cults, continues to find favor, based on imagery of phalli and female genitalia (Bonanno 1986; Haaland and Haaland 1996:297; Tusa 1997:190). Proponents argue that such a cult is likely from the Neolithic onward, when agricultural fertility and productivity were of crucial importance. Other scholars caution against too quickly applying contemporary notions of fertility to the past, with the risk of conflating fertility and sexuality, and female with fertile (Tringham and Conkey 1998).

Locating Ritual

A crucial component in understanding ritual activities of all kinds is considering the space in which they occur. This is methodologically essential, as a means of distinguishing, for example, between inclusionary and exclusionary feasts, or between cults and other sorts of rituals. Moreover, studying these spaces can enrich our understanding of the activities themselves, with space taken as a material artifact of these practices rather than the passive backdrop against which they unfold. Once the residues of a ritual activity have been identified, determining its nature may be the next challenge: Does it pertain to a funeral or other rite of passage? Is it secular and political? Is it a seasonal celebration? Is it in honor of a deity? Here the location of the ritual might provide the only evidence for its purpose.

The space of the ritual may also shed light on the identities and numbers of participants at the event, and is thus important for understanding social relations. The spaces in which rituals occur are often liminal, having the condition of being between two worlds: the everyday world, and the "other." In funerary contexts these spaces might bridge the worlds between the living and the dead; in other cult contexts, it might be a space in which to contact the divine. The location of cults may be socially determinative, that is to say, it will have an impact on the structures of power within a society. For these reasons, and because the temporal sequences across the Mediterranean vary widely, I have organized the discussion of cult and ritual by context rather than chronologically. The examples begin in the Neolithic: although the peoples of the Paleolithic practiced rituals, the richest material residues date from the Neolithic period onward, when sedentism and the domestication of plants and animals brought great changes to the outlook and cosmology of people everywhere (see Hodder 1991). These changes in lifestyle entailed the elaboration of ritualized behaviors in new ways. The examples do not represent a comprehensive, or even geographically balanced, sampling of sites. The Levant is particularly neglected here, with no real justification other than the fact that, while "Mediterranean," it is also "Near Eastern," and so the reader is encouraged to turn to books on the Ancient Near East for its coverage. The sites discussed in this chapter are either among the better known examples of each particular type or, in the case of the Italian examples, simply better known by the author than examples from elsewhere.

Mortuary contexts

Rites and feasts in funerary contexts are perhaps the most carefully studied of prehistoric rituals, both for what they tell us in specific cases about beliefs in the afterlife or ancestor worship, and what these rites in general terms indicate about the construction and maintenance of social structure and social identities (see Chapman et al. 1981; Morris 1992; Saxe 1970). There are certain accepted inferences to be made from rituals in mortuary contexts. First, rituals at a communal burial site apparently belonging to a single family or kin group would seem to underscore the kin identities of the participants. Second, scholars have long argued that mortuary rites serve a social purpose of reestablishing the status quo after the disruption caused by death. Activities in funerary contexts include rites of passage to facilitate the transition of the deceased to a possible "realm of the ancestors," and this transition may be organized into three stages, marked by accompanying rites: separation; a liminal, transitional period; and aggregation or return to normalcy for both the living and the deceased (van Gennep 1960). The space in front of the tomb entrance, which may have been perceived as a liminal space between the living and the dead, was often the site of such activities. At some Mycenaean tholos tombs, for example, the deliberate smashing of drinking cups at the tomb's entrance passage would seem to be a liminal rite (Cavanagh 1998:106–107). Initial rituals may involve the preparation of the deceased's body, including anointing, dressing, and placement in the chamber with associated objects. Later, after decomposition, the bones may be disarticulated and cleaned of flesh, with the removal of some or all of the bones or their reordering into anonymous piles. These actions may serve to make way for new bodies in the tomb, or as a way of acknowledging the completion of the deceased's transit, or both (see Murphy 1998 for discussion of these rites of passage with regard to Pre-Palatial Minoan tholos tombs). Similar traces of skeletal disarticulation and the rearrangement of the bones are evident at Copper Age chamber tombs in south-east Spain, notably at Los Millares and El Barranquete. In contrast to the examples from Crete, however, the end of the tombs' use was marked by the sealing off of the entrances and forecourt areas (Chapman 1990:184–185).

Ritual activities at funerary sites are common in the Mediterranean from the Neolithic through the Bronze Age. In the western Mediterranean, these activities become increasingly important in the Copper Age (third millennium B.C.). On Sardinia, throughout much of the Neolithic and Copper Age the evidence of religious activity is limited to funerary contexts, in particular from the Middle

Neolithic (4000–3500 B.C.) on, in rock-cut tombs. Depositions with the deceased include small female figurines with stylized carving reminiscent of Cycladic fig-urines and Maltese examples. Also in the tombs are wall carvings in the form of bulls' horns as well as designs of spirals and half-circles (Lilliu 1988:199–221). At the entrances to the tombs, cupules, possibly for libation offerings, are sometimes present in the entrance floor (Figure 5.1). These rock-cut tombs continue in use throughout the Copper Age, and even into the Early Bronze Age, although by then new, free-standing megalithic tombs were proliferating. These new tombs, the so-called "giants' tombs," have yielded evidence of feasting activities in their forecourt. Hearths and pits containing the remnants of burnt animal bones and broken pottery have been found at a number of sites (Bittichesu 1989; Castaldi 1968). The fore-court spaces themselves, and in particular the continuous stone benches lining the interior walls of some of them, are further evidence that communal activities were carried out in these spaces.

In peninsular Italy, it is not until the Copper Age and Early and Middle Bronze Ages (ca. 3500–1300 B.C.) that burial sites involving cult activities are visible, con-temporary to ongoing use of earlier cave sites (see below). This change corresponds to the appearance, in a few isolated areas, of standing stones and megaliths in small pockets of southeast Italy. These suggest new, more prominent foci for cult activities than the caves. Whitehouse (1995:85) contends that this new visibility represents a more explicit expression of the cult power of a few members of society. The prevalence of cults in funerary contexts may be attributed to a growing impor-tance of kin relations and ancestral linkages, with participant identities emphasiz-ing familial roles.

Sicily shows a similar pattern in the Copper Age (3500–2500 B.C.), where ritual activities at cemeteries are evident from hearths near the burials, as well as at pits and shafts containing what appear to be the remnants of sacrifices, including ashy soil, axe-hammers, pots containing ochre and seeds, and burnt animal bones. Small clay figures, both anthropomorphic and zoomorphic, are also known from these contexts, in some cases deliberately broken before being deposited (Leighton 1999:96). The Early Bronze Age (ca. 2500–1500 B.C.) sees an elaboration of rites in funerary contexts on Sicily. The addition of forecourts to the rock-cut chamber tomb facades, sometimes with benches carved out of the rock and designs etched on the walls, points to a use of the space for more formalized cult activities focused on the deceased, a trend also evident in Sardinia, described above (Leighton 1999:123). In both Sicily and Sardinia, the material remains are often buried on one side of the forecourt, although in the Sicilian examples, the left side of the fore-court is favored, while in the Sardinian examples, the right side is preferred (Castaldi 1969:148, 156). Clearly in both cases the objects used in the activities of the forecourt retained enough significance to need to be disposed of with care. The formalization of the rites in these spaces is further emphasized by more distinct vessels, relating to libations: these are primarily chalice vases with high pedestals, and in some cases dippers (Maniscalco McConnell 1996:84–86).

Tholos tombs offer the main evidence for communal ritual on Early Bronze Age Crete before the emergence of the peak sanctuaries in Middle Minoan IA (ca. 2100–1900 B.C.), although individual items of cultic significance are known

Figure 5.1 Rock-cut tomb entrance viewed from tomb interior. Sant' Andrea Priu, Sardinia. (Photo: E. Blake)

(Branigan 1991:183; and see Peatfield 1990:123–125 for temporal relationship between tombs and peak sanctuaries). The tholos tombs from the Mesara show evidence for curation of the bones. These tombs contained multiple burials, and the rearrangements of the bones inside, or removal of certain bones altogether, may point to an ancestor cult, or simply a way of asserting control over death and the dead (Branigan 1991). Animal bones and other food remains, drinking cups and pouring vessels of all kinds, eating vessels (in fewer numbers), and adjacent activity areas have been found at these modest tombs, and similar residues are known, later, from the impressive Mycenaean tholoi and chamber tombs (Hamilakis 1998:119–126). Hamilakis (1998:121–122) suggests that tombs would have been the sites for bodily activities of feasting, dancing, and possibly the consumption of narcotics, as well as the clearance of the bones into disarticulated and anonymous piles, all serving as part of the structured and communal remembering-and-forgetting of the deceased, which may be a good way of characterizing the activities at the earlier Minoan tholoi as well. At the Mesara tholoi, in the Early Minoan II period (ca. 2900–2300 B.C.), annex-rooms and paved areas are added to some of the tholoi, suggesting a formalizaton of activities beyond simply the deposition of the deceased. The annex-rooms in some cases contained just bones and seem to have functioned as ossuaries, while others contained such objects as pottery, stone bowls, and figurines, as well as built-in benches, leading scholars to surmise ritual functions, or perhaps repositories for offerings (Murphy 1998:36). The paved area (or, in some cases, beaten earth) near the tomb points likewise to a gathering place, possibly for dancing (Branigan 1991:187). Stone slabs tentatively identified as altars are also known from some tombs. By the Middle Minoan I period (ca. 2100–1900 B.C.), the prevalence of these adjacent areas suggests that activities at the tombs were further cemented and formalized. Murphy notes a correspondence between wealthier tombs (based on grave goods) and the elaboration of these adjacent activity areas, and infers that the elites were by this stage drawing legitimacy from emphasizing associations with ancestors through such rites (Murphy 1998:36–39). Branigan (1991:187) cautions against assuming that the activities of the paved areas were solely mortuary in nature: at Koumasa, a wall even separates the paved area from the tombs, raising the possibility of activities disconnected from the tombs.

Caves

Enclosed spaces, such as caves and rock shelters, are common sites of cult activities, particularly in the Neolithic. Ruth Whitehouse notes that in the Middle to Late Neolithic (fifth millennium B.C.) and through the Copper Age up to 2000 B.C., characterized on the Italian peninsula by small-scale segmentary societies, the cult practices tended to take place in enclosed natural spaces: caves, crevices, and the like, rather than open-air sites. There are variations in the details. At some sites there is evidence of a "hunting cult" marked by cave paintings of animals and the deliberate, structured deposition of wild animal bones. Elsewhere, the emphasis is on water, such as springs or pools, stalactites, and stalagmites, that Whitehouse labels "abnormal water." The consistent features of all these sites are the restrictive nature of the space (often small and cramped) and the fact that they are not easily visible, with hidden entrances and in hard-to-find locations. These two elements point to the esoteric nature of this cult, which was being practiced either by only a few members of these societies, or by all members but only very infrequently in their lives. An example of activities occurring at punctuated moments in the life cycle would be coming-of-age rites. Given the hidden nature of the sites, these rites must have been organized by individuals with exclusive control over the knowledge of the location of the sites (Whitehouse 1995:84; see also Whitehouse 1992).

In Sicily during the Neolithic, similar esoteric cult activity to that identified on the mainland in secret underground places is suggested at a few sites. Wall paintings in the Grotta dei Genovesi, a cave on the island of Levanzo, just off western Sicily, provide an example of how such sites were frequented for cult purposes. The paintings are tentatively dated to the fourth or early third millennia B.C. and consist of mainly anthropomorphic figures, as well as animals and some unrecognizable symbols. Located in the dark recesses of the inner chamber of the cave, only visible by torchlight, access to these paintings must have been restricted. Another set of cave paintings on Sicily, in the Grotta dei Cavalli in the north-western part of the island, is thought to date to between the Middle Neolithic and Early Copper Age on stylistic grounds of comparison with the Porto Badisco cave in Apulia. Although differing in style from the Levanzo examples, the Grotta dei Cavalli paintings' position in the small and dark inner chamber of the cave points to the limited number of participants in the activities there. Caves continued to be the sites of cult activity throughout the Copper Age on Sicily, even though they also served as habitations (Leighton 1999:82–85, 102).

Such esoteric sites are not exclusive to Italy. Similarly remote and hidden caves, decorated with rock art, are known from north-west Iberia, dating to the fourth and third millennia B.C. One decorated cave in northern Portugal contained evidence of feasting, including, interestingly, opium. Another had two stone platforms in front of it, suggesting an activity space of a less secluded nature (Bradley et al. 2001:499–500). Likewise, on the island of Menorca, a cave that can only be reached by boat or by scaling down a cliff was apparently a sanctuary ca. 1200–1000 B.C. The chamber contained a carved wooden head and some ceramic lamps, and could only have accommodated a few people at a time (Chapman 2004: personal communication). Dark and inaccessible caves, often with the same sorts of "abnormal" water features, were also used as cult sites during the Minoan period in the Early and Middle Bronze Ages on Crete. Ashy remains of feasts, libation tables, as well as figurines in bronze and clay, double axes in gold, and other weapons are testimony to the activities in one of the most impressive examples, at Psychro (Tyree 1974). Independent of the secluded nature of the cave sites, the role of such sites as places of contact with chthonic deities seems highly likely, given their underground setting.

Open-air sites

Cult activities in open-air settings take numerous forms, many of which leave only faint traces archaeologically, and are not easily recovered. Cult activities in natural settings that have undergone no distinct human modification must have been frequent, but are invisible now. Under the heading of open-air sites we may also

include those places where permanent features such as altars and standing stones
are present, but which lack a permanent building, or if there is a building, it is of
ancillary importance to the activities. The transitional Early-Middle Bronze (ca.
2100–1900 B.C.) clay model from the cemetery of Vounous on Cyprus may represent such an open-air sanctuary: it depicts standing and seated figures gathered
around a space where three plank-shaped figures wearing bulls' masks and snakes
are represented. An animal pen and other figures in the model are not, according
to Peltenburg, part of the discreet cult zone (Peltenburg 1994).

Larger open-air sanctuaries suggest large-scale community-level activities where
the participants are redefined in communal terms rather than the familial categories
of the mortuary sites, or the narrowly framed participant identities of the caves. The
emergence of large open-air sanctuaries, therefore, may indicate the emergence of
a ranked society. This seems to be the case in central Italy, in the Late Bronze Age
and Iron Age – with the shift away from activities in funerary contexts (Whitehouse
1995:85–86) – and is also true in Iron Age Sardinia.

Among the more simple open-air sites is the "pit" sanctuary, focused around a
hollow or crevice in the ground or rock that serves as a focal point and repository
for offerings, presumably to chthonic deities. An elaborate version of the "pit" sanctuary is the site of Pian di Civita in central Italy, near the later city of Tarquinia.
There, a natural cavity in the rock was the apparent focus of cult activities for many
centuries, from the tenth through the sixth centuries B.C. Ash and charcoal point
to sacrificial fires, and the layers of ash contain fragments of deer antlers. In the
ninth century the body of a boy was deposited on the surface, with a few bronze
objects, and then covered with soil mixed with the ash and antler pieces. Late in
the successive century three infant burials were placed near the boy, similarly
unburied, and similarly covered with ash and soil mixed with antler pieces. In the
early seventh century a building was constructed that shared an alignment with the
cavity and with the boy's burial. Inside there was an altar platform and a channel
possibly to receive the blood of sacrificed animals, which would have flowed to the
underground cavity, suggesting sacrifices to chthonic deities. Burnt bones of pigs,
sheep, and cows, as well as tortoise shells, date from the eighth and seventh centuries. Trenches in front of the building produced an axe, a shield, and a trumpet,
all carefully decorated and in bronze, and in the case of the latter two objects, deliberately broken. There were also undecorated plates and cups, likewise intentionally
broken (Bonghi Jovino 2001:22–29). These successive modifications of the site that
seem to refer back to the site's earlier history suggest that a social memory of the
earlier phases was perpetuated for many centuries.

Other open-air sanctuaries were associated with fresh water, at wells or springs.
In the Copper Age of southern France (4000–3500 B.C.), riverine cult sites are
known. At one such site, St. Michel du Touche near Toulouse, "long spreads of
cobble flooring with plentiful traces of burning defy easy interpretation, but
may represent some kind of sauna or communal facilities at sites of ceremonial
significance" (Sherratt 1994:183). These sites appear to have been the settings for
a type of water-based cult with possible healing or purification rituals for its
participants.

Several central Italian cult sites were also associated with water. One is known at Banditella, near what would later become the Etruscan town of Vulci. There a spring was the site of offerings from the Middle Bronze Age (17th century B.C.) until the sixth century B.C. These offerings began as pottery and worked bone discs in the early stages but came to include bronze and silver rings and a small bronze statue of a horse. The abandonment of the site seems to coincide with the rise of Vulci, and a shift to urban sanctuaries (D'Ercole and Trucco 1992). This trend is repeated elsewhere in Italy. With the rise of urban state-level societies, we see a corresponding state religion emerge, and the sanctuaries shift into the urban sites by the sixth century B.C. (Whitehouse 1995: 86). The Laghetto del Monsignore spring, near Campoverde in Latium, is a similar site with votive depositions, including pottery of both regular and miniature size, and anthropomorphic figures in sheet bronze, and dates from the tenth through seventh centuries B.C. (Crescenzi 1978:52–53; Guidi 1980:149).

Just a few kilometers away is the site of Le Ferriere-Satricum, on a hilltop, where small hut-pits, presumably covered with thatched roofs and arranged in a semi-circular formation, frame an apparent sacred space, inside of which a shallow natural depression would have periodically been filled with water. Assemblages of votive objects were deposited in the adjacent pits from the tenth century B.C. onwards. In the eighth or seventh century B.C. the natural depression was carved out into a round pond 12 meters in diameter, and the nature of the deposits changed, with the addition of personal effects (jewelry and perfume pots) suggesting both an increasing artificial manipulation of the sacred, and a shift in emphasis to even more personal associations with the divine. The excavators suggest that visiting groups prepared and consumed sacral meals at the site, and made offerings of that food in miniature vessels to the gods (Maaskant-Kleibrink 1995; 1992:13–19).

Hilltop sites like the one above are particularly well represented on Crete in the Minoan period, where they constitute a distinct class of cult site (Figure 5.2). Some twenty-five of these so-called peak sanctuaries are known, appearing in Middle Minoan IA, ca. 2100 B.C. The more elaborate ones linked to the palaces featured an altar, stone libation table, chalices, offering stands, and cache of bronze double axes, while the more modest and early examples have little in the way of installations and may not have been the sites of animal sacrifice (see Peatfield 1992:66). All peak sanctuaries have votive offerings in the form of terracotta figurines, of animals, people, and body parts (usually limbs). The first peak sanctuaries date to before the palaces were founded. Cherry (1986:32) has argued that the sanctuaries' presence in the period of state formation on Crete (emerging in Middle Minoan I, and disappearing by the Late Minoan period) suggests that they aided the consolidation of power by certain elites (Cherry 1986:32). Peatfield (1990; 1992) has suggested instead that these early rural sanctuaries, scattered on the hills away from settlements yet accessible from them, were initially a popular cult of local communities. Peatfield (1992:61) sees a progressive centralization of the peak sanctuaries in the Second Palace Period (ca. 1650–1425 B.C.) as the cult is effectively appropriated by the palace elites.

Figure 5.2 View toward peak sanctuary at Ketsophas, Crete. The sanctuary is located just below the summit of the mountain in the distance. (Photo: J. Cherry)

Complex open-air sites are also known in the western Mediterranean. Monte d'Accoddi, in north-central Sardinia, is one such site. It consists of a trapezoidal platform on an artificial mound, reached by a sloped causeway. At one time a rectangular structure sat atop the platform. The site was frequented from the Middle Neolithic on, but the platform dates to the Copper Age (ca. 2700–2000 B.C.), with some minor subsequent activity in the Early Bronze Age (ca. 2000–1600 B.C.). Near the mound are several standing stones, and a large limestone slab, now at the foot of the mound, might have served as an altar. A large spherical stone with small grooves on its surface has also been found. These sorts of "pock-marked" slabs are known from other sites on Sardinia, near megalithic tombs and in other apparently sacred areas, and indeed cup-marks of various sizes are a feature of megalithism throughout Europe. The Sardinian site, suggesting by its scale a cult place of regional importance, is surprising in light of the society that produced it: small villages and hamlets, scattered across the countryside, with little evidence of an extra-village level of political organization (Lilliu 1988:222–226; Webster 1996:52).

Open-air post-Paleolithic rock-art sites might also be understood as places of ritual activity, some or all of it cult-based. Both in the formal act of producing the art, and in subsequent visits to the art or even pilgrimages, these sites must have held a special, sacral significance. Such sites in the Mediterranean region are particularly known from northwest Iberia and the Alpine regions (Bradley et al. 2001:494–495). There are some twenty to thirty open-air rock-art sites in the Alps, predominantly in the southern Alps, spanning later prehistory. The two most famous sites of this type are Valcamonica and Valtellina, adjacent valleys in northern Italy, with some 300,000 images between them. They may be studied as a unit, and are tentatively dated to 5500–16 B.C. (the latter date marking the region's absorption into the Roman Empire); thus they were in use for an extraordinarily long time. Imagery includes humans with arms raised as if in worship (Bradley et al. 2001:510–513). The remote site of Mont Bego in France is another notable site, with over 30,000 figures dating to a narrower time range: 2500–1700 B.C. (Bradley et al. 2001:504). How such sites may relate to cult activities has been only recently explored, with the bulk of the research on rock art focusing on the classification of motifs. The designs, both painted and carved, include abstract images as well as animals, weapons, and people. In the case of the weapons, it has been suggested that these represent votive deposits of metalwork, as contemporary hoards have been found with similar items (Bradley 1998). The open-air rock art points to both a prosaic concern with territoriality, but also to an ascription of sacredness on the landscape that extends beyond the spatially contained ritual contexts discussed throughout this chapter.

In North Africa, the most archaeologically visible expression of cult is the rock art, which extends from around 5000 B.C. down to the late first millennium B.C. and spans the entire Saharan and pre-Saharan zone. Styles and subject matter vary regionally and through time, but two main periods can be delineated. Up until 3000 B.C., during a wet climatic period, the images are products of Neolithic pastoral societies. Along with scenes of animals and people, there are images several meters high that presumably signify deities or other mythical, non-human beings. They offer clear evidence of a richly textured cosmology whose content is now lost. After a hiatus during the arid second millennium B.C., rock art is again produced throughout the first millennium B.C., this time characterized by fewer overtly symbolic or mythological scenes, and replaced by images of warriors, horses and chariots introduced from Egypt and the East, and at the very end, of camels (Muzzolini 2001). While efforts to interpret this art are fraught with difficulties, they point to the presence of a highly charged spiritual world, and we can ascribe to the very production of that art some degree of ritualism.

Some objects, such as hoards or standing stones (stelae), may point to open-air cult activities, because, if *in situ*, they mark what must have been a place of significance in the past (Figure 5.3). Statue-menhirs have also been found in relation to rock-art sites in the Alpine region, as at Valcamonica and Valtellina, as well as in southern Italy, southern France, Corsica, and, outside the scope of this study, throughout much of northern Europe. The Iberian peninsula has yielded a rich and varied assortment of decorated stelae, including the statue-menhirs, dating from the Copper Age and by some accounts even earlier, through the Late Bronze Age (ca. 3000–900 B.C.). Although notoriously difficult to date, there appears to be an evolution in the carved images on the slabs through time, and with regional stylistic groupings as well. It is in the Middle Bronze Age that weapons such as axes,

Figure 5.3 Row of three menhirs. Perda Longa, Sardinia. (Photo: E. Blake)

swords, and halberds are thought to have been first engraved on slabs from south-west Spain, the so-called Alentejo-type stelae. Many of the Iberian examples are found in funerary contexts and are assumed to be grave markers (Oliveira Jorge 1999a:121). With regard to a later sequence of decorated stelae from southwest Spain from the Late Bronze Age, the ninth and eighth centuries B.C. (Fernandez Castro 1995:148–58, although Oliveira Jorge [1999a:117] suggests they begin as early as the mid-second millennium B.C.), it has been suggested that these were territorial markers, placed along natural communication routes (Galán Domingo 1993:77–81). Contemporary with these Late Bronze Age stelae are hoards, deposits of wealthy bronze and gold objects (Oliveira Jorge 1999a:122). Although hoards often have prosaic functions, they may in some cases be votive offerings to a particular deity.

Many standing stones, including statue-menhirs, have been found on Corsica, apparently a feature of the island's megalithism of the Copper and Bronze Ages, in the third and second millennia B.C. Whereas many are located near dolmens and other tombs, they are also found far from tombs and, similarly to the Iberian exam-ples, are thought to mark routes and territorial boundaries (Bonifay 1990:73–101). Sometimes associated with the stelae, megalithic enclosures are a form of open-air site found in Iberia, and on many of the western Mediterranean islands, such as Sardinia, Corsica, and the Balearics (see Kolb this volume). One such site in what is now Portugal, Cabeço da Mina, consisted of a stone ring surrounding a low hill, with statue-menhirs – the largest concentration in Iberia – arranged within the ring, on the hill (Oliveira Jorge 1999b). The purpose of these enclosures, framed by their own (usually undecorated) large standing slabs, remains unclear (Webster 1996:54; Moravetti 1981).

Domestic cults

The kinds of individual and household rituals that presumably would have occurred on a regular basis are difficult to detect archaeologically. Nonetheless we may group foundation offerings, in the form of items deliberately buried under or near domestic structures, as evidence of these domestic contexts of cult. Examples include the Early Bronze Age deposit of miniature vessels in the floor at Fogliuto (Adrano) in Sicily (Leighton 1999:118), or the burial of human skulls under the floor of huts in southern France in the Late Bronze Age and Early Iron Age, as at Camp-Redon (Py 1993:70). On Cyprus in the Neolithic period (ca. 7000 B.C.), in villages such as Khirokitia, the dead were buried within the houses, under the floors, and offerings suggest some domestic cult with ancestral focus (Le Brun 1989). These sorts of residues would seem to demonstrate a need for spiritual approbation of the domestic sphere. Also in the domestic realm, there are many examples of cosmological imperatives determining the structure of seemingly secular space, so that domestic buildings follow alignment along cardinal points (see for example the layout of Balkan Neolithic and Copper Age communities – Sherratt 1994:172–173).

In social terms, rituals in households or settlements imply a minimum of external control or mediation between individuals and the divine, and a degree of autonomy in the performance of rituals. It is perhaps no wonder, then, that domestic shrines are particularly visible in relatively egalitarian societies. On Malta, prior to the emergence of the monumental temple complexes, limited cult activity is evident by the mid to late fifth millennium B.C., when Maltese society shows little evidence of ranking. From this time, a domestic shrine containing terracotta figurines and animal bones has been excavated at Skorba, highlighting the localized nature of cult practices (Trump 1966). Such localized activities on Malta vanish in later periods, replaced first with elaborate collective underground burial sites, and then by the temple complexes themselves (see below), pointing to widening spheres of ritual authority.

Cult sites within settlement areas that have little to distinguish them architecturally from the dwellings themselves may be tentatively labeled as domestic. In the Neolithic period (ca. 7000–4000 B.C.) within the Mediterranean, as in much of Europe, the evidence of cult activities in agricultural villages is largely limited to the extensive finds of clay anthropomorphic and zoomorphic figurines, with a few large buildings that may have served as religious centers. At the Early Neolithic (ca. 7000–5500 B.C.) village site of Nea Nikomedeia in Macedonia, a large building set amongst small houses might have had a religious function, and figurines were found there. Elsewhere, clay building models from this time might also be representations of cult places for which we have no actual remains. Figurines from this period are found often in household contexts and suggest a broad-based, non-hierarchically structured religion: "The wide distribution of figurines implies some kind of spiritual or conceptual unity among early farming communities in the region [Greece and the Balkans]" (Whittle 1994:140–144). In the Middle Neolithic (ca. 5500–5000 B.C.), the figurines continued to be popular, although the emergence of larger settlements points to a site hierarchy that might have led to some individuals within the community overseeing the practice of ritual (Whittle 1994:144).

Sometimes the finds from domestic cults may be surprisingly numerous: the Iron Age settlement at Lavinium in central Italy has yielded a deposit of some 30,000 miniature vessels, mostly representing two-handled pots. The deposit dates to the second half of the seventh to early sixth century B.C. Its location in a habitation area has led the excavators to suggest a domestic cult (Fenelli and Guaitoli 1990:184–185). These miniature vessels are not unusual: Bronze Age votive deposits in Italy frequently take the form of miniature vessels, miniature weapons, and small-scale figurines, particularly in Latium (Maaskant-Kleibrink 1995:124). These miniatures point to symbolic offerings to the gods or, in funerary contexts, to the deceased.

The earliest known Minoan shrine has been characterized as domestic, and was found in the Cretan Early Bronze Age Pre-Palatial village of Myrtos Pyrgos. The shrine contained a bench altar with a ceramic statuette of a female, probably a deity, as well as ceramic containers for liquid and food offerings (Warren 1988:4–5). Minoan house shrines are known from the Palatial period as well, such as the example of the probable shrine inside the Late Minoan I country house at Pyrgos (Cadogan 1981). More impressive are the shrine rooms attached to the Minoan palaces, and later, within the Mycenaean palaces. Late Minoan I B (ca. 1450 B.C.) destruction layers have preserved the contents of the shrine area at the palace of Kato Zakros, which yielded numerous cups, a wall painting depicting horns of consecration, a lustral basin, and the shrine treasury filled with numerous vessels in alabaster, obsidian, serpentine, red marble, and rock crystal. "Huge sheet bronze double axes engraved as papyrus heads, miniature ivories and faiences, and stone ritual hammers" were also found (Warren 1988:7). The location of this shrine and others like it within the palaces points to the explicit associations of political and religious power in this state-level society, a situation that continues to be evident in slightly later Mycenaean contexts. Indeed, the evidence that shrine personnel had administrative control of certain industrial workshops may indicate that economic power was also a factor in embedding them within the palaces, or at least suggests that all three sources of power were interpolated (Lupack 1999).

Temples

The construction of buildings devoted to cult activity independent of households or funerary sites occurs most often in complex societies. The phenomenon sometimes goes hand in hand with an increased codification of religion, particularly when the inspiration for these buildings is external. The transformations of the Etruscan religion under Greek influence in the seventh and sixth centuries B.C. fit this pattern (Barker and Rasmussen 1998:219). It is little wonder, then, that there are few examples of temples before the Bronze Age outside the eastern Mediterranean. One exception is the Maltese archipelago, whose great temple complexes offer ample evidence of formalized and codified rituals in a structured space. Temple-building and associated ritual activity began in the Ggantija phase, ca. 3600–3000 B.C. Stoddart et al. (1993:7) have attributed this unique development to insular competition in this isolated location. The full fluorescence of temple construction comes in the subsequent Tarxien phase, ca. 3000–2500 B.C., resulting in labor-intensive, highly spatially structured communal sites, and associated underground mortuary spaces. Both the temples and hypogea are lobed, divided into separate rooms or modules with irregular, curved walls, hidden from the exterior by a concave façade. The structures were modified over time, and have variable layouts, but they tend to be oriented northwest. The finds associated with them are consis-tent: ritual paraphernalia, including stone statues of corpulent figures, stone and ceramic bowls, amulets, altars, architectural features composed of upright stones with a capstone, and remains of burnt sacrifice. Caches of equipment point to the presence of ritual specialists, and the small size of the modules would have restricted access, with the cult participants for the most part presumably gathered outside the temples (Stoddart et al. 1993; Grima 2001).

Built sanctuaries proliferate in the Middle and Late Bronze Age in the eastern Mediterranean. The Late Bronze Age Mycenaean sanctuary at Phylakopi, in use during the 13th and 12th centuries B.C., is an important example of these free-standing temple complexes (Renfrew 1985). The Late Bronze Age Cypriot sanctuaries such as those at Enkomi and Kition are similarly complex, and, with the frequent appearance of horns of consecration, are closely tied to contemporary Aegean counterparts (see Webb 1999).

At the end of the Late Bronze Age and in the Iron Age on Sardinia (ca. 1000–500 B.C.), new cult sites unrelated to funerary activities appear. These include new cave sanctuaries, megaron structures, and, most notably, the so-called "sacred well" temples, vaulted structures with forecourts and steps descending to underground water sources. Ancillary buildings and enclosures in some cases cover a vast area and point to a regional role for these sites. Within the settlements, there are also large bench-lined huts known as "reunion huts," some with models of the earlier stone towers known as *nuraghi* serving as a focal point in the center (Lilliu 1988:521–544). This diversification in ritual sites almost certainly relates to the emergence of a site hierarchy dominated by vast tower complexes and proto-urban settlements, and an increasingly complex social structure (Webster 1996:190–194).

The correlation between temples and social complexity is echoed in the emer-gence of exclusionary feasts. In the Bronze Age eastern Mediterranean, a new emphasis is placed on the vessels associated with feasting and drinking ceremonies (Sherratt 1997:403–430). No longer simply the standard receptacles used in daily meals, a new repertoire of bronze and even gold feasting equipment is found in the wealthiest graves of those societies, the ones most affected by the new prestige goods economies and networks of exchange (e.g., South 2000, Kalavossas *Ayios Dhimitrios* in Cyprus). The rarity of these luxury vessels: cauldrons, buckets, goblets, and the like, suggests that the feasts at which these vessels were used were restricted to a select social group, and were thus exclusionary in purpose (Steel 2002). As the cuisine itself was unlikely to have been qualitatively different from daily meals (apart from probably greater proportions of meat), the difference lay in the presentation of the feast: how it was consumed, and on what vessels (Dietler 1996:106).

In the Iron Age, the trend of exclusive, elite feasting becomes even more pronounced in certain regions. In Greece, where feasting, occurring primarily at festivals, had long been a unifying activity for a community, the new elite drinking parties, the symposia, now exclude the general populace from participation (Murray 1990; Schmitt-Pantel 1992). This shift is evident in the western Mediterranean as well. The latter cases, for example in Italy among the Villanovans and later the Etruscans, and in central France, are heavily influenced by the practices of Greek colonizers (Dietler 1996). These Italian feasts, like the Greek symposia that were their inspiration, revolve largely around the consumption of wine, a growing alternative to beer. Dietler examined the distribution patterns of these goods in France. He noted that in the southern region, which experienced a lot of foreign contact but only partly stratified societies, the drinking paraphernalia are more widely distributed, while in the more stratified interior Hallstatt zone, only the very wealthiest burials contain these objects, which are themselves of the highest quality (Dietler 1996:110–111). This suggests that in the less complex society of the south, feasting was open to a larger segment of the community. In the more hierarchical regions inland, feasting remained a privileged activity as it had been in the Bronze Age, and the luxurious nature of the associated vessels points to the use of material culture in reinforcing the exclusivity of this activity. Other examples of Iron Age feasting include the "princely tombs" from central Italy with elaborate banquet services such as the Bernardini Tomb from Latium and the Regolini Galassi Tomb from Cerveteri, both dated to the seventh century B.C. and showing both Greek and Near Eastern influences in the art and in the feasting practices (Curtis 1919; Rathje 1995; Winther 1997). In these Orientalizing period feasts, as prehistory comes to a close, the emphasis is almost certainly on the differentiation of the elite from the rest of society.

Conclusion

In this selective survey of the material remnants of prehistoric rituals I have avoided analyzing the beliefs themselves, out of concern that any reconstruction based on the partial material remains is virtually impossible, as Hawkes (1954) famously observed, and would do an injustice to these belief systems. Yet the material remains of rituals are nevertheless full of information about the societies that produced them. Although there is no evidence of a common religion practiced throughout the Mediterranean in any period of prehistory, people in the region still drew from the similar features of their surroundings: hilltops, caves, springs, groves, stone, and the like, to express in material form their beliefs. These parallels in practices, settings, and materials of the cult, unwittingly shared across the region, reaffirm the validity of the prehistoric Mediterranean as an object of study, in spite of the obvious internal heterogeneity.

Prehistoric ritual practices have been presented here in terms of the cult places themselves and their associated paraphernalia. Yet these actions are not easily limited to a single type of cult place: they would have permeated all areas of prehistoric life. As Connerton (1989:45) notes, "Although demarcated in time and space, rites are also as it were porous. They are held to be meaningful because rites have significance with respect to a set of further non-ritual actions, to the whole life of a community." Let us look again at the ritual actions that Warren (1988) identified in Minoan contexts. We see, for example, that the robe rituals in which a gown is made and presented to a female deity must have begun long before the final presentation, involving spinning, dying, and weaving, all taking place elsewhere. The same is true for the presentation of flowers to the deity, possibly amassed from a wide surrounding area and arranged before presentation in a domestic context. In the case of the sacrifice of animals, the mundane raising of the animals for years before may have been continuously inflected with the expectation of this subsequent sacrifice. If the settings for the final stages of some of these actions, in forecourts, caves, temples, or at altars, were "sacred," then the earlier preparations must equally have imbued their settings with a sacred character, which perhaps they forever retained. We can thus imagine the spiritual world of the ancient Mediterranean as immanent, and the divine and human spheres spilling over into each other. From this perspective, the notion of the "liminality" of the recognizably sacred spaces may be no more than a matter of degree.

ACKNOWLEDGMENTS

I would like to thank Bob Chapman, Bernard Knapp, Lyun Meskell, Ian Morris, and Rob Schon for reading earlier drafts of this chapter and making excellent suggestions.

REFERENCES

Barker, Graeme, and Tom Rasmussen, 1998 The Etruscans. Oxford: Blackwell.
Barrett, John, 1991 Towards an Archaeology of Ritual. *In* Sacred and Profane: Proceedings of a Conference on Archaeology, Ritual, and Religion. Oxford, 1989. P. Garwood, D. Jennings, R. Skeates and J. Toms, eds. pp. 1–9. Oxford: Oxbow Books.
Bell, Catherine, 1992 Ritual Theory, Ritual Practice. Oxford.
Bietti Sestieri, Anna Maria, 1992 The Iron Age Community of Osteria dell'Osa: A study of Socio-Political Development in Central Tyrrhenian Italy. Cambridge: Cambridge University Press.
Bittichesu, C., 1989 La Tomba di Busoro a Sedilo e l'Architettura Funeraria Nuragica. Sassari: Lorziana.

Blegen, Carl, and Marion Rawson, 1966 The Palace of Nestor at Pylos in Western Messenia. Volume I: The Buildings and Their Contents. Princeton: Princeton University Press.

Bonanno, Anthony, ed., 1986 Archaeology and Fertility Cult in the Ancient Mediterranean: Papers Presented at the First International Conference on Archaeology of the Ancient Mediterranean. The University of Malta, 2–5 September 1985. Amsterdam: B. R. Gruner.

Bonghi Jovino, Maria, 2001 "Area Sacra/Complesso Monumentale" della Civita. In Tarquinia Etrusca: Una Nuova Storia. A. M. Moretti Sgubini, ed. pp. 21–29. Rome: L'Erma di Bretschneider.

Bonifay, Eugene, 1990 Préhistoire de la Corse. Ajaccio: C.R.D.P. de la Corse.

Bourdieu, Pierre, 1977 Outline of a Theory of Practice. Cambridge: Cambridge University Press.

Bradley, Richard, 1998 Daggers Drawn: Depictions of Bronze Age Weapons in Atlantic Europe. In The Archaeology of Rock Art. C. Chippindale and P. Tacon, eds. pp. 130–145. Cambridge: Cambridge University Press.

Bradley, Richard, Christopher Chippindale, and Knut Helskog, 2001 Post-Paleolithic Europe. In Handbook of Rock Art Research. D. S. Whitley, ed. pp. 482–529. Walnut Creek: Altamira Press.

Branigan, Keith, 1991 Funerary Ritual and Social Cohesion in Early Bronze Age Crete. Journal of Mediterranean Studies 1(2):183–192.

Cadogan, Gerald, 1981 A Probable Shrine in the Country House at Pyrgos. In Sanctuaries and Cults in the Aegean Bronze Age. R. Hagg and N. Marinatos, eds. pp. 169–171. Stockholm: Paul Astroms Forlag.

Castaldi, Editta, 1968 Nuove Osservazioni sulle "Tombe di Giganti." Bollettino di Paletnologia Italiana 77:7–91.

——1969 Tombe di Giganti nel Sassarese. Origini 3:119–274.

Cavanagh, William, 1998 Innovation, Conservatism and Variation in Mycenaean Funerary Ritual. In Cemetery and Society in the Aegean Bronze Age. K. Branigan, ed. pp. 103–114. Sheffield: Sheffield Academic Press.

Chapman, Robert, 1990 Emerging Complexity. The Later Prehistory of South-East Spain, Iberia and the West Mediterranean. Cambridge: Cambridge University Press.

Chapman, Robert, Ian Kinnes, and Klaus Randsborg, eds., 1981 The Archaeology of Death. Cambridge: Cambridge University Press.

Cherry, John F., 1986 Polities and Palaces: Some Problems in Minoan State Formation. In Peer Polity Interaction and Socio-political Change. Colin Renfrew and John F. Cherry, eds. pp. 19–45. Cambridge: Cambridge University Press.

Connerton, Paul, 1989 How Societies Remember. Cambridge: Cambridge University Press.

Crescenzi, Livio, 1978 Campoverde. Archeologia Laziale 1:51–55.

Curtis, C. D., 1919 The Bernardini Tomb. Memoirs of the American Academy in Rome 3:9–90.

Davidson, James, 1999 Courtesans and Fishcakes: The Consuming Passions of Classical Athens. New York: Perennial.

D'Ercole, Vincenzo, and Flavia Trucco, 1992 Canino (Viterbo). Località Banditella. Un Luogo di Culto all'Aperto Presso Vulci. Bollettino di Archeologia 13–15:77–84.

Dietler, Michael, 1996 Feasts and Commensal Politics in the Political Economy. Food, Power and Status in Prehistoric Europe. In Food and the Status Quest: An Interdisciplinary Perspective. P. Wiessner and W. Schiefenhovel, eds. pp. 87–125. Providence and Oxford: Berghahn Books.

——2001 Theorizing the Feast: Rituals of Consumption, Commensal Politics, and Power in African Contexts. In Feasts: Archaeological and Ethnographic Perspectives on Food,

Politics, and Power. M. Dietler and B. Hayden, eds. pp. 65–114. Washington and London: Smithsonian Institution Press.

Dietler, Michael, and Brian Hayden, eds., 2001 Feasts: Archaeological and Ethnographic Perspectives on Food, Politics, and Power. Washington and London: Smithsonian Institution Press.

Doumas, Christos, 2002 Silent Witnesses: Early Cycladic Art of the Third Millennium. New York: Alexander S. Onassis Public Benefit Foundation.

Fenelli, Maria, and Marcello Guaitoli, 1990 Nuovi Dati degli Scavi di Lavinium. Archeologia Laziale 10:195–201.

Fernández Castro, Maria C., 1995 Iberia in Prehistory. Oxford: Blackwell.

Galán Domingo, Eduardo, 1993 Estelas, Paisaje y Territorio en el Bronce Final del Suroeste de la Peninsula Iberica. Complutum Extra no. 3. Madrid: Universidad Complutense.

Garwood, P., D. Jennings, R. Skeates, and J. Toms, 1991 Introduction. In Sacred and Profane: Proceedings of a Conference on Archaeology, Ritual and Religion, Oxford, 1989. P. Garwood, D. Jennings, R. Skeates, and J. Toms, eds. pp. i–xi. Oxford: Oxbow Books.

Gimbutas, Marija, 1982 The Goddesses and Gods of Old Europe. Berkeley: University of California Press.

Goodison, Lucy, and Christine Morris, 1998 Beyond the "Great Mother": The Sacred World of the Minoans. In Ancient Goddesses: The Myths and the Evidence. L. Goodison and C. Morris, eds. pp. 113–132. Madison: University of Wisconsin Press.

Goody, Jack, 1982 Cooking, Cuisine and Class: A Study in Comparative Sociology. Cambridge: Cambridge University Press.

Grima, Reuben, 2001 An Iconography of Insularity: A Cosmological Interpretation of Some Images and Spaces in the Late Neolithic Temples of Malta. Papers of the Institute of Archaeology 12:48–65.

Guidi, A., 1980 Luoghi di Culto dell'Età del Bronzo Finale e della Prima Età del Ferro nel Lazio Meridionale. Archeologia Laziale 3:148–155.

Haaland, Gunnar, and Randi Haaland, 1996 Levels of Meaning in Symbolic Objects. In Viewpoint: Can We Interpret Figurines? Cambridge Archaeological Journal 6(2):295–300.

Hamilakis, Yannis, 1998 Eating the Dead: Mortuary Feasting and the Politics of Memory in the Aegean Bronze Age Societies. In Cemetery and Society in the Aegean Bronze Age. K. Branigan, ed. pp. 115–132. Sheffield: Sheffield Academic Press.

Hamilton, Naomi, 1996 The Personal is Political. In Viewpoint: Can We Interpret Figurines? Cambridge Archaeological Journal 6(2):282–285.

Hawkes, Christopher, 1954 Archaeological Theory and Method: Some Suggestions from the Old World. American Anthropologist 56:155–168.

Hodder, Ian, 1991 The Domestication of Europe. Oxford: Blackwell.

Jorda, Francisco, 1991 The Cults of the Bull and of a Feminine Divinity in Spanish Levantine Art. Journal of Mediterranean Studies 1(2):295–305.

Knapp, A. Bernard, 1996 Power and Ideology on Prehistoric Cyprus. In Religion and Power in the Ancient Greek World. P. Hellstrom and B. Alroth, eds. pp. 9–25. Uppsala and Stockholm: Department of Archaeology and Ancient History and Almqvist and Wiksell.

Knapp, A. Bernard, and Lynn Meskell, 1997 Bodies of Evidence on Prehistoric Cyprus. Cambridge Archaeological Journal 7:183–204.

Le Brun, Alain, 1989 Le Traitement des Morts et les Représentations des Vivants à Khirokitia. In Early Society in Cyprus, E. J. Peltenburg, ed. pp. 71–81. Edinburgh: Edinburgh University Press.

Leighton, Robert, 1999 Sicily Before History: An Archaeological Survey from the Paleolithic to the Iron Age. Ithaca, NY: Cornell University Press.

Lewis, Gilbert, 1980 Day of Shining Red: An Essay on Understanding Ritual. Cambridge: Cambridge University Press.

Lilliu, Giovanni, 1988 La Civiltà dei Sardi dal Paleolitico all'Età dei Nuraghi. Turin: Nuova ERI.

Lo Schiavo, Fulvia, 1999 The Nuragic Bronze Statuettes. In Gods and Heroes of the European Bronze Age. K. Demakopoulou, C. Eluere, J. Jensen, A. Jockenhovel, and J.-P. Mohen, eds. pp. 123–124. London: Thames and Hudson.

Lukes, Steven, 1975 Political Ritual and Social Integration. Sociology 9:289–308.

Lupack, Susan, 1999 Palaces, Sanctuaries, and Workshops: The Role of the Religious Sector in Mycenaean Economics. In Rethinking Mycenaean Palaces: New Interpretations of an Old Idea. M. L. Galaty and W. A. Parkinson, eds. pp. 25–34. Los Angeles: The Cotsen Institute of Archaeology.

Maaskant-Kleibrink, Marianne, 1992 Settlement Excavations at Borgo Le Ferriere (< Satricum >) Vol. II, Groningen: Egbert Forsten.

——1995 Evidence of Households or of Ritual Meals? Early Latin Cult Practices: A Comparison of Finds at Lavinium, Campoverde and Borgo Le Ferriere (Satricum). In Settlement and Economy in Italy 1500 B.C. to A.D. 1500. Oxbow Monographs 41. Neil Christie, ed. pp. 123–143. Oxford: Oxbow Books.

Malone, Caroline, 1998 God or Goddess: The Temple Art of Ancient Malta. In Ancient Goddesses: The Myths and the Evidence. L. Goodison and C. Morris, eds. pp. 148–163. Madison: University of Wisconsin Press.

Maniscalco McConnell, Laura, 1996 Early Bronze Age Funerary Ritual and Architecture: Monumental Tombs at Santa Febronia. In Early Societies in Sicily. New Developments in Archaeological Research. Accordia Specialist Studies on Italy 5. R. Leighton, ed. pp. 81–87. London: Accordia Research Institute.

Mann, Michael, 1986 The Sources of Social Power. Volume I: A History of Power from the Beginning to A.D. 1760. Cambridge: Cambridge University Press.

Meskell, Lynn, 1995 Goddesses, Gimbutas and "New Age" Archaeology. Antiquity 69:74–85.

——1998 Oh My Goddesses: Archaeology, Sexuality and Ecofeminism. Archaeological Dialogues 5:126–142.

Moravetti, Alberto, 1981 Nota agli Scavi nel Complesso Megalitico di Monte Baranta (Olmedo, SS). Rivista di Scienze Preistoriche 36:281–290.

Morris, Ian, 1992 Death-Ritual and Social Structure in Classical Antiquity. Cambridge: Cambridge University Press.

Morris, Ian, Trinity Jackman, Emma Blake, and Sebastiano Tusa, 2002 Stanford University Excavations on the Acropolis of Monte Polizzo, Sicily II: Preliminary Report on the 2001 Season. Memoirs of the American Academy at Rome 47:153–198.

Murphy, Joanne, 1998 The Nearness of You—Proximity and Distance in Early Minoan Funerary Landscapes. In Cemetery and Society in the Aegean Bronze Age. K. Branigan, ed. pp. 27–40. Sheffield: Sheffield Academic Press.

Murray, Oswyn, ed., 1990 Sympotica. A Symposium on the Symposion. Oxford: Clarendon.

Muzzolini, Alfred, 2001 Saharan Africa. In Handbook of Rock Art Research. D. S. Whitley, ed. pp. 605–636. Walnut Creek: Altamira Press.

Oliveira Jorge, Susana, 1999a Bronze Age Stelai and Menhirs of the Iberian Peninsula: Discourses of Power. In Gods and Heroes of the European Bronze Age. K. Demakopoulou, C. Eluere, J. Jensen, A. Jockenhovel, and J.-P. Mohen, eds. pp. 114–122. London: Thames and Hudson.

—— 1999b Cabeco da Mina (Vila Flor, Portugal): A Late Prehistoric Sanctuary with "Stelai" of the Iberian Peninsula. *In* Gods and Heroes of the European Bronze Age. K. Demakopoulou, C. Eluere, J. Jensen, A. Jockenhovel, and J.-P. Mohen, eds. pp. 137–144. London: Thames and Hudson.

Peatfield, Alan A. D., 1990 Minoan Peak Sanctuaries: History and Society. Opuscula Atheniensia 18:117–131.

—— 1992 Rural Ritual in Bronze Age Crete: The Peak Sanctuary at Atsipadhes. Cambridge Archaeological Journal 2.1:59–87.

Peltenburg, Edgar J., 1994 Constructing Authority: The Vounous Enclosure Model. Opuscula Atheniensia 20:157–162.

Py, Michel, 1993 Les Gaulois du Midi: de la Fin de l'Age du Bronze à la Conquête Romaine. Paris: Hachette.

Rathje, Annette, 1995 Il Banchetto in Italia Centrale: Quale Stile di Vita? *In* In Vino Veritas. O. Murray and M. Tecusan, eds. pp. 167–175. London: British School at Rome in Association with American Academy at Rome.

Renfrew, Colin, 1985 The Archaeology of Cult: The Sanctuary at Phylakopi. London: British School at Athens and Thames and Hudson.

—— 1986 The Prehistoric Maltese Achievement and its Interpretation. *In* Archaeology and Fertility Cult in the Ancient Mediterranean. A. Bonanno, ed. pp. 118–130. Amsterdam: B. R. Gruner.

Saxe, Arthur, 1970 Social Dimensions of Mortuary Practices. Unpublished Ph.D. thesis, University of Michigan.

Schmandt-Besserat, Denise, 2004 'Ain Ghazal Monumental Figures: A Stylistic Analysis. Electronic Document. http://link.lanic.utexas.edu/menic/ghazal/ChapVI/dsb.html.

Schmitt-Pantel, Pauline, 1992 La Cité au Banquet. Histoire des Repas Publics dans les Cités Grecques. Rome: Ecole Française de Rome.

Sherratt, Andrew, 1991 Sacred and Profane Substances: The Ritual Use of Narcotics in Later Neolithic Europe. *In* Sacred and Profane: Proceedings of a Conference on Archaeology, Ritual, and Religion. Oxford, 1989. P. Garwood, D. Jennings, R. Skeates and J. Toms, eds. pp. 50–64. Oxford: Oxbow Books.

—— 1994 The Transformations of Early Agrarian Europe: The Later Neolithic and Copper Ages, 4500–2500 B.C. *In* The Oxford Illustrated History of Prehistoric Europe. B. Cunliffe, ed. pp. 167–201. Oxford: Oxford University Press.

—— 1995 Alcohol and its Alternatives: Symbol and Substance in Pre-Industrial Cultures. *In* Consuming Habits: Drugs in History and Anthropology. J. Goodman, P. Lovejoy, and A. Sherratt, eds. pp. 11–46. London and New York: Routledge.

—— 1997 Economy and Society in Prehistoric Europe. Changing Perspectives. Edinburgh: Edinburgh University Press.

Smith, Adam, 2001 The Limitations of Doxa: Agency and Subjectivity from an Archaeological Point of View. Journal of Social Archaeology 1:155–171.

South, A., 2000 Late Bronze Age Burials at Kalavasos Ayios Dhimitrios. *In* Acts of the Third International Congress of Cypriot Studies. G. C. Ioannides and S. A. Hadjistellis, eds. pp. 345–364. Nicosia: Society of Cypriot Studies.

Steel, Louise, 2002 Wine, Women and Song: Drinking Ritual in Cyprus in the Late Bronze and Early Iron Ages. *In* Engendering Aphrodite: Women and Society in Ancient Cyprus. D. Bolger and N. Serwint, eds. pp. 105–119. Cyprus American Archaeological Research Institute Monograph 3. Boston: American Schools of Oriental Research.

Stoddart, Simon, Anthony Bonanno, Tancred Gouder, Caroline Malone, and David Trump, 1993 Cult in an Island Society: Prehistoric Malta in the Tarxien Period. Cambridge Archaeological Journal 3:3–19.

Thomas, Julian, 1991 Rereading the Body: Beaker Funerary Practice in Britain. *In* Sacred and Profane: Proceedings of a Conference on Archaeology, Ritual, and Religion. Oxford, 1989. P. Garwood, D. Jennings, R. Skeates and J. Toms, eds. pp. 33–42. Oxford: Oxbow Books.

Trigger, Bruce G., 2003 Understanding Early Civilizations: A Comparative Study. Cambridge: Cambridge University Press.

Tringham, Ruth, and Margaret Conkey, 1998 Rethinking Figurines. *In* Ancient Goddesses: The Myths and the Evidence. L. Goodison and C. Morris, eds. pp. 22–45. Madison: University of Wisconsin Press.

Tronchetti, Carlo, 1986 Nuragic Statuary from Monte Prama. *In* Studies in Sardinian Archaeology, Vol. 2: Sardinia in the Mediterranean. M. Balmuth, ed. pp. 41–59. Ann Arbor: University of Michigan Press.

Trump, David, 1966 Skorba. Research Reports of the Society of Antiquaries of London 22. London: Society of Antiquaries.

Tusa, Sebastiano, 1997 Origine della Società Agro-Pastorale. *In* Prima Sicilia: Alle Origini della Societa Siciliana. S. Tusa, ed. pp. 173–191. Palermo: Ediprint.

Tyree, E. Loeta, 1974 Cretan Sacred Caves: Archaeological Evidence. Unpublished Doctoral Dissertation, University of Missouri-Columbia. University Microfilm.

Ucko, Peter, 1968 Anthropomorphic Figurines of Predynastic Egypt and Neolithic Crete with Comparative Material from the Prehistoric Near East and Mainland Greece. Royal Anthropological Institute Occasional Paper 24. London: Szmidla.

van Gennep, Arnold, 1960. The Rites of Passage. Translated by M. B. Vizedom and G. L. Caffee. Chicago: University of Chicago Press.

van Leuven, J. C., 1981 Problems and Methods of Prehellenic Naology. *In* Sanctuaries and Cults in the Aegean Bronze Age. R. Hagg and N. Marinatos, eds. pp. 11–25. Stockholm: Paul Astroms Forlag.

Warren, Peter, 1988 Minoan Religion as Ritual Action. Goteborg: Gothenberg University.

Webb, Jennifer, 1999 Ritual Architecture, Iconography and Practice in the Late Cypriot Bronze Age. Studies in Mediterranean Archaeology Pocket-book 75. Jonsered: Paul Astroms Forlag.

Webster, Gary S., 1996 A Prehistory of Sardinia 2300 to 500 B.C. Monographs in Mediterranean Archaeology 5. Sheffield: Sheffield Academic Press.

Whitehouse, Ruth, 1981 Megaliths of the Central Mediterranean. *In* The Megalithic Monuments of Western Europe. C. Renfrew, ed. pp. 42–63. London: Thames and Hudson.

—— 1992 Underground Religion. Cult and Culture in Prehistoric Italy. London: University of London, Accordia Research Centre.

—— 1995 From Secret Society to State Religion: Ritual and Social Organisation in Prehistoric and Protohistoric Italy. *In* Settlement and Economy in Italy 1500 B.C. to AD 1500. Oxbow Monograph 41. N. Christie, ed. pp. 83–88. Oxford: Oxbow Books.

Whittle, Alasdair, 1994 The First Farmers. *In* The Oxford Illustrated History of Prehistoric Europe. B. Cunliffe, ed. pp. 136–166. Oxford: Oxford University Press.

Wiessner, Polly, and Wulf Schiefenhovel, eds., 1996 Food and the Status Quest: An Interdisciplinary Perspective. Providence and Oxford: Berghahn Books.

Wilfong, Terry, 1997 Women and Gender in Ancient Egypt from Prehistory to Late Antiquity. Ann Arbor: Kelsey Museum of Archaeology.

Winther, Helene Caroline, 1997 Princely Tombs of the Orientalizing Period in Etruria and Latium Vetus. *In* Acta Hyperborea 7: Urbanization in the Mediterranean in the 9th to 6th Centuries B.C. H. Damgaard Andersen, H. W. Horsnaes, S. Houby-Nielsen, and A. Rathje, eds. pp. 423–446. Copenhagen: Museum Tusculanum Press.

6

The Gendered Sea: Iconography, Gender, and Mediterranean Prehistory

Lauren E. Talalay

Introduction

Systematic attempts to "engender" prehistory are a comparatively recent phenomenon. First seriously proposed less than twenty years ago, the notion that archaeologists could retrieve information about gender from the prehistoric record was initially dismissed within the academy as naïve and suspect, motivated more by feminist politics than clear intellectual agendas. Gradually, however, gender archaeologists have proved their critics wrong. Although this branch of archaeological research continues to retain some of the ghettoized status that marked its emergence, gender is now generally regarded as a legitimate conceptual and analytic category of archaeology. Publications on ancient gender roles, sexuality, sexual difference, and the gendered division of labor presently number in the hundreds.[1] Women, once barely visible members of past societies, are slowly being rewritten into prehistory, while essentialist gender types are gradually being written out. Discussions on the subject of masculinity in past cultures are also slowly finding their way into print (e.g., Knapp 1998). On the theoretical front, thoughtful if occasionally tortured discussions about the meanings of gender, sex, and the materiality of gender surface with increasing regularity. While feminist-inspired inquiries have not produced the radically revisionist past that some had anticipated, they have fundamentally altered the way we think about the ancient world.

Mediterranean prehistorians, including scholars working in southeastern Europe, began to incorporate feminist concerns into their work in the early 1990s. Those efforts have produced both provocative and problematic results. Although important aspects of Mediterranean prehistory previously elided or ignored in traditional discourse have found a forum, the studies are variable in quality. Indeed, the difficulties of effectively translating theoretical conviction into practical application still loom large (Sørenson 2000:3). This problem notwithstanding, gender archaeology in Mediterranean prehistory is a burgeoning and stimulating field, still immersed in critical self-reflection. Given the recent gender-inflection of much research, it is instructive at this point to take stock of where we stand. What kinds of studies have been undertaken and how successful have they been? What have we learned in our endeavors to "engender" the Mediterranean, and what might we have lost if such research had never been attempted?

As a first step in answering these questions, I review here recent research on gender and iconography, focusing on Neolithic, Chalcolithic, and Bronze Age societies of the Mediterranean, principally Italy, Greece, and Cyprus. What emerges is not a unified narrative or holistic view of gender in these cultures. Rather, the following discussion offers glimpses into how scholars have approached the topic, how they have interpreted the "vernacular" and "official" iconographies of men and woman, and how they imagine these early societies might have perceived the human body and defined gender and sexual ideologies. These studies range from broad sweeping investigations into the emergence of gender inequality to tightly focused studies on sexuality, figurines, and gender roles, to articles that simply raise questions and unmask biases. The lack of readable prehistoric texts has forced Mediterranean prehistorians to probe various classes of mute evidence, especially the glyptic material, the scrappy but instructive remains of wall paintings, the mortuary data, and where relevant, architectural information. Archaeologists who have attempted to recover gender from the archaeological record have, however, most frequently interrogated anthropomorphic imagery. Depictions of the human form are often seen as mediating, authorizing, reflecting, or mobilizing certain social and gendered categories. Consequently, the following review and discussion focus principally on research that has grappled with interpreting anthropomorphic portrayals, in various forms and contexts. Before turning to these case studies, however, some relevant observations about gender and material culture may be instructive.

Gender, Sex, and Material Culture

Gender is not a fixed set of categories, nor is it determined by a universal understanding of biology. Indeed, current literature in the social sciences contains lengthy debates about the definitions of gender and its relationship to sex (e.g., Butler 1990; 1993; Laqueur 1990). Although a review of that dispute falls outside the purview of this chapter, it is important to note that, with few exceptions, Mediterranean prehistorians have failed to define these concepts clearly. When they do, they tend to distinguish between sex and gender in coarse-grained terms. "Sex" refers to categories based on observable biological characteristics of females, males, and intersexed individuals, and "gender" to the cultural values inscribed on sex (Hays-Gilpin and Whitley 1998:glossary). While these reductive definitions allow archaeologists to parse their research into tidy categories – sex is biologically determined, gender is socially constructed – the sex:gender paradigm is, in fact, no longer well supported (see Gilchrist 1999:9; Meskell 1999:69–77). As one scholar correctly observed, there is a blurring of the borders between sex and gender, which may forever defy clarification (Kampen 1996:1).

Although Mediterranean prehistorians have not been eager participants in this deliberation on definition, they have been quick to grasp the instructive value that cross-cultural studies of sex and gender can provide archaeologists. Even the most superficial perusal of the anthropological literature reveals that the definitions of male and female, masculine and feminine, are part of a continuum that is historically and culturally contingent, susceptible to ongoing negotiation and alteration. For many societies, "sex is not so much given at birth as accreted" (Bender 2000:xx). Among the Hua of Papua New Guinea, for example, males and females are classified by their bodily fluids, which are viewed as changing as one ages (Moore 1994:24), and for several New Guinean groups, such as the Sambia and the Etoro, the definition of one's sexual identity is a continuing process, created through life, especially in rites of passage (Herdt 1987; 1994).

Equally edifying are the well-known "third sex" individuals detailed by ethnographers and anthropologists. The "two-spirit" of Native America – biological males who adopt female roles – have a sex/gender status distinct from that of either males or females in their society (Whitehead 1981; Williams 1986; Roscoe 1994). Indian Hijars, biological males who describe themselves as "neither woman nor man," often have their penis and testicles surgically removed and assume very specific female roles (Nanda 1990). And the "sworn virgins" of North Albania are biological females who fully embrace the roles, dress, and behaviors of men for a variety of social reasons (Grémaux 1994). These intriguing reports stand as bold warnings that, as archaeologists, we should not approach sexual and gender identities in past societies within the rigid dyadic frameworks of Western discourse. As anthropologists long ago pointed out, not all cultures form beliefs about the sexes based on "logical oppositions or complementarities; the sexes appear more as gradations on a scale" (Ortner and Whitehead 1981:6–7).

Just as compelling is the fact that discourses on gender and sex vary widely across cultures. The spectrum embraces unitary notions of sex and gender wherein undivided genders have ways of dividing themselves from each other, composite ideologies in which males and females are seen as naturally contrasted but complementary, and divided identities where the sexes and genders are viewed as radically different and separate. In all likelihood, the range was no less broad or complex in antiquity.

Intimately related to these discussions about the nature of gender and sex (and of paramount importance to archaeologists) is the matter of how these concepts are expressed and communicated through material culture. Most archaeologists would agree that objects are not inherently gendered; nor do they simply *reflect* gendered norms in a society. Rather, gendered meanings are invested in objects over time by the people who use them. While the instability of an object's meaning or identity, gendered or other, invariably complicates archaeological interpretation, it is difficult to escape the conclusion that objects have complex "biographies" – their significance can shift over time and, as repositories of multiple meanings, they are open to divergent readings. In some sense, then, objects behave as "partners" in the construction of gender. While not every object colludes in this partnership or management of relations, many classes of material culture do. Maureen MacKenzie's exceptional book *Androgynous Objects* (1991), a study of string bags designed by the

Telefol of Papua New Guinea, brings clearly into focus how these alliances can evolve. The Telefol bags are "multi-authored," produced by both men and women, and move through different social contexts and transactions throughout their life-times. They successfully acquire and negotiate different meanings, serving as powerful metaphors for gender difference and gender relationships. As MacKenzie's work demonstrates, just as gender is open to negotiation and reproduction, so too is the relationship between objects and gender construction. Both are dynamic and discursive parts of daily life.

These brief introductory comments on gender, sex, and their relationship to material culture serve as a background against which to place recent research in Mediterranean prehistory. Bearing these layered constructions in mind, we can consider what kind of a testing ground the Mediterranean has become over the past decade.

Gender and Iconography: Recent Research

Mediterranean prehistory has not historically resided in a "gender-neutral zone," nor have archaeologists ignored the iconographic (or limited textual) evidence for gender construction. Indeed, researchers have often noted the relative percentages of males and females in burials, the seeming predominance of females in the production of Neolithic and Bronze Age figurines, and the presence or absence, relative size, and elaboration of images of males and females in wall paintings, cult equipment, seals, and sealings. None of these early studies, however, was theoretically informed by research in gender studies, nor were underlying assumptions made explicit. Consideration of anthropomorphic images, for example, was often superficial, more descriptive than analytic, with archaeologists usually assigning all images to the realm of a Mother Goddess cult, regardless of sex, posture, gesture, costume, and ornamentation.[2] The human form was never perceived as a distinct source of theoretical discussion, and in most cases, the sex of an image was unproblematized, determined by the researcher on the basis of primary (or secondary) sexual characteristics as male, female, or questionable.

Recently, scholars have adopted less normative and more nuanced approaches, exploring the possible range and variability of sexual and gender identities, individual experiences, and the contingencies of daily life. As the sections below indicate, studies now concentrate on sexual coding and ambiguity in figurines, the role of the body, performance, the individual in gender constructions, the iconographic evidence for gendered space, and arguments about gender roles and social asymmetries.

Sexual Coding and Anthropomorphic Images

Within the past decade Mediterranean prehistorians have begun to question various aspects of sexual coding on anthropomorphic figurines, contending that our determination of a figure's sex is distorted by modern cultural filters, that the depiction of sex on a figurine may not have held primary importance to the makers and users, or that the absence of explicit indicators may reflect a deliberate attempt to emphasize sexual ambiguity.

Naomi Hamilton, for example, has taken a critical look at traditional sexual classifications of prehistoric anthropomorphic figurines from Eastern Europe, the Mediterranean, and the Near East. She argues that these images have been subjected to methodologies that categorize them by sex and then translate sex "into stereotyped Western gender roles which may have no relevance to prehistory" (2000:17; see also Sarenas 1998 for a critique of sexual classifications of Neolithic figurines from southeastern Europe). Hamilton's work reveals how deeply ethnocentric our gender biases are, starting with the identification of sexual attribution. Her examples are telling: prehistoric images of human figures with breasts and beards that are summarily identified as male on the basis of their beard, while breasts are dismissed as insignificant; large, well-modeled, enthroned human images designated male, despite the absence of any indications of sex; and two-headed figurines presumed to depict a male and a female, despite explicit indicators to the contrary. Moreover, Hamilton questions the prevalent assumption that these early societies necessarily divided human groups into two mutually exclusive categories: male and female. As she observes, both the figurines, which often defy straightforward sexing, and ethnographic analogues suggest instead that early Mediterranean cultures may have held "different gender concepts and structures from our own" (Hamilton 2000:28).

Talalay (1993; 2000) noted similar biases in earlier studies of roughly twelve hundred Greek Neolithic figurines. The corpus predominantly represents females, but also includes a substantial number of sexless or (to the modern eye) sexually indeterminate pieces, a handful of images with male attributes, and a few that incorporate *both* male and female sexual characteristics in a single image. The relatively high percentage of sexless or sexually indeterminate pieces and the existence of dual-sexed examples raise questions about Greek Neolithic constructions of gender and sexuality that have been ignored previously. Can we assume that the sexless images were viewed as truly neuter, possibly embodying gender-free concepts? Did they transcend sexual classifications altogether? Or were they seen as subsuming male and female (and possibly other) categories? If so, could they have been capable of moving in and out of various sexual or gendered categories, depending, perhaps, on their use? The dual-sexed images inspire similar kinds of questions: were they conceived as hermaphroditic or, again, as a kind of fluid representation that moved along a spectrum and fluctuated with the piece's function? While the data are insufficient to answer these questions, this study, like Hamilton's, encourages us to reevaluate the extent to which traditional Western notions of binary sexuality may be applicable to early societies.

Similar kinds of queries are pertinent to the Bronze Age, particularly for the hundreds of small terracotta anthropomorphic figures found in Mycenaean contexts, the limited but intriguing examples of human and hybrid depictions in wall paintings, and the large corpus of glyptic images. Louise Hitchcock (2000), for example, has focused on the problem of determining the sex of the most famous fresco image from Knossos, the so-called "Priest-King." Variously reconstructed from several fragments found at different levels, the "Priest-King" – long assumed to be a male ruler – exhibits attributes associated with both males and females (e.g., white skin typically used to portray females, kilt and cod-piece typical of males, and special plumed hat reserved for women and sphinxes). In her paper amusingly subtitled "It's a Drag to be a King," Hitchcock argues that scholarly thinking about this figure has been constrained by modern notions of gender. The possible inversion or confusion of color conventions and the mixture of male and female attributes on this very public fresco may have intentionally broadcast the message that multiple genders and sexual ambiguity played a sanctioned role in the dominant social order of Minoan Crete. The "Priest-King" may be a "Priest-Queen" (for a recent exploration of ancient "queens" see Nelson 2003), or, if the figure was indeed intended as male, official iconography purposely appropriated certain female attributes as a way of empowering the image by subsuming both sexes (see Joyce 1992 and Looper 2002 for a comparable phenomenon in Classic Maya society).[3]

Intentional gender ambiguity in human figurines has also been investigated in recent research on Early and Middle Bronze Age plank figurines from Cyprus (Talalay and Cullen 2002; see also Knapp and Meskell 1997). These large, distinctive, and often elaborately decorated figures are most frequently recovered from mortuary contexts (collective burials) and rarely exhibit characteristics that permit unproblematic identifications as male or female. Rather than argue, as others have, for a specific meaning and sexual identity of these figures, Talalay and Cullen suggest that plank figures were intended to project a kind of sexual ambiguity that served specific purposes for members of an emerging hierarchical society.

As they note, plank figures are chronologically limited to a time when Cyprus was experiencing growing tensions, the beginnings of metallurgy, and burgeoning social inequalities. Within such contexts, ritual would likely have played an important role in broadcasting and legitimizing the power and influence of competing social groups. Talalay and Cullen suggest that the distinctive nature and sexual uncertainty of the plank figures would have accorded well with the demands of ritual which, as anthropologists (e.g., Turner 1967:27–29) have long observed, frequently underscore mystification and ambiguity, and employ symbols that unify and condense disparate meanings within a single form. Plank figures – perhaps newly designed insignia for an emerging elite – would have provided an ideal symbol. This striking, and, to our eyes, exotic image could have embraced a range of multi-valent allusions, materially embodying a reference to the human body – male, female, or other – and to divine or ancestral authority. The plank figures, which are found with secondary burials of both men and women, would have been capable of conveying cultural messages that subsumed the notion of male and female, stressing instead the collectivity and ancestral ties of the community, a message of particular power for an emerging elite, who may have needed to secure their lines of descent within the larger collective.

Holmes and Whitehouse (1998), in one of the first systematic investigations of free-standing anthropomorphic figurines in Neolithic Italy, adopt a slightly different approach to interpreting sexually ambiguous human images. The small Neolithic corpus of approximately 60 images is predominantly female; only two images can be unequivocally labeled as male, and none can be classified as "sexless." According to Holmes and Whitehouse, however, there are clear indications of mixed sexual symbolism (e.g., explicitly phallic-shaped heads on otherwise female figures), and a hybrid category, which seems to meld human and animal or human and bird characteristics. Single-sex (female) images derive mostly from domestic contexts, while combined-sex (male/female) and hybrid (human/animal or human/bird) figures are found primarily in cult caves or burials. Holmes and Whitehouse do not conceive of these images as depicting "third" or "other" genders, nor do they dwell on the validity of Western dyadic conceptions. Rather, they offer a model based on Marilyn Strathern's work in Melanesia (1988), where sexual and gendered identities are viewed as flexible and separable. Among certain Melanesian groups, gender does not reside in or adhere unequivocally to the individual. Rather, gender is conceived as an essence – invariably male or female – that separates, interacts, unites, and combines in either same-sex or cross-sex combinations. Individuals are not viewed as "irreducibly unique" components, but as composite sites of relation-ships. Identities are therefore not complete in themselves but are unbounded and divisible.

Using that model as a springboard, Holmes and Whitehouse imagine a belief system in prehistoric Italy that is rooted in the notion of shifting male and female essences. Same-sex manifestations are expressed by the female figurines found in domestic contexts and cross-sex manifestations are depicted in the melded images, most often confined to cultic contexts.

Although their conclusions are highly speculative, Holmes and Whitehouse, along with other scholars cited above, have taken important steps to restructure the intel-lectual scaffolding that has traditionally supported the study of anthropomorphic depictions. These new studies acknowledge that prehistoric anthropomorphic images from the Mediterranean do not lend themselves to simple sexual identifi-cations that can be cast facilely within Western discourse. Figurines were probably inscribed with a kind of sexual "shorthand" that could accommodate and subsume a range of polymorphous identities, and function effectively in a number of social contexts. If we accept this basic premise, the next step is to bridge the complex array of visual portrayals and their possible gendered meanings in these early soci-eties. Why, for example, are single-sexed female images only found in domestic con-texts of Neolithic Italy, while multi-sexed or hybrid images are confined to burials or cultic contexts? What are the contexts of dual-sexed or sexless images in the Greek Neolithic? How can we account for the evolution of mixed and purposely ambiguous depictions, or explain the opposition of "male" and "female" in the first place? And, as Ribiero (2002) and others (see Moore and Scott 1997:part 3) have observed, how were children, the invisible people of the ancient world, depicted and perceived; were they deemed a pre-sexual gender group or a neutral collective as our term "children" implies? None of these queries is easy to answer but they are vitally important for the future of gender studies. In the meantime, it is clear that recent studies have permanently altered the ways in which we discuss sexual coding, and carry consequences for how we interpret gender in the early archaeological record of the Mediterranean.

Gender, Gesture, Dress, and Performance

Not all recent studies on prehistoric figurines and gender have focused on overt sexual characteristics. Indeed, some scholars protest that such research is ultimately restrictive, fixated on the notion that biological sex predetermines gender. Gendered identities, they argue, are neither signaled nor negotiated exclusively via primary sexual attributes, but through more subtle dimensions such as gesture, dress, performance, and particularities in the overall depiction of the body. Recent studies on pre-Hispanic Costa Rican sculptures, for example, suggest that hands, more than genitalia, were the locus of gender identification (see Joyce 1998).

Alberti's consideration of figurative art in Late Bronze Age (LBA) Knossos and the aesthetics of sexual difference stands as a salient case (2001; 2002). For Alberti, the binary sexual structure normally assumed to underlie most cultures was not perceived, *a priori*, in LBA art. Rather, he argues, the sex and gender of LBA images were carefully (re)constructed in the visual record through a complex layering of factors: aesthetic, formal, contextual, and performative. Art objects, and the responses people had to them in the Late Bronze Age, served as conduits for agency and social relations, including gendered identities.

Part of Alberti's argument rests on the well-known work of Judith Butler, who purports that there is no fixed core to a person's gendered identity (Butler 1990:7–10; 24–25). According to Butler, gender (and sex) is discursively constituted, accruing to an individual through everyday activities and gestures, which are repeatedly performed or acted out in a variety of contexts. Consequently, gender is regarded as a fluid and context-driven phenomenon that reflects a relative point of convergence among various cultural and social relations (Butler 1990:10). Using Butler's basic premise as part of his theoretical framework, Alberti submits that the sexed/gendered body at Knossos was materialized iconographically by the artist taking a basic body template, combining it with particular types of garments and ornamentations, situating it in certain contexts, and utilizing it in certain ways. As he writes, "a gendered body does not pre-exist its representation in Knossian imagery: rather, the costumes, adornments, acts, body position and medium of representation combine to produce gender performatively in the figurines" (Alberti 2001:200).

Alberti uses as his examples the well-known faience snake goddess figurines from the "Temple Repositories" and the (male) ivory bull-leaper figurines from the "Domestic Quarter." Attempting to tease out the similarities and differences between the two types, Alberti analyzes the posture, context, medium, processes of production, possible aesthetic effects, and social functions of each. He notes that each is built on a basic Knossian body type, a singular form that cuts across other distinctions. Within the parameters of that basic template are conceived or grafted a particular posture, a selected array of colors, garments, materials, accoutrements, and bodily features (such as female breasts, which Alberti argues are never shown on naked bodies at Knossos, but only in combination with certain types of dress and ornamentation). Moreover, he observes that "snake goddesses" and bull-leapers are associated with very different kinds of assemblages and used in distinctly dissimilar contexts, the former deliberately arranged in repositories that were possibly accessible to a particular but restricted group, the latter in a more casual and secluded context. Different social functions for these two types are also suggested – the faience figures serving perhaps as iconic representations of divinities, the ivories holding mere mortal status.

For Alberti, the faience and ivory figurines represent two related deployments of bodily representations, both deriving from a basic Knossian bodily template. To label simplistically one male and the other female on the basis of sexual attributes (although the bull-leaper is devoid of sexual features) undermines what Alberti sees as the complex, nuanced, and ongoing construction of gender identities in LBA society. Representations of the body and sexuality were highly contextualized, dependent upon an image's aesthetic qualities, the significance attached to its placement in certain physical spaces, the mobility of the depiction, and the potential visibility of the portrayal – all factors that were ultimately tethered to a kind of performative or active life of the figure.

While processualists might disapprove, Alberti, along with a small but growing roster of prehistorians, has taken important steps in exploring the relationships among personal adornment, dress, gesture, performance, media, and gender (for Bronze Age Greece see Morris and Peatfield 2002; Barber 1994; 1997; Lee 2000; German 2000; Hughes-Brock 1999; Hitchcock 1997; Younger 1995; Marinatos 1987; 1993; and Koehl 1986; for Stone Age Italy, see Pluciennik 1998; 2002). Since the mid-1990s Paul Rehak has also made significant contributions to the study of gender in LBA Greece by considering a broad range of attributes, including body morphology, jewelry, hairstyles, dress, scale, gesture, posture and, where relevant, evidence from Linear B tablets (e.g., 1994; 1995; 1998; 1999; 2002). His most recently published work (2002) concentrates on Late Minoan art, particularly the spectacular frescoes from Xeste 3 at Akrotiri on Thera. Marshaling data from various sectors, Rehak suggests that the main theme of Xeste 3 is a female rite of passage, reflecting all stages of a woman's life, centering on the medicinal use of saffron. Moreover, he proposes that these rites of passage fostered same-sex relations in Theran society, helping to construct and maintain a homoerotic element among women in early Greece.

Although some of these recent studies tend to the nebulous and are indeed speculative, they raise provocative new questions, moving well beyond what traditionally has been a largely descriptive sub-field of Mediterranean prehistory. Dress, gesture, and bodily marking (which are all broadly linked to the notion of performance) have long been seen in other disciplines as emblematic of ethnic identities or as expressions of boundary maintenance. There is little reason to doubt that throughout Mediterranean prehistory these aspects of human corporeality also helped construct, broadcast, and maintain definitions of gender.

What is required now are more detailed and informed investigations into the kinds of ornamentation, dress, and bodily activities signified in anthropomorphic imagery. Do ornaments that are easily separable from the body perhaps signify gender in ways different from more permanent markings? Is the choice of media perceived as having "gendered" signification? How often do certain gestures appear in selective contexts at given sites, or across regions? Is there anything in the construction of figurines to suggest possible detachable body parts or clothing, indicating their use in rites?[4] How, in essence, did various groups within these cultures "perform" their gender? Equally important, it would benefit us to reflect specifically on *levels* of meaning within the categories of dress, gesture, and bodily signification. As Stig Sørensen (1998) has noted, for example, dress can be divided into three distinct categories: cloth (the actual textile), clothing (the cutting and designing of cloth), and costume (the final assemblage of clothing and ornaments). Each one of these categories serves as a useful heuristic device, helping us recognize that we often conflate our data in unproductive ways. Different stages in the creation of a product, as well as the media selected, can have different statuses in the discourse surrounding identity (see also Barber 1994; 1997).

As the studies cited here reveal, the gradual transformation of the body into a social signifier and the different levels of meanings that must have surrounded the development of a "social skin" (Turner 1980) probably represented key expressions of gender and sex in the ancient Mediterranean. These are important new avenues of research for gender studies in archaeology that are likely to produce valuable insights in the future.

Gender Asymmetries and Tensions

As thought-provoking as these recent studies of sexual coding, dress, gesture, and performance are, they do not directly confront the complex subject of gender *relationships* and the inevitable shifts in social and political power that can arise between the sexes over time. Studies suggest that sexual and gendered relationships are rarely static – associations among male, female, or other are continually redefined and renegotiated. It is critical, therefore, that we not only tease out what it meant to be classified "male" or "female" in a given society, but also consider the kinds of relationships that were constructed and negotiated *between* the sexes. How were the assigned roles of men and women perceived and valued in relation to one another? Can ancient iconography help archaeologists identify ideological shifts in power balances or tensions that may have emerged over the *longue durée*? These kinds of questions pose challenges, and mortuary data, rather than iconographic details, tend to offer better evidence from which to draw reliable inferences. Difficulties notwithstanding, a limited number of broad-based evolutionary studies of gender inequality, taking iconography into account, have been attempted for Mediterranean prehistory, specifically in Italy and Cyprus. A few are briefly summarized here.

For Italy, John Robb (1994a; 1994b) suggests that the roots of gender asymmetries extend back as early as the Eneolithic and evolve through the Iron Age. According to Robb, sexual/gender ideology moves from fairly unelaborated differences between male and females in the earlier part of the Neolithic to publicly expressed distinctions in the Eneolithic and Bronze Age in which males are defined iconographically by daggers and hunting prowess, and females by their biological attributes. Sexual asymmetry, therefore, is marked by a valued prestige item for men and the apparent lack of any equivalent for women, signaling perhaps that men had access to prestige while women did not. As Robb observes, however, these attributes may also indicate that women were not so much devalued by such a system as left unvalued (1994a:37). By the Iron Age, iconographic elaborations become more varied, the lines between the sexes more strongly delineated. Parietal art now shows preferences for male warriors and combat scenes, as well as a mythological vocabulary. Stelae exhibit instructive shifts as well, carved with more complex attributes for both men and women. For males, the typical attribute is no longer the dagger but a combination of a long sword, shield, and military clothing. For females, depictions that invariably included breasts are replaced by a variety of finery, suggesting that women too now had access to prestige items and were subject to internal differences. Essentially, Robb offers a broad evolutionary scheme wherein gender hierarchy and differences are increasingly institutionalized over time. The evidence for the Neolithic suggests a general balanced complementarity between the sexes; the Chalcolithic and Bronze Ages are marked by a dominant male ideology based on warfare and hunting; and the Iron Age sees even greater asymmetries, with the emergence of more class-based distinctions, an empowered female elite, and a growing and powerful male class. Although this summary cannot do justice to Robb's well-conceived and complex arguments, it underscores the value in adopting a long view. By using iconography as one element in a range of convergent data, Robb has been able to track shifting and evolving gender ideologies over time in a given area.

Different approaches have been taken in Cyprus where investigations into emerging asymmetries have sparked debate about the nature of complexity in early Cypriot society. Bolger (e.g., 1992; 1993; 1996; 2002; 2003) argues, for example, that women's roles were radically restructured from the Neolithic to the Bronze Age, with women's position in society gradually downgraded from one of prominence to one of subordination. In earlier periods women were prized for their procreative abilities, and often depicted in images associated with birth and birthing rituals (see Peltenburg 1991:chapter 4). By the Bronze Age, however, the long tradition of important birthing rituals seems to have ended. Indeed, at Middle Chalcolithic Kissonerga *Mosphilia* there is intriguing evidence for the public destruction and ritual burial of an unusual collection of birthing figurines. As the Bronze Age evolves, a marked decrease in the production of female figurines can be seen as well as signs of intensified agricultural production, perhaps greater control (by men?) over the distribution of stored foods, and possible transformations in kinship relationships. It is during this time of important transitions that, according to Bolger, women seem to be represented primarily as caretakers and accorded a low status (Mateu [2002] suggests a related scenario for the Neolithic of eastern Spain, based on figurative art in Levantine rock art).

David Frankel, on the other hand, posits that emerging inequalities, gendered or other, are not archaeologically defensible during the Cypriot Bronze Age (Frankel 1997; 2002). As he observes, even if increasing social stratification can be demonstrated, it does not necessarily imply an increasing imbalance in gender relations and social power. Frankel prefers to see interpersonal and gender relations on the island marked by the temporary and egalitarian coexistence of two ethnic groups, one indigenous, the other migrant. Frankel suggests that we decouple gender from the longstanding notions of evolving hierarchy and status on Cyprus and attempt to reconsider, instead, the processes of acculturation and assimilation through a gendered lens.

Surprisingly, few other studies on the evolution of gender asymmetries exist in the literature of Mediterranean prehistory. It would not be unexpected, however, if more publications begin to emerge. Women's inequality and the devalued nature of their work were, after all, among the prime movers of early feminism. Despite changes in feminist research, the analysis and understanding of gender tensions and power relations are likely to remain a cornerstone of the discipline. Moreover, exploration of social and political hierarchies has dominated processual archaeology for many years and it is difficult to imagine that those research agendas will vanish soon. While Mediterranean prehistorians have only just begun their investigations into this area of inquiry, the studies cited above suggest that explorations linking iconographic data with other types of evidence hold promise for understanding shifting asymmetries in early Mediterranean societies.

Iconography, Gender Roles, and Gendered Space

The topics discussed so far, namely sexual coding, dress, and performance, and evolving gender asymmetries, relate in the broadest sense to ideology – the ways in which gender is conceptualized in society. Gender, however, can be approached through other material correlates that shed light on more daily and routine activities. In most societies, different tasks are assigned to men and women and at least some of those activities are conducted in jurally, symbolically, or behaviorally designated areas. For some areas of Mediterranean prehistory debates about the roles, professions, and activities of men and women have been ongoing since the 1980s. In Greece, for example, readings of Linear B texts have long suggested a society with distinct task differentiations between men and women, as well as children, and possible segregation of work environments. The related question of *where* certain activities and behaviors may have been played out has, on the other hand, only been addressed in recent years. Given these recent preoccupations, it is timely to review briefly the literature on gender roles and the gendered landscape.

Current research suggests that early Mediterranean societies did indeed assign separate activities and roles to men and women, with the relative status of those roles and the asymmetrical organization of power probably becoming increasingly pronounced over time. These conclusions are based on a suite of data, including limited iconographic information. Unlike Egypt, however, with its rich scenes of daily life, other areas of the Mediterranean offer few depictions of quotidian activities. Scholars are more often confronted with mystifying figures painted or incised on pottery, etched into seals, or painted on caves or the walls of built structures. These problems notwithstanding, edifying readings of the data have been offered in the past few years. Rehak's studies (1994; 1995; 1998), for example, of Greek Bronze Age gender roles are particularly extensive (for discussions of gender roles and craft activities in the Greek Bronze Age see articles by Barber, Kopaka, Nordquist, and Gregerson, in Laffineur and Betancourt 1997). He observes that men and women are seldom shown together, and when they are, they tend to form separate groups, with women depicted at a larger scale, and more elaborately outfitted. When portrayed separately, men can be shown as musicians, sailors, hunters, and warriors. Males and females are shown both as bull-leapers and boar hunters and as officiating at or participating in various religious rites. Individuals most easily identified as divinities, however, seem to be women (see Marinatos 1987 and 1993 for detailed discussions about gender and religion in the Bronze Age). In addition, women, not men, are depicted in roles related to child-care. Unlike men, women seem to be represented at all stages of sexual development. Interestingly, Rehak also notes that no depictions exist of tiny babies, individuals of advanced age or with physical deformities, overt or covert (e.g., kissing) sexual activities, or childbirth.

The iconographic depictions from Bronze Age Greece are not always coincident with the textual evidence. As Olsen (1998) observes, Linear B tablets from both the Mycenaean and Minoan worlds clearly assign child-care to women, but the repertoire of mother-child imagery differs between the two cultures. Mycenaean imagery provides a systematic reinforcement of women as child-rearers and an investment on the part of Mycenaean society to envision women within the household context. Minoan artists, on the other hand, seem to eschew those kinds of images, supplanting them with representations of women outside domestic contexts. Other archaeologists (see Rehak 1995) have identified additional contradictions between text and iconography, most notably that the Linear B tablets attest to a *wanax* or male ruler in Mycenaean society who seems virtually absent from iconographic representations.

In recent years, scholars have also investigated the topic of gender roles and activities in prehistoric Cyprus, particularly during the third millennium (e.g., Frankel 2002; Webb 2001; 2002; Peltenburg 1994; for the Neolithic, see articles by McCartney and Clarke in Bolger and Serwint 2002; for Late Bronze Age, see articles by Smith and Steel in the same volume). Webb (2001), for example, notes that the Cypriot iconographic record during the Early Bronze Age regularly depicts women in one of three categories: as lovers or partners, mothers, or as sources of productive labor, involved principally in grinding, pounding, baking, and making pots. Men are rarely represented in those roles, suggesting a clear division of labor in Early Bronze Age Cyprus, at least as broadcast by the visual record. Webb proposes that as the primary practitioners of certain technologies, particularly pot-making and probably weaving, women must have served as the main conduits through which these often complicated technologies were transferred from one generation to the next. These issues of technological transmissions become critical in discussing the origins and development of the Cypriot Early Bronze Age. Most Cypriot scholars agree that the island is marked by visible changes at the beginning of the Bronze Age, not least in cooking practices, ceramic technology, and textile production. Whether these changes are the result of migrant arrivals mixing with indigenous populations or internal evolution is a matter of debate. As Webb has shown, however, the evolution and transmission of these technologies and the ways in which these practices affected the social and economic structures of early societies in Cyprus may have had strong sex-linked elements that warrant further investigation.

Directly related to the subject of gender roles are discussions about *where* sex-linked activities may have been conducted. Scholars in several disciplines have long argued that particular spatial organization creates a medium for both experiencing and structuring social relations, including the differences between male and female. If appropriate data are available, archaeologists can answer an array of relevant questions: Which areas of a community are seen as gender neutral or gender specific? What kinds of identities are forged within those domains? Are the activities carried out within and around houses designated by age or sex? Do people work in gendered groups? Can one gender pollute the area of another gender? Where are artifacts kept when they are not used and do those storage areas mark gendered spaces (Nelson and Rosen-Ayalon 2002:119)?

Currently, the most detailed research in Mediterranean prehistory that concentrates on iconographic evidence and gendered space has been conducted in Italy (especially by Whitehouse 1992; 2002; cf. Skeates 1994; Morter and Robb 1998; Pluciennik 1998). Whitehouse, whose work focuses on the use of caves, crevices, and rock shelters for cult purposes during the Neolithic and Chalcolithic periods, proposes that several of the larger sites were utilized in male initiation rites. Her study of Grotta di Porto Badisco (1992) reveals meaningful gendered spatial patterns among complex figurative scenes. Female images are confined to the outer areas of the cave, near the entrance, while male images occur both near the entrance and deeper within the inner "sancta," along with more abstract designs. Most of the figurative images of men relate to hunting large game, although archaeological remains from roughly contemporary settlements clearly show that the consumption of wild animals was of little economic importance. Whitehouse proposes that caves like Porto Badisco functioned as sites of initiation into a secret male cult of elders, where hunting took on a ritual dimension, exploited as a source of esoteric male knowledge. Women, she argues, are likely to have been excluded from these rites, confined possibly to the outer zones of the cave and prohibited from the deeper precincts, where more arcane knowledge was expressed via the abstract images. While women may indeed have had their own cults, they appear to have been unwelcome members in these areas, at least as inferred from the anthropomorphic imagery (another ritual site with figurines that suggest possible sexual segregation is the peak sanctuary at Atsipades, Crete; see Rehak and Younger 2001:467).

Morter and Robb (1998), following Whitehouse, have adopted a broader perspective, concentrating on general settlement patterns throughout southern Italy during the Neolithic. The authors divide the Neolithic "world" into zones ranging from domestic village compounds to intervillage catchment areas to marginal lands. Each of these zones is, according to the authors, linked to nested social identities.

Having established these spatial categories, Morter and Robb use various kinds of data to allocate these zones to either male or female activities. The authors conclude that males carried out at least two symbolically elaborated activities, hunting and ritual, in the outer zones. Women, on the other hand, seem to have been more closely tethered to the household, while both men and women would have conducted activities in the village and the immediate catchment area. Part of their argument rests on evidence from anthropomorphic images – female images are found most frequently in domestic units, in contrast to male-oriented symbols, which are most often associated with zones beyond daily experience. According to Morter and Robb, these spatial distinctions in iconography may indicate that the household (*domus*) was a center for female-associated domestic activities, while more male-dominated zones lay in the periphery (*agros*) (Hodder 1990).

Although Morter, Robb, and Whitehouse have made pioneering contributions to the topic of gendered space in the early Mediterranean, their work leaves one with the simplistic impression that females were associated with "domesticity" and males with "wildness" – the kind of essentialism decried by most feminists (though as Whitehouse [2002:39] has commented, gender archaeology is not required to be politically correct). They are not alone in this tendency and there is, in fact, a penchant in the literature to impose modern Western notions on ancient evidence. Archaeologists, for example, often attempt to distinguish public and private spaces, with the former linked to men in roles of power and the latter associated with women working in the domestic sphere and devalued roles. The division between public and private was probably much more layered in antiquity than is suggested in some of the literature.

Other Mediterranean and European prehistorians who have begun to explore possibilities of behaviorally or symbolically gendered space in prehistoric contexts include Tringham (1991a; 1991b; 1994); Bailey (1994); Peltenburg (1991; 1998; 2002); Chapman (1997); Hayden (1998); Pluciennik (1998); Webb (2001); Frankel (2002); and Rehak (2002). Bailey (1994) suggests, for example, that some communities of the Bulgarian Chalcolithic maintained visible spatial divisions among the sexes, although society was not structured along simple male-female alignments, but in more complex and graded frameworks. In southeastern Europe, Chapman (1997) has argued for an increasing divergence of female and male economic power from the Neolithic to the Copper Ages of eastern Hungary, with men visibly appropriating the burial domain and women, less visibly, controlling the domestic sphere. In Cyprus, Peltenburg (2002) proposes that evidence from Middle Chalcolithic levels at Kissonerga may indicate an area of dominance by male elders in one sector of the site. And several scholars in addition to Morter and Robb have envisioned

women as the main players within the household context of the built environment
(e.g., Hayden 1998; Webb 2002). Tringham follows a slightly different path by fash-
ioning an imaginative narrative from archaeological data. Her detailed work at the
Neolithic site of Opovo in the former Yugoslavia suggests that the settlement was
subjected to a series of intentional conflagrations. Attempting "to people" the landscape at Opovo, Tringham recasts that evidence into a thoughtful narrative of one
woman who sets her house ablaze and contemplates its demise. The monologue
is set as a gendered social act that is neither fiction nor science, but somewhere
between the two worlds (Tringham 1991a).

Conclusions

Having briefly surveyed some of the current research on sex and gender, I return
to the questions posed at the beginning of this chapter: what have we learned by
attempting to "engender" Mediterranean prehistory and have those efforts altered
our understanding of ancient perceptions and behaviors? As suggested above, the
first decade of a gender-conscious archaeology in the Mediterranean has indeed
changed our perspective, generating productive debate. The studies, however, are
often speculative and variable in quality, reflecting the fragmentary and layered
nature of such an enterprise, which essentially seeks to map relationships in the
ancient world, not to re-create or isolate total systems. And, as anyone who has
studied the literature would agree, there are not only a myriad of ways to find indications of gendered lives in the archaeological record, but also multiple notions
about how to define gender (Nelson and Rosen-Ayalon 2002:1).

Given the relatively young age of gender studies in Mediterranean prehistory,
scholars have yet to establish a consensual set of guidelines or conclusions. Nor
have Mediterranean prehistorians truly engaged with the range of sophisticated and
theoretically informed frameworks that are now well represented in gender studies
of other disciplines. There are, for example, few references to important theoretical works on the notion of agency (see, however, the recent manuscript by Nanoglou
[n.d.]) or Bourdieu's concept of "doxa," both of which have relevance to the study
of gendered relations in society (see also Lazzari [2003] for an interesting discussion of gender and "optic knowledge" and the dangers of constructing gender as a
disciplinary fortress). Rather, the strength of this particular feminist-inspired
archaeology lies in the nature of the basic questions posed and the provocative –
though admittedly tentative and provisional – answers proffered. As Natalie
Kampen observed in her introduction to a recent volume on the burgeoning interest in ancient art and sexuality, scholars who are involved in this new, heightened
self-consciousness serve "as 'resistant readers,' demanding to know 'who is seeing,'
'who is interpreting,' along with who and what are seen" (Kampen 1996:9).
Mediterranean prehistorians currently delving into the topic of gender and iconography, particularly as expressed through anthropomorphic imagery, are asking
comparable questions: How clearly or intentionally were these images coded sexually? Who created and used them? Did men and women see or use these depictions

differently? What kinds of gender information are broadcast by the gestures, pos-
tures, dress, ornamentation, size, media, and color of these images? Were certain
sexed (or unsexed) figures reserved for use in designated domestic, public, private,
or ritual contexts (and do these kinds of terms accurately reflect ancient ideologies)? Can these images, when used in conjunction with other sources of data,
inform us about which kinds of activities devolved to men or women? And, what
happens when we reassign the sex of images that have long been identified as male
or female, but are, in fact, still undetermined?

What is clear from recent scholarship is that we can no longer think of these
early images in simple sexual terms – figures may depict males, females, perhaps
some kind of "third gender" hybrids, intentionally ambiguous representations, or
even images that moved in and out of traditional sexual categories. Early Mediterranean taxonomies appear to have embraced multiple or ambiguous genders, a kind
of general messiness that rubs against the grain of Western discourse.

Nor can we continue to examine these human depictions without some awareness of their performative roles in ancient contexts. Like other objects in ancient
communities, human images were probably made, used, and viewed in a variety of
contexts, rendering them part of the society's discursive apparatus. As Brumfiel's
study of Late Post Classic figures from Mexico (1996) suggests, different classes of
anthropomorphic images can broadcast contradictory messages, depending on who
made them, who viewed them, who used them, and who controlled their use. Official images from the Late Post Classic period embody very different gender
ideologies from those intended as popular representations.

Each time human images were seen or employed they had the potential to reinforce, transmute, reverse, or question a range of ideas, strategies, or rules of social
behavior. As discussed above, for example, the Theran frescoes in Xeste 3 may have
underscored a homoerotic element in prehistoric Greek society during special rites
for women; the so-called "Priest-King" at Knossos may have served to remind visitors to the great Cretan center that official iconography was empowered by subsuming both sexes; the anthropomorphic figurines from Neolithic Italy may have
helped reinforce the prevailing notion that male and female were regarded as fluid
essences in that society; and the restriction of female images to the entrance of a
cave in Italy may have signaled the exclusion of women from male rites held within
the cave. Each one of these images reflected and shaped gender ideologies of the
society, on both a daily and episodic basis.

Moreover, reconsideration of anthropomorphic images in conjunction with
spatial organization has produced intriguing results. When scholars insert questions
of gender into their investigation of Mediterranean settlement patterns, the result
is a more subtle attunement to the environment. The studies cited above suggest
that separate gender domains could be detected in Neolithic Italy, Chalcolithic
Bulgaria, and Chalcolithic-Early Bronze Age Cyprus, with women and men
working in or appropriating specific and separate areas.

Finally, an explicitly gendered archaeology has led us to contemplate emerging
asymmetries between the sexes over the *longue durée*. While we need to be wary of

adopting simple evolutionary schemes, it is possible to identify broadly evolving trends in gender relations over time.

Nearly all the works cited here underscore the notion that gender is a complex and metaphorical discourse. Definitions of gender, which are inherently unstable in any society, are continually resituated and recast. Indeed gender is subject to constant production and manipulation. Gender is, however, only one of several social and occasionally contradictory identities that people in ancient societies must have adopted. Given the existence of multiple identities, isolating gender as a category distinct from cross-cutting domains such as class, age, and ethnicity can create problems. Meskell (2001:200) and others (e.g., Ashmore 2002; Ardren 2002) suggest that we situate gender within the framework of life cycles, paying particular attention to overlapping and shifting identities that may have coalesced or divided over time. Gender and sex are not then classed as separate privileged categories, but become part of a larger, more complex and multidimensional picture that takes on a dynamic element as one moves through life.

In the introduction of this book, the editors raise questions about the value in conceptualizing the Mediterranean in holistic terms. Why, despite the enormous variety in social lives and histories ("the differences that resemble"), are we justified in recognizing it as an entity, more than simply the southern edge of Europe or the northern edge of Africa? Did the Mediterranean of the past, with its possibly fluid boundaries, provide some kind of overarching social identities that linked and distinguished the inhabitants, particularly with respect to their material and mental histories? And, how do we approach the issue of an identity defined by a sea? Although this chapter has provided a selective review of recent gender studies, focused particularly on Italy, Greece, and Cyprus, there are sufficient data to suggest that the ancient Mediterranean was a highly gendered society. Certain tasks seem to have been allocated to men rather than to women, though they may not be ones typically associated with Western ideals. Various parts of the landscape are likely to have projected gendered meanings, and the processes through which sexual and gendered identities were expressed and maintained – by dress, gesture, performance, and anthropomorphic imagery – appear to have some coherency throughout the region. Precisely how gender ideologies and gender roles differed throughout the Mediterranean is difficult to assess at this point. Whether a Late Bronze Age traveler from Cyprus to Crete would find the divisions of activities and sense of gender ideology coincident between the two regions is unknowable. We are, however, on fairly safe ground arguing that gendered identities encompassed broader and more fluid notions than those encapsulated by modern Western societies.

As we move forward in the study of gender in Mediterranean prehistory, it is important to keep in mind that, for gender archaeologists, ongoing research inevitably generates paradoxes. This self-consciously postmodern view has, unfortunately, earned gender archaeology a reputation as unrigorous, susceptible to a kind of epistemological relativism that makes it impossible to choose between competing hypotheses. While these criticisms may be partially true, the counterargument is equally valid – a gendered archaeology (of the kind now practiced in the Mediterranean) produces a more self-critical and socially situated perspective (Gilchrist 1999:27; Conkey and Gero 1997). Admittedly, ambivalent and even contradictory conclusions will arise out of these non-traditional approaches, but they may more accurately reflect the complex realities of life that existed in early Mediterranean societies.

ACKNOWLEDGMENTS

I would like to extend my warmest thanks to Tracey Cullen for her insights, advice, and patience, to Paul Rehak for his thoughtful comments and inspired musings, to Jenny Webb and David Frankel for unpublished material, to Kathryn Talalay and Nina Callahan for their ongoing support, and to Steve Bank for his unwavering sense of humor. I am also very grateful to Emma Blake and Bernard Knapp for encouraging me to write this chapter and for their editorial comments. This article is dedicated to the memory of Paul Rehak, a pioneering thinker and a creative voice in the field of gender and Aegean prehistory.

NOTES

1   Some basic and/or pioneering "texts" of the last two decades, many of which contain detailed bibliographies, include Conkey and Spector 1984; Bertelsen et al. 1987; Gero and Conkey 1991; Conkey and Williams 1991; Walde and Willows 1991; Wylie 1991; 1992; Engelstad 1991; Dommasnes 1992; Claassen 1992; du Cros and Smith 1993; Archer et al. 1994; Balme and Beck 1995; Wright 1996; Conkey and Gero 1997; Classen and Joyce 1997; Moore and Scott 1997; Casey et al. 1998; Wyke 1998; Gilchrist 1999; Sørensen 2000; and Arnold and Wicker 2001. For seminal texts on sexuality and the body, see Foucault 1980 and Laqueur 1990; see also Meskell and Joyce 2003 for a recent and comparative study on embodiment in the ancient Egyptian and Mayan cultures.

2   For detailed discussions on the Mother Goddess, most of which discredit the notions espoused by Gimbutas, see Ucko 1968; Fleming 1969; Hayden 1986; Talalay 1993; 1994; 2000; Conkey and Tringham 1995; Meskell 1995; Hamilton et al. 1996; Goodison and Morris 1998.

3   Paul Rehak (personal communication) has correctly observed that the problem of reconstructing this image needs to be addressed before scholars can accurately debate the matter of gender attribution. The white/red color of the pieces is still being debated, there are few convincing joins among the fragments, and no one has yet to agree on how many figures were actually represented in the original fresco.

4   There is compelling though limited evidence from the Mediterranean and southeastern Europe that figurines and other objects, often found in association with house models, may have served active roles in some kind of staged performance; see in particular Bolger and Peltenburg's (1991:22–27) summary discussion of house models and associated objects.

REFERENCES

Alberti, Benjamin, 2001 Faience Goddesses and Ivory Bull-Leapers: The Aesthetics of Sexual Difference at Late Bronze Age Knossos. World Archaeology 33:189–205.

——2002 Gender and the Figurative Art of Late Bronze Age Knossos. *In* Labyrinth Revisited: Rethinking "Minoan" Archaeology. Y. Hamilakis, ed. pp. 98–117. Oxford: Oxbow Books.

Archer, Leonie, Susan Fischler, and Maria Wyke, eds., 1994 Women in Ancient Societies: An Illusion of the Night. London: Macmillan.

Ardren, Traci, 2002 Women and Gender in the Ancient Maya World. *In* Ancient Maya Women. T. Ardren, ed. pp. 1–11. Walnut Creek, CA: AltaMira Press.

Arnold, Bettina, and Nancy L. Wicker, 2001 Gender and the Archaeology of Death. New York: AltaMira Press.

Ashmore, Wendy, 2002 Encountering Maya Women. *In* Ancient Maya Women. T. Ardren, ed. pp. 229–245. New York: AltaMira Press.

Bailey, Douglass W., 1994 Reading Prehistoric Figurines as Individuals. World Archaeology 25:321–31.

Balme, Jane, and Wendy Beck, eds., 1995 Gendered Archaeology: Proceedings of the Second Australian Women in Archaeology Conference, Research Papers in Archaeology and Natural History 26. Canberra: Australian National University.

Barber, Elizabeth W. J., 1994 Women's Work: The First 20,000 Years. New York: W.W. Norton.

——1997 Minoan Women and the Challenges of Weaving for Home, Trade, and Shrine. *In* TEXNH: Craftsmen, Craftswomen and Craftsmanship in the Aegean Bronze Age. R. Laffineur and P. Betancourt, eds. pp. 515–519. Aegaeum 16. Liège and Austin: Université de Liège and University of Texas.

Bender, Barbara, 2000 Introduction. *In* Representations of Gender from Prehistory to Present. M. Donald and L. Hurcombe, eds. pp. xix–xxix. London: Macmillan.

Bertelsen, Reider, Arnvid Lillehammer, and Jenny-Rita Naess, eds., 1987 Were They all Men? An Examination of Sex Roles in Prehistoric Society. Norway: Stavanger.

Bolger, Diane, 1992 The Archaeology of Fertility and Birth: A Ritual Deposit from Chalcolithic Cyprus. Journal of Anthropological Research 48:145–164.

——1993 The Feminine Mystique: Gender and Society in prehistoric Cypriot studies. Report of the Department of Antiquities, Cyprus: 29–42.

——1996 Figurines, Fertility and the Emergence of Complex Society in Prehistoric Cyprus. Current Anthropology 37:365–372.

——2002 Gender and Mortuary Ritual in Chacolithic Cyprus. *In* Engendering Aphrodite: Women and Society in Ancient Cyprus. D. Bolger and N. Serwint, eds. pp. 67–86. Boston: ASOR.

——2003 Gender in Ancient Cyprus. Narratives of Social Change on a Mediterranean Island. New York: AltaMira Press.

Bolger, Diane, and Edgar Peltenburg, 1991 The Building Model. *In* A Ceremonial Area at Kissonerga, Lemba Archaeological Project. E. Peltenburg, ed. pp. 12–27. SIMA LXX: 3. Göteborg: Paul À6ströms Förlag.

Bolger, D., and N. Serwent, eds., 2002 Engendering Aphrodite: Women and Society in Ancient Cyprus. Cyprus American Archaeological Research Institute, Monograph 3. ASOR Archaeological Reports 7. Boston: American Schools of Oriental Research.

Brumfiel, Elizabeth M., 1996 Figurines and the Aztec State: Testing the Effectiveness of Ideological Domination. *In* Gender and Archaeology. R. P. Wright, ed. pp. 143–166. Philadelphia: University of Pennsylvania Press.

Butler, Judith, 1990 Gender Trouble: Feminism and the Subversion of Identity. New York: Routledge.

——1993 Bodies that Matter: On the Discursive Limits of "Sex." New York: Routledge.

Casey, Mary, Denise Donlon, Jeannette Hope, and Sharon Wellfare, eds., 1998 Redefining Archaeology: Feminist Perspectives. Canberra: ANH Publications.

Chapman, John, 1997 Changing Gender Relations in the Later Prehistory of Eastern Hungary. *In* Invisible People and Processes. Writing Gender and Childhood into European Archaeology. J. Moore and E. Scott, eds. pp. 131–149. New York: Leicester University Press.

Claassen, Cheryl, ed., 1992 Exploring Gender through Archaeology: Selected Papers from the 1991 Boone Conference. Madison: Prehistory Press.

Claassen, Cheryl, and Rosemary A. Joyce, eds., 1997 Women in Prehistory: North America and Mesoamerica. Philadelphia: University of Pennsylvania Press.

Conkey, Margaret W., and Janet Spector, 1984 Archaeology and the Study of Gender. Archaeological Method and Theory 7:1–38.

Conkey, Margaret W., with Sarah H. Williams, 1991 Original Narratives: The Political Economy of Gender in Archaeology. *In* Gender at the Crossroads of Knowledge: Feminist Anthropology in the Postmodern Era. M. Di Leonardo, ed. pp. 102–139. Berkeley: University of California Press.

Conkey, Margaret W., and Joan Gero, 1997 Programme to Practice: Gender and Feminism in Archaeology. Annual Review of Anthropology 26:411–437.

——eds., 1991 Engendering Archaeology: Women and Prehistory. Oxford: Blackwell.

Conkey, Margaret W., and Ruth E. Tringham, eds., 1995 Archaeology and the Goddess: Exploring the Contours of Feminist Archaeology. *In* Feminisms in the Academy. D. C. Stanton and A. J. Stewart, eds. pp. 199–247. Ann Arbor: University of Michigan Press.

Dommasnes, Lev H., 1992 Two Decades of Women in Prehistory and in Archaeology in Norway: A Review. Norwegian Archaeological Review 25:1–14.

du Cros, Hilary, and Laurajane Smith, eds., 1993 Women in Archaeology: A Feminist Critique. Canberra: Australian National University.

Engelstad, Erika, 1991 Images of Power and Contradiction: Feminist Theory and Post-Processual Archaeology. Antiquity 65:502–514.

Fleming, Andrew, 1969 The Myth of the Mother Goddess. World Archaeology 1:247–261.

Foucault, Michel, 1980 The History of Sexuality, vol. 1. R. Hurley, trans. New York: Vintage.

Frankel, David, 1997 On Cypriot Figurines and the Origins of Patriarchy. Current Anthropology 38:84.

——2002 Social Stratification, Gender and Ethnicity in Third Millennium Cyprus. *In* Engendering Aphrodite: Women and Society in Ancient Cyprus. D. Bolger and N. Serwint, eds. pp. 171–179. Boston: ASOR.

German, Senta C., 2000 The Human Form in the Late Bronze Age Aegean. *In* Reading the Body. A. E. Rautman, ed. pp. 95–110. Philadelphia: University of Pennsylvania Press.

Gero, Joan M., and Margaret W. Conkey, eds., 1991 Engendering Archaeology: Women and Prehistory. Oxford: Blackwell.

Gilchrist, Roberta, 1999 Gender and Archaeology. Contesting the Past. London: Routledge.

Goodison, Lucy, and Christine Morris, eds., 1998 Ancient Goddesses: The Myths and the Evidence. Madison: University of Wisconsin Press.

Grémaux, René, 1994 Woman becomes Man in the Balkans. *In* Third Sex, Third Gender: Beyond Sexual Dimorphism in Culture and History. G. Herdt, ed. pp. 241–281. New York: Zone Books.

Hamilton, Naomi, 2000 Ungendering Archaeology: Concepts of Sex and Gender in Figurine Studies in Prehistory. *In* Representations of Gender from Prehistory to the Present. Moira Donald and Linda Hurcombe, eds. pp. 17–30. London: Macmillan.

Hamilton, N., J. Marcus, D. Bailey, G. and R. Haaland, and P. J. Ucko 1996 Can we interpret figurines? Cambridge Archaeological Journal 6:281–307.

Hayden, Brian, 1986 Old Europe: Sacred Matriarchy or Complementary Opposition?. *In* Archaeology and Fertility Cult in the Ancient Mediterranean. A. Bonnano, ed. pp. 17–30. Amsterdam: B.R. Gruner.

Hayden, Christopher, 1998 Public and Domestic: The Social Background to the Development of Gender in Prehistoric Sardinia. *In* Gender and Italian Archaeology: Challenging Stereotypes. R. D. Whitehouse, ed. pp. 127–141. London: Accordia Research Institute, University of London and Institute of Archaeology, University College London.

Hays-Gilpin, Kelly, and David S. Whitley, eds., 1998 Reader in Gender Archaeology. London: Routledge.

Herdt, Gilbert H., 1987 The Sambia: Ritual and Gender in New Guinea. New York: Holt, Rinehart, and Winston.

——ed., 1994 Third Sex, Third Gender: Beyond Sexual Dimorphism in Culture and History. New York: Zone Books.

Hitchcock, Louise A., 1997 Engendering Domination: A Structural and Contextual Analysis of Minoan Neopalatial Bronze figurines. *In* Invisible People and Processes: Writing Gender and Childhood into European Archaeology. J. Moore and E. Scott, eds. pp. 113–130. London: University of Leicester Press.

——2000 Engendering Ambiguity in Minoan Crete: It's a Drag to Be a King. *In* Representations of Gender from Prehistory to Present. M. Donald and L. Hurcombe, eds. pp. 69–86. London: Macmillan.

Hodder, Ian, 1990 The Domestication of Europe: Structure and Contingency in Neolithic Societies. Oxford: Blackwell.

Holmes, Katie, and Ruth D. Whitehouse, 1998 Anthropomorphic Figurines and the Construction of Gender in Neolithic Italy. *In* Gender and Italian Archaeology: Challenging Stereotypes. R. D. Whitehouse, ed. pp. 95–126. London: Accordia Research Institute, University of London and Institute of Archaeology, University College London.

Hughes-Brock, Helen, 1999 Mycenaean Beads: Gender and Social Contexts. Oxford Journal of Archaeology 18:277–295.

Joyce, Rosemary A., 1992 Images of Gender and Labor Organization in Classic Maya Society. *In* Exploring Gender through Archaeology. Cheryl Claassen, ed. pp. 63–70. Madison: Prehistory Press.

——1998 Performing the Body in Pre-Hispanic Central America. *In* Anthropology and Aesthetics. Theme issue. RES 33:147–166.

Kampen, Natalie B., ed., 1996 Sexuality in Ancient Art: Near East, Egypt, Greece and Italy. Cambridge: Cambridge University Press.

Knapp, A. Bernard, 1998 Who's Come a Long Way Baby: Masculinist Approaches to a Gendered Archaeology. Archaeological Dialogues 5:91–106.

Knapp, A. Bernard, and Lynn Meskell, 1997 Bodies of Evidence on Prehistoric Cyprus. Cambridge Archaeological Journal 7:183–204.

Koehl, Robert, 1986 The Chieftain Cup and a Minoan Rite of Passage. Journal of Hellenic Studies 106:99–110.

Laffineur, Robert, and Philip Betancourt, eds., 1997 TEXNH: Craftsmen, Craftswomen and Craftsmanship in the Aegean Bronze Age. Aegaeum 16. Liège and Austin: Université de Liège and University of Texas.

Laqueur, Thomas, 1990 Making Sex: Body and Gender from the Greeks to Freud. Cambridge, MA: Harvard University Press.

Lazzari, Marisa, 2003 Archaeological Visions: Gender, Landscape and Optic Knowledge. Journal of Social Archaeology 3:194–222.

Lee, Mireille M., 2000 Deciphering Gender in Minoan Dress. In Reading the Body. A. E. Rautman, ed. pp. 111–123. Philadelphia: University of Pennsylvania Press.

Looper, Matthew G., 2002 Women-Men (and Men-Women): Classic Maya Rulers and the Third Gender. In Ancient Maya Women. T. Ardren, ed. pp. 171–202. New York: AltaMira Press.

Mackenzie, Maureen A., 1991 Androgynous Objects. Philadelphia: Harwood Academic Publishers.

Marinatos, Nanno, 1987 Role and Sex Division in Ritual Scenes of Aegean Art. Journal of Prehistoric Religion 1:23–34.

——1993 Minoan Religion. Ritual, Image, and Symbol. Columbia, S.C.: University of South Carolina Press.

Mateu, Trinidad E., 2002 Representations of Women in Spanish Levantine Art: An Intentional Fragmentation. Journal of Social Archaeology 2: 81–108.

Meskell, Lynn, 1995 Goddesses, Gimbutas, and the "New Age" Archaeology. Antiquity 69:74–86.

——1999 Archaeologies of Social Life. Age, Sex, Class et cetera in Ancient Egypt. Oxford: Blackwell.

——2001 Archaeologies of Identity. In Archaeological Theory Today. Ian Hodder, ed. pp. 187–213. Cambridge: Polity Press.

Meskell, Lynn, and Rosemary A. Joyce, 2003 Embodied Lives: Figuring Ancient Maya and Egyptian Experience. London: Routledge.

Moore, Henrietta, 1994 A Passion for Difference. London: Blackwell.

Moore, Jennifer, and Elizabeth Scott, eds., 1997 Invisible People and Processes: Writing Gender and Childhood into European Archaeology. London: Leicester University Press.

Morris, Christine, and Alan Peatfield, 2002 Feeling through the Body: Gesture in Cretan Bronze Age Religion. In Thinking through the Body: Archaeologies of Corporeality. Yannis Hamilakis, Mark Pluciennik, and Sarah Tarlow, eds. pp. 105–120. New York: Kluwer Academic/Plenum Publishers.

Morter, Jon, and John Robb, 1998 Space, Gender, and Architecture in the Southern Italian Neolithic. In Gender and Italian Archaeology. Challenging Stereotypes. Ruth D. Whitehouse, ed. pp. 83–94. London: Accordia Research Institute, University of London and Institute of Archaeology, University College London.

Nanda, Serena, 1990 Neither Man nor Woman: The Hijras of India. Belmont: Wadsworth.

Nanoglou, Stratos, n.d. Subjectivity and Material Culture in Thessaly, Northern Greece: The Case of Neolithic Anthropomorphic Imagery. Unpublished manuscript.

Nelson, Sarah M., ed., 2003 Ancient Queens: Archaeological Explorations. Walnut Creek, CA: Altamira Press.

Nelson, Sarah M., and M. Rosen-Ayalon, eds., 2002 In Pursuit of Gender: Worldwide Archaeological Approaches. Walnut Creek, CA: AltaMira Press.

Olsen, Barbara A., 1998 Women, Children and the Family in the Late Bronze Age: Differences in Minoan and Mycenaean Constructions of Gender. World Archaeology 29: 380–392.

Ortner, Sherry B., and Harriet Whitehead, 1981 Introduction: Accounting for Sexual Meaning. *In* Sexual Meanings: The Cultural Construction of Gender and Sexuality. Sherry B. Ortner and H. Whitehead, eds. pp. 1–27. Cambridge: Cambridge University Press.

Peltenburg, Edgar, 1991 Contextual Implications of the Kissonerga Rituals. *In* A Ceremonial Area at Kissonerga, Lemba Archaelogical Project. E. Peltenburg, ed. pp. 85–108. SIMA LXX: 3. Göteborg: Paul Åströms Förlag.

—— 1994 Constructing Authority: The Vounous Enclosure Model. Opuscula Atheniensia 20:157–162.

—— 2002 Gender and Social Structure in Prehistoric Cyprus: A Case Study from Kissonerga. *In* Engendering Aphrodite: Women and Society in Ancient Cyprus. D. Bolger and N. Serwint, eds. pp. 53–63. Boston: ASOR.

Peltenburg, Edgar, et al., 1998 Lemba Archaeological Project, vol. II: IA. Excavations at Kissonerga-Mosphilia, 1979–1992. Jonsered: Paul Åströms Förlag.

Pluciennik, Mark, 1998 Representations of Gender in Prehistoric Italy. *In* Gender and Italian Archaeology. Challenging Stereotypes. Ruth D. Whitehouse, ed. pp. 57–82. London: Accordia Research Institute, University of London and Institute of Archaeology, University College London.

—— 2002 Art, Artefact, Metaphor. *In* Thinking through the Body: Archaeologies of Corporeality. Yannis Hamilakis, Mark Pluciennik, and Sarah Tarlow, eds. pp. 217–232. New York: Kluwer Academic/Plenum Publishers.

Rehak, Paul, 1994 The Aegean "Priest" on CMS 1223. Kadmos 33:76–84.

—— 1995 Enthroned Figures in Aegean art and the Function of the Mycenaean Megaron. *In* The Role of the Ruler in the Prehistoric Aegean. Paul Rehak, ed. pp. 95–117. Aegaeum 11. Liège and Austin: Université de Liège and University of Texas.

—— 1998 The Construction of Gender in Late Bronze Age Aegean Art – A Prolegomenon. *In* Redefining Archaeology: Feminist Perspectives. Proceedings of the Third Australian Women in Archaeology Conference. Mary Casey, Denise Donlon, Jeannette Hope, and Sharon Wellfare, eds. pp. 191–198. Canberra: Australia National University Publications.

—— 1999 The Aegean Landscape and the Body: A New Interpretation of the Thera Frescoes. *In* From the Ground Up: Beyond Gender Theory in Archaeology: Proceedings of the Fifth Gender & Archaeology Conference, University of Wisconsin-Milwaukee. N. L. Wicker and B. Arnold, eds. pp. 11–21. London: BAR International Series, 812. Oxford: British Archaeological Reports.

—— 2002 Imag(in)ing a Women's World in Bronze Age Greece: The Frescoes from Xeste 3 at Akrotiri, Thera. *In* Among Women: From the Homosocial to the Homoerotic in the Ancient World. N. S. Rabinowitz and L. Auanger, eds. pp. 34–59. Austin: University of Texas Press.

Rehak, Paul, and John G. Younger, 2001 Addendum: 1998–1999. *In* Aegean Prehistory: A Review. T. Cullen, ed. pp. 466–473. Boston: Archaeological Institute of America.

Ribeiro, E., 2002 Altering the Body: Representations of Pre-Pubescent Gender Groups on Early and Middle Cypriot 'Scenic Compositions'. *In* Engendering Aphrodite: Women and Society in Ancient Cyprus. D. Bolger and N. Serwint, eds. pp. 197–209. Cyprus American Archaeological Research Institute, Monograph 3. ASOR Archaeological Reports 7. Boston: American Schools of Oriental Research.

Robb, John, 1994a Gender Contradictions, Moral Coalitions and Inequality in Prehistoric Italy. Journal of European Archaeology 2:20–49.

—— 1994b Burial and Social Reproduction in the Peninsular Italian Neolithic. Journal of Mediterranean Archaeology 7:29–75.

Roscoe, Will, 1994 How to Become a Berdache: Toward a Unified Analysis of Gender Diversity. *In* Third Sex, Third Gender. Beyond Sexual Dimorphism in Culture and History. G. Herdt, ed. pp. 329–372. New York: Zone Books.

Sarenas, M. 1998 Unveiling the "Female" Figurines: Critiquing Traditional Interpretations of Anthropomorphic Figurines. *In* Redefining Archaeology: Feminist Perspectives. Proceedings of the Third Australian Women in Archaeology Conference. Mary Casey, Denise Donlon, Jeannette Hope, and Sharon Wellfare, eds. pp. 154–64. Canberra: Australia National University Publication.

Skeates, Robin, 1994 Burial, Context and Gender in Neolithic South-Eastern Italy. Journal of European Archaeology 2:199–214.

Stig Sørensen, M. L., 1998 Women's Culture in Bronze Age Europe: Social Categories or 'Symbolic Capital'. *In* Redefining Archaeology: Feminist Perspectives. Proceedings of the Third Australian Women in Archaeology Conference. Mary Casey, Denise Donlon, Jeannette Hope, and Sharon Wellfare, eds. pp. 84–89. Research Papers in Archaeology and Natural History 29. Canberra: ANH Publications, Australian National University.

Sørenson, Marie Louise S., 2000 Gender Archaeology. Cambridge: Cambridge University Press.

Strathern, Marilyn, 1988 The Gender of the Gift. Berkeley: University of California Press.

Talalay, Lauren E., 1993 Deities, Dolls, and Devices: Neolithic Figurines from Franchthi Cave, Greece. Bloomington: Indiana University Press.

——1994 A Feminist Boomerang: The Great Goddess of Great Prehistory. Gender & History 6:165–183.

——2000 Archaeological Ms.conceptions: Contemplating Gender and the Greek Neolithic. *In* Representations of Gender from Prehistory to the Present. Moira Donald and Linda Hurcombe, eds. pp. 3–16. London: Macmillan.

Talalay, Lauren E., and Tracey Cullen, 2002 Sexual Ambiguity in Plank Figures from Bronze Age Cyprus. *In* Engendering Aphrodite: Women and Society in Ancient Cyprus. D. Bolger and N. Serwint, eds. pp. 181–195. Boston: ASOR.

Tringham, Ruth E., 1991a Households with Faces: The Challenge of Gender in Prehistoric Architectural Remains. *In* Engendering Archaeology: Women and Prehistory. Joan Gero and Margaret W. Conkey, eds. pp. 93–131. Oxford: Blackwell.

——1991b Men and Women in Prehistoric Architecture. Traditional Dwellings and Settlements Review 111:9–28.

——1994 Engendered Places in Prehistory. Gender, Place and Culture 1:169–203.

Turner, Terence S., 1980 The Social Skin. *In* Not Work Alone. J. Cherfas and R. Lewin, eds. pp. 112–140. Beverly Hills, CA: Sage Publications.

Turner, Victor, 1967 The Forest of Symbols: Aspects of Ndembu Ritual. Ithaca, N.Y.: Cornell University Press.

Ucko, Peter J., 1968 Anthropomorphic Figurines. Royal Anthropological Institute Occasional Papers, no 24. London: A. Szmidla.

Walde, Dale, and Noreen D. Willows, eds., 1991 The Archaeology of Gender. Calgary: University of Calgary Archaeological Association.

Webb, Jennifer M., 2001 Tracking Gender and Technology in Prehistory. A Case Study From Bronze Age Cyprus. Paper presented at the Annual Meeting of the Society for the History of Technology, San Jose, CA.

——2002 Engendering the Built Environment: Household and Community in Prehistoric Cyprus. *In* Engendering Aphrodite: Women and Society in Ancient Cyprus. D. Bolger and N. Serwint, eds. pp. 87–101. Boston: ASOR.

Whitehead, Harriet, 1981 The Bow and the Burden of the Strap: A New Look at Institutionalized Homosexuality in Native North America. *In* Sexual Meanings: The Cultural
Construction of Gender and Sexuality. Sherry B. Ortner and H. Whitehead, eds. pp.
80–115. Cambridge: Cambridge University Press.

Whitehouse, Ruth W., 1992 Underground Religion: Cult and Culture in Prehistoric Italy.
London: University of London, Accordia Research Centre.

——2002 Gender in the South Italian Neolithic: A Combinatory Approach. *In* In Pursuit
of Gender: Worldwide Archaeological Approaches. S. M. Nelson and M. Rosen-Ayalon,
eds. pp. 15–42. Walnut Creek, CA: AltaMira Press.

Williams, Walter L., 1986 The Spirit and the Flesh: Sexual Diversity in American Indian
Culture. Boston: Beacon Press.

Wright, Rita P., ed., 1996 Gender and Archaeology. Philadelphia: University of
Pennsylvania Press.

Wyke, Maria, ed., 1998 Gender and the Body in the Ancient Mediterranean. Oxford:
Blackwell.

Wylie, Alison, 1991 Gender Theory and the Archaeological Record: Why is There no Archaeology of Gender? *In* Engendering Archaeology: Women and Prehistory. Joan M. Gero and
Margaret W. Conkey, eds. pp. 31–54. Oxford: Blackwell.

——1992 Feminist Theories of Social Power: Some Implications for a Processual Archaeology. Norwegian Archaeological Review 25:51–68.

Younger, John G., 1995 The Iconography of Rulership–a Conspectus. *In* The Role of the
Ruler in the Prehistoric Aegean. Paul Rehak, ed. pp. 151–211. Aegaeum 11. Liège and
Austin: Université de Liège and University of Texas.

7

The Genesis of Monuments among the Mediterranean Islands

Michael J. Kolb

Introduction

One of the most essential ways archaeologists examine past social relationships is through the study of durable monuments. Monuments, such as elaborate tombs, large temples, and elite palaces, are usually the product of complex societies, where they serve as testimonies of social authority and prestige. They express in a public and very enduring fashion the accomplishment of past builders to combine materials, human labor, and specialized knowledge, creating something greater than the sum of their products. Even today's modern visitor, accustomed to tall buildings of steel and concrete, cannot help but be awed and inspired by the magnitude and durability of many ancient monuments. Perhaps it is the laborious effort by which these primeval stones were carved and stacked by hand. Perhaps it is the lingering, virtually eternal presence of our oldest places of veneration. Maybe it is the way these monuments shaped and synchronized the lives of our ancestors. Or perhaps it is the audacity and brashness of the builders who commanded so much power during the infancy of civilization. Whatever the reasons, these monuments stir the imagination and offer a very tangible medium by which we might explore our human past.

In Mediterranean prehistory, the most outstanding examples of monumentality are the colossal tombs, temples, and palaces present on Crete, Malta, Gozo, Sardinia, Corsica, and the Balearic islands (Figure 7.1). Archaeologists have routinely utilized these monuments to help monitor and explain political transformations within Mediterranean societies (e.g., Bonnano et al. 1990; Knappett and Schoep 2000; Patton 1996; Renfrew 1974; Webster 1991), and rightly so, given that monuments served to negotiate relationships between dominant and consenting groups in class-structured societies. Yet a number of questions still remain. What are the functional and morphological similarities and differences between these monument types? Why does monumental elaboration occur at different times

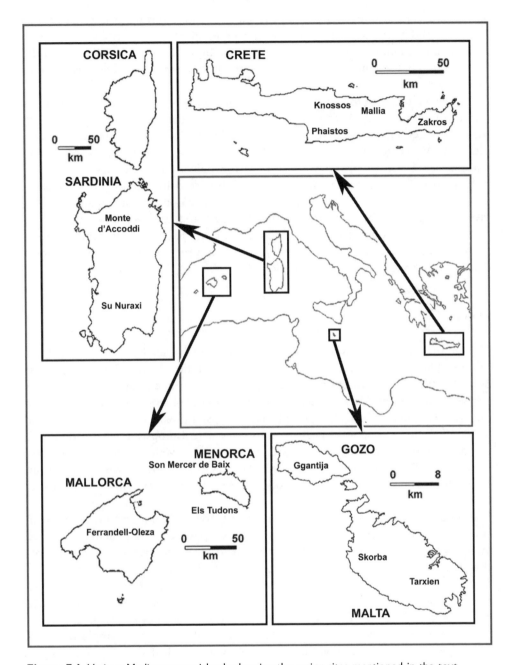

Figure 7.1 Various Mediterranean islands showing the major sites mentioned in the text

among different island groups (from the Late Neolithic through the Final Bronze Age ca. 3600–800 B.C.)? How do certain types of social and ritual elaboration assume monumental proportions? What was the basis of power associated with the construction of these monuments? The answers to these questions are worth further exploration.

The specific aim of this chapter is to examine and compare a series of Mediterranean monuments in order to understand some of the variables associated with their construction and elaboration. These include: (1) the temple and funerary complexes of Malta and Gozo; (2) the palaces of Minoan Crete; (3) the Sardinian *nuraghi* and Corsican *torre* towers; and (4) the Balearic *talayot, naveta,* and *taula* monuments. Each monumental type will be discussed in detail, with a focus on architecture, function, chronology, and social organization. Special attention is also given to ongoing debates regarding their building and use over time. Finally, the records of these monuments are synthesized in order to assess better the nature of monumental elaboration in the Mediterranean, and thereby the nature of political discourse and the rise of social complexity.

Malta

The monuments of the Maltese islands predate any other built in the Mediterranean. These temple and funerary complexes, built in the Copper Age (ca. 3600–2500 B.C.), represent some of the earliest monuments ever built. Little is known about the builders of these monumental sites. The original inhabitants of the Maltese Islands had clear affinities to the Stentinello culture of Sicily (ca. 5000–4500 B.C.), and were farmers who grew cereal crops and raised domestic livestock. A number of syntheses exist regarding the Maltese temples and their chronology (Bonnano et al. 1990; Evans 1984; Grima 2001; Lewis 1977; Patton 1996; Robb 2001; Stoddart 1999; Stoddart et al. 1993; Tilley 2004; Trump 1972; 2002).

About 40 temples are distributed on the islands of Malta and Gozo, often in clusters. The seven largest complexes consist of a perimeter wall encircling two or more adjacent temples. Each is distinct in layout and size, but all use the apsidal chamber as a basic architectural element. The typical apse averages 6 meters in diameter and is a curved hemispheric room, broad at the base but tapered toward the top (Figure 7.2). It has a horizontal arch entryway consisting of a post-and-lintel trilithon. An apse had no stone roof, but was probably covered with suspended rafters covered in thatch, wattle and daub, or animal hides. Each temple was built with multiple apses, usually laid out in paired or trefoil (leaf-shape) groups. Styles ranged from three to six apses per temple.

The Ggantija (or giantess' tower) temple complex of Gozo is the largest and best preserved. Two neighboring temples are constructed of undressed coralline limestone boulders rising to a height of 6 meters. The rough interior surfaces of these stones were originally coated with clay and lime plaster. The southern temple was constructed about 3400 B.C., and is 27 meters long. It has five large chambers, the

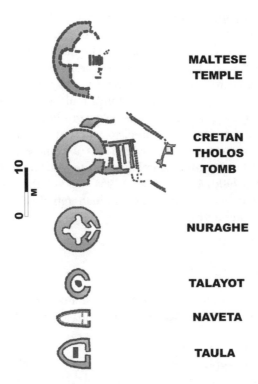

MALTESE
TEMPLE

CRETAN
THOLOS
TOMB

NURAGHE

TALAYOT

NAVETA

TAULA

Figure 7.2 Plans of typical Mediterranean monuments. The tholos tomb is the site of Moni Odigitria (after Myers and Cadogan 1992)

innermost one being the largest and highest. The northern temple was constructed around 3000 B.C., and is 19.5 meters long. It has four chambers, and a fifth central chamber the size of a small niche. A massive curvilinear perimeter surrounds both temples, constructed of gargantuan slabs up to 5.5 meters long. The space between the temple walls and the perimeter wall is filled with earth and rubble.

The most elaborate temple complex is at Tarxien (pronounced Tar-sheen) on Malta, consisting of three temple structures built after 3100 B.C. A large central six-apse temple was built last. The remains of an older abandoned temple lie nearby. The Tarxien temples contained significant numbers of "cult" objects found in the innermost apses. These include major concentrations of pottery, carved female figurines, and animal bones. These same apses had doorjambs and holes use to restrict access. A number of statues and spiral wall carvings were also present, the best-known statue being an oversized female torso.

The earliest ritual structure found on Malta is located at Skorba. This small shrine dates to 4100 B.C., and is considered the precursor to the later monumental structures. The shrine was the largest building of a small village. The main room was D-shaped, with paved courtyards to the east and west. The shrine contained female figurines, polished cow bones, and mutilated goat skulls. The later temple was of the typical three-lobed design, with a closed-off central apse and altars.

Two large funerary complexes are also associated with the Maltese temples. Both are below ground, but follow the same modular design as the temples, being composed of carved rock niches and cavities. The Hal Saflieni Hypogeum at Tarxien is an expansive subterranean structure with large uprights of coralline limestone. It remains the most extensively excavated funerary complex, and was built in three successive phases. The first was a simple tomb built around 3000 B.C., about 2 meters in diameter and averaging 2 meters below ground. This space was extended both above and below ground over time, to where it became the most complex of all the Maltese monuments. It was used as a cemetery. The Xaghra Stone on Gozo is centered between two temple complexes, including the Ggantija group (see Bonnano et al. 1990; Malone et al. 1995). One of the excavated niches was filled with articulated and disarticulated human remains, and small terracotta female figurines and statuettes.

Chronology and origins

The chronology of construction for the Maltese temple and funerary complexes is long (see Stoddart et al. 1993). Major building phases include:

1.   Skorba (ca. 4500–4100 B.C.)
2.   Zebbug (ca. 4100–3800 B.C.)
3.   Ggantija (ca. 3600–3000 B.C.)
4.   Tarxien (ca. 3000–2500 B.C.)
5.   Tarxien Cemetery (ca. 2500–1500 B.C.).

The temples and funerary complexes were first constructed during the Ggantija phase, and expanded and elaborated during the Tarxien phase. The antecedents of these monuments may be traced back to smaller shrines and upright menhir stones used during the Skoba and Zebbug phases. The temples were abandoned during the Tarxien Cemetery phase, at which time funerary rituals switched to the use of new cremation cemeteries.

Temple styles changed over time as well. The earliest temple style was a simple lobed design, with a central court and irregular-shaped apses (Figure 7.2). Then followed the trefoil temple with three apses opening symmetrically off the central court. Five-apse temples were also built, combining a three-apse group with an additional pair of apses at the front. By 3000 B.C., four-apse structures were being built, where the central apse of a five-apse structure was walled off or reduced in size to a small niche. It was at this time that many of the central apses of earlier trefoil temples were walled off. One large six-apse temple was also built at Tarxien, consisting of three paired apses and a small central niche.

The Maltese monuments represent some of the best evidence regarding the nature of emerging elite religious power (e.g., Stoddart 1999; Stoddart et al. 1993; Grima 2001). Current debate has focused on the monuments' role in controlling sacred knowledge and ritual practice, and/or as territorial centers for rival and competing social groups (Stoddart et al. 1993:17). Renfrew and Level (1979) argue that these temples represent the centralization of political power based upon inter-group competition. As population increased (perhaps as many as 2,000 utilized each temple group), competing groups built successively larger monuments (Renfrew 1974). Emerging elites would increasingly organize and direct the activities associated with the construction and use of such temples, thus coming into power. The similarities between funeral and temple architecture support the argument of centralization. Others have argued that ritual power was instead decentralized with competing religious factions (Meillassoux 1964; 1967). The lack of any single central place, and the recurrent pairing of temples, supports the argument for decentralization, with intra-group social competition occurring as well as group rivalries (Bonnano et al. 1990). Whatever the nature of the elite hierarchy, it is clear that a certain segment of society had increased control over ritual practice, particularly the ceremonies associated with the afterlife.

Another major debate centers on the Tarxien Cemetery phase (see Bonnano et al. 1990; Stoddart et al. 1993; Trump 1977). After 2500 B.C., the temples are abandoned, monumental construction ceases, and cremation cemeteries begin to be utilized. The temple complex at Tarxien continues to be used, but only as a cremation cemetery. Imported metal objects begin appearing as well. This shift in religious architecture and practice suggests an important change in social organization. A popular argument is that this shift represents the abandonment of Malta and Gozo altogether, and the eventual migration of new peoples to the islands (Trump 1977). Stratigraphic evidence at Tarxien has revealed a long period of abandonment before the conversion to a cemetery. Another argument is that these changes represent only an internal shift in religious expression (Bonnano et al. 1990). A third possibility is that this shift represents a new way that elites are doing business, with religious control "giving way" to a broader-based economic control of external trade (Stoddart et al. 1993). The Maltese elite may have found their power slowly waning in the wake of increasing external trade contacts and had to redefine the ways in which they defined themselves. Following their peers on Crete, they reemphasized control by focusing on trade goods.

Crete

Perhaps the best-known monuments of the Mediterranean are the majestic labyrinthine structures of Bronze Age Crete that have been dubbed "palaces" (Driessen 2003). Their true function remains obscure and debated, although they present a tantalizing mystery regarding the society of Middle to Late Bronze Age Crete (ca. 2200–1200 B.C.). It was during this period that the "Minoan" culture flourished; that culture is named after the King Minos mentioned in Homeric legend. The Minoans are regarded as the Mediterranean's first large-scale complex society, implementing such key innovations as political centralization, organized government, literacy and record-keeping, specialization of labor, and mass-produced trade goods. Although space does not permit a comprehensive discussion

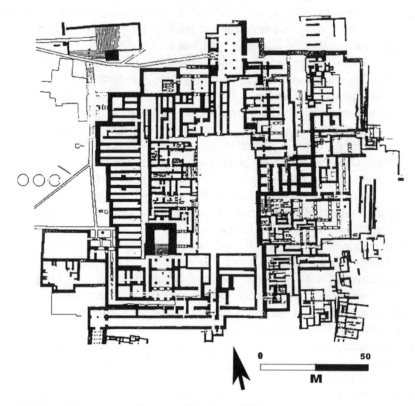

0   50

M

Figure 7.3 Plan of the palace at Knossos (after Evans 1921)

of Minoan society, this analysis will focus on the origin and evolution of the monuments themselves. There are of course a number of excellent syntheses that provide a more in-depth investigation of the Minoans, their palaces, and the archaeologists who made the discoveries (e.g., Driessen et al. 2002; Graham 1987; Hägg and Marinatos 1987; Hamilakis 2002; MacGillivray 2000; Manning 1994; Patton 1996; Rehak and Younger 1998; Renfrew 1972; Watrous 1994).

Four classical labyrinthine palaces had already been built on Crete by 1900 B.C. The largest was Knossos with an area of 13,000 square meters, followed by Malia (7,600 square meters), Phaistos (6,500 square meters), and Kato Zakros (2,800 square meters). They were built using cut-stone masonry, recessed façades, and stylistic embellishments such as engraved decoration, painted stucco, veneering, and clay ornamentation. Each palace was a multi-story building consisting of a series of recessed and projecting rectilinear architectural units, giving the entire structure an irregular shape and a labyrinthine appearance (Figure 7.3). Vertical pillars included a startling variety of forms, often clustered in particular combinations. A foreign visitor would be impressed by both the sheer bulk of the building as well as its architectural variety. These palaces were located on the coast and in the interior, at places thought to have religious significance and/or to provide easy access to the sea.

Most share prominent architectural features such as: (1) a central court; (2) a paved western plaza/entrance; (3) west-side sunken cult rooms; (4) storage magazines and grain silos; (5) clusters of similar room/hall elements; (6) large second-floor reception halls; and (7) an auditorium.

The most prominent of these features is the rectangular central court. This court represents the most distinguishing feature of a Minoan palace, adding an important public quality to this monument type. The courts of all the palaces are oriented slightly east of a north-south axis, and their dimensions are 2:1 in size proportion. The three largest courts average 50 × 25 meters. The court at Zakros is 30 × 12 meters. This similarity of form suggests a standardized function so crucial that it dictated the general layout of the surrounding building complex, perhaps for providing optimal sunlight exposure, recognizing sacred mountains and caves, or facing certain rooms along the west side to the rising sun (Shaw 1973). The specific function of these courts is equally puzzling; did they serve as arenas for exclusionary rituals that only served the elite such as ritual sacrifice or the legendary Minoan bull games? Or were they used for more public rituals such as feasting, dancing, astronomical observation, or ceremonial displays? Minoan art and miniature frescoes suggest a variety of scenarios, in particular bull leaping and group dancing (Davis 1987; Sipahi 2001; Younger 1995). Certainly the imposing size of these courts suggests more inclusive rituals, since these large courts could accommodate major segments of the population at a single event. For example, the central court at Knossos was large enough to have held up to 5,435 people, assuming two and one-half square feet per person (Gesell 1987). This is equivalent to about one-quarter of the total estimated population of Neopalatial Knossos (14–18,000 individuals according to Whitelaw 2001:27).

The three main complexes at Knossos, Malia, and Phaistos also contain a second spacious paved plaza located on the western side of the palace (Marinatos 1987). This western plaza contains raised stone walkways, crisscrossing the paved court at various angles. At Knossos this western plaza contains other features, such as circular pits and small raised altars. It is possible that the western plaza was the formal approach and entrance to the palace, with the walkways being used as processional routes. This area may have also been associated with a "sacred grove," as depicted in a fresco found at Knossos. The fresco depicts at least two trees, a walkway, and a public gathering that includes representation of female participants and male and female observers (see Davis 1987; Marinatos 1987; cf. Driessen et al. 2002).

Another prominent feature of these palaces is the cult rooms known as "pillar crypts," sunken rooms with single or double pillars (see Graham 1987). These pillars frequently bear carved mason insignia, particularly the double axe. The double axe is a prominent Minoan cult symbol, depicted in many different media such as fresco paintings, carvings, gold votive offerings, and in stalactite/stalagmite worship within sacred caves. At least fourteen of the pillar crypts identified have contained double-axe engravings and/or pyramidal stone stands for mounting double axes or other cult emblems. Most of these cult rooms are closely associated with storage magazines (see below), although at both Knossos and Malia these crypts may be found on the ground floor west of the central court. In fact cult rooms take up most of the western face of the central court at Knossos, including prominent rooms such as the Temple Repositories, Tripartite Shrine, and the Throne Room complex identified and named by Arthur Evans (Evans 1921). A similar arrangement of rooms may have been present at Malia, while some of the odd rooms along the west side of the court at Phaistos may also have served religious functions. Cult paraphernalia was stored in rooms west of the central court at Zakros as well. Pillar crypts have also been found at some nearby buildings, such as the South House, Southeast House, and Royal Villa at Knossos.

A large proportion of the total ground floor area of a palace was devoted to storage magazines. These long and narrow rooms were located in the west and north wings. At Knossos, Malia, and Phaistos, the magazines form the external west façade of the palace, a carefully built wall characterized by major projections and recesses that correspond to groups or "blocks" of magazines. Malia has the largest proportion of magazines, while Zakros has the smallest. These magazines commonly contained *pithoi*, large clay storage jars often several feet tall (see Christakis 1999). Typical storage items probably included grain, wine, olive oil, textiles, and smaller pottery vessels. In addition to the magazines, large semi-subterranean grain silos were also used. These cylindrical structures were rubble-built and lined with plaster on the interior side. Three are preserved at Knossos, built over older houses and then filled in with debris from later collapse. Eight shallow silos are preserved at Malia, in two rows of four, and surrounded by a wall. At all three of the main palaces these silos were placed in prominent locations outside the west façade in or near the west plaza, suggesting they served an important ritual or symbolic function as well as a practical one.

Another notable feature of Minoan architecture is a series of functionally equivalent architectural units that give the palace its maze-like appearance (see Graham 1987). These units, dubbed "Minoan halls," consist of two unequally sized rectangular rooms. These rooms were separated by a row of pillars and a set of piers in which a retractable door was set, serving as an effective means of permitting or restricting the access of movement, air, or light. A light well was located at one end of the partition along the side of the hall. Some halls also include a third, more private room that contains a short flight of doglegged stairs leading to a toilet and a "lustral basin." The basin typically has gypsum veneering and fresco decoration. Its function has been interpreted as a place for ritual initiation, purification, symbolic descent into the earth, or simple bathing. The Minoan hall was probably multifunctional, depending on specific need or the time of day or season. Suggested functions include general living space, meeting area, or ceremonial space. At Knossos, a large multi-storied monumental staircase was used to gain access to the Minoan halls. A stairway fresco depicts a ritual procession, suggesting these halls were the endpoint of important rituals or economic transactions. In several instances, these halls are located near small rooms containing tablet or sealing archives, suggesting they may have been used as a meeting place for bureaucratic record keepers. Certainly literacy was a specialized skill tied to ritual use, and so there would have been a need to practice record keeping in a controlled and restricted setting.

Archaeological evidence for the presence of a large reception hall is also present at all of the major palaces. They were originally situated above the western storage magazines, except at Zakros where the hall was placed on the ground floor directly west of the central court. Residual evidence of these halls from the three main palaces includes the presence of western stairways leading over the magazines, architectural collapse from above the magazines, and the presence of regularly spaced support piers in the magazines themselves.

A third sort of public area is present at both Knossos and Phaistos. It is a small open area accessed by shallow steps on either side, and postulated to be an auditorium or theater. At Knossos, the auditorium is located at the northwest corner of the palace, while at Phaistos it is on the north end of the western plaza, dividing the plaza into a lower and upper level. The steps are believed to be too shallow to accommodate a seated audience. At Malia, no similar structure is preserved, but it may have been located at the northwest corner of the site. There is no preserved auditorium at Zakros. Possible activities may have included political assemblies, religious gatherings, sporting events, or simple entertainment.

Chronology and origins

The chronology of construction for these structures is long and complex. Bronze Age Crete is broken down into the Early, Middle, and Late Minoan periods, approximately corresponding to the Early, Middle, and Late Bronze Ages. Each period is further subdivided into three or more phases (e.g., Late Minoan III). The Subminoan period is the earliest phase of the Iron Age. More useful is the broad scheme used to clarify the major building and abandonment phases of the major palaces. These are:

1. Pre-Palatial Period-EM I-MM IA (ca. 3100–1900 B.C.)
2. Protopalatial (or Old Palace) Period-MM IB-MM IIB (ca. 1900–1720 B.C.)
3. Neopalatial (or New Palace) Period-MM IIIA-LM IB (ca. 1720–1470 B.C.)
4. Post-Palatial Period–LM II-IIIC (ca. 1470–1050 B.C.).

The palaces were first constructed during the Protopalatial Period, at the beginning of Middle Minoan IB (ca. 1900 B.C.). Many were rebuilt or heavily modified at the beginning of the Neopalatial Period (ca. 1720 B.C.), but all sustained significant damage early in the fifteenth century B.C. The Post-Palatial period is marked by decline and eventual abandonment (see Driessen and Macdonald 1997). Knossos continued to serve as a Mycenaean administrative center until the end of the Late Minoan IIIA (ca. 1330 B.C.).

Two major theories have been developed regarding the origins of the palaces around 1900 B.C. (see Graham 1987): (1) an earlier generation of scholars argued that Minoan architecture was influenced and inspired by Near Eastern palatial structures; (2) more recent arguments consider the palaces an indigenous development of the Minoans themselves. Unfortunately, the poor understanding of earlier Pre-Palatial and Protopalatial structures has hampered both arguments. Nonetheless, it is clear that Minoan palatial culture represented a unique expression of local complex society, quite distinctive from Egypt, Mesopotamia, or the Greek mainland (see Cherry 1983). The labyrinthine architecture and an emphasis on naturalistic rather than militaristic iconography suggest a bold departure from many contemporaneous societies.

It is for these reasons that the debate about palatial origins has shied away from architectural studies and rather focused on explaining the social, economic, and political factors attributed to this emergence (e.g., Cherry 1986; Hägg and Marinatos 1987; Hamilakis 1999; Hansen 1988; Knappett and Schoep 2000; Manning 1994; Renfrew 1972; Schoep 2002; Sherratt 1981). Colin Renfrew initiated this debate in 1972, arguing that the growth of these palaces helped an emerging elite class to accumulate and to redistribute vital resources such as food and specialized craft items. Others have continued the discussion, arguing for various economic and social motivations behind these elites, including: forced specialization, environmental instability, economic control, or trade monopolization.

Obviously more work is needed on these earlier time periods. One potential forerunner of the palaces is the rectangular-shaped "house tomb" and beehive-shaped "*tholos* tomb" of the Pre-Palatial Period (e.g., Branigan 1993; Goodison 2001; Watrous 1994:715). These slab-lined collective-style tombs are built on a monumental scale, with house tombs averaging over 1,000 square meters and *tholos* tombs often built with adjacent enclosed courts and an annex of auxiliary rooms built against the circular wall near the entrance (Figure 7.2). Burial goods include personal adornments and ritual offerings of food and drink. Drinking paraphernalia, statues, and altars have been found in some of the room annexes adjacent to the *tholos* tomb, suggesting some sort of worship tied to the dead (Murphy 1998; and see Blake this volume). Neighboring tombs were often utilized simultaneously, signifying multiple parallel social groups such as families, clans, or political factions. Obviously some sort of social organization and coordination was needed for the construction and maintenance of these large tombs, organization that may have served as a foundation for the eventual construction of the Minoan palaces. This burgeoning Minoan elite class may have been bolstered economically by trade contacts with Egypt and Mesopotamia, rousing them to create a series of administrative and religious "palaces" that followed their own culturally distinctive design.

Sardinia and Corsica

The most prominent feature of the Sardinian archaeological landscape is the *nuraghe* tower. Over 7,000 of these monuments are still preserved today, attesting to important social developments in Sardinian Bronze Age society. The Sardinian word *nuraghe* means "heap" or "hollow," and derives from its mound-like appearance of stacked rock. A number of key syntheses have been published on the nuragic towers (Balmuth 1992; Balmuth and Rowland 1982; Blake 1998; 2001; Lilliu 1982; Tore 1984; Webster 1991; 1996; 2001).

The *nuraghi* are truncated conical or sub-rectangular towers built using large basalt or granite rocks. The walls may be over a meter thick, built with dry-laid stone stacked either into concentric rows or cyclopean style. The typical *nuraghe* is between 11 and 16 meters in diameter, and ranges up to 18 meters in height (Figure 7.2). A lintel-style doorway, often facing south, opens to a short entrance passage that in turn leads to a central chamber. A small window may be present above the lintel. The central chamber averages 4 meters in diameter, has a corbelled roof, and has several niches set into the walls. The entrance passage usually has a niche (the *garetta*) to the right of the doorway, and if a second-story floor or rooftop balcony is present, a circular stairway leads upward to the left of the door. The conical *nuraghi* usually have more than one story, while the sub-rectangular towers have flat roofs and a central corridor with radiating side chambers. Often several *nuraghi* might be joined together to form a larger tower complex with connecting structures and walls.

The *nuraghi* appear to have served as residences, though their monumentality suggests some sort of role for community defense. Excavations have produced abundant material evidence for domestic activity, including cooking and manufacturing. Different workshop areas have been identified as well, for the manufacture of pottery, textiles, and metallurgy. Votive offerings have also been recovered, such as bronze human and animal figurines. One of the largest and best-preserved complexes is Su Nuraxi (see Tore 1984), which possesses a central tower surrounded by four smaller bastion towers. This central complex is also surrounded by a hexagonal circuit wall with additional towers, out-walls, and two entrances. Numerous huts and other structures were located outside the circuit wall. A carved stone model of a *nuraghe* was discovered in one of these huts, interpreted as a large public meetinghouse because of the presence of benches.

The many existing *nuraghi* are dispersed across the local landscape in varying densities determined in part by the nature of the terrain (Blake 2001). They are predominantly located in strategic positions, often visible to neighboring *nuraghi*. The size and complexity of the larger *nuraghi* clusters are dependent on local topography. The dispersed spacing suggests autonomous territorial control, while the inter-visibility speaks of broader social networking.

Other affiliated monumental architecture includes nuragic-style tombs, sacred wells, and megaron-temples (Balmuth 1992). Nuragic tombs are called *tombe di giganti* (giants' tombs), and were constructed with large upright stones forming an enclosed corridor chamber. This semi-subterranean chamber averages ten square meters (5 by 2 meters). A carved stone slab is placed at one end, usually before a crescent forecourt defined by more upright stones. Up to sixty individuals were collectively interred in these tombs, along with ample grave goods. The sacred wells were paved and benched constructions built around springs and used for ritual activities. The megaron-temples are rectangular nuraghi with multiple chambers and large caches of bronze items.

The Corsican *torre* tower is similar in design, layout, and chronology to the *nuraghe* tower, averaging 12 meters in diameter and with a 5-meter-high corbelled roof (de Lanfranchi and Weiss 1997). These towers seem never to have reached a level of elaboration comparable to that of the later *nuraghi* (Lewthwaite 1984; Chapman 1985:145). Indeed, given Corsica's proximity to Sardinia, and the fact that most of the *torre* are in the southern part of the island, close to Sardinia, it is generally believed that the *torre* was not an independent development but directly inspired by their Sardinian neighbors to the south (Chapman 1985:144). The *torre* were built as single conical structures with narrow entry passages, and were relatively simple architecturally. Less evidence exists regarding the function of these Corsican counterparts, although we assume they too had a residential function. However, the reuse and incorporation of older menhir standing stones suggests an important religious significance as well.

Chronology

The chronology of construction for the Sardinian *nuraghi* includes the:

1.   Bonnanaro Period (Early Bronze Age–ca. 1750–1500 B.C.)
2.   Nuragic Period (Middle and Late Bronze Age–ca. 1500–900/510 B.C.)
3.   Phoenician Period (Early Iron Age–ca. 900–510 B.C.)
4.   Punic/Carthaginian Period (ca. 510–238 B.C.)
5.   Roman Period (ca. 238 B.C.–A.D. 455).

Single-tower *nuraghi* first appear in the Bonnanaro or Nuragic I period, with both the conical and sub-rectangular designs dating to this period, but with a slightly earlier date for the appearance of the sub-rectangular "*proto-nuraghi*"). Tower construction peaked during the Nuragic Period, when large multi-towered complexes were built, many of them elaborations or expansions of existing single-tower structures. For example, four separate building phases have been identified at Su Nuraxi. It was during this period that residential huts were constructed adjacent to or nearby these nuragic complexes. The *tombe di giganti* were utilized during both these periods.

    The origins of the *nuraghi* and *torre* towers seem to be rooted in earlier megalithic monuments and tombs of the Late Neolithic (ca. 3500 B.C.). Menhirs, or standing stones, were arranged in various rows around one or more chamber tombs. Many of these upright menhir stones were carved with various decorations. The chamber tombs were either rock-cut or made of stacked stones. The most famous pre-nuragic monument is Monte d'Accoddi on Sardinia, a massive stepped stone platform with an entrance ramp and accompanying shrine on top. This structure was about 40 meters in size, and was constructed in two separate phases.

    The most fascinating aspect of nuragic construction is their sustained use (see Blake 1998), which has encouraged a number of discussions regarding their function. They have been variously interpreted as fortresses, watchtowers, shrines, family prestige symbols, or fortified residences for local elites. Although the apex of nuragic construction was over by 900 B.C., many continued to be modified and occupied until medieval times. Several *nuraghi* were burned or destroyed after Phoenician contact, but others were transformed into cult sites. During the era of Carthaginian rule (510–238 B.C.) many interior *nuraghi* continued to be occupied, while others were abandoned for a few centuries before being reoccupied. Material culture during this time period was fairly modest, but included Punic ceramics. Roman nuragic activity increases with a number of abandoned *nuraghi* being reoccupied as residences. Other documented activities include grain storage, cult observances, and mortuary practices. A number of churches were attached to *nuraghi* during the early medieval period. The *nuraghi* thus served a variety of functions over time. It is unclear to what extent the Corsican *torre* were constructed and reused after 1000 B.C.

Another important debate centers on the degree of political centralization during the Late Nuragic Period (see Lilliu 1988:574–579; Trump 1992; Webster 1991; 1996b). Clear evidence exists for increased social stratification, including the sub-nucleation of villages around existing *nuraghi*, the elaboration of some *nuraghi* into large monumental complexes, and a hierarchy of settlements with at least three major nuragic centers. The burning and abandonment of some *nuraghi* also suggests a restructuring of the hierarchical landscape. One argument is that the *nuraghi* represent "proto-castles" of a quasi-feudal elite. Another is that they represent fortified family towers utilized during a heightened period of inter-clan feuding (for discussion of these different theories, see Webster 1996a). The modest labor needed to build a *nuraghe* (an average of 3,600 person-days for a single tower) and the lack of social specialization that would be necessary to support a feudal elite argues for less rather than more political centralization. The symbolic component of their "monumentality," however, should not be overlooked. As with Crete and Malta, religious power was definitely a component of the power of emerging elite, coupled with evidence of growing extra-island trade, more intensive agriculture, and flourishing craft production. During this time period the archeological record reveals a vast increase in copper working on Sardinia, as well as the influx of eastern Mediterranean trade goods to the island (Lo Schiavo et al. 1985), though the quantity of copper exported from Sardinia is hard to calculate (Giardino 1992:307).

The Balearic Islands

The monumental phase of the Balearic Islands is called the Talayotic Period and spans a broad period between about 1800 B.C. and 800 B.C. Less work has been done on these monuments than on those from other island groups, but a number of important syntheses do exist (Calvo Trias et al. 2001; Bellard 1995; Gasull et al. 1984; Patton 1996; Plantalamor and Rita 1984; Rita 1988; Waldren 1982; 1992). Three specific monumental types characterize this phase: (1) the *talayot* watchtower; (2) the *naveta* burial tomb; and (3) the *taula* sanctuary. The most common of the three is the *talayot*, a tower-like structure that is similar to the Sardinian nuragic towers (Waldren 1982). A *talayot* may be square, round, oval, or stepped. The typical *talayot* is between 12 and 20 meters in diameter with a massive central pillar to support the roof (Figure 7.2). *Talayots* are commonly found in or near the center of a settlement, or built adjacent to defensive walls. Some of these settlements are quite large and have more than one *talayot*. Over 300 of the structures are still preserved on both Mallorca and Menorca.

The *naveta* is a dry-laid stone mound with a shape similar to an inverted boat (Waldren 1982). In plan view the *naveta* is horseshoe shaped. The *naveta* were built up with stacked stones over 2 meters in height. The interior was accessible via a narrow entrance, and consisted of a lower room for the placement of disarticulated bones and an upper shelf, probably used for the drying of recently placed corpses. The roofing stones are slightly ajar to permit the access of light. Over thirty of these structures are still preserved on Menorca. The largest and best-preserved *naveta* is located at Es Tudons, where more than 100 individuals were recovered, along with various personal accoutrements such as tools and jewelry (Serra-Belabre 1964).

The *taula* is a massive table-like pillar with a single capstone. It is surrounded by a horseshoe-shaped walled open-air enclosure lined with large menhir stones on its interior side. The typical *taula* is about 6 square meters in size with a capstone of about 2 meters in height. With the exception of a single monument on Mallorca, the *taula* is only known from Menorca. Most scholars consider the *taula* to have functioned as a small open-air shrine or sanctuary because several excavations have produced large quantities of animal remains, reminiscent of ritual sacrifice or communal feasting (Pericot García 1972; Waldren 1982).

Chronology

The monuments of the Balearic Islands follow this general chronology (Waldren 1992):

1. Pretalayotic Period (Chalcolithic/Early Bronze Age–ca. 3400–1700 B.C.)
2. Talayotic Period (Middle/Late Bronze Age/Iron Age–ca. 1700–123 B.C.)
3. Roman Period (after 123 B.C.).

Similar to the monuments of Sardinia and Corsica, the Balearic structures trace their origins to megalithic chamber tombs, fortified enclosures, and standing menhir stones of the Pretalayotic Period (Bellard 1995; Rita 1988). Many rectangular-style tombs are present on Mallorca, although circular ones exist as well. Settlements from the Pretalayotic Period, such as Ferrandell-Oleza on Mallorca, often incorporate central tower-like structures and other circular buildings (Waldren 1982). Boat-shaped houses are present at the site of Son Mercer de Baix on Menorca (Plantalamor and Rita 1984; Rita 1988), suggesting a clear link to the *naveta* structures. The link between Pretalayotic boat-shaped houses and later *naveta* architecture illustrates an important continuity between past and present, and life and death. All these early settlements document an intensification of human presence on the island, although material culture demonstrates clear links to the Iberian mainland, and includes such things as metal and Bell-Beaker pottery (Chapman 1985:145).

There has been some discussion regarding the chronological sequence of the *talayot*, and it is argued that the circular style was developed earliest and eventually evolved into the square and stepped forms (Waldren 1982). Unfortunately, the function of the *talayot* is not clear. Perhaps they served as a defensive structure, or perhaps as a community storage area. It has also been suggested that they served as loci for ceremonial community feasting, based on food remains (see Gasull et al. 1984). Less is known about the chronology of the *taula*, although archaeological finds suggest they were used as late as Roman times (Waldren 1982).

Unfortunately, ancient looting and a paucity of modern systematic excavations hinder our understanding of the Talayotic Period. The chronology of these monuments is still somewhat imprecise, being based on evidence from a very small number of excavated sites. We do know that that the majority of these three monument types were built in the late Bronze Age, between 1400 and 800 B.C., and so they were therefore used simultaneously. The *talayot* does bear some architectural and possibly functional resemblance to the towers of Sardinia and Corsica. However, the material remains found in the Balearic Islands have much clearer parallels to that of the Iberian mainland, even though none of the monuments have any convincing mainland analogues (Patton 1996:94).

Comparisons

Three distinct trajectories of monumental proliferation appear to exist. The earliest and most unusual are the impressive temple and funerary complexes of Malta and Gozo. They flourish from 3600–2600 B.C. on two of the most remote islands in the Mediterranean, and are functionally, chronologically, and stylistically unique. The Minoan palaces represent the second trajectory, rising into prominence in the eastern Mediterranean from 1900–1000 B.C. These labyrinthine buildings represent the largest and most elaborate monuments. The Sardinian *nuraghi*, the Corsican *torre*, and the Balearic monuments (*talayot*, *naveta*, and *taula*) represent the third trajectory. Although smaller in scale and construction than the Minoan palaces or the Maltese temples, these monuments all share similar architectural and functional qualities, dominating the landscape of the central and western Mediterranean islands from at least 1700–200 B.C.

At first glance, these trajectories appear to have very little in common. They span vast distances in time, space, and architectural execution, suggestive of distinctly local processes of social and ritual elaboration. Upon closer inspection, however, it is clear that they also share three commonalities: (1) they trace their architectural origins to Neolithic burial architecture; (2) they occur on relatively isolated islands; and (3) they represent early expressions of social power relationships.

Origins

The architectural origins of these monumental trajectories may be traced to the megalithic chamber tomb, a type of funerary monument used for collective or group burial during the Late Neolithic and Early Bronze Age. These tombs, sometimes called dolmens, are circular or squared stone chambers, often covered by earth or stone mounds. They served as communal burial places, often with a variety of special grave goods, and were sometimes marked with large upright menhir stones. The social context in which these structures developed during the Late Neolithic was characterized by significant Mediterranean-wide changes, including rising populations, increased subsistence production, and economic differentiation (Wells and Geddes 1986). Local economies were increasingly based on a mixed economy of plow agriculture and sheep/cattle herding, with a greater emphasis being placed on "secondary animal products" such as wool, leather, and milk (Sherratt 1983). Nucleated settlements of larger populations were more common, although smaller seasonal dwellings were still utilized in order to take advantage of other available resources.

The first chamber tombs appear in the central and western Mediterranean, covering the coasts of Spain, France, Italy, Corsica, and Sardinia (Grinsell 1975; cf. Hoskin 2001). They date to the fourth millennium B.C. (Late Neolithic), and are similar in chronology and style to the tombs of Atlantic Europe. By 2200 B.C. these tombs fall out of favor on the mainland, being progressively replaced by smaller collective graves or single tombs. Megalithic chamber tombs and beehive *tholos* tombs are present in Greece as well, but these were constructed at the end of the third millennium and continued well into the second millennium B.C. (Branigan 1970; 1993).

Certainly these tombs are the architectural precursors to the three monumental trajectories. For example, the same vaulted megalithic chamber of these earlier tombs served as a common architectural element for the Malta temples and cemeteries, the apse. The apse is simply utilized on a monumental scale, built in clusters and used repeatedly to form large and more complex structures. The incorporation of standing menhir stones into their configuration represents another link to the past. The towers of Sardinia, Corsica, and the Balearics are of similar origins, in that all three were preceded by a rich megalithic funerary culture, but also possess unique architectural elaborations such as multiple floors, niches, and passageways. In the case of the Sardinian *nuraghi*, they too are clustered to form larger monumental structures. Even the Minoan palaces seem to trace their origins to burial architecture as well. The Pre-Palatial Cretan tombs, with their galleries, room annexes, and multiple functions, seem to prominently influence the development of the palatial room/hall complexes, the basic architectural unit most commonly repeated.

Insularity

A second trait common to these three trajectories is that a clear correlation exists between island insularity and monumental elaboration. All of these monumental examples are found on islands that are more than 48 kilometers away from the mainland, and all are large enough to support stable populations (an area of over 200 square kilometers). Other large islands that are closer to the mainland, such as Sicily or Rhodes, lack this monumental phase. So also do the many smaller and isolated islands located around the Mediterranean. It has been argued therefore that island insularity, and the environmental and social isolation it caused, influenced monumentality. This would include the increased use of monuments as territorial markers (Renfrew 1976), or the elaboration of peculiar or local monumental styles (Evans 1973; Patton 1996), or the enhanced use of monuments for religious or ideological control (Stoddart et al. 1993).

The importance of island insularity with respect to monumentality, however, has probably been overemphasized (see Rainbird 1999). Transport distances of under 50 kilometers are rather minimal compared to other areas of the world at this time; take for example the second millennium expansion of the Lapita culture of Near Remote Oceania, maintaining a trade network spanning thousands of kilometers (Irwin 1992; Kirch 2000). Moreover, archaeological evidence clearly indicates that farmers and foragers easily traversed back and forth through the Mediterranean islands for millennia (see Barker, this volume). Nonetheless, it is still curious that monumental elaboration is indeed present upon some of the Mediterranean's more remote islands. Perhaps isolation played a minor factor, or perhaps it is time to come full circle and reconsider Renfrew's territoriality argument. It is certainly easier to view these islands not so much as isolated environments, but rather as circumscribed environments, where we might imagine a scenario of heightened social competition for limited land as populations increased, resulting in the various expressions of monumental elaboration.

Social power

The third commonality of these monuments deals with the nature of status relationships and how they are expressed materially. Two social phenomena coincide with the rise of monumental architecture in the Mediterranean: the appearance of social inequality and increasing economic intensification. Unlike the individualized tombs and palaces of Egypt and the Near East which are indicators of the authoritative power held by elites, the Mediterranean monuments document a more corporate-based strategy for maintaining social power. Corporate strategies are social relations that emphasize collective unity rather than personal aggrandizement, and serve to suppress economic differentiation and de-emphasize access to personal wealth (e.g., Feinman 1995). Moreover, the architectural labor used to reinforce corporate cooperation of religious rituals, food production, and boundary maintenance are all activities that enhance corporate social power (see Kolb 1997).

The Maltese temples represent an excellent example of corporate social power; not only did their construction require collective organized labor, but they also hosted important group-oriented rituals that allowed emerging elites to exercise political, spiritual, and economic control within their society. As these structures became more architecturally complex over time, they served as markers for expressing territorial conflagrations and social dissent among and perhaps within social groups. It is unclear whether power became centralized under one or more elites and their social groups over time, but it does seem that social friction was on the rise. The eventual shift from temples to cremation cemeteries during the Tarxien Cemetery phase may indicate a breakdown of corporate power, and a shift to more authoritative rule where the access to external exchange goods such as metal objects played a more important role for elites to maintain power (see Stoddart et al. 1993).

The Sardinian and Corsican towers together with the Balearic monuments were built on a much smaller scale than the Maltese temples, but it is clear that they too were group-oriented expressions of power. Although they served a variety of functions, their symbolic importance speaks to important corporate power. The subsequent elaboration of the Sardinian *nuraghi* and their associated evidence for economic intensification speak again to growing social tensions and a subsequent shift to more authoritative (yet decentralized) rule.

The Minoan palaces represented the greatest departure from the corporate strategy of elite power. On Crete, a focus on the long-distance trade of prestige goods seems to have fostered more authoritative control. This exchange served to enhance the social and ideological stature of local elites, artistically reinforced by the magnificent Minoan frescos. Undoubtedly the rapid changes experienced in the east Mediterranean during the second millennium (increasing population, more intensive farming, extensive trade contacts, rise of metallurgy) stressed collective group cohesion by enhancing social distinctions among individuals. There is, however, most certainly a degree of corporate-based power that functioned on Crete as well. The diverse set of palatial functions, the public spaces and processional ways, the decentralized use of space, and the lack of elite spaces seem to indicate the expression of group-oriented control, even if it was a vestige of the past.

Conclusions

The goal of this chapter has been to examine the genesis and elaboration of some of the Mediterranean world's most impressive monuments. Although substantial differences exist in the construction, chronology, and location of these monuments, a number of key similarities also exist. First, the origins of these monuments may be traced to the same Late Neolithic pan-Mediterranean social fabric. Second, island insularity may have served to stimulate a divergence in the way these monuments were utilized. And finally, those who built and used them made logical choices for negotiating social consensus. As social inequality and economic intensification increased over time, communities struggled with ways to maintain their collective unity in the face of emerging elites. These monuments represent a variety of expressions for economically and ideologically enhancing long-term authority. Political and territorial cohesion result in very tangible economic benefits not only for emerging elites, but for all members of a community who helped build and use these monuments.

REFERENCES

Balmuth, Miriam S., 1992 Archaeology in Sardinia. American Journal of Archaeology 96:663–687.

Balmuth, Miriam S., and R. J. Rowland, eds., 1984 Studies in Sardinian Archaeology. Ann Arbor: University of Michigan Press.

Bellard, C. G., 1995 The First Colonization of Ibiza and Formentera (Balearic Islands, Spain): Some More Islands out of the Stream? World Archaeology 26:442–445.

Blake, Emma, 1998 Sardinia's Nuraghi: Four Millennia of Becoming. World Archaeology 30(1):59–71.

——2001 Constructing a Nuragic Locale: The Spatial Relationship between Tombs and Towers in Bronze Age Sardinia. American Journal of Archaeology 105:145–162.

Bonnano, Anthony, Tancred Gouder, Caroline Malone, and Simon Stoddart, 1990 Monuments in an Island Society: The Maltese Context. World Archaeology 22:90–205.

Branigan, Keith, 1970 The Tombs of Mesara: A Study of Funerary Architecture and Ritual in Southern Crete, 2800–1700 B.C. London, Duckworth.

——1993 Dancing with Death: Life and Death in Southern Crete c. 3000–2000 B.C. Amsterdam: Adolf M. Hakkert.

Calvo Trias, M., V. M. Guerrero Ayuso, and B. Salvà Simonet, 2001 Arquitectura Ciclópea del Bronce Balear. El Tall del Temps 37. Mallorca: El Tall.

Chapman, Robert W., 1985 The Later Prehistory of Western Mediterranean Europe: Recent Advances. In Advances in World Archaeology 4. F. Wendorf and A. Close, eds. pp. 115–187. New York: Academic Press.

Cherry, John F., 1983 Evolution, Revolution and the Origins of Complex Society in Minoan Crete. In Minoan Society. O. Krzyszkowska and L. Nixon, eds. pp. 33–45. Bristol: Bristol Classical Press.

——1986 Polities and Palaces: Some Problems in Minoan State Formation. In Peer Polity Interaction and Socio-political change. Colin Renfrew and John F. Cherry, eds. pp. 19–45. Cambridge: Cambridge University Press.

Christakis, K. S., 1999 Pithoi and Food Storage in Neopalatial Crete: A Domestic Perspective. World Archaeology 31:1–20.

Davis, E. N., 1987 The Knossos Miniature Frescoes and the Function of the Central Courts. In The Function of the Minoan Palaces. R. Hägg and N. Marinatos, eds. pp. 157–161. Stockholm: Svenska Institutet i Athen.

de Lanfranchi, François, and Michel-Claude Weiss, 1997 L'Aventure Humaine Préhistorique en Corse. Ajaccio, Corsica: Les Éditions Albiana.

Driessen, Jan, 2003 The Court Compounds of Minoan Crete: Royal Palaces or Ceremonial Centers? Athena Review 3(3):57–61. (Full section on Aegean Palaces in this issue).

Driessen, J., and C. Macdonald, 1997 The Troubled Island. Minoan Crete before and after the Santorini Eruption. Aegaeum 17. Liège: Université de Liège.

Driessen, J., I. Schoep, and R. Laffineur, eds., 2002 Monuments of Minos: Rethinking the Minoan Palaces. Aegaeum 23. Liège: Université de Liège.

Evans, A., 1921 The Palace of Minos. London: Macmillan.

Evans, J. D., 1973 Island Archaeology in the Mediterranean: Problems and Opportunities. World Archaeology 9:12–26.

——1984 Maltese Prehistory: A Reappraisal. In The Deyà Conference of Prehistory. Early Settlement in the West Mediterranean Islands and the Peripheral areas. W. H. Waldren, R. Chapman, R. J. Lewthwaite, and R. C. Kennard, eds. pp. 489–497. Oxford: British Archaeological Reports S229.

Feinman, G. M., 1995 The Emergence of Inequality: A Focus on Strategies and Processes. In Foundations of Social Inequality. T. D. Price and G. M. Feinman, eds. pp. 255–280. New York: Plenum Press.

Gasull, P., V. Lull, and M. E. Sanahuja, 1984 Son Fornes I: La Fase Talayotica. Ensayo de Reconstruccion Socio-Economica de una Comunidad Prehistórica de la Isla de Mallorca. Oxford: British Archaeological Reports, International Series, no. 209.

Gesell, G. C., 1987 The Minoan Palace and Public Cult. In The Function of the Minoan Palaces. R. Hägg and N. Marinatos, eds. pp. 123–128. Stockholm: Svenska Institutet i Athen.

Giardino, Claudio, 1992 Nuragic Sardinia and the Mediterranean: Metallurgy and Maritime Traffic. In Sardinia in the Mediterranean: A Footprint in the Sea. R. H. Tykot and T. K. Andrews, eds. pp. 304–316. Sheffield: Sheffield Academic Press.

Goodison, Lucy, 2001 From Tholos Tomb to Throne Room: Perceptions of the Sun in Minoan Ritual. In Potnia. Deities and Religion in the Aegean Bronze Age, Aegaeum 22. R. Laffineur and R. Hägg, eds. pp. 77–88. Liège: University of Liège.

Graham, J. W., 1987 The Palaces of Crete. Princeton: Princeton University Press.

Grima, Reuben, 2001 An Iconography of Insularity: A Cosmological Interpretation of Some Image and Spaces in the Late Neolithic Temples of Malta. Papers of the Institute of Archaeology 12:48–65.

Grinsell, Leslie V., 1975 Barrow, Pyramid, and Tomb: Ancient Burial Customs in Egypt, the Mediterranean, and the British Isles. London: Thames and Hudson.

Hägg, Robin, and Nanno Marinatos, eds., 1987 The Function of Minoan Palaces. Proceedings of the Fourth International Symposium at the Swedish Institute at Athens. Göteborg, Paul Åströms Förlag.

Hamilakis, Yannis, 1999 Food Technologies/Technologies of the Body: The Social Context of Wine and Oil Production and Consumption in Bronze Age Crete. World Archaeology 31:38–54.

——ed., 2002 Labyrinth Revisited: Rethinking Minoan Archaeology. Oxford: Oxbow Books.

Hansen, J. M., 1988 Agriculture in the Pre-Historic Aegean: Data versus Speculation. American Journal of Archaeology 92:39–52.

Hoskin, Michael A., 2001 Tombs, Temples and Their Orientations: A New Perspective on Mediterranean Prehistory. Bognor Regis: Ocarina.

Irwin, G., 1992 The Prehistoric Exploration and Colonisation of the Pacific. Cambridge: Cambridge University Press.

Kirch, P., 2000 On the Road of the Winds. Berkeley: University of California Press.

Knappett, Carl, and I. Schoep, 2000 Continuity and Change in Minoan Palatial Power. Antiquity 74:365–371.

Kolb, Michael J., 1997 Labor, Ethnohistory, and the Archaeology of Community in Hawai'i. Journal of Archaeological Method and Theory 4:265–286.

Lewthwaite, James, 1984 The Neolithic of Corsica. In Ancient France: Neolithic Societies and Their Landscapes, 6000–2000 BC. C. Scarre, ed. pp. 146–181. Edinburgh: Edinburgh University Press.

Lilliu, Giovanni, 1982 La Civiltà Nuragica. Sassari: Carlo Delfino.

——1988 La Civiltà dei Sardi dal Paleolitico all'Età dei Nuraghi. Turin: Nuova ERI.

Lewis, H., 1977 Ancient Malta; A Study of its Antiquities. Gerrards Cross: Smythe.

Lo Schiavo, Fulvia, Ellen Macnamara, and Lucia Vagnetti, 1985 Late Cypriot Imports to Italy and their Influence on Local Bronzework. Papers of the British School at Rome 53:1–71.

MacGillivray, J. A., 2000 Minotaur. Sir Arthur Evans and the Archaeology of the Minoan Myth. New York: Hill & Wang.

Malone, C., A. Bonnano, T. Gouder, S. Stoddart and D. Trump, 1995 Mortuary Ritual of 4th Millennium Malta: The Zebbug Period Chartered Tomb from the Brochtorff Circle at Xaghra (Gozo). Preceedings of the Prehistoric Society 61:303–345.

Manning, Sturt, 1994 The Emergence of Divergence: Development and Decline on Bronze Age Crete and the Cyclades. In Development and Decline in the Mediterranean Bronze Age. C. Mathers and S. Stoddart, eds. pp. 221–270. Sheffield: Sheffield University, Sheffield Archaeology Monographs 8.

Marinatos, Nanno, 1987 Public Festivals in the West Courts of the Palaces. In The Function of the Minoan Palaces. R. Hägg and N. Marinatos, eds. pp. 135–143. Stockholm: Svenska Institutet i Athen.

Meillassoux, C., 1964 Anthropologie Économique des Gouro de Côte d'Ivoire; de l'Économie de Subsistance à l'Agriculture Commerciale. Den Haag: Mouton.

——1967 Récherche d'un Niveau de Détermination dans la Société Cynégétrique. L'Homme et la Société 6:24–36.

Murphy, Joanne, 1998 The Nearness of You–Proximity and Distance in Early Minoan Funerary Landscapes. In Cemetery and Society in the Aegean Bronze Age. K. Branigan, ed. pp. 27–40. Sheffield: Sheffield Academic Press.

Myers, Eleanor E., and Gerald Cadogan, eds., 1992 The Aerial Atlas of Ancient Crete. Berkeley: University of California Press.

Patton, M., 1996 Islands in Time: Island Sociogeography and Mediterranean Prehistory. London: Routledge.

Pericot García, Luis, 1972 The Balearic Islands. London: Thames & Hudson.

Plantalamor, L., and M. C. Rita, 1984 Formas de Poblacion durante el Segundo y Primero Milenio BC en Menorca: Son Merver de Baix, Transicion entre la Cultura Pretalayotica y Talayotica. In The Deyà Conference of Prehistory. Early Settlement in the West Mediterranean Islands and the Peripheral areas. W. H. Waldren, R. Chapman, R. J. Lewthwaite, and R. C. Kennard, eds. pp. 797–826. Oxford: British Archaeological Reports S229.

Rainbird, P., 1999 Islands out of Time: Towards a Critique of Island Archaeology. Journal of Mediterranean Archaeology 12:216–234.

Rehak, P., and J. G. Younger, 1998 Review of Aegean Prehistory VII: Neopalatial, Final Palatial, and Postpalatial Crete. American Journal of Archaeology 102:91–173.

Renfrew, Colin, 1972 The Emergence of Civilisation. The Cyclades and the Aegean in the Third Millennium B.C. London: Methuen.

——1974 Beyond a Subsistence Economy. In Reconstructing Complex Societies. C. B.

Moore, ed. pp. 69–96. Cambridge, MA: Supplement to the Bulletin of American School of Prehistoric Research 20.

——1976 Megaliths, Territories, and Populations. *In* Acculturation and Continuity in Atlantic Europe. S. DeLaet, ed. pp. 198–220. Ghent: Dissertationes Archaeologicae Gandenses 16.

Renfrew, Colin, and E. V. Level, 1979 Exploring Dominance: Predicting Polities from Centers. *In* Transformations: Mathematical Approaches to Culture Change. A. C. Renfrew and K. L. Cooke, eds. pp. 145–167. New York: Academic Press.

Rita, C., 1988 The Evolution of the Minorcan Pretalayotic Culture as Evidenced by the Sites of Morellet and Son Mercer de Baix. *Proceedings of the Prehistoric Society* 54:241–247.

Robb, John, 2001 Island Identities: Travel and the Creation of Difference in Neolithic Malta. European Journal of Archaeology 4:175–202.

Schoep, Ilse 2002 Social and Political Organization on Crete in the Proto-Palatial Period: The Case of Middle Minoan II Malia. Journal of Mediterranean Archaeology 15:101–132.

Serra-Belabre, M. L., 1964 La Naveta d'Es Tudons, Mahon. Madrid, Congreso Nacional de Arqueologica 10.

Shaw, J. W., 1973 The Orientation of the Minoan Palaces. Antichità Cretesi Studi in onore di Doro Levi 2:47–59.

Sherratt, Andrew, 1981 Plough and Pastorialism: Aspects of the Secondary Products Revolution. Pattern of the Past: Studies in Honour of David Clark. I. Hodder, G. Isaac, and N. Hammond, eds. pp. 261–305. Cambridge: Cambridge University Press.

——1983 The Secondary Exploitation of Animals in the Old World. World Archaeology 15:90–104.

Sipahi, T., 2001 New Evidence from Anatolia regarding Bull-Leaping Scenes in the Art of the Aegean and the Near East. Anatolica 27:107–125.

Stoddart, Simon, Anthony Bonnano, Tancred Gouder, Caroline Malone, and David Trump, 1993 Cult in an Island Society: Prehistoric Malta in the Tarxien Period. Cambridge Archaeological Journal 3:3–19.

Stoddart, Simon, 1999 Long-Term Dynamics of an Island Community; Malta 5500 B.C.–2000 A.D. *In* Social Dynamics of Prehistoric Central Mediterranean. R. H. Tykot, J. Morter, and J. E. Robb, eds. pp. 137–147. Accordia Specialist Studies on the Mediterranean 3. London: Accordia Research Institute, University of London.

Tilley, Christopher, 2004 From Honey to Ochre: Maltese Temples, Stones, Substances and the Structuring of Experience. *In* the Materiality of Stone: Explanations in Landscape Phenomenology I. Christopher Tilley, with assistance of Wayne Bennett, pp. 87–145. London: Berg.

Tore, Giovanni, 1984 Per una Rilettura del Complesso Nuragico di S'Uraki, Loc. Su Pardu, S. Vero Milis, Oristano (Sardegna). *In* The Deyà Conference of Prehistory. Early Settlement in the West Mediterranean Islands and the Peripheral Areas. W. H. Waldren, R. Chapman, R. J. Lewthwaite, and R. C. Kennard, eds. pp. 703–723. Oxford: British Archaeological Reports S229.

Trump, David H., 1972 Malta: An Archaeological Guide. London: Faber and Faber.

——1977 The Collapse of the Maltese Temples. *In* Problems in Economic and Social Archaeology. G. d. G. Sieveking, I. H. Longworth, and K. E. Wilson, eds. pp. 605–609. Boulder: Westview.

——1992 Militarism in Nuragic Sardinia. *In* Sardinia in the Mediterranean: A Footprint in the Sea. R. Tykot and T. Andrews, eds. pp. 198–203. Sheffield: Sheffield Academic Press.

——2002 Malta: Prehistory and Temples. Valetta, Malta: Midsea Books.

Waldren, William H., 1982 Balearic Prehistoric Ecology and Culture. Oxford: British Archaeological Reports S149.

—— 1992 Radiocarbon and Other Isotopic Age Determinations from the Balearic Islands: A Comprehensive Inventory. Deyà Archaeological Museum and Research Centre, vol. 26. Deyà, Mallorca: Deyà Archaeological Museum and Research Centre.

Watrous, L.V., 1994 Review of Aegean prehistory III: Crete from Earliest Prehistory through the Protopalatial Period. American Journal of Archaeology 98:695–753.

Webster, Gary S., 1991 Monuments, Mobilization, and Nuragic Organization. Antiquity 65:840–856.

—— 1996a A Prehistory of Sardinia 2300–500 B.C. Sheffield: Sheffield Academic Press.

—— 1996b Social Archaeology and the Irrational. Current Anthropology 37:609–627.

—— 2001 Duos Nuraghes: A Bronze Age Settlement in Sardinia. Oxford: British Archaeological Reports International Series, no. 949.

Wells, P. S., and D. S. Geddes, 1986 Neolithic, Chalcolithic, and Early Bronze in West Mediterranean Europe. American Antiquity 51:763–778.

Whitelaw, Todd, 2001 From Sites to Communities: Defining the Human Dimensions of Minoan Urbanism. In Urbanism in the Aegean Bronze Age. K. Branigan, ed. pp. 15–37. Sheffield: Sheffield Studies in Aegean Archaeology.

Younger, J. G., 1995 Bronze Age Aegean Representations of Aegean Bull-Games, III. In Politeia: Society and State in the Aegean Bronze Age. R. Laffineur and W.-D. Neimeier, eds. 507–545. Aegaeum 12 Liège: Université de Liège.

8

Lithic Technologies and Use

Evagelia Karimali

Introduction

Long before pottery came into use, stone functioned as an essential component of the technology of early human groups in the Mediterranean. Its use for tools in game hunting, plant collecting and grain processing activities, as well as in a multitude of manufacturing activities (drilling, scraping, cutting, etc.) during the Pleistocene and the early Holocene left indelible imprints on the human landscape of the Mediterranean Basin, for example in stone quarries, flake scatters, and other types of deposit.

As a consequence, stone tools have long played a primary role in the process of identifying human presence, movement, and communication. In fact, without the aid of their stone tools, it would never have been possible to track the presence of humans or to reconstruct their movements and intentional displacements (e.g., colonizations) in the Mediterranean. Nor would it ever be possible to reconstruct the socio-economic base of their foraging and settled life. Because of the enduring character of stone, it has been possible not only to recover but to construct a diverse series of taxonomies of stone implements, upon which chronologies of various areas in the Mediterranean and Europe have been built. Thus it would not be an exaggeration to speak of a "stone-based" history of the human species during the Pleistocene and early Holocene periods, without which the earlier "pre-pottery" human developments would have been lost. Stone continued to be used throughout the later Neolithic and Bronze Age, following the appearance of pottery and metals. The replacement of stone tools and weapons by metals took place in several sequential stages, depending on various contextual, social, and cultural factors. For certain classes of tools (e.g., milling instruments), replacement never occurred and these implements continued to be manufactured in stone throughout antiquity and right down to the pre-industrial era. Chert continued to be used until the 1960s in various Mediterranean settings, where chert flakes were set as cutting tools into threshing sledges (e.g., Karimali 1994). For all these reasons, stone and stone tools hold a prominent place in any discussion about human presence in the Mediterranean.

This chapter summarizes efforts to understand the history and social uses of stone and stone tools, mainly during the Holocene era (from 10,000 B.P. onward). Rather than serving as a comprehensive overview, an overwhelming task, this chapter provides an introduction to lithic use in the prehistoric Mediterranean, and to the myriad theoretical issues surrounding its study. In this narrative, lithics are not severed from their links to production, function, and meaning. These stone tools themselves also have "histories," as they undergo several stages of procurement, exchange, and manufacture until they are transformed into tools and discarded. Stone tools were made to be used and they were used in a meaningful way. Accordingly a history of lithics cannot be envisioned as distinct from the social history of their use by human beings.

Chipped and Ground Stone Tools: Two Complementary Industries

Stone tools comprise a distinct analytical category, distinguished from other toolkits by material (e.g., bone tools). They are divided into two categories, chipped stone and ground stone, on the basis of differences in production techniques and the mechanical properties of the materials used for their production. Silicates (obsidian included) exhibit a concoidal fracture and thus are suitable to flint-knapping, whereas igneous and metamorphic rocks are more suitable to pecking, polishing, and flaking as well (Table 8.1; Runnels 1985c).

This distinction, echoing a shift of interest toward issues of production over recent decades in Europe, is adopted strictly for analytical purposes, in order to

Table 8.1 Chipped and ground stone industries: raw materials and production techniques

Raw materials	Production techniques	Lithic categories
I. Silicates (e.g., flint, chert, jasper, chalcedony, obsidian)	1. Percussion 2. Indirect percussion 3. Pressure	Chipped or flaked stone tools (sickles, drills, end-scrapers, projectile points, etc.)
IIa. Igneous and altered volcanics (e.g., andesite, basalt, serpentinite, diabase, microgabbro, gabbro, diorite, microdiorite etc.)	1. Pecking 2. Flaking 3. Grounding 4. Polishing 5. Perforating	Ground-stone tools (axes, adzes chisels, hammers, querns, mortars, polishers, whetstones, etc.)
IIb. Metamorphics (marble, amphibolite)		
IIc. Sedimentary (e.g., sandstone, limestone)		

stress differences in the technological infrastructure (the "know-how") underlying the manufacture of the two industries. All tools, however, were used in a continuum of economic and consumption behavior that pertained to a set of different but integrated activities (for example, the activities involved in farming) of the prehistoric community (Table 8.2). Specifically, chipped and ground stone tools:

- had complementary uses, as they were sequentially employed in integrated economic activities (e.g., the farming cycle); thus sickle elements made of flint (chipped stone) were used for harvesting, whereas millstones made of igneous or metamorphic rocks (ground stone) were used in grinding cereal to flour;
- were both elements of more complex, synthetic implements (e.g., flint blades or ground stone tools hafted in antler sleeves); and
- were sometimes employed for the production of each other (e.g., hand-stones were used in flint-knapping as percussion tools, hammerstones for pecking and manufacturing ground stone tools and metal (Astruc 2001).

Chipped Stone Technologies

Raw materials and exchange networks

Chipped stone tools comprise a distinct tool category, with manufacture characterized by flaking techniques. The most common materials used were obsidian, flint and chert, jasper, chalcedony, and, more rarely, quartz.

Obsidian, a natural volcanic glass of amorphous crystalline structure, stems from a limited number of geological sources in the Mediterranean (Melos and Giali in the Aegean; Lipari, Sardinia, Pantelleria, and Palmarola in the central Mediterranean; Göllü Dağ and Nenezi Dağ in Cappadocia, central Anatolia, and Nemrut Dağ in eastern Anatolia; modern Ethiopia and Eritrea – Renfrew et al. 1968; Tykot 1996; M.-C. Cauvin et al. 1998; Betancourt 1999; see Figure 8.1); this configuration has been demonstrated by characterization studies carried out over the past forty years (Williams-Thorpe 1995). Obsidian was extensively traded in prehistory through interregional networks in the form of prepared cores or pressure-ready blades to be used as cutting and hunting implements (knives, razors, bifacial arrowheads, etc.). Mediterranean obsidian networks never formed a single unified system, but remained regional and "self-contained" cultural zones with minimal overlaps (see Renfrew et al. 1965; Tykot 1996).

As a result of its successful "fingerprinting," obsidian has been particularly applicable for use in exchange modeling. Several exchange mechanisms have been proposed, based on fall-off patterns of quantitative and qualitative variables against the distance of a site from a source (Renfrew et al. 1968; Torrence 1986; Perlès 1990). Current work is revising central concepts used in past studies (e.g., distance calculated in kilometers), instead favoring time and region-specific models (Ammerman and Polglase 1993; Karimali 2000; 2001).

Table 8.2 The main tool types encountered in Mediterranean assemblages, the type of activity involved, and the type of raw material used

Motion	Tool type	Raw material	Activity
I. Reaping	I. Sickle elements	Silicates	I. Harvesting
II. Grinding, milling	II. Millstones, querns, grinding stones	Igneous, metamorphics, sedimentary	II. Pre-Pottery Neolithic: Grinding (red ochre, minerals and plant foods [seeds, vegetable etc.], Wright 1993). Neolithic, Bronze Age: Grinding grain to flour, mineral pigments, clay, salt, or for sharpening and smoothing celts, shells, and bone implements (Kardulias and Runnels 1995).
III. Pounding	III. Mortars, pestles		III. • Pounding spices, salt, coloring matter, drugs, etc. (Runnels 1988) • Dehusking emmer (Samuel 1999)
IVa. Cutting	IVa. Axe, adze, chisel	Igneous and volcanics	IVa. Axes: Pre-Pottery Neolithic A: • Cutting, paring, wedging wood (Roodenberg 1983) Neolithic: • Carpentry, hide and bone working (Roodenberg 1983; Wright 1993; Perlès 2001:232) • Tree clearance • Deliberate breakage ("ritual" function? Stroulia 2003).
	"shaft-hole" axe		Early Bronze Age Aegean, Anatolia, and Italy: • Ore mining/crushing and metalworking.

Table 8.2 *Continued*

Motion	Tool type	Raw material	Activity
			Middle Bronze Age: • Axes reused as chisels or wedges for quarrying of building stone material, or for cutting of tomb chambers and dromoi (Mogelonsky 1996; Aston et al. 2000:7). Chisels Neolithic:
		Silicates	• Carpentry and other crafts. Bronze Age:
		Silicates	• Stone vase manufacture (Evely 1980).
IVb. Cutting	IVb. Retouched/truncated/backed/unretouched blades/flakes		IVb. Cutting (meat, fish, hide etc). Light domestic tasks.
IVc. Cutting	IVc. "Glossed blades and segments"		IVc. Cutting plants (reeds, grasses, bushes etc.) for: roof and house building activities, basketry for storage etc. (Anderson-Gerfaud 1983; Perlès and Vaughan 1983).
V. Drilling (shell, stone bone, ivory etc.)	V. Borers (drills), microdrills	Silicates	V. • Beadmaking (Grace, 1989–1990; Rosen, 1997; Perlès 2001:223). • Wood joinery (Keeley 1983). • Soft stone vase making (el-Khouli 1978). • Seal cutting (Evely 1993:157). • Stone architecture (Arnold 1991:265). etc.
VI. Engraving/Incising (bone, ivory, soft materials)	VIa. Gravers	Silicates	VIa. Ivory, stone carving (Rosen 1997; Kardulias 1992).
	VIb. Burins		VIb. Bone working

Table 8.2 *Continued*

Motion	Tool type	Raw material	Activity
VII. Polishing (pots)	VII. Polishing stone (polishers)	Pebble, natural stones	VII. Ceramic vessel finishing
VIII. Hammering	VIIIa. Hammer-stones	Metamorphics, siliceous limestones, metamorphosed chert	VIIIa. Neolithic: Flintknapping, chert mining, wedging, producing other tools (e.g., axes) by pecking, chiseling, etc.
			Bronze Age: stone dressing, smoothing (Shaw 1973:52), stone quarrying (Arnold 1991; Aston et al. 2000:7), metal ore mining (Wagner and Weisgerber 1985), metal sheet hammering (Evely 1993).
	VIIIb. Perforated hammers or "hammer-axes" (EBA II and on)		VIIIb. Mining and crushing ores (Branigan 1974; Leighton, 1992:26), metal beating.
	VIIIc. Grooved hammers		VIIIc. Metal and flint mining (Michailidou 1993–1994; Leighton 1992; Maggi et al. 1994).
	VIIId. Ritual hammers		VIIId. Ritual function (Shaw 1973).
IX. Scraping	IX. End-scrapers	Silicates	IX. PPNA: Wood chopping, bone and leather working (Coqueugniot 1983).
			Neolithic/Bronze Age: Leather processing (Coqueugniot 1991; Runnels 1985a; Barker 1995).
X.	X. Backed bladelets, projectile points, arrowheads, trapezes, tranverse arrowheads	Silicates	X. Hunting, fishing, warfare.
XI. Wedging	XI. *Pièces Esquillées*	Obsidian, chert	XI. Splitting bone or wood; striking fire? (Runnels 1985a:374).

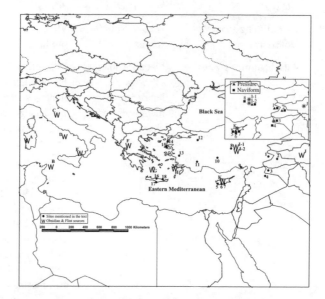

Figure 8.1 Map of the Mediterranean with stone material sources and sites mentioned in the text. Inset: Distribution of pressure and naviform techniques in the Eastern Mediterranean during the Pre-Pottery Neolithic period

Nos. 1–8: Pre-Pottery Neolithic/Aceramic sites
1. Cafer Höyük
2. Çayönü
3. Mureybet
4. Abu Hureyra
5. Mylouthkia
6. Shillourokambos
7. Kalavasos-Tenta
8. Aşikli Höyük

Nos. 9–11: Neolithic sites
9. Mersin
10. Çatalhöyük
11. Hacilar
Nos. 12–18: Bronze Age sites
12. Demirci Höyük
13. Aphrodisias
14. Troy
15. Poliochni
16. Knossos
17. Phaistos
18. Mochlos

Obsidian sources
A. Monte Arci, Sardinia
B. Pantelleria
D. Palmarola
E. Lipari
G. Melos
H. Giali
I-1. Göllu Dağ (central Anatolian sources)
I-2. Nenezi Dağ
J. Nemrut Dağ (eastern Anatolian sources)
Flint sources
C. Apennines
F. Pindos Mountains
K. Troodos Mountains

Other stones of cryptocrystalline structure (radiolarian cherts, "honey flint," chalcedony), collected as nodules from secondary deposits such as river beds, or extracted from beds outcropping from natural formations, were used alongside obsidian. The most fine-grained ones were processed by sophisticated punch and hammer or pressure techniques and were traded in the form of prepared cores or blades to distant sites through interregional and regional networks (e.g., "Canaanean" blades [Rosen 1997; Anderson et al. 2004] honey-flint blades). Subsequently, at the local level, they were turned into various formal (e.g., sickles, scrapers, pointed tools) or non-formal (e.g., notched, truncated, retouched) tools, simply by applying retouch on their edge. Rarely, they were traded at greater distances as formal tools such as projectile points and arrowheads, possibly encoded with special or symbolic meanings. Among the best-known Mediterranean flint sources used in prehistory were those of northern Italy, in the Alps and the Apennines (Barfield 1999); the jasper beds from Valle Lagorara at Liguria (Maggi et al. 1994); the chert outcrops of the Lefkara formation surrounding the Troodos Mountains on Cyprus (Kardulias and Yerkes 1998; McCartney 2002); and the secondary river deposits of "chocolate" jasper cobbles lying at the foot of the Pindos Mountains in the Aegean (Figure 8.1; for possible sources of honey flint in western Greece or Albania, see Perlès 1992).

Lastly, coarse-grained flint and chert sources were processed in a non-specialized, opportunistic manner (hammer techniques), for producing various everyday blade and flake tools. In general, selection of raw materials of appropriate flaking quality was deliberate in prehistory. Moreover, there was always an inextricable link between the quality of the raw material used and the technical "know-how" invested: the better the quality of the flint traded, the more likely that its processing was in the hands of specialized and skillful producers.

Symbolic aspects of raw materials

Raw materials were endowed with symbolic properties of which we understand all too little today. As gifts from the earth, stone materials are often associated metaphorically with other socio-cultural values (Whittle 1995). The possible association of the name of obsidian with the Roman name Obsius, for example, suggests a relation with the Greek word opsi ("one's appearance"). This link is indirectly confirmed by the use of obsidian in the eyes of prehistoric figurines (J. Cauvin 1998) and in the so-called "mirrors" (Conolly 1999). Ancient sources provide references to obsidian's medico-magical use in antiquity, for example to cure eye diseases, to foresee the future, or even to bring luck to sea travelers (Decourt 1998). Obsidian had similar properties and cosmological associations in Egypt and the Near East. Deposition of obsidian blades in graves and the application of sophisticated blade production pressure techniques have been linked to ritual and ceremonial behavior in Minoan contexts on Crete (Carter 1994). Although used in what today appears to be a "utilitarian" context, stones and stone-tool use retained metaphorical connotations in prehistory, making our modern dichotomy between "utilitar-ian" and "symbolic" almost meaningless (Karimali 2000).

Stone-tool production

Because it is a reductive technique whose stages leave clear vestiges in the archaeo-logical record, chipped stone technology is particularly appropriate to studies of production. Reconstruction of the manufacturing process on a site typically is under-taken with the *"chaine operatoire"* approach ("reduction sequence"), which operates at three levels of analysis: conceptual, behavioral, and practical. At the conceptual level, this approach examines the knapping operations in succession, in order to deduce the cognitive and motor strategies that obtained during its actualization (Pélegrin 1990). At the behavioral level, it views all stages amenable to stone pro-cessing as sequential, from material procurement and production, to exchange, tool use and discard; emphasis is placed on the way in which these stages interact to leave "meaningful patterns" in the archaeological record. At the practical level, when com-bined with debitage and attribute analysis, it allows the identification of debitage categories such as cores, debris, and so on, linked to the various stages of manu-facture, and consequently it permits the reconstruction of the reduction sequence itself. In this way, several questions related to modes of material importation, con-tinuous or discontinuous production, and specialization can be addressed.

One of the major issues put forward in lithic production studies is the identifi-cation of specialization. Different levels of technical "know-how" were implemented in different manufacturing techniques, as not every technique required the same degree of skill. Pressure, for example, employed during the Neolithic and the Bronze Age, required in-depth understanding of the mechanics of force applied during the core preparation stage. The same is true for the more elaborate varieties of indirect percussion techniques (e.g., naviform, "Canaanean" blade technology) used in dif-ferent periods within the Mediterranean (see below).

What was the character of specialization among such early, pre-monetary societies and how is it to be measured archaeologically? Traditional views have regarded specialization as a factor of the labor and time invested (energy expendi-ture), as measured by quantitative variables such as debitage quantity, blade stan-dardization, and special segregation of debris. Ethnographic studies, however, have expressed caution if not concern about the "economic" character of this phenom-enon, emphasizing its ties with the socio-cultural context in which it operates. Emphasis is now given to the technical "know-how" embodied in production. Such studies also point out that among non-hierarchical groups, specialization is orga-nized at the "community" level, is restricted to a few, and is often mantled with a divining character (Perlès and Vitelli 1999). In line with these latter views, current claims about specialized production are based on qualitative parameters, such as the degree of complexity and standardization of the operative strategies employed and the amount of skill embodied in production (for an example in the Early Bronze Aegean, see Karabatsoli 1997).

Cognitive and motor skills ("know-how") are transmitted from generation to generation through long apprenticeship, visual inspection, and imitation (Roux and Gorbetta 1989). In this way, they form part of the conscious or subconscious cultural apparatus, embedded in cultural traditions. Obviously technological know-how cannot be superficially linked to ethnic or cultural groups. It can be transmitted widely or restricted to certain groups, depending on its role in the process of identity definition and negotiation within specific historical contexts. By being transferred, adopted, or avoided, technologies – along with their end products – act as active or passive carriers of cultural traditions. Such processes are particularly interesting in periods of acculturation and/or colonization, as in the Pre-Pottery Neolithic of the Near East, whereby spatial discontinuities in technological traditions give insights into the movement of people, ideas, and cultures over vast geographical areas. In the later periods of consolidated farming (the Neolithic and Bronze Ages), distribution of "know-how" was carried out through participation in extensive exchange networks, in which specialists and specialized products were circulated (see below).

Production techniques across time and space

Upper Paleolithic – Pre-Pottery Neolithic (PPN)
Flake and blade technologies have a long history in Europe and the Mediterranean. Although blade techniques were already known from several episodes in northern Europe during earlier periods, the typical volumetric blade core in a fully-fledged form appeared only during the Upper Paleolithic (ca. 40,000–10,000 B.P.) (J. Kozlowski 2001). Blade-flaking techniques used at that time included direct (hammer striking) and indirect (punch) percussion, both employed for backed bladelets and geometrics to be used as projectile inserts (Perlès 1999).

By the beginning of the Holocene, when Italy and the Aegean area were still engaged in what are regarded as Mesolithic technologies (Perlès 1999; Binder 2000), pressure flaking, and a new technique, bipolar/naviform (Calley 1985), developed into highly sophisticated and specialized techniques in the eastern Mediterranean (but see also the use of pressure flaking in the Late Mesolithic of Europe). The two techniques exhibited clearly distinct regional distribution patterns in this region. In a few sites, however, products of the two techniques spatially overlapped (e.g., at the early Aceramic Neolithic site of Paraklessia *Shillourokambos*, Cyprus; see below). In most of the cases, cores worked by these techniques coexisted with cores worked by simpler flaking techniques. The naviform/bipolar technique became the diagnostic marker ("*fossil directeur*") of the PPNB period in the Levant (8200–6200 cal. B.C.; Figure 8.2.1). It spread as part of the cultural/techno-PPNB complex to other parts of the eastern Mediterranean Basin, as a result of colonization (Paraklessia *Shillourokambos*, Kissonerga *Mylouthkia*, Kalavasos *Tenta*, Cyprus – Peltenburg et al. 2001) or "acculturation" (Çayönü, southeastern Anatolia – Cavena et al. 1998; see Figure 8.1, inset). This technique was probably in the hands of groups with specialized knowledge (male

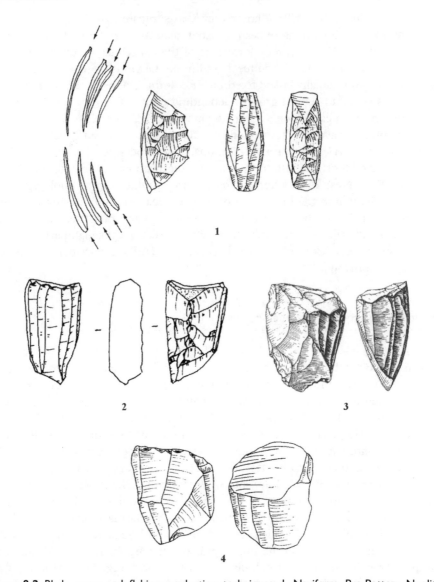

Figure 8.2 Blade cores and flaking production techniques: 1. Naviform, Pre-Pottery Neolithic Levant (after Calley 1985); 2. Pressure, Bronze Age Aegean (after Karabatsoli 1997); 3. "Canaanean," Early Bronze Aegean Levant (after Rosen 1997); 4. Direct percussion, Aegean (after Reinders et al. 2003; in press)

hunters? – Nishiaki 2000), and it was always applied on good-quality flint (but see "naviform" bidirectional flaking on obsidian from Kalatepe, Cappadocian sources – Balkan-Atli and Aprahamian 1998) for making cutting tools and arrowheads. Given the widespread occurrence of high quality flint in the Levant, it was knowledge rather than resources that was distributed over long distances. Regional variations in technical traditions also existed (see, e.g., "Kaletepe" style for getting pointed blades, central Anatolia, *supra*; "Douara" type, northern Syria–Nishiaki

2000). The technique disappeared gradually from the Levant in the subsequent, Pottery Neolithic period, possibly as one result of the decrease in hunting and the changing social roles of male-hunters associated with it (Nishiaki 2000). Knowledge of this technique had also fallen into disuse earlier on Cyprus (end, early Aceramic Neolithic, 7600–7000 cal. B.C.), as the island gradually lost contact with the Levantine mainland (Peltenburg et al. 2001).

Pressure flaking, on the other hand (Figure 8.1, inset and Figure 8.2.2), appeared in the upland regions of southeastern Anatolia at Pre-Pottery Neolithic sites such as Çayönü and Cafer Höyük (Inizan and Lechevallier 1994; Cavena et al. 1998; J. Cauvin et al. 1999). In central Anatolia, pressure flaking was probably used for prismatic bladelet production at the Cappadocian source of Göllü Dağ (e.g., Kömürcü-Kalatepe, Trench P-C4 and Kayirli-Bitlikeler workshops; Balkan-Atli et al. 1999; Balkan-Atli et al. 2001). Recent studies suggest that similar Kalatepe prismatic pressure blades were exported at several PPN sites of Syria (e.g., Mureybet, see Pernicka et al. 1997; Binder and Balkan-Atli 2001:12–14) and Cyprus (e.g., *Shillourokambos*, Gomez et al. 1995; Briois et al. 1997). Pressure was not applied on flint in the Levant during the Pre-Pottery Neolithic period, however, as only bipolar/naviform and simpler percussive techniques were applied on flint in this region. Thus, it is proposed that pressure was an Anatolian import to the Levantine area (for a discussion, see Binder and Balkan-Atli 2001).

Neolithic (7000/6500–3200/3000 B.C.)

During the Neolithic, a two-tier production system was established in the Mediterranean, related to the deliberately differential exploitation of raw materials of diverse quality and origin. The first tier was linked to the specialized procurement, production, and exchange of fine-quality stone resources of limited physical distribution (obsidian, radiolarites); the second tier was connected with the non-specialized manipulation of local chert resources. In most cases, the materials circulated by the two subsystems were deliberately used toward different ends: cutting and harvesting needs in the former case, scraping, boring, and other domestic needs in the latter case. For more on this notion of "the economy of raw material," see Perlès (1990; 1992).

In the first case, because of increasing sedentism, fine-grained stone materials of limited spatial occurrence were circulated in the form of prepared cores or blades to sedentary communities located several kilometers from the sources through long-distance, overlapping exchange networks. In most cases, specialized production, restricted to a few communities or persons who possessed the necessary "know-how," lay behind these networks. Depending on the distribution (limited vs. widespread) of fine-grained resources over the landscape and other spatial factors, such interregional, regional, and local production systems developed.

In the Aegean, Anatolia, and Italy, where high-quality resources were of limited distribution, specialized production and interregional exchange systems flourished, focusing on the manipulation of sophisticated techniques (for Anatolia, see Conolly 1999 and Baykal-Seeher 1996; for the Aegean, see Perlès 1990; for Italy, see Tykot 1996 and Luglie 2000). Pressure flaking, one such technique, required exceptional levels of technical competence. It was often applied on obsidian and fine-grained flints (e.g., "chocolate flint," western Thessaly, Karimali 1994; "honey-flint," Perlès 2001:202). Other sophisticated punch and hammer techniques were applied to fine and medium quality flints, which were available on a regional scale through exchange networks or direct procurement. Examples of these flints include *Biancone* and *Scaglia variegata* types (Barfield 1999); silicified limonite and the volcanic "honey" type (Skourtopoulou 1999; see also Holmes 1988; Gatsov 2000). Specialized production centers have not yet been identified with certainty (Ammerman 1985:65), and so little can be said about the organization of production and exchange systems in the Neolithic. Sites retained differential access to obsidian and production skills depending on their location (e.g., coastal vs. inland) and their status in the social networks (Carter 1998; Karimali 2000). Parallel to these networks, local production of chert flakes by simpler direct or bipolar hammer techniques also occurred, aimed at the production of everyday tools of domestic function (Figure 8.2.4).

On Cyprus, where chert varieties were available locally within the Troodos Mountains (Kardulias and Yerkes 1998), production retained a distinctly local character, with the use of less sophisticated percussive techniques. Many of the chert tools produced, however, were involved in the manufacture of stone objects characterized by an impressive technical quality (Astruc 2001). In some cases, specialized production activities cannot be precluded (Papagianni 1997). In the Levant, because of the decreasing specialization in the production of hunting tools and the increasing need for expedient tools for domestic uses (Nishiaki 2000), naviform techniques were replaced by simpler flake percussion techniques (Gopher 1994).

Bronze Age

During the Bronze Age (ca. 3500/3000–end of second millennium B.C.), heavy reliance on the earlier Neolithic, long-distance exchange networks of fine-grained flint declined in several areas, notably the Aegean and Italy. Nonetheless, flints of lower quality remained in circulation to satisfy a constant need for sickles and expedient tools. At the same time, obsidian production systems consolidated in some places, which then emerged as new regional centers of specialization.

During the Early Bronze Age (ca. 3200–2000 B.C.), just such a regional production center was established in the Aegean, and was involved in the restricted manipulation of sophisticated metal and stone processing techniques. Whereas sites in the northeastern Aegean (Poliochni, Troy) specialized in the exploitation of metal (Nakou 1995), several southern coastal Aegean sites, notably Manika and sites in the Argolid, evolved into centralized obsidian processing depots, procuring prepared cores for distant sites (Kardulias 1992; Karabatsoli 1997; Hartenberger and Runnels 2001). Obsidian pressure-flaking techniques reached a high level of sophistication (Karabatsoli 1997) in terms of the standardized procedures and resulting products (Figure 8.2.2). Melian obsidian products were exported as far as the northeastern Aegean (Troy; Pernicka et al. 1996) and western Anatolia

(Aphrodisias; Blackman 1986). In various phases of the Minoan period (from about 2900–1600 B.C.), obsidian was unequally distributed, with larger sites such as Knossos and Phaistos and coastal sites such as Mochlos retaining wider access (Carter 2004). During the Late Helladic/Mycenaean period (ca. 1600–1180 B.C.) production remained in the hands of peripheral sites, as the palaces seem to have had little interest in controlling obsidian production and incorporating it into the realm of the palatial economy (Parkinson 1999). At sites on the periphery of the Mycenean world, such as Epirus in northwestern Greece, lithic industries retained a local and unspecialized character (Tartaron et al. 1999).

In Anatolia, obsidian from central Anatolian sources (Göllü Dağ) was exported to a number of Anatolian and Levantine sites (Renfrew et al. 1966; Pernicka et al. 1996). The obsidian pressure technique is attested at Early Bronze Age sites such as Demircihüyük (although not securely dated; see Baykal-Seeher 1996). On Cyprus, production of blades/flakes and flakes through percussive techniques continued throughout the Bronze Age (Kingsnorth 1996; Given and Knapp 2003: 305–311). In the Levant and eastern Anatolia, new flint production networks developed during the Early Bronze Age (3500–2200 B.C.), based on the application of an elaborated metal-bitted punch or pressure technique, known as "Canaanean" (Pélegrin and Otte 1992; Rosen 1997; Hartenberger et al. 2000; Anderson et al. 2004; see Figure 8.2.3). This technique was used to produce long and symmetrical flint blades, snapped and traded as segments to be used as sickle elements. Specialized production and manipulation of "know-how" took place at the village level, and thus the system continued unbroken, despite the collapse of "urban" sites from the Early Bronze II period onward (post-2200 B.C.: Rosen 1997).

In central Italy, during the Copper Age (ca. 3500/3000–2500/2100 B.C.) a switch to bifacial technology took place (Barfield 1999). The bifacial technique seems to have been developed for making arrowheads and daggers from jasper, to be used by newly emerging, competitive social groups (Maggi et al. 1994). In line with these social developments, copper assumed a higher value, whereas obsidian use declined on the mainland (Tykot 1999). Hard-hammer techniques continued until the end of the Bronze Age (Phillips 1986).

Concomitant with the need for blades, there developed a parallel need for flakes (Moundrea-Agrafioti 1997). Flake production techniques such as hammering remained largely opportunistic, applied by non-specialists on flint and chert of mediocre quality and local origin. By the end of the Bronze Age, chipped stone industries declined in most of the Mediterranean region, but never became extinct, as local chert resources continued to be in use for making sickles and expedient tools down to the historical periods (see further below).

The use of stone and stone tools

Questions and methods

Three approaches to lithic tools currently dominate the field: the typological, the functional, and the technological. The construction of tool-type taxonomies has been a useful device in reconstructing cultural histories in the Mediterranean (e.g., for the Paleolithic and PPN typologies of the Near East, see S. K. Kozlowski 1999). Yet recent views question the criteria on which tool typologies have been formed. Often one observes a disjuncture between those tool categories that would have been constructed by prehistoric peoples themselves and those established by archaeologists. Formal tools, for example "sickles," are often defined on the basis of morphological characteristics or use-wear ("silica sheen"), the function of which is neither precise nor conclusive unless demonstrated by use-wear or functional analysis. Aided by microscopic techniques, such analysis is a promising field for clarifying the use of stone tools and the relationship between tool form and function (see J. Cauvin 1983 for fuller discussion). Use-wear studies have successfully tackled many questions raised in the field of Mediterranean prehistory, such as the wide use of "lustred blades" in cutting reeds for various domestic purposes rather than for harvesting during the PPN (Anderson-Gerfaud 1983), or the use of scrapers for chopping wood in the late PPNA (ca. early to mid-ninth millennium B.C.; Coqueugniot 1983). Alternative methods, such as "attribute analysis," which define tool categories on the basis of tool edge morphology and assumed function, are also employed (Conolly 1999).

Tool types exhibit variability in frequency and form at both diachronic and synchronic levels. The earliest typological approaches (e.g., by François Bordes) interpreted differences in the frequency or the presence/absence of tool types ("*fossils directeurs*") between assemblages as the result of cultural differences between ethnic groups. This view was later challenged by Lewis Binford, who interpreted such differences as the result of inter-site functional differences. Recently, inter-site differences in tool representation have been linked to task differentiation on the basis of gender or context, for example, "domestic" vs. "non-domestic" (McCartney 2002).

Another interrelated topic is why certain formal tools such as sickles and points exhibit either typological uniformity or variation in different contexts over space and time. Is it a matter of style preference, or is it tied to the more general socio-economic conditions in which tool management belongs? Various interrelated factors lie behind tool-form variability or uniformity, leading to the spread or neglect of particular types and styles: access to fine-grained materials, hafting technologies, the socio-economic level at which production runs, technological traditions, the mode of cultural interaction leading to the transmission of such traditions, and finally the symbolic connotation of tools. Tools, especially formal tools, are produced within a framework of specific technological, culturally transmitted traditions, operating at different levels of socio-economic organization (village/city) and at different time-scales (long/short span). In this way, their presence or absence provides indices of the particular ways in which human groups with these traditions at their disposal interacted. For example, the spread or neglect of a particular tool type may be tied to the inclusion or exclusion of the use-group from culturally defined networks sharing similar production traditions, or circulating materials and/or ready products to specific cultural (but not strictly ethnic) groups (Rosen 1997:143). Thus stylistic typology is far from signaling simple aesthetic preferences strictly tied to particular cultural-ethnic groups. Rather, its choice lies at the heart of human relations: "who is producing, transmitting and receiving typological or stylistic messages, and in what contexts" (Rosen 1997:149).

Evolution of stone tools

A variety of tools were employed for cutting, scraping, piercing, hunting/killing, and other activities during the prehistoric period. Because of the different subsistence strategies employed by the groups under discussion (e.g., early sedentary or semi-sedentary Natufian hunters, PPNB hunters/early cultivators, Neolithic and Bronze Age agro-pastoralists), patterns of chipped stone use exhibited a great deal of variation through time.

As far as tool form and function are concerned, however, a general evolutionary development may be seen from the Neolithic onward. Whereas in the Upper Paleolithic and the earlier phases of the Holocene specific tool forms such as burins and scrapers were employed by hand for a variety of uses and on different materials (e.g., scrapers at Mureybet III – Coqueugniot 1983, see Table 8.2), from the Neolithic on hafting systems became more elaborate, tools were more frequently of the composite type, and, consequently, tool use became more standardized in relation to specific ecological contexts (see J. Cauvin 1983 for a full discussion).

Tool types (see Table 8.2)

"Lustred blades," bearing gloss and striations along their edge, were used in a wide range of production activities related to increasing sedentism in the earlier Pre-Pottery Neolithic period; gradually they became the main agricultural tools (sickles) for reaping siliceous grasses and cereal grain (see Figure 8.3.16). Being composite tools, that is, blades/blade segments fixed in wooden or bone hafts by mastic or lime plaster, sickles exhibited a wide typological diversity across time and space. Haft typological changes are less well documented (Mortensen 1970; Bar-Yosef 1987), but are often reconstructed on the basis of macro-wear blade features (M.-C. Cauvin 1983). The whole or segmented, unilaterally or bilaterally retouched blade or blade/flake (Figure 8.3.1) was the most common sickle type used, at least until the later phases of the Bronze Age (end of second millennium B.C.). It was then replaced by the bifacial, serrated flint flake throughout the Mediterranean (Coqueugniot 1991; Karimali 1994; Waldren et al. 1984; see Figure 8.3.2). Other tool variants also existed (Crowfoot-Payne 1993; Moundrea-Agrafioti 1997; Peltenburg et al. 2001). In a few cases, blades to be used as sickles were the products of specialized production (e.g., "Canaanean" blades – Rosen 1997; Anderson et al. 2004).

Changes in sickle tool morphology were not only a function of the type of retouch adopted, but of the technological traditions on which the sickle tool product depended, as in the case of naviform blades in the PPNB, and Canaanean blades in the Early Bronze Age Levant). Depending on the organizational level (village/urban, multicultural/ethno-cultural) at which such traditions run, changes

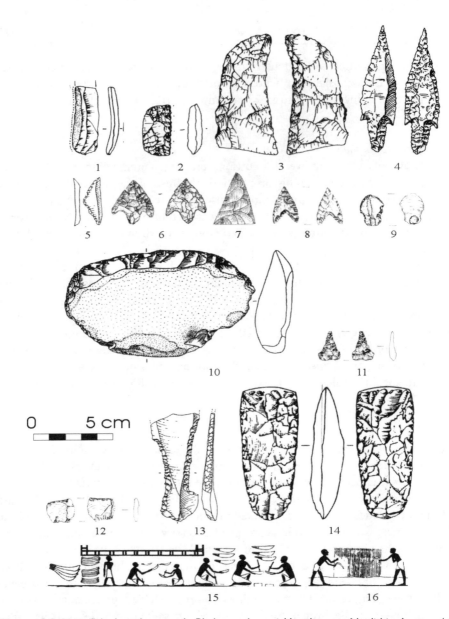

Figure 8.3 Main flaked tool types: 1. Blade used as sickle element, Neolithic Aegean (after Moundrea-Agrafioti 1983: fig. 1.14); 2. Bifacially-flaked sickle element, Bronze Age Pefkakia, Aegean (after Karabatsoli 1997: fig. 70.3); 3. Egyptian Bifacial Knife (after Rosen 1997: fig. 3.39.1); 4. Pre-Pottery Neolithic "Jericho" point, from Jericho (after Gopher in Kozlowski 1999: 127, fig. D). 5. Microlith, Aceramic Anatolia (after Balkan-Atli 1994: figs. 2, 4). 6. Barbed and tanged projectile point, Neolithic Halai, Aegean (personal observation); 7. Triangular bifacially-flaked arrowhead, Final Neolithic Pefkakia, Aegean (Karimali 1994); 8. Hollow-based projectile point, Bronze Age Lerna, Aegean (after Runnels 1985a: fig. 11C); 9. End-scraper, Bronze Age Lerna, Aegean (after Runnels 1985a: fig. 12B); 10. Tabular scraper, Bronze Age Levant (after Rosen 1997: fig. 3.30.3); 11. Piercing tool, Bronze Age Lerna, Aegean (after Runnels 1985a: fig. 15D); 12. *Pièce esquillé*, Bronze Age Lerna, Aegean (after Runnels 1985a: fig. 12E); 13. Obsidian "Çayönü" tool, Pre-Pottery Neolithic eastern Anatolia (after Anderson and Formenti 1994: fig. 1, 1); 14. Flaked axe, Neolithic Levant (after Rosen 1997: fig. 3.49.3); 15–16. Early Twelfth-Dynasty (Middle Bronze Age) tomb of Amenmhat at Beni Hasan with scenes of Egyptian knife manufacture and harvesting with curved sickles (after Newberry 1893: plate XI)

in sickle morphology often took place in discontinuous steps, cross-cutting periodization. In general, being tied to specific cultural, yet subconscious, routine traditions, sickle technologies and styles must have often acted as passive carriers of cultural messages (Rosen 1997:133–134).

A plethora of other ad hoc cutting implements (retouched, backed, truncated, and/or non-retouched but utilized blades and flakes) were in everyday use, linked to the performance of "domestic" activities such as plant processing and craft activities (McCartney 2002). A distinctive type of knife was produced by highly specialized mastercraftsmen in a uniform manner in pre-dynastic Egypt (Naqada II/Gerzean), indicating "a strong tradition of formalized education and training" (Kelterborn 1984:452; see Figures 8.3.3 and 8.3.15).

Various types of points and arrowheads were used as hunting/fishing or fighting implements (Table 8.2, Figure 8.3.4–8.3.8). There is a great deal of variability in the forms of these tools, well placed in temporal and spatial contexts (Anderson-Gerfaud 1983; Runnels 1985a; Crowfoot-Payne 1993; Maggi et al. 1994; Barker 1995; Baykal-Seeher 1996; Nicoletti 1996; Rosen 1997; Conolly 1999; S. K. Kozlowski 1999; Perlès 1999; Luglie 2000; Balkan-Atli et al. 2001; McCartney 2002). No linear typological and stylistic development of these forms existed throughout the Mediterranean, as they alternated or coexisted, depending on local conditions of use.

Function and style are but two of the many reasons lying behind point variability, but the specifics are not always well understood. Clearly, the exact function (e.g., hunting, warfare – Clark et al. 1974) of these tools was context-specific through time. Absence of such implements from a site or a region may be indicative of radical changes in hunting practices such as the use of traps (Perlès 1999), or the decline of hunting (Rosen 1997). Absence also may be related to site function, with, for example, industrial or hunting activities performed at open-air sites only (McCartney 2002). On the other hand, style encodes information, and in the case of hunting implements, the information encoded is expected to be relevant to the position of hunting or hunters in the general cosmology and in the social structure. Stylistic parameters are more visible when viewed at smaller, regional scales. This is the case, for example, of the series of standardized point types (Figure 8.3.4) spread across the Levantine and Anatolian regions during the PPNB. The remarkable uniformity and diffusion of such implements has been seen as the result of continuous interactions and the exchange of information (regarding, for example, territorial alliances or competition) between different hunting groups across extensive distances (Gopher 1994). To us today, such tools are helpful *fossils directeurs* for establishing lines of diffusion and acculturation (Peltenburg et al. 2001). In another case, high-quality bifacial flint arrowheads, with no evidence of use, were transported over large distances in the southern Balkans during the Final Neolithic, possibly carrying symbolic information related to hunting and/or the status of hunters (Carter and Ydo 1996:164–165).

Other tools were used for scraping, drilling, engraving, chopping, and wedging (see Table 8.2). Conventionally identified by the abrupt retouch on their convex edge (Figure 8.3.9), end-scrapers are usually linked to leather working, although other uses are also possible (Table 8.2). The so-called "tabular scrapers" (Figure 8.3.10) were probably used as knives (for cutting reeds or shearing wool?), although a ritual function cannot be excluded (Rosen 1997).

Boring and engraving tools were used in a variety of tasks (Figure 8.3.11). Drilling, either by hand (Perlès 2001:223) or with a composite tool (bow drill – Grace 1989–1990; Rosen 1997) is often associated with specialized production. The introduction of the bow drill (Fifth Dynasty, third millennium B.C. Egypt) made possible the boring of regular circular holes on stone and other material with the aid of abrasive materials (sand, emery) and lubricating agents (water, oil) (Evely 1993). Burins comprised another tool category associated with engraving activities in the earlier prehistoric periods (Rosen 1997; Nishiaki 2000:24). Lastly, *pièces esquillées* (or splintered pieces, see Figure 8.3.12) are commonly found in all periods (Runnels 1985a). Other tool groups of limited distribution include the "Çayönü" tools (Anderson and Formenti 1996; see Figure 8.3.13) and flaked axes or adzes, mainly limited to the Levant and Egypt (Coqueugniot 1983; Holmes 1990; Rosen 1997; see Figure 8.3.14). Although widely known in pre-industrial times (Pearlman 1984; Kardulias and Yerkes 1998; Whittaker 1999; Karimali in press), the use of threshing-sledges (*tribuli, doukani*) in prehistory still remains under investigation (Anderson and Inizan 1994; Shakun 1999).

Ground Stone Technologies

This category includes stone tools produced mostly by grinding, although other techniques were employed (see Tables 8.1 and 8.2). Ground stone technology had evolved in the Levant already by the Upper Paleolithic period, possibly deriving from the earlier use of hammerstones and anvils (Wright 1993). Selection of raw materials depended on the physical properties of the stone such as hardness and workability. Most ground stone tools did not undergo major morphological changes across time and space, and thus are of limited chronological value. Although employed in "utilitarian" contexts, ground stone tools often were endowed with symbolic meanings (see below).

The most common tool category is that of cutting tools (axes, adzes, and chisels) hafted into antler or wooden sleeves, or pierced hafts (see Figure 8.4.1). Axes (with symmetrical, convergent working edges) and adzes (with asymmetrical, beveled cutting edges) were used with direct percussion for chopping wood and chipping activities, whereas chisels with use-wear traces on their butts were used with indirect percussion, that is, hammered by stone pounders or wooden mallets. Class boundaries between these groups, however, are not always rigid, and functional groups – recognized by use-wear analyses – cross-cut morphologically defined groups (Tsountas 1908; Roodenberg 1983; Moundrea-Agrafioti and Gnardellis 1994). Typology is further complicated in cases of tool recycling (e.g., adzes and axes used as chisels or hammerstones in secondary use).

Axes were made by pecking, grinding, and polishing. Full tool coverage by polish depended on tool type, function, and hafting techniques (Moundrea-Agrafioti

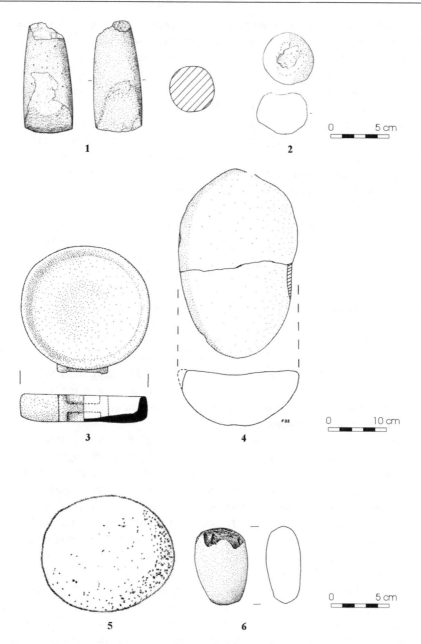

Figure 8.4 Main ground stone tools: 1. Axe, Neolithic Aegean (after Reinders et al. 1997: fig. 9a); 2. Hammerstone, metamorphic rock, Early Bronze Age Karystos, S. Euboia, Aegean (Karimali, personal observation); 3. Reconstruction of mortar, Bronze Age Aegean (after Runnels 1988: fig. 7); 4. Andesite saddle quern, Early Bronze Age Aegean (after Kardulias and Runnels 1995: fig. 100); 5. Grinding stone, Neolithic Aegean; 6. Celt reused as handstone, Final Neolithic Aegean (after Kardulias and Runnels 1995: fig. 106)

1992). In some areas, as in the Aegean and on Cyprus, the selection of stones from local riverbeds and their subsequent manufacture was a pre-planned but non-specialized activity. In cases of distant sources, well-organized systems of rock acquisition developed (Elliott 1981; Leighton 1989). Drawing on ethnographic examples, gender specialization in the production or use of these tools can also be argued (McCartney 2002; Stroulia 2003).

Axes are ethnographically known as deforestation implements (Pétrequin and Pétrequin 1993). In prehistory, however, they were employed in a variety of wood-working and light duty activities. Only larger axes were suitable for shrub clearing and tree-felling tasks, and such implements became more numerous only during later Neolithic phases (Perlès 2001:232). Deliberate breakage, possibly for marking ceremonial events and for creating lasting bonds in periods of tension, has also been suggested for small-sized, broken axes (Stroulia 2003). When the use of metal axes became common from the Middle Bronze Age onward, stone axes were oriented toward new uses (see Table 8.2).

In the western Mediterranean, where elaborate, long-distance exchange systems of axes had developed along local networks, axes made of fine materials traveled far from their sources, often acquiring high symbolic value, as was the case for axes of "jadeite" and "nephrite," imported from northern Italy and the Alpine regions to southern Italy and Sicily (Leighton and Dixon 1992). On Malta, it has been argued that axes were encoded with symbolic meaning linked to cultural identity, spiritual power, and visual display (Skeates 2002). In Portugal, the production and distribution of axes made of "amphibolite" was carried out at a few sites, and this exclusive control of these products contributed to the unequal distribution of power during the Copper Age (Lillios 1997).

In sum, it is hard to separate a strictly "utilitarian" from a symbolic use of axes in prehistory (Whittle 1995). Drawing on a large corpus of ethnographic parallels, Lillios has argued that axes were often considered by their users as "powerful symbols (usually male) of authority, wealth and prestige. (They) are often mythified or personified, their manufacture and use is associated with taboos, and they are so highly valued that their theft can be a cause for battle" (Lillios 1997:31).

Another common ground stone group found in prehistoric contexts was the hammering tools. Simple hammer stones show up in all periods, engaged in a wide range of direct and indirect percussive tasks (Evely 1993; Maggi et al. 1994). Made from river cobbles and pebbles of various shapes and sizes, such implements are recognized by their battered and pitted appearance (see Figure 8.4.2). During the Bronze Age, they were employed in new manufacturing activities (Table 8.2).

Pounding tools (vessel-mortars, pestles) were among the first ground stone tools encountered in the archaeological record of the Levant, appearing already in the Upper Paleolithic period; their use coincided with the processing of wild cereals (Wright 1991; see Figure 8.4.3). Grinding tools outnumbered pounding tools in the Pre-Pottery Neolithic Levant, perhaps one result of the transition to farming (Wright 1993). Saddle querns along with handstones remained typical grinding implements throughout the Neolithic and Bronze Age (Runnels 1985b; 1992; Kardulias and Runnels 1995; Samuel 1999; see Figure 8.4.4–8.4.6). In some cases, they were made of imported material transferred over long distances because of the scarcity in suitable resources. This was true at Kitsos Cave in the Aegean, where andesite from Aigina was used for grinding implements (Cohen and Runnels 1981).

Mortars of various shapes (e.g., ring-based, spouted) were put into use in a variety of agricultural and domestic pounding tasks (Runnels 1988; see Figure 8.4.3). Substances were pounded by pestles, that is, stone implements of elongated shape (tapered cylindrical, conical, circular). Although largely utilitarian implements, several Natufian and PPN examples, decorated with carved motifs of goat heads and bovid horns, may have had a symbolic value, used in public feasts for reinforcing inter-communal social ties (Özdogan 1999) or linked to religious beliefs regarding animal domestication.

Other common stone tools include: maceheads, often endowed with symbolic meaning related to status and prestige (Evely 1984; Leighton 1989; Crowfoot Payne 1993; Moundrea-Agrafioti 1996); polishing stones ("polishers") used for pot burnishing, hide softening, etc.; whetstones for sharpening bone, stone, and metal tool edges with the aid of oil or abrasive substances (Evely 1984); molds for casting precious metals and making tools, weapons, sickles, and jewelry (Branigan 1974); "gaming" stones, found in Egypt, the Levant, and Cyprus (Swiny 1980); and various stationary, outsized stone implements such as basins, spouted press beds, slab anvils, and pivot bases for supporting doorposts (Elliot 1991; Blitzer 1995). Other stone artifacts, from the Late Bronze Age, included miniature axes, bow drill cups, spindle whorls, balance weights, and anchors. Lastly, stone vases, figurines, and jewellery (beads, pendants) are found in all periods. Particularly on Cyprus, beads, pendants, small vessels, and figurines were often made of picrolite, a soft, blue and green stone transferred through exchange networks from the Aceramic period onward (Peltenburg 1991). On Minoan Crete several fine stone vases were made from obsidian from Giali in the Aegean, a type of translucent obsidian with white spherules (Betancourt 1999; see Fig. 1).

The Impact of Metal on Stone Technology

What was the impact of the appearance and increasing use of metals, first copper and then bronze, on the long-term use of stone tools? Did stone tools disappear, slowly fade, or continue in use? This issue has been tackled several times in the past, but only occasionally has it been discussed analytically (cf. Runnels 1982; Rosen 1984; 1996; 1997). The key role played by metals and metallurgical technologies in the rise of complex societies is the main reason behind the excessive focus given to metals and the omission of stone technologies in developing models of social change (Renfrew 1967; Heskel 1983). The issue has been examined thoroughly from the perspective of metals (e.g., Hauptmann et al. 1989; Pare 2000; see also the chapter by Kassianidou and Knapp, this volume), whereas usually the lithic perspective is ignored. The presence of obsidian and chert specimens in Geometric and Classical contexts in Greece and Italy, on the other hand, raises the question of whether the tradition of stone use continued down to the pre-industrial era

(Runnels 1982). In the following discussion, I reconsider the same question by placing the stone-metal relationship into a diachronic perspective. The impact of metal on stone technologies can be measured on two levels: first, the impact can be traced physically, by recording the physical or numerical representation (presence/decline) of each of the tool types (Rosen 1996; 1997). The following questions may be addressed: which types disappeared, which types coexisted in both materials, and which continued in stone with no important changes? Different tool types reacted differently to metal through time, and it is critical to understand this temporal aspect of material preference. Secondly, the impact on the kind of activities involved in tool use can be assessed in order to determine which aspects of any given society or economy benefited from the presence and use of metals. These two levels are examined briefly in what follows.

Case I: coexistence of stone and metal types

The following stone tools coexisted with metal finds mainly during the Bronze Age, but in later periods as well: axes and chisels, micro-drills and borers, projectile points and sickles.

Axes and chisels, along with pins and needles, were the earliest tools encountered in metal. Even so, metal examples were neither numerically significant nor widespread during the Late Neolithic and Chalcolithic periods: axes and chisels from pure copper were only found sporadically at sites throughout these periods (Rosen 1997; Zachos and Dousougli 1999), some of them serving as prestige items, transferred through long-distance exchange networks. During the Early Bronze Age (ca. third millennium B.C.), stone axes (flat and shaft-hole) and chisels continued to be used even in sites involved in metals production, for example Poliochni (Bernabo-Brea 1976). In the meantime, a range of new metal types (e.g., the double axe, single axe, flat axe, axe-adze, chisel) came into use. These new types mostly benefited carpentry (for architecture, furniture, shipbuilding), stone dressing, stone bowl carving, and weaponry (Shaw 1973; Killen 1980; Evely 1993; Downey 2001). In the Middle Bronze Age (beginning of second millennium B.C.), stone axes and chisels continued as complementary implements, or were directed to new uses (see Table 8.2). Toward the end of the Late Bronze Age (end of second millennium B.C.), their use seems to have been primarily symbolic (Elliott 1985; 1991). Reused Neolithic or Chalcolithic stone tool specimens continued in use into the Iron Age and Classical and Hellenistic periods, up to the first century B.C. (Leighton 1989; Kardulias and Runnels 1995).

Microlithic stone drills, hafted onto the shafts of bow drills, remained in use during the Early Bronze Age (Rosen 1997). They were gradually replaced by metal drills from the Middle Bronze Age onward (Shaw 1973; Evely 1993; Rosen 1997). The latter benefited seal stone carving (Evely 1993), architecture (Shaw 1973), bead perforation, and timber construction (Killen 1980).

Flint sickle elements of the geometric, denticulated type continued to be used to the end of the Bronze Age, coexisting with metal types especially during the Late

Bronze Age (Branigan 1974). Being more easily accessible through specialized networks, flint sickles lasted in many areas until the Iron Age (ca. tenth-ninth century B.C.) and perhaps down to the historical periods (Runnels 1982).

Stone projectile points coexisted with metal types in many areas. In the Aegean, for example, although metal examples appeared early (e.g., the mica-schist mold for four metal arrowheads in Troy II, Early Bronze Age – Branigan 1974), stone points of the hollow-base type continued into Middle and Late Bronze Age contexts. In Italy, stone arrowheads were collectively made at jasper quarries during the Copper and Early Bronze Ages (Maggi et al. 1994) and continued throughout the Bronze Age. Only in the Levant had flint arrowheads fallen into disuse prior to the Bronze Age, a phenomenon possibly linked to the decline in the importance of hunting (Rosen 1997).

Case 2: the continuation of stone tool types

This category includes ad hoc chipped stone (notched and denticulated flakes, borers, scraping flakes), as well as agricultural and domestic ground stone implements (querns, mortars, polishers, stationary stones, etc.). Other tools continuing in use included whetstones, *pièces esquillées*, abrasive stones, polishers, and stationary stones.

Notched and denticulated flakes as well as flint borers, gravers, and pointed flakes continued to be used throughout the Bronze Age in a variety of domestic activities: light scraping, cutting, drilling, or incising hard or soft materials such as stone, ivory, pottery sherds, and so on (Rosen 1997; Kardulias 1992). The number of notched flakes is surprisingly high in Late Bronze Age contexts (Moundrea-Agrafioti 1990; Coqueugniot 1991; Barker 1995).

Scrapers dropped numerically (Rosen 1997), although they were still present in small numbers after the Early Bronze Age (Runnels 1985a; Coqueugniot 1991; Barker 1995). Hammers were the least frequently replaced implements, given that the basic forms continued in stone and wood (e.g., wooden mallets, known from Egyptian contexts – Killen 1980:18) down into the Bronze Age. The rarity of metal types in Bronze Age contexts (e.g., on Crete–Shaw 1973) is also suggestive of the continuous use of stone types. This is to be expected, given the suitability of stone for hammering tasks.

Lastly, grinders and querns were the longest-lasting stone tool implements. Querns remained the chief agricultural implement, and one of the least inexpensive implements used for grain grinding in any household throughout the Bronze Age and the Classical and Hellenistic periods, and indeed, right down to the present day (Kardulias and Runnels 1995). In these latter periods, saddle querns were carefully hammer-dressed, whereas new, more specialized milling instruments such as hopper mills and rotary querns were introduced (Kardulias and Runnels 1995). Mortars were also long-lasting stone tools, displaying increased standardization over time.

Synthesis

Although stone tools continued to play a role throughout the Bronze Age, their importance responded to the transformation of the meaning of metal in different historical contexts. In the Late Neolithic and Chalcolithic periods, given the limited number and the "symbolic" value of some of the first metal implements (the result of their circulation in long-distance exchange networks – Nakou 1995), metal had almost no effect on stone technology. Most early metal types (axes, chisels, needles, awls, pins, daggers) were metal imitations of already known tool types of stone and bone, used in domestic industries such as wood- and leather-working, as well as for hunting or fighting (Renfrew 1967; Yakar 1984; Gale 1991; Skeates 1993; Zachos and Douzougli 1999). During the Bronze Age, the explosion of metallurgy, followed by transformations in the symbolic connotations of metal objects (e.g., means of personal display – Nakou 1995), led to the production of a variety of new types of axes and chisels, as well as swords, daggers, and spearheads. The three activities that benefited most from this explosion were carpentry, stone dressing, and warfare. As the expansion in metals' use encouraged the rise of new elites and vice versa, certain groups of tools first employed in metal form were directly related to elite interests, notably shipbuilding, architecture, furniture, and weaponry. Because of the relatively "cheap" character of stone, however, several tool types continued to be used alongside and complementary to metal types throughout the Bronze Age. A large portion of other tools, such as querns and mortars, remained unaffected by the introduction and use of metals, because of the suitability of stone (its hardness and polishing action) for grinding, breaking, and building activities. Tools of expedient and domestic function such as borers and denticulates continued to be manufactured in stone (Phillips 1986; Barker 1995). Lastly, plain obsidian and chert blades and flakes may have been reused or made also during the historical periods, an issue that needs further attention (Runnels 1982). In sum, the "replacement" process was a sequential one, carried out in several phases (Rosen 1997). Manipulated by people and social systems in the Bronze Age, the use of metals alternated with stone tool use in various ways through time, depending on several diverse parameters that included metal cost, flint availability, the functional efficiency of metal and stone, and the socio-economic context of production. Future work should help to fill in the details of this interactive process within specific historical contexts.

Conclusion

In sum, this chapter presents the different patterns of exchange, production, and use of chipped and ground stone tools in the Mediterranean during prehistory. Silicates, metamorphics, sedimentary, igneous, and altered volcanics were the main stone types chosen for tool manufacture based on size, mechanical properties, and aesthetic qualities. Fine-grained materials (obsidian, flint of high quality) were transferred as highly prized artifacts to be used as tools through long-distance exchange networks. In several cases these networks were linked to specialized communities or skillful producers (Karabatsoli 1997). Thanks to these networks, brought to light through recent advances in characterization studies (e.g., central Anatolian obsidian sources, M.-C. Cauvin et al. 1998), it is possible to reconstruct movements of people (colonizations), and of artifacts and ideas (trade, acculturation) in the earlier periods, where other types of information (e.g., linguistic, architectural) are lacking. This is the case for the colonization of Cyprus, for example (Peltenburg et al. 2001), or for the exploitation of Anatolian obsidian from two different cultural groups during the PPN period (Binder and Balkan-Atli 2001). Stone tools were used for cutting, drilling, scraping, hammering, grinding, pounding, engraving, reaping, and hunting. Tool forms became more specialized and standardized in the Neolithic and Bronze Age (J. Cauvin 1983; Runnels 1988), but tools were gradually replaced by metal depending on local conditions. Yet, several tool types, being cheaper than their metal counterparts, continued to be used until the pre-industrial period.

The foregoing presentation underscores the many and diverse meanings embedded in stone materials and stone tools during their entire life cycle in prehistory. Because they were products of the earth, and often of mysterious origin, stone materials often were imbued with a mystical character. As products of culturally defined technical traditions, stone tools acted as markers of socio-cultural boundaries or discontinuities. Often they were products of specialized manufacture and use. Because they were transferred through long-distance exchange networks, they were almost certainly regarded as exotic items, ascribing status to their owners. Lastly, when used in non-utilitarian contexts, many of them embodied a high symbolic value. Firmly embedded in their cultural contexts, the meanings of stone tools and stone materials still remain open fields for exploration.

ACKNOWLEDGMENTS

I am grateful to Curtis Runnels and the editors for providing me with the opportunity to write this manuscript. My special gratitude goes to a number of colleagues – R. Tykot, B. Hartenberger, I. Gatsov, N. Kardulias, T. Carter, M. Özdogan, J. Gonzalez Urquijo, D. Papagianni, K. Skourtopoulou, L. Astruc, L. Kassianidou, M. Rosenberg, and S. Chlouveraki – for providing me with references during the course of this research. I also wish to thank A. Hadji for our fruitful discussions on metal technologies, as well as C. Perlès and T. Carter for brief discussions related to Near Eastern lithic industries. This chapter has also benefited during its final stage of preparation from J. Coleman, whom I thank for his valuable comments. Finally, many thanks go to A. Karabatsoli, D. Papagianni, K. Glinou, and Kerill O' Neill for helping me to resolve several translation issues and to A. Sarris and E. Kavountzis for providing me practical assistance during the course of this research. Italian texts were translated by T. Karvounaki. Responsibility for the ideas presented in this chapter belongs entirely to the author.

REFERENCES

Ammerman, Albert J., 1985 The Acconia Survey: Neolithic Settlement and the Obsidian Trade. London: Institute of Archaeology.

Ammerman, Albert J., and Christopher Polglase, 1993 The Exchange of Obsidian at Neolithic Sites in Italy. *In* Trade and Exchange in European Prehistory. F. Healy and C. Scarre, eds. pp. 101–107. Oxbow Monograph 33. Oxford: Oxbow Books.

Anderson-Gerfaud, Patricia C., 1983 A Consideration of the Uses of Certain Backed and "Lustred" Stone Tools from Late Mesolithic and Natufian Levels of Abu Hureyra and Mureybet (Syria). *In* Traces d'Utilisations sur les Outils Neolithiques du Proche-Orient, M.-C. Cauvin, ed. pp. 77–105. Lyon: GIS, Maison de l'Orient.

Anderson, Patricia, Jacques Chabot, and Annelou van Gijin, 2004 The Functional Riddle of 'Glossy' Canaanean Blades and the New Eastem Threshing Sledge. Journal of Mediterranean Archaeology 17:87–130.

Anderson, Patricia C., and M.-L. Inizan, 1994 Utilisation du Tribulum au Début du IIIe Millénaire: des Lames "Cavanéennes" Lustrées à Kutan (Ninive V) dans la Region de Mossoul, Iraq. Paléorient 20(2):85–101.

Anderson, Patricia C., and Françoise Formenti, 1996 Exploring the Use of Abraded Obsidian "Çayönü tools" Using Experimentation, Optical and SEM Microscopy, and EDA Analysis. *In* Archaeometry 94. The Proceedings of the 29th International Symposium on Archaeometry, Ankara, 9–14 May 1994. Ş. Demirci, A. M. Özer, and G. D. Summers, eds. pp. 554–559. Ankara: Tübitak.

Arnold Dieter, 1991 Building in Egypt. Pharaonic Stone Masonry. Oxford: Oxford University Press.

Aston, Barbara G., J. A. Harrell, and Ian Shaw, 2000 Stone. *In* Ancient Egyptian Materials and Technology. P. T. Nicholson and I. Shaw, eds. pp. 5–77. Cambridge: Cambridge University Press.

Astruc, Laurence, 2001 Lithic Tools Involved in the Manufacture of Stone Ornaments and Utilitarian Products at Khirokitia (Cyprus). *In* Beyond Tools. Redefining the PPN Lithic Assemblages of the Levant. Proceedings of the Third Workshop on PPN Chipped Lithic Industries. I. Caneva, C. Lemorini, D. Zampetti, and P. Biagi, eds. pp. 113–127. Berlin: Ex Oriente.

Balkan-Atli, Nur, and G. Der Aprahamian, 1998 Les Nucléus de Kalatepe et Deux Ateliers de Taille en Cappadoce. *In* L'Obsidienne au Proche et Moyen Orient. Du Volcan à l'Outil. M.-C. Cauvin, A. Gourgaud, B. Gratuze, N. Arnaud, G. Poupeau, J.-L. Poidevin, and C. Chataigner, eds. pp. 241–258. British Archaeological Reports, International Series 738. Oxford: Archaeopress.

Balkan-Atli, Nur, Didier Binder, and Marie-Claire Cauvin, 1999 Obsidian: Sources, Workshops and Trade in Central Anatolia. *In* Neolithic in Turkey, the Cradle of Civilization. Mehmet Özdogan and Nezih Başgelen, eds. pp. 133–145. Istanbul: Arkeologi ve Sanat Yayinlari.

Balkan-Atli, Nur, Nurcan Kayacan, Mihriban Özbaşaran, and Semra Yildirim, 2001 Variability in the Neolithic Arrowheads of Central Anatolia (Typological, Technological and Chronological aspects). *In* Beyond Tools. Redefining the PPN Lithic Assemblages of the Levant. Proceedings of the Third Workshop on PPN Chipped Lithic Industries. I. Caneva, C. Lemorini, D. Zampetti, and P. Biagi, eds. pp. 27–43. Berlin: Ex Oriente.

Barfield, Lawrence H., 1999 Neolithic and Copper Age Flint Exploitation in Northern Italy. Universitätsforschungen zur prähistorischen Archäologie 55:245–252.

Barker, Graeme, 1995 A Mediterranean Valley: Landscape Archaeology and Annales History in the Biferno Valley. Leicester: Leicester University Press.

Bar-Yosef, Ofer, 1987 Direct and Indirect Evidence for Hafting in the Epi-palaeolithic and Neolithic of the Southern Levant. In La Main et l'Outil. Manches et Emmanchements Préhistoriques. D. Stordeur, ed. pp. 155–164. Paris: Maison de l'Orient.

Baykal-Seeher, Ayşe, 1996 Die Lithischen Kleinfunde. In Demircihüyük, Volume 4. Die Kleinfunde. pp. 7–206. Mainz: Verlag Phillip Von Zabern.

Bernabò-Brea, Luigi, 1976 Poliochni. Città Preistorica Nell' Isola di Lemnos. Volume 2,1 TESTO. Roma: L'Erma di Bretschneider.

Betancourt, Philip, 1999 The Trade Route for Ghyali Obsidian. In Meletemata. Studies in Aegean Archaeology Presented to Malcolm H. Wiener as He Enters his 65th Year. Philip P. Betancourt, Vassos Karageorghis, Robert Laffineur, and Wolf-Dietrich Niemeier, eds. pp. 171–174. Aegeaum 20. Liège: Université de Liège.

Binder, Didier, 2000 Mesolithic and Neolithic Interaction in Southern France and Northern Italy: New Data and Current Hypotheses. In Europe's First Farmers. T. Douglas Price, ed. pp. 117–143. Cambridge: Cambridge University Press.

Binder, Didier, and Nur Balkan-Atli, 2001 Obsidian Exploitation and Blade Technology at Kömürcü-Kalatepe (Cappadocia, Turkey). In Beyond Tools. Redefining the PPN Lithic Assemblages of the Levant. Proceedings of the Third Workshop on PPN Chipped Lithic Industries. I. Caneva, C. Lemorini, D. Zampetti, and P. Biagi, eds. pp. 1–16. Berlin: Ex Oriente.

Blackman, J., 1986 The Provenience of Obsidian Artifacts from Late Chalcolithic Levels at Aphrodisias. In Prehistoric Aphrodisias. An Account of the Excavations and Artifact Studies. M. Sharp Joukowsky, ed. pp. 279–285. Archaeologia Transatlantica, 3. Louvain: Université Catholique de Louvain.

Blitzer, Harriet, 1995 Minoan Implements and Industries. In Kommos I. The Kommos Region and Houses of the Minoan Town, Part 1. The Kommos Region, Ecology, and Minoan Industries. J. W. Shaw and M. C. Shaw, eds. pp. 403–535. Princeton, NJ: Princeton University Press.

Branigan, Keith, 1974 Aegean Metalwork of the Early and Middle Bronze Age. Oxford: Clarendon Press.

Briois, F., B. Gratuze, and J. Guilaine, 1997 Obsidiennes du Site Néolithique Précéramique de Shillourokambos (Chypre). Paléorient 23:95–112.

Calley, S., 1985 Les Techniques de Taille dans l' Industrie Lithique de Mureybet. Thèse de Doctorat. Lyon: Université de Lyon.

Carter, Tristan, 1994 Southern Aegean Fashion Victims: An Overlooked Aspect of Early Bronze Age Burial Practices. In Stories in Stone. N. Ashton and A. David, eds. pp. 127–144. Occasional Paper 4. London: Lithics Society.

——1998 Through a Glass Darkly: Obsidian and Society in the Southern Aegean Early Bronze Age. Unpublished Ph.D. Dissertation, University College London.

——2004 Mochlos and Melos: A Special Relationship? Creating Identity and Status in Minoan Crete. In Crete beyond the Palaces: Proceedings of the Crete 2000 Conference. P. M. Day, M. S. Mook and J. D. Muhly, eds. Philadelphia: INSTAP Academic Press.

Carter, Tristan, and Mark Ydo, 1996 The Chipped and Ground Stone. In Continuity and Change in a Greek Rural Landscape: The Laconia Survey, Volume 2. W. Cavanagh, J. Crouwel, R. W. V. Catling, and G. Shipley, eds. pp. 141–182. London: British School at Athens.

Cauvin, Jacques, 1983 Typologie et Fonctions des Outils Préhistoriques. Apports de la Tracéologie a un Vieux Débat. *In* Traces d'Utilisations sur les Outils Néolithiques du Proche-Orient. M.-C. Cauvin, ed. pp. 259–274. Lyon: GIS, Maison de l'Orient.

—— 1998 La Signifaction Symbolique de l'Obsidienne. *In* L'Obsidienne au Proche et Moyen Orient. Du Volcan à l' Outil. M.-C. Cauvin, A. Gourgaud, B. Gratuze, N. Arnaud, G. Poupeau, J.-L. Poidevin, and C. Chataigner, eds. pp. 379–382. British Archaeological Reports, International Series 738. Oxford: Archaeopress.

Cauvin, Jacques, Olivier Aurenche, M.-C. Cauvin, and Nur Balkan-Atli, 1999 The Pre-Pottery Site of Cafer Höyük. *In* Neolithic in Turkey, the Cradle of Civilization. Mehmet. Özdogan and Nezih Başgelen, eds. pp. 87–103. Istanbul: Arkeologi ve Sanat Yayinlari.

Cauvin, M.-C., 1983 Les Faucilles Préhistoriques du Proche-Orient. Données Morphologiques et Fonctionnelles. Paléorient 9(1):63–76.

Cauvin, M.-C., A. Gourgaud, B. Gratuze, N. Arnaud, G. Poupeau, J.-L. Poidevin, and C. Chataigner, eds., 1998 L'Obsidienne au Proche et Moyen Orient. Du Volcan à l'Outil. British Archaeological Reports, International Series 738. Oxford: Archaeopress.

Cavena, Isabella, Christina Lemorini, and Daniela Zampetti, 1998 Chipped Stones at Aceramic Çayönü: Technology, Activities, Traditions, Innovations. *In* Light on Top of the Blackhill. Studies Presented to Halet Çambel. G. Arsebük, Machteld Mellink and W. Schirmer, eds. pp. 199–205. Istanbul: Ege Yayinlari.

Clark, J. D., James L. Philips, and P. Staley, 1974 Interpretations of Prehistoric Technology from Ancient Egypt and Other Sources. Paléorient 2:323–388.

Cohen, Ronald, and Curtis Runnels, 1981 The Source of the Kitsos Millstones. *In* La Grotte Préhistorique de Kitsos (Attique). Recherche sur les Grandes Civilisations. N. Lambert, ed. pp. 233–239. Paris: École Française d'Athènes.

Conolly, James, 1999 The Çatalhöyük Flint and Obsidian Industry. Technology and Typology in Context. British Archaeological Reports, International Series 787. Oxford: Archaeopress.

Coqueugniot, Éric, 1983 Analyse Tracéologique d'une Série de Grattoirs et Herminettes de Mureybet (Syrie). *In* Traces d'Utilisations sur les Outils Néolithiques du Proche-Orient. M.-C. Cauvin, ed. pp. 163–176. Lyon: GIS, Maison de l'Orient.

—— 1991 Outillage de Pierre Taillée au Bronze Récent, Ras Shamra 1978–1988. *In* Arts et Industries de la Pierre, Ras-Shamra-Ougarit 6. M. Yon, ed. pp. 127–173. Paris: Éditions Recherche sur les Civilisations.

Crowfoot Payne, Joan, 1993 Catalogue of the Predynastic Egyptian Collection in the Ashmolean Museum. Oxford: Clarendon Press.

Decourt, Jean-Claude, 1998 L'Obsidienne dans les Sources Anciennes. Notes sur l'Histoire du mot et l'Utilisation de la Roche dans l'Antiquité. *In* L'Obsidienne au Proche et Moyen Orient. Du Volcan à l' Outil. M.-C. Cauvin, A. Gourgaud, B. Gratuze, N. Arnaud, G. Poupeau, J.-L. Poidevin, and C. Chataigner, eds. pp. 363–377. British Archaeological Reports, International Series 738. Oxford: Archaeopress.

Downey, C. J., 2001 Prehistoric Tools and the Bronze Age Woodworking Industry. *In* Archaeometry Issues in Greek Prehistory and Antiquity. Y. Bassiakos, E. Aloupi, and Y. Facorellis, eds. pp. 791–797. Athens: Hellenic Society of Archaeometry and Society of Messenian Archaeological Studies.

Elliott, Carolyn, 1981 Observations on Ground Stone Adzes and Axes from Lemba *Lakkous*. Report of the Department of Antiquities Cyprus: 1–23.

—— 1985 Ground Stone Tools from Kition Areas I and II. *In* Excavations at Kition, Volume 5. The Pre-Phoenician Levels, Part 2. Vassos Karageorghis, ed. pp. 295–316. Nicosia: Department of Antiquities, Cyprus.

——1991 The Ground Stone Industry. *In* Arts et Industries de la Pierre, Ras-Shamra-Ougarit 6. M. Yon, ed. pp. 9–80. Paris: Éditions Recherche sur les Civilisations.

Evely, R. D. G., 1980 Some Manufacturing Processes in a Knossian Stone Vase Workshop. British School of Athens 75:127–137.

——1984 The Other Finds of Stone, Clay, Ivory, Faience, Lead etc. *In* The Minoan Unexplored Mansion at Knossos. M. R. Popham, ed. pp. 223–260. London: Thames and Hudson.

——1993 Minoan Crafts: Tools and Techniques. An Introduction. Studies in Mediterranean Archaeology 92.1. Göteborg: Paul Åströms Förlag.

Gale, Noël H., 1991 Metals and Metallurgy in the Chalcolithic Period. Bulletin of the American Schools of Oriental Research 282(2):37–62.

Gatsov, Ivan, 2000 Chipped Stone Assemblages from South Bulgaria and North-West Turkey. *In* Technology, Style and Society. L. Nikolova, ed. pp. 1–28. British Archaeological Reports, International Series 854. Oxford: Archaeopress.

Given, M. and A. Bemard Knapp, 2003 The Sydney Survey Project: Social Approaches to Regional Archaeological Survey. Monumenta Archaeologica 21. Los Angeles, Cotsen Institute of Archaeology, UCLA.

Gomez, B., M. D. Glascock, M. J. Blackman, and I. A. Todd, 1995 Neutron Activation Analysis of Obsidian From Kalavasos-*Tenta*. Journal of Field Archaeology 22:503–508.

Gopher, Avi, 1994 Pottery Neolithic/6th–5th Millennia B.C. Industries of the Southern Levant seen through PPN Glasses. *In* Neolithic Chipped Stone Industries of the Fertile Crescent. H. G. Gebel and S. K. Kozlowski, eds. pp. 563–566. Berlin: Ex Oriente.

Grace, R., 1989–1990 The Use-wear Analysis of Drill Bits from Kumartepe. Anatolica 16:145–150.

Hartenberger, Britt, Steve Rosen, and Timothy Matney, 2000 The Early Bronze Age Blade Workshop at Titris Höyük: Lithic Specialization in an Urban Context. Near Eastern Archaeology 63(1):51–58.

Hartenberger, Britt, and Curtis Runnels, 2001 The Organization of Flaked Stone Production at Bronze Age Lerna. Hesperia 70:255–283.

Hauptmann, Andreas, Ernst Pernicka, and Gunther A. Wagner eds., 1989 Old World Archaeometallurgy. Die Anschnitt, Beiheft 7. Bochum: Deutsches Bergbaumuseum.

Heskel, Dennis, 1983 A Model for the Adoption of Metallurgy in the Ancient Middle East. Current Anthropology 24:362–366.

Holmes, D. L., 1988 The Predynastic Lithic Industries of Badari, Middle Egypt: New Perspectives and Inter-regional Relations. World Archaeology 20:70–86.

——1990 The Flint Axes of Nagada, Egypt: Analysis and Assessment of a Distinctive Predynastic Tool Type. Paléorient 16:1–21.

Inizan, Marie-Louise, and Monique Lechevallier, 1994 L'Adoption du Débitage Laminaire par Pression au Proche-Orient. *In* Neolithic Chipped Stone Industries of the Fertile Crescent. H. G. Gebel and S. K. Kozlowski, eds. pp. 23–32. Berlin: Ex Oriente.

Karabatsoli, Anna, 1997 La Production de l'Industrie Lithique Taillée en Grèce Centrale pendant le Bronze Ancien. These. Paris: Université de Paris X.

Kardulias, P. Nicholas, 1992 The Ecology of Flaked Stone Tool Production in Southern Greece: The Evidence from Agios Stephanos and the Southern Argolid. American Journal of Archaeology 96:421–442.

Kardulias, P. Nicholas, and Curtis Runnels, 1995 Artifact and Assemblage: The Finds from a Regional Survey of the Southern Argolid, Greece. Stanford: Stanford University Press.

Kardulias, P. Nicholas, and Richard W. Yerkes, 1998 Defining the Cypriot Aceramic Neolithic: The Lithic Evidence. Lithic Technology 23:124–138.

Karimali, Evagelia, 1994 The Neolithic Mode of Production and Exchange Reconsidered: Lithic Production and Exchange Patterns in Thessaly, Greece, During the Transitional Late Neolithic-Bronze Age period. Unpublished PhD Dissertation. Boston: Boston University.

——2000 Decoding Inferences in Models of Obsidian Exchange: Contexts of Value Transformation in the Neolithic Aegean. *In* Trade and Production in Premonetary Greece. Acquisition and Distribution of Raw Materials and Finished Products. C. Gillis, C. Risberg, and B. Sjoberg, eds. pp. 9–27. Jonsered: Paul Åströms Förlag.

——2001 Redefining the Variables of Material Abundance and Distance in the Fall-off Models: The Case of Neolithic Thessaly. *In* Archaeometry Issues in Greek Prehistory and Antiquity. Y. Bassiakos, E. Aloupi, and Y. Facorellis, eds. pp. 753–761. Athens: Hellenic Society of Archaeometry and Society of Messenian Archaeological Studies.

——In preparation Inferences and Limitations in Chipped-Stone Modelling: Learning from an Ethnoarchaeological Case (Threshing-Sledge Production in Thessaly, Greece). *In* Acts of the 14th UISPP.

Keeley, Lawrence, 1983 Neolithic Novelties: The View from Ethnography and Microwear Analysis. *In* Traces d'Utilisations sur les Outils Néolithiques du Proche-Orient. M.-C. Cauvin, ed. pp. 251–258. Lyon: GIS, Maison de l'Orient.

Kelterborn, Peter, 1984 Towards Replicating Egyptian Predynastic Flint Knives. Journal of Archaeological Science 11:433–453.

el-Khouli, A., 1978 Egyptian Stone Vessels: Predynastic Period to Dynasty III. Mainz: Philip von Zabern.

Killen, G., 1980 Ancient Egyptian Furniture 4000–1300 B.C. Volume 1. Warminster: Aris and Phillips Ltd.

Kingsnorth, A., 1996 Chipped Stone. *In* Alambra. A Middle Bronze Age Settlement in Cyprus. John E. Coleman, Jane A. Barlow, Marcia K. Mogelonsky, and Kenneth W. Schaar, eds. pp. 178–196. Studies in Mediterranean Archaeology 118. Jonsered: Paul Åströms Förlag.

Kozlowski, Janusz K., 2001 Origin and Evolution of Blade Technologies in the Middle and Early Upper Paleolithic. Mediterranean Archaeology and Archaeometry 1(1):3–18.

Kozlowski, Stefan Karol, 1999 The Eastern Wing of the Fertile Crescent. Late Prehistory of Greater Mesopotamian Lithic Industries. British Archaeological Reports, International Series 760. Oxford: Archaeopress.

Leighton, Robert, 1989 Ground Stone Tools from Serra Orlando (Morgantina) and Stone Axe Studies in Sicily and Southern Italy. Proceedings of the Prehistoric Society 55:135–159.

——1992 Stone Axes and Exchange in South Italian Prehistory: New Evidence from Old Collections. Accordia Research Papers 3:1–28.

Leighton, Robert, and John E. Dixon, 1992 Jade and Greenstone in the Prehistory of Sicily and Southern Italy. Oxford Journal of Archaeology 11:179–200.

Lillios, Katina T., 1997 Groundstone Tools, Competition, and Fission: The Transition from the Copper to the Bronze Age in the Portuguese Lowlands. *In* Encounters and Transformations. The Archaeology of Iberia in Transition. Miriam Balmuth, Antonio Gilman, and L. Prados-Torreira, eds. pp. 25–32. Monographs in Mediterranean Archaeology 7. Sheffield: Sheffield Academic Press.

Luglie, C., 2000 L'Industria su Pietra Scheggiata (vetrine A-B). *In* Le Collezioni Litiche Preistoriche dell' Universita di Cagliari. E. Atzeni, ed. pp. 17–27. Cagliari: Edizioni AV.

Maggi, Roberto, Nadia Campana, Fabio Negrino, and Caterina Ottomano, 1994 The Quarrying and Workshop Site of Valley Lagorara (Liguria–Italy). *In* Accordia Research

Paper 5. Elizabeth Herring, Ruth Whitehouse, and John Wilkins, eds. pp. 73–96. London: Accordia Research Centre.

McCartney, Carole, 2002 Women's Knives. *In* Engendering Aphrodite. Women and Society in Ancient Cyprus. Diane Bolger and Nancy Serwint, eds. pp. 237–249. Cyprus American Archaeological Research Institute, Monograph 3. ASOR Archaeological Reports 7. Boston: American Schools of Oriental Research.

Michailidou, Anna, 1993–1994 Investigating Metal Technology in a Settlement. The Case of Akrotiri at Thera. Archaegnosia 8:165–180.

Mogelonsky, Marcia K., 1996 Ground Stone. *In* Alambra. A Middle Bronze Age Settlement in Cyprus. *In* Alambra. A Middle Bronze Age Settlement in Cyprus. J. E. Coleman, J. A. Barlow, M. K. Mogelonsky, and K. W. Schaar, eds. pp. 143–177. Studies in Mediterranean Archaeology 118. Jonsered: Paul Åströms Förlag.

Mortensen, Peter, 1970 Chipped Stone Industry. *In* Excavations at Hacilar. James Mellaart, ed. pp. 153–157. Edinburgh: Edinburgh University Press.

Moundrea-Agrafioti, H. Antikleia, 1990 Akrotiri, the Chipped Stone Industry: Reduction Techniques and Tools of the LC I Phase. *In* Thera and the Aegean World III. Volume 1. D. A. Hardy, Christos G. Doumas, and J. A Sakellarakis, eds. pp. 390–406. London: The Thera Foundation.

—— 1992 Ergaleia apo Leiasmeno Litho. *In* Minoikos kai Ellinikos Politismos apo tin Sillogi Mitsotaki, pp. 174–80. Athina: Idrima Goulandri-Mouseio Kikladikis Texnis.

—— 1996 Tools. *In* Neolithic Culture in Greece. G. A. Papathanassopoulos, ed. pp. 103–106. Athens: Nicholas P. Goulandris Foundation, Museum of Cycladic Art.

—— 1997 I Lithotexnia tis Poliochnis kai I Thesi tis os pros tis Ergaliotexnion tou Apokrousmenou Lithou tis Proimis Epoxis tou Xalkou. *In* I Poliocni kai I Proimi Epoxi tou Xalkou sto Vorio Aigaio. Christos G. Doumas and V. La Rosa, eds. pp. 168–194. Athens: Scuola Archaeologica Italiana di Atene, University of Athens.

Moundrea-Agrafioti, H. Antikleia, and Charalambos Gnardellis, 1994 Classification des Outils Tranchants Thessaliens en Pierre Polie par les Méthodes Multidimensionnelles. *In* La Thessalie. Quinze Années de Recherches Archéologiques, 1975–1990. Bilans et Perspectives, Vol. 1. pp. 189–200. Athens: Ministère de la Culture, Éditions Kapon.

Nakou, Georgia, 1995 The Cutting Edge: A New Look at Early Aegean Metallurgy. Journal of Mediterranean Archaeology 8:1–32.

Nicoletti, Fabrizio, 1996 Le Industrie Litiche Oloceniche: Forme, Materie Prime e Aspetti Economici. *In* Early Societies in Sicily: New Developments in Archaeological Research. Robert Leighton, ed. pp. 57–70. London: Accordia Research Centre.

Nishiaki, Yoshihiro, 2000 Lithic Technology of Neolithic Syria. British Archaeological Reports, International Series 840. Oxford: Archaeopress.

Özdogan, Asli, 1999 Çayönü. *In* Neolithic in Turkey, the Cradle of Civilization. M. Özdogan and N. Başgelen, eds. pp. 35–64. Istanbul: Arkeologi ve Sanat Yayinlari.

Papagianni, Dimitra, 1997 Late Neolithic Flint Technologies in Cyprus. Lithics: The Newsletter of the Lithic Studies Society 17/18:70–81.

Pare, Christopher F. E., ed., 2000 Metals Make the World Go Round: The Supply and Circulation of Metals in Bronze Age Europe. Oxford: Oxbow Books.

Parkinson, William A, 1999 Chipping away at a Mycenean Economy. Obsidian Exchange, Linear B and Palatial Control in Late Bronze Age Messenia. *In* Rethinking Mycenean Palaces: New Interpretations of an Old Idea. W. Parkinson and M. Galaty, eds. pp. 73–85. Los Angeles: UCLA Institute of Archaeology.

Pearlman David, 1984 Threshing Sledges in the Eastern Mediterranean: Ethnoarchaeology with Chert Knappers. Unpublished MA Thesis. Minneapolis: University of Minnesota.

Pélegrin, Jacques, 1990 Prehistoric Lithic Technology: Some Aspects of Research. Archaeological Review from Cambridge 9:116–125.

Pélegrin, Jacques, and M. Otte, 1992 Einige Bemerkungen zur Präparations- und Ausbeuttechnik der Kernsteine aus Raum 29. *In* Hassek Höyük. Naturwissenschaftliche Untersuchungen und Lithische Industrie. M. R. Behm-Blancke, ed. pp. 219–224. Tübingen: Ernst Wasmuth Verlag.

Peltenburg, Edgar, 1991 Local Exchange in Prehistoric Cyprus: An Initial Assessment of Picrolite. Bulletin of the American Schools of Oriental Research 282/283:107–126.

Peltenburg, Edgar, Paul Croft, Adam Jackson, Carole McCartney, and Mary Anne Murray, 2001 Well-Established Colonists: Mylouthkia 1 and the Cypro-Pre-Pottery Neolithic B. *In* The Earliest Prehistory of Cyprus. From Colonization to Exploitation. S. Swiny, ed. pp. 61–86. Cyprus American Archaeological Research Institute, Monograph 3. ASOR Archaeological Reports 7. Boston: American Schools of Oriental Research.

Perlès, Catherine, 1990 L'Outillage de Pierre Taillée Néolithique en Grèce: Approvisionnement et Exploitation des Matières Premières. Bulletin de Correspondance Hellénique 114:1–42.

—— 1992 Systems of Exchange and Organization of Production in Neolithic Greece. Journal of Mediterranean Archaeology 5:115–164.

—— 1999 Long-term Perspectives on the Occupation of the Franchthi Cave: Continuity and Discontinuity. *In* The Paleolithic Archaeology of Greece and Adjacent Areas. G. N. Bailey, E. Adam, E. Panagopoulou, C. Perlès, and K. Zachos, eds. pp. 311–319. London: British School at Athens.

—— 2001 The Early Neolithic in Greece. Cambridge: Cambridge University Press.

Perlès, Catherine, and Patrick Vaughan, 1983 Pièces Lustrées, Travail des Plantes et Moissons à Franchthi (X^e-IVe Millénium B.C.). *In* Traces d'Utilisations sur les Outils Néolithiques du Proche-Orient. M.-C. Cauvin, ed. pp. 209–224. Lyon: GIS, Maison de l'Orient.

Perlès, Catherine, and K. D. Vitelli, 1999 Craft Specialization in the Greek Neolithic. *In* Neolithic Society in Greece. P. Halstead, ed. pp. 96–107. Sheffield: Sheffield Academic Press.

Pernicka, E. J. Keller, G. Rapp, and T. Ercan, 1996 Provenance of late Neolithic and Early Bronze Age Obsidian Artifacts from the Troad. *In* Archaeometry 94. The Proceedings of the 29th International Symposium on Archaeometry, Ankara, 9–14 May 1994. Ş. Ok. Demirci, A. M. Özer and G. D. Summers, eds. pp. 515–519. Ankara: Tübitak.

Pernicka E., J. Keller, and M.-C. Cauvin, 1997 Obsidian from Anatolian Sources in the Neolithic of the Middle Euphrates Region (Syria). Paléorient 23:113–122.

Pétrequin, P., and A.-M. Pétrequin, 1993 Ecologie d'un Outil: la Hache de Pierre en Irian Jaya (Indonésie). Monographies du CRÁ 12. Paris: Editions de CNRS.

Phillips, Patricia, 1986 Sárdara (Cagliari). Preliminary Report of Excavations 1975–1978 of the Nuraghe Ortu Còmidu. Notizie degli Scavi 37:353–410.

Renfrew, Colin, 1967 Cycladic Metallurgy and the Aegean Early Bronze Age. American Journal of Archaeology 71:1–20.

Renfrew, Colin, J. R. Cann, and J. E. Dixon, 1965 Obsidian in the Aegean. Annual of the British School at Athens 60:225–247.

—— 1966 Obsidian and Early Cultural Contact in the Near East. Proceedings of the Prehistoric Society 32:30–72.

Renfrew, Colin, J. E. Dixon, and J. R. Cann, 1968 Further Analysis of Near Eastern Obsidians. Proceedings of the Prehistoric Society 34:319–331.

Roodenberg, J. J., 1983 Traces d'Utilisation sur les Haches Polies de Bouqras (Syrie). *In* Traces d'Utilisations sur les Outils Néolithiques du Proche-Orient. M.-C. Cauvin, ed. pp. 177–188. Lyon: GIS, Maison de l'Orient.

Rosen, Steven A., 1984 The Adoption of Metallurgy in the Levant: A Lithic Perspective. Current Anthropology 25:504–505.

—— 1996 The Decline and Fall of Flint. *In* Stone Tools, Theoretical Insights into Human Prehistory. G. H. Odell, ed. pp. 129–158. Beersheva, Israel: University of the Negev.

—— 1997 Lithics after the Stone Age. A Handbook of Stone Tools from the Levant. Thousand Oaks, CA: Altamira Press.

Roux, Valentine, and Danièla Corbetta, 1989 The Potter's Wheel. Craft Specialization and Technical Competence. Oxford: Oxford and IBH Publishing Company.

Runnels, Curtis, 1982 Flaked Stone Artifacts in Greece during the Historical Period. Journal of Field Archaeology 9:363–373.

—— 1985a The Bronze-Age Flaked-stone Industries from Lerna: A Preliminary Report. American Journal of Archaeology 54:357–391.

—— 1985b Trade and the Demand for Millstones in Southern Greece in the Neolithic and the Early Bronze Age. *In* Prehistoric Production and Exchange. The Aegean and Eastern Mediterranean. A. Bernard Knapp and Tamara Stech, eds. pp. 30–43. Monograph 25. Los Angeles: Institute of Archaeology, University of California, Los Angeles.

—— 1985c Lithic Studies: Some Theoretical Considerations. Lithic Technology 14(3):100–106.

—— 1988 Early Bronze-Age Stone Mortars from the Southern Argolid. Hesperia 57: 257–272.

—— 1992 The Millstones. *In* Well Built Mycenae. The Helleno-British Excavation within the Citadel at Mycenae, 1959–1969. William D. Taylour and Elizabeth B. French, eds. pp. 35–38. Fascicule 27. Oxford: Oxbow Books.

Samuel, Delwen, 1999 Bread Making and Social Interactions at the Amanda Workmen's Village, Egypt. World Archaeology 31:121–124.

Shakun, Natalia, 1999 Evolution of Agricultural Techniques in Eneolithic (Chalcolithic) Bulgaria: Data from Use-wear Analysis. *In* Prehistory of Agriculture: New Experimental and Ethnographic Approaches. Patricia C. Anderson, ed. pp. 199–210. Los Angeles: University of California Press.

Shaw, Joseph W., 1973 Minoan Architecture: Materials and Techniques. Annuario Della Scuola Archeologica di Atene e Delle Missioni Italiane in Oriente 33:5–256.

Skeates, Robin, 1993 Early Metal-Use in the Central Mediterranean Region. Accordia Research Paper 4. Elizabeth Herring, Ruth Whitehouse, and John Wilkins, eds. pp. 5–36. London: Accordia Research Centre.

—— 2002 Axe Aesthetics: Stone Axes and Visual Culture in Prehistoric Malta. Oxford Journal of Archaeology 21:13–22.

Skourtopoulou, Katerina, 1999 The Chipped Stone from Makriyalos: A Preliminary Report. *In* Neolithic Society in Greece. Paul Halstead, ed. pp. 121–127. Sheffield: Sheffield Academic Press.

Stroulia, Anna, 2003 Ground Stone Celts from Franchthi Cave. A Close Look. Hesperia 72:1–30.

Swiny, Stuart, 1980 Bronze Age Gaming Stones From Cyprus. Report of the Department of Antiquities Cyprus. pp. 54–78.

Tartaron, Thomas, Curtis Runnels, and Evagelia Karimali, 1999 Prolegomena to the Study of Bronze Age Flaked Stone in Southern Epirus. Meletemata. Studies in Aegean

Archaeology Presented to Malcolm Wiener as He Enters his 65th Year. Philip P. Betancourt, Vassos Karageorghis, Robert Laffineur, and Wolf-Dietrich Niemeier, eds. pp. 819–825. Aegeaum 20. Liège: Université de Liège.

Torrence, Robin, 1986 Production and Exchange of Stone Tools. Prehistoric Obsidian Exchange. Cambridge: Cambridge University Press.

Tsountas, Chistos, 1908 Ai Proistorikai Akropoleis Diminiou kai Sesklou. Athens: Sakellariou.

Tykot, Robert H., 1996 Obsidian Procurement and Distribution in the Central and Western Mediterranean. Journal of Mediterranean Archaeology 9:39–82.

—— 1999 Islands in the Stream. Stone Age Cultural Dynamics in Sardinia and Corsica. In Social Dynamics of the Prehistoric Central Mediterranean. Robert H. Tykot, Jonathan Morter, and John E. Robb, eds. pp. 67–77. Accordia Specialist Studies on the Mediterranean, Vol. 3. London: Accordia Research Centre.

Wagner, Gunther, and Gerd Weisgerber, 1985 Silber, Blei and Gold auf Sifnos. Bochum: Deutsches Bergbaumuseum.

Waldren, William, Edward Sanders, A. C. Conesa, and Jaume Coll, 1984 The Lithic Industry of the Balearic Islands. In The Deya Conference of Prehistory. Part 3: Early Settlement in the Western Mediterranean Islands and their Peripheral Areas. William H. Waldren, Robert Chapman, James Lewthwaite, and Rex-Claire Kennard, eds. pp. 859–869. British Archaeological Reports, International Series, 229. Oxford: British Archaeological Reports.

Whittaker, John C., 1999 Alonia: The Ethnoarchaeology of Cypriot Threshing Floors. Journal of Mediterranean Archaeology 12:7–25.

Williams-Thorpe, Olwyn, 1995 Obsidian in the Mediterranean and the Near East: A Provenancing Success Story. Archaeometry 37:217–248.

Whittle, Alasdair, 1995 Gifts from the Earth: Symbolic Dimensions of the Use and Production of Neolithic Flint and Stone Axes. Archaeologia Polona 33:247–259.

Wright, Katherine I., 1991 The Origins and Development of Ground Stone Assemblages in Late Pleistocene Southwest Asia. Paléorient 17:19–45.

Wright, Katherine I., 1993 Early Holocene Ground Stone Assemblages in the Levant. Levant 25:93–111.

Yakar, Jak, 1984 Regional and Local Schools of Metal Work in Early Bronze Age Anatolia. Part I. Anatolian Studies 34:59–86.

Zachos, Konstantinos, and Angelika Douzougli, 1999 Aegean Metallurgy: How Early and how Independent? In Meletemata. Studies in Aegean Archaeology Presented to M. Wiener as He Enters his 65th Year. Philip P. Betancourt, Vassos Karageorghis, Robert Laffineur, and Wolf-Dietrich Niemeier, eds. pp. 959–968. Aegeaum 20. Liège: Université de Liège.

9

Archaeometallurgy in the Mediterranean: The Social Context of Mining, Technology, and Trade

*Vasiliki Kassianidou
and A. Bernard Knapp*

Introduction

Throughout the Mediterranean world, mainland zones of mineral wealth and islands of volcanic origin often enjoyed special prominence because of their raw materials. Other islands and mainland ports became important because of their strategic location – whether as convenient stopovers for merchants involved in long-distance trade, or as stepping stones to other islands and ports. Such places often retained their status long after demand for certain resources dried up, or when the focus and direction of regional trade shifted. Viable and ongoing external links usually required not just surplus products or resources available for exchange, but more importantly community alliances and even kin-based relations. As often as not, long-distance contacts resulted in foreign domination and the relentless exploitation of both mainland and insular resources. The overexploitation of metals and other minerals particularly affected Mediterranean islands, both large and small, whose inhabitants otherwise did not exceed the carrying capacity of the land that sustained them. The Mediterranean "triad" of olives, grapes, and figs, as well as wheat, may have served as commodities in their own right, but the more common and most profitable items of trade throughout the Mediterranean were minerals, raw materials, essential goods, and luxury items in demand.

In this chapter, we examine two components of these Mediterranean systems of production, distribution, and consumption: mining and metallurgy – and some of their social, technological, and spatial aspects. We begin with a brief overview of the origins of metallurgy in Anatolia and subsequent developments in the Mediterranean. We continue with detailed consideration of the empirical evidence for the production and use of specific metals throughout the Mediterranean. We then attempt to integrate these material factors of Mediterranean metallurgy by considering their social and technological contexts – including the mining community, and by viewing prehistoric landscapes of mining and metallurgical production. We discuss the role of metallurgy within prehistoric Mediterranean societies – including the Bronze Age trade in metals – and conclude with some more general statements on the role and impact of metals and metallurgy on Mediterranean peoples, production, and trade.

Background: Anatolia and the Mediterranean

The archaeometallurgy of the Old World has long formed a topic of specialized interest for metallurgists and historians as well as archaeologists (e.g., Hauptmann et al. 1989; Maddin 1988; Muhly 1973; Pigott 1999a; Stöllner et al. 2003; Yalçin 2000a; 2002). The primacy of Anatolia, and in particular the eighth millennium B.C. site of Çayönü Tepesi, in the emergence and development of metallurgy currently is not in question (Çambel and Braidwood 1980; Maddin et al. 1991; Muhly 1989a; Stech 1999:60–61; Yalçin 2000b). Yener (2000), moreover, maintains that copper sulphide ores were being smelted in Anatolia by the fifth millennium B.C. In neighboring Mesopotamia and on the Iranian Plateau, finds are not so numerous as in Anatolia, and date to the seventh-sixth millennia B.C. In all three areas, however, early developments in the exploitation and use of native copper led from a sophisticated reduction of copper oxides and arsenical ores (fifth-fourth millennia B.C.) to a full-fledged pyrotechnological era (third millennium B.C.) when copper was smelted and alloyed, first with arsenic and later with tin, to produce bronze on a much more widespread and intensive scale. Recent studies by Stech (1999), Pigott (1999b), Yalçin (2000b) and Yener (2000) have very usefully outlined the processes that form the technological backdrop and overall context in which we must consider mining and metallurgy in the Bronze Age Mediterranean. Although we will not pursue here specific questions of origin or diffusion (Muhly 1988:2–3), present evidence indicates that the production and use of copper and its alloys spread throughout the Mediterranean from east to west. Several lines of argument, however, suggest independent developments of metallurgy in the Balkans (and thence to the Aegean – Muhly 1988:8–9; 1999:15), and in southeast Spain (Delibes de Castro et al. 1996; Diaz-Andreu and Montero Ruiz 2000:116) as well as the Balearics (Calvo Trias and Guerrero Ayuso 2002; Ramis et al., n.d.).

In contrast to Anatolia and the Near East, the earliest stages in the development of Mediterranean metallurgy appear only after about 5500 B.C. Muhly (1985a:109; 1996b; 1999:15; 2002:77–79) maintains that Aegean metallurgy has its roots and closest parallels in the Balkans, where a strong metalworking tradition had developed much earlier. During the Late Neolithic of the Aegean (ca. 5500–4500 B.C.), pins of copper turn up at Dikili Tash, Paradeissos, and Kitsos Cave, while two small daggers have been recovered from Ayia Marina in Phocis (Muhly 2002:77). It was only during the following, Final Neolithic period (ca. 4500–3700 B.C. – Johnson

1999), however, that Aegean metallurgy began to flourish (Muhly 1996b; 2002:77). Copper, gold, silver, and lead artifacts have been recovered from at least twelve different sites of this period, including large assemblages of metal finds at sites such as Zas Cave on Naxos (Demoule and Perlès 1993:395; Zachos 1999:154, 158–161; Muhly 2002:77–79). Slag and crucibles from Sitagroi III, together with crucibles from Kephala and Giali, provide clear evidence from the Final Neolithic for metalworking and perhaps even smelting (Muhly 1985a:110–114; 2002:77). Gold beads, pendants, and ear-rings have been recovered from Sitagroi, Sesklo, Dikili Tas, Dimitra, Alepotrypa, and other Final Neolithic sites within the Aegean (Demakopolou 1998:17–18; McGeehan Liritzis 1996; Muhly 1985a:112, 2002:78). The extraordinary discovery of a hoard containing 53 pieces of gold jewelry – looted from its archaeological context – has increased dramatically the known number of Neolithic gold artifacts from Greece (Demakopolou 1998:15; Mangou et al. 1998:45).

By the beginning of the Bronze Age (about 3000 B.C.), in tandem with developments in seafaring, the intensification of trade, and the emergence of the Cycladic culture, metallurgy truly began to flourish in the Aegean. In the Levant (Jordan), excavations at Khirbat Hamra Ifdan in the mining district of Feinan have revealed evidence of an Early Bronze Age workshop dedicated to the production of (unalloyed) copper (Levy et al. 2002), while analytical work on a small hoard of axes from Early Bronze II Pella indicates that they were made from copper consistent with production from ore deposits in Cyprus and Anatolia, as well as the southern Levant (Philip et al. 2003). These new discoveries highlight both the complexity and extent of the ores and metals circulating in the early third millennium B.C. (also Genz and Hauptmann 2002), and suggest that the internationalism usually associated with the metals trade in the second millennium B.C. actually had much earlier antecedents (Philip 1999:50).

On Cyprus, the earliest copper artifacts (about 3500 B.C.) include a small hook and a plaque from the settlement at Kissonerga *Mylouthkia*, and a spiral spacer bead from the cemetery of Souskiou *Vathyrkakas* (Muhly 1991a:357). From Late Chalcolithic Kissonerga *Mosphilia* (period 4), six metal objects, ore consistent with production from local sources, and two possible crucibles suggest that extractive metallurgy and metalworking from local ores was under way by this time (Peltenburg et al. 1998:188–189). Fewer than twenty metal artifacts can be dated to the Chalcolithic period overall, between about 3900 and 2600 B.C. (Muhly 1989a:1; 1991a:358–359). Although this situation may result from the limited number of excavated Chalcolithic sites, it seems clear that Cyprus played no significant role in the inception of Mediterranean metallurgy. Only when the technology for smelting sulphide ores was developed, early in the second millennium B.C., would Cyprus begin to assume its preeminent role in copper production and trade throughout the Mediterranean.

In the central Mediterranean, with the exception of two axes from Italian Middle Neolithic contexts, the introduction of metalworking is dated to the Late and Final Neolithic (4300–3500 B.C.), when copper awls are found throughout the Italian mainland (Pearce 2000:67–68). During the Final Neolithic, the discovery in the south Alpine Trentino area of ancient mines and metallurgical debris – slag, furnaces, crucibles and tuyères – indicates a flourishing metallurgical industry exploiting local mineral resources (Giardino 2000a:57).

The beginning of metals' use in Sardinia is contemporary with developments on mainland Italy and in the Aeolian islands, areas with which Sardinia was closely linked because of the earlier, well-developed trade in obsidian (Lo Schiavo 1988:92). The earliest metal artifacts from Sardinia date to the Late Neolithic Ozieri culture, late fifth or early fourth millennium B.C. (Lo Schiavo 1986:231; Sanna et al. 2003). The discovery of silver artifacts from this period implies very early smelting practice (Lo Schiavo 1986:232). Although Sardinia only began to produce and use metal artifacts at a relatively late date, like Cyprus it became an important metallurgical center during the Bronze Age, when an abundance of high quality metalwork, metallic artifacts, crucibles, and molds is found in nearly every excavated Nuragic site (Lo Schiavo 1988:98–101, 1998).

On the Iberian peninsula, one of Europe's richest metal-producing regions, metallurgy probably developed independently. Although Renfrew (1967a:276–278, 284) argued long ago that Iberian metallurgy had no connection with colonization from the eastern Mediterranean, only recently have new excavations and archaeometallurgical studies provided the evidence to support his argument (e.g., Delibes de Castro et al. 1996). Rescue excavations at Cerro Virtud in the Almeria area (first half of the fifth millennium B.C.) recovered fragments of a ceramic vessel, argued to have been used for smelting copper ores (Ruiz Tabaoda and Montero Ruiz 1999:897). This discovery pushes back the earliest evidence for metalworking in Iberia by 1,000 years; even so, Chapman (1990:46, 2003:114, 119) maintains that the developed Iberian Copper Age only began with the advent of the Los Millares culture in the second half of the third millennium B.C. Recent evidence from the Balearics, in particular Mallorca, indicates that the initial stages of copper metallurgy developed there during the "Chalcolithic" period (around 2000 B.C.) (Calvo Trias and Guerrero Ayuso 2002; Ramis et al., n.d.). From the Copper Age onwards, the region's rich and varied archaeometallurgical record shows that metallurgy continued to thrive in Iberia.

Metals and Metal Technology

Copper and bronze

Excavations throughout the Mediterranean have revealed hundreds of mines and smelting workshops as well as the debris associated with the prehistoric extraction of copper from its minerals (Figure 9.1). Copper ore deposits are found in several regions that flank the Mediterranean, most of which were exploited already in prehistoric times. Amongst Anatolia's 91 recorded copper ore deposits, 36 reveal evidence of prehistoric mining (Wagner and Öztunali 2000:31). The main deposits are concentrated in the Troad in the northwest, in the Pontus region along the Black Sea coast, and in central-eastern Anatolia (Wagner and Öztunali 2000:35–53;

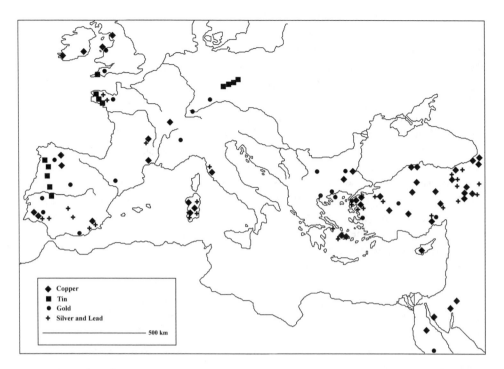

Figure 9.1 Map of the Mediterranean showing the location of principal ore deposits. Map drawn by Vasiliki Kassianidou

Wagner et al. 2003). Recent excavations in eastern Thrace suggest that this area – intermediate between Anatolia, the Balkans, and the Aegean – may also have been an early center in the exploitation of copper minerals, especially malachite (Özdogan and Parzinger 2000).

In the Levant, there are rich copper sources in Jordan's area of Feinan, east of the Wadi Arabah, and in Timna in Israel, which lies 150 kilometers south of Feinan and west of the same wadi. Mining and smelting started at least as early as the Chalcolithic period in Feinan (Genz and Hauptmann 2002:150–152; Hauptmann 1989:122). This area has impressive remains of both prehistoric mines and smelting workshops (Hauptmann 2000) and became one of the most important sources of Near Eastern copper during the Early Bronze Age, about 2900–2200 B.C. (Levy et al. 2002:427). Timna is one of the most intensively and systematically studied copper-producing regions, with mines, copper smelting workshops, mining settlements, and sanctuaries, many of which are prehistoric (Rothenberg 1988; 1999). Also in the Sinai, but to the southwest of Timna, lies Serabit el Khadim, an important source of copper (as well as turquoise) exploited by the Egyptians from the Old Kingdom onward. In Egypt proper there are copper deposits along the whole length of the eastern desert and south into Nubia (Ogden 2001:149–150).

The island of Cyprus is still considered today one of the richest countries in copper per surface area in the world, with the main ore deposits located in the foothills of the Troodos Mountains (Constantinou 1982:15). Because these are sulphide ore deposits, their exploitation came late in comparison with neighboring regions. By the Late Bronze Age (after about 1600 B.C.), however, once the technology of treating such ores had become widely known and practiced, Cyprus emerged as one of the most important sources of copper throughout the Mediterranean (Knapp 1989; 1990b; Muhly 1989b; 1991b; 1996a).

The Aegean region is also rich in copper. The Cycladic islands of Andros, Syros, Paros, Seriphos, and Kythnos all have copper ore deposits that were exploited in antiquity (Gale et al. 1985:82). The remains of an Early Bronze Age smelting site on Kythnos have now been very thoroughly examined (Bassiakos and Philaniotou-Hadjianastasiou in press; Stos Gale et al. 1988). Because the island of Crete has no copper deposits, the ore smelted at Chrysokamino – a Final Neolithic-Early Bronze Age smelting workshop on the northeast coast (Betancourt et al. 1999:363) – most likely originated in one of the Cycladic islands. On the Greek mainland, it has been suggested that limited amounts of copper were exploited during the Bronze Age from mines at Laurion in Attica, best known for their argentiferous lead (Gale et al. 1985:82; Gale and Stos Gale 1982). Although copper mineralization exists at Laurion, no archaeological evidence (e.g., copper slag or the remains of copper smelting furnaces) has yet been found to indicate that it was exploited at any time in antiquity.

On the Italian peninsula, important copper deposits exist in Tuscany (Tylecote 1992:27). Sardinia is also rich in copper, with substantial deposits in the southwest and the center of the island (Lo Schiavo 1988:98; Sanna et al. 2003). Copper metalworking was highly developed on Sardinia during the Late Bronze Age, as is evident from numerous finds of ingots, molds, and bronze artifacts (Webster 1996:136). Although the copper industry was most likely based on the exploitation of local ore deposits (Lo Schiavo 1988:101), Sardinia has yet to reveal a single smelting site and has produced only small amounts of slag, none of which was clearly the result of smelting.

In France, copper ore deposits are known in the Central Massif and in Jura near Geromagny but the best evidence for prehistoric copper mining comes from Cabrières in Hérault, near Montpelier (Forbes 1972:16; Tylecote 1987:33). The Iberian peninsula is also very rich in copper, with important deposits in the area of Rio Tinto in Andalusia, in the provinces of Asturias and Leon in the north, in the southern Meseta (Diaz-Andreu and Montero Ruiz 2000:118–121), and in the Almeria region in the southeast (Montero Ruiz 1993). The last is also the region where Iberian copper metallurgy seems to have originated, presumably independently (Ruiz Taboada and Montero Ruiz 1999:902). Detailed discussion of prehistoric copper mines in Spain is presented in a forthcoming paper by Montero Ruiz and Rodriguez de la Esperanze (in press).

The Mediterranean archaeometallurgical record shows an astonishing variety of installations and instruments used to extract copper from its minerals. The materials used, typically local refractory clays and stones, are the same but the shapes of the diverse components used in the installation – furnaces, tuyères, bellows – vary considerably.

It has been suggested that the Early Bronze Age furnaces from the Feinan may have been wind operated (Hauptmann 2000:148–155). Intriguing, perforated ceramic fragments found at the copper smelting site of Chrysokamino on Crete (Betancourt et al. 1999:354) and similar finds reported from prehistoric smelting sites on the Cycladic island of Kythnos (Bassiakos and Philaniotou-Hadjianastasiou, in press) have been seen as components of the furnace wall. Muhly (personal communication, August 2003) now regards these as chimneys that would have been placed on top of the furnaces. Whatever the truth may be about these wind-operated installations, archaeological evidence shows that, by the Bronze Age, tuyères were used in combination with bellows to induce a draft in the furnace and raise the temperature required for smelting. Again there is great variety in the shapes of tuyères (Tylecote 1987:115–123): in Late Bronze Age Timna the tuyères were short, wide cones made of refractory material and incorporated in the furnace wall (Rothenberg, 1990:8). Contemporary smelting furnaces in Cyprus, however, were operated with the help of long tubular ceramic tuyères, some of which were bent and presumably introduced air into the furnace from the top (Knapp et al. 1999:139–140; Tylecote 1987:118) (Figure 9.2). Foot-operated, ceramic pot bellows are shown on Egyptian tomb wall paintings, the best example being a scene from the 15th century B.C. tomb of Rekhmire which portrays the casting of bronze doors for the temple of Amun (Tylecote 1992:23). Similar examples have been found at several sites in the eastern Mediterranean, but their shape and size suggest that they would have been hand-operated (Davey 1979:104–105, 110).

The need to produce a final product of standard quality, shape, and weight was understood early on and ingot molds dating to the Early Bronze Age have been found at several sites. Excavations at Khirbat Hamra Ifdan in Jordan's Feinan mining district, for example, have revealed a well-organized copper-producing workshop. Among the finds were numerous molds for casting crescent-shaped ingots (Levy et al. 2002:430), one of many different ingot types used in the Bronze Age. Ingots from the Bronze Age show variety not only in shape but also in weight, depending on the standard used in the areas where they were produced. This is perhaps best exemplified by the cargo of the 14th century B.C. Uluburun shipwreck, off the southern coast of Turkey: the finds include oxhide ingots (the most characteristic shape of the Late Bronze Age) (Figure 9.3), round plano-convex ingots, several oval plano-convex ingots, and some ingot shapes previously unattested, for example, two-handled oxhide ingots (Pulak 1998:193; 2000: 140–145).

From the beginning of the Bronze Age onward, in certain areas of the Mediterranean, copper metal came to be mixed with arsenic and later with tin to produce an alloy that had much better mechanical and physical properties. But were these arsenical bronzes intentionally or accidentally produced? How was arsenical bronze prepared, since native arsenic is rare and the metal could not have been produced in antiquity (Tylecote 1987:43; Craddock 1995:284)? Two schools of thought have attempted to answer these key questions. The first argues that arsenical bronze was

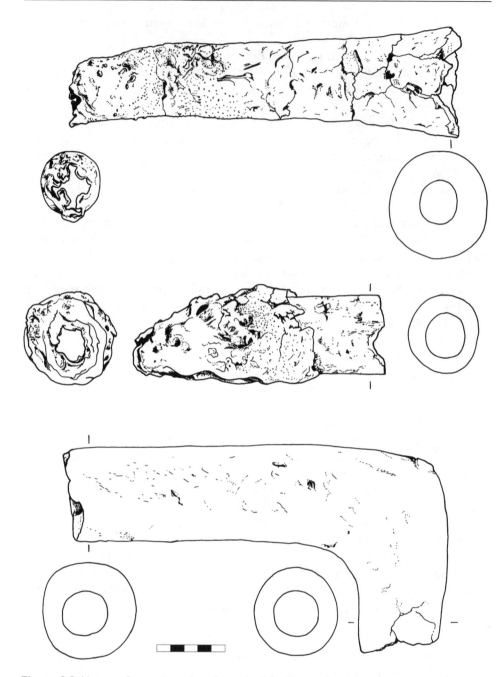

Figure 9.2 Variety of ceramic tuyères from the Late Bronze Age primary copper smelting site Politiko *Phorades* in Cyprus. (Drawing: Glynnis Fawkes)

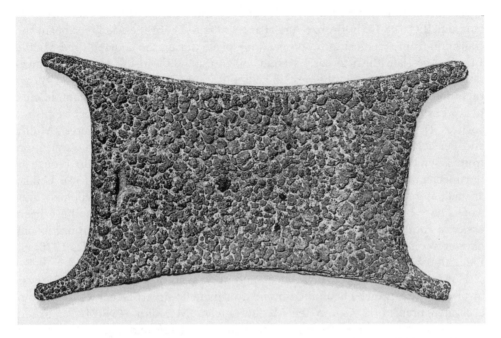

Figure 9.3 Copper ox-hide ingot dating to the Late Bronze Age, from the site of Enkomi in Cyprus. (Photo: Xenophon Michael, Department of Antiquities, Cyprus)

a product of mixing copper ores with arsenic-rich ores during the smelting process; the second maintains that arsenical ores were added to molten metallic copper (discussion in Zwicker 1991; Charles 1980:168–170).

Copper alloys were used to produce not just weapons, tools, vessels, and dress ornaments (pins, pendants, fibulae) but also works of art. The craft of casting intricate objects seems to have developed quite early if we are to judge from the extraordinary crowns, staffs, maceheads, and other objects found at Chalcolithic Nahal Mishmar in Israel (Tadmor et al. 1995). By the Late Bronze Age, the technique of lost-wax casting was widespread in the eastern Mediterranean, and is well exemplified in the size of cast statues (the Enkomi "Horned God" stands 55 centimeters tall) as well as the intricate designs of four-sided Cypriot stands (Papasavvas 2003).

Tin

Many issues and questions related to tin sources, technology, and trade have long challenged archaeologists and archaeometallurgists. For example, why and when does the transition to tin bronze take place? How was tin bronze produced? Where did tin come from and in what form was it traded? Who were the primary producers and consumers of tin?

Tin bronze first appeared in Mesopotamia and Anatolia during the third millennium B.C., or Early Bronze Age (Pare 2000a:6–7). In the Mediterranean, the transition from arsenical to tin bronze took place during the course of the Middle Bronze Age (late third to early second millennium B.C. in the eastern Mediterranean, somewhat later in the west). The implication (Renfrew 1972:313–319) that tin bronze was an independent development in the northeast Aegean is contradicted by lead isotope analyses which show that most copper or bronze objects from sites such as Troy, Poliochni, and Kastri were not produced from local ores (Muhly and Pernicka 1992; Pernicka 1998:140–141). Exactly what caused the transition from arsenical to tin bronze is not well understood: as an alloy, tin bronze is not mechanically superior to arsenical copper (Pernicka 1998:135–136). Unlike arsenic, moreover, tin is not widely available as a mineral, and new trade networks would have been required to enable its distribution. However, it may have been easier to control the quality of tin bronze, and the production of tin bronze would have overcome the problem of working with toxic arsenic fumes (Charles 1978:30; Pare 2000a:7).

How, then, was tin bronze produced and in what form was it traded? Who was involved in this trade? The limited number of metallic tin artifacts recovered from excavated prehistoric sites in the Mediterranean (Meredith 1998:21–22) would seem to indicate that metallic tin was not widely available, and that tin bronze was produced (much like arsenical bronze) by mixing molten metallic copper with cassiterite, the principal ore of tin which is an oxide and is usually found in alluvial deposits (Tylecote 1987:36–37). The near complete absence of tin smelting slag (Meredith 1998:19) and the discovery of a badly decomposed paste of tin (cassiterite?) on the Cape Gelidonya shipwreck (Turkey) also would seem to support this notion (Charles 1978:26, 31). Maddin et al. (1977:44–45) pointed out, however, that slag does not result in cases where the ore being smelted is extremely pure, as is the case with cassiterite (Tylecote 1987:307). The rarity of metallic tin objects may be ascribed to the physical properties of the metal, which decomposes in most burial conditions (Maddin 1989:102). Finally, two key investigations demonstrate that, at least during the Late Bronze Age, tin was traded as a metal and not as a mineral (Bass 1991:71). First is the discovery of metallic tin ingots off the coast of Haifa in Israel (Galili et al. 1986:25; Raban and Galili 1985:327); second is the extraordinary recovery of one ton of tin in various ingot types on the Uluburun shipwreck (Pulak 2000:150–151).

Given the limited number of tin deposits in the region, the source(s) of tin used in the prehistoric eastern Mediterranean has always been a highly controversial issue. The suggestion that Afghanistan served as a prime source of tin for Bronze Age eastern Mediterranean societies is based in part on the existence of its rich tin resources (Muhly and Pernicka 1992:315; Weeks 1999:60–61). Muhly (1999:21) recently argued that Afghanistan or central Asia provided the tin that supplied the bronze industries of Mesopotamia, Anatolia, and the eastern Mediterranean, including Cyprus. Cuneiform documents from the early second millennium B.C., moreover, point to a trade network that brought tin from the east to the early states of Anatolia and Mesopotamia (Maddin et al. 1977:41: Weeks 1999), and thence to the Mediterranean. Weisgerber and Cierny (2002, with fuller references) now maintain that prehistoric tin mining (second millennium B.C.), attested at the sites of Karnab (Uzbekhistan) and Musciston (Tajikistan), provided an important source of tin for Anatolia and Mesopotamia, if not for the Mediterranean. In contrast, Yener and Vandiver (1993) have argued that (very limited) tin deposits in the Taurus Mountains of southern Turkey were exploited during the Early Bronze Age. Their argument has been challenged by several scholars (e.g., Muhly 1993; Weisgerber and Chierny 2002:180–181; papers in *Journal of Mediterranean Archaeology* 5 [1995]) who maintain that the archaeological evidence is unclear, and far too limited to demonstrate anything beyond local use. Even if tin from the Taurus were mined during the Early Bronze Age, it now seems more likely that central Asia provided at least some of the tin used during the Middle-Late Bronze Ages, when tin bronze was far more widely produced, traded, and consumed in the Mediterranean.

In the central and western Mediterranean, tin deposits are found in Tuscany, a rich metalliferous region of Italy, and ancient workings have been unearthed in one of the area's tin mines (general discussion in Pare 200a:23–24). These workings, however, are not dated securely and in fact may derive from a much later time period (Meredith 1998:33). Small tin deposits are also found on the island of Sardinia (Meredith 1998:33), which may explain why Cypriot and/or Mycenaean traders – seeking tin sources for the production of bronze – established close links with the island (Knapp 1990b:150–152; Kassianidou 2001:110). There is no archaeological evidence, however, for the Bronze Age exploitation of these Sardinian tin deposits. Sardinia's role in the Bronze Age metals trade thus may have been as an intermediary (but see below).

Major tin deposits are also located in Brittany and Cornwall (Needham et al. 1989), but more important for the present discussion are those in the Iberian peninsula (Meredith 1998:29–31). Tin bronze alloys are now attested from the north of Spain by the mid-third millennium B.C., but their use did not become predominant in the peninsula for another millennium (Diaz-Andreu and Montero Ruiz 2000; Pare 2000a:20–21). Recent excavations at Logrosan have revealed for the first time the remains of Bronze Age tin mines and smelting sites (Rodriguez Diaz et al. 2001). Although it is uncertain if any of this tin was exported beyond the Iberian Peninsula, two Mycenaean sherds found at Montaro on the Guadalquivir River (Martin de la Cruz 1990) may indicate that the rich tin deposits of Iberia provided certain people in the Mediterranean – perhaps via Sardinia as an intermediary – with this metal in such high demand.

Lead and silver

Native silver is rare, and the most important sources of this precious metal in antiquity were the argentiferous ores of lead – mainly cerussite (lead carbonate), galena (lead sulphide), and other polymetallic ores (Craddock 1995:211). The history of silver thus is intrinsically linked with that of lead, and here we discuss issues concerning both metals. In the earliest stages of developing metallurgy, and in some areas such as Egypt, electrum – a natural alloy of gold and silver – provided another source for silver (Ogden 2001:170). The color of electrum is determined by the proportions of the two metals: where the silver content is 20 percent or above the nugget is silvery in color (aurian silver), otherwise it is golden (Tylecote 1987:81).

The process of separating silver from lead – called cupellation – is based on the principle that lead, a base metal, oxidizes readily while silver does not (Craddock 1995:223). Cupellation takes place in an open fire so that oxidizing conditions are attained at the necessary temperature of 1,000°C (Tylecote 1987:198). The lead is placed in a cupellation dish and soon oxidizes to form litharge (lead oxide), which is either poured out or absorbed by the dish, leaving behind the refined silver.

The most important sources of silver in the eastern Mediterranean are located in Anatolia (Forbes 1950:190; Moorey 1994:235). With the exception of Egyptian aurian silver (Moorey 1994:235), Cyprus, the Levant, and Egypt have no other significant silver deposits. Moving west, a number of the Aegean islands, such as Siphnos, have rich argentiferous deposits, which were exploited by the Early Bronze Age (early third millennium B.C.) (Pernicka et al. 1985:195). The most important Aegean deposit, however, is in Attika. Silver production at the site of Thorikos began during the Late Bronze Age (second half of the second millennium B.C.) (Conophagos 1980:58). In the Peloponnese, silver artifacts dating to the Final Neolithic (see below) argue for a much earlier exploitation of argentiferous deposits on the Greek mainland (see also Maran 2000). Farther west, in Italy, silver deposits are found in Tuscany and Sardinia; in France important deposits exist in Brittany and Auvergne. The Iberian peninsula also has important argentiferous deposits in the Sierra Morena in Andalusia, and in the areas of Linares, Ciudad Real, Murcia, and Cartagena (Aubet 2001:279–285; Forbes 1950:199). These Iberian deposits are believed to have attracted Phoenician traders to the peninsula during the Iron Age, in the first millennium B.C. (Aubet 2001:283–285).

Because lead occurs only very rarely as a native metal, it is assumed that all very early lead objects were the result of smelting. In Anatolia, beads made of galena (lead sulphide) are attested at Çatalhöyük about 7000 B.C., but the earliest date for lead smelting is indicated by a bracelet made from a massive lead rod, dated to the sixth millennium and found at Yarim Tepe in Iran (Merpert et al. 1977:82). Lead objects dated to the fifth millennium B.C. have been recovered from Naqada and other sites in Egypt (Gale and Stos-Gale 1981:178).

Silver first appears in the Mediterranean, and most dramatically, in the form of a hoard of silver jewelry found in a Final Neolithic (ca. 4500–3700 B.C.) deposit at the Alepotrypa Cave in southern Greece (Muhly 2002:78). A metal hoard that included a silver ring (De Jesus 1980:76) derives from Late Chalcolithic levels (after ca. 3500 B.C.) at Beycesultan in southwest Anatolia. Other early silver objects, all dating to the late fourth millennium B.C., are reported from various sites in the southern Levant (e.g., Prag 1978; Rehren et al. 1996). Analysis of some objects from Naqada in Egypt indicates that they were made of cupelled silver (Gale and Stos-Gale 1981:180). More secure evidence for early cupellation comes from Late

Uruk (late fourth millennium B.C.) contexts at Habuba Kabira South in Syria (Pernicka et al. 1998), and from the third millennium B.C. site of Mahmaltar in Anatolia (Wertime 1973:883). As noted above, lead and silver objects began to appear frequently in Cycladic and mainland Greek sites of the third millennium B.C. (Renfrew 1967b:4–6). Isotopic analysis of some Early Bronze Age lead arti-facts at first indicated that they were consistent with production from ores on Siphnos (Gale 1978:541). As more ore sources (e.g., Laurion in Attica, the north Aegean, western Anatolia) and more objects (e.g., from Poliochni, Amorgos, Naxos, and Syros) were analyzed, however, the overlap between the different isotopic fields made it much more difficult to distinguish the origin of the ores exploited during the Early Bronze Age (Pernicka et al. 1990:278–280).

Like most other metals, the earliest use of lead involved the manufacture of per-sonal ornaments: beads, bracelets, and the like. Unlike copper, however, lead is intrinsically soft and malleable, and does not become harder with cold working (Krysko 1979:470). These physical properties therefore render lead worthless for fabricating weapons and tools. Its low melting point, high specific gravity, and resis-tance to corrosion resulted in different applications, like the manufacture of weights and sinkers, flat strips of lead that were bent over the strings of fishing nets. Lead was also used to repair broken pottery (Renfrew 1967b:4). Associated with chthonic deities and cults, lead was often used for magical tablets containing inscribed curses or prayers for the sick (Forbes 1950:178; Moorey 1994:295). It is also important to note that lead was added to copper, tin-bronzes, and other copper alloys to create leaded tin-bronzes. This means that any effort to provenance the copper in a leaded bronze by the lead isotope method is futile. Although pointed out repeatedly by all those critical of the way lead isotope analysis has been used (e.g., Budd et al. 1995; Kassianidou 2001:106–107; Knapp 2000; Muhly 1985b), attempts continue to provenance objects containing lead in the region of 1–20 percent. In any case, the most important application of lead was in producing silver; many of the objects mentioned here were made of de-silvered lead derived from recycling litharge, a by-product of cupellation.

By the second millennium B.C., when trade became more international in outlook, silver and silver objects are found widespread throughout the eastern Mediterranean. As a precious metal, silver was used to manufacture jewelry as well as vessels, statuettes, and other prestige items, for example a silver trumpet from the tomb of Tutankhamun (Moorey 1994:238; Ogden 2001:170). The techniques used are the same as those for other metals: casting with the lost-wax process and raising sheet metal to produce vessels of different forms. The main use of silver, however, was as a standard against which the value of other raw materials and objects was measured. Throughout the Middle and Late Bronze Ages, silver was traded in the form of bars or rings with a standardized weight: cuneiform economic texts from various Anatolian and Near Eastern sites describe exchanges and list the prices of various goods relative to silver (e.g., Dercksen 1996; Moorey 1994:237; Veenhof 1988) (Figure 9.4). In the absence of documentary evidence from Bronze Age sites in the central and western Mediterranean, it is uncertain if silver was used there in a similar way. The first century B.C. historian Diodorus Siculus, however,

Figure 9.4 Silver ingots, from the Late Bronze site of Pyla *Kokkinokremos* in Cyprus. (Photo: Xenophon Michael, Department of Antiquities, Cyprus)

portrays an interesting contrast between the east and west Mediterranean: In the eighth century B.C., the Phoenicians found in Iberia abundant sources of silver (Aubet 2001:198–199), a metal whose use – according to Diodorus – was unknown to local peoples. As a result, the Phoenicians were able to exchange small, insignificant goods for large amounts of silver, and even larger profits.

Gold

Gold stands apart from all other metals: it has a strikingly different color and a specific gravity almost double that of most other metals. It is also highly ductile and malleable, and thus can be hammered easily into extremely thin sheets or drawn into very fine wire. Gold is chemically inert, which is why it will not corrode, even in adverse depositional contexts. Unlike all other metals (excepting electrum, the natural alloy of gold and silver), gold is commonly found as a native metal (Tylecote 1987:69). Gold, however, is a very uncommon element in the earth's crust (Patterson 1971:297), a factor that added to its status as a precious metal from the Late Neolithic-Chalcolithic periods onward.

The most important sources of gold in the eastern Mediterranean are located in Egypt and Nubia (Müller and Thiem 1999:36–41). That this was common knowledge in antiquity is illustrated by the Amarna Letters (EA) from Egypt, in particular EA 19, sent to Pharaoh from the king of Mitanni: "In my brother's country, gold is as plentiful as dirt" (Moran 1992:44–45). Important deposits of gold are also located in Anatolia, within Lydia (home of Midas, mythical king of the golden touch), and along the Black Sea coast in the Pontus area (ancient Colchis, where Jason and the Argonauts sought the golden fleece) (Williams and Ogden 1994:13). No significant sources of gold are known from the Levant or Cyprus (Moorey 1994:220), but in the Aegean deposits are known from the Cycladic islands of Siphnos and Thasos, and in Macedonia and Thrace (Williams and Ogden 1994:13). Gold deposits are also found in Italy's Alpine and Apennine Mountains, with alluvial deposits in the Aosta and the Po Valley (Lehrberger 1995:129). The main auriferous zones in France are located in eastern Brittany, in the southern and northwestern parts of the Central Massif, and in the eastern Pyrenees. The Iberian Peninsula is also particularly rich in gold, with the most significant deposits concentrated in the regions of Porto in Portugal, and Galicia, Extramedura, and Almeria in Spain (Lehrberger 1995:119).

Pure gold is extremely soft and to make it practical for use it was typically alloyed with silver and/or copper. Goldsmiths used different ratios of the three metals to achieve different colors (red, silver, gold) of the final product (Tylecote 1987:80–81). The availability of different types of gold alloys – in terms of color, physical properties, and value – is reflected in the numerous terms used to describe these alloys in the languages and scripts of ancient Western Asia (e.g., Edzard 1960; Forbes 1971:172). The diversity of gold alloys made it essential to develop techniques of determining gold content, and therefore the value of a "gold" object, because gold, like all other metals, was continuously recycled (Moorey 1994:221). Although different techniques were used in antiquity for assaying gold, there is little agreement about when such techniques were first employed (Moorey 1994:218–219; Ogden 2001:163).

Gold objects were produced either by casting in the lost-wax technique, or more commonly by the mechanical treatment of sheet metal (Ogden 2001:165). Gold jewelry often combines numerous components, and different gold-working techniques include granulation (motifs with minute globules) and filigree work (motifs with metal wire). Almost all these techniques were well developed by the Bronze Age (see further Moorey 1994:226–231; various papers from the *Temple University Aegean Symposium* 8 [1983], Philadelphia – "Gold in the Bronze Age Aegean").

The malleability of gold meant that it could be turned into thin sheets used to cover furnishings and even parts of a building. Diverse and prestigious objects from Tutankhamun's tomb in Egypt, the "Treasure of Priam" and others like it from Troy, as well as the "royal" tombs of Mycenae all demonstrate the use of gold as the ultimate status symbol. Temples and other ceremonial structures often were endowed with abundant golden offerings, which of course meant that they were subject to looting. This situation is shown clearly in another Amarna Letter (EA 137) sent to the Egyptian Pharaoh by a desperate Canaanite vassal whose city (Byblos) was in danger of falling into enemy hands: "May the king, my lord, not neglect the city. Note there is much gold and silver in it, and much is the property belonging to its temples" (Moran 1992:218).

Hittite texts from Anatolia (e.g., Siegelova 1993:117) that spell out the value of different goods indicate that gold was the most precious of all metals. Because of its great value, gold was continuously and systematically recycled (Moorey 1994:219–221). Again the Amarna Letters prove particularly enlightening (e.g., EA 3 – Moran 1992:3): it seems that, almost immediately upon their arrival in Egypt, some gold vessels and jewelry sent as regal gifts were melted down to produce gold bullion. Such practice may also have served to test the quality of the metal: the dynasts of the Amarna period often complained that the gold they received was not suitably pure (e.g., EA 7 and EA 10 – Moran 1992:14, 19).

Archaeometallurgy and Society in the Prehistoric Mediterranean

Given this broad array of evidence for the production, distribution, and consumption of copper, tin, lead, silver, and gold throughout the Mediterranean, what can we say about the role of metals, and the impact of metallurgical production and trade, on its prehistoric societies?

By the Late Neolithic period (ca. 4800–3100 B.C.), most people living in the Mediterranean region produced their own food, lived the year round in sedentary communities and increasingly were involved in intricate social and economic exchanges. By the beginning of the Bronze Age, certain alliances, special-interest groups, or even individual local leaders came to control access to raw materials in demand: obsidian, precious or semi-precious stones, metals such as gold, silver, copper, and tin, and a range of more perishable goods. From about 3000 B.C. onward – corresponding to the Chalcolithic period (Argaric culture) in Spain, the Final Neolithic in Italy, and the Early Bronze Age in the Aegean and eastern Mediterranean – the production and trade in metals increasingly became a key factor in promoting social change (Giardino 2000b; Knapp 1990a; Levy et al. 2002; Manning 1994; Ruiz Taboada and Montero Ruiz 1999).

The social context of mining and early metallurgy

In order to consider the social context of mining and metallurgy during the Mediterranean Bronze Age, it is instructive to look at historical or ethnographic contexts where the mining and production of metals was carried out (also Stöllner 2003). Godoy (1985:205–206) pointed out, for example, that physical and social isolation, along with labor requirements and the harsh working conditions involved in extracting and producing metal ores, shaped the social structure and economic organization of metallurgical production in historical and more recent mining communities. Despite the isolation that typified their existence, mining communities provided raw materials in demand to wider economic networks and thus were always linked into broader communication and transport systems (Stöllner 2003:417–418). The resulting interactions – material, social, ideological, and symbolic (Hardesty 1988:1–5) – are often visible archaeologically in the form of settlement layout, trash dumps, skeletal remains, mass-produced goods, and so on. Moreover, the variability and individuality in ethnicity, origin, status, and class in most historically attested mining communities often translate into material visibility (Fenenga 1967) and thus form a focus of interest for studying prehistoric mining and metallurgy.

During the early phases of the Bronze Age (third millennium B.C.) in the eastern Mediterranean, archaeological evidence reveals not only an increased number and size of sites but a marked differentiation between sites in terms of their spatial extent and material splendor. Although the existence of site hierarchies becomes more obvious in the later phases of the Bronze Age, most known production sites were located in close proximity to ore deposits, and consequently were quite isolated from the more dynamic social, organizational, and economic developments that took place in population centers, usually located along the seacoast. Such developments were linked at least in part to the increased production of metals and the expansion of long-distance trade, itself bound up with the acquisition of imported prestige goods.

From at least the mid-third millennium B.C., the city-states and kingdoms of the Levant also became key players in the production, bulk exchange, and consumption of both ores and finished metal products (Greenberg 2002:117–121). In the Aegean, metallurgical production flourished – copper on Kythnos; silver/lead and gold on Siphnos – with the emergence of the Cycladic culture and the expansion of interregional trade. On Cyprus, the third millennium B.C. was a time of major social change, when indigenous elites – let us call them Cypriots rather than Frankel's (2000) imagined Anatolian colonists – seized the opportunity to formalize, legitimize, and integrate the copper industry that became so critical in all of the political, social, and urban developments of the Middle-Late Bronze Ages. Although Cyprus never had palatial economies like those that characterized communities in the Aegean and the Levant, once some person or group managed to organize all the factors involved in producing, transporting, and distributing the island's copper resources, including the subsistence needs of miners and metalsmiths, Cyprus rapidly assumed a prominent economic and political position in what was to become a Mediterranean-wide trade in metals and other luxury goods in demand.

Farther west, also during the Early Bronze Age, the widespread occurrence of mass-produced Beaker pottery (Lewthwaite 1987; Waldren and Kennard 1987; Waldren 1998) – whether the result of human migrations, social exchanges, or trade – makes it clear that there was a significant amount of interaction throughout the central and western Mediterranean at this time. Because copper daggers are often associated with Beakers, the link between the increased movement of people and the exploitation of copper resources seems evident. Metal goods, however, remained quite rare at this time. In southeast Spain, the emergence of fortified hilltop settlements such as El Argar signaled further social inequality alongside increasingly specialized economic activities, including the production of metals (Chapman 2003:131–146).

Technologies of mining and metallurgy

Technology as a social process involves people's daily practices and abilities, their beliefs, and their capacity to negotiate complex spatial, economic, and political relationships (Childs and Killick 1993). Innovations in technology affected not just the environment but also the social practices of those who mined and produced metals; they promoted more extensive mining operations and often led to the intensified production of metals (Stöllner 2003:430–432). The cost of intensified production decreased with greater investment in metallurgical technology. With smelting technology, for example, the introduction of sulphide ore dressing and roasting during the second millennium B.C. facilitated the production of copper on a major, commercial scale (Hauptmann and Weisgerber 1981). Weisgerber (1982:27–28) maintained that this sort of smelting operation was the key technological development in the intensification of Cypriot copper production by the Late Bronze Age (cf. Muhly et al. 1988:287–288), and consequently in the increased presence of Cypriot copper throughout the Mediterranean. This kind of technological advance also required a sophisticated communication system, efficient organization of copper mining and distribution, and an adequate shipping capacity to meet overseas demand (Knapp 1986b; 1997).

Technological innovations may be seen as progressive by managers and elites, but for the people who mined ores or smelted metals they were also potentially disruptive, forming the backdrop for social change as well as social abuse (Heskel and Lamberg-Karlovsky 1980:260–261; Stöllner 2003:427–429). Miners and metalsmiths often use ideology as a means to maintain, resist, or change their power base within society. Because elites who control and organize metallurgical production often use material culture to restructure relations of power (Gamble 1986:39), we may also expect such transformations to be visible in the archaeological record. For example: on Late Bronze Age Cyprus, various "paraphernalia of power" associated with the newly developed technology of smelting sulphide ores not only served ideological functions and symbolized political or economic aspirations, they also helped entrepreneurs and metal producers to establish their social position and legitimize their authority (Knapp 1988; Knapp et al. 2001; Stöllner 2003:440).

The conspicuous quality of metals such as copper or gold, and the prestige that resulted from owning or displaying them, often invoked a rich body of symbolism with multiple, historically situated images (e.g., Knapp 1986a; Budd and Taylor 1995; Schmidt and Mapunda 1997). Ancient documentary sources reveal that gold was used mainly for prestige and ceremonial purposes, from jewelry and metal vessels to idols and death masks. From situations such as the erection of a temple dedicated to the goddess Hathor by an Egyptian mining expedition in the remote copper-producing area of Timna (Negev) during the Late Bronze Age (Rothenberg 1988:276–277), or Galen's chilling description of his second century AD visit to the mines near Soli on Cyprus, or the use of child labor in the Roman mining districts of the Iberian peninsula (Stöllner 2003: 428), it is clear that the mining and production of metals had profound social implications that impacted on the natural order of things and served to structure and alter people's lives.

In this respect, we may also consider the operational tactics of metallurgists, for example in the case where copper had to be extracted from sulphide ores (Kassianidou et al., in Given and Knapp 2003:301–305). The concept of the *chaîne opératoire* (Pfaffenberger 1992; Schlanger 1994:143; Stöllner 2003:418–420, and figure 1) engages the extant material remains with the technological processes and social actions involved in their production; it also helps us to understand better the spatial organization of production units like mining adits, roasting and slag heaps, and smelting installations (Pfaffenberger 1998:294–295). In Early Bronze Age Crete, for example, only one specialized component – the actual smelting of copper – of a much larger metallurgical operation was carried out at the site of Chrysokamino. Both the morphology of the furnaces and the location of the site – on the tip of a steep promontory overlooking the Bay of Mirabello – suggest that the prevailing northerly winds facilitated the natural draft employed in the smelting process (Betancourt et al. 1999). From individual enterprise to collective operation, the social organization of production largely determines technological strategies.

Archaeometallurgical remains reflect a wide range of activities, from the mining of ores to the casting of metals. Tools and implements such as hammers, tongs, tuyères, or even furnaces acquire meaning only by being used in a technically efficient manner. The wind-operated furnaces from Early Bronze Age sites in Jordan (Feinan) and on Kythnos (if not on Crete at Chrysokamino), for example, eventually were replaced by furnaces equipped with tuyères and bellows, which meant that metallurgical production no longer had to rely on the weather. Even the most rudimentary use of tools necessitates some degree of prior knowledge and socialization, which means that tool-use is at once a social and a material phenomenon (Pfaffenberger 1998:294). Technology involves not only material things but also human actions, which in turn affect social organization and require the application of knowledge. By identifying certain technical characteristics or assessing certain features of technological design, we can attempt to reconstruct not just the production process but also its social and spatial organization, in particular as it may be reflected in an ancient industrial landscape.

Landscapes of Mining and Metallurgy

In attempting to understand the configuration of an ancient metallurgical landscape, we must consider how the physical makeup of the land conditioned the location of mines, ore beneficiation installations, primary and secondary smelting sites, and distribution centers. In addition, we need to evaluate how mining or archaeometallurgical enterprises transformed the natural landscape into an industrial landscape.

The material culture of the mining enterprise impacts heavily on the configuration of industrial landscapes (Hardesty 1988; Knapp 1999:236–237). Because unprocessed ores are by nature both bulky and weighty, metals were almost always produced near the ore deposits. Basal geology is thus a key factor in selecting such a deposit for exploitation and mining. Other factors affect social production and economic demand: the nature of the labor force (free or servile), the availability of water (for energy or drinking), the difficulties in exploiting ore sources and transporting the end product, and the micro-environments where ores were refined and smelted. Constantinou (1992) points out that other "natural" features – for example the bright gossan "cap" that distinguishes many copper ore deposits, or a specific type of vegetation associated with certain ore bodies – are well known to prospectors and miners. Other factors influence where the ores are prepared for smelting or refining. If, for example, washing ores forms part of the beneficiation process, then either a fresh water source must be available, or water must be collected from elsewhere and stored for use, or the ores must be transported to a water source. In some cases, the primary stages in smelting ores take place in the immediate vicinity of a mine; in other cases, the determining factor may be the availability of fuel. Because certain metals are also highly valued commodities, production sites or workshops may be established in secure and easily defensible places, especially when economic organization is lax or political unity is lacking. One of the best examples of such a prehistoric industrial landscape is the intensively studied and excavated area around Timna in the Negev, which includes mines, shafts and adits, copper smelting installations, habitational remains, and a "sanctuary," as well as a likely outer fortification wall (Muhly 1984; Rothenberg 1988).

The smelting of copper required staggering amounts of wood or charcoal (Constantinou 1982:22–23; 1992:69–72; Stöllner 2003:423). Based on a more recent Mediterranean analogy (on the island of Elba), Weisgerber (1982:28) argued that deforestation for fuel so completely denuded primary copper production areas on Cyprus that evidence of prehistoric metallurgical activities would only be found buried deep beneath alluvial deposits triggered by widespread erosion. Constantinou (1992:72), however, pointed out that the climatic regime (rainfall, winds, temperature distribution) imposed by Cyprus's Troodos Mountains allowed for the regeneration of forests every 80–100 years, thus mitigating the environmental impact of the long-term exploitation and production of copper. Moreover, the recent discovery and excavation of a Late Bronze Age smelting site at Politiko *Phorades* – with evidence for unprecedented archaeometallurgical and pyrotechnological developments (Kassianidou 1999; Knapp et al. 2001; Knapp 2003) – also shows that prehistoric metallurgical sites are not all buried deep under alluvial deposits. It is also interesting to note that, according to ancient documentary sources, the care as well as the exploitation of Cyprus's forests – a valuable natural resource not only for fuel but for shipbuilding material – was under the strict control of the kings of Iron Age Cyprus (Theophrastus – *Historia Plantarum* 5.8.1; see also Meiggs 1998:377).

Despite the wealth of historical documentation available on mining, deforestation, overgrazing, manuring, and intensive agricultural practices, we still understand very little about the complex relationship between land use, resource exploitation, and landscape change in the Mediterranean Basin. Geomorphological investigations carried out by the Sydney Cyprus Survey Project (Noller, in Given and Knapp 2003:295–299) have demonstrated two major agents of landscape change: running water and human beings. The two have interacted over the past five millennia both to embellish and to alter the "naturally" occurring landforms. Consequently, there is little room to doubt that innovations in technology had deep-seated and long-lasting social and ecological effects, placing constraints as well as conferring benefits on Bronze Age mining and metallurgical production. In social terms, whereas the intensified production of copper employing an advanced technology did not preclude a strong sense of local community, such factors served to increase social distinctions between those at the top of the control structure and those at the bottom (Hardesty 1988:102, 116; Knapp 1986b; 2003).

Mining communities

The mining community is the focal point of human activity in an industrial landscape. Such communities typically are situated near the ore bodies being worked, and often in proximity to water, timber, agricultural land, access roads, and transport systems (Hardesty 1988:108; Stöllner 2003:422–423). Both mining communities and archaeometallurgical sites offer diverse types of evidence – industrial or habitational features, the tools and artifacts of daily life and work, utilitarian or prestige goods – that provide insights into the social relations that developed in these communities. Rescue excavations at the Late Bronze Age Cypriot site of Apliki *Karamallos* (Du Plat Taylor 1952; Muhly 1989b:306–310), for example, revealed not only clear evidence of primary copper smelting activity but also abundant pottery finds, stone tools (pestles, rubbers, querns), spindle whorls and loomweights, structural remains, and two charred fiber baskets with grain. Arguably the remains from Apliki are those of a miners' community that included living space as well as many of the accoutrements of daily life. Because the variety of plant remains found at Apliki would have been quite difficult to cultivate on the igneous, rocky slopes in this region (Helbaek 1962:185–186), the miners must have relied at least in part on agricultural support villages for subsistence.

In order to discuss the social organization of mining communities, it is necessary to relate their visible material remnants to the more abstract or "imagined" concept of a community (Anderson 1991; Amit 2002; Knapp 2003; see also the chapter by Sollars, this volume). Such communities are not just physical places but the mental space in which the social and material conditions of life are developed and transformed (Brück and Goodman 1999:13). Archaeological concepts of community (e.g., Verhoeven 1999; Canuto and Yaeger 2000; Gerritsen 2003; 2004) have considered how people and place are integrated socially, and how the community fosters a sense of shared identity. Knapp (2003) has presented evidence from the Late Bronze Age Cypriot smelting site of Politiko *Phorades* that portrays an imagined regional community involving miners, metalworkers, and the farmers who provided their daily subsistence.

With respect to mining communities, recent research (Knapp et al. 1998; Stöllner 2003) indicates that we need to look beyond seasonality, isolation, economic orientation, and household makeup to consider the social factors that impacted on daily practices, community location, and inter-community links. Because mining and metallurgical production sites typically were established in isolated settings close to the mineral resources in demand, or at some distance from population centers, miners and metallurgists may have formed a "community without a locus" (Douglass 1998); their living space and subsistence base often would have been situated elsewhere in the wider regional community. The social organization of these small mining communities was typically expedient, and often of a seasonal nature since mining would have alternated with the demands of the agricultural cycle (Given and Knapp 2000; Knapp et al. 2001; Stöllner 2003:419–420). Mining as a political or economic activity served to establish social relations between individuals and groups that went beyond the local community and at times even transformed regional community relations. The archaeological concept of a mining community thus may be considered more dynamically by analyzing its material and social patterns and integrating them into the wider social and economic landscape.

The Trade in Metals

Within the Mediterranean, the study of prehistoric trade often has focused on a quest for the origins of imported or exotic goods, or on the production and distribution of single artifact types, be they metal goods, stone tools, pottery, or faience vessels (Perlès 1992). Attempts to model the spatial extent of Mediterranean trade by considering the role of "central places" and the spatial distribution of artifacts (e.g., Renfrew 1975) are problematic in the Bronze Age Mediterranean, where several different types and regimes of trade overlapped with one another (Knapp 1993; Knapp and Cherry 1994:126–151).

The trade in metals during the Chalcolithic period was carried out on a very limited scale, and most metals were certainly consumed in the same area where they were produced (cf. Gale 1991). During the Early Bronze Age (third millennium B.C.), technological innovations like the longboat and sail facilitated the bulk transport of raw materials or manufactured goods on a much larger scale than ever before (Broodbank 1989). Silver produced in the Cyclades became an important commodity, and the products of early Aegean metallurgists helped to expand trade rapidly throughout the Aegean and along the coasts of western Anatolia and the Levant. That the circulation of metals was already highly developed in the east Mediterranean is revealed by recent lead isotope analysis of a small hoard from Early Bronze Age II at Pella in Jordan. Of the five artifacts analyzed, three were consistent with production from copper sources in Feinan or Timna, one with Cypriot copper ores, and one with ores from the Taurus Mountains of southern Turkey (Philip et al. 2003). A multitude of harbors and the potential diversity of trading routes further promoted a growing sense of internationalism. In the Argaric Bronze Age (ca. 2250–1550 B.C.) of southeast Spain, despite a debate over intensified copper production and its impact on social structure (Chapman 2003:139–142; cf. Díaz-Andreu and Montero Ruiz 2000:116–118), there is no reason to doubt that copper was traded widely *within* the Iberian peninsula.

During the Middle-Late Bronze Ages (ca. 2000–1200 B.C.) in the eastern Mediterranean, port cities and palatial centers took part in a lucrative international trade, and found their political positions enhanced as a result (Knapp 1998; Stager 2001). Fleets from Egypt, the Levantine city-states, Cyprus, Anatolia, and the Aegean were active in this region. The palatial economies that propelled and supported the Minoan and Mycenaean cultures were involved in the production and exchange of copper and other precious metals on a widespread, interregional level. The rich and diverse cargo recovered from the Uluburun shipwreck – hundreds of copper oxhide ingots, tin and cobalt ingots, a range of Cypriot and Aegean pottery, various organic goods, and much more – has fundamentally altered our understanding of the scope and extent of Late Bronze Age Mediterranean trading systems (Bass 1991; Pulak 1998; 2000). In the central Mediterranean, by the end of the Middle Bronze Age, some town centers in Calabria, Apulia, and Sicily increasingly became involved in the long-distance trade in metals (Giardino 2000a; 2000b).

Amongst the more prominent Late Bronze Age centers involved in the metals trade were Ugarit (Syria), Enkomi and Hala Sultan Tekke (Cyprus), Tel Nami and Tel el-'Ajjul (Israel), Troy (Anatolia), Kommos (Crete), Mycenae and Pylos (Greece), Nuraghe Antigori (Sardinia), Thapsos and Cannatello (Sicily), and Scoglio del Tonno (Apulia, Italy). Such polities increasingly became involved in the production, exchange, and consumption of raw materials, foods and spices, as well as utilitarian and luxury goods (copper and tin, silver and gold, metal artifacts, precious and semi-precious stones, ivory, pottery, and glass), all within a broad but loosely linked interregional system. The primarily sea-borne trade in metals was complex in nature and diverse in structure, with state-dominated as well as entrepreneurial aspects (Knapp 2000). Many factors conditioned the mechanics of Mediterranean trade: cooperation and competition, the nature of the goods traded, social or economic status, even the ideology of exchange. Miners, metalworkers, and craft specialists, along with merchants and political elites, were all loosely integrated in an interregional system that linked exchanged goods, ideology, iconography, and socio-political status.

The Late Bronze Age witnessed a quantum leap in the production and trade of copper ingots and metal artifacts. Standardized values and mediated exchange rates not only facilitated interregional trade, but may also have served as a stabilizing influence in a system where social alliances and economic relationships were constantly changing. Copper oxhide ingots, which consistently weigh around 30 kilograms and have been recovered in contexts from the Black Sea and Babylonia to Sicily, Sardinia, and Marseilles (Lo Schiavo et al. 1985; Muhly et al. 1988; Domergue and Rico 2002:141–144), suggest a Mediterranean standard for value, weight, and exchange during the Late Bronze Age (ca. 1600–1000 B.C.). A set of bronze and stone weights from *Ayios Dhimitrios* on Cyprus, a set of disk weights from Akrotiri on Thera, and their possible (regional) intercalation make it likely that interrelated systems of weights and measures helped to facilitate Mediterranean trade (Courtois 1983; Michailidou 1990; 2001; Petruso 1984).

Over the course of the Bronze Age, trade in a limited number of high-value, low-bulk, convertible luxury goods (e.g., precious metals, semi-precious stones, or ivory) expanded to incorporate the bulk-exchange of commodities that could not be converted into anything else (storage jars, textiles, glass), and that were locally produced for export on an interregional scale (Sherratt and Sherratt 1991). The real determinants of regional politico-economic power, however, were convertible resources such as copper ingots and metals, which may never have been exchanged on the open market but instead traded exclusively by formal gift-exchange. Another major incentive in Middle-Late Bronze Age Mediterranean trade was the desire by new leaders to acquire goods from afar, the direct effect of the ideological link between distance and the exotic (Broodbank 1993; Knapp 1998; n.d.). To enhance and consolidate their position, elites often imported goods that could only be acquired through the production of certain other goods – whether raw materials (e.g., metal, wood, or ivory) or finished products (e.g., bronzes, textiles, or decorated inlaid chests).

Mediterranean trade was in a continuous state of flux as new opportunities arose or long-established systems broke down. Interregional trade may have been centered on palatial regimes in some regions, but individual acts of exchange helped to mobilize more specific demand for imports and exports. Even if powerful elites controlled the local economies, the dynamics of production and trade freed up resources for entrepreneurial activities within a generally more structured political economy. Consumer or supplier demand and maritime technology increasingly enabled regional exchange networks to be linked to a wider, common circulation system that moved not only commodities and high-value goods (most notably metals), but also ideas and iconographies between participating units.

Conclusion: Metals, Metallurgy and Mediterranean Society

In the increasingly interconnected and acculturated region that made up the Mediterranean from the early third millennium B.C. onward, the interplay of social and economic forces with spatial and resource diversity helped to shape the entire history of shipping and commerce, the emergence and divergence of political regimes, the configuration of ideologies, and the implementation and spread of religious doctrines. The multiple *mentalités* of ancient and recent miners, metalsmiths, merchants, entrepreneurs, traders, and raiders set the stage for individual exchanges, community relations, social alliances, regional polities, interregional systems of production and exchange, and imperial regimes of exploitation and consumption. The knowledge of and control over resources, the circulation of valued goods in demand, expertise in navigation and maritime technology, and the impact of distance and the exotic on local people and ideologies – all of which could be, and often were, tightly controlled – served to shape and continually reform social conventions, economic connections, and power relations.

Metals and metallurgy wielded an immense impact on Mediterranean Bronze Age societies, clearly evident in all the fundamental changes seen in the archaeological record from the end of the Chalcolithic period (Copper Age) onward. During the Bronze Age, innovations in maritime transport and the earliest cultivation of olives and vines stimulated the economy of the Mediterranean region and spurred some of its inhabitants to produce metals, take part in maritime trade, manufacture distinctive artifacts, and build domestic and public structures that represented the earliest towns and ceremonial complexes in the Mediterranean. The advent and spread of metallurgy promoted greater social distinctions, as certain individuals or groups acquired new wealth and prestige items. Because tin had to be imported in order to produce bronze, long-distance trade was stimulated. During the second millennium B.C., gold, silver, copper, and tin came to represent what Sherratt (2000:83) has termed "convertible" value, both in an economic sense and in the literal sense that they could be consumed, stored, redistributed, or recycled in diverse forms and for various symbolic or ideological ends. Such documentary evidence as exists, exclusively in the eastern Mediterranean, is frequently preoccupied with these self-same metals (Liverani 1990:205–223, 247–266; Moran, in Knapp 1996:21–25).

A remarkable series of social and economic changes thus were linked closely to all the innovative developments in extractive and metallurgical technologies, and to the increasingly widespread and intensified production and distribution of metals and metal objects. These changes include but are not limited to: (1) the proliferation of settlements and the emergence of town centers; (2) the development and expansion in interregional trade; (3) the growth of palatial regimes and city-state kingdoms, with their attendant writing systems (notably in the eastern Mediterranean); (4) the development and refinement of craft specialization and the spread of an iconographic *koine*; (5) the elaboration of mortuary rituals and burials with large quantities of precious metal goods; (6) the widespread occurrence of metal hoards and the related trade in recycled and scrap metal. The circulation of goods, ideas, and ideologies across geographic, cultural, and economic boundaries represents a social transaction, one that entangled producers, distributors, and consumers in wider relations of alliance and dependence, patronage and privilege, prestige and debt (Thomas 1991:123–124). Certain occupational identities came to be focused around metallurgical production and trade, and Cyprus even gave its name to the island's most prominent product: copper ore (Muhly 1973:174–175). The coming of the Age of Iron, subsequent to all the developments discussed in this study, itself relied on extractive and smelting technologies developed during the Bronze Age, together with the use of carburization, all of which are linked directly (albeit over the millennia) to the dramatic social and economic changes that ushered in the Industrial Revolution and the beginnings of the modern era. If it is indeed the case that "metals make the world go round" (Pare 2000b), nowhere can this slogan be better and more widely illustrated than in the prehistoric Bronze Age of the Mediterranean.

ACKNOWLEDGMENTS

The authors would particularly like to thank James Muhly for his careful reading of the manuscript, and for suggesting further relevant references. Robert Chapman also provided references and materials in press relevant to the western Mediterranean.

REFERENCES

Amit, Vered, ed., 2002 Realizing Community: Concepts, Social Relationships and Sentiments. London: Routledge.

Anderson, Benedict, 1991 Imagined Communities: Reflections on the Origin and Spread of Nationalism. 2nd edition. London: Verso.

Aubet, Maria Eugenia, 2001 The Phoenicians and the West: Politics, Colonies, and Trade. Cambridge: Cambridge University Press.

Bass, George F., 1991 Evidence of Trade from Bronze Age Shipwrecks. *In* Bronze Age Trade in the Mediterranean. Noel H. Gale, ed. pp. 69–82. Studies in Mediterranean Archaeology 90. Göteborg: Paul Åströms Förlag.

Bassiakos, Yannis, and Olga Philaniotou-Hadjianastasiou, In press Early Copper Production on Kythnos: Archaeological Evidence – Material and Analytical Reconstruction of Metallurgical Processes. *In* Neolithic and Early Bronze Age Metallurgy. Peter M. Day, ed. Sheffield Studies in Aegean Archaeology 6. Sheffield: Sheffield Academic Press.

Betancourt, Philip P., James D. Muhly, William R. Farrand, Carola Stearns, Lada Onyshkevych, William B. Hafford, and Doniert Evely, 1999 Research and Excavation at Chrysocamino, Crete, 1995–1998. Hesperia 68:343–371.

Broodbank, Cyprian, 1989 The Longboat and Society in the Cyclades in the Kyros-Syros Culture. American Journal of Archaeology 93:319–337.

—— 1993 Ulysses Without Sails: Trade, Distance, Knowledge and Power in the Early Cyclades. World Archaeology 24:315–331.

Brück, J., and M. Goodman, 1999 Introduction: Themes for a Critical Archaeology of Prehistoric Settlement. *In* Making Places in the Prehistoric World. J. Brück and M. Goodman, eds. pp. 1–19. London, UCL Press.

Budd, Paul, A. Mark Pollard, Brett Scaife, and Richard G. Thomas, 1995 Oxhide Ingots, Recycling and the Mediterranean Metals Trade. Journal of Mediterranean Archaeology 8:1–32.

Budd, Paul, and Timothy Taylor, 1995 The Faerie Smith Meets the Bronze Industry: Magic versus Science in the Interpretation of Prehistoric Metal-Making. World Archaeology 27:133–143.

Calvo Trias, Manuel, and Víctor M. Guerrero Ayuso, 2002 Los Inicios de la Metalurgia en Baleares el Calcolítico (c.2500–1700 cal. B.C.). El Tall del temps maior 9. Mallorca: El Tall.

Çambel, Halet, and Robert J. Braidwood, 1980 The Joint Istanbul-Chicago Universities' Prehistoric Research in Southeastern Anatolia. Istanbul University, Faculty of Letters, Publication 2589. Istanbul: University of Istanbul.

Canuto, Marcello A., and Jason Yaeger, eds., 2000 The Archaeology of Communities: A New World Perspective. London: Routledge.

Chapman, Robert, 1990 Emerging Complexity. The Later Prehistory of South-East Spain, Iberia and the West Mediterranean. Cambridge: Cambridge University Press.

—— 2003 Archaeologies of Complexity. London: Routledge.

Charles, James A., 1978 The Development of the Usage of Tin and Tin Bronze: Some Problems. In The Search for Ancient Tin. Alan D. Franklin, Jacqueline S. Olin, and Theodore A. Wertime, eds. pp. 25–32. Washington, DC: U.S. Government Printing Office.

—— 1980 The Coming of Copper and Copper-Base Alloys and Iron. In The Coming of the Age of Iron. Theodore A. Wertime and James D. Muhly, eds. pp. 151–181. New Haven: Yale University Press.

Childs, S. Terry, and David Killick, 1993 Indigenous African Metallurgy: Nature and Culture. Annual Review of Anthropology 22:317–337.

Conophagos, Constantinos, 1980 To Arxaio Laurion (Ancient Laurion). Athens: Ekdotike Ellados.

Constantinou, George, 1982 Geological Features and Ancient Exploitation of the Cupriferous Sulphide Orebodies of Cyprus. In Early Metallurgy in Cyprus 4000–500 B.C. James D. Muhly, Robert Maddin, and Vassos Karageorghis, eds. pp. 13–23 Nicosia: Pierides Foundation.

—— 1992 Ancient Copper Mining in Cyprus. In Cyprus, Copper and the Sea. A. Marangou and K. Psillides, eds. pp. 43–74. Nicosia: Government of Cyprus.

Courtois, Jacques-Claude, 1983 Le Trésor de Poids de Kalavasos-Ayios Dhimitrios 1982. Report of the Department of Antiquities, Cyprus: 117–130.

Craddock, Paul T., 1995 Early Metal Mining and Production. Edinburgh: Edinburgh University Press.

Davey, Christopher J., 1979 Some Ancient Near Eastern Pot Bellows. Levant 11:101–111.

De Jesus, Prentiss S., 1980 The Development of Prehistoric Mining and Metallurgy in Anatolia. British Archaeological Reports, International Series 74(I). Oxford: BAR.

Delibes de Castro, Germàn, Ignacio Montero Ruiz, and S. Rovira Llorens, 1996 The First Use of Metals in the Iberian Peninsula. In The Copper Age in the Near East and Europe. B. Bagolini and F. Lo Schiavo, eds. pp. 19–34. Forli: ABACO Edizioni.

Demakopoulou, Kaite, 1998 The Neolithic Hoard. In Jewelry of Greek Prehistory: The Neolithic Hoard. Kaite Demakopoulou, ed. pp. 15–19. Athens: Tameio Arxaiologikon Poron kai Apallotrioseon (in Greek).

Demoule, J.-P., and Catherine Perlès, 1993 The Greek Neolithic: A New Review. Journal of World Prehistory 7:355–416.

Dercksen, J. G., 1996 The Old Assyrian Copper Trade in Anatolia. Nederlands Historisch-Archaeologisch Instituut te Istanbul, Uitgaven 75. Amsterdam: Nederlands Historisch-Archaeologisch Instituut.

Diaz-Andreu, Margarita, and Ignacio Montero Ruiz, 2000 Metallurgy and Social Dynamics in the Later Prehistory of Mediterranean Spain. In Metals Make the World Go Round: The Supply and Circulation of Metals in Bronze Age Europe. C. F. E. Pare, ed. pp. 116–132. Oxford: Oxbow Books.

Domergue, Claude, and Christian Rico, 2002 À propos de Deux Lingots de Cuivre Antiques Trouvés en Mer sur la Côte Languedocienne. In Vivre, Produire et Échanger: Reflets Méditerranéens. Mélanges Offerts à Bernard Liou. L. Rivet and M. Sciallano, eds. pp. 141–152. Montagnac: Éditions Monique Mergoil.

Douglass, William A., 1998 The Mining Camp as Community. In Social Approaches to an Industrial Past: The Archaeology and Anthropology of Mining. A. Bernard Knapp, Vincent C. Pigott, and Eugenia Herbert, eds. pp. 97–108. London: Routledge.

Du Plat Taylor J., 1952 A Late Bronze Age Settlement at Apliki, Cyprus. Antiquaries Journal 32:133–167.

Edzard, Deitz Otto, 1960 Die Beziehungen Babyloniens und Ägyptens in der Mittelbabylonischen Zeit und das Gold. Journal of the Economic and Social History of the Orient 3:38–55.

Fenenga, F., 1967 Post-1800 Mining Camps. Historical Archaeology 1:80–82.

Forbes, Robert James, 1950 Metallurgy in Antiquity. A Notebook for Archaeologists and Technologists. Leiden: Brill.

——1971 Studies in Ancient Technology 8. Leiden: Brill.

——1972 Studies in Ancient Technology 9. 2nd revised edition. Leiden: Brill.

Frankel, David, 2000 Migration and Ethnicity in Prehistoric Cyprus: Technology as *habitus*. European Journal of Archaeology 3:167–187.

Gale, Noel H., 1978 Lead Isotopes and Aegean Metallurgy. *In* Thera and the Aegean World, Vol. 1. C. Doumas, ed. pp. 529–545. London: Aris and Phillips.

——1991 Metals and Metallurgy in the Chalcolithic Period. Bulletin of American Schools of Oriental Research 282(2):37–62.

Gale, Noel. H., and Sophia A. Stos-Gale, 1981 Cycladic Lead and Silver Metallurgy. Annual of the British School at Athens 76:169–224.

——1982 Bronze Age Copper Sources in the Mediterranean: A New Approach. Science 216(4541):11–18.

Gale, Noel H., Artemis Papastamataki, Sophia Stos-Gale, and K. Leonie, 1985 Copper Sources and Copper Metallurgy in the Aegean Bronze Age. *In* Furnaces and Smelting Technology in Antiquity. Paul T. Craddock and M. J. Hughes, eds. pp. 81–102. British Museum Occasional Paper 48. London: British Museum Press.

Galili, Ehud, N. Shmueli, and Michal Artzy, 1986 Bronze Age Ship's Cargo of Copper and Tin. The International Journal of Nautical Archaeology and Underwater Exploration 15:25–37.

Gamble, Clive, 1986 Hunter-Gatherer Studies and the Origin of States. *In* States in History. John A. Hall, ed. pp. 22–47. London: Blackwell.

Genz, Hermann, and Andreas Hauptmann, 2002 Chalcolithic and EBA Metallurgy in the Southern Levant. *In* Anatolian Metal II. Ünsal Yalçin, ed. pp. 149–157. Der Anschnitt, Beiheft 15. Bochum: Deutsches Bergbau-Museum.

Gerritsen, Fokke, 2003 Local Identities: Landscape and Community in the Late Prehistoric Meuse-Demer-Scheldt Region. Amsterdam Archaeological Series 9. Amsterdam: University of Amsterdam Press.

——2004 Archaeological Perspectives on Local Communities. *In* A Companion to Archaeology, J. Bintliff, ed. pp. 141–154. Oxford: Blackwell.

Giardino, Claudio, 2000a The Beginning of Metallurgy in Tyrrhenian South-Central Italy. *In* Ancient Italy in its Mediterranean Setting. Studies in Honour of Ellen Macnamara. David Ridgway, Francesca R. Serra Ridgway, Mark Pearce, Edward Herring, Ruth D. Whitehouse, and John B. Wilkins, eds. pp. 49–73. Accordia Specialist Studies on the Mediterranean 4. London: Accordia Research Institute, University of London.

——2000b Sicilian Hoards and Protohistoric Metal Trade in the Central West Mediterranean. *In* Metals Make the World Go Round: The Supply and Circulation of Metals in Bronze Age Europe. C. F. E. Pare, ed. pp. 99–107. Oxford: Oxbow Books.

Given, Michael, and A. Bernard Knapp, 2000 The Sydney Cyprus Survey Project and the Archaeology of Mining. *In* Acts of the Third International Congress of Cypriot Studies. G. C. Ioannides and S. A. Hadjistellis, eds. pp. 281–287. Nicosia: Society of Cypriot Studies.

——2003 The Sydney Cyprus Survey Project: Social Approaches to Regional Archaeological Survey. Monumenta Archaeologica 21. Los Angeles: Cotsen Institute of Archaeology, UCLA.

Godoy, R., 1985 Mining: Anthropological Perspectives. Annual Review of Anthropology 14:199–217.

Greenberg, Raphael, 2002 Early Urbanizations in the Levant: A Regional Narrative. London and New York: Leicester University Press.

Hardesty, Donald L., 1988 The Archaeology of Mining and Miners: A View from the Silver State. Society for Historical Archaeology, Special Publication 6. Pleasant Hill, CA: Society for Historical Archaeology.

Hauptmann, Andreas, 1989 The Earliest Periods of Copper Metallurgy in Feinan, Jordan. In Old World Archaeometallurgy. Andreas Hauptmann, Ernst Pernicka, and Günther A. Wagner, eds. pp. 119–135. Der Anschnitt Beiheft 7. Bochum: Deutsches Bergbau-Museum.

——2000 Zur Frühen Metallurgie des Kupfers in Fenan/Jordanien. Der Anschnitt Beiheft 11. Bochum: Deutsches Bergbau-Museum.

Hauptmann, Andreas, Ernst Pernicka, and Günther A. Wagner, eds., 1989 Old World Archaeometallurgy. Die Anschnitt, Beiheft 7. Bochum: Deutsches Bergbau-Museum.

Hauptmann, Andreas, and Gerd Weisgerber, 1981 The Early Bronze Age Metallurgy of Shari-i Sokhta. Paleorient 6:120–123.

Helbaek, Hans, 1962 Late Cypriot Vegetable Diet at Apliki. Opuscula Atheniensia 4:171–186.

Heskel, Denis, and Carl Clifford Lamberg-Karlovsky, 1980 An Alternative Sequence for the Development of Metallurgy: Tepe Yahya, Iran. In The Coming of the Age of Iron. Theodore A. Wertime and James D. Muhly, eds. pp. 229–265. New Haven: Yale University Press.

Johnson, Mats, 1999 Chronology of Greece and South East Europe in the Final Neolithic and Early Bronze Age. Proceedings of Prehistoric Society 65:319–336.

Kassianidou, Vasiliki, 1999 Bronze Age Copper Smelting Technology in Cyprus – The Evidence from Politico Phorades. In Metals in Antiquity. Suzanne M. M. Young, A. Mark Pollard, Paul Budd, and Rob A. Ixer, eds. pp. 91–97. British Archaeological Reports, International Series 792. Oxford: Archaeopress.

——2001 Cypriot Copper in Sardinia. Yet Another Case of Bringing Coals to Newcastle? In Italy and Cyprus in Antiquity: 1500–400 B.C. Larissa Bonfante and Vasses Karageorghis, eds. pp. 97–119. Nicosia: Costakis and Leto Severis Foundation.

Knapp, A. Bernard, 1986a Copper Production and Divine Protection: Archaeology, Ideology and Social Complexity on Bronze Age Cyprus. Studies in Mediterranean Archaeology and Literature, Pocket-book 42. Göteborg: P. Åströms Förlag.

——1986b Production, Exchange and Socio-Political Complexity on Bronze Age Cyprus. Oxford Journal of Archaeology 5:35–60.

——1988 Ideology, Archaeology and Polity. Man 23:133–163.

——1989 Copper Production and Mediterranean Trade: The View from Cyprus. Opuscula Atheniensia 18:109–116.

——1990a Production, Location and Integration in Bronze Age Cyprus. Current Anthropology 31:147–176.

——1990b Entrepreneurship, Ethnicity, Exchange: Mediterranean Inter-Island Relations in the Late Bronze Age. Annual of the British School at Athens 85:115–153.

——1993 Thalassocracies in Bronze Age Eastern Mediterranean Trade: Making and Breaking a Myth. World Archaeology 24:332–347.

—— 1996 Near Eastern and Aegean Texts from the Third to the First Millennia B.C. Sources for the History of Cyprus II. Altamont, NY: Greece/Cyprus Research Center.

—— 1997 Mediterranean Maritime Landscapes: Transport, Trade and Society on Late Bronze Age Cyprus. *In* Res Maritimae: Cyprus and the Eastern Mediterranean from Prehistory through the Roman Period. Stuart Swiny, Robert Hohlfelder, and Helena W. Swiny, eds. pp. 153–162. Cyprus American Archaeological Research Institute, Monograph 1. Atlanta: ASOR/Scholars Press.

—— 1998 Mediterranean Bronze Age Trade: Distance, Power and Place. *In* The Aegean and the Orient in the Second Millennium: Proceedings of the 50th Anniversary Symposium, Cincinnati 18–20 April 1997. Eric H. Cline and Diane Harris-Cline, eds. pp. 260–280. Aegaeum 18. Liège: Université de Liège.

—— 1999 Ideational and Industrial Landscape on Prehistoric Cyprus. *In* Archaeologies of Landscapes: Contemporary Perspectives. Wendy Ashmore and A. Bernard Knapp, eds. pp. 229–252. Oxford: Blackwell.

—— 2000 Archaeology, Science-Based Archaeology and the Mediterranean Bronze Age Metals Trade. European Journal of Archaeology 3:31–56.

—— 2003 The Archaeology of Community on Bronze Age Cyprus: Politiko *Phorades* in Context. American Journal of Archaeology 107:559–580.

—— n.d. Orientalisation and Prehistoric Cyprus: The Social Life of Oriental Goods. *In* Orientalisation in Antiquity. Corinna Riva and Nicholas Vella, eds. Monographs in Mediterranean Archaeology 10. London: Equinox Press.

Knapp, A. Bernard, and John F. Cherry, 1994 Provenance Studies and Bronze Age Cyprus: Production, Exchange, and Politico-Economic Change. Monographs in World Archaeology 21. Madison: Prehistory Press.

Knapp, A. Bernard, Vasiliki Kassianidou, and Michael Donnelly, 1999 Excavations At Politiko Phorades – 1998. Report of the Department of Antiquities, Cyprus, pp. 125–146.

—— 2001 The Excavations at Politiko *Phorades*, Cyprus: 1996–2000. Near Eastern Archaeology 64:202–208.

Knapp, A. Bernard, Vincent Pigott, and Eugenia Herbert, eds., 1998 Social Approaches to an Industrial Past: The Archaeology and Anthropology of Mining. London: Routledge.

Krysko, Wladimir W., 1979 Lead in History and Art. Stuttgart: Riederer Verlag.

Lehrberger, Gerhard, 1995 The Gold Deposits of Europe: An Overview of the Possible Metal Sources for Prehistoric Gold Objects. *In* Prehistoric Gold in Europe. Giuolio Morteani and Jeremy P. Northover, eds. pp. 115–144. NATO Advanced Science Institutes Series 280. Dordrecht: Kluwer.

Levy, Thomas E., Russell B. Adams, Andreas Hauptmann, Michael Prange, Sigrid Schmitt-Strecker, and Mohammad Najjar, 2002 Early Bronze Age Metallurgy: A Newly Discovered Copper Manufactory in Southern Jordan. Antiquity 76:425–437.

Lewthwaite, James G., 1987 The Braudelian Beaker: A Chalcolithic Conjuncture in Western Mediterranean Prehistory. *In* Bell Beakers of the Western Mediterranean. W. H. Waldren and R. C. Kennard, eds. pp. 31–60. British Archaeological Reports, International Series 331. Oxford: British Archaeological Reports.

Liverani, Mario, 1990 Prestige and Interest: International Relations in the Near East ca. 1600–1100 B.C. Padua: Sargon Press.

Lo Schiavo, Fulvia, 1986 Sardinian Metallurgy: The Archaeological Background. *In* Studies in Sardinian Archaeology 2: Sardinia in the Mediterranean. Miriam S. Balmuth, ed. pp. 231–250. Ann Arbor: University of Michigan Press.

—— 1988 Early Metallurgy in Sardinia. *In* The Beginnings of the Use of Metals and Alloys. Robert Maddin, ed. pp. 92–103. Cambridge, MA: MIT Press.

——1998 Zum Herstellung und Distribution bronzezeitlicher Metallgegenstaende im nuragischen Sardinien. *In* Mensch und Umwelt in der Bronzezeit Europas. B. Hänsel, ed. pp. 193–216. Kiel: Oetker-Voges Verlag.

Lo Schiavo, Fulvia E., Ellen MacNamara, and Lucia Vagnetti, 1985 Late Cypriot Imports to Italy and their Influence on Local Bronzework. Papers of British School at Rome 53:1–71.

McGeehan-Liritzis, Veronica, 1996 The Role and Development of Metallurgy in the Late Neolithic and Early Bronze Age of Greece. Studies in Mediterranean Archaeology, Pocketbook 122. Jonsered: Paul Åströms Förlag.

Maddin, Robert, ed., 1988 The Beginning of the Use of Metals and Alloys. Cambridge, MA: MIT Press.

Maddin, Robert, 1989 The Copper and Tin Ingots from the Kas Shipwreck. *In* Old World Archaeometallurgy. Andreas Hauptmann, Ernst Pernicka, and Günther A. Wagner, eds. pp. 99–105. Der Anschnitt-Beiheft 7. Bochum: Deutsches Bergbau-Museum.

Maddin, Robert, Tamara Stech Wheeler, and James D. Muhly, 1977 Tin in the Ancient Near East. Old Questions and New Finds. Expedition 19(2):35–47.

Maddin, Robert, Tamara Stech, and James D. Muhly, 1991 Cayönü Tepesi. *In* Découverte du Métal. J.-P. Mohen and C. Éluère, eds. pp. 375–386. Amis du Musée des Antiquités Nationales Millénaires, Dossier 2. Paris: Picard.

Mangou, Eleni, Yannis Maniatis, Themistocles Paradellis, and Andreas Karydas, 1998 Archaeometric Study of the Neolithic Hoard of the National Archaeological Museum. *In* Jewelry of Greek Prehistory: The Neolithic Hoard. Kaite Demakopoulou, ed. pp. 44–47. Athens: Tameio Arxaiologikon Poron kai Apallotrioseon (in Greek).

Manning, Sturt W., 1994 The Emergence of Divergence: Bronze Age Crete and the Cyclades. *In* Development and Decline in the Bronze Age Mediterranean. Clay Mathers and Simon Stoddart, eds. pp. 221–270. Sheffield Archaeological Monographs 8. Sheffield: John Collis Publications.

Maran, Joseph, 2000 Das aegaeische Chalkolithikum und das erste Silber in Europa. *In* Studien zur Religion und Kultur Kleinasiens und des Aegeischen Bereiches. Festschrift Baki Ogun. C. Isik, ed. pp. 179–193. Asia Minor Studien 39. Bonn: R. Habelt.

Martin De La Cruz, J. C., 1990 Die erste Mykenische Keramik von der Iberischer Halbinsel. Prähistorischer Zeitschrift 65:49–52.

Meiggs, Russell, 1998 Trees and Timber in the Ancient Mediterranean World. Oxford: Clarendon Press.

Meredith, Craig, 1998 An Archaeometallurgical Survey of Ancient Tin Mines and Smelting Sites in Spain and Portugal. British Archaeological Reports, International Series 714. Oxford: Archaeopress.

Merpert, N. I., R. M. Munchaev and N. O. Bader, 1977 The Most Ancient Metallurgy of Mesopotamia. *Sovetskaya Arkheologiya* 1977(3):154–163.

Michailidou, Anna, 1990 The Lead Weights from Akrotiri: The Archaeological Record. *In* Thera and the Aegean World, Vol. 3.1. D. A. Hardy, C. G. Doumas, J. A. Sakellarakis, and P. M. Warren, eds. pp. 407–419. London: The Thera Foundation.

——2001 Script and Metrology: Practical Processes and Cognitive Inventions. *In* Manufacture and Measurement: Counting, Measuring and Recording Craft Items in Early Aegean Societies. Anna Michailidou, ed. pp. 53–82. Meletemata 33. Paris, Athens: Diffusion de Boccard.

Montero Ruiz, Ignacio, 1993 Bronze Age Metallurgy in South-east Spain. Antiquity 67:46–57.

Montero Ruiz, Ignacio, and Maria Jesus Rodriguez de la Esperanza, In press Prähistorische Kupferbergbau in Spanien: ein Überblick über die Forschungsstand. Der Anschnitt.

Moorey, Peter Roger Stuart, 1994 Ancient Mesopotamian Materials and Industries: The Archaeological Evidence. Oxford: Clarendon Press.

Moran, William, 1992 The Amarna Letters. Baltimore: John Hopkins University Press.

Müller, Hans Wolfgang, and Eberhard Thiem, 1999 The Royal Gold of Ancient Egypt. London: I. B. Tauris.

Muhly, James D., 1973 Copper and Tin: The Distribution of Mineral Resources and the Nature of the Metals Trade in the Bronze Age. Transactions of the Connecticut Academy of Arts and Sciences 43:155–535. Hamden, CT: Archon Books.

—— 1984 Timna and King Solomon. Bibliotheca Orientalis 41:275–292.

—— 1985a Beyond Typology: Aegean Metallurgy in its Historical Context. In Contributions to Aegean Archaeology: Studies in Honor of William A. McDonald. Nancy C. Wilkie and William D. E. Coulson, eds. pp. 109–141. Minneapolis: Center for Ancient Studies, University of Minnesota.

—— 1985b Lead Isotope Analysis and the Problem of Lead in Copper. Report of the Department of Antiquities, Cyprus, pp. 78–82.

—— 1988 The Beginnings of Metallurgy in the Old World. In The Beginning of the Use of Metals and Alloys. Robert Maddin, ed. pp. 2–20. Cambridge, MA: MIT Press.

—— 1989a Cayönü Tepesi and the Beginnings of Metallurgy in the Old World. In Old World Archaeometallurgy. Der Anschnitt 7. A. Hauptmann, E. Pernicka, and G. A. Wagner, eds. pp. 1–11. Bochum: Deutsches Bergbau-Museum.

—— 1989b The Organisation of the Copper Industry in Late Bronze Age Cyprus. In Early Society in Cyprus. Edgar Peltenburg, ed. pp. 298–314. Edinburgh: Edinburgh University Press, Leventis Foundation.

—— 1991a Copper in Cyprus: The Early Phase. In Découverte du Métal. Jean-Pierre Mohen and Christiane Éluère, eds. pp. 357–374. Amis du Musée des Antiquités Nationals Millénaires, Dossier 2. Paris: Picard.

—— 1991b The Development of Copper Metallurgy in Late Bronze Age Cyprus. In Bronze Age Trade in the Mediterranean. Noel H. Gale, ed. pp. 180–196. Studies in Mediterranean Archaeology 90. Jonsered: Paul Åströms Förlag.

—— 1993 Early Bronze Age Tin and the Taurus. American Journal of Archaeology 97:239–254.

—— 1996a The Significance of Metals in the Late Bronze Age Economy of Cyprus. In The Development of the Cypriot Economy: From the Prehistoric Period to the Present Day. Vassos Karageorghis and Demetrios Michaelides, eds. pp. 45–60. Nicosia: University of Cyprus and the Bank of Cyprus.

—— 1996b The First Use of Metals in the Aegean. In The Copper Age in the Near East and Europe. B. Bagolini and F. Lo Schiavo, eds. pp. 75–84. 13th International Congress of Prehistoric and Protohistoric Sciences, Colloquium XIX (Metallurgy: Origins Technology), Vol. 10. Forlì, Italy: A.B.A.C.O. Edizioni.

—— 1999 Copper and Bronze in Cyprus and the Eastern Mediterranean. In The Archaeometallurgy of the Asian Old World. University Museum Monograph 89; University Museum Symposium Series 7; MASCA Research Papers in Science and Archaeology 16. V.C. Pigott, ed. pp. 15–25. Philadelphia: University Museum, University of Pennsylvania.

—— 2002 Early Metallurgy in Greece and Cyprus. In Anatolian Metal II. Ünsal Yalçin, ed. pp. 77–82. Der Anschnitt, Beiheft 15. Bochum: Deutsches Bergbau-Museum.

Muhly, James D., Robert Maddin, and Tamara Stech, 1988 Cyprus, Crete and Sardinia: Copper Oxhide Ingots and the Bronze Age Metals Trade. Report of the Department of Antiquities, Cyprus, pp. 281–298.

Muhly James D., and Ernst Pernicka, 1992 Early Trojan Metallurgy and Metals Trade. *In* Heinrich Schliemann: Grundlagen und Ergebnisse moderner Archäologie 100 Jahre nach Schliemanns Tod. J. Herrmann, ed. pp. 309–318. Berlin: Akademie Verlag.

Needham, Stuart P., M. N. Leese, D. R. Hook, and M. J. Hughes, 1989 Developments in the Early Bronze Age Metallurgy of Southern Britain. World Archaeology 20:383–402.

Ogden, Jack, 2001 Metals. *In* Ancient Egyptian Materials and Technology. Paul T. Nicholson and Ian Shaw, eds. pp. 148–176. Cambridge: Cambridge University Press.

Özdogan, Mehmet, and Hermann Parzinger, 2000 Asagipinar and Kanligeçit Excavations – Some New Evidence on Early Metallurgy from Eastern Thrace. *In* Anatolian Metal I, Ünsal Yalçin, ed. pp. 83–91. Der Anschnitt, Beiheft 13. Bochum: Deutschen Bergbau-Museums.

Papasavvas, Georgios, 2003 Cypriot Casting Technology I: The Stands. Report of the Department of Antiquities, Cyprus.

Pare, Christopher F. E., 2000a Bronze and the Bronze Age. *In* Metals Make the World Go Round: The Supply and Circulation of Metals in Bronze Age Europe. Christopher Pare, ed. pp. 1–38. Oxford: Oxbow Books.

——ed., 2000b Metals Make the World Go Round: The Supply and Circulation of Metals in Bronze Age Europe. Oxford: Oxbow Books.

Patterson, Clair C., 1971 Native Copper, Silver, and Gold Accessible to Early Metallurgists. American Antiquity 36:286–321.

Pearce, Mark, 2000 What this Awl Means. Understanding the Earliest Italian Metalwork. *In* Ancient Italy in its Mediterranean Setting. Studies in Honour of Ellen Macnamara. David Ridgway, Francesca R. Serra Ridgway, Mark Pearce, Edward Herring, Ruth D. Whitehouse, and John B. Wilkins, eds. pp. 67–73. Accordia Specialist Studies on the Mediterranean 4. London: Accordia Research Institute, University of London.

Perlès, Catherine, 1992 Systems of Exchange and Organisation of Production in Neolithic Greece. Journal of Mediterranean Archaeology 5:115–164.

Peltenburg, E. J., et al., 1998 Lemba Archaeological Project, vol. II.1A. Excavations at Kissonerga-Mosphilia 1979–1992. Studies in Mediterranean Archaeology 70:2. Jonsered: P. Åströms Förlag.

Pernicka, Ernst, 1998 Die Ausbreitung der Zinnbronze em 3. Jarhtausend. *In* Mensch und Umwelt in der Bronzezeit Europas. B. Hänsel, ed. pp. 135–147. Kiel: Oetker-Voges Verlag.

Pernicka, Ernst, Cristiane Lutz, Hans Gert Bachmann, Günther A. Wagner, C. Elitzsch, and E. Klein, 1985 Alte Blei-Silber-Verhüttung auf Sifnos. *In* Silber, Blei und Gold auf Sifnos. Günther A. Wagner and Gert Weisgerber, eds. pp. 185–199. Der Anschnitt, Beiheft 3. Bochum: Deutsches Bergbau-Museum.

Pernicka, Ernst, F. Begeman, S. Schmitt-Strecker, and A. P. Grimanis, 1990 On the Composition and Provenance of Metal Artefacts from Poliochni on Lemnos. Oxford Journal of Archaeology 9:263–298.

Pernicka, Ernst, Thilo Rehren, and Sigrid Schmitt-Strecker, 1998 Late Uruk Silver Production by Cupellation at Habuba Kabira, Syria. *In* Metallurgica Antiqua: In Honour of Hans-Gert Bachmann and Robert Maddin. Thilo Rehren, Andreas Hauptmann, and James D. Muhly, eds. pp. 123–134. Der Anschnitt, Beiheft 8. Bochum: Deutsches Bergbau-Museum.

Petruso, Karl M., 1984 Prolegomena to Late Cypriot Weight Metrology. American Journal of Archaeology 88:293–304.

Pfaffenberger, Brian, 1992 The Social Anthropology of Technology. Annual Review of Anthropology 21:491–516.

—— 1998 Mining Communities, Chaînes Opératoires and Sociotechnical Systems. In Social Approaches to an Industrial Past: The Archaeology and Anthropology of Mining. A. Bernard Knapp, Vincent C. Pigott, and Eugenia W. Herbert, eds. pp. 291–300. London: Routledge.

Philip, Graham, 1999 Complexity and Diversity in the Southern Levant during the Third Millennium B.C.: The Evidence of Khirbet Kerak Ware. Journal of Mediterranean Archaeology 12:26–57.

Philip, Graham, Philip W. Clogg, David Dungworth, and Sophia Stos, 2003 Copper Metallurgy in the Jordan Valley from the Third to the First Millennia B.C.: Chemical, Metallographic and Lead Isotope Analysis of Artefacts from Pella. Levant 35:71–100.

Pigott, Vincent C., ed., 1999a The Archaeometallurgy of the Asian Old World. University Museum Monograph 89; University Museum Symposium Series 7; MASCA Research Papers in Science and Archaeology 16. Philadelphia: University Museum, University of Pennsylvania.

—— 1999b The Development of Metal Production on the Anatolian Plateau: An Archaeometallurgical Perspective. In The Archaeometallurgy of the Asian Old World. University Museum Monograph 89; University Museum Symposium Series 7; MASCA Research Papers in Science and Archaeology 16. V. C. Pigott, ed. pp. 73–106. Philadelphia: University Museum, University of Pennsylvania.

Prag, Kay, 1978 Silver in the Levant in the Fourth Millennium B.C. In Archaeology in the Levant: Essays for Kathleen Kenyon. Roger Moorey and Peter J. Parr, eds. pp. 38–45. Warminster: Aris and Philips.

Pulak, Çemal, 1998 The Uluburun Shipwreck: An Overview. International Journal of Nautical Archaeology and Underwater Excavation 27:188–224.

—— 2000 The Copper and Tin Ingots from the Late Bronze Age Shipwreck at Uluburun. In Anatolian Metal I, Ünsal Yalçin, ed. pp. 137–157. Der Anschnitt, Beiheft 13. Bochum: Deutschen Bergbau-Museums.

Raban, Avner, and Ehud Galili, 1985 Recent Maritime Archaeological Research in Israel – a Preliminary Report. The International Journal of Nautical Archaeology and Underwater Exploration 14:321–356.

Ramis, Damià, Andreas Hauptmann, and Jaume Coll, n.d. Réduction de Cuivre dans la Préhistoire de Majorque, n.d. In Colloque Internationale: La Première Métallurgie en France et dans les Pays Limitrophes (Carcassonne, 28–30 Septembre 2002). P. Ambert, J. Vaquer, and A. Boisslier, eds. Paris: Société Préhistorique de France.

Rehren, Thilo, K. Hess, and Graham Philip, 1996 Auriferous Silver in Western Asia: Ore or Alloy? Journal of the Historical Metallurgy Society 30:1–10.

Renfrew, Colin, 1967a Colonialism and Megalithismus. Antiquity 41:276–288.

—— 1967b Cycladic Metallurgy and the Aegean Early Bronze Age. American Journal of Archaeology 71:1–20.

—— 1973 Trade and Craft Specialization. In Neolithic Greece. Demetrios Theocharis, ed. pp. 179–191. Athens: National Bank of Greece.

—— 1975 Trade as Action at a Distance: Questions of Integration and Communication. In Ancient Civilization and Trade. J. A. Sabloff and C. C. Lamberg-Karlovsky, eds. pp. 3–59. Albuquerque: University of New Mexico Press.

Rodriguez Diaz, A., I. Pavon Soldevilla, C. Meredith, and J. Juan I Tresseras, 2001 El Cerro de San Cristobal, Logrosan, Extremedura, Spain. The Archaeometallurgical Excavation of a Late Bronze Age Tin-Mining and Metalworking Site. First Excavation Season 1998. British Archaeological Reports, International Series 922. Oxford. Archaeopress.

Rothenberg, Beno, 1988 The Egyptian Mining Temple at Timna. Researches in the Arabah 1959–1984. Vol. 1. London: Institute of Archaeometallurgical Studies, University of London.

—— 1990 The Ancient Metallurgy of Copper. Researches in the Arabah 1959–1984, Vol. 2. London: Institute of Archaeometallurgical Studies, University of London.

—— 1999 Archaeometallurgical Researches in the Southern Arabah, 1959–1990. Part 2: Egyptian New Kingdom (Ramesside) to Early Islam. Palestine Exploration Quarterly 131:149–175.

Ruiz Taboada, Arturo, and Ignacio Montero Ruiz, 1999 The Oldest Metallurgy in Western Europe. Antiquity 73:897–903.

Sanna, U., R. Calera, and Fulvia Lo Schiavo, eds., 2003 Archeometallurgia in Sardegna dalle Origini al Primo Ferro. Cagliari: Università degle Studi di Cagliari e Consiglio Nazionale delle Richerche.

Schlanger, Nathan, 1994 Mindful Technology: Unleashing the Chaîne Opératoire for an Archaeology of the Mind. In The Ancient Mind: Elements of Cognitive Archaeology. Colin Renfrew and Ezra B. W. Zubrow, eds. pp. 143–151. Cambridge: Cambridge University Press.

Schmidt, P. R., and B. B. Mapunda, 1997 Ideology and the Archaeological Record in Africa: Interpreting Symbolism in Iron Smelting Technology. Journal of Anthropological Archaeology 16:73–102.

Sherratt, Andrew G., and Susan Sherratt, 1991 From Luxuries to Commodities: The Nature of Mediterranean Bronze Age Trading Systems. In Bronze Age Trade in the Mediterranean. Noel H. Gale, ed. pp. 351–386. Studies in Mediterranean Archaeology 90. Göteborg, Sweden: P. Åströms Förlag.

Sherratt, Susan, 2000 Circulation of Metals and the End of the Bronze Age in the Eastern Mediterranean. In Metals Make the World Go Round: The Supply and Circulation of Metals in Bronze Age Europe. Christopher F. Pare, ed. pp. 82–98. Oxford: Oxbow Books.

Siegelova, J., 1993 Metalle und Metallurgie in den hethitischen Texten. In Reallexikon der Assyriologie und Vorderasiatischen Archäologie 8.1(2). Dietz Otto Edzard ed. pp. 112–119. Berlin: Walter de Gruyter.

Stager, Lawrence E., 2001 Port Power in the Early and Middle Bronze Ages: The Organization of Maritime Trade and Hinterland Production. In Studies in the Archaeology of Israel and Neighboring Lands in Memory of Douglas L. Esse. S. R. Wolff, ed. pp. 625–638. Studies in Ancient Oriental Civilizations 59. Boston: American Schools of Oriental Research.

Stech, Tamara, 1999 Aspects of Early Metallurgy in Mesopotamia and Anatolia. In The Archaeometallurgy of the Asian Old World. University Museum Monograph 89; University Museum Symposium Series 7; MASCA Research Papers in Science and Archaeology 16. Vincent C. Pigott, ed. pp. 59–71. Philadelphia: University Museum, University of Pennsylvania.

Stöllner, Thomas, 2003 Mining and Economy – A Discussion of Spatial Organisations and Structures of Early Raw Material Exploitation. In Man and Mining–Mensch und Bergbau: Studies in Honour of Gerd Weisgerber. Thomas Stöllner, Gabriele Körlin, Gero Steffens, and Jan Cierny, eds. pp. 415–446. Der Anschnitt, Beiheft 16. Bochum: Deutsches Bergbau-Museum.

Stöllner, Thomas, Gabriele Körlin, Gero Steffens, and Jan Cierny, eds., 2003 Man and Mining–Mensch und Bergbau: Studies in Honour of Gerd Weisgerber. Der Anschnitt, Beiheft 16. Bochum: Deutsches Bergbau-Museum.

Stos-Gale, Sophia, Noel H. Gale, and Artemis Papastamataki, 1988 An Early Bronze Age Copper Smelting Site on the Aegean Island of Kythnos. *In* Aspects of Ancient Mining and Metallurgy: Acta of a British School at Athens Centenary Conference at Bangor, 1986. J. Ellis Jones, ed. pp. 23–30. London: British School at Athens and University of North Wales.

Tadmor, Miriam, Dan Kedem, Friedrich Begemann, Andreas Hauptmann, Ernst Pernicka, and Sigrid Schmitt-Strecker, 1995 The Nahal Mishmar Hoard from the Judean Desert: Technology, Composition and Provenance. Atiqot 27:95–148. Jerusalem: Israel Exploration Society.

Theophrastus (translated by Arthur Hort), 1916 Enquiry into Plants and Minor Works on Odours and Weather Signs. The Loeb Classical Library 70, Vol. I. Series editor G. P. Goold. Cambridge, MA: Harvard University Press.

Thomas, Nicholas, 1991 Entangled Objects: Exchange, Material Culture, and Colonialism in the Pacific. Cambridge, MA: Harvard University Press.

Tylecote, Ronald F., 1987 The Early History of Metallurgy in Europe. Essex: Longman.

——1992 A History of Metallurgy. 2nd Edition. London: Institute of Materials.

Veenhof, K. R., 1988 Prices and Trade. Altorientalische Forschungen 15:243–263.

Verhoeven, Marc, 1999 An Archaeological Ethnography of a Neolithic Community: Space, Place, and Social Relations in the Burnt Village at Tell Sabi Abyad, Syria. Istanbul: Nederlands Historisch-Archaeologisch Instituut te Istanbul.

Wagner, Günther A., and Önder Öztunali, 2000 Prehistoric Copper Sources in Turkey. *In* Anatolian Metal I. Ünsal Yalçin, ed. pp. 31–61. Der Anschnitt, Beiheft 13. Bochum: Deutsches Bergbau-Museum.

Wagner, Günther A., Irmtud Wagner, Önder Öztunali, Sigrid Schmitt-Strecker, and Friedrich Begemann, 2003 Archäometallurgischer Bericht über Feldforschung in Anatolien und bleiisotopische Studien an Erzen und Schlacken. *In* Man and Mining–Mensch und Bergbau: Studies in Honour of Gerd Weisgerber. Thomas Stöllner, Gabriele Körlin, Gero Steffens, and Jan Cierny, eds. pp. 475–494. Der Anschnitt, Beiheft 16. Bochum: Deutsches Bergbau-Museum.

Waldren, William H., 1998 The Beaker Culture of the Balearic Islands. British Archaeological Reports, International Series 709. Oxford: Archaeopress.

Waldren, William, and R. C. Kennard, eds., 1987 Bell Beakers of the Western Mediterranean: Definition, Interpretation, Theory and New Site Data. British Archaeological Reports, International Series 331. Oxford: BAR.

Webster, Gary S., 1996 A Prehistory of Sardinia, 2300–500 B.C. Monographs in Mediterranean Archaeology 5. Sheffield: Sheffield Academic Press.

Weeks, Lloyd R., 1999 Lead Isotope Analyses from Tell Abraq, United Arab Emirates: New Data Regarding the "Tin Problem" in Western Asia. Antiquity 73(279):49–64.

Weisgerber, Gerd, 1982 Towards a History of Copper Mining in Cyprus and the Near East: Possibilities of Mining Archaeology. *In* Early Metallurgy in Cyprus, 4000–500 B.C. James D. Muhly, Robert Maddin, and Vassos Karageorghis, eds. pp. 25–32. Nicosia: Pierides Foundation.

Weisgerber, Gerd, and Jan Cierny, 2002 Tin for Ancient Anatolia? *In* Anatolian Metal II. Ünsal Yalçin, ed. pp. 179–186. Der Anschnitt, Beiheft 15. Bochum: Deutsches Bergbau-Museum.

Wertime, Theodore A., 1973 The Beginnings of Metallurgy: A New Look. Science 182(4115):875–887.

Williams, Dyfri, and Jack Ogden, 1994 Greek Gold. Jewellery of the Classical World. London: British Museum Press.

Yalçin, Ünsal, ed., 2000a Anatolian Metal I. Der Anschnitt, Beiheft 13. Bochum: Deutsches Bergbau-Museum.

Yalçin, Ünsal, 2000b Anfänge der Metallverwendung in Anatolien. *In* Anatolian Metal I. Ünsal Yalçin, ed. pp. 17–30. Der Anschnitt, Beiheft 13. Bochum: Deutsches Bergbau-Museum.

Yalçin, Ünsal, ed., 2002 Anatolian Metal II. Der Anschnitt, Beiheft 15. Bochum: Deutsches Bergbau-Museum.

Yener, K. Aslihan, 2000 The Domestication of Metals: The Rise of Complex Metal Industries in Anatolia. Culture and History of the Ancient Near East 4. Leiden: Brill.

Yener, K. Aslihan, and Pamela B. Vandiver, 1993 Tin Processing at Göltepe, an Early Bronze Age Site in Anatolia. American Journal of Archaeology 97:207–238.

Zachos, Kostas L., 1999 Zas Cave on Naxos and the Role of Caves in the Aegean Late Neolithic. *In* Neolithic Society in Greece. Paul Halstead, ed. pp. 153–163. Sheffield Studies in Aegean Archaeology 2. Sheffield: Sheffield Academic Press.

Zwicker, Ulrich, 1991 Natural Copper-Arsenic Alloys and Smelted Arsenic Bronzes in Early Metal Production. *In* Découverte du Métal. Jean-Pierre Mohen and Christiane Éluère, eds. pp. 331–340. Paris: Picard.

10

Settlement in the Prehistoric Mediterranean

Luke Sollars

Introduction

Fernand Braudel, the most notable historian ever to write on the wider Mediterranean world, would not venture to discuss *the* Mediterranean town (Horden and Purcell 2000:101). Following his example, Horden and Purcell simply indicate some "characteristic features of Mediterranean *settlement*." I, in turn, following these precedents, will not attempt to present an exhaustive chronological catalog of prehistoric settlement throughout the Mediterranean region, but instead have chosen some of Horden and Purcell's characteristics for discussion and illustration.

Settlement, in one form or another, is an inevitable consequence of human presence in the landscape and, as such, has been studied for as long as archaeologists have been active. In the past, however, settlements have often been investigated as discrete entities, and archaeologists have focused on sites and the reconstruction of sites, rather than considering the broader picture of how they might fit into local, regional, and wider networks. The term "settlement archaeology" (summarized in Knapp 1997:2) has been applied to these approaches, and its proponents, for the most part, ignored inter-site relationships. Relationships between settlements and the surrounding landscape also received little attention, and site distributions were generally treated as static patterns to pinpoint extant remains on a map.

Settlement is one of the basic blocks from which archaeological patterns are built and should never be forgotten, for without these patterns any attempt at an interpretation of the landscape is futile. But as Darvill (1997:74–75) notes, overemphasizing the importance of sites and monuments can obscure the fact that archaeological evidence is everywhere and not restricted to the more obvious loci of activity. Anschuetz et al. (2001:170) move beyond site descriptions and hierarchy to interpret the underlying meaning of archaeologically observed patterns across space and time. Approaches such as these are typical of landscape archaeology which, unlike settlement archaeology, focuses not just on sites but on entire

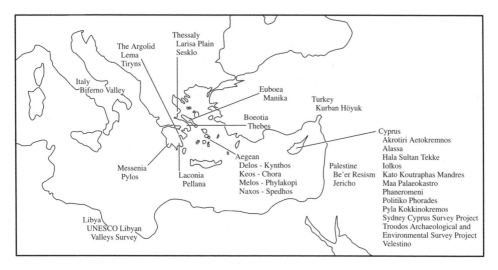

Figure 10.1 Map of regions, places, projects, and sites mentioned in the text

landscapes, taking into account the beliefs and practices of past populations, as well as elements of social structure and physical space (Knapp and Ashmore 1999), of which settlement and settlements are inevitably a part. This wider, more integrated view is being adopted by an increasing number of archaeologists, and regional survey projects, rather than more traditional excavations, are gathering the broad-ranging data that they need. Intensive surveys offer a combination of the wide-ranging extent of earlier, "site-hunting" surveys and the localized detail retrieved by excavation. Compromises, of course, have to be made, but projects such as the Northern Keos Survey (Cherry et al. 1991), the Biferno Valley Survey (Barker 1995), the UNESCO Libyan Valleys Archaeological Survey (Barker 1996), the Sydney Cyprus Survey Project (Given and Knapp 2003) and the Troodos Archaeological and Environmental Survey Project (Given et al. 2002) have all produced data and interpretations in accord with the landscape approach (Figure 10.1).

What Is Settlement?

The village has been with us for at least 9,000 years (Zubrow and Robinson 1999:133). Hall (1998:4) argues that no two cities are the same, while Banning (1997:283) points out that urbanism does not necessarily mean homogeneity. If we are to study settlement distribution across any landscape, or the interactions of one settlement with another, it is essential first to understand what "settlement" means. Surprisingly, there is little discussion in either settlement archaeology or landscape studies as to just what makes up a settlement. Simply put, a settlement is a place where people have chosen to live. However, there is a bewildering array of examples that fit this simple definition, each one shaped by a diverse set of social processes and factors unique to the time and place that it occupies, which only serves to make the task of defining them all the more difficult.

If permanence is associated with settlement then we must rule out temporary camps or resting places set up by pastoralists, nomads, or individuals engaged in short-term activities such as hunting or herding. Such sites, in any case, are often ephemeral and archaeologically elusive. It seems unlikely that Akrotiri *Aetokremnos*, fast eroding into the sea in southern Cyprus, was a permanent dwelling place, but the butchered remains of over 300 pygmy hippopotami and the tools with which the work was carried out attest to considerable activity there around 10,000 years ago (Simmons 1989; 1992; 1999). To give another example, temporary summer camps were established on high ground in Italy's Biferno Valley by animal herders, in the late fifth millennium B.C. (Barker 1995:114). Neither the evidence from Akrotiri *Aetokremnos* nor that from the Biferno Valley constitutes settlement in themselves, for although they indicate occupation and activity, settlement necessitates a structure or group of structures and indicators of agricultural or industrial use, in association with evidence of various daily activities and practices: sleeping, eating, cooking – in a word, living. Permanence alone, then, is an insufficient criterion to define settlement: a single, permanent field shelter might indicate the presence of a nearby settlement, but would not represent a settlement in itself.

Perhaps the most compelling image of settlement is a collection of basic living and working structures – a village or a town, or a city. One of the features of such a collection is the pooling of shared activities and the establishment of "communal facilities" such as chapels, springs, quarries, and limekilns (Whitelaw 1991:425). As settlement size increases, the balance between living and working units and these other, ancillary, facilities changes, just as the nature of a settlement changes: this, at least in part, reflects the shift between rural and urban modes of living.

The Urban/Rural Distinction

Distinguishing between what is rural and what is urban is not as straightforward as it may seem. Blouet (1972:12) talks of a settlement hierarchy, progressing from isolated dwelling through hamlet and village to town; his general assumption is that as centers of settlement increase in size, they move from being rural to being urban; thus villages are inevitably associated with rural life and towns with urban life. But the transition from one to the other is not a simple, linear process (MacKay 1994:283; Hall 1998:14), and using a checklist like Wheatley's (1972:622) – temple, baths, mosque, market, and seat of power – to differentiate between town and country may be too simplistic.

The primary requirements for rurality appear to be small, dispersed settlements primarily dependent on agriculture (Alcock 1993:33) – Wilkinson (1999:50) certainly equates urbanism in the Levant and Near East with a move in the opposite direction. But agriculture is not the only occupation of those who live in the countryside – pottery production and mining, for example (Knapp 1997: 48), are also practiced and must be taken into account when considering the rural landscape and its settlements. The countryside is not simply a collection of farming villages that happen to be in the fields around a town.

When dealing with a pre-industrial past, a population of greater than about 10,000 has often been taken to comprise an urban situation, but size alone is an unreliable measure and regional, political, legal, social, and architectural considerations will always play a part in a settlement's definition (Horden and Purcell 2000:93). In some cases, there is no inconsistency between these criteria for urbanism. It has been estimated that, in the first part of the 12th century B.C., Hala Sultan Tekke (Åström 1986), in southern Cyprus, had a population of 11,000–14,000 inhabitants. It was a large and thriving port town, its streets laid out in a grid pattern, and many of the buildings were well built with fine-dressed ashlar masonry. There is evidence for large-scale copper production as well as gold and silver working, and the manufacture of arrow heads, armor, and jewelry. In addition, tools have been found that were used in the processing of grapes, olives, and wool – grinders and presses, spindle whorls, and loom weights. This town by all criteria is an urban site.

Kurban Höyük (Algaze 1990), on the other hand, probably only had a population of just over 1,000 at its peak in the Middle to Late Early Bronze Age. Nevertheless, at this time it was a small town with a fortified inner quarter containing buildings of a quality and size that suggest they were either public amenities or dwellings for an elite class. Kurban Höyük was typical of settlements in the region at this time, albeit one of the smaller examples, with no smaller, satellite settlements. Later, in the Early to Middle Bronze Age, it had shrunk in size and is described as a small village, and yet it had an entrance complex of gates, doors, steps, and stone-built structures quite out of keeping with the scale of the rest of the settlement. On current evidence, this does not seem to have been an ordinary village in any case – despite expectations to the contrary, no material remains have been recovered to indicate that important economic activities such as agriculture, leather-working, textile manufacture, or associated activities took place at the site (Algaze 1990:431). So, whilst its size might have indicated a village, communal amenities such as the entrance way and the lack of evidence for practical activities do not.

Geographers, in particular, have agonized over the difference between *urban* and *rural*: some have even imposed indexes of rurality (Cloke 1979) or urban indicators (OECD 1997), but there is no straightforward way to define or describe what makes a settlement urban or what makes it rural and it may not always be helpful to do so in any case. The "urban variable," that feature of town or city life that distinguishes it from other types of settlements, is all but impossible to define (Horden and Purcell 2000:96); more importantly, it is very difficult to apply universally. It is more important to be aware of a settlement's existence within an urban/rural continuum, and to consider it with respect to other settlements, the landscape, the population, and the time periods under study (Horden and Purcell 2000:93–94).

Settlement Boundaries

The basic shape of a settlement is one of its more obvious attributes. The way that a settlement occupies space – its size and its shape – is defined by both internal and external boundaries. External boundaries can mark both the full extent of the main center of habitation, and a settlement's wider territory, signaling the transition from one settlement to another. The latter is not necessarily evident in the archaeology; it is the kind of boundary that today is marked on maps and often used by authorities for administrative divisions of a region. External boundaries defining the main agglomeration of habitation tend to be far more evident, whether marked by town walls or simply the limits of building concentrations.

Walls, or the lack of them, often evoke terms such as "defended" or "open" settlement. With its connotations of warfare, defended is a loaded term, but there is, of course, no denying that some strong walls were primarily concerned with defense, aggression, or warfare. A fortification wall, with a fortified building behind it, dating from the Early Helladic period, has been excavated at Thebes (Aravantos 1986). Its efficacy may be judged by the fact that the evidence shows it was finally abandoned, rather than destroyed by nature or humanity. However, the massive defensive wall and tower of Neolithic Jericho – once thought to make it the earliest city in the world – have been reinterpreted and are now thought to be concerned with flood defenses and ceremony respectively (Herzog 1997:20). Evidence from mid-third millennium BC Aegean settlements at Spedhos on Naxos and Kynthos on Delos shows that, here too, hilltops and slopes were used as defenses not just against hostile, human forces but also against natural factors such as floods (Doumas 1972:228).

While, at times, stout city walls would indeed serve to defend against both human and natural agents, at other times they might be associated more with display, control, and, of course, the demarcation of territory. The impressive entrance to Kurban Höyük (Algaze 1990:192) during the Middle to Late Bronze Age was perhaps part of just such a boundary, as it guided those using it through a succession of passageways, doorways, and chambers. The early Helladic town of Manika covered such an extensive area that it seems unlikely an enclosing wall would have been a practical undertaking; moreover, fortification does not seem to have been considered important to developing settlements in this period (Sampson 1986:48). Swiny (1981) records Bronze Age settlements in Cyprus with no real evidence of defensive walls; they are situated on plateaux and, whether or not the slopes offered natural defenses, their edges provided very clear boundaries to the settlement. The lower slopes and resources beyond lay outside this inner external boundary, but within a wider boundary or boundaries that marked the settlement's territory.

Internal boundaries are perhaps less confrontational, less suited than external barriers to the term defensive, but still they mark divisions, whether planned or organic. While the term town planning may conjure images of streets laid out on a grid system, as in Hala Sultan Tekke (Åström 1986), it manifests itself in other, less geometric, though no less uniform ways. At the Early Bronze Age village of Be'er

Resism in Palestine (Dever 1985), patterns have been identified that, while not the result of deliberate planning, show marked similarities between individual clusters of structures; the clusters were divided into three social levels, which have been identified by the standard of construction of the buildings in them. There was a differentiation between living, storage, and preparation areas in each cluster and an area of animal enclosures separate from the settlement to its south. But just as settlement planning does not require a regular layout of structures, so the regular layout of a town need not necessarily imply centralized town planning. It was not a primary concern in early Helladic Euboea and yet all the houses in Manika are on the same alignment (Sampson 1986:48).

Whether it was planned or not, internal and external boundaries changed in settlements in southeast Iberia between the Copper and Bronze Ages. Loosely arranged, ovoid and circular dwellings were favored in the Copper Age, while in the Bronze Age settlements were smaller, more tightly packed, and made up of rectangular buildings. The shift appears to have been due simply to a different use of space rather than a drop in the population or any external pressures (Mathers 1994:32; though see Chapman this volume for discussion of social changes in this period). Whatever deeper significance might later be inferred from a settlement's physical layout, it is quite possible that it grew out of practical need – for example, the central agglomeration of an agricultural village may be bounded by threshing floors and positioned close to the center of the agricultural land it exploits. Because many settlements subsist and exist in broadly similar ways, it may be possible to discern patterns that are helpful in identifying settlements. The evidence for much of Bronze Age Cyprus, for example, suggests that villages adopted an open plan layout, with houses separated by small gardens and orchards (Swiny 1981:79). Such arrangements are equivalent to what geographers (e.g., Hornby and Jones 1991; Roberts 1996) – with their battery of descriptive categories – would label as regular, agglomerated settlements.

Location

The location of a settlement may well have significant bearing upon its boundaries and its morphology. Although it may be tempting, or indeed quite useful, to divide these physical elements for initial study, it should be kept in mind that they exist in combination, not in isolation. To study one factor, such as location, without assessing its impact upon and relationships with other factors, such as size or morphology, would be to view only a partial image of settlement. Here I consider issues that affect both the position and the extent of individual settlements in the landscape; in the next section I look at the question of multiple settlements in the landscape.

Essentially the choice of settlement location, like so much of life, must be a compromise struck in consideration of all the various influences that may affect a population, whether that be the dominant, day-to-day activities of its members, physical factors arising from the surrounding landscape, or wider social influences from beyond the single population in question. The lifestyle of any given community is closely tied to environmental considerations. Topography, for example, will dictate the practicality of building in a certain area, whether it be flat ground or a place where access to distant water supplies or exploitable resources is required (Swiny 1981:80–81): the acropolis of Pellana, in Greek Laconia, at the climax of its prosperity in the 13th century B.C., stood above a well-watered, fertile plain (Spyropoulos 1998). In contrast, there is no clear evidence of a permanent water supply within the boundaries of the Late Bronze Age Cypriot sites of Pyla *Kokkinokremos* (Karageorghis and Demas 1984:5) or Maa *Palaeokastro* (Karageorghis and Demas 1988:1), which does not sit easily with the generally accepted opinion that they were defensive settlements (Karageorghis 2001). If a population were forced by conflict, for example, to move from the plains to settle in a mountainous region, their lifestyle would, of necessity, come to reflect their location, rather than influence their choice of it. Their choice of location would reflect the broader social situation of conflict.

Although it need not be a primary factor, the dominant activity carried out by the occupants of a settlement, be it agriculture or manufacture, is an important consideration in determining its location. The temporary summer camps established on high ground in the Biferno Valley, Italy, in the late fifth millennium B.C. were occupied by herders of sheep and goats; associated, permanent settlements devoted to systematic farming were situated on lower ground (Barker 1995:113–114). Manufacturing settlements would have different requirements of their surroundings; mining and metallurgy, for example, demand a location close to sources of ore and other raw materials as well as considerable supplies of water and fuel (Knapp et al. 2001). Technologies such as these leave distinct traces of their practice in the landscape, such as adits, shafts, galleries, and slag heaps. Legacies of agricultural activity are less obvious perhaps, but ancient field systems and threshing floors can be identified. So, while the landscape may have influenced the initial choice of location, settlements in turn affect the landscape in which they have been established.

Whatever activity dominated the lives of a population may have affected not only the location of a settlement, but also its layout and, further, the situation of other sites in the vicinity. Clearly it is less desirable to live directly downwind of or next to a furnace or a mine than a threshing floor, and this is a preference that is well reflected in the archaeological record (Barker et al. 1999:262–269; Given 2002a). The archaeological interpretation of such activities in the landscape, in turn, demands special care: Osborne (1992:22) points out that evidence of agricultural activity does not necessarily imply residence; Knapp et al. (2001) demonstrate that many industrial sites reveal no traces of habitation. However, any permanent exploitation of the landscape will require a population to sustain it, and that population will require somewhere to live – a settlement. They may not be in the same place, but they will likely be close.

I have, thus far, considered basic elements of production that might influence a settlement's location: the practical side of life. Considerations of control, however, were also important in choosing a site to settle, whether that was control of production centers, of the populations exploiting the resources, or access to and through the exploited and settled landscape. Both the Cypriot sites mentioned above – Pyla *Kokkinokremos*, situated atop a plateau on a plain and Maa *Palaeokastro*, located on a peninsula – combined natural and constructed fortifications to control access to the settlements and to the nearby sea. The Early Bronze Age Greek town of Manika, to cite another example, was built on a promontory between two fertile areas, evidently giving it control over all of central Euboea and the straits of Euripos (Sampson 1986:47).

One final point worth remembering about the location of settlements is that in many cases it represents a choice that does not have to be made; for the most part life continues with a minimum of disruption and settlements remain in just about the same place. Populations continue to be settled and develop what Rowlands (1972:453) termed emotional and historical ties of tradition with a particular place. They have no wish to move or to establish settlements in new locations.

Distribution

The factors influencing settlement distribution across the landscape are similar to those affecting the location of individual settlements; the former is a development of the latter. By shifting our viewpoint slightly and broadening our scope we can incorporate the spacing, layout, and strategic position of other settlements in the landscape and consider them with respect to one another. Settlements seldom, if ever, exist in absolute isolation, and it is important to keep in mind their context, made up of the landscape around them and the other settlements in it.

A major distinction is made in the distribution of settlements across a landscape, between nucleated and dispersed; both were favored throughout the Mediterranean at different times throughout the prehistoric period. Late Neolithic settlement in Thessaly, central Greece, tended to be dispersed (Halstead 1994:200), consisting of small, short-lived hamlets on the arid Larisa plain. Expansion during the Early Bronze Age saw a tendency toward a more nucleated pattern, with individual settlements increasing markedly in size from less than 0.5 hectare to between 7 and 15 hectares. This expansion continued through into the Late Bronze Age, when marginal colonization began again and settlement leaned once more toward a dispersed pattern, despite its nucleated centers. Further south there was also a tendency toward nucleation in the Early Bronze Age as Neolithic villages and hamlets grew into settlements such as Lerna, Tiryns, and Thebes (Halstead 1994:203). Evidence on the ground, however, can be confusing; numerous occupation sites have been found across the island of Melos, but given the likely occupation span of such sites and the length of the prehistoric period it is unlikely that many of them were contemporary. It seems more likely that Melos supported a tiny population until the decline of the small rural sites and the advent of the first large nucleated village at Phylakopi in the Middle Bronze Age (Bintliff et al. 1999:141; Cherry 1982; 1979).

The distribution of settlement cannot, alone, reveal the nature of society, economy, or contemporary events, but at times there are clues. Just as the two styles of settlement on the uplands and lowlands in the Biferno Valley indicate a mixed agricultural and pastoral lifestyle (Barker 1995:113–114), so the distribution of farms on Keos suggests differing levels of land use in different areas of the island (Whitelaw 1991:437). Around Chora, in northwest Keos, lay scattered farmsteads. The regular density of farmhouses close to the nucleated village suggests the full exploitation of the landscape, while the low ratio of farms to fields farther out, toward the coast, suggests a less intense level of exploitation with farmers traveling some distance from the center of population to work on this peripheral land.

Wider economic, social, and political relationships can be reflected in the physical distribution of settlements. In Late Bronze Age Iberia, for example, there is some evidence of a regional hierarchy, based on settlement size (Mathers 1994). There is even clearer evidence of stratified settlement around the Greek kingdom of Pylos during the Late Bronze Age, where each of three levels interacted in a system that would appear to have involved more than simple physical distribution. The palace formed the center of a large community that controlled several large towns situated around it, while dependent satellite villages housed the majority of the working population (Davis et al. 1997:483–484).

It can be tempting, when looking at settlements in a landscape, to represent them as a scatter of dots across the map, with each one assigned a size appropriate to its economic, social, or political importance. Such a view can be useful to provide an initial overview of a region or landscape, but is limiting and obscures the multifaceted nature of the individual elements and the differing levels of interconnections that exist between settlements in any given area. Another temptation to avoid is seeing settlements as no more than a series of contiguous yet discrete entities fitting together neatly to fill all the available space in a landscape. This approach is, perhaps, encouraged by considerations of boundaries and reference to historical maps showing the world divided up into a series of interlocking shapes. But, as Horden and Purcell (2000:103) suggest, it would be simplistic if not erroneous to divide the Mediterranean landscape into neat regional or functional packages, and the diversity of factors involved makes it impossible to reduce settlements to the geometry and mathematics of dots, lines, and polygons.

Change

Despite the fact that stability is probably the most common state, a change in any of the factors that originally configured a settlement could well override the influence of tradition and inaction. Change is inevitable, whether initiated by human activity or instigated by natural events. The ascendance of one settlement over others in a region may cause a realignment of social and political relationships, or a climatic shift may force a change in local subsistence practices or other aspects of the economy, or increased conflict in an area may trigger a change from an open, dispersed settlement plan to a more nucleated, possibly defended one (Rowlands 1972:458). Settlements come and go, and as they do settlement patterns change.

During the Neolithic period in Italy's Biferno Valley, for example, the general movement to the lower valley through time has been associated with a decrease in the variety of locations chosen for settlement (Barker 1995:104). This movement reflects a growing dependence on agriculture as opposed to pastoralism, which exploited more of the uplands farther up the valley (see also the chapter by Barker, this volume). Presumably the reduction in variety of location resulted from people being confined to one part of the valley, rather than exploiting its whole range. It is difficult, however, to distinguish cause from effect. In the southern Argolid of Greece during the Early Bronze Age, erosion had stripped soil from hill-slopes and plain margins, and the number of inhabited sites dropped dramatically from twenty-eight to two by the end of Early Helladic III (Peltenburg 2000:192). It is not clear, however, if topographical degradation resulting from human exploitation or natural causes prompted the population to seek more productive land, or if the land began to deteriorate once the bulk of the people had moved away and ceased to manage it.

Change does not necessarily imply relocation; simply by shifting its center of habitation a settlement changes. The remnant pattern of a single settlement can give impressions ranging from a concentrated, multi-period site to a number of dispersed single-period sites ranging across a broad time frame (Dewar and McBride 1992:234, figure 1). At Phaneromeni in Cyprus the main center of occupation in the Late Bronze Age was well separated from the area inhabited during the Middle Bronze Age. The combination of material evidence from these two centers resulted in scatters of pottery that gave the impression of a much larger settlement than Phaneromeni ever was during any one given period of occupation (Swiny 1981:79). On a broader scale, Melos appeared, at first glance, to have been liberally populated throughout the prehistoric period, until the short-lived nature of the settlements was taken into account and a clearer picture of a sparse, constantly shifting population emerged (Bintliff et al. 1999:141; Cherry 1979; 1982).

Growth is often taken for granted, as if settlements followed a linear evolutionary path from isolated farmstead, through hamlet and village to town. The settlements in the Biferno Valley certainly tended to become larger as people moved, over time, toward the lower ground (Barker 1995:108). Growth, of course, tends to promote growth, while smaller settlements in the system tend to decline and die out (Blouet 1972:7). And yet, while very small settlements often do fade and fail over time, the situation is not as inevitable or as frequent as much of the literature suggests (Zubrow and Robinson 1999:144). Moreover, a reduction in size does not necessarily spell the inevitable demise of a settlement. For example, after a protracted period of dominance over Euboea in the early Bronze Age, wider economic circumstances led to a contraction in settlement size at Manika to a small area at the end of the promontory it had previously covered. However, despite this reduction in size, the settlement continued to be viable and evidence shows that the promontory was inhabited, apparently without interruption, well into the late Bronze Age (Simpson and Dickinson 1979:226; Sampson 1986:49).

Stasis may also form an important component in broader circumstances of change; settlements and settlement patterns often remain unchanged and unchanging for protracted periods. Roberts (1996:120) defines settlements that undergo no major change within one generation of human life as "stable." Such a situation, however, precludes neither constant, small-scale changes nor the possibility of larger changes in a settlement's past or future. Few aspects of human demography are ever completely stable and continuity of occupation on a site need not imply stagnation. The landscape around Pylos, in Greece's western Messenia region, has been occupied for thousands of years, but there is clear evidence of development and change, from the relatively low level of settlement in the third millennium B.C. to major land-clearance around 2000 and a palatial enterprise in the 13th century B.C., right down to the present day (Davis et al. 1997:483).

Even when settlements fail and are abandoned, they do not necessarily disappear from the landscape or fall from the consciousness of the people remaining in the general area. Although their functions may change, such settlements continue to be a part of the landscape patterning, landscape change, and human memory.

Community

Thus far discussion has concentrated on the material aspects of settlement, while simply acknowledging the human input. This is deliberate because settlements consist of the buildings, gardens, paths or roads, and such territory as they occupy. Obviously settlements do not exist without the input of their inhabitants, but once people are introduced into the equation the material aspects combine with them to create communities. There is no easy formula for adding people to a settlement to produce a community; communities are far too fluid for such treatment. The links are inescapable, the elements indivisible, but the relationship is not a simple one. Archaeological evidence of a settlement might indicate the locus of a past community, but the terms settlement and community are not interchangeable; the nature of a community cannot be extrapolated directly from the form and function of the material evidence (Yaeger and Canuto 2000:3). In Middle Neolithic Thessaly at Sesklo, an unusually large settlement for the period, communities based on the social hierarchy were clear in the material evidence; well-built houses containing abundant painted pottery spoke of an elite community based in a central acropolis-like area, while flimsier structures with less fine wares indicated a lower stratum of community in the outlying areas (Halstead 1994:203). This physical division of communities was also evident, elsewhere in the region, into the Bronze Age at Velestino and Iolkos. Frankel and Webb (1999:6) have sought to identify the extent of communities in Early and Middle Bronze Age Cyprus by plotting the decrease in density of favored motifs in the pottery record around a central concentration, but it is even more difficult to draw a line on the map around a community than it is to define a settlement.

Some take community to be a measure of size, a point on a scale between "family" and "larger scale social networks" (Kolb 1997:266), or between "household" and "region" (Lightfoot et al. 1998:206). These are "natural communities," static in nature and tied to a particular place (Kolb and Snead 1997:611; Isbell 2000:245). A more flexible, and useful, concept is that of the "imagined community," first coined by Anderson (1987), that grows out of human relationships and is dependent upon the people that make it up, rather than the place in which they live (Isbell 2000:248–250). Communities are fluid; a single community may occupy more than one settlement and, indeed, one settlement can be home to more than a single community. Relationships and the relative status of individuals or groups within the population shift in different social or working situations, and the communities that they comprise change to reflect these shifts. At Alassa, in Cyprus, at least four communities are identified by occupation: farmers and metalworkers, by the remains of their work; and, less certainly, warriors and scribes by the contents of their tombs (Hadjisavvas 1989:40–41). At Politiko *Phorades*, Knapp (2003) has presented detailed evidence for the existence of an imagined community that combined the activity-defined community of miners and metalworkers with that of the farmers who provided their daily subsistence. There is no suggestion that membership of one community excluded membership of another and, just as in Kato Koutraphas *Mandres* in the 20th century A.D. (Given 2002b), the community to which an individual belonged – be it farmer, pastoralist, or metalworker – could easily be dependent upon the turn of the season.

Static populations may consist of different levels of community, from the relationship within families and working groups, to the wider community of a settlement and beyond to the community of related settlements distributed across the landscape. Communities may be centered on or resident in a settlement, but they are neither defined by the physical limits of a settlement nor dependent upon it for their existence. Thus while there may be no direct equation between "community" and "site," we can begin to infer the social process of community from the spatial clusters of material evidence that we recover (Yaeger and Canuto 2000:9).

Discussion and Conclusion

If the "settlement" is taken to be the basic building block that enables further study of social, political, and economic activities of people distributed throughout a landscape, then it is sensible to identify what is meant by "settlement." And yet, while rigid labels and defining criteria may be comforting, they can become shortcuts that, if used thoughtlessly, will deceive and ultimately cloud discussions with side issues, rather than ease their flow.

It is evident that settlements come in many forms and it is futile to propose anything more than the most fundamental criteria for their identification. Essentially, a settlement requires evidence of closely associated structures connected with long-term, albeit not necessarily continual occupation, employment, and the minutiae of daily life. Larger settlements may display signs of communal facilities such as water fountains, bread ovens, storage facilities, workshops, or ceremonial places. Without wishing to gainsay all efforts to categorize, the division of settlement between urban and rural is also fraught with difficulty. "A town is what each age takes it to be" (Horden and Purcell 2000:93), as is any settlement – hamlet, village, town, or city – and they should always be studied with due consideration of their past status. What is considered to be a village in the 21st century may, in its heyday, have been thought of as a town. It is more useful to envisage a rural/urban continuum (Cloke 1979) and to consider specific settlements in relation to it, in the context of their location and periods of occupation, rather than to lay down a set of criteria against which they may be defined or judged. It seems more fruitful to accept the differences, however extreme, without seeking to explain the definitive transition from rural to urban.

The urban/rural debate often employs size as a distinguishing feature, but the factors that contribute to a settlement's extent are usually more informative, and more interesting, than simple measurement. External boundaries describe a settlement's outer limits, but the reasons for the form and the course of that boundary vary enormously. The boundary that marks the territorial limits of an agricultural village will be very different from that which encloses a fortified town; the reasons for establishing a settlement – domination, defense, exploitation of resources – can often be surmised from its outer border. The relationship of internal to external boundaries within a settlement may also be of interest but the one need not necessarily dictate the extent of the other. Clearly the outer edge of a hilltop settlement is so well defined that it must be the dominant partner, but on a broad, open plain, internal boundaries and the spaces they enclose may determine the shape and size of a settlement.

In determining the limits of a settlement, whether of a city or a hamlet, it would be a mistake to consider only the spread of bricks and mortar. A settlement may, and a community almost certainly will, stretch far beyond its physical remnants. One of the prime goals of landscape archaeology and settlement studies is to gain a broader picture of a settlement's regional context. Landscape archaeologists consider all settlements in a region in combination rather than as isolated elements; equally they step beyond the purely physical to consider the "imagined" community or communities within a given area. Even if it is essential to plot the static distribution patterns of settlement as derived from such physical criteria as size and location, it is much more informative to study interactions within these distributions and between the people that inhabited them. The topography of a landscape may be the matrix in which archaeological remains are preserved, but it is by no means immutable (Stafford and Hajic 1992:138–140). More and more archaeologists now take into account the fact that topography might degrade as easily as remain stable. Thus the landscape we see today may not be the same as the landscape of the past; it might, indeed, bear no resemblance to it at all. Rather more quickly changing than the underlying topography, vegetation – appearing as patches of energy or nutrients – will support settlement or indicate suitable areas for cultivation. Whether animal, vegetable, or mineral, and for whatever kind of consumption, the raw materials available in a landscape will have a direct bearing on its suitability for settlement. Moving beyond the purely material evidence may introduce uncertainty and speculation, and overly fluid definitions can be unhelpful, but it should be clear from this study that even physical settlements cannot be described in purely prescriptive terms. Given this certainty, Isbell's (2000) imagined community offers a far more dynamic concept of study than the natural community, which gives primarily a prescriptive, physical indicator of place or scale. Imagined communities allow us to envision changing peoples, social relations, and interconnections within and between physical settlements and to ponder the nature of places where no clear trace of settlement survives.

In sum, it is all but impossible to identify any single, clear pattern or trend in settlement or settlement distribution across so wide a geographical area as the Mediterranean and within a temporal sweep as broad as the prehistoric period. The only realistic approach to understanding Mediterranean settlements is to be aware of their broad, characteristic features within the broader scope of prehistory and to use such characteristics to inform the study of settlements, both individually and within a defined region. Moreover, it is absolutely clear that such specific study should always be informed by the temporal and geographic context of each individual settlement or community, as Horden and Purcell (2000) suggest.

REFERENCES

Alcock, Susan E., 1993 Graecia Capta: The Landscapes of Roman Greece. Cambridge: Cambridge University Press.

Algaze, Guillermo, ed., 1990 Town and Country in Southeastern Anatolia, vol. II. The Stratigraphic Sequence at Kurban Höyük, Text. The University of Chicago Oriental Institute Publications, vol. 10. Chicago: The Oriental Institute of the University of Chicago.

Anderson, Benedict, 1987 Imagined Communities: Reflections on the Origin and Spread of Nationalism. London: Verso.

Anschuetz, Kurt F., Richard H. Wilshusen, and Cherie L. Scheick, 2001 An Archaeology of Landscapes: Perspectives and Directions. Journal of Archaeological Research 9:157–207.

Aravantinos, Vassilis L., 1986 The EHII Fortified Building at Thebes and Some Notes on its Architecture. *In* Early Helladic Architecture and Urbanisation. Proceedings of a Seminar held at the Swedish Institute in Athens, June 8, 1985. Studies in Mediterranean Archaeology 76. Robin Hägg and Dora Konsola, eds. pp. 47–50. Göteborg: Paul Åströms Förlag.

Åström, Paul, 1986 Hala Sultan Tekke – An International Harbour Town of the Late Bronze Age. Opuscula Atheniensia XVI:7–17.

Banning, E. B., 1997 Spatial Perspectives on Early Urban Development in Mesopotamia. *In* Urbanism in Antiquity from Mesopotamia to Crete. Walter E. Aufrecht, Neil A. Mirau, and Steven W. Gauley, eds. pp. 17–34. Sheffield: Sheffield University Press.

Barker, Graeme, 1995 A Mediterranean Valley: Landscape Archaeology and Annales History in The Biferno Valley. Leicester: Leicester University Press.

——1996 Farming The Desert: The UNESCO Libyan Valleys Archaeological Survey, vol. 1. Synthesis. Paris: UNESCO.

Barker, G. W., R. Adams, O. H. Creighton, D. Crook, D. D. Gilbertson, J. P. Grattan, C. O. Hunt, D. J. Mattingly, S. J. McLaren, H. A. Mohammed, P. Newson, C. Palmer, F. B. Pyatt, T. E. G. Reynolds, and R. Tomber, 1999 Environment and Land Use in the Wadi Faynan, Southern Jordan: The Third Season of Geoarchaeology and Landscape Archaeology (1998). Levant 31:255–292.

Bintliff, John, Phil Howard, and Anthony Snodgrass, 1999 The Hidden Landscapes of Prehistoric Greece. Journal of Mediterranean Archaeology 12(2):139–168.

Blouet, Brian W., 1972 Factors Influencing the Evolution of Settlement Patterns. *In* Man, Settlement and Urbanism: Proceedings of a Meeting of the Research Seminar in Archaeology and Related Subjects Held at the Institute of Archaeology, London University. Peter J. Ucko, Ruth Tringham, and G. W. Dimbleby, eds. pp. 3–15. London: Duckworth.

Cherry, John F., 1979 Four Problems in Cycladic Prehistory. *In* Papers in Cycladic Prehistory, Monograph 14. J. L. Davis and J. F. Cherry, eds. pp. 22–47. Los Angeles: UCLA Institute of Archaeology.

—— 1982 A Preliminary Definition of Site Distribution on Melos. *In* An Island Polity: The Archaeology of Exploitation in Melos. C. Renfrew and M. Wagstaff, eds. pp. 10–23. Cambridge: Cambridge University Press.

Cherry, John F., Jack L. Davis, and Eleni Mantzourani, eds., 1991 Landscape Archaeology As Long-Term History: Northern Keos in the Cycladic Islands from Earliest Settlement until Modern Times. Monumenta Archaeologica 16. Los Angeles: UCLA Institute of Archaeology.

Cloke, Paul, 1979 Key settlements in Rural Areas. Methuen: London.

Darvill, T., 1997 Landscapes and the Archaeologist. *In* Making English Landscapes: Changing Perspectives. Bournemouth University, School of Conservation Sciences, Occasional Papers 3. Oxbow Monograph 93. K. Barker and T. Darvill, eds. pp. 70–91. Oxford: Oxbow.

Davis, Jack L., Susan E. Alcock, John Bennet, Yannos G. Lolos, and Cynthia W. Shelmerdine, 1997 The Pylos Regional Archaeological Project Part I: Overview and The Archaeological Survey. Hesperia 66:391–494.

Dever, William G., 1985 Village Planning at Be'er Resism and Socio-Economic Structure in Early Bronze Age IV Palestine. *In* Eretz-Israel: Archaeological, Historical and Geographical Studies, vol. 18. B. Mazar and Y. Yadin, eds. pp. 18–28. Jerusalem: The Israel Exploration Society in cooperation with the Institute of Archaeology, The Hebrew University.

Dewar, Robert E., and Kevin A. McBride, 1992 Remnant Settlement Patterns. *In* Space, Time, and Archaeological Landscapes. Jacqueline Rossignol and LuAnn Wandsnider, eds. pp. 227–255. New York and London: Plenum Press.

Doumas, Christos, 1972 Early Bronze Age Settlement Patterns in the Cyclades. *In* Man, Settlement and Urbanism: Proceedings of a Meeting of the Research Seminar in Archaeology and Related Subjects Held at the Institute of Archaeology, London University. Peter J. Ucko, Ruth Tringham, and G. W. Dimbleby, eds. pp. 227–230. London: Duckworth.

Frankel, David, and Jennifer M. Webb, 1999 Three Faces of Identity: Ethnicity, Community and Status in the Cypriot Bronze Age. Mediterranean Archaeology 11:1–12.

Given, Michael, ed., 2002a Troodos Archaeological and Environmental Survey Project, TS02: Xyliatos *Mavrovouni*. Electronic document. http://www.taesp.arts.gla.ac.uk/Landscape/SIA/TS02.htm Last updated 7 February 2003. Last accessed 22 March 2003.

—— 2002b Troodos Archaeological and Environmental Survey Project, TS07: Kato Koutraphas *Mandres*. Electronic document. http://www.taesp.arts.gla.ac.uk/Landscape/SIA/TS07.htm Last updated 7 February 2003. Last accessed 22 March 2003.

Given, Michael, Vasiliki Kassianidou, A. Bernard Knapp, and Jay Noller, 2002 Troodos Archaeological and Environmental Survey Project, Cyprus: Report on the 2001 Season. Levant 34:25–38.

Given, Michael, and A. Bernard Knapp, 2003 The Sydney Cyprus Survey Project: Social Approaches to Regional Archaeological Survey. Monumenta Archaeologica 21. Los Angeles: Cotsen Institute of Archaeology.

Hadjisavvas, Sophocles, 1989 A Late Cypriot Community at Alassa. In Early Society in Cyprus. Edgar Peltenburg, ed. pp. 32–42. Edinburgh: Edinburgh University Press.

Hall, Tim, 1998 Urban Geography. London: Routledge.

Halstead, Paul, 1994 The North-South Divide: Regional Paths to Complexity in Prehistoric Greece. In Development and Decline in the Mediterranean Bronze Age. C. Mathers and S. Stoddart, eds. pp. 195–217. Sheffield: Sheffield University, Sheffield Archaeology Monographs 8.

Herzog, Ze'ev, 1997 Archaeology of the City: Urban Planning in Ancient Israel and its Social Implications. Tel Aviv: Emery and Claire Yass Archaeology Press.

Horden, Peregrine, and Nicholas Purcell, 2000 The Corrupting Sea: A Study of Mediterranean History. Oxford: Blackwell.

Hornby, William Frederic, and Melvyn Jones, 1991 An Introduction to Settlement Geography. Cambridge: Cambridge University Press.

Isbell, William H., 2000 What Should We Be Studying: The "Imagined Community" and the "Natural Community." In The Archaeology of Communities: A New World Perspective. Marcello A. Canuto and Jason Yaeger, eds. pp. 243–266. London: Routledge.

Karageorghis, Vassos, 2001 Patterns of Fortified Settlement in the Aegean and Cyprus ca.1200 B.C. In Defensive Settlements of the Aegean and the Eastern Mediterranean after ca.1200 B.C. Proceedings of an International Workshop held at Trinity College Dublin, 7th–9th May, 1999. Nicosia.

Karageorghis, Vassos, and Martha Demas, 1984 Pyla-Kokkinokremos: A Late 13th Century B.C. Fortified Settlement in Cyprus. Nicosia: Department of Antiquities.

—— 1988 Excavations at Maa-Palaeokastro 1979–1986. Nicosia: Department of Antiquities.

Knapp, A. Bernard, 1997 The Archaeology of Late Bronze Age Cypriot Society: The Study of Settlement, Survey and Landscape. Occasional Paper 4. Glasgow: Department of Archaeology, University of Glasgow.

—— 2003 The Archaeology of Community on Bronze Age Cyprus: Politiko Phorades in Context. American Journal of Archaeology 107:559–580.

Knapp, A. Bernard, and Wendy Ashmore, 1999 Archaeological Landscapes: Constructed, Conceptualized, Ideational. In Archaeologies of Landscape: Contemporary Perspectives. Wendy Ashmore and A. Bernard Knapp, eds. pp. 1–30. Malden, MA; Oxford: Blackwell Publishers.

Knapp, A. Bernard, Vasiliki Kassianidou, and Michael Donnelly, 2001 The Excavations at Politiko Phorades, Cyprus: 1996–2000. Near Eastern Archaeology 64:202–208.

Kolb, M. J., 1997 Labor Mobilization, Ethnohistory, and the Archaeology of Community in Hawai'i. Journal of Archaeological Method and Theory 4:265–285.

Kolb, Michael J., and James E. Snead, 1997 It's A Small World After All. American Antiquity 62:609–628.

Lightfoot, Kent G., Antoinette Martinez, and Ann M. Schiff, 1998 Daily Practice and Material Culture in Pluralistic Social Settings: An Archaeological Study of Culture Change and Persistence from Fort Ross, California. American Antiquity 63:199–222.

MacKay, D. Bruce, 1994 A View from the Outskirts: Realignments from Modern to Postmodern in the Archaeological Study of Urbanism. In Urbanism in Antiquity from

Mesopotamia to Crete. Walter E. Aufrecht, Neil A. Mirau, and Steven W. Gauley, eds. pp. 278–285. Sheffield: Sheffield University Press.

Mathers, Clay, 1994 Good Bye to All That? Contrasting Patterns of Change in the Southeast Iberian Bronze Age c.24/2200–600 BC. *In* Development and Decline in the Mediterranean Bronze Age. C. Mathers and S. Stoddart, eds. pp. 21–71. Sheffield: Sheffield University, Sheffield Archaeology Monographs 8.

OECD, 1997 Better Understanding Our Cities: The Role of Urban Indicators. Paris: Organisation for Economic Co-operation and Development.

Osborne, Robin, 1992 "Is it a Farm?" The Definition of Agricultural Sites and Settlements in Ancient Greece. *In* Agriculture in Ancient Greece: Proceedings of the Seventh International Symposium at the Swedish Institute at Athens, 16–17 May, 1990. Berit Wells, ed. pp. 21–27. Stockholm: Swedish Institute in Athens.

Peltenburg, Edgar, 2000 From Nucleation to Dispersal. Late Third Millennium BC Settlement Transformations in the Near East and Aegean. Subartu 7:183–206.

Roberts, Brian K., 1996 Landscapes of Settlement: Prehistory to the Present. London: Routledge.

Rowlands, Michael J., 1972 Defence: A Factor in the Organisation of Settlements. *In* Man, Settlement and Urbanism: Proceedings of a Meeting of the Research Seminar in Archaeology and Related Subjects Held at the Institute of Archaeology, London University. Peter J. Ucko, Ruth Tringham, and G. W. Dimbleby, eds. pp. 447–462. London: Duckworth.

Sampson, Adamantios, 1986 Architecture and Urbanisation in Manika, Chalkis. *In* Early Helladic Architecture and Urbanisation. Proceedings of a Seminar held at the Swedish Institute in Athens, June 8, 1985. Studies in Mediterranean Archaeology 76. Robin Hägg and Dora Konsola, eds. pp. 47–50. Göteborg: Paul Åströms Förlag.

Simmons, A., 1989 Preliminary Report on the 1988 Test Excavations at Akrotiri-Aetokremnos. Report of the Department of Antiquities, Cyprus, pp. 1–5.

——1992 Preliminary Report on the Akrotiri Peninsula Survey, 1991. Report of the Department of Antiquities, Cyprus, pp. 9–11.

——1999 Faunal Extinction in an Island Society: Pygmy Hippopotamus Hunters of Cyprus. Dordrecht, Boston: Kluwer Academic/Plenum.

Simpson, R. Hope, and O. T. P. K. Dickinson, 1979 A Gazetteer of Aegean Civilisation in the Bronze Age, vol. 1. The Mainland and Islands. Göteborg: Paul Åströms Förlag.

Spyropoulos, Thedoros G., 1998 Pellana, the Administrative Centre of Prehistoric Laconia. *In* Sparta in Laconia: Proceedings of the 19th British Museum Classical Colloquium held with the British School at Athens and Kings and University Colleges London 6–8 December 1995. W. G. Cavanagh and S. E. C. Walker, eds. pp. 28–38. London: British School at Athens.

Stafford, C. Russel, and Edwin R. Hajic, 1992 Landscape Scale: Geoenvironmental Approaches to Prehistoric Settlement Strategies. *In* Space, Time, and Archaeological Landscapes. Jacqueline Rossignol and LuAnn Wandsnider, eds. pp. 137–161. New York; London: Plenum Press.

Swiny, Stuart, 1981 Bronze Age Settlement Patterns in Southwest Cyprus. Levant 13:51–87.

Wheatley, Paul, 1972 The Concept of Urbanism. *In* Man, Settlement and Urbanism: Proceedings of a Meeting of the Research Seminar in Archaeology and Related Subjects Held at the Institute of Archaeology, London University. Peter J. Ucko, Ruth Tringham, and G. W. Dimbleby, eds. pp. 601–637. London: Duckworth.

Whitelaw, Todd M., 1991 The Ethnoarchaeology of Recent Rural Settlement and Land Use in Northwest Keos. *In* Landscape Archaeology As Long-Term History: Northern Keos in the Cycladic Islands from Earliest Settlement until Modern Times. Monumenta Archaeologica 16. John F. Cherry, Jack L. Davis and Eleni Mantzourani, eds. pp. 403–454. Los Angeles: UCLA Institute of Archaeology.

Wilkinson, Tony, 1999 Demographic Trends from Archaeological Survey: Case Studies from the Levant and Near East. *In* The Archaeology of the Mediterranean Landscape, vol. 1. Reconstructing Past Population Trends in Mediterranean Europe (3000 B.C.–A.D. 1800). John Bintliff and Kostas Sbonias, eds. pp. 45–64. Oxford: Oxbow Books.

Yaeger, Jason, and Marcello A. Canuto, 2000 Introducing an Archaeology of Communities. *In* The Archaeology of Communities: A New World Perspective. Marcello A. Canuto and Jason Yaeger, eds. pp. 1–15. London: Routledge.

Zubrow, Ezra, and Jennifer Robinson, 1999 Chance and the Human Population: Population Growth in the Mediterranean. *In* The Archaeology of the Mediterranean Landscape, vol. 1. Reconstructing Past Population Trends in Mediterranean Europe (3000 B.C.–A.D. 1800). John Bintliff and Kostas Sbonias, eds. pp. 133–144. Oxford: Oxbow Books.

11

Maritime Commerce and Geographies of Mobility in the Late Bronze Age of the Eastern Mediterranean: Problematizations

Sturt W. Manning and Linda Hulin

Introduction

One of the main and longstanding areas of study and interest in the archaeology of the Late Bronze Age (LBA, ca.1700–1200 B.C.[1]) east Mediterranean concerns the manifest evidence for extensive interregional trade and contact. Whereas early work tended to perceive evidence of "imports" and influences in terms of migration and conquest (Adams 1968), subsequently such movements of items and influences were conceived more within economic models – what we today can label as trade. Attention to imports/exports has been obsessive throughout the last century; such items speak of some form of social contacts, of exchange processes, of values and aspirations, and, in general, give some materialization to evidence for crafting and trade available in the ancient Near East from texts and iconographic sources (e.g., Zaccagnini 1977; Bickel 1998). Evidence for orientalizing and occidentalizing imports, exports, or influences abound (e.g., Evans 1921–45; Pendlebury 1930; Kantor 1947; Stubbings 1951; Lambrou-Phillipson 1990; Cline 1994; Leonard 1994; Wijngaarden 2002). Hundreds of site reports proudly highlight such items while a few "glamor" shipwreck excavations materialize aspects of such trade "in action" (Bass 1967; Pulak 1997), and are the subject of awed attention by the entire field. Today even the contents of many ceramic containers are starting to be revealed (e.g., Evershed et al. 1992; Serpico et al. 2003).

The question of what all these lovingly assembled data mean is less clear. The simple existence of most "imports" is universally accepted. However, the importance of imports in their deposition context – typically but a tiny fraction of total recovered assemblage – is often simply assumed, rather than argued. We shall argue that the static object recovered from the dirt fails to convey almost entirely the potentially rich, polyvalent, and multivocal cultural/social life of both the class of object and the specific artifact: its roles and associations in life, the biographies acquired between manufacture and eventual discard (Gosden and Marshall 1999); and what is, and is not, perceived as special, valuable, or exotic by consumers/recipients as opposed to being perceived as just a class of items or contents either largely or partly irrespective of provenance. We will show that local concepts of value are related to the means of acquisition open to consumers, and the prejudices that they bring to them. Some expensively acquired scientific provenance data may therefore in fact be almost irrelevant to a social archaeology of material culture, since they highlight patterns of production and distribution rather than consumption. There is a tendency for archaeologists to treat all non-local items as largely similar, whereas in reality some come from easily accessible locations (even if from overseas and thus deemed "imports"), while others are truly exotic and/or require specialist skills or costs in the acquisition, something which can be used to build and to signify status, roles, and associations (Helms 1988; 1993). In some cases the act of acquisition or ability to associate persons with such distance and/or local crafting may have been more valuable than any actual import. The latter are now widely recognized as offering an esoteric value resource, and esoteric concepts/knowledge (Broodbank 1993). But, at the same time, it is important also to remember that in many prehistoric and early pre-modern established societies (in contrast to emergent societies) the travelers/traders/merchants themselves were usually not of high status, despite providing key resources and information (Trigger 2003:349–350, 629). Elites controlled and employed the outcomes of trade and movement, with the corollary that they had to control and downplay the role of their agents. Status was founded within a society's internal/local criteria. We will reexamine concepts of distance in terms of concepts of local and distant, and the effects that these had on the generation of "exotic" as opposed to simply imported.

Historiography

The practical mechanics of trade as a system, beyond culture history, have occupied archaeologists for over fifty years. The modern agenda was set by Colin Renfrew (1969), who, in line with the mood of "archaeology-as-science" of the time, pleaded for a wide variety of burgeoning scientific analyses to fingerprint a range of materials, in order to reveal the movement of materials and help to delineate patterns of production and consumption. His work on the provenance and trading modes of obsidian offers a classic example (e.g., Renfrew and Shackleton 1970).

Considerations of the role of trade in the cultural process as a whole, and for urban development in particular, were not new; they had in fact occupied classical scholars for some time. Battle (sometimes astonishingly fierce) was drawn between the "modernists" (or formalists), inspired by Weber (1968), who sought the origins of capitalism in medieval and pre-medieval economies, versus the "primitivists" (or substantivists), inspired by Sombart (1916–27), Bücher (1901), and Hasebroek (1933), who regarded ancient economies as fundamentally different from modern-day systems, requiring their own models. Polanyi (1957) revitalized the minimalist debate by emphasizing that economies are always embedded in non-economic institutions and shaped by socially prescribed activities. Classical archaeology continues to house similar minimalist positions (Finley 1973; Snodgrass 1991). Mauss's definition of exchange as a "total social phenomenon" (1990) was every bit as embedded in the psychological and political fabric of the community as was Polanyi's definition of redistribution. Although, in Bronze Age contexts, it is usually restricted to considerations of high-level gift exchange (see below), equivalencies of value lay at the centre of many discussions of ancient trade (Heltzer 1978; Janssen 1975).

Renfrew (1975) considered Polanyi's ideas in relation to prehistory, focusing in particular on state formation. *Contra* Childe (1951), White (1959), and others who held that social growth depended upon an increase in agricultural production, which supported craft specialization which in turn permitted more developed social systems, Renfrew argued that it was interregional trade that provided the engine for social development, by stimulating producers to organize and intensify production, and by generating wealth and economic disparities leading to social stratification.

The Study of East Mediterranean Trade in the Bronze Age

For the east Mediterranean, studies of trade have been of two basic types:

(i) reliance upon some "historical" reconstruction of events, therefore tending to emphasize the shifting prominences (even thalassocracies) of a Minoan, Mycenaean, Egyptian, or Syrian cast of players (critiqued by Knapp 1993; Knapp and Cherry 1994:128–134), and
(ii) following Renfrew, development of anthropology and economics-based models, but without necessarily integrating historical detail into the general picture.

There has been extensive work on the fingerprinting of copper (e.g., Gale 1991) and its role in the eastern Mediterranean economy (e.g., Muhly et al. 1988). In Egypt, the types and distribution of Minoan (Kemp and Merrillees 1980), Cypriot (Merrillees 1968), and Mycenaean (Hankey 1981; Bell 1991) pottery have been studied in detail, as has the profile of Mycenaean (Yannai 1983; Leonard 1987; 1994; Yon et al. 2000) and Cypriot (Gittlen 1981; Bergoffen 1989; Artzy 2001) pottery in the Levant. Cline (1994) and Lambrou-Phillipson (1990) have documented Near Eastern goods in the Aegean, and Jacobsen (1994) has cataloged Egyptian objects found on Cyprus. There have also been some attempts at identifying, inter alia, the place of manufacture of Aegean Marine Style pottery, Canaanite jars, Bichrome ware and some other Cypriot products or finds,

Mycenaean pottery, and much more (e.g., Knapp and Cherry 1994; Hein et al. 1999; Mountjoy and Ponting 2000; Serpico et al. 2003).

Anthropological studies of exchange and consumption were brought to bear upon the east Mediterranean stage (Knapp and Cherry 1994). The rich tributes referred to in the Amarna Letters (EA) (Moran 1992) were reinterpreted as high-level gift exchange between the dominant powers and, on a more one-way level, between the great powers and their vassals (Liverani 1990). But gift exchange, glittering or not, was by definition restricted and, by nature of the distances involved between polities, could not, in strictly commercial terms, have accounted for the bulk of trade, certainly not enough to have provided the engine for social change accepted by theorists. Clearly a commercial network also operated, sometimes on a considerable scale, as attested to by the richness of the Uluburun shipwreck (Pulak 1997) and the vast quantities of copper therein (although just how vast or abnormal a cargo this was depends upon whether the emphasis is placed upon the metal [= royal/elite] or the pottery and scrap [= merchant]). The exact nature of long-distance east Mediterranean commercial trade is still highly uncertain given current evidence. It undoubtedly operated even at a state level (e.g., EA 35), but at the same time merchants seemed to be able to operate on their own account to a certain extent. Artzy (1985; 1988) suggested that state and freelance trade can be distinguished by the type of shipping utilized: long boats for the former and round, that is, shorter, vessels for private ventures.

However, a more ad hoc trade system can also be distinguished, in which individuals on state or large-scale commercial missions conducted small-scale transactions on their own account (Artzy 1997). The activities at "Bates Island," a seasonal revictualing station off Marsa Matruh in Egypt, bear witness to this: pins and other small metal items were cast on the spot and doubtless on demand, presumably in return for food, water, and ostrich egg shells (White et al. 2003). It is also important to note that it was possible for all types of exchange – gift giving, state and individual trading – to occur (as argued by Knapp and Cherry 1994), sometimes in the same venture: this is demonstrated by the massive quantities of copper found on the Uluburun shipwreck (10 tons), alongside timber, scrap metal, and pottery, plus small balance scales.

Prestige, status, and imported goods

The possibilities for individuals to accumulate wealth and status independent of the patronage of the state – and specifically elite individuals – is germane, given the standard argument that the incentive for long-distance trade was fueled by the desire for emergent elites to acquire goods through which to express status and prestige. Sherratt and Sherratt (1991) refined Renfrew's model by focusing upon consumption, rather than production, arguing that the demand for convertible resources (especially metal) provided the incentive to intensify and further organize production, which led to surplus wealth on the part of the producers, who became consumers of goods themselves. The "prestige market" was initially fed by low-bulk essential and prestige/luxury goods, but expanded with the success of the metals trade to include other "non-convertible" and to a certain extent archaeologically invisible commodities, for example pottery and their contents, textiles, and so on (for such perishable goods: Knapp 1991): all these became part of the language of status expression. On the other hand, Horden and Purcell (2000:123–172) stress the significance of short-hop ad hoc low-value commodity trade (Braudel's "cabo-tage"). In fact they regard the high-prestige trade as an outgrowth of ordinary trade, and not vice versa, and argue that the vicissitudes of the former say nothing about either the persistence or importance of the latter. This appears not to be the case when considering the first development of regional and long-distance trade in the prehistoric context, where the evidence indicates that such trade began with portable low-bulk essential (if utilitarian) goods (Perlès 1992), as well as pres-tige/luxury/esoteric goods (Broodbank 1993), even if the latter served as symbols enabling access to subsistence-related resources (Halstead 1989). On an inter-regional scale across the east Mediterranean and Aegean, there is no evidence for large(r) deep draft ocean-going sailing ships with plank-built hulls, masts, and rigging until around 2000 B.C. (Broodbank 2000:342–243); this change in tech-nology represents (potential) access to maritime worlds of entirely differing orders of magnitude. The first is local to regional, the second is regional and inter-regional. The first is small scale; the second is bulk. The first has limited operating times and directional flexibility; the second has year-round capability in all directions. The first requires few facilities; the second requires anchorages and ports and a supporting complex society capable of providing capital investment and specialists (Broodbank 2000:345–347). For the Aegean, such interregional trade seems likely to correlate with the emergence of the first palaces on Crete and, as often argued, it is proba-ble that elites centered in these structures initiated and controlled (and restricted) such early long-distance trade (Niemeier 1998:36). A likely key resource for Proto-palatial, or Old Palace, Crete (Watrous 2001:198–212) (ca. 1900–1750 B.C.) acquired via this new long-distance maritime avenue was tin from the far western end of an established Near Eastern distribution route (Niemeier 1998:36–37). At this time (and within the context of a moderate level of complexity, typically labeled complex chiefdom, or heterarchy, or early state, or the like), we have moved to the potential for commodity trade, and for specialist traders (merchants) operating within some form of administrative-bureaucratic context.

Thus we must distinguish system creation from subsequent persistence. Consideration of early long-distance trade immediately brings us to the "other" – something held to have almost independent explanatory force in a number of recent studies. We stress the need to consider "other" only as locally constructed and relevant.

The Other

The history of early modern to modern (colonial) Europe led to the creation of an "other" in the Orient: Said (1978) famously conceptualized this as "orientalism" –

an imposed set of "western" views which sought to isolate, control, and explain "Orientals" (Said 1978:1). The dangerous allure and magic of the orient, controlled and distanced in the colonial world, could be given free reign in the archaeology of the distant past: *ex Oriente lux*. It was therefore all too inevitable in earlier archaeological work to explain history in terms of the spread/diffusion of civilization out from the Orient and to highlight all and any instances of imports/exports between the core and periphery, as if they explained by their mere existence. Such exchanges and links from periphery back to the core even provided the chronological framework for history – in an entirely circular reinforcing process (Leonard 1988).

But such processes were neither passive nor static nor arbitrary. Today it is regularly argued that "secondary" entities such as the major centers in the Aegean and on Cyprus were motivated in seeking and developing contacts with the ancient Orient at least partly because local elites sought to enhance their social and political position through such associations and material correlates (e.g., Knapp 1998; Knapp and Cherry 1994; Manning 1994; Sherratt and Sherratt 1991; Keswani 1989). They were thus active receptors and manipulators. A predominance of luxury goods (crafted or the exotic raw materials) as foreign imports would therefore be anticipated (e.g., Lambrou-Phillipson 1990:164). In reverse, the "primary/core" states of western Asia sought these same contacts because they too were stimulated by their own economic and political concerns to secure new and different resources (both primary and crafted). Networks of inter-elite contacts and exchanges sought effectively similar signifiers. Thus, while distinct, the exchange of luxury goods and commodities was often linked (and/or complementary). The "other" became sets of reciprocal relationships in which certain iconography, images, objects, artists, or ideas were exchanged into local contexts. The encoded elements and values traded rested on the contradiction of both common inter-elite modalities and recognized transferences of skills and renown, as well as the use of acquisition from a distance to create localized "otherness" and exclusivity. In developed form, we see this in the artistic and ideological koiné linking dispersed elites around the east Mediterranean in the Late Bronze Age (e.g., Keswani 1989; Knapp 1998; Feldman 2002), with different and limited forms of local trickle-down processes.

A common problem with the literature discussing long-distance trade and the other is to discuss regional areas, or even just overall groupings we (modern scholars) define, as if they were seen as centralized or corporate entities within modern states and economies: thus "the Minoans" or "the elite" are said to do this or that. In reality, all the evidence we have available indicates that in the secondary regions, like the Aegean and Cyprus, and in large areas of western Asia (e.g., the Levant), the political formations were multiple and plural within the larger regions, and also inside even what we usually consider to be "states" or "polities" of some level or other (Wright; 1995; Cherry 1986; Keswani 1996; Hamilakis 2002; Schoep 2002). In turn, different groups (or factions) or families within particular centers engaged in a multiplicity of different and/or competitive practices as part of their own local political and economic arenas. Nonetheless, common themes and contexts may be noted: for example, both certain individuals/groups at Akrotiri on Thera in a wall painting (landscape frieze, east wall room 5, West House), and others at near-contemporary Mycenae in a "Nilotic" cat-chasing-ducks in a papyrus marsh design on an inlaid dagger from Shaft Grave V (Negbi 1994:74–75, with further refs.), sought to identify themselves with the esoteric value of "Nilotic" landscapes and exotic knowledge. Meanwhile, other groups all around the eastern Mediterranean employed the wall-painting medium, per se, as a key form of encoded expression.

The example of wall paintings nicely highlights an additional real problem with the "other," and perceived value and status in eastern Mediterranean prehistory. Now famous wall paintings were discovered just over a decade ago at Tell el-Dab'a in Egypt (Bietak 1992). Because these paintings looked broadly similar to Aegean examples, this art was attributed to "Minoan" style or similar production. But more sober reflection has led to several questions. Although the Tell el-Dab'a examples are often linked to the unique body of art from Thera buried by the volcanic eruption (Bietak 2003:29), in fact some now speculate that later Late Minoan (LM) IB/II or indeed Mainland Greek art may also offer as good or better associations. Others note that the wall paintings at Tell el-Dab'a exhibit some characteristics not easily paralleled in Minoan art or Aegean art and thus the idea emerged of their being in some way the product of hybridization (Shaw 1995), along with clear Egyptian antecedents/influence for some elements (e.g., Morgan 1995:38). Finally, there is the fundamental question of whether the Aegeanocentric identification was ever the only possibility. Elaborate and figural wall paintings have a long ancestry in the Near East (e.g., Frankfort 1996:424) and in Egypt (e.g., Newberry and Griffith 1893–1900). We are largely ignorant of the Levantine tradition, except as known from the major sites of Alalakh, Tel Kabri, and Tell el-Dab'a (Niemeier and Niemeier 2000; Bietak 2000b). As E. Sherratt (1994:237–238) suggests, one wonders if it is but the fortuitous pattern and history of extant data recovered by archaeology that led us to seeing this art as unquestionably a Minoan export (Bietak 2000a:195–200; 2000c), rather than perhaps seeing the Aegean as the western edge of a common zone of expression that maybe had its home in western Asia (E. Sherratt 1994:237–238; Knapp 1998). Shaw (1967; 1970) and also Immerwahr (1990) have long noted the probable influence of Egyptian painting in the creation of the Aegean tradition. We are perhaps seeing part of that extraordinary fusion that occurred in the Near East broadly during the Second Intermediate Period (ca. 1800–1550 B.C.); in this regard one may note with interest a recent report on an Egyptianizing mural in a Middle Bronze public building at Tell Sakka (Taraqji 1999). Thus the direction of otherness, and the role of which/whose "other," needs careful analysis on a case-by-case basis.

Space, Place, and the Other

In the case of the Mediterranean, it is important to recognize the sea as a facilitator, as much as a barrier. Adapting a well-known map of Mediterranean intervisibility (Chapman 1990: figure 262; Broodbank 2000: figure 4; and Horden and Purcell 2000:127), our Figure 11.1 shows the eastern Mediterranean in terms of

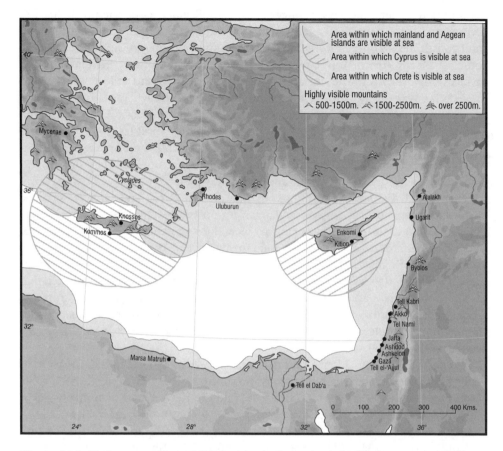

Figure 11.1 Maximum maritime visibility: plain shading around the Mediterranean and Aegean coastline indicates sea areas from which the mainland is potentially visible, while hatched areas around Crete and Cyprus indicate sea areas from which those islands are potentially visible. Areas of overlap show where a sailor could see both his origin and his destination at the same time. White areas are out of sight of land.

visibility from land/sea. This highlights that only the central eastern Mediterranean was an isolating sea, entirely out of sight of land; in contrast, the entire Aegean offers sight of land (unless in bad weather). The nature of "distance" between the Aegean (and especially Crete, the nearest point in the Aegean) and the Near East involves a large expanse of remote sea. A direct (i.e., shortest) and favorable (in terms of wind directions and sea currents) sea voyage from Crete to Egypt involves considerable travel out of sight of land, and thus requires more sophisticated navigation skills – not to mention a certain *mentalité* – to achieve a target (Wachsmann 1998:299–301). Even the route leading down to North Africa, although facilitated by direct, if seasonal winds, involves sailing clear of sight of land and only seems "easy" in retrospect, once the route has been achieved and is known (clearly the case in the LB 3 period – but here we are describing initial route creation). The conceptually easier route, if far longer, is east via Rhodes along the north coast of Cyprus and then down the Levant, with at no time the need to leave sight of land (and constitutes a concrete route map once done a first time). Critically, unlike the route to North Africa, this could be explored and developed incrementally; it involves no voyage into the unknown (in either direction, and indeed Wachsmann argued this was always the necessary return route, although he also regarded a journey from Marsa Matruh to western Cyprus as "feasible": Wachsmann 1998:299). But it is much farther and with intermediary polities.

The map highlights the relative isolation of Egypt and the distance between it and the Aegean (and vice versa): Pharaonic trade had to move through the Levant, since it was bounded to the north and northwest by large stretches of water from which no land was visible; southbound trade from Cyprus and Crete required a smaller leap of faith, for ships would fetch up on the North African cost eventually, and could then (once it was known) tack along the coast (hence the existence of the facilities at Marsa Matruh); overall, the balance of knowledge would not have swung in Egypt's favor. Horden and Purcell (2000:123–172) emphasize that geographical knowledge was sequential; thus ports would have been known in relation to where the ships had just been, rather than where a captain intended to trade. Thus the inhabitants of Tel Nami advertised their presence by carving ships into the surrounding hills which were, according to its excavator, easily visible from the sea (Artzy 1997:7–9).

It is perhaps no coincidence that the earliest Aegean exports/influences seem to occur along such a chain running from the southeast Aegean to northern Cyprus (Manning 1995:88–91, 108–110, 197–198) and the Levant, and then finally Egypt (Branigan 1966; 1967; Warren and Hankey 1989:130–135; Merrillees 2003). Whether either "end" of this chain met directly before the middle of the second millennium B.C. is debated – representations of *Keftiu* (Minoans/Aegeans) from the reign of Tuthmosis III (ca. 1479–1425 B.C.) (Vercoutter 1956; Wachsmann 1987) would seem unquestionably to indicate some form of direct contact by the 15th century B.C., and the evidence from Kommos in south Crete likewise points by the Late Minoan (LM) III period (ca. 1400–1200 B.C.) to direct trade between Crete and Egypt and vice versa (Watrous 1992:172–173, 175–178). Some scholars have advocated that the Minoans mastered the open ocean route earlier, at least during the first half of the second millennium B.C. (Warren 1995:10–11), and that this perhaps made them special in this regard (Wachsmann 1998:297–299); others have argued the opposite. The "miniscule amount of Minoan pottery" at the site of Marsa Matruh (Warren 1995:11), the obvious "drop down" route from Crete to North Africa/Egypt, or the "across and up" route from Egypt/North Africa to Crete, and "the only natural harbor between Alexandria and Tobruk" (Wachsmann 1998:299) argue rather strongly against significant Minoan trade via this route – especially when contrasted with the plentiful Cypriot, Egyptian, and some Mycenaean and Levantine material at the site.

In general, the notable aspect of Aegean relations with the eastern Mediterranean is their very scarcity in archaeological terms until the Late Bronze (LB) 3 period (ca. 1400–1200 B.C.), even for Crete (Niemeier 1998:38). It can be argued that the Aegean entered the periphery (versus being a margin) of the greater Near Eastern and Levantine world late in the third millennium B.C., when bronze started to be imported into the region, presumably from Anatolia (Nakou 1997), but it went little further. Contacts between Protopalatial, or Old Palace, Crete (ca. 1900–1750 B.C.) and the region are much discussed (e.g., Wiener 1987:261–264; Watrous 2001:211), with finds especially of Kamares pottery in Egypt providing a fundamental building block of the chronology and history of the greater region. But the reality is that this evidence consists of little more than a handful of objects from a time-span of a couple of centuries (Merrillees 2003). Other connections are also quite limited when one quantifies the data, rather than just lovingly describes them (e.g., Warren 1995:1–3). Minoan influence, for example, extends across the southern Aegean and to southwest Anatolia, but even Cyprus sees only very limited physical evidence for Aegean contact until after LM I (after ca. 1700–1500 B.C.) (less than two dozen items to date from four or five centuries: Warren and Hankey 1989:115–116; Wijngaarden 2002:191). Conversely, there are but a handful of Cypriot imports to the Aegean up to and including LM I (Cadogan 1979), and little evidence of definite Cypriot copper exports until later (Knapp 1990; Niemeier 1998:36–37). Moreover, as is the case in the wider Near East, when things change it is not Minoan, but mainland, Mycenaean objects that herald a change, starting in the Late Helladic (LH) IIA period (ca. 1600–1500 B.C.) (Graziadio 1995). Distance may therefore have operated as a powerful and valuable force in the peripheral Aegean in the period up to and including LM I – until its annihilation in the region-wide "palatial" era of LB 3 (ca. 1400–1200 B.C.), when the scale and range and commoditization of exchanges stretching from the Near East to the Aegean (with the central and western Mediterranean becoming the new "margin/periphery") indicate an entirely new trading reality. In this LB 3 era one may envisage a period of region-wide organized commodity exchanges. This picture offers a potentially important context when considering the much earlier development of both Old Palace (Protopalatial) and New Palace (Neopalatial) Crete (ca. 1900–1750 B.C., ca. 1750–1500 B.C. respectively) at the western periphery of the ancient world system. However, in both these situations, it is important to note that local manipulation is central, because these international objects/images are de-contextualized in order that they may travel, and they only weakly and stereotypically refer back to the originating culture. Such "foreign" or "exotic" goods become currency only in terms of the external local context (and not on their own terms/criteria).

In general, however, it is also important to note that Cyprus was quite different from the Aegean. As regular maritime trade networks developed in the eastern Mediterranean during the course of the Middle Bronze Age (MBA) (ca. 2000–1600 B.C.), an external world was entirely manifest and potentially available. For example, on Cyprus's north coast, with visibility across to the mainland, and a constrained plain between mountain and sea, Cypriots will have seen any passing ship, and vice versa, and it seems no coincidence that nearly all early long-distance imports occur in this northern zone. Elites and emergent rivals had both opportunity and competitive requirement in this regard as contact spread. Cyprus also offered a key raw resource in copper; exports to Syria are known from the 19th century B.C. and perhaps earlier (Knapp 1996a:16, 18–19; Niemeier 1998:36). Maritime opportunity was expressed by the Middle Cypriot (MC) period both via significant quantities of exports (pottery being the most easily identified material remnant – e.g., Johnson 1982; Maguire 1990), and by some "boat" models (Westerberg 1983: 9–11). The transition to the Late Cypriot (LC) period (around 1700–1600 B.C.) saw a well-known settlement shift to coastal locations in many areas (Catling 1962; Knapp 1997), and the island was very much better connected to the contemporary eastern Mediterranean than to the Aegean. Cyprus, in other words, was a periphery engaged to the core, versus a margin, as was the position of Crete.

Routes and Movement of Goods

If, as we would argue, the proper focus of trade is consumption, then it is necessary to form an idea of the role of imports in indigenous systems, a role dependent upon the degree of familiarity of a product, and social constructs of alien/exotic. Opportunities for trade are formed by geographical possibility, and shaped by the exigencies of wind, current, and landfall. Such factors lent a seasonality to the endeavor which bad weather could sabotage entirely. An important point is that outward and return routes were frequently different: indeed Braudel (1972:107) argued that destination-conscious shipping is a relatively recent phenomenon. The resulting ad hoc nature of trade has been highlighted by likening the enterprise to tramping (similar to Hasebroek's 1933 "sideline trading"), with multiple transactions along the route as need required (Artzy 1997; Sherratt and Sherratt 1991:357). At the same time, however, it must be recognized that such ad hoc movement is mainly plausible within an already broadly established system of destinations; furthermore, core-periphery and vice versa trade may have been more direct. Altman (1988) has also doubted the scenario of multiple stop routes along the Egyptian and Canaanite coast, at least by Aegean ships, arguing that taxation and pilfering (combined with navigational difficulties) would have proved a deterrent. In his view, Cyprus and the cities along the Lebanese coast provided the main distribution points for Aegean goods.

The determining variables of distance and visibility, as discussed above, are both factors in what might be termed common knowledge, the absence of which defines the mysterious and exotic – which Knapp (1998), following Helms (1988), argued lent an air of prestige to foreign goods. But distance is also a cast of mind. Broodbank (2000:16) introduced the concept of "habitat islands," comparable to Braudel's "islands that the sea does not surround" (1972:160–1), or Veth's "islands of the interior" (1993), that is, locations isolated by virtue of being surrounded by inhospitable or uninhabited land. Certainly parts of Egypt, like Marsa Matruh, may be viewed in this way. But is it possible that, from a mariner's point of view, many of the Levantine ports were also terrestrial islands, worlds largely separate from hinterlands (ports and key urban sites can also function as partial islands)? Renfrew

(1975), in developing the concept of the "Early State Module," suggested that the practical radius of a terrestrial staple finance system was perhaps 50 kilometers, or typically a territory of ca. 1,500 square kilometers; Mann (1986) likewise stressed the limitations of direct rule and transport technologies for prehistoric polities. Although there was clearly much variation (Trigger 2003:92–113), such limits are inherent. Thus local knowledge gained of anywhere outside the territorial boundaries would have been second hand at best, and arguably unnecessary. Accordingly, the "other" would probably have extended to areas which archaeologists might consider to be local. Gillis (1996) suggested that the bulk of long-distance Mediterranean trade was in the hands of middlemen traders (Artzy 1997; Hirschfeld 1992; 2000), and the Mycenaeans may not have had a fleet at all, certainly not one of any significance. This would further restrict knowledge of foreign parts, although it could have increased a general sense of otherness and prestige for the few involved and for the imports they offered. The difference between the east and southeast of Cyprus, but one day's sail away from the Levantine centers, and the "distant" Aegean, while not obvious to the modern world, would have been significant in prehistory.

Another important element is how local markets receiving goods might work. Hodder and Ukwu (1969), building upon Polanyi's view of long-distance trade, argued that the local markets which develop around distant parent markets are disembedded from the local economy, and have nothing to do with the communities near them. Knapp (1997:27) argued that "the waterfront . . . often reveals a unique human openness to outside impulses," but it could equally have been seen as dangerous, a pollutant to be contained (Sherratt and Sherratt 1998:337–338; Barr 1970).

The likely low level of interregional knowledge in the ancient world has an impact upon the way in which foreigners, and foreign goods, are viewed. It may be that goods arriving in port were assigned the category of "other" relative to local wares, but it is as well to remember that "other" is, in itself, a local category, and that items which are not relevant or relatable to indigenous systems will simply not be visible to them and thus will not succeed. For example, Welsch and Terrell (1998) documented a clearly differentiated distribution of glass beads and shell rings along the Sepik coast of New Guinea: glass beads were highly prized amongst the western groups of villages studied, where they formed a necessary part of the bride-price, but shell-rings were not common. In contrast, in villages to the east, wives were acquired through sister exchange and glass beads had no appeal, whereas shell rings were used as marks of wealth and prestige; other items were traded between the two zones (resource/social groups) but these items were not.

Thus imports must always tread the line between exotic and familiar. This tension can be resolved in a number of ways. High-level gift exchange can be seen as dealing with the familiar: prestige items of precious metals tended to be one-off "designer" items or else they belonged to a very small stylistic range: design variability and/or unfamiliarity mattered less than the materials from which they were made, which carried a universal (expensive) message. In such a way emerged the "international style" of the Late Bronze Age (e.g., Keswani 1989; Knapp 1998;

Feldman 2002): the whole adds up to a shared vocabulary. An equivalence of value was established, recognizable not only to those in the group, but also, most likely, to those who were not, that is, local non-elites.

Sometimes the categories of same/different could indeed be manipulated by producers. For example, Mycenaean kraters decorated with chariots, a style uncommon on the mainland, were aimed directly at the Syrian and Cypriot emergent elites for whom horse and chariot teams had social and symbolic importance (Steel 1998; 2002a; 2002b). But the appeal was not automatic: those self-same warrior elites living farther south, in areas under Egyptian control, favored Egyptian-style bronze drinking sets over Mycenaean ones. Furthermore, and not withstanding the difficulties in identifying "ethnicity" in archaeological data (Jones 1997), Hodder (1982) noted that ethnic boundaries may be maintained by a limited range of material culture, while other forms and styles may be shared across group boundaries. In this context, E. Sherratt (1999:177) was right to suggest that the trade in pottery (routinely assigned a high status by excavators) was successful partly because it lay outside the elite value system. Sherratt and Sherratt (2000) noted that the range of pottery and metal goods imported by sub-elites supported local social display through the consumption of wine, oil, and incense, and Hulin (in press) has argued that the popularity of Cypriot and Mycenaean oil containers should be seen in this light.

The Evidence for Trade and its Limitations

There is the large hidden corpus of evidence – perishable goods and the like – that simply does not exist from the work at most archaeological excavations. Textual data, the odd depiction (and now some scientific analyses, as well as the infrequent, extraordinary find like a shipwreck) give us reason to think we are seeing only the tip of the iceberg (e.g., Knapp 1991; Wachsmann 1987; Pulak 1997). We tend to focus on elite exchanges on the grounds that they are critical to political processes (and they also have a near monopoly over the "good stuff" that most archaeologists lust to find). Reference to textual evidence indicates very well how little we observe archaeologically.

When we come to the agents of Mediterranean maritime trade, we are also poorly informed. Despite various textual and iconographic data from the Near East, we know surprisingly little about these key mobile persons – including their ethnicity and gender. For the east Mediterranean and Aegean, a critical group appears to be the independent merchants (Knapp and Cherry 1994:142–145), and especially those christened "nomads of the sea" (Artzy 1997), an important collection of people (by the LB 3 era especially, i.e., ca. 1400–1100 B.C.) outside the state elite structure who were hired or bought to provide, and take on the risks of, ships, shipping, and maritime expertise. These people became the agents and actors between centers and elites. Here we have extreme mobility and maritime geography beyond the state, reaching from the east to the central Mediterranean in the LB 3 era, and yet largely hidden (or requiring teasing out) in the textual records. In archaeological terms a few trading sites may be noted, otherwise such polymorphic groupings are largely invisible except as proposed for various palimpsests of material from mixed origins. Furthermore, Artzy highlights a dual-trade world conveyed and carried out by these same agents, with a main inter-elite cargo trade, complemented by captains' or sailors' trade on the side (Braudel's 1972:107 "tramping"). The modes and motivations of acquisition and consumption in any local context will have been very different between these two economies, even if involving the same boat.

But perhaps most alarming is the temporal and spatial dimension. Cline (1994) assembled 1,118 imports of varying certainty and contextual association, and proceeded to try to derive trade patterns from this corpus. This sounds like quite a lot of evidence, but it comes from a period of almost 600 years (Cline 1994:7) – so this purportedly large number of imports in fact is equivalent to about 1.9 objects per year on average from a large and variegated region! More seriously, examination reveals that fully 277 items, almost 25 percent of the total, come from just two "instantaneous" shipwrecks (Cape Gelidonya and Uluburun), leaving only about 1.4 objects per year for the rest of the six centuries at stake. Even this is misleading as just 149 objects cover the first three centuries of the LBA study period (Cline 1994:13 tables 2, 3), so what Cline documented in 1994 was the exchange of about 0.5 objects per year from the entire Aegean for these crucial six centuries. When one considers the massive haul of material culture evidence from surveys and excavations at any site in the eastern Mediterranean, not to mention the entire world of perishable and other evidence not represented in recovered artifact finds, this evidence base of 1,118 items becomes an inadequate, if not misleading basis from which to analyze trade.

Moreover, even if we acknowledge that this is the sort of data we must work with, then several stark problems confront us. Does a lot of Mycenaean pottery in the east Mediterranean mean extensive Mycenaean trade, or rather material traveling – and not necessarily as key items – with Levantine or Cypriot merchants returning from the east Aegean, or west Anatolia, or the Greek mainland (e.g., Catling 1964; Knapp and Cherry 1994:128–130; Bass 1991)? And, if these trade items were important, then to whom – and how did this vary in time and space? The very small volume of Minoan pottery found in Egypt, for example, hardly indicates significant commercial relations, and its find-spots tend (where a context is known) to derive from what Merrillees termed "middle class" or at least non-elite contexts (Merrillees 1972; 1998; Kemp and Merrillees 1980). Even the more plentiful corpus of Mycenaean pottery largely comprises one cache from Tell el-Amarna. In turn, the impressive 616 Mycenaean pottery imports from Ugarit (combining Ras Shamra and Minet el-Beida) (Wijngaarden 2002:43) take on a different complexion when considered in terms of time and space (data from Wijngaarden 2002:37–73, 330–342). Roughly speaking, these finds come from about 5.7 hectares of excavations – the total site area is ca. 27.4 hectares+ (Wijngaarden 2002:37 and n. 5). Ignoring the obvious concentration in existing work on the main elite areas, this still works out at approximately 1 Mycenaean import per 92.5 square meters of surface area. The material covers the temporal range of LH II/IIIA1-

LHIIIB (ca. 1600–1200 B.C.), or somewhere around 250+ years (Wijngaarden 2002:10 figure 2.1). Thus we have at Ugarit around 2.5 foreign items per year on average – hardly overwhelming. Of the 294 vases with a known find circumstance (237 are unknown), 70 percent were found in tombs.

Wijngaarden (2002:24) states that the "sheer quantity of Mycenaean vessels distributed outside the Aegean appears to be incompatible" with ideas that long-distance trade was not important to the Mycenaean economy. This may well be, but it would seem from Hirschfeld's study of pot marks on Mycenaean wares in Cyprus and the east Mediterranean that it was not the Mycenaeans who acted as the prime distributors of Helladic wares to the east Mediterranean, but the Cypriots (Hirschfeld 1992; 2000). In support of such ideas, one may note both a well-recognized rule of thumb that there tends to be about three Cypriot pots to every one Mycenaean pot at Levantine sites (e.g., Bourke and Sparks 1995:156), and the relatively meager quantities of Cypriot material in the Aegean. It is, therefore, easy to make too much of the evidence of the easily recognizable Mycenaean pottery exports of LHIIIA-B, without weighting such finds against the much greater evidence for other east Mediterranean trade. In any event, Wijngaarden (2002:7) instead adopts the viewpoint that the Mycenaeans took part in large, diverse, multifaceted trade networks in which there were many participants and several modes of exchange. He identified 348 sites outside the Aegean with Mycenaean pottery. On examination, however, 72.1 percent of these sites have yielded 1–10 imports, and 89 percent yielded fewer than 50 imports (across LHI-IIIB or almost 400 years: Wijngaarden 2002:10 figure 2.1 uses the dates ca. 1600–1200 B.C.). Any space/time analysis would again find that the significance of these imports is perhaps less than obvious. The simple ability of pottery to survive and thus to produce an end-of-period "pile" of data is misleading scholarship.

In contrast to this sort of spatial-temporal minimalism, some documentary and some rare iconographic evidence likely referring to Aegeans, or depicting Aegean-style items in the context of royal-level offerings or gifts with other peoples in some Theban wall paintings (Sakellarakis and Sakellarakis 1984; Knapp 1985; Wachsmann 1987; Matthäus 1995; Rehak 1998), seem to evidence and hint at very different connections by the mid-15th century B.C., although, even then, Wachsmann (1987:42) did not regard these *Keftiu* representations in paintings from the Theban tombs as in fact necessarily indicating an Aegean presence in Egypt. Moreover, even assuming this evidence *is* taken on face value, it must be put in context: as Bass (1998:186–187) notes, depictions of Aegeans in Egypt are limited to just six tombs, and this therefore compares very minimally to the totality of evidence.

It is all too easy to make far too much of the very limited Aegean-Oriental connections in the second millennium B.C., and much previous scholarship has undoubtedly done just this on quite meager evidence (e.g., Kantor 1947). Even in the LB 3 era, when undeniably an international style/koiné is evident across a wide region of the east Mediterranean, the role of the Aegean remains less than clear. There is some textual evidence, but Linear B records notoriously fail to mention overseas trade or merchants, despite mentions of ships, personal names associated with maritime activities, and foreigners or captives from overseas locations

(Wachsmann 1998:123–128), and despite the existence of goods/items that must have originally been imports, or items ("of export quality") that were, plausibly, intended to be exports (see Knapp 1991:41–44). Thus how far such a model of an international style/koiné and of serious interconnectedness translates beyond the Near Eastern core into the wider eastern Mediterranean, and for which time periods, is unclear.

For example, when one examines the Aegean evidence, one perhaps finds that the well-known Nilotic wall painting in the West House at Akrotiri on Thera (see above) derives its local justification and value from the very lack of general Aegean familiarity with Egypt and the Levant; it is instead part of an exclusionary political economy possible on the periphery of the east Mediterranean world (Manning et al. 1994:221–222, 228). The situation clearly does change in LB 3, when we can see a common pool of regal/power symbols (e.g., leonine creatures, sphinxes, griffins, chariots) employed in local contexts across the wider east Mediterranean region. The objects themselves are malleable and transferable (within recognized social and cultural biographies of classes of objects), as local elites sought to develop status through reference to a repertoire of symbols that were linked to the extensive and shared power/status-laden eastern Mediterranean and Near East. It is only in such a connected elite world that the specific biographic value of objects can also come significantly into play – before this they are at best an exotic (and perhaps very socially valuable) class. A nice example of the LB 3 world in action is represented by the exotic source Near Eastern lapis lazuli cylinder seals reworked with gold foil on Cyprus and then transported to a Mycenaean ruler at Thebes (Porada 1982:68–70). Perhaps in the LB 3 period (only) we may see the Aegean as firmly engaged within the periphery of the east Mediterranean interaction sphere.

Three shipwrecks are known from this period, broadly: Cape Gelidonya, Uluburun, and Point Iria (Bass 1967; Pulak 1997; Phelps et al. 1999). A key question is whether these are the tip of the iceberg of a huge such body of evidence (well beyond the textual evidence of inter-kingly exchanges), or whether they may have been somewhat special – detritus from a restricted number of elite exchanges. The fact that these known Bronze Age shipwrecks all date to the LB 3 period (from roughly two centuries ca. 1400–1200 B.C.), and given their random find circumstances, also raises the question of whether the absence of any firm MB or LB 1 evidence (from some five centuries ca. 2000–1500 B.C. – but cf. Bass 1998:187) indicates much less regular and less commoditized trade in those earlier periods. Known (non-shipwreck) imports concentrate into this same LB 3 period, supporting the reality of the pattern. Finds of stone anchors also provide some indication: whereas significant numbers of these have been recognized off, or at, LBA sites in Cyprus, the Levant, and Egypt – at least consistent with a moderate level of shipping – such finds are much scarcer to date in the Aegean realm (Wachsmann 1998:258–275). The distribution of bulk transport vessels such as Canaanite Jars or Cypriot *pithoi* (storage jars) or Plain White jars offers another measure, as these items indicate trade well beyond the knick-knack level. Again, although finds are known in the Aegean from LMIA onward (e.g., Leonard 1996), it is fair to say they pale into insignificance compared to the copious import/export numbers found respectively in Cyprus, the Levant, or Egypt. One might speculate, as above, that the connected world of the Near East included Cyprus, but only partly the Aegean, at least until the LB 3 period.

Elites and Others: Consumption and Identity

The link between elites and long-distance contact and trade in material or intangible goods and ideas is ubiquitous in the archaeological and ethnographic record. The linkage from there to the rest of society, however, remains less clear. For example, Wijngaarden (2002:199–200) argues that because most published/described tombs found in an area of Cyprus (Maroni *Tsaroukkas*) contained some evidence of Mycenaean imports, therefore such items are unlikely to indicate elite status (contra Manning and Monks 1998; Manning 1998; Steel 1998). Hence he implies that imported Mycenaean pottery penetrated widely into Cypriot society (or at least the few major coastal sites – Aegean imports to Cyprus are strongly biased to certain loci: Portugali and Knapp 1985). Yet this logic only applies if one can argue that all or at least much of the population at these notable sites were buried in the tombs in question – whereas we know for the case referred to that there were a significant unknown number of other tombs without such imports. At issue are just over 40 tombs (Johnson 1980; Manning and Monks 1998) covering some 400–500 years (MC/LCI transition through LCIIC, ca. 1700–1200 B.C.). A total number of burials in these tombs of 100–400, give or take, seems plausible, but is a very much smaller number than the likely overall population for this major site area across the 400–500 years in question. Hence the known and conspicuous tombs represent but a tiny fraction of the real mortuary record.

Given the extent of research on the nexus of elites and long-distance imports, the relation and relevance of such elite items to a wider social world is now perhaps the key issue. This issue is more complicated than it seems to modern archaeologists, who "recognize" imports very readily as a category. It is important to realize that this was not necessarily straightforward in the relevant prehistoric contexts, and certainly not for the majority of potential consumers in such societies. We see only successes. Imported goods faced the problem of product recognition. Hence, for example, we may cite the move in Late Cypriot II to a standardized package – the Base Ring juglet – for low-bulk liquid goods, compared to the range of juglets exported to the Levant in MCIII-LC I (Maguire 1990).

The "otherness" that made an import not "local" is also complex. Distance alone cannot be the sole indicator of the "other." Otherness depends to a large extent on the permeability of social boundaries, that is, the willingness of a culture to embrace innovation at all (itself a complex outcome of context and history – see, for example, the contrasting attitudes and consumption histories between England and Germany when coffee was introduced: the former society adopted coffee drinking in public as a dynamic innovation which formed part of a wider social restructuring in the 17th century A.D., whereas the latter society did not, and only belatedly subsumed coffee drinking conservatively into its domestic status quo [Schivelbusch 1992]). On a theoretical level, this subject is rarely addressed head-on. The question of visibility in the material culture record, however, devolves upon the interpretation of style – be it style as object, as technology, or as decoration. Unfortunately, as Hegmon (1998) pointed out, the interest in the maintenance of boundaries means that more attention has been paid to differences across boundaries than to differences within.

Another important problem concerns whether trade was elite-oriented with simply a limited trickle-down effect, as some analyses of reported evidence would indicate (e.g., Portugali and Knapp 1985), or whether there was interregional trade at different levels that permeated more widely than a few main centers/emporia and the regional elites. Most work to date has formalized the elite-centered view, but with an inevitable circularity of logic as elite-oriented contexts and data have dominated much archaeological research until very recently (and the advent in particular of intensive regional survey projects). Archaeological studies still derive directly or indirectly from the view that consumption is an aspect of the political economy of societies. Economists (e.g., Sombart 1967; Frank 1993), anthropologists (e.g., Appadurai 1986, Kopytoff 1986), and sociologists (e.g., Baudrillard 1968) have concentrated upon the conditions under which economic objects circulate in different regimes of value in space and time. Such approaches in archaeology inherently tend to dichotomize elite and popular culture, with the assumption that the wealthier elements of society control power and knowledge for their own ends, and are arbiters of tastes (see also Foucault 1972; Berger and Luckmann 1966), which then trickle down to the rest of society.

There are, however, other ways of approaching the analysis and construction of society and trade – especially by focusing on individuals and their choices. Economic psychologists (e.g., Ajzen and Fishbein 1980; Lea et al. 1987; Lunt and Livingstone 1992) have sought to move the focus of studying goods away from their role as expressions of status (still the concern of much archaeology) to the ways in which they express self and personal relations. Csikszentmihalyi and Rochberg-Halton (1981) argue that the symbolic meaning of objects balances between differentiation (social individuality) and similarity (social integration), in much the same way as Douglas and Isherwood (1979 – respectively an anthropologist and an economist) argue that goods are explicable only in their total context as represented by the full range of possible behaviors. Ajzen and Fishbein's (1980) interest in the relationship between normative beliefs and consumption behavior finds an echo in the assertion of Douglas and Isherwood (1979) – itself based upon a long tradition of anthropological thought concerning the polarities of individualist and conformist behaviors (e.g., Durkheim 1893; Weber 1976) – that the degree of latitude afforded to individuals by the groups to which they belong determines the freedom with which they embrace innovation across the whole spectrum of their activities. These scholars argued that the level of expectation placed upon an individual, both as an individual and as a member of a group, determines his/her willingness to embrace innovation. We differ from this perspective only inasmuch as where they saw such social forces to be constraining, we apply an agency perspective and argue that social forces simply stake out an individual's room to maneuver by determining what is appropriate.

Part of the problem and reason for the dichotomy of elite/other in existing studies stems from the fact that much existing literature on LBA trade derives from, or is influenced by, ethnographic parallels that are not necessarily compatible with the international city-state arena of the LBA eastern Mediterranean and its peripheral elements. For example, studies of the Melanesian kula system have heavily influenced a number of views of eastern Mediterranean exchange (e.g., Portugali and Knapp 1985; Knapp 1988–1989). In contrast, it might be as useful to examine analogies with trade between colonial powers and those colonies that have achieved a social development comparable to that of the imperial power (e.g., Riden 1980), and other non-western state-complex society maritime interactions (e.g., Junker 1999).

Acquisition as Expression

The standard argument is that individuals acquire goods through which to build and express status and prestige, with most work focused on elite activities in this regard. Shipwreck sites such as Uluburun provide rich testament to the possible range of even a single consignment, much of which would ordinarily not otherwise be evident in the material record. The ten tons of copper (more oxhide ingots than the rest of the region put together), one ton of tin, and the gold and silver scrap would have been reprocessed over the centuries, with but a small proportion surviving, as would the glass ingots and beads. The organic material would also have perished; the fate of the various beads, swords, and other luxury items would have been as random as for most in the Near East.

Metals and pottery provide the key indicators for ancient trade in the existing evidence and in current trends of scholarship. Metal is overemphasized partly because the minerals trade is inevitably prominent in high-level correspondence, since it was the literate elites who controlled the organization of production and export of bulk items. As Horden and Purcell pointed out (2000: 350), however, the usefulness of certain metals in the definition of an elite does not imply their scarcity, because metals were also utilitarian. Moreover, while few would doubt the importance of the copper/metals industry to Cyprus, the Aegean, and Sardinia, areas with a built-in advantage by virtue of access to these resources, the assumption that the metals trade was the driving force behind economic development is both simplistic and particularist.

Cyprus is a case in point. Knapp (1996b; 1986), Keswani (1996; 1993) and Peltenburg (1996) all have regarded the mining and production of copper on a scale, by LC II, that far outweighed local needs, and so argued that external demand drove a shift in the island's economy from a regional, agricultural, and village-based society to a complex, urban, and international one. But the evidence remains less than overwhelming, excepting the textual mentions of *Alashiya* and its copper, and the supply of a few significant cargoes by its king. An earlier LBA copper production site is now known in the Troodos foothills at Politiko *Phorades*, but this site and community was very small and was perhaps only seasonally exploited (Knapp 2003); similarly the much discussed "Fortress" at Enkomi (e.g., Muhly 1989: 298–305) is impressive only because of the lack of other evidence, and is in fact hardly overwhelming in scale. From LCI through LCIIC there is a lack of unambiguous evidence for a significant organized structure to the Cypriot economy compatible with island-wide large-scale metal production (Manning and De Mita 1997 – cf. Webb 1999 who argues the case for more unified ideological structures). External agency might be suggested to be crucial, but much of the best evidence for a major Cypriot metals industry and its linkage to power and ideology on Cyprus is notably late, from the 12th century B.C. in particular (see Webb 1999:298–299 with refs.), although Knapp (1986:35–37; 1988) has argued forcefully to push the evidence of a copper-based ideology back into the 14th century B.C. Thus it is arguably an outcome of complex engagement with the eastern Mediterranean, rather than necessarily its prime or only cause. In several cases agriculturally based activities, rather than metallurgy, appear central to various prominent sites: for example, Kalavasos *Ayios Dhimitrios* (South 1995; 1997), or Alassa *Paliotaverna* (Hadjisavvas 1996; 2003). Muhly (1986) also noted Cyprus/*Alashiya*'s significance as a major source of wood and a center for shipbuilding, at least in the Greco-Roman period, although the references to Alashiyan timber (EA 35, 36 and 40) in the Amarna Letters suggest that it was a source for wood much earlier.

In any event, such arguments center on production, rather than consumption, and the role of metals in indigenous economies is still unexplored. Clearly precious metals, to be converted either into objects of desire or used as a means of payment, had a readily identifiable and translatable value across the region. Copper was expensive precisely because it was shipped in bulk; its distribution within a system, in terms of the status of the items produced, has been little studied. Obviously it is not comparable to the precious metals, which were intrinsically valuable because of their practical disadvantages as much as their aesthetic appeal. Metal objects may have been items to aspire to, but would have been within the grasp of a larger section of the population than is sometimes supposed (see, for example, in Egypt, where a bronze razor cost about the same as a goat: Janssen 1975).

If the role of supposedly high value goods in local economies is sketchy, the role of pottery is more firmly established in many minds as makeweights alongside "real" cargo, necessary containers for higher value goods, space-fillers, or items for petty trade, but never as items in their own right. E. Sherratt (1999) disagreed, but noted that pottery never seemed to make up more than 20 percent of a cargo on bulk carriers. Arguably true as far as it goes, this observation is of value only if one assumes that pottery always piggy-backed on shipments of bulk items, such as copper and timber, and along routes set up and controlled by merchants in those commodities. If this were indeed the case, then the huge quantities of Cypriot and Mycenaean pottery in the Levant imply a hidden trade in bulk commodities (usually taken in the literature to mean metals, but also including timber, *pithoi*, and Canaanite jars) of staggering proportions. Certainly it should be remembered that pottery could comprise the bulk of cargo on smaller ships, as was the case with the Point Iria shipwreck, for example (Phelps et al. 1999).

Consumption as Alternative Logic

In former days largely functionalist ideas often underpinned concepts of trade/exchange (e.g., Renfrew 1972). The assumption was that the bases of trade consisted of trading what you have for things that you do not (mutual complementarity). Merrillees (1974:7), for example, doubted the significance of Cyprus in the Aegean markets principally because he regarded the resources of the two regions as being too similar to make exchange desirable. In fact, in money-less economies, a wide variety of subsidiary goods may be exchanged to make up an abstract notion of value. Thus while the presence of Cypriot copper on Sardinia (or even Crete) is seen as problematic, it would have been perfectly possible for a consignment to include a quantity of copper as makeweight within a broader transaction, as long as the recipient was a merchant/consumer and not a producer, whose need for copper would be the same whether locally acquired or not. Certainly on a smaller scale, pottery would have moved up and down the line as part of a barter system, distorting deposition patterns. Need, value, and negotiation must be conceived in localized and social and symbolic terms, not solely in macro-economic and functionalist terms.

Douglas and Isherwood (1979) also made the point that status consumption relates to the entire repertoire open to the individual. They introduced the archaeologically useful – and measurable – concept of consumption periodicities: that is, how often an object is used and displayed relative to everyone and everything else. This brings us back to the work of economic psychologists (above), who have sought to direct attention to the way choice of consumption expresses self and personal relations (which can include status, etc., as in the traditional archaeological approach, but is wider and, critically, can encompass the non-elite as well). It is of course difficult to judge whether one Cypriot jar containing unguents for personal use at a public event would signal a higher status than a host of plain local cups used at the feast. On the other hand, comparing like with like, a Mycenaean drinking set would certainly send a different message than would a local one. In this regard, it is interesting to note that the take-up of "cheaper" imports (Base Ring juglets, for example, or Mycenaean drinking sets) appealed to the sub-elite classes in Egypt, and possibly the southern Levant (above). Such objects may initially have circulated in the elite sphere, but as their popularity spread to sub-elites, they would, by definition, have lost their elite status. We therefore gain different windows into the entirety of local cultures – and can start to shake off the solely elite-centered focus of most existing work. Kopytoff (1986) argued for a biographical approach to specific commodities, in order to tease out the expectations placed upon any given item by the communities it passes through. Appadurai (1986) agreed, but broadened the focus to include the "social history" of things, which includes whole classes of objects, arguably an approach more relevant to the bulk of the archaeological record. Both scholars emphasized the way objects may be restricted ("enclaved") in circulation in order to enhance either their value or their owner's prestige. Archaeology offers the further ability to address how such roles and values can also transmute over time.

Conclusions

We have deliberately sought to take a somewhat minimalist and "problem"-oriented view, seeking to identify and to suggest issues in need of investigation, consideration, and clarification. We are particularly concerned with what we do not (yet) know but, at the same time, it is true that "the archaeological record is always minimalist" (Horden and Purcell 2000:269), and so we must seek to find a middle path. We suggest that a consumption-oriented approach may offer a useful conceptual and explanatory future for eastern Mediterranean trade/exchange studies. We have tried to highlight inadequacies of the current data for anything other than such a social and relative approach. Much "quantification" is at present meaningless in either historical-temporal, or spatial, or human, terms. We have tried to highlight that the majority of society was localized and not directly involved in trade and geographies of movement, and to argue that the Aegean, especially, was peripheral at most to the main part of the eastern Mediterranean world – engaged (on the margins) only in LB 3. While noting that distance and exotic status can offer power resources, as regularly argued in recent literature, we stress the issue of receptivity and, equally important, the local negotiation of values and meanings. Indeed, a key feature of many exports/imports is their generic, de-contextualized nature (viz. the "international style" and similar labels) – this is what enables them to travel, and to then be capable of the necessary local reception and manipulation. References back to a point of origin are thus weak and stereotypical at most. Until recently, too much of the scholarly literature in the Mediterranean field has been in effect anachronistic (not that we deny the limited relevance of nascent capitalism). We recognize the many problems and limitations identified with the primitivist and minimalist schools, but believe the modern challenge should be to reconfigure an ancient viewpoint through considerations of consumption/reception, in order to break away from both the inherently modern formalist positions, or aesthetic and ideological positions, still largely dominant in scholarship today concerning trade in the second millennium B.C. Mediterranean.

NOTE

1. Dates given in this chapter are rounded versions of the chronology in Manning (1995); Manning and Bronk Ramsey (2003); and Bronk Ramsey et al. (in press). For the middle of the second millennium B.C. an alternative "lower" chronology is also current, see for example Warren and Hankey (1989).

REFERENCES

Adams, William Y., 1968 Invasion, Diffusion, Evolution. Antiquity 42:194–215.

Ajzen, Icek, and Martin Fishbein, 1980 Understanding Attitudes and Predicting Social Behavior. Englewood Cliffs: Prentice-Hall.

Altman, A., 1988 Trade between the Aegean and the Levant in the Late Bronze Age: Some Neglected Questions. *In* Society and Economy in the Eastern Mediterranean (ca. 1500–1000 B.C.). Michael Heltzer and Edward Lipínski, eds. Leuven: Uitgeveru Peeters.

Appadurai, Arjun, 1986 Introduction: Commodities and the Politics of Value. *In* The Social Life of Things: Commodities in Cultural Perspective. Arjun Appadurai, ed. pp. 3–63. Cambridge: Cambridge University Press.

Artzy, Michal, 1985 Merchandise and Merchantmen: On Ships and Shipping in the Late Bronze Age Levant. *In* Acts of the Second International Cyprological Congress. T. Papadopoulos and S. Hadjistylli, eds. pp. 135–140. Nicosia: A. G. Leventis Foundation.

—— 1988 Development of War/Fighting Boats of the IInd millennium B.C. in the Eastern Mediterranean. Report of the Department of Antiquities, Cyprus, pp. 181–186.

—— 1997 Nomads of the Sea. *In* Res Maritimae. Cyprus and the Eastern Mediterranean from Prehistory to Late Antiquity. Stuart Swiny, Robert L. Hohlfelder, and Helena W. Swiny, eds. pp. 1–16. CAARI Monograph Series I. Atlanta: Scholars Press.

—— 2001 A Study of Cypriote Bronze Age Bichrome Ware: Past, Present and Future. *In* The Chronology of Base-Ring and Bichrome Wheel-made Ware. Paul Åström, ed. pp. 157–174. Konferenser 54. Stockholm: The Royal Academy of Letters, History and Antiquities.

Barr, Pat, 1970 Foreign Devils: Westerners in the Far East. Harmondsworth: Penguin.

Bass, George F., 1967 Cape Gelidonya: A Bronze Age shipwreck. Transaction of the American Philosophical Society 57, Part 8. Philadelphia: American Philosophical Society.

—— 1991 Evidence of Trade from Bronze Age Shipwrecks. *In* Bronze Age Trade in the Mediterranean. Noel H. Gale, ed. pp. 69–82. Studies in Mediterranean Archaeology 90. Jonsered: Paul Åströms Förlag.

—— 1998 Sailing between the Aegean and the Orient in the Second Millennium B.C. *In* The Aegean and the Orient in the Second Millennium. Eric H. Cline and Diane Harris-Cline, eds. pp.183–189. Aegaeum 18. Liège and Austin: Université de Liège and University of Texas at Austin.

Baudrillard, Jean, 1968 Le Système des Objets. Paris: Gallimard.

Bell, Martha Rhodes, 1991 The Tutankhamun Burnt Group from Gurob, Egypt: Bases for the Absolute Chronology of LH IIIA and B. Ph.D. Dissertation, University of Pennsylvania.

Berger, Peter L., and Thomas Luckmann, 1966 The Social Construction of Reality: A Treatise in the Sociology of Knowledge. Garden City: Doubleday.

Bergoffen, Celia J., 1989 A Comparative Study of the Regional Distribution of Cypriote Pottery in Canaan and Egypt in the Late Bronze Age. Ph.D. Dissertation, Institute of Fine Arts, New York.

Bickel, Susanne, 1998 Commerçants et Bateliers au Nouvel Empire. Mode de Vie et Statut d'un Groupe Social. *In* Le Commerce en Égypte Ancienne. Nicolas Grimal and Bernadette Menu, eds. pp. 157–172. Cairo: Institut Français d'Archéologie Orientale.

Bietak, Manfred, 1992 Minoan Wall-Paintings Unearthed at Ancient Avaris. Egyptian Archaeology 2:26–28.

——2000a Rich beyond the Dreams of Avaris: Tell el-Dab'a and the Aegean World – a Guide for the Perplexed. A Response to Eric H. Cline. Annual of the British School at Athens 95:185–205.

——2000b Minoan Paintings in Avaris, Egypt. *In* The Wall Paintings of Thera. Elizabeth S. Sherratt, ed. pp. 33–42. Athens: Petros M. Nomikos and The Thera Foundation.

——2000c The Mode of Representation in Egyptian Art in Comparison to Aegean Bronze Age Art. *In* The Wall Paintings of Thera. Elizabeth S. Sherratt, ed. pp. 209–24. Athens: Petros M. Nomikos and The Thera Foundation.

——2003 Science versus Archaeology: Problems and Consequences of High Aegean Chronology. *In* The Sychronisation of Civilisations in the Eastern Mediterranean in the Second Millennium B.C. II. Manfred Bietak, ed. pp. 23–33. Wien: Verlag der Österreichischen Akademie der Wissenschaften.

Bourke, Stephen J., and Rachel T. Sparks, 1995 The Daj Excavations at Pella in Jordan 1963/64. *In* Trade, Contact and the Movement of Peoples in the Eastern Mediterranean. Studies in Honour of J. Basil Hennessy. Stephen J. Bourke and Jean-Paul Descoeudres, eds. pp. 149–167. Mediterranean Archaeology Supplement 3. Sydney: Meditarch.

Branigan, Keith, 1966 Byblite Daggers in Cyprus and Crete. American Journal of Archaeology 70:123–126.

——1967 Further Light on Prehistoric Relations between Crete and Byblos. American Journal of Archaeology 71:117–121.

Braudel, Ferdinand, 1972 The Mediterranean and the Mediterranean World in the Age of Philip II. London: Collins.

Broodbank, Cyprian, 1993 Ulysses without Sails: Trade, Distance, Knowledge and Power in the Early Cyclades. World Archaeology 24:315–331.

——2000 An Island Archaeology of the Early Cyclades. Cambridge: Cambridge University Press.

Bronk Ramsey, Christopher, Sturt W. Manning, and Mariagrazia Galimberti, In press Dating the Volcanic Eruption at Thera. Radiocarbon.

Bücher, Karl, 1901 Industrial Evolution. London: Bell.

Cadogan, Gerald, 1979 Cyprus and Crete ca. 2000–1400 B.C. *In* Acts of the International Archaeological Symposium 'The Relations between Cyprus and Crete ca. 200–500 B.C.'. Vassos Karageorghis, ed. pp. 63–68. Nicosia: Department of Antiquities.

Catling, Hector W., 1962 Patterns of Settlement in Bronze Age Cyprus. Opuscula Atheniensia 4:129–169.

——1964 Cypriot Bronzework in the Mycenaean World. Oxford: Oxford University Press.

Chapman, Robert W., 1990 Emerging Complexity: The Later Prehistory of South-east Spain, Iberia and the West Mediterranean. Cambridge: Cambridge University Press.

Cherry, John F., 1986 Polities and Palaces: Some Problems in Minoan State Formation. *In* Peer Polity Interaction and Socio-Political Change. Colin Renfrew and John F. Cherry, eds. pp. 19–45. Cambridge: Cambridge University Press.

Childe, V. Gordon, 1951 Social Evolution. London: Watts.

Cline, Eric H., 1994 Sailing the Wine-Dark Sea. International Trade and the Late Bronze Age Aegean. BAR International Series 591. Oxford: BAR.

Csikszentmihalyi, Mihaly, and Eugene Rochberg-Halton, 1981 The Meaning of Things: Domestic Symbols and the Self. Cambridge: Cambridge University Press.

Douglas, Mary, and Baron Isherwood, 1979 The World of Goods: Towards an Anthropology of Consumption. New York: Basic Books.

Durkheim, Emile, 1893 De la Division du Travail Social. Paris: Alcan.

Evans, Arthur J., 1921–1945 The Palace of Minos at Knossos, vols. I-IV plus index. London: Macmillan.

Evershed, Richard P., C. Heron, S. Charters, and L. J. Goad, 1992 The Survival of Food Residues: New Methods of Analysis, Interpretation and Application. *In* New Developments in Archaeological Science. A. Mark Pollard, ed. pp. 187–208. Proceedings of the British Academy 77. Oxford: Oxford University Press for the British Academy.

Feldman, Marilyn H., 2002 Luxurious Forms: Redefining a Mediterranean 'International Style', 1400–1200 B.C.E. Art Bulletin 84:6–29.

Finley, Moses I., 1973 The Ancient Economy. London: Chatto & Windus.

Foucault, Michel, 1972 The Archaeology of Knowledge. London: Tavistock.

Frank, A. Gunder, 1993 Bronze Age World System Cycles. Current Anthropology 34:383–429.

Frankfort, Henri, 1996 The Art and Architecture of the Ancient Orient. Fifth edition. New Haven: Yale University Press.

Gale, Noel H., 1991 Copper Oxhide Ingots: Their Origin and Their Place in the Bronze Age Metals Trade in the Mediterranean. *In* Bronze Age Trade in the Mediterranean. Noel H. Gale, ed. pp. 197–239. Studies in Mediterranean Archaeology 90. Jonsered: P. Åströms Förlag.

Gillis, Carole, 1996 Trade in the Late Bronze Age. *In* Trade and Production in Premonetary Greece: Aspects of Trade. Carole Gillis, Christina Risberg, and Birgitte Sjöberg, eds. pp. 61–86. Studies in Mediterranean Archaeology and Literature Pocket-book 134. Jonsered: P. Åströms Förlag.

Gittlen, Barry M., 1981 The Cultural and Chronological Implications of the Cypro-Palestinian Trade during the Late Bronze Age. Bulletin of the American Schools of Oriental Research 241:49–59.

Gosden, Chris, and Yvonne Marshall, 1999 The Cultural Biography of Objects. World Archaeology 31:169–78.

Graziadio, Giampaolo, 1995 Egina, Rodi e Cipro: Rapporti Inter-Insulari agli Inizio del Tardo Bronzo? Studi Micenei ed Egeo-Anatolici 36:7–27.

Hadjisavvas, Sophocles, 1996 Alassa: A Regional Centre of Alasia? *In* Late Bronze Age Settlement in Cyprus: Function and Relationship. Paul Åström and Ellen Herscher, eds. pp. 23–38. Studies in Mediterranean Archaeology and Literature Pocket-book 126. Jonsered: P. Åströms Förlag.

——2003 Dating Alassa. *In* The Sychronisation of Civilisations in the Eastern Mediterranean in the Second Millennium B.C. II. Manfred Bietak, ed. pp. 431–436. Wien: Verlag der Österreichischen Akademie der Wissenshaften.

Halstead, Paul, 1989 The Economy has a Normal Surplus: Economic Stability and Social Change among Early Farming Communities of Thessaly, Greece. *In* Bad Year Economics. Cultural Responses to Risk and Uncertainty. Paul Halstead and John O'Shea, eds. pp. 68–80. Cambridge: Cambridge University Press.

Hamilakis, Yannis, 2002 Too Many Chiefs?: Factional Competition in Neopalatial Crete. *In* Monuments of Minos: Rethinking the Minoan Palaces. Jan Driessen, Ilse Schoep, and Robert Laffineur, eds. pp. 179–199. Aegaeum 23. Liège and Austin: Université de Liège and University of Texas at Austin.

Hankey, Vronwy, 1981 The Aegean Interest in el-Amarna. Journal of Mediterranean Anthropology and Archaeology 1:38–49.

Hasebroek, Johannes, 1933 Trade and Politics in Ancient Greece. London: G. Bell and Sons.

Hegmon, M., 1998. Technology, Style and Social Practices: Archaeological Approaches. *In* The Archaeology of Social Boundaries. Miriam T. Stark, ed. pp. 264–277. Washington: Smithsonian Institution Press.

Hein, A., H. Mommsen, and J. Maran, 1999 Element Concentration Distributions and Most Discriminating Elements for Provenancing by Neutron Activation Analyses of Ceramics from Bronze Age Sites in Greece. Journal of Archaeological Science 26:1053–1058.

Helms, Mary W., 1988 Ulysses' Sail: An Ethnographic Odyssey of Power, Knowledge, and Geographical Distance. Princeton: Princeton University Press.

——1993 Craft and the Kingly Ideal: Art, Trade, and Power. Austin: University of Texas Press.

Heltzer, Michael, 1978 Goods, Prices and the Organization of Trade in Ugarit. Wiesbaden: Reichert.

Hirschfeld, Nicolle E., 1992 Cypriot Marks on Mycenaean Pottery. *In* Mykenaïka. Jean-Paul Olivier, ed. pp. 315–319. BCH Suppl. XXV. Paris: Diffusion de Boccard.

——2000 Marked Late Bronze Age Pottery from the Kingdom of Ugarit. *In* Céramiques Mycéniennes. Ras-Shamra-Ougarit XII. Margeurite Yon, Vassos Karageorghis, and Nicolle E. Hirschfeld, pp. 163–200. Nicosia: A. G. Leventis Foundation.

Hodder, Bramwell W., and U. I. Ukwu, 1969 Markets in West Africa: Studies of Markets and Trade among the Yoruba and Ibo. Ibadan: Ibadan University Press.

Hodder, Ian, 1982 Symbols in Action: Ethnoarchaeological Studies of Material Culture. Cambridge: Cambridge University Press.

Hulin, Linda, In press Embracing the New: The Perception of Cypriot Pottery in Egypt. *In* Egypt and Cyprus. Robert S. Merrillees, Dhimitri Michaelides, and Maria Iacovou, eds. Oxford: Oxbow Books.

Horden, Peregrine, and Nicholas Purcell, 2000 The Corrupting Sea. A Study of Mediterranean History. Oxford: Basil Blackwell.

Immerwahr, Sara A., 1990 Aegean Painting in the Bronze Age. University Park, Pennsylvania State University: Pennsylvania State University Press.

Jacobsen, Inga, 1994 Aegyptiaca from Late Bronze Age Cyprus. Studies in Mediterranean Archaeology 112. Jonsered: P. Åströms Förlag.

Janssen, Jac J., 1975 Commodity Prices from the Ramessid Period. An Economic Study of the Village Necropolis Workmen at Thebes. Leiden: E. J. Brill.

Johnson, Jane, 1980 Maroni de Chypre. Studies in Mediterranean Archaeology 59. Gothenburg: Paul Åströms Förlag.

Johnson, P., 1982 The Middle Cypriote Pottery Found in Palestine. Opuscula Atheniensia 14:49–72.

Jones, Siân, 1997 The Archaeology of Ethnicity: Constructing Identities in the Past and Present. London: Routledge.

Junker, Laura L., 1999 Raiding, Trading, and Feasting: The Political Economy of Philippine Chiefdoms. Honolulu: University of Hawaii Press.

Kantor, Helene J., 1947 The Aegean and the Orient in the Second Millennium B.C. American Journal of Archaeology 51:1–103.

Kemp, Barry J., and Robert S. Merrillees, 1980 Minoan Pottery in Second Millennium Egypt. Mainz am Rhein: Philipp von Zabern.

Keswani, Priscilla S., 1989 Dimensions of Social Hierarchy in Late Bronze Age Cyprus: An Analysis of the Mortuary Data from Enkomi. Journal of Mediterranean Archaeology 2:49–86.

——1993 Models of Local Exchange in Late Bronze Age Cyprus. Bulletin of the American Schools of Oriental Research 292:73–83.

—— 1996 Hierarchies, Heterarchies, and Urbanization Processes: The View from Bronze Age Cyprus. Journal of Mediterranean Archaeology 9:211–250.

Knapp, A. Bernard, 1985 Alashiya, Caphtor-Keftiu, and Eastern Mediterranean Trade: Recent Studies in Cypriote Archaeology and History. Journal of Field Archaeology 12:231–250.

—— 1986 Copper Production and Divine Protection: Archaeology, Ideology and Social Complexity on Bronze Age Cyprus. Studies in Mediterranean Archaeology and Literature Pocket-book 42. Göteborg: P. Åströms Förlag.

—— 1988–89 Paradise Gained and Paradise Lost: Intensification, Specialization, Complexity, Collapse. Asian Perspectives 28:179–214.

—— 1990 Cyprus, Crete, and Copper: A Comment on Catling's Paradox. Report of the Department of Antiquities, Cyprus: 55–63.

—— 1991 Spice, Drugs, Grain and Grog: Organic Goods in Bronze Age Eastern Mediterranean Trade. In Bronze Age Trade in the Mediterranean. Noel H. Gale, ed. pp. 21–68. Studies in Mediterranean Archaeology 90. Jonsered: P. Åströms Förlag.

—— 1993 Thalassocracies in Bronze Age Eastern Mediterranean Trade: Making and Breaking a Myth. World Archaeology 24:332–347.

—— 1996a Near Eastern and Aegean Texts from the Third to the First Millennia B.C. Sources for the History of Cyprus II. Paul W. Wallace and Andreas G. Orphanides, eds. Altamont, NY: Greece/Cyprus Research Center.

—— 1996b The Bronze Age Economy of Cyprus: Ritual, Ideology, and the Landscape. In The Development of the Cypriot Economy from the Prehistoric Period to the Present Day. Vassos Karageorghis and Dhimitri Michaelides, eds. pp. 71–94. Nicosia: University of Cyprus and the Bank of Cyprus.

—— 1997 The Archaeology of Late Bronze Age Cypriot Society: The Study of Settlement, Survey and Landscape. Glasgow: Department of Archaeology, University of Glasgow.

—— 1998 Mediterranean Bronze Age Trade: Distance, Power and Place. In The Aegean and the Orient in the Second Millennium. Eric H. Cline and Diane Harris-Cline, eds. pp. 193–207. Aegaeum 18. Liège and Austin: Université de Liège and University of Texas at Austin.

—— 2003 The Archaeology of Community on Bronze Age Cyprus: Politiko Phorades in Context. American Journal of Archaeology 107:559–580.

Knapp, A. Bernard, and John F. Cherry, 1994 Provenance Studies and Bronze Age Cyprus: Production, Exchange, and Politico-Economic Change. Monographs in World Archaeology 21. Madison: Prehistory Press.

Kopytoff, Igor, 1986 The Cultural Biography of Things: Commoditization as Process. In The Social Life of Things: Commodities in Cultural Perspective. Arjun Appadurai, ed. pp. 64–91. Cambridge: Cambridge University Press.

Lambrou-Phillipson, Connie, 1990 Hellenorientalia: The Near Eastern Presence in the Bronze Age Aegean ca. 3000–1100 B.C. plus Orientalia: A Catalogue of Egyptian, Mesopotamian, Mitannian, Syro-Palestinian, Cypriot and Asia Minor Objects from the Bronze Age Aegean. Göteborg: P. Åströms Förlag.

Lea, Stephen E. G., Roger M. Tarpy, and Paul Webley, 1987 The Individual in the Economy: A Textbook of Economic Psychology. Cambridge: Cambridge University Press.

Leonard, Albert Jr., 1987 The Significance of the Mycenaean Pottery Found East of the Jordan River. In Studies in the History and Archaeology of Jordan, vol. 3. Adnan Hadidi, ed. pp. 261–266. Amman: Department of Antiquities.

—— 1988 Some Problems Inherent in Mycenaean/Syro-Palestinian Synchronisms. In Problems in Greek Prehistory. Elizabeth B. French and Kenneth A. Wardle, eds. pp. 319–330. Bristol: Bristol Classical Press.

—— 1994 An Index to the Late Bronze Age Aegean Pottery from Syria-Palestine. Studies in Mediterranean Archaeology 114. Jonsered: Paul Åströms Förlag.

—— 1996 "Canaanite Jars" and the Late Bronze Age Aegeo-Levantine Wine Trade. *In* The Origins and Ancient History of Wine. Patrick E. McGovern, Stuart J. Fleming, and Solomon H. Katz, eds. pp. 233–254. Philadelphia: Gordon and Breach.

Liverani, Mario, 1990 Prestige and Interest: International Relations in the Near East ca.1600–1000 B.C. Padua: Sargon Press.

Lunt, Peter K., and Sonia M. Livingstone, 1992 Mass Consumption and Personal Identity: Everyday Economic Experience. Buckingham: Open University Press.

Maguire, Louise C., 1990 The Circulation of Cypriot Pottery in the Middle Bronze Age. Ph.D. dissertation, University of Edinburgh.

Mann, Michael, 1986 The Sources of Social Power, vol. I: A History of Power from the Beginning to A.D. 1760. Cambridge: Cambridge University Press.

Manning, Sturt W., 1994 The Emergence of Divergence: Development and Decline on Bronze Age Crete and the Cyclades. *In* Development and Decline in the Mediterranean Bronze Age. Clay Mathers and Simon Stoddart, eds. pp. 221–270. Sheffield: John Collis.

—— 1995 The Absolute Chronology of the Aegean Early Bronze Age: Archaeology, Radiocarbon and History. Monographs in Mediterranean Archaeology 1. Sheffield: Sheffield Academic Press.

—— 1998 Changing Pasts and Socio-Political Cognition in Late Bronze Age Cyprus. World Archaeology 30:39–58.

Manning, Sturt W., and Christopher Bronk Ramsey, 2003 A Late Minoan I-II Absolute Chronology for the Aegean – Combining Archaeology with Radiocarbon. *In* The Synchronisation of Civilisations in the Eastern Mediterranean in the Second Millennium B.C. (II). Manfred Bietak, ed. pp. 111–133. Wien: Österreichischen Akademie der Wissenschaften.

Manning, Sturt W., and Frank A. De Mita Jr., 1997 Cyprus, the Aegean and Maroni-Tsaroukkas. *In* Proceedings of the International Archaeological Conference Cyprus and the Aegean in Antiquity from the Prehistoric Period to the Seventh Century A.D. Nicosia 8–10 December 1995. Dimos Christou et al., eds. pp. 101–142. Nicosia: Department of Antiquities.

Manning, Sturt W., Frank A. De Mita Jr., Sarah J. Monks, and Georgia Nakou, 1994 The Fatal Shore, the Long Years, and the Geographical Unconscious. Considerations of Iconography, Chronology and Trade in Response to Negbi's 'The "Libyan Landscape" from Thera: A Review of Aegean Enterprises Overseas in the Late Minoan IA Period' (JMA 7.1). Journal of Mediterranean Archaeology 7:219–235.

Manning, Sturt W., and Sarah J. Monks, with contributions by Louise Steel, Elinor C. Ribeiro, and James M. Weinstein, 1998 Late Cypriot Tombs at Maroni Tsaroukkas, Cyprus. Annual of the British School at Athens 93:297–351.

Matthäus, Hartmut, 1995 Representations of Keftiu in Egyptian Tombs and the Absolute Chronology of the Aegean Late Bronze Age. Bulletin of the Institute of Classical Studies 40:177–194.

Mauss, Marcel, 1990 The Gift: The Form and Reason for Exchange in Archaic Societies. London: Routledge.

Merrillees, Robert S., 1968 The Cypriote Bronze Age Pottery found in Egypt. Studies in Mediterranean Archaeology 18. Göteborg: Paul Åströms Förlag.

——1972 Aegean Bronze Age Relations with Egypt. American Journal of Archaeology 76:281–294.

——1974 Trade and Transcendence in the Bronze Age Levant. Studies in Mediterranean Archaeology 39. Paul Åströms Förlag.

——1998 Egypt and the Aegean. *In* The Aegean and the Orient in the Second Millennium. Eric H. Cline and Diane Harris-Cline, eds. pp. 149–155. Aegaeum 18. Liège and Austin: Université de Liège and University of Texas at Austin.

——2003 The First Appearances of Kamares Ware in the Levant. Ägypten und Levant 13:127–142.

Moran, William, 1992 The Amarna Letters. Baltimore: The Johns Hopkins University Press.

Morgan, Lyvia., 1995 Minoan Painting and Egypt: The Case of Tell el-Dabᶜa. *In* Egypt, the Aegean and the Levant: Interconnections in the Second Millennium B.C. W. Vivian Davies and Louise Schofield, eds. pp. 29–53. London: British Museum Publications.

Mountjoy, Penelope A., and Matthew J. Ponting, 2000 The Minoan Thalassocracy Reconsidered: Provenance Studies of LH II A/LM I B pottery from Phylakopi, Ay. Irini and Athens. Annual of the British School at Athens 95:141–184.

Muhly, James D., 1986 The Role of Cyprus in the Economy of the Eastern Mediterranean. *In* Acts of the International Archaeological Symposium 'Cyprus between the Orient and the Occident, Nicosia, 8–14 September 1985'. Vassos Karageorghis, ed. pp. 45–62. Nicosia: Department of Antiquities.

——1989 The Organisation of the Copper Industry in Late Bronze Age Cyprus. *In* Early Society in Cyprus. Edgar J. Peltenburg, ed. pp. 298–314. Edinburgh: Edinburgh University Press.

Muhly, James D., Robert Maddin, and Tamara Stech, 1988 Cyprus, Crete and Sardinia: Copper Oxhide Ingots and the Bronze Age Metals Trade. Report of the Department of Antiquities, Cyprus, pp. 281–298.

Nakou, Georgia, 1997 The Role of Poliochni and the North Aegean in the Development of Aegean Metallurgy. *In* H Poliochni kai he proimi epoche tou Chalkou sto Voreio Aigaio / Poliochni e l'Antica Età del Bronzo nell'Egeo Settentrionale. V. La Rosa and C. Doumas, eds. pp. 634–648. Athens: Scuola archeologica italiana di Atene and Panepistimio Athenon.

Negbi, Ora, 1994 The 'Libyan Landscape' from Thera: A Review of Aegean Enterprises Overseas in the Late Minoan IA period. Journal of Mediterranean Archaeology 7:73–112.

Newberry, Percy E., and Frank L. Griffith, 1893–1900 Beni Hasan I-IV. London: Egypt Exploration Fund.

Niemeier, Wolf-Dietrich, 1998 The Minoans in the South-Eastern Aegean and in Cyprus. *In* Eastern Mediterranean: Cyprus-Dodecanese-Crete 16th-6th century B.C. Vassos Karageorghis and Nicolas Stampolidis, eds. pp. 29–47. Athens: The University of Crete and A. G. Leventis Foundation.

Niemeier, Barbara, and Wolf-Dietrich Niemeier, 2000 Aegean Frescoes in Syria-Palestine: Alalakh and Tel Kabri. *In* The Wall Paintings of Thera. Elizabeth S. Sherratt, ed. pp. 763–802. Athens: Petros M. Nomikos and The Thera Foundation.

Pendlebury, John D. S., 1930 Aegyptica: A Catalogue of Egyptian Objects in the Aegean Area. Cambridge: Cambridge University Press.

Perlès, Catherine, 1992 Systems of Exchange and Organization of Production in Neolithic Greece. Journal of Mediterranean Archaeology 5:115–164.

Peltenburg, Edgar J., 1996 From Isolation to State Formation in Cyprus, ca. 3500–1500 B.C. *In* The Development of the Cypriot Economy from the Prehistoric Period to the

Present Day. Vassos Karageorghis and Dhimitri Michaelides, eds. pp. 17–43. Nicosia: University of Cyprus and the Bank of Cyprus.

Phelps, William, Yiannis Lolos, and Yiannis Vichos, eds., 1999 The Point Iria Wreck: Interconnections in the Mediterranean ca. 1200 B.C. Athens: Hellenic Institute of Marine Archaeology.

Polanyi, Karl, 1957 Marketless Trading in Hammurabi's Time. *In* Trade and Market in the Early Empires: Economies in History and Theory. Karl Polanyi, C. M. Arensberg, and H. W. Pearson, eds. pp. 10–26. Glencoe: Free Press & Falcon's Wing Press.

Porada, Edith, 1982 The Cylinder Seals Found at Thebes in Boeotia. Archiv fur Orientforschung 28:1–70.

Portugali, Yuval, and A. Bernard Knapp, 1985 Cyprus and the Aegean: A Spatial Analysis of Interaction in the 17th-14th Centuries B.C. *In* Prehistoric Production and Exchange: The Aegean and Eastern Mediterranean. A. Bernard Knapp and Tamara Stech, eds. pp. 44–78. Institute of Archaeology Monograph 25. Los Angeles: University of California.

Pulak, Cemal, 1997 The Uluburun Shipwreck. *In* Res maritimae: Cyprus and the Eastern Mediterranean from Prehistory to Late Antiquity. Stuart Swiny, Robert L. Hohlfelder, and Helena Wylde Swiny, eds. pp. 233–262. Atlanta: Scholars Press.

Rehak, Paul, 1998 Aegean Natives in the Theban Tomb Paintings: The Keftiu revisited. *In* The Aegean and the Orient in the Second Millennium. Eric H. Cline and Diane Harris-Cline, eds. pp. 39–51. Aegaeum 18. Liège and Austin: Université de Liège and University of Texas at Austin.

Renfrew, Colin, 1969 Trade as Culture Process in European Prehistory. Current Anthropology 10:151–169.

—— 1972 The Emergence of Civilization. The Cyclades and the Aegean in the Third Millennium B.C. London: Methuen.

—— 1975 Trade as Action at a Distance: Questions of Integration and Communication. *In* Ancient Civilization and Trade. Jeremy A. Sabloff and Carl C. Lamberg-Karlovsky, eds. pp. 3–59. Albuquerque: University of New Mexico Press.

Renfrew, Colin, and N. Shackleton, 1970 Neolithic Trade Routes Realigned by Oxygen Isotope Analyses. Nature 228:1062–1065.

Riden, Philip, ed., 1980 Probate Records and the Local Community. Gloucester: Alan Sutton.

Said, Edward W., 1978 Orientalism. New York: Pantheon.

Sakellarakis, Efi, and Yiannis Sakellarakis, 1984 The Keftiu and the Minoan Thalassocracy. *In* The Minoan Thalassocracy: Myth and Reality. Robin Hägg and Nanno Marinatos, eds. pp. 197–203. Skrifter Utgivna av Svenska Institut i Athen, 4°, 35. Stockholm: Paul Åströms Förlag.

Schivelbusch, Wolfgang, 1992 Tastes of Paradise. A Social History of Spices, Stimulants and Intoxicants. New York: Pantheon Books.

Schoep, Ilse, 2002 The State of the Minoan Palaces or the Minoan Palace-State? *In* Monuments of Minoa: Rethinking the Minoan Palaces. Jan Driessen, Ilse Schoep and Robert Laffineur, eds. pp.15–33. Aegaeum 23. Liège and Austin: Université de Liège and University of Texas at Austin.

Serpico, Margaret, Janine Bourriau, L. Smith, Yuval Goren, B. Stern, and C. Heron, 2003 Commodities and Containers: A Project to Study Canaanite Amphorae Imported into Egypt during the New Kingdom. *In* The Sychronisation of Civilisations in the Eastern Mediterranean in the Second Millennium B.C. II. Manfred Bietak, ed. pp. 365–375. Wien: Verlag der Österreichischen Akademie der Wissenshaften.

Shaw, Maria, 1967 An Evaluation of Possible Affinities between Egyptian and Minoan Wall Paintings before the New Kingdom. Ph.D. dissertation, Bryn Mawr.

——1970 Ceiling Patterns from the Tomb of Hepsefa. American Journal of Archaeology 74:25–30.

——1995 Bull Leaping Frescoes at Knossos and Their Influence on the Tell el-Dab'a Murals. Ägypten und Levante 5:91–120.

Sherratt, Andrew G., and Elizabeth S. Sherratt, 1991 From Luxuries to Commodities: The Nature of Mediterranean Bronze Age Trading Systems. In Bronze Age Trade in the Mediterranean. Noel H. Gale, ed. pp. 351–386. Studies in Mediterranean Archaeology 90. Jonsered: Paul Åströms Förlag.

——1998 Small Worlds: Interaction and Identity in the Ancient Mediterranean. In The Aegean and the Orient in the Second Millennium. Eric H. Cline and Diane Harris-Cline, eds. pp. 329–343. Aegaeum 18. Liège and Austin: Université de Liège and University of Texas at Austin.

——2000 Technological Change in the East Mediterranean Bronze Age: Capital, Resources and Marketing. In The Social Context of Technological Change. Egypt and the Near East, 1650–1550 B.C. A.J. Shortland, ed. pp. 15–38. Oxford: Oxbow Books.

Sherratt, Elizabeth S., 1994 Comment on Ora Negbi, The "Libyan Landscape" from Thera: A Review of Aegean Enterprises Overseas in the Late Minoan IA Period. Journal of Mediterranean Archaeology 7:237–240.

——1999 E pur si muove: Pots, Markets and Values in the Second Millennium Mediterranean. In The Complex Past of Pottery. Production, Circulation and Consumption of Mycenaean and Greek Pottery (Sixteenth to Early Fifteenth Centuries B.C.). J. P. Crielaard, V. Stissi, and Gert J. van Wijngaarden, eds. pp. 163–211. Amsterdam: J. C. Gieben.

Snodgrass, Anthony M., 1991 Bronze Age Exchange: A Minimalist Position. In Bronze Age Trade in the Mediterranean. Noel H. Gale, ed. pp. 15–20. Studies in Mediterranean Archaeology 90. Jonsered: Paul Åströms Förlag.

Sombart, W. (trans. W. R. Dittmar), 1967 Luxury and Capitalism. Ann Arbor: University of Michigan Press.

Sombart, Werner, 1916–1927 Der Moderne Kapitalismus, vols. 1–3. Second edition. Munich: von Duncker und Humbolt.

South, Alison K., 1995 Urbanism and Trade in the Vasilikos Valley in the Late Bronze Age. In Trade, Contact and the Movement of Peoples in the Eastern Mediterranean. Studies in Honour of J. Basil Hennessy. Stephen Bourke and Jean-Paul Descoeudres, eds. pp. 187–197. Theme issue. Mediterranean Archaeology Supplement 3. Sydney: Meditarch.

——1997 Kalavasos-Ayios Dhimitrios 1992–1996. Report of the Department of Antiquities, Cyprus, pp. 151–176.

Steel, Louise, 1998 The Social Impact of Mycenaean Imported Pottery in Cyprus. Annual of the British School at Athens 93:285–296.

——2002a Consuming Passions: A Contextual Study of the Local Consumption of Mycenaean pottery at Tell el-'Ajjul. Journal of Mediterranean Archaeology 15:25–51.

——2002b Changing Places: The Transmission of Mycenaean Pictorial Pottery. In Proceedings of the First International Congress on the Archaeology of the Ancient Near East 2. Paola Matthiae, A. Enea, L. Peyronel, and F. Pinnock, eds. pp. 1557–1571. Rome: Università degli studi di Roma 'La Spienza', Dipartimento di scienze storiche, archeologiche e antroplogiche dell'antichità.

Stubbings, F. H., 1951 Mycenaean Pottery from the Levant. Cambridge: Cambridge University Press.

Taraqji, A., 1999 Nouvelles Découvertes sur les Relations avec l'Egypte à Tell Sakka et à Keswé dans la Région de Damas. Bulletin de la Societe Française d'Egyptologie 144:27–43.

Trigger, Bruce G., 2003 Understanding Early Civilizations: A Comparative Study. Cambridge: Cambridge University Press.

Vercoutter, Jean, 1956 L'Égypte et le Monde Égéen Préhellénique. Bibliothèque d'Étude 22. Cairo: Institut Français d'Archéologie Orientale.

Veth, Peter M., 1993 Islands of the Interior: The Dynamics of Prehistoric Adaptations within the Arid Zone of Australia. International Monographs in Prehistory Archaeological Series 3. Ann Arbor: International Monographs in Prehistory.

Wachsmann, Shelley, 1987 Aegeans in the Theban Tombs. Orientalia Lovaniensia Analecta 20. Leuven: Peeters.

——1998 Seagoing Ships & Seamanship in the Bronze Age Levant. London: Texas A&M University Press.

Warren, Peter, 1995 Minoan Crete and Pharaonic Egypt. *In* Egypt, the Aegean and the Levant: Interconnections in the Second Millennium B.C. W. Vivian Davies and Louise Schofield, eds. pp. 1–18. London: British Museum Publications.

Warren, Peter, and Vronwy Hankey, 1989 Aegean Bronze Age Chronology. Bristol: Bristol Classical Press.

Watrous, Livingston V., 1992 Kommos III: The Late Bronze Age Pottery. Princeton: Princeton University Press.

——2001 Review of Aegean Prehistory III: Crete from Earliest Prehistory through the Protopalatial Period. *In* Aegean Prehistory: A Review. Tracey Cullen, ed. pp. 157–223. Boston: Archaeological Institute of America.

Webb, Jennifer M., 1999 Ritual Architecture, Iconography and Practice in the Late Cypriote Bronze Age. Studies in Mediterranean Archaeology Pocket-book 75. Jonsered: Paul Åströms Förlag.

Weber, Max, 1968 Economy and Society: An Outline of Interpretive Sociology. New York: Bedminster Press.

——1976 The Protestant Ethic and the Spirit of Capitalism. London: George Allen & Unwin.

Welsch, R. L., and J.E. Terrell, 1998 Material Culture, Social Fields and Social Boundaries on the Speik Coast of New Guinea. *In* The Archaeology of Social Boundaries. M. T. Stark, ed. pp. 50–77. Washington: Smithsonian Institution Press.

Westerberg, Karin, 1983 Cypriot Ships from the Bronze Age to ca. 500 B.C. Studies in Mediterranean Archaeology Pocket-book 22. Gothenburg: Paul Åströms Förlag.

White, Donald, et al., 2003 Marsa Matruh I-II. The University of Pennsylvania Museum of Archaeology and Anthropology's Excavations on Bates's Island, Marsa Matruh, Egypt 1985–1989. Prehistory Monographs 1 and 2. Philadelphia: The Institute for Aegean Prehistory Press.

White, Leslie, 1959 The Evolution of Culture. New York: McGraw-Hill.

Wiener, Malcom H., 1987 Trade and Rule in Palatial Crete. *In* The Function of the Minoan Palaces. R. Hagg and N. Marinatos, eds. pp. 261–267. Skrifter Utgivna av Svenska Institutet i Athen 35. Stockholm: Svenska Institutet i Athen.

——1991 The Nature and Control of Minoan Foreign Trade. *In* Bronze Age Trade in the Mediterranean. Noel H. Gale, ed. pp. 325–350. Studies in Mediterranean Archaeology 90. Jonsered: Paul Åströms Förlag.

Wijngaarden, Gert J. van, 2002 Use and Appreciation of Mycenaean Pottery in the Levant, Cyprus and Italy (1600–1200 B.C.). Amsterdam: Amsterdam University Press.

Wright, James C., 1995 From Chief to King in Mycenaean Greece. *In* The Role of the Ruler in the Prehistoric Aegean. Paul Rehak, ed. pp.63–80. Aegaeum 11. Liège and Austin: Université de Liège and University of Texas at Austin.

Yannai, Anita, 1983 Studies on Trade between the Levant and the Aegean in the 14th to 12th Centuries B.C. Ph.D. dissertation, Oxford.

Yon, Marguerite, Vassos Karageorghis, and Nicolle E. Hirschfeld, 2000 Céramiques Mycéniennes. Ras-Shamra-Ougarit XII. Nicosia: A. G. Leventis Foundation.

Zaccagnini, Carlo, 1977 The Merchant at Nuzi. Iraq 39:171–189.

12

Museum Archaeology and the Mediterranean Cultural Heritage

Robin Skeates

Introduction

The prehistory collections of museums represent an often overlooked but arguably significant manifestation of the cultural heritage of the Mediterranean. Famous works, prized as art and contested as heritage, include the "Dama de Elche," the Iceman, the Maltese Ladies, the Vucedol pot, Cycladic figurines, the Treasures of Aidona and of Priam, Haçilar pottery, the Çatalhöyük frescoes, the Cesnola Collection, the plastered skulls of Jericho, and the lime plaster figurines of Ain Ghazal in Jordan. Most Mediterranean prehistory collections in world museums, however, comprise large numbers of anonymous artifacts, ranging widely in material, size, and age, many of which never see the light of display cases. Together, these collections and their collectors raise a number of questions that scholars have only recently begun to address. The first concerns our chosen analytical approaches: How should we evaluate them? The second set concerns the current state of our knowledge: How much information is publicly available about them, how useful is it, and what areas require further investigation? The third relates to their development: How have they fared since the 19th century, in what condition are they today, and how might they be developed in the future, particularly compared to museums in the UK and North America? The fourth considers their differences: How regionally diverse are they, and what factors contribute to their diversity? The final question concerns their significance to different interest groups: What is their social value, who needs them, who does not, and why or why not?

Despite its restricted scale, the existing literature relating to Mediterranean museum archaeology reveals a wide variety of analytical approaches to these questions. Such questions can be broadly divided into "professional" and "academic."

Professional publications place an emphasis on museography (i.e., professional museum practice). They are generally written by senior museum staff and government officials, often published by the International Council of Museums (ICOM), and are characterized by qualitative (and even self-congratulatory) accounts of professional principles, practice, and prospects relating to particular institutions or countries (e.g., Ali 1994; Kirigin 1994; Sadek 1994). A recent exception has been the publication of some more quantitative assessments of museum institutions and visitors in Italy, involving performance evaluations and questionnaire surveys, undertaken by specially commissioned social scientists (e.g., Solima 2000; Zan 2000). Academic approaches are more varied, but they can be divided into artifact studies and museum studies or museology (i.e., the theory as well as the practice of museums). Archaeological and art historical studies of artifacts housed in museum collections are well established, and have often resulted in the publication of scholarly (and sometimes lavish) exhibition and museum catalogs (e.g., Currelly 1913; Andrews 1981; Hammade 1987; Antonova et al. 1996; Papathanassopoulos 1996; Karageorghis 2000). More recent sociology-based museum studies also examine the history of collections, archaeologists, and institutions, particularly in southern and southeast Europe. Some take the form of narrative histories (e.g., Schnapp 1996), while the majority comprise critical histories, with an emphasis on deconstructing cultural politics in the past and present (e.g., MacConnell 1989; Hamilakis and Yalouri 1996; Holo 1999; Rountree 1999; Skeates 2000a; Meskell 2001; Preziosi 2002; Vella and Gilkes 2001; Tahan 2002). Related to these are some critical exposés of the history and ethics of antiquities collecting (e.g., Butcher and Gill 1993; Gill and Chippindale 1993; Moffitt 1994; Traill 1995).

I draw upon these studies and other published information below to provide an overview of the history and present-day state of museum archaeology relating to Mediterranean prehistory, and I offer some preliminary answers to the questions posed above. It is worth noting, however, that the latter clearly depend upon the definitions – chosen for the purposes of this chapter – of some problematic key words, including "museum," "heritage," "Mediterranean," and "prehistory." "Museums" were clearly defined in 1998, by the UK's Museums Association, as "institutions that collect, safeguard and make accessible artifacts and specimens, which they hold in trust for society" (Museums Association 1998). Some heritage managers claim that all archaeological sites and monuments fall within this definition, but for the purposes of this chapter they are excluded, except where they have associated permanent collections or exhibitions. "Cultural heritage" is used here, with an archaeological slant, to mean both the material culture of past societies and the process through which that material is reused and reevaluated in the present (Skeates 2000b:9–18). The "Mediterranean" is defined not only as an ecological unit, comprising the sea and its hinterlands, but also as a fragmented interaction zone in which cultural relations and differences have developed over time (cf. Magnarella 1992; Horden and Purcell 2000). Finally, "prehistory" refers (conventionally if awkwardly) to those periods of the human past undocumented by written records, which appear as early as 3000 B.C. in Egypt, but as late as 600 B.C. in other parts of the Mediterranean.

The Making and Breaking of Prehistory Collections

Prehistoric artifacts have been collected in the Mediterranean region for at least 500 years, for a variety of reasons relating to the aesthetic, scholarly, social, and even patriotic motivations of their collectors (e.g., Daniel 1975; Groenen 1994; Skeates 2000a). In the Italian states, for example, small quantities of stone arrowheads and axe blades began to be incorporated into the encyclopedic natural history collections of humanist scholars in the 16th century. In this context, they were interpreted both as natural thunder-stones and as man-made arrow-stones and knives. During the following century, their value was elaborated into that of museological curiosities, within eclectic cabinets of strange and rare objects. Then, in the 18th century, their status was reassessed again, particularly by antiquarians working under the influence of French Enlightenment scholarship, who interpreted them more confidently as the weapons and tools of ancient barbarians.

It was only from the mid-19th century, however, that prehistoric artifacts began to be collected in any significant quantity and range. In Italy, their value was enhanced in particular by a new generation of ambitious liberal scholars. They displayed them in new typological series as historical and scientific "paleo-ethnographic" evidence, in support of their newly acquired comparative and evolutionary interpretations of ancient human origins and development. They also ascribed to them an added value, as tokens of patrimonial history, wealth, and status, which were collected and displayed in public museums in support of provincial and nationalist political agendas. This process reached a crescendo in the 1860s and 1870s, with the establishment of national museums of antiquities in France and Spain (in 1867), the display of national prehistory collections at the Universal Exposition in Paris (also in 1867), and the foundation of a unique National Prehistoric and Ethnographic Museum in Rome (in 1875). The latter was instituted by the Ministry of Public Education, at the initiative of Luigi Pigorini, who became both the preeminent prehistorian in Italy and the patriotic servant of the nationalist government. Their stated intention was to establish a great museum that would rival the scientific institutions of other, more established, European nations.

New forms of nationalism contributed to the reevaluation and reorganization of prehistory collections under the dictatorships of the northern Mediterranean in the 1930s and 1940s. In Turkey, Mustafa Kemal ("Atatürk"), the nation's "father," expected history and archaeology to provide a cultural heritage for the new Turkish state, which would develop the idea of a pre-Ottoman Turkish heritage, unify the heterogeneous population of Anatolia, improve the image of Turkey in Europe, and counter territorial claims of the Greeks, Armenians, and Nazi Germany (MacConnell 1989). As a consequence, Atatürk founded the Turkish Historical Society, which mounted a lavish exhibition in 1937 that combined prehistoric artifacts with displays on advances in the economy, public administration, and civic life under the new regime. He also initiated the establishment of a central Hittite Museum in Ankara, which opened to the public as the Museum of Anatolian Civilizations in 1943. In Spain, General Franco also exploited the famous sculpture of the "Dama de Elche" (then assumed to be pre-Roman in date) as a national emblem (Ramírez Domínguez 1994; Holo 1999:19). It became especially useful to Franco, as a "demonstration" of the great, pre-Roman antiquity and venerability of civilized Spain, and as a tool to deflect attention from his political humiliation, when he publicly accepted it from the Vichy government in France in 1941 (along with other Spanish art), which sought to appease Franco after he had been denied his territorial ambitions by Hitler in French Morocco and Gibraltar. The "Dama de Elche" was then exhibited in the national art gallery (the Prado) as a masterpiece of ancient Iberian art, and was even pictured on paper money issued by the Bank of Spain in 1948. In fascist Italy, too, nationalist propaganda was promoted by Ugo Rellini, the Professor of Paleoethnology and Director of the Museum of Origins and Tradition at the University of Rome, which was formally inaugurated in 1942. Both the name of the museum, and the ordering of the prehistory collections according to successive Italian "cultures," expressed Rellini's concern with "demonstrating" the indigenous prehistoric origins of the Italic peoples, and hence the antiquity, originality, and continuity of ancient Roman culture and its fascist reincarnation.

Colonialism also played a significant part in the establishment of national and university-based archaeological museums with prehistory collections in capital cities in the eastern Mediterranean and North Africa during the late 19th and early 20th centuries. This process was embedded in locally and historically specific colonial situations, in which members of local élites (of both foreign and native origin) interacted to create a variety of museum institutions, with diverse administrative and architectural forms (see van Dommelen 1997). British colonial authorities tended to establish national archaeological museums as monuments to imperial possession and power, in prominent positions in capital cities, and to maintain control over them by dominating their management committees. They also shared their administration, however, with local (albeit British-trained) archaeologists. In Malta, for example, the British Governor established a Museum Department in 1903, and an archaeological museum in Valetta on Empire Day of the following year (Vella and Gilkes 2001). The governor also appointed Sir Themistocles Zammit, the founding father of Maltese archaeology, to be their first Director and Curator. A similar situation was also established soon after in relation to the management of the Cyprus Museum in Nicosia, built as a memorial to the late Queen Victoria, and curated by the Cypriot archaeologist Menelaos Markides (Karageorghis 1985; 1989). The development of the Palestine Museum of Archaeology between the 1920s and 40s, under the British Mandate, was somewhat different (Taha 2001). It was funded by the wealthy American John D. Rockefeller, and administered by an International Council. Westerners dominated the membership of this council (five British, two American, one French, and one Swedish). Two members, however, were appointed by mutual agreement between Egypt, Syria, Lebanon, Iraq, and Jordan, and another represented the Hebrew University of Jerusalem. The French also helped to establish a variety of colonial museum situations, with varying degrees of local involvement. The best-known example is the National Museum of Egyptian Antiquities, established in Boulak by the determined

French archaeologist Auguste Mariette in 1859, despite the reluctance of the Khedive; this collection was later rehoused in Cairo in a monument to European Egyptology (Daniel 1975:161–164; Reid 2002:2–7). Another example is the National Museum of Beirut in the Lebanon, founded at the initiative of a group of local enthusiasts, but built according to a French-inspired, Orientalist vision of Egyptian architecture (Tahan 2000).

The colonial period also saw the formation of large collections of prehistoric artifacts by foreign archaeologists working in the Mediterranean region, and their dispersal to public museums and private collections, particularly in northern Europe and the USA. This diaspora was facilitated by the generosity of colonial and early post-independence governments, whose relatively weak antiquities legislation allowed foreign archaeologists to remove a substantial share of the finds from their excavations, often to the disadvantage of emergent local museums. It was also fueled by the acquisitive demands of international museums, dealers, and private collectors, who were often prepared to pay large sums of money to archaeologists in order to build up large and prestigious collections of antiquities. The archaeologists, for their part, often depended financially on this relationship, and some were even prepared to compromise established scientific standards (and local laws) in order to profit from the discovery and export of valuable "art" and "treasure." A classic example is provided by the German archaeologist Heinrich Schliemann who, in 1873, illegally smuggled from Turkey to Athens the Early Bronze Age hoard of precious metalwork known as "Priam's Treasure," which he had discovered during his excavations at Hissarlik (ancient Troy) (Easton 1981; Traill 1995:102–140). Historical research has shown that Schliemann clearly thought he was entitled to keep the more valuable finds from his excavations as compensation for his own fieldwork expenses, and that he removed these in violation of Ottoman law and the terms of his excavation permit. Schliemann later donated most of his finds from Troy to the German nation in 1880, on the understanding that a wing of a museum would be dedicated to his collection and display his name. It was eventually displayed, under these terms, in the prestigious Museum for Pre- and Early-History in Berlin. Schliemann's wife, Sophia, also donated a small collection of antiquities from Troy to the National Archaeological Museum in Athens, two years after her husband's death in 1890 (Konsola 1990).

Schliemann's contemporary and rival, General Luigi Palma di Cesnola, the first American consul on Cyprus, also amassed a huge collection of antiquities from unscientific excavations carried out all over the island from 1865, unhindered by the Ottoman authorities (Karageorghis 2000:3–11). In 1872, he sold his Cypriot collection to the Metropolitan Museum of Art in New York, having previously haggled with representatives from museums in St. Petersburg, Berlin, Paris, and London. He was then paid by the museum to repair and display his finds, and to collect more from Cyprus, and was eventually appointed as the first director of the museum in 1879. A substantial quantity of Cypriot antiquities was also "lost" to museums such as the Berlin Antiquarium, the British Museum, and the Museum of Mediterranean and Near Eastern Antiquities in Stockholm. These losses occurred despite the belated enactment of an Antiquities Law by the Ottoman

Government in 1874, its strengthening by the British administration from 1878, and the establishment of the Cyprus Museum in Nicosia in 1888 (Karageorghis 1985; Knapp and Antoniadou 1998). Because foreign archaeologists were still allowed to keep and export a large portion of the finds from any excavation for which a permit was granted, such a situation was almost inevitable.

Similar arrangements benefited British archaeologists and museums collecting in other parts of the Mediterranean region during the late 19th and early 20th centuries. Well-known collectors include Sir Arthur Evans in Crete, Sir Flinders Petrie in Palestine, and Sir Max Mallowan in Syria (e.g., Boardman 1961:v; Butcher and Gill 1993; Ucko 1998; Nunn 1999:v). It is perhaps inevitable, in this dynamic context, that some expensive fakes were also acquired by major Western museums, including the recently exposed "Minoan" statuette known as the "Fitzwilliam Goddess," bought by the Fitzwilliam Museum in Cambridge in 1926, and the "Iberian" "Dama de Elche" sculpture, sold to the Louvre in 1897 (Butcher and Gill 1993; Moffitt 1994).

World War II set the stage for the looting and further dispersal of museum collections of Mediterranean prehistory. In 1945, for example, the Red Army removed three boxes containing Schliemann's Trojan gold (as well as other artworks) from their place of safe keeping in the fortified Flakturm Zoo tower of Berlin to the Pushkin Museum in Moscow, where they remained hidden until the 1990s (Meyer 1993; Moorehead 1994:245–293). The rest of Schliemann's collection was dispersed to a variety of hiding places during the war, and much remains lost.

Contemporary Patterns and Problems

Over the past fifty years, new patterns have emerged in the organization, status, and management of museums with prehistory collections in the Mediterranean area. Regional differences have increased as a result of old and new political and economic concerns, surrounding issues such as cultural identity (national, postcolonial, regional, local), public education and access, and cultural tourism. Contrasts have also increased between rich and poor countries, particularly in terms of museum provision (Figure 12.1). There are, for example, some 1,897 museums in Italy, compared to 74 in Egypt, and just 16 in the Lebanon (Zils 2001).

In post-war southern Europe (Spain, France, Italy, Malta, Greece), relatively substantial public and private investment has led to the renovation, expansion, and modernization of old archaeology museums, and to an exponential growth in the establishment of new ones (e.g., Skeates 2000a:63–90). All levels of government, from the state to the municipalities, have invested in their museums, and sponsorship has also been provided by private sector institutions such as businesses, foundations, and banks. In addition, recent changes in cultural heritage legislation (notably in Italy and Malta) have encouraged museums to raise revenue themselves, particularly by adopting more business-like approaches to marketing and merchandising. This has been accompanied by efforts to improve museum management. In France, this strategy has promoted moves to tighten up poorly defined

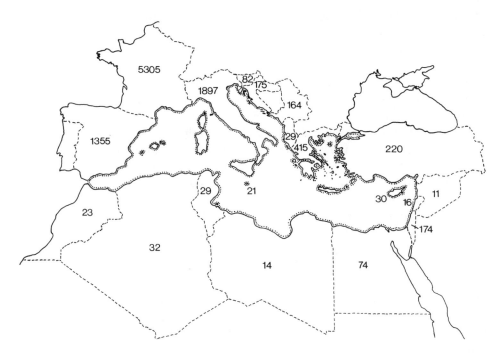

Figure 12.1 Total numbers of museums in different Mediterranean countries (based on details published by Zils 2001)

museum acquisition policies and practice relating to the curation of archaeological excavation archives (Marin 1994). And in Italy it has involved clarifying the administrative status of local museums, simplifying budgeting processes, enhancing visitor facilities, and involving volunteers in the day-to-day running of small museums (e.g., Maggi 2000; Zan 2000).

The greatest expansion has been in local museums, which focus on a specific territory or archaeological site. This reflects a broader social and political process, in which a growth in the value of archaeological remains, as endangered tokens of local cultural patrimony and identity, has contributed to a shift in government heritage policies toward decentralization and state-sponsored regionalism. This is particularly evident in Italy and Greece, although much less so in France, where a high degree of centralism remains (Schnapp 1996). The Herakleion Museum in Crete provides a good example of this change of policy. In 1979, thousands of people successfully protested against the Greek government's decision to forcefully remove some Minoan artifacts from the museum for an international touring exhibition on Aegean civilization (Hamilakis and Yalouri 1996). By contrast, in 2002, the Greek government widely publicized its handing over of the recently rediscovered "Minos Ring," originally found by Sir Arthur Evans at Knossos, to the museum. The Minister of Culture announced that the ring "will be turned over to its natural owners, the people of Crete, the people of Herakleion [. . .] the Archaeological Museum of

Herakleion, which is entering a new period as an autonomous unit of the Ministry of Culture" (reported by the Macedonian Press Agency). Despite this overall pattern of museum growth in southern Europe, however, some fundamental organizational problems persist, especially when compared to the museum sector in the United Kingdom. Of particular note are the relatively low numbers of museum archaeologists employed in France (Schnapp 1984), and the lack of clearly defined administrative accountability and evaluation in Italian museums (Zan 2000). In addition, prehistoric remains and prehistorians rarely have enjoyed the same prestige as that accorded to their counterparts in Classical archaeology.

The pace of change has been slower in southeast Europe (Slovenia, Croatia, Montenegro, Albania). In the Communist era, state funding helped to develop established archaeological museums, particularly as dynamic research institutions, which continued to curate archaeological artifacts as study collections, participate in fieldwork, and publish their own journals (e.g., Chapman 1981; Kirigin 1994). In the post-Communist era, however, museums have begun to suffer from under-funding, the loss of staff, the maintenance of traditional museological practices, and low visitor numbers (e.g., Hodges 2000). The Balkan wars of the 1990s also led to the damage of many museum buildings and the removal of prehistory collections. In Croatia, by contrast, the recent restoration of museums such as that of Vukovar (which has an important prehistoric site nearby) has served to provide national symbols of post-war continuity, resistance and reconstruction (Maroevic 1996).

In the eastern Mediterranean (Turkey, Cyprus, Syria, Lebanon, Israel), recent museum developments have been variable, with the nature and degree of government involvement again being a key factor. In Israel and Turkey, for example, where museums come under the auspices of Ministries of Culture and Education, there has been a steady growth in the number of archaeology museums, together with professional museum archaeologists. The connection is particularly clear in Israel, where archaeology museums have flourished since the foundation of the state of Israel, particularly at kibbutzim (Gonen 1992; Inbar 1992). One striking example is the Ma'ayan Baruch Kibbutz Museum of Prehistory in Upper Galilee, which deals with the prehistory of the Chula valley and its surrounding area: here archaeological remains have been used "educationally" (and ideologically) to establish and strengthen a connection between the land and its Jewish settlers, and to support the search for an Israeli national identity. Such museums have also been accused of excluding the history and culture of the indigenous Palestinian people, who instead wish to exploit the same prehistoric remains as a symbol of political resurgence (Taha 2001). In post-colonial Cyprus, Syria, and the Lebanon, on the other hand, where museums tend to be associated more with foreign scholars and tourism, prehistory collections have been loaned to overseas touring exhibitions, as evidence of "original" "civilizations" and as tokens of international diplomacy, while only a few new museums have been established locally (e.g., Alaoui 1999; Fortin 1999).

Despite these national differences, cultural heritage legislation has generally been strengthened throughout the region. For example, in Cyprus, the antiquities law of the colonial era was modified in 1964 in favor of the Cyprus Museum (Karageorghis, 1985), and in Israel a Museums Act was passed in 1983 (Inbar 1992). All legislation, however, has proved ineffective at times of war. In 1974, for instance, the Turkish Army's occupation of northern Cyprus led to the looting of public and private collections (Ministry of Culture and Sciences, 1985; Knapp and Antoniadou 1998). Artifacts stolen from the Famagusta District Museum and from the private Hadjiprodromos collection included Chalcolithic figurines, which were then exported illicitly to European cities such as London, where they have appeared on the antiquities market. Civil war in the Lebanon, between the 1970s and 1990s, also resulted in the damage of museum buildings and the emigration of curatorial staff (Asmar 1994).

Relatively limited museological developments have occurred in postcolonial North Africa (Egypt, Libya, Tunisia, Algeria, Morocco), where museums have tended, until recently, to be regarded as foreign, colonial institutions, of relevance to wealthy tourists rather than to locals. As a consequence, government investment has been restricted, and "modernization" fairly conservative. In Tunisia, for example, most of the funds allocated to museums are spent on building maintenance and daily running costs, rather than to fulfill a long-term national strategy relating to museum education (Khader 1991). The professional training of museum staff is clearly another priority, as is recognized by the Department of Antiquities of Libya (Ali 1994). Egypt's archaeological museums, however, comprise a partial exception to this general pattern of underdevelopment. Since the 1960s, the Egyptian government has successfully promoted its antiquities as "world heritage," and its archaeological museums have consequently benefited from significant international expertise, financial investment, and tourist visits. A good example is provided by the Luxor Museum of Ancient Egyptian Art, whose catalog and display labels were prepared by an American researcher, funded by the Smithsonian Institution through the American Research Center in Egypt (Bothmer and Romano 1979:vii).

On a Mediterranean scale, then, these regional variations in museum organization and status highlight a pattern of considerable diversity. Such a situation might be regarded as healthy, were it not accompanied by an inevitable inequality, which has recently begun to be tackled by targeted international funding and projects. These supportive interventions have sought to increase the sharing of expertise and skills between local museum professionals in different countries, and to raise public awareness of the fragile shared archaeological heritage. ICOM, for example, founded in 1946 to promote and develop museums and the museum profession at an international level, has, since the 1990s, actively sought to address the needs of museums in newly independent and developing African and Arab countries (Baghli et al. 1998). The European Union (EU) has also funded a variety of international cultural heritage projects, particularly through their European Bronze Age, Raphael, and Framework 5 programs. A recent example was an exhibition on "Burial Practices and Traditions of the Mediterranean from 1100 B.C. to A.D. 400," which toured museums in Cyprus, Rhodes, Marsala, and Marseilles. The revealing (federalist) aims of this exhibition were – according to a statement issued by the

Hellenic Ministry of Culture – not only "to make the Greek and European citizens more sensitive toward the significance of the conservation, preservation and promotion of their rich cultural heritage," but also "*to demonstrate the common cultural roots of the Mediterranean peoples*, through the study of burial customs, while at the same time acknowledging the individuality of each region" (emphasis added). Archaeological site museums in the Mediterranean region, including their management and public presentation, are also currently the focus for international study and workshops sponsored by ICOM's International Committee for Museums and Collections of Archaeology and History and by the EU's Euromed Heritage II program.

Another set of problems faced by stakeholders in the region's prehistoric heritage, particularly in southern Europe and the eastern Mediterranean, stems from the international (and often illicit) trade in antiquities, in both the past and the present. Requests for the repatriation of antiquities illegally removed in the 19th and early 20th centuries continue to be pursued by a number of countries, but with limited success. Ownership of "Priam's Treasure," for example, which recently surfaced in Russia, is being claimed by Germany, Turkey, and even Greece. According to press reports, however, it is currently set to remain in Russia, following a ruling by Russia's Constitutional Court in 1999 that it is not obliged to return works of art seized during World War II to "aggressor nations" such as Germany. A request from Israel for the return of Petrie's Palestinian Lachish collection was also turned down in 1980 by the University of London's Institute of Archaeology, which sold it instead to the British Museum for £15,000 (Ucko 1998). At the same time, wealthy private collectors and public museums continue to fuel the looting of prehistoric sites, the illicit trade in antiquities, and the production of fakes, by acquiring unprovenanced prehistoric artifacts for their collections. Recently, a broken and unprovenanced Cycladic figure was the prize object offered for sale, at a guide price of $50,000–80,000, at Sotheby's antiquities auction in New York (December 2002). The transformation of marble Cycladic figurines into saleable "masterpieces," and the destruction of their archaeological sites since the 1960s, is particularly well documented and debated (e.g., Broodbank 1992; Elia 1993; Gill and Chippindale 1993; Chippindale and Gill 1995; Renfrew 1991; 1993).

In this illicit process, looters, dealers, private collectors, modernist artists, museum curators, and even archaeologists are all implicated in the de-contextualization of cultural artifacts. In response, a variety of measures are now being taken to tackle such problems. Scientific techniques, such as thermoluminescence, have been used to identify fakes, including copies of Haçilar ceramics produced in the 1960s (Jones 1990:286–289). Antiquities legislation has been strengthened and enforced in "exporting" countries, such as the Lebanon, where Ministerial decrees in 1988 banned the export of antiquities and suspended the permits of antiquities dealers (Asmar 1994). The governments of Greece and Turkey have also aggressively pursued stolen antiquities in a series of well-publicized international legal cases. A recent example (publicized by the Hellenic Ministry of Culture) concerns the Aidonia Treasure. This collection of Mycenaean jewelry and seals, looted from the Late Bronze Age cemetery of Aidonia, was put up for auction at the Michael Ward Gallery in New York in 1993, but later returned to Greece, following the legal intervention of the Greek government (Cherry 1999). Archaeologists, museum curators, and international cultural organizations are also increasingly highlighting the damage to the Mediterranean's cultural heritage caused by factors such as the antiquities trade, resource exploitation, and poor planning. But it is far too early to claim that the tide is turning.

Turning to museum communication, curators remain divided on how best to present prehistoric remains to visitors in contemporary museum exhibitions. Traditional displays survive, particularly in older museums dominated by poorly documented archaeological collections. These are often curated as study collections, in which prehistoric objects are ordered serially, according to their relative chronology, provenance, typology, and archaeological "culture." But despite their intended scientific objectivity, the diffusionist and culture-historical interpretations of these displays often perpetuate politically biased claims about ethnic and national origins (e.g., Kaiser 1996). "Modern" displays are diverse, but can be broadly divided into two types. On the one hand we find displays that place a didactic emphasis on the artifacts and their archaeological contexts. A good example is provided by the newly established South Tyrol Museum of Archaeology in Bolzano (Italy), which houses the body and equipment of the famous Copper Age "Iceman" (Skeates 1999). The permanent exhibition, targeted at visitors of all ages and levels of education, is intended to be both informative and entertaining. It successfully achieves this aim by employing a wide range of display media, including bilingual text panels, uncrowded cases of well-lit artifacts, two- and three-dimensional reconstructions, photographs, videos, and touch-screen computers, all of which are ordered both chronologically and thematically. Another successful example comprises the recently "modernized" Prehistoric Collection in Malta's National Museum of Archaeology (Martin 1999; Buhagiar 2000). Here, hundreds of freshly conserved prehistoric artifacts have been redisplayed in new showcases, together with graphics, models, and bilingual explanatory texts, with the help of a $150,000 grant awarded by the J. P. Getty Foundation.

On the other hand we find "modernist" displays that favor the aesthetic appreciation of ancient "art." This display style is common in Greece, at institutions such as the Goulandris Museum of Cycladic and Ancient Greek Art in Athens, which opened in 1986 (Renfrew 1985–86; 1991; Papathanassopoulos 1996). Here, in a purpose-designed building, with a plate glass and marble façade and marble-lined interior passages, artifacts are exhibited as artistic "masterpieces." Significantly, the Cycladic figurines are displayed vertically, with the aid of transparent supports, despite the fact that most were not made to stand on their own feet (Gill and Chippindale 1993:655–656). Similar displays of these figures are found throughout the world's art museums, ranging from the Louvre to the Sainsbury Centre for Visual Arts at the University of East Anglia (Figure 12.2). Some of these institutions, however, are at least beginning to redisplay their collections more accessibly. In the new Prehistoric to Early Greek Galleries of the Metropolitan Museum of Art, for example, artifacts including Cycladic figurines are now grouped according to period

Figure 12.2 Cycladic figurines in the Robert and Lisa Sainsbury Collection displayed in the Sainsbury Centre for Visual Arts at the University of East Anglia, Norwich. (Photo: John Donat. Reproduced with the kind permission of Kate Carreno and Nichola Johnson)

rather than by medium, together with contextualizing "wall chats," drawings, and photographs (Bonfante 1996).

Developments such as these, which enhance the accessibility of prehistory collections and displays, are symptomatic of a broader and growing concern throughout the Mediterranean with identifying and catering for the diverse needs of consumers of cultural heritage. Visitor surveys have identified significant demographic and seasonal variations in museum visiting. In Italy, for example, recent studies have revealed that parties of school children comprise the largest share of the audience of the Archaeological Museum of Bologna, while more than half the visitors to state museums in June and July are foreign tourists (Solima 2000; Zan 2000). Qualitative and quantitative evaluations have also identified visitors' perceptions of museums, and the factors that discourage others from visiting at all. The Italian studies show that museums are widely perceived as temples of learning and preservation, rather than as places of social interaction, distanced from the public by unchanging exhibitions, unapproachable staff, limited educational resources, and inconvenient opening hours. In Malta, another recent survey of cultural participation, undertaken by the National Statistics Office, found that 70.2 percent of the Maltese population never visited a museum or monument between November 1999 and October 2000. These figures reflect what politicians now accept: that Maltese citizens have been alienated from their cultural heritage, with museums and monuments perceived as places for foreign scholars and tourists (Grima 1998). The same attitude toward museums is widespread in North Africa. In response to these criticisms, and growing political pressure, increasing numbers of museums are trying out new approaches to improve their visitor services and attract local audiences. In Egypt, for example, the manager of the Luxor Museum of Ancient Egyptian Art recently recognized that "the museum constitutes nothing of value to the townspeople" (El Mallah 1998:18). He is therefore now attempting to involve local residents in museum meetings, educational programs, and exhibition evaluations. Elsewhere, tried and tested approaches have included curating popular temporary exhibitions, enabling groups of blind and deaf visitors to handle artifacts, involving the public in experimental archaeology workshops, providing new visitor facilities such as toilets and elevators, and reducing or abolishing museum entrance charges for citizens. The Internet is also being used, increasingly, to advertise information about museum collections and services (e.g., Avenier 1999; Atagok and Ozcan 2001). There is still a long way to go, however, before old attitudes toward cultural heritage and related institutions, held by professionals as well as the public, change significantly.

Conclusion

The study of the cultural heritage of the Mediterranean, and of Mediterranean prehistory museum collections in particular, is still in its infancy. Perhaps the most successful studies so far have been those that have adopted a critical historical approach, drawing upon personal experience and other informal sources of information. These studies confirm that prehistoric remains have been valued as a small but significant aspect of the Mediterranean's cultural heritage for over 150 years. They have been collected and displayed, in increasing quantity and range, and in a diversity of institutional and cultural contexts, throughout the Mediterranean and beyond. They have also been exploited by a variety of interest groups: as scholarly specimens, museological curiosities, saleable artworks, patrimonial tokens of origins and civilization, symbols of political oppression and resistance, and as economic resources. Their fortunes have varied greatly, in different periods and countries, particularly in relation to the degree of government patronage that they and their collectors have attracted. But they have often been marginalized as "archaic," appropriated by foreigners, and overshadowed by interest in the more obvious archaeological remains and literature of the historical era. As a consequence, public appreciation of them remains limited, and their potential as accessible cultural heritage has yet to be fully developed. Future studies will therefore need to gather more detailed primary data about all aspects of the prehistoric cultural heritage of the Mediterranean, from politicians, professionals, and the public, particularly in non-European countries. This development will involve more rigorously constructed qualitative and quantitative surveys and evaluations, and painstaking archival research. We may then learn how best to exploit, present, and preserve the remains of the Mediterranean's prehistoric past in the present.

REFERENCES

Alaoui, Brahim, 1999 An Ongoing Dialogue: The Museum of the Institute of the Arab World in Paris. Museum International 51(3):38–42.

Ali, Ali Emhemed, 1994 Of the Importance of Training Archaeologists and Museum Staff. *In* Museums, Civilization and Development: Proceedings of the Encounter, Amman, Jordan, 26–30 April 1994. International Council of Museums, ed. pp. 217–219. Paris: International Council of Museums.

Andrews, Carol A. R., 1981 Catalogue of Egyptian Antiquities in the British Museum VI. Jewellery I: From the Earliest Times to the Seventeenth Dynasty. London: British Museum Press.

Antonova, Irina, Vladimir Tolstikov, and Mikhail Treister, 1996 The Gold of Troy: Searching for Homer's Fabled City. London: Thames and Hudson.

Asmar, Camille, 1994 La Protection du Patrimoine dans un Pays en Guerre. *In* Museums, Civilization and Development: Proceedings of the Encounter, Amman, Jordan, 26–30 April 1994. International Council of Museums, ed. pp. 203–206. Paris: International Council of Museums.

Atagok, Tomur, and Ozcan Oguzhan, 2001 Virtual Museums in Turkey. Museum International 53(1):42–45.

Avenier, Philippe, 1999 Putting the Public First: The French Experience. Museum International 51(4):31–34.

Baghli, Sid Ahmed, Patrick Boylan, and Yani Herreman, 1998 History of ICOM (1946–1996). Paris: International Council of Museums.

Boardman, John, 1961 The Cretan Collection in Oxford: The Dictaean Cave and Iron Age Crete. Oxford: The Clarendon Press.

Bonfante, Larissa, 1996 The Belfer Court at the Metropolitan Museum of Art: The New Prehistoric to Early Greek Galleries. Apollo 413:3–5.

Bothmer, Bernard V., and James F. Romano, 1979 The Luxor Museum of Ancient Egyptian Art: Catalogue. Cairo: American Research Center in Egypt.

Broodbank, Cyprian, 1992 The Spirit is Willing. Antiquity 66:542–546.

Buhagiar, C. Michelle, 2000 National Museum of Archaeology News: 1998 & 1999. Malta Archaeological Review 4:44–50.

Butcher, Kevin, and David W. J. Gill, 1993 The Director, the Dealer, the Goddess, and her Champions: The Acquisition of the Fitzwilliam Goddess. American Journal of Archaeology 97:383–401.

Chapman, John C., 1981 The Value of Dalmatian Museum Collections to Settlement Pattern Studies. *In* The Research Potential of Anthropological Museum Collections. Anne-Marie E. Cantwell, James B. Griffin, and Nan A. Rothschild, eds. pp. 529–555. New York: Annals of The New York Academy of Sciences.

Cherry, John F., 1999 After Aidonia: Further Reflections on Attribution in the Aegean Bronze Age. *In* Meletemata: Studies in Aegean Archaeology Presented to Malcolm H. Weiner as He Enters his 65th Year. Philip P. Betancourt, Vassos Karageorghis, Robert Laffineur, and

Wolf-Dietrich Niemeier, eds. pp. 103–110. Aegaeum 20(1). Liège and Austin: Histoire de l'Art et Archeologie de la Grèce Antique, Université de Liège, and Program in Aegean Scripts and Prehistory, University of Texas.

Chippindale, Christopher, and David W. J. Gill, 1995 Cycladic Figurines: Art vs Archaeology? In Antiquities: Trade or Betrayed: Legal, Ethical and Conservation Issues. K. W. Tubb, ed. pp. 131–142. London: Archetype Publications.

Currelly, Charles T., 1913 Catalogue Général des Antiquités Égyptiennes du Musée du Caire. Nos. 63001-64906. Stone Implements. Cairo: L'Institut Français d'Archéologie Orientale).

Daniel, Glyn, 1975 A Hundred and Fifty Years of Archaeology. London: Duckworth.

Easton, Donald F., 1981 Schliemann's Discovery of "Priam's Treasure": Two Enigmas. Antiquity 55:179–183.

Elia, Ricardo J., 1993 A Seductive and Troubling Work. Archaeology 46(1):64–69.

El Mallah, Madline Y., 1998 The Luxor Museum of Ancient Egyptian Art: The Challenge of Abundance. Museum International 50(2):16–22.

Fortin, Michel, 1999 Syria: Land of Civilizations. Québec: Musée de la Civilisation de Québec.

Gill, David W. J., and Christopher Chippindale, 1993 Material and Intellectual Consequences of Esteem for Cycladic Figurines. American Journal of Archaeology 97:601–659.

Gonen, Rivka, 1992 In Search of Identity: The Role of the Museum in a Dynamic Society. In The Museum and the Needs of People: ICOM CECA Annual Conference, Jerusalem, Israel, 15–22 October 1991, Israel National Committee of International Council of Museums, ed. pp. 35–40. Jerusalem: Israel National Committee of the International Council of Museums.

Grima, Reuben, 1998 Ritual Spaces, Contested Places: The Case of the Maltese Prehistoric Temple Sites. Journal of Mediterranean Studies 8(1):33–45.

Groenen, Marc, 1994 Pour une Histoire de la Préhistoire: le Paléolithique. Grenoble: Éditions Jérôme Millon.

Hamilakis, Yannis, and Yalouri, Eleana, 1996 Antiquities as Symbolic Capital in Modern Greek Society. Antiquity 70:117–129.

Hammade, Hamido, 1987 Cylinder Seals from the Collections of the Aleppo Museum, Syrian Arab Republic, 1: Seals of Unknown Provenience. Oxford: British Archaeological Reports.

Hodges, Richard, 2000 Archaeology in Albania after Kosovo. History Today 50(3):3–4.

Holo, Selma Reuben, 1999 Beyond the Prado. Museums and Identity in Democratic Spain. Liverpool: Liverpool University Press.

Horden, Peregrine, and Nicholas Purcell, 2000 The Corrupting Sea: A Study of Mediterranean History. Oxford: Blackwell.

Inbar, Judith, 1992 On the History and Nature of Museums in Israel. In The Museum and the Needs of People: ICOM CECA Annual Conference, Jerusalem, Israel, 15–22 October 1991. Israel National Committee of International Council of Museums, ed. pp. 28–34. Jerusalem: Israel National Committee of the International Council of Museums.

Jones, Mark, ed., 1990 Fake? The Art of Deception. London: British Museum Publications.

Kaiser, Timothy, 1996 Archaeology and Ideology in Southeast Europe. In Nationalism, Politics and the Practice of Archaeology. Philip L. Kohl and Clare Fawcett, eds. pp. 99–119. Cambridge: Cambridge University Press.

Karageorghis, Vassos, 1985 The Cyprus Department of Antiquities, 1935–1985. In Archaeology in Cyprus, 1960–1985. Vassos Karageorghis, ed. pp. 1–10. Nicosia: A.G. Levantis Foundation.

Karageorghis, Vassos, 1989 The Cyprus Museum. Nicosia: C. Epiphaniou Publications.

—2000 Ancient Art from Cyprus: The Cesnola Collection in the Metropolitan Museum of Art. New York: The Metropolitan Museum of Art.

Khader, Aïcha Ben Abed-Ben, 1991 Museum Management: The Tunisian Example. In What Museums for Africa? Heritage in the Future. Proceedings of the Encounters. Benin, Ghana, Togo, November 18–23, 1991. International Council of Museums, ed. pp. 29–30. Paris: International Council of Museums.

Kirigin, Branko, 1994 Archaeological Museums in Croatia: Past, Present and Future. In Museum Archaeology in Europe: Proceedings of a Conference Held at the British Museum, 15–17th October 1992. David Gaimster, ed. pp. 147–154. Oxford: Oxbow Books.

Knapp, A. Bernard, and Sophia Antoniadou, 1998 Archaeology, Politics and the Cultural Heritage of Cyprus. In Archaeology under Fire: Nationalism, Politics and Heritage in the Eastern Mediterranean and Middle East. Lynn Meskell, ed. pp. 13–43. London: Routledge.

Konsola, Dora, 1990 The Trojan Collection in the National Archaeological Museum. In Troy, Mycenae, Tiryns, Orchomenos. Heinrich Schliemann: The 100th Anniversary of his Death. Katie Demakopoulou, ed. pp. 79–87. Athens: Ministry of Culture of Greece, Greek Committee ICOM, and Ministry of Culture of the German Democratic Republic.

MacConnell, Brian E., 1989 Mediterranean Archaeology and Modern Nationalism: A Preface. Revue des Archéologues et Historiens d'Art de Louvain 22:107–113.

Maggi, Maurizio, 2000 Innovation in Italy: The a.muse Project. Museum International 52(2):50–53.

Magnarella, Paul J., 1992 Conceptualizing the Circum-Mediterranean for Purposes of Social Scientific Research. Journal of Mediterranean Studies 2(1):18–24.

Marin, Jean-Yves, 1994 L'Acquisition des Objets Archéologiques par les Musées en France. In Museum Archaeology in Europe: Proceedings of a Conference Held at the British Museum, 15–17th October 1992. David Gaimster, ed. pp. 107–116. Oxford: Oxbow Books.

Maroevic, Ivo, 1996 Museums and the Development of Local Communities after the War. Museums, Catalysts for Community Development. Proceedings of the Annual Meeting, ICOM International Committee for the Training of Personnel. Gary Edson and Claudia Cory, eds. pp. 136–143. Lubbock, Texas: Museum of Texas Tech University.

Martin, David, 1999 Maltese Revival. Museum Practice 10(4):31–37.

Meskell, Lynn, 2001 The Practice and Politics of Archaeology in Egypt. In Ethics and Anthropology: Facing Future Issues in Human Biology, Globalism, and Cultural Property. Anne-Marie Cantwell, Eva Friedlander, and Madeleine Lorch Tramm, eds. pp. 146–169. New York: Annals of the New York Academy of Sciences 925.

Meyer, Karl E., 1993 The Hunt for Priam's Treasure. Archaeology 46(6):26–32.

Ministry of Culture and Sciences, 1985 Cyprus: The Plundering of a 9000 Year Old Civilization. Athens: Akademia Athenon.

Moffitt, John Francis, 1994 Art Forgery: The Case of the Lady of Elche. Gainesville: University Press of Florida.

Moorehead, Caroline, 1994 The Lost Treasures of Troy. London: Weidenfeld and Nicolson.

Museums Association, 1998 Museum Definition. London: Museums Association.

Nunn, Astrid, 1999 Stamp Seals from the Collections of the Aleppo Museum, Syrian Arab Republic. Oxford: British Archaeological Reports.

Papathanassopoulos, George A., ed., 1996 Neolithic Culture in Greece. Athens: N. P. Goulandris Foundation.

Preziosi, Donald, 2002 Archaeology as Museology: Re-Thinking the Minoan Past. *In* Labyrinth Revisited: Rethinking "Minoan" Archaeology. Yannis Hamilakis, ed. pp. 30–39. Oxford: Oxbow Books.

Ramírez Domínguez, J.A., 1994 The Situation of the Dama de Elche in Post-Franco Spain. *In* Art Forgery: The Case of the Lady of Elche. John Francis Moffitt, pp. xv–xxi. Gainesville: University Press of Florida.

Reid, Donald Malcolm, 2002 Whose Pharaohs? Archaeology, Museums and Egyptian National Identity from Napoleon to World War I. Berkeley: University of California Press.

Renfrew, Colin, 1985–86 The Goulandris Museum of Cycladic and Ancient Greek Art. Archaeological Reports 32:134–41.

——1991 The Cycladic Spirit: Masterpieces from the Nicholas P. Goulandris Collection. New York: Harry N. Abrams.

——1993 Collectors are the Real Looters. Archaeology 46(2):16–17.

Rountree, Kathryn, 1999 Goddesses and Monsters: Contesting Approaches to Malta's Neolithic Past. Journal of Mediterranean Studies 9(2):204–231.

Sadek, Mohammed-Moain, 1994 Archaeological Museums in Palestine: Reality and Prospects. *In* Museums, Civilization and Development: Proceedings of the Encounter, Amman, Jordan, 26–30 April 1994. International Council of Museums, ed. pp. 287–291. Paris: International Council of Museums.

Schnapp, Alain, 1984 France. *In* Approaches to the Archaeological Heritage: A Comparative Study of World Cultural Resource Management Systems. Henry Cleere, ed. pp. 48–53. Cambridge: Cambridge University Press.

——1996 French Archaeology: Between National Identity and Cultural Identity. *In* Nationalism and Archaeology in Europe. Margarita Díaz Andreu and Timothy C. Champion, eds. pp. 48–67. London: University College London Press.

Skeates, Robin, 1999 Rest in Peace? The Iceman Display in the South Tyrol Museum of Archaeology, Bolzano, Italy. A Museum Review. Palaeo-Express 4:21–23.

——2000a The Collecting of Origins: Collectors and Collections of Italian Prehistory and the Cultural Transformation of Value (1550–1999). Oxford: British Archaeological Reports.

——2000b Debating the Archaeological Heritage. London: Duckworth.

Solima, Ludovico, 2000 Il Pubblico dei Musei: Indagine sulla Comunicazione nei Musei Statali Italiani. Roma: Ministero per i Beni e le Attività Culturali.

Taha, Hamdan, 2001 The History and Role of Museums in Palestine. *In* ICOM International Committee for Museums and Collections of Archaeology and History, Study Series 9. Jean-Yves Marin, ed. pp. 25–27. Paris: International Council of Museums.

Tahan, L. G., 2000 Lebanese Museums of Archaeology: Will the Past be Part of the Future? *In* SOMA 2001 Symposium on Mediterranean Archaeology. G. Muskett, A. Koltsida, and M. Georgiadis, eds. pp. 241–247. British Archaeological Reports International Series 1040. Oxford: Archaeopress.

Tahan, Lina Gebrail, 2002 Lebanese Museums of Archaeology: Will the Past Be Part of the Future? *In* SOMA 2001: Symposium on Mediterranean Archaeology. Proceedings of the Fifth Annual Meeting of Postgraduate Researchers. The University of Liverpool, 23–25 February 2001. Georgina Muskett, Aikaterini Koltsida and Mercourios Georgiadis, eds. pp. 241–247. Oxford: British Archaeological Reports.

Traill, David A., 1995 Schliemann of Troy: Treasure and Deceit. New York: St. Martin's Press.

Ucko, Peter J., 1998 The Biography of a Collection: The Sir Flinders Petrie Palestinian Collection and the Role of University Museums. Museum Management and Curatorship 17(4):351–399.

Van Dommelen, Peter, 1997 Colonial Constructs: Colonialism and Archaeology in the Mediterranean. World Archaeology 28(3):305–323.

Vella, Nicholas C. and Oliver Gilkes, 2001 The Lure of the Antique: Nationalism, Politics and Archaeology in British Malta (1880–1964). Papers of the British School at Rome 79:353–384.

Zan, Luca, 2000 Managerialisation Processes and Performance in Arts Organisations: The Archaeological Museum of Bologna. Scandinavian Journal of Management 16(4): 431–454.

Zils, Michael, 2001 Museums of the World: 8th Edition, 2 vols. München: K. G. Sauer.

Index

Page references in *italics* denote figure/table

adzes 29, 198
Aegean
  chipped stone production 192
  copper ore deposits 220
  distance between Near East and routes
    to 277–8
  interregional trade 274
  metallurgy 216–17, 231
  relations and trade with Near East 26,
    278–9, 284–5
  silver sources 226
  society, material representation and the
    state in 87–95
Aegina 93, 96
Afghanistan 224
agriculture 46–67, 83
  crop cultivation 55–6, 57, 63, 65
  development of animal husbandry 51,
    55, 56, 57, 63, 65–6
  development of polyculture 56, 57, 63,
    65
  features of by third millennium B.C. 57
  Minoan/Mycenaean palace societies
    57–8
  plant gathering in early Holocene 49–50
  small scale and intensive 55, 64–5
  transition from foraging to farming
    51–4, 64

Aidonia Treasure 303, 312–13
Ain Ghazal (Jordan) 108, 303
Ajzen, Icek 287
Akrotiri *Aetokremnos* (Cyprus) 51, 254
Akrotiri (Thera) 138, 146, 275, 285
Alashiyan timber 289
Alassa (Cyprus) 263
Alberti, Benjamin 137–8
Alepotrypa Cave (Greece) 226
Almeria 56–7, 63, 220
Alps
  rock-art sites 118
Altamira (Spain) 14
Altman, A. 280
Amarna Letters 229–30, 273, 289
Ammerman, Albert J. 37
Anatolia
  copper ore deposits 218–19
  exporting of obsidian 193
  gold sources 229
  origins of metallurgy in 216
  silver sources 226
Anderson, Benedict 263
animal husbandry 51, 55, 56, 57, 63, 65–6
animals
  hunted in early Holocene 49
  sacrifice of 124
  trade in 31

Anschuetz, Kurt *et al* 252
anthropomorphic images
  and sexual coding 133–7
antiquities
  illicit trade in 312
Apliki *Karamallos* (Cyprus) 235
Appadurai, Arjun 290
apse 158, 172
Apulia (Italy) 53, 54
Archaeological Museum (Bologna) 314
"Archaeomedes" project 15
Argos (Greece) 93
arrowheads *196*, 197, 203
arsenical bronze 221, 223, 224
art, Late Bronze Age 137
Artzy, Michael 273, 283
Asfaka (Greece) 53
Assiros (Thessaly) 55, 95
Atatürk (Mustafa Kemal) 305
Atsipades (Crete) 144
axes *183–4*, 198, *199*, 200
  circulation and trade of 27–8, 29, 33,
    38, 39, 200
  double 163
  functions *183–4*, 200
  metal 202

Bailey, Douglass W. 144
Balearic Islands
  metallurgy 218
  monuments 169–71, 174
Banditella (Italy) 116
Banning, E. B. 253
Barrett, John 105
Base Ring juglet 286
Bass, George F. 284
Bates Island (Egypt) 273
Beaker pottery 231
Be'er Resism (Palestine) 257
Bernardini Tomb (Latium) 123
bifacial technique 193
Biferno Valley (Italy) 53–4, 59–60, 67, 254,
    258, 261
Biferno Valley Survey 253
Binford, Lewis 194
bipolar/naviform technique 189–91
blades 37–8, 189, 195, *196*
Blouet, Brian W. 254
boats, Neolithic 25–6

Bogucki, Peter 54
Bolger, Diane 140, 141
Bourdieu, Pierre 27, 105, 145
bow drill 198
bracelets 30
Branigan, Keith 113
Braudel, Fernand 2, 11, 46, 78, 252, 280
Brochtorff Circle (Gozo) 160
Broglio (Italy) 61–2
Broodbank, Cyprian 89, 95, 280
Brumfiel, Elizabeth 146
Bücher, Karl 272
Bulgaria 144
"Burial Practices and Traditions of the
    Mediterranean" exhibition 311–12
burials
  communal 81, 82, 89
  wealth items deposited with 94
  see also mortuary rituals; tombs
Butler, Judith 137

Cabeço da Mina (Portugal) 119–20
Cabezo Juré 85
Calabria 28
  use of obsidian *34*, 37
Calabrian axes 29
Camp-Redon (France) 120
"Canaanean" 193
Cape Gelidonya shipwreck (Turkey) 224,
    283, 285
Carter, Tristan 38
Carthage 5
cassiterite 224
Çatalhöyük 226, 303
cattle 65
caves
  as site for cult activities 113–14, 148
Çayönü Tepesi (Anatolia) 216
cereals 49–50, 53, 55, 57, 63
Cerro Virtud (Almeria) 218
Cesnola Collection 303
Chapman, John 144, 218
cheese-making 56
Cherry, John F. 16, 116
chert 28, 31, 180–1, 187, 192, 193
chiefdoms 79, 86
child-care 142
chipped stone technologies 27–8, 181–2,
    183–98, 203

activity involved and types of raw
    material used *183–5*
blade cores and flaking production
    techniques 189–91, *190*
evolution of tools 195
factors behind tool-form variability or
    uniformity 194
map of sources *186*
production 188–9
production techniques 189–93
raw materials and exchange networks
    182–7, 204–5
and specialization 188, 191
symbolic aspects of raw materials 187–8
types of tools 195, *196*
use of 193–8
chaîne opératoires 233
Chalandriani-Kastri 89
Chalcolithic figurines 107, 311
Chalcolithic societies 56–7
chisels 29, 198, 202
Chrysokamino (Crete) 220, 221, 233
Cierny, Jan 225
cinnabar 30
Clark, Grahame 26
class system 84, 86
climate 7, 47
Cline, Eric 272, 283
colonialism
    part played in establishment of museums
        306–7
coming-of-age ceremonies 105, 114
communal burials 81, 82, 89
communities 262–3, 264, 265
Connerton, Paul 124
Constantinou, George 234
consumption 286–8, 290–1
copper 193, 216, 217, 218–23, 288, 289
    ingots 221, *223*, 237
    instruments and installations for
        extracting from minerals 220–1
    mixing of with arsenic to produce
        arsenical bronze 221, 223
    smelting of 234
    sources of ore deposits 218–19, *219*, 220
    trade in 236–7
Corsica 7, 30, 49, 119
    torre tower 167–8, 169, 171
Crete 95, 96, 135, 174, 279

caves as cult sites 114
clay figurines in 108
copper smelting 233
Minoan palaces *see* Minoan palaces
peak sanctuaries 116, *117*
relations with eastern Mediterranean
    279
third millennium B.C. societies 89–92
tholos tombs 94, 111–13, *159*, 166,
    172
transition from foraging to farms 52, 64
see also Minoan society
Croatia 36, 310
crop cultivation 55–6, 57, 63, 65
Csikszentmihalyi, Mihaly 287
Cullen, Tracey 135
cult personnel 105
cult rooms (pillar crypts) 163–4
cults 102–24
    archaeological evidence for 103
    associated with water 115–16
    caves as site for activities 113–14, 143
    definition 102
    domestic 120–1
    fertility 109
    figurines and statues 107–9
    in funerary contexts 111
    mother goddess 108–9
    open-air settings 114–20
    peak sanctuaries in Crete 116, *117*
    and rock-art sites 117–18
    and sacrifice 102–3
    and temples 121–3
cultural heritage
    definition 304
cultural heritage legislation 310–11
cupellation 226, 227
Cycladic figurines 107, 108, 303
    display of in museums 313–14, *314*
    illicit trade in 312
Cycladic islands 87–9, 95, 220
Cyprus 7, 49, 67, 96, 290
    agro-pastoralism 51
    chipped stone production 192, 193
    copper production 217, 220, 231, 232,
        234, 288–9
    losses of antiquities 307–8
    museums 310
    plank figurines 135

Cyprus (cont'd)
    settlements 257
    trade with eastern Mediterranean
        279–80
Cyprus Museum (Nicosia) 306, 308
Cyrene 5

Dalmatia 54, 67
"Dama de Elche" 303, 306, 308
dance 104
Darvill, T. 252
Daskaleio-Kavos 89
deforestation 25, 66, 234
Dietler, Michael 123
Dilofos (Thessaly) 95
Diodorus 227–8
direct procurement 38, 39
    cultural heritage legislation 310–11
    domestic cults 120
    forests 234
    gender roles and asymmetries 140–1,
        142–3
    and gendered space 144–5
"ditched villages" (Apulia) 53, 54
Dixon, John 37
domestic cults 120–1
donkeys 57, 65
double axe 163
Douglas, Mary 287, 290
"down the line" exchange 38, 39
dress
    and gender 137–9

East/West divide 4, 5
Egypt 226
    archaeological museums 311
    copper deposits 219
    gold sources 228–9
    trade with Aegean 278
einkorn 51
El Argar (Spain) 231
El Barranquete (Spain) 110
electrum 226, 228
elites
    and long-distance contact 286–8
    Minoan/Mycenaean dynastic 57–8
emmer 51
end-scrapers 185, 196, 197
Enkomi 97, 122, 289

erosion 7, 13, 25, 66
Es Tudons (Menorca) 170
Etruria (Italy) 59
Euboea 261
European Union 14, 311
Evans, Sir Arthur 164, 308, 309
exchange 10, 24 see also gift exchange;
    trade

fakes 312
feasting 106–7, 113, 122–3
Feinan 219, 221
Ferrandell-Oleza (Mallorca) 170
fertility cults 109
Fezzan Project 5
Fiavè (Italy) 60
figs 57, 65
figurines 20, 111, 121, 133, 140
    association with cult activities 107–9
    Chalcolithic 107, 311
    Cycladic see Cycladic figurines
    Cypriot plank 135
    sexual coding on anthropomorphic
        133–6
fish/fishing 31, 49, 50–1, 52–3
Fishbein, Martin 287
"Fitzwilliam Goddess" 308
flint 31, 33, 192
    circulation of 28, 28, 29, 192
    mines 29
    production of 193
    sources 186, 187
Fogliuto (Sicily) 120
Font-Juvénal (France) 62–3
food 106–7
    trade in 31, 33
foraging 64
    in early Holocene 47–51
    transition to farming from 51–4
Forbes, Hamish 66
Fournou Korifi Myrtos 89
France 27, 56
    copper ore deposits 220
    expansion of agricultural landscape
        during second millennium in southern
        62–3
    gold sources 229
    materials traded 29
    museums 306–7, 308–9, 310

riverine cult sites 115
silver deposits 226
Franchthi Cave (Greece) 26, 30, 36, 49, 50–1, 52–3
Franco, General 305–6
Frankel, David 141, 262
Frattesina (Italy) 61
Fuente Alamo (Spain) 80–1, 83, 84
funerary complexes, Maltese 160
funerary practices
  Crete 89, 90
  and rituals 110–13
  see also burials; mortuary rituals; tombs
furnaces 221

Gaione (Emilia-Romagna) 39
"gaming" stones 201
Gargano peninsula (Puglia) 28, 29
Gatas (Spain) 80–1, 83
gender 130–48
  asymmetries and tensions 139–41, 146–7
  and gesture, dress, and performance 137–9
  and material culture 132–3
  roles 141–3
  and sex 131, 137
  sexual coding and anthropomorphic images 133–7, 145–6
gendered space 143–5, 146
gift exchange 272, 273, 281
Gillis, Carole 281
Gimbutas, Maria 108, 109
glass beads 281
goats 50, 57, 63
Godoy, R. 230
gold 217, 228–30, 232
  sources of ore deposits 219
Goody, Jack 106
Goulandris Museum of Cycladic and Ancient Greek Art (Athens) 313
Gozo 158, 171
Graziadio, Giampaolo 93
Greece 261
  farming communities 55
  feasting 123
  and gender 138
  gender roles 141
  and obsidian 38

societies in third millennium B.C. southern 92–4, 95
grinders 203
grinding stones 30, 83
grinding tools 200–1
Grotta dei Cavalli (Sicily) 114
Grotta dei Genovesi (Sicily) 114
Grotta dell' Uzzo (Sicily) 49, 51
Grotta di Porto Badisco (Italy) 143
ground stone technologies 181–2, 198–201, 199, 203
Guadalquivir Valley 85

Habuba Kabira South (Syria) 227
Hal Safliena Hypogeum (Tarxien) 160
Hala Sultan Tekke (Cyprus) 255, 256–7
halberds 83
Hall, Tim 253
Halstead, Paul 66
Hamilakis, Yannis 113
Hamilton, Naomi 134
hammering tools 200
hammers 185, 203
Hasebroek, Johannes 272
Hawkes, Christopher 123
Hegmon, M. 287
Helms, Mary 280
Herakleion Museum (Crete) 309–10
Herzfeld, Michael 2, 3, 11, 12
Hitchcock, Louise 134–5
Hodder, Bramwell 281
Holmes, Katie 135–6
Holocene 64
  foraging seascapes in early 47–51, 64
honey flint 187, 192
Horden, Peregrine 2, 3, 12, 15, 27, 46–7, 64, 77, 252, 260, 265, 274, 278, 288
"house tomb" 166
Hua 132
Hungary 144
hunting 49, 58, 197

Iberia 30, 85, 119, 260
Iberian peninsula 51, 56
  copper ore deposits 220
  gold sources 229
  metallurgy 218
  silver deposits 226
  tin deposits 225

Iceman 27, 33, 35, 57, 303, 313
iconography
   and gender 130–48
identity, Mediterranean 11
imagined communities 263, 264, 265
Immerwahr, Sara 276
Impressed Wares 25, 30
Indian Hijars 132
"initial class societies" 85
International Council of Museums
   (ICOM) 304, 311, 312
Isbell, William 265
Isherwood, Baron 287, 290
Isis 103
island insularity 9–10
   and monuments 173, 174–5
Israel, museums 310
Italy 56, 59, 306
   anthropomorphic figurines in Neolithic
      135–6
   chipped stone production 193
   cult sites associated with water 116
   expansion of agricultural landscape
      during second millennium 59–62
   feasting 123
   gender asymmetries 140
   and gendered space 143–4
   gold sources 229
   materials traded 28
   metallurgy 217–18
   museums and artifact collections 305,
      309, 310, 314
   Polada lakeside villages 60
   and polyculture 65
   ritual activities at funerary sites 111
   settlements 59–61
   silver deposits 226

Jacobsen, Inga 272
jasper 193
Jericho 256
   plastered skulls of 303
Journal of Mediterranean Archaeology 2

Kampen, Natalie 145
Kato Koutraphas Mandres 263
Keros-Syros culture 88–9
Keswani, P. S. 97, 288
Khirbat Hamra Ifdan (Jordan) 217, 221

Khirokitia (Cyprus) 120
Kissonerga (Cyprus) 144–5
Kissonerga Mosphilia (Cyprus) 217
Kissonerga Mylouthkia (Cyprus) 51, 217
Kition (Cyprus) 122
Kitsos Cave 201
Knapp, A. Bernard 96–7, 235, 258, 263,
   280, 281, 288, 289
Knappett, Carl 91, 92
knives 197
Knossos 90, 92, 137
   Late Bronze Age art and gender 137–8
   palace at 162, 162, 163, 164
   "Priest-King" fresco 135, 146
Kolonna 93, 96
Kommos (Crete) 278
Kopytoff, Igor 290
Koumasa 113
Krahtopoulou, Athanasia 66
kula system 24, 288
Kurban Höyük (Turkey) 255, 256
Kynthos (Delos) 220, 221, 231, 256

La Defensola 29
La Marmotta (Italy) 26
La Starza (Campania) 27
Laghetto del Monsignore spring 116
Lambrou-Phillipson, Connie 272
landscape 46–67, 234–5
   changes during Late Neolithic and
      Chalcolithic 56–7
   divergent views of 46–7
   features of by third millennium B.C.
      57
   formation of 64–7
   of second millennium 57–63
Lapita culture 173
Las Pilas (Spain) 81
Laurion (Attica) 220
Lavinium (Italy) 121
Le Ferriere-Satricum (Italy) 116
lead 225–8
Lebanon museums 310, 311
legumes 49, 51, 55, 57, 63
Lerna 92
Levant 51, 192, 217, 219, 231, 278
Level, E. V. 161
Levi, Carlo 46
Lewthwaite, James 50

Libiola (Italy)
  copper mines of 65
Libyan Valley Project 5, 15
Liguria (Italy) 30, 54
Lillios (Katina) 200
Linear B tablets 57, 58, 95, 142
Lipari 26, 28, 30
  circulation of obsidian *34*, 36–7, 40
Lisbon (Portugal) 29
livestock 51, 52, 53
location
  and settlement 257–9, 264
log boats 25–6
longue durée 11, 46
Los Millares (Spain) 80–1, *81*, 82, 110,
  218
lost-wax technique 229
Ludwig, Emil 5
Lukes, Steven 104
lustred blades 195
Luxor Museum of Ancient Egyptian Art
  (Egypt) 311, 315

Maa *Palaeokastro* (Cyprus) 258, 259
Ma'ayan Baruch Kibbutz Museum (Israel)
  310
Macedonia 95
maceheads 201
MacKenzie, Maureen *Androgynous Objects*
  132–3
Maddin, Robert *et al* 224
Malia (Crete) 91–2, *91*, 162, 163, 164, 165
Mallorca 170, 170–1, 218
Mallowan, Sir Max 308
Malone, Caroline *et al* 85
Malta 28, 306
  and axes 200
  domestic cults 120
  funerary complexes 160
  monuments 158–61
  museums 314–15
  National Museum of Archaeology 313
  temples 14, 31, 33, 108, 120, 122,
    158–61, *159*, 171, 172, 174
  trade in 40
Maltese Ladies 303
Mandalo (Macedonia) 36
Manika (Euboia) 92–3, 192, 256, 257,
  259, 261

Mann, Michael 281
Manning, Sturt 90
Mariette, Auguste 307
marine shells 30
Markides, Menelaos 306
Maroni *Tsaroukkas* (Cyprus) 286
Marroquíes Bajos (Jaén) 84–5
Marsa Matruh (Egypt) 278, 280
Mauss, Marcel 272
Mediterranean
  arrival of first people 8
  cultural heritage of 13–15, 16
  history of prehistory in 4–5
  insularity and maritime interaction
    9–10
  landscape and physical environment 6–8,
    25, 27, 46
  tradition, change and identity 10–12
  unity and diversity 12–13
Mediterranean Sea 6
  currents 7–8
  impact of 1
  and Neolithic trade 25–6
  visibility of 276–7, *277*
Megaceros cazioti (deer) 49
megalithic tombs 78, 111, 117, 168, 172
Melanesia 136
Melos 36, 49, 259–60, 261
Menorca 114, 170
merchants 282
Merrillees, Robert 290
Meskell, Lynn 147
Mesolithic 36, 49, 50
Mesopotamia 216
Messenia 94
metals/metallurgy 78, 215–39, 289
  factors influencing where ores are
    prepared for smelting/refining 234
  impact on society 230–3, 238–9
  impact on stone technology 180,
    201–4
  landscapes of 233–6
  mining communities 235–6
  overview of origins 216–18
  social and economic changes linked to
    developments in 239
  social implications for production of
    232–3
  technological innovations 232

metals/metallurgy (cont'd)
    trade in 236–8, 274, 288
    see also copper; gold; lead; silver; tin
Metropolitan Museum of Art (New York)
    307, 313–14
Mexico 146
mines/mining 29, 233–6
mining communities 230–1, 236–7, 258
Minoan palaces 87, 161–6, 171, 172, 174,
    274
    chronology and origins 165–6
    courts of 163
    cult rooms (pillar crypts) 163–4
    destruction of 58, 92
    at Knossos 162, *162*, 163, 164
    Minoan halls 164
    rituals held at 163
    shrine rooms 121
    storage magazines 164
Minoan society 57–8, 87, 161–2
    elites 57–8
    "horns of consecration" in cult sites
        104–5
    and women 142
"Minos Ring" 309–10
Mochlos 90
Mont Bego (France) 118
Monte d'Accoddi (Sardinia) 117, 168
Monte Polizzo (Sicily) 105
Monte Prama cemetery (Sardinia) 108
monuments 156–75
    and island insularity 173, 174–5
    origins 172, 174
    purpose of 156
    and social power 173–4, 175
    see also individual types
Morris, Sarah 12
mortars *183*, 201, 203, 204
Morter, Jon 144
mortuary rituals 83, 89, 92, 94, 95,
    110–13
Mother Goddess 108–9, 133
mountains 56, 57
Muhly, James 216, 221, 224, 289
Mulino Sant'Antonio (Campania) 39
Murphy, Joanne 90, 113
Museum of Origins and Traditions
    (University of Rome) 306
museums 303–16

contemporary patterns and problems
    308–15
contrast between countries 308
definition 304
display of prehistoric remains to visitors
    in exhibitions 313–14
in eastern Mediterranean 310
expansion of local 309
growth of in southern Europe 308–10
making and breaking of collections
    305–8
part played in establishment of by
    colonialism 306–7
in postcolonial North Africa 311
problem of illicit trade in antiquities 312
professional and academic approaches
    303–4
in southeast Europe 310
total numbers of *309*
visitors to 314–15
Mycenae 57–8, 87, 95, 142
    culture 57–8
    palaces 121
    pottery 283–4, 286
    Shaft Graves at 93–4
    tholos tombs 110
    and trade 284
Myotragus Balearicus 8
Myrtos 121
Myrtos Pyrgos 91

Nahal Mishmar (Israel) 223
narcotics 104, 113
National Museum of Beirut (Lebanon)
    307
National Museum of Egyptian Antiquities
    (France) 306–7
National Prehistoric and Ethnographic
    Museum (Rome) 305
naveta burial tomb *159*, 169, 170
New Guinea 281
Nocete, Francisco 85
North Africa 4–5, 118
North-South divide 4–5
Northern Keos Survey 253
Nubia 228–9
Nuraghe Trobas 86
nuraghi towers (Sardinia) 122, *159*, 166–7,
    168–9, 171, 172, 174

obsidian 26, 35–8, 39, 49, 182, 192–3, 201
    blades/bladelets made from 37–8
    change in functional niche and meaning
        in movement of *34*, 37
    characteristics 35, 38
    circulation of and trade in 28, *28*, 29,
        32, 182, 192
    sources of 182, *186*
    symbolic aspect of 187
    uses for 38
ochre 30
olives/olive oil 6–7, 56, 57, 61, 63, 65, 239
    naviform/bipolar technique 189–91
    navigation 27
    Nea Nikomedeia (Macedonia) 120–1
    Neolithic trade *see* trade (Neolithic)
Olsen, Barbara 142
open-air sites
    for cult activities 114–20
Opovo (former Yugoslavia) 145
orientalism 274–75
ornaments 83
    and gender 139
Osborne, Robin 258
Osteria dell'Osa 105
other, the 274–6, 281, 286

palaces *see* Minoan palaces
Palagruza 33
Palaikastro 90
Palestine Museum of Archaeology 306
Palestinian Lachish collection 312
Palma di Cesnola, General Luigi 307
Pantelleria 36
Paraklessia *Shillourokambos* 51
Passo di Corvo (Italy)
    local trade networks *32*
pastoralism 55, 57, 63
peak sanctuaries 116, *117*
Peatfield, Alan 116
Pella (Jordan) 236
Pellana (Laconia) 258
Peltenburg, Edgar 115, 144, 288
Peñalosa (Spain) 80–1, 85
Perlès, Catherine 27, 36, 39
pestles *183*
Petrie, Sir Flinders 308
Phaistos (Crete) 162, 163, 164, 165
Phaneromeni (Cyprus) 261

Phylakopi 122, 260
Pian di Civita (Italy) 115
picks 29
picrolite 201
pièces esquillées 185, *196*, 198, 203
Pigorini, Luigi 305
Pigott, Vincent 216
pillar crypts *see* cult rooms
Piña-Cabral, Joao de 2, 3, 12
"pit" sanctuary 115
plank figures, Cypriot 135
plants 49–50, 51
Po Valley (Italy) 54
Podere Tartuchino farm (Italy) 65
Point Iria shipwreck 285
points 197, 203
Polada "lake villages" 60
Polanyi, Karl 272
polishing stones *185*, 201, 203
Politiko *Phorades* (Cyprus) 234, 235, 263, 289
polyculture 56, 57, 63, 65, 78
Portugal
    axes 29, 200
    caves and cult activity 114
pottery 38, 40, 283, 289–90
    Beaker 231
    Mycenaean 283–4, 286
    trade of 29–30, 282
pounding tools 200, 201
practical mastery theory 27
prayer 102–3
pressure flaking 189, 191, 191–2, 192
prestige goods 37, 38, 39, 89, 90, 174,
    273–4, 281
"Priam's Treasure" 303, 307, 312
"Priest-King" fresco (Knossos) 135, 151
Prolagus sardus 49
property relations 80
Psychro (Crete) 114
Purcell, Nicholas 2, 3, 12, 15, 27, 46–7,
    64, 77, 252, 260, 274, 278, 288
pygmy elephant 49
pygmy hippopotamus 49
Pyla *Kokkinokremos* (Cyprus) 258, 259
Pylos (Greece) 260, 262
    palace 58, 260
Pyrgos 121

querns 203, 204

Rainbird, Paul 49
regional survey projects 2, 16
Regolini Galassi Tomb (Cerveteri) 123
Rehak, Paul 138, 142
Rellini, Ugo 306
Renfrew, Colin 6, 37, 38, 55, 56, 57, 87,
    90, 103, 109, 161, 166, 173, 218, 271,
    272, 281
Ribeiro, E. 136
Risch, Roberto 84
rituals 11, 102, 135
    archaic elements of 105
    definitions 103, 104
    and feasting 106–7
    in funerary contexts 110–13
    location and space of 109–10
    and Maltese temples 160–1
    and Minoan palaces 163
    and narcotics 104
    private and public 106
    repeating of 104
    and society 104–6
    see also cults
riverine cult sites 115
Robb, John 9, 85, 140, 144
robe rituals 124
Roberts, Brian 262
Robertson Smith 107
Rochberg-Halton, Eugene 287
rock-art sites
    and cults 117–18
rock carvings 60, 61, 62
rock-cut tombs 111, 112
Rowley-Conwy, Peter 54
Ruiz, Matilde et al 57, 63
rural settlements 254–5

sacrifice 102–3, 104, 106, 115, 124
Said, Edward 274–5
sailing ships 274
Sainsbury Centre for Visual Arts
    (University of East Anglia) 313, 314
St Michel du Touche (France) 115
salt
    production and trade in 31
San Marco 54
Sant' Andrea Priu (Sardinia) 112
Santorini volcano 58
Sardinia 7, 30, 36, 49, 86

copper ore deposits and industry 220
cult sites 122
metallurgy 218
nuraghi towers 122, 159, 166–7, 168–9,
    171, 172, 174
ritual activities at funerary sites 110–11
"sacred well" temples 122
society 169
tin deposits 225
Schliemann, Heinrich 307, 308
Schoep, Ilse 90, 91, 92
scrapers 203
    tabular 196, 197–8
seafaring 26, 27
Serabit el Khadim 219
Serpentine bracelets 30
Sesklo (Thessaly) 262
settlements 252–5
    boundaries 256–7, 264
    changing in patterns of 260–2
    and communities 262–3
    distribution 259–60, 264
    fortification 256
    location 257–9, 264
    meaning of 253–4, 263–4
    urban/rural distinction 254–5, 264
sex
    and gender 131, 137
sexual coding
    and anthropomorphic images 133–7
Shaft Graves (Mycenae) 93–4
Shaw, Maria 276
sheep 50, 57, 63, 66
shell rings 281
shells, marine 30
Sherratt, Andrew 104, 239, 273, 282
Sherratt, Elizabeth 276, 282, 289
shipwrecks 290 see also Cape Gelidonya
    shipwreck; Uluburun shipwreck
Sicily 7, 28
    caves as site of cult activities 114
    ritual activities at cemeteries 111
    society in 85–6
    trade with Malta 40
sickles 194, 195, 196, 196, 202–3
silver 225–8
    ingots 228
    objects of 226–7
    separating from lead process 226

sources 225–6
trade in 227, 236
use of 227
Siphnos 231
Skorba (Malta) 159
smelting technology 232
Smilcic (Dalmatia) 53
Smith, Adam 105
social power
and monuments 173–4, 175
societies 77–97
Aegean 87–95
concepts and ambiguities 77–80
conflict, exploitation, and coercion in the
west 80–7
impact of metallurgy on 230–3, 238–9
levels of complexity 78
Sombart, Werner 272
Son Mercer de Baix (Menorca) 170
Sørensen, Stig 139
Sorgenti della Nova (Fiora Valley) 59
Souskiou *Vathyrkakas* (Cyprus) 217
South Tyrol Museum of Archaeology (Italy)
313
Spain 30, 96, 231, 305–6
copper production and trade 236–7
Neolithic agricultural communities in
southeast 81
olive cultivation 65
sequence of change toward increasing
complexity 84–5
societies in southeast 63, 80–5
specialization
and stone-tool production 188, 191
Spedhos (Naxos) 256
standing stones 118, 119
statue-menhirs 107–8, 118, *119*, 120
Stech, Tamara 216
stelae 118–19, 140
stone tools 11, 180–205
coexistence with metal types 202–3
continuation of use 203
impact of metal on 180, 201–4
primary role in process of identifying
human presence and movements
180
trade of 29
types of, activity involved and raw
material used *183–5*

see also chipped stone technologies;
ground stone technologies
storage magazines 164
Straits of Messina 26, 29
Strathern, Marilyn 136
Su Nuraxi (Sardinia) 167, 168
Swiny, Stuart 256
swords 83
"sworn virgins" 132
Sydney Cyprus Survey Project 235, 253
Symposium on Mediterranean Archaeology
(SOMA) 2
Syrian museums 310

tabular scrapers *196*, 197–8
Talalay, Lauren E. 134, 135
talayot 159, 169–70, 171
Tarxien temples (Malta) 108, 159, 160,
161
taula 159, 169, 170, 171
Tel el-Dab'a (Egypt) 276
Tel Nami 278
Telefol 133
Tell Sakka (Egypt) 276
tell villages 52
temples
and cult activity 121–3
golden offerings in 229
Maltese *see* Maltese temples
terracing 56, 57, 63
Terrell, J. E. 281
Thapsos (Sicily) 86
Thebes 92, 93, 256
Thessaly (Greece) 52, 92, 95, 259, 262
"third sex" individuals 132
tholos tombs 94, 111–13, *159*, 166,
172
Thomas, Julian 105
threshing-sledges 198
Timna (Israel) 219, 221, 234
tin 223–5, 239
production of 224
sources of *219*, 224–5
trade of 224, 274
transition from arsenical to tin bronze
224
tin bronze 223, 224
tombe di giganti 167, 168
tombs 84, 110

tombs (cont'd)
    evidence for inequalities in society 82,
        84
    megalithic 78, 111, 117, 168, 172
    naveta 159, 169, 170
    nuragic (*tombe di giganti*) 167, 168
    rock-cut 111, *112*
    tholos 94, 111–13, *159*, 166, 172
torre tower (Corsica) 167–8, 169, 171
Toumba Thessalonikis 95
tourism 14
trade 10
trade (Late Bronze Age) 270–91
    acquisition as expression 288–90
    consumption as alternative logic 290–1
    elites and long-distance contact 286–8
    evidence for and its limitation 282–6
    historiography 271
    interregional 274
    in metals 236–8, 274, 288
    other and long-distance 274–6
    prestige and status goods 273–4
    role of in cultural process 271–2
    routes from Aegean to Near East 277–8
    routes and movement of goods 280–2
    types of 273
    working of local markets receiving goods
        281
trade (Neolithic) 24–41
    binding together and separation of
        people by traded materials 40
    general pattern 31–3
    intensification in 40–1
    knowledge of surroundings and
        navigation 27
    local trade networks at Passo di Corvo
        32
    networks 39
    objects and materials transported 27–31,
        28
    obsidian case study 35–8
    sea as avenue for and sailing routes
        25–6
    social context 38–41
Trigger, Bruce 102–3
Tringham, Ruth 145
Troodos Archaeological and Environmental
    Survey Project 253
Trypeti 89

Tunisian museums 311
Turkey 7, 225, 305
    museums 310
Turkish Historical Society 305
Tuscany (Italy) 220, 225
tuyères 221, *222*, 233

Ugarit 283–4
Ukwu, U.I. 281
Uluburun shipwreck 33, 221, 224, 237,
        273, 283, 285, 288
UNESCO
    "Blue Plan" 6
    Libyan Valleys Archaeological Survey
        253
urban settlements 55, 254–5

Valcamonica (Italy) 60, 118
Valencina de la Concepción (Seville)
        84–5
Valtellina (Italy) 118
Vandiver, Pamela 225
variscite 30–1
Vasiliki 89
Vera Basin 63, 67, 81, 82
Vera Valley Survey 56
vines 57, 61, 65, 239
Vita-Finzi, Claudio 67
Vounous cemetery (Cyprus) 115
Voutsaki, Sofia 94
Vulci (Italy) 116

Wachsmann, Shelley 284
wall paintings 275–6, 284
Warren, Peter 104, 124
water
    cults associated with 115–16
Watrous, Vance 90
Webb, Jennifer 97, 142–3, 262
Weber, Max 271
Webster, Gary 86
Weisgerber, Gerd 225, 232, 234
Welsch, R. L. 281
whetstones 205, 203
Whitehouse, Ruth 105, 111, 113, 135–6,
        143, 144
Whitelaw, Todd 89, 90
Whittle, Alasdair 52
Wiessner, Polly 79

Wijngaarden, Gert 284, 286
Wilkinson, Tony 254
wind-operated furnaces 233
wine 55–6, 57, 58, 63, 65
women
  and gendered space 143–4
  relationship with men 140
  roles of 140–3
  see also gender
woodland management 57

Yalçin, Ünsal 216
Yener, K. Aslihan 216, 225

Zakros (Crete) 162, 163, 164, 165
  palace of Kato 121
Zammit, Sir Themistocles 306
Zas Cave (Naxos) 217
Zohar, I. *et al* 31
Zvelebil, Marek 54